Lecture Notes in Computer Sc

Lecture Notes in Computer Science

Commenced Publication in 1973
Founding and Former Series Editors:
Gerhard Goos, Juris Hartmanis, and Jan van Leeuwen

Editorial Board

Rémi Bastide Philippe Palanque
Jörg Roth (Eds.)

Engineering Human Computer Interaction and Interactive Systems

Joint Working Conferences EHCI-DSVIS 2004
Hamburg, Germany, July 11-13, 2004
Revised Selected Papers

Volume Editors

Rémi Bastide
LIIHS-IRIT, Université Toulouse I
Place Anatole France, 31042 Toulouse Cedex, France
E-mail: bastide@irit.fr

Philippe Palanque
LIIHS-IRIT, Université Paul Sabatier
118, route de Narbonne, 31062 Toulouse Cedex, France
E-mail: palanque@irit.fr

Jörg Roth
Universität Hagen
Praktische Informatik II
Universitätsstr. 1, 58084 Hagen, Germany
E-mail: Joerg.Roth@Fernuni-hagen.de

Library of Congress Control Number: 2005928449

CR Subject Classification (1998): H.5.2-3, H.5, I.3, D.2, H.3, H.4, K.4, F.3

ISSN 0302-9743
ISBN-10 3-540-26097-8 Springer Berlin Heidelberg New York
ISBN-13 978-3-540-26097-4 Springer Berlin Heidelberg New York

Springer is a part of Springer Science+Business Media

springeronline.com

Printed in Germany

Typesetting: Camera-ready by author, data conversion by Boller Mediendesign
Printed on acid-free paper SPIN: 11431879 06/3142 5 4 3 2 1 0

Preface

As its name suggests, the EHCI-DSVIS conference has been a special event, merging two different, although overlapping, research communities: EHCI (Engineering for Human-Computer Interaction) is a conference organized by the IFIP 2.7/13.4 working group, started in 1974 and held every three years since 1989. The group's activity is the scientific investigation of the relationships among the human factors in computing and software engineering.

DSVIS (Design, Specification and Verification of Interactive Systems) is an annual conference started in 1994, and dedicated to the use of formal methods for the design of interactive systems. Of course these two research domains have a lot in common, and are informed by each other's results. The year 2004 was a good opportunity to bring closer these two research communities for an event, the 11th edition of DSVIS and the 9th edition of EHCI. EHCI-DSVIS was set up as a working conference bringing together researchers and practitioners interested in strengthening the scientific foundations of user interface design, specification and verification, and in examining the relationships between software engineering and human-computer interaction.

The call for papers attracted a lot of attention, and we received a record number of submissions: out of the 65 submissions, 23 full papers were accepted, which gives an acceptance rate of approximately 34%. Three short papers were also included. The contributions were categorized in 8 chapters:

Chapter 1 (Usability and Software Architecture) contains three contributions which advance the state of the art in usability approaches for modern software engineering. Bonnie John and her colleagues discuss that, in contrast to other software quality attributes such as performance, reliability and maintainability, usability is not usually tackled at the software architecture level. Their contribution is to propose usability-supporting architectural patterns, assorted with sample solutions. The second paper, by Brinkman et al., proposes three usability measures designed to be applied in a component-based environment. These measures can be objective, based on event logs, or subjective, obtained through questionnaires. An experimental study assessing the value of these measures is also described. The third paper, by Folmer and her colleagues, also deals with the relationships between usability and software architecture. They show how explicit evaluation of usability during architectural design may reduce the risk of building a system that fails to meet its usability requirements and may prevent high costs incurring adaptive maintenance activities once the system has been implemented.

Chapter 2 is devoted to issues regarding task modelling, which is a traditional topic of choice for both the EHCI and DSVIS series of conferences. The paper by Dittmar et al. investigates the slow adoption of task modelling by software practitioners. A thorough examination of the leading-edge tools for task modelling reveals how this situation can be improved by better integration of scenario-based design elements. The work of Clerckx et al. investigates the improvement that can be brought to usual task, environment and dialogue models by tackling the new application domain of context-sensitive user interfaces. The paper by Eicholz et al. explores the relationships between task modelling and workflow, or business process modelling.

Chapter 3 is concerned with the "browsing and searching" application domain, which is of high industrial relevance considering the current interest in Web-based applications. Ormerod et al. present new browser concepts to support the sharing of digital photographs and also report on the combined use of ethnographic, experimentation and design methods they used for their project. Gonçalves and Jorge propose a new classification scheme for document retrieval systems, where users "tell a story" about their document, in order to make the later retrieval of the document more natural.

Chapter 4 deals with model-based approaches. It is made up of six contributions, making it the longest chapter of the book, witness to the fact that the definition and use of models is at the core of the EHCI-DSVIS community. Campos and Nunes, in this chapter's first paper, emphasize the need for a better integration of models and tools. They present a new UI specification language bridging the gap between envisioned user behavior and concrete user interfaces. Macías and Castells bring the field of programming-by-example to the domain of Web-based applications by detecting iteration patterns in user behavior and generating a programmatic representation of a user's actions. Navarre et al. integrate two different notations in order to offer a tool-supported approach for the prototyping of advanced multimodal applications. Limbourg and his colleagues apply their USIXML language to show how a user interface can be specified and produced at and from different, and possibly multiple, levels of abstraction while maintaining the mappings between these levels. The chapter is concluded by two short contributions: In the paper by Schaefer et al., a novel dialogue model for the design of multimodal user interfaces is proposed. Ziegler and Specker conclude by proposing the use of "Navigation Patterns," pattern systems based on structural mappings.

Chapter 5 is devoted to a rapidly developing application domain, ubiquitous computing. Borkowski et al. propose several software tools with the assorted interaction techniques to develop multisurface computer-augmented environments. Evreinov and his colleagues explore the use of vibro-tactile interaction, especially useful for new mobile devices such as palmtop computers.

Chapter 6 is called "Bridging Viewpoints": this refers to an ongoing activity of the IFIP 2.7/13.4 working group, which is to find ways to reconcile the fundamental paradigms of user-centered design and software engineering. For instance, Blandford, Green and Connel analyze the misfits between the user's conceptualization of the domain and device with which they are working and the conceptualization implemented within those systems. Barbosa et al. discuss the role of an enhanced extended lexicon as a shared communicative artefact during software design. They describe how it may act as an interlingua that captures the shared understanding of both stakeholders and designers. López-Jaquero et al. contribute a short paper on a design process for adaptive interfaces.

Chapter 7 is concerned with the emerging application domain of plastic and adaptive interfaces. Increasingly often, the same application has to be delivered on widely different platforms, ranging from a complete workstation to a PDA or a cell phone. Clearly, advances in design approaches are needed to avoid redesigning the user interface from scratch for each platform. Dobson's work is concerned with laying out such principles, in particular for pervasive computing systems. Calvary and her colleagues present a software widget explicitly dealing with plasticity of the user interface. Gilroy and Harrison propose the incorporation of interaction style into abstract UI specification, in order to accommodate with different UI platforms. Correani et al. present a new version of the TERESA tool supporting flexible development of multidevice interfaces.

Chapter 8 (Groupware) concludes the book with two papers, both concerned with supporting collaborative software construction. Wu and Graham present the Software Design Board, a prototype collaborative design tool supporting a variety of styles of collaboration and facilitating transitions between them. Gutwin et al. explore ways to improve group awareness in collaborative software design.

The conference was held in the beautiful, quiet and secluded Tremsbüttel Castle, near Hamburg, Germany, providing a studious atmosphere propitious to after-hours discussion. As usual for the EHCI conference series, the discussion that followed each paper presentation was transcribed, revised and appended to the edited version of the paper. From these, the reader may catch a glimpse of the lively debates that were held at the conference.

Rémi Bastide
Philippe Palanque
Jörg Roth

Programme Committee

Conference Chairs

Rick Kazman	SEI, Carnegie Mellon University, USA
Philippe Palanque	LIIHS-IRIT, France

Programme Committee Chairs

Rémi Bastide	LIIHS-IRIT, France
Nick Graham	Queen's University, Kingston, Canada
Jörg Roth	University of Hagen, Germany

Programme Committee Members

Len J. Bass	SEI, Carnegie Mellon University, USA
Ann Blandford	University College London, UK
Annie Chabert	GPS Pilot, France
Stéphane Chatty	Intuilab, France
Joëlle Coutaz	Université Joseph Fourier, France
Anke Ditmar	University of Rostock, Germany
Alan Dix	Lancaster University, UK
Gavin Doherty	Trinity College, Dublin, Ireland
Peter Forbrig	University of Rostock, Germany
Phil Gray	University of Glasgow, UK
Morten Borup Harning	Open Business Innovation, Denmark
Michael Harrison	University of York, UK
Rob Jacob	Tufts University, USA
Bonnie John	HCII, Carnegie Mellon University, USA
Chris Johnson	University of Glasgow, UK
Joaquim Jorge	Instituto Superior Técnico, Lisbon, Portugal
Reed Little	SEI, Carnegie Mellon University, USA
Quentin Limbourg	Catholic University of Louvain, Belgium
Panos Markopoulos	University of Eindhoven, The Netherlands
Laurence Nigay	Université Joseph Fourier, France
Nuno Jardim Nunes	Universidade da Madeira, Portugal
Fabio Paternò	ISTI-CNR, Italy
Oscar Pastor	Universidad Politécnica de Valencia, Spain
Greg Phillips	Royal Military College, Canada
Chris Roast	Sheffield Hallam University, UK
Daniel Salber	CWI, The Netherlands
Kevin Schneider	University of Saskatchewan, Canada
Helmut G. Stiegler	STI Consulting, Germany
Halvard Trætteberg	NTNU, Norway
Claus Unger	University of Hagen, Germany
Jean Vanderdonckt	Université Louvain-La-Neuve, Belgium
Leon Watts	UMIST, UK

Table of Contents

Usability

Task Modelling

Browsing and Searching

Model-Based Approaches

Ubiquitous Computing

Bridging Viewpoints

Plastic and Adaptive Interfaces

Groupware

Bringing Usability Concerns to the Design of Software Architecture[1]

Bonnie E. John[1], Len Bass[2], Maria-Isabel Sanchez-Segura[3], Rob J. Adams[1]

[1] Carnegie Mellon University, Human-Computer Interaction Institute, USA
{bej, rjadams}@cs.cmu.edu
[2] Carnegie Mellon University, Software Engineering Institute, USA
ljb@sei.cmu.edu
[3] Carlos III University of Madrid, Computer Science Department, Spain
misanche@inf.uc3m.es

Abstract. Software architects have techniques to deal with many quality attributes such as performance, reliability, and maintainability. Usability, however, has traditionally been concerned primarily with presentation and not been a concern of software architects beyond separating the user interface from the remainder of the application. In this paper, we introduce usability-supporting architectural patterns. Each pattern describes a usability concern that is not supported by separation alone. For each concern, a usability-supporting architectural pattern provides the forces from the characteristics of the task and environment, the human, and the state of the software to motivate an implementation independent solution cast in terms of the responsibilities that must be fulfilled to satisfy the forces. Furthermore, each pattern includes a sample solution implemented in the context of an overriding separation based pattern such as J2EE Model View Controller.

1. Introduction

For the past twenty years, software architects have treated usability primarily as a problem in modifiability. That is, they separate the presentation portion of an application from the remainder of that application. This separation makes it easier to make modifications to the user interface and to maintain separate views of application data. This is consistent with the standard user interface design methods that have a focus on iterative design – i.e. determine necessary changes to the user interface from user testing and modify the system to implement these changes. Separating the user interface from the remainder of the application is now standard practice in developing interactive systems.

Treating usability as a problem in modifiability, however, has the effect of postponing many usability requirements to the end of the development cycle where they are overtaken by time and budget pressures. If architectural changes required to

* This work supported by the U. S. Department of Defense and the NASA High Dependability Computing Program under cooperative agreement NCC-2-1298.

R. Bastide, P. Palanque, and J. Roth (Eds.): EHCI-DSVIS 2004, LNCS 3425, pp. 1-19, 2005.

implement a usability feature are discovered late in the process, the cost of change multiplies. Consequently, systems are being fielded that are less usable than they could be.

Recently, in response to the shortcomings of relying exclusively on separation as a basis for supporting usability, several groups have identified specific usability scenarios that are not well supported by separation, and have proposed architectural solutions to support these scenarios [2,3,5,6,11]. In this paper, we move beyond simply positing scenarios and sample solutions by identifying the forces that conspire to produce such scenarios and that dictate responsibilities the software must fulfill to support a solution. Following Alexander [1], we collect these forces, the context in which they operate, and solutions that resolve the forces, into a *pattern*, in this case a *usability-supporting architectural pattern.*

In the next section, we argue that software architects must consider more than a simple separation-based pattern in order to achieve usability. We then discuss why we are focusing on forces and why the forces that come from prior design decisions play a special role in software creation. In section 4, we describe our template for these patterns and illustrate it with one of the usability scenarios previously identified by several research groups. We also comment on the process for creating these patterns. Finally, we conclude with how our work has been applied and our vision of future work.

2. Usability Requires More than Separation

The J2EE Model-View-Controller (J2EE-MVC) architectural pattern [12], appears in Fig. 1. This is one example of a separation based pattern to support interactive systems. The model represents data and functionality, the view renders the content of a model to be presented to the user, and the controller translates interactions with the view into actions to be performed by the model. The controller responds by selecting an appropriate view. There can be one or more views and one controller for each functionality.

The purpose of this pattern is explained by Sun as follows [12]: "By applying the Model-View-Controller (MVC) architecture to a Java™ 2 Platform, Enterprise Edition (J2EE™) application, you separate core business model functionality from the presentation and control logic that uses this functionality. Such separation allows multiple views to share the same enterprise data model, which makes supporting multiple clients easier to implement, test, and maintain." Modifications to the presentation and control logic (the user interface) also become easier because the core functionality is not intertwined with the user interface. A number of such patterns have emerged since the early 1980s including the original Smalltalk MVC and Presentation Abstraction Control (PAC) [8] and they have proven their utility and have become common practice.

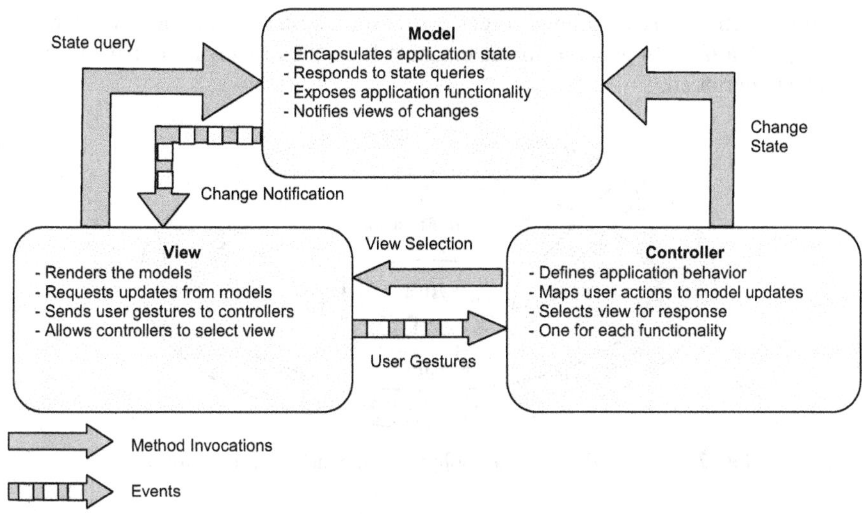

Fig. 1. J2EE-MVC structure diagram (adapted from [12]).

The problem, however, is that achieving usability means more than simply getting the presentation and control logic correct. For example, consider cancelling the current command, undoing the last command, or presenting progress bars that give an accurate estimate of time to completion. Supporting these important usability concerns requires the involvement of the model as well as the view and the controller. A cancellation command must reach into the model in order to terminate the active command. Undo must also reach into the model because, as pointed out in [10], command processing is responsible for implementing undo and command processing is carried out in the model in J2EE-MVC. Accurate time estimates for progress bars depend on information maintained in the model. This involvement of multiple subsystems in supporting usability concerns is also true for the other separation based patterns. Thus, usability requires more than just separation.

3. The Forces in Usability-Supporting Architectural Patterns

The patterns work pioneered by Christopher Alexander in the building architecture domain [1] has had a large impact on software engineering, e.g. [8,10]. Following Alexander's terminology, a pattern encompasses three elements: the context, the problem arising from a system of clashing forces, and the canonical solution in which the forces are resolved. The concept of forces and their sources plays a large role in defining the requirements that a solution must satisfy.

As we mentioned above, previous work [2,3,5,6,11] focused on identifying usability scenarios not well served by separation and providing an example solution, architectural or OOD. These solutions did indeed support the scenarios, but included design decisions that were not dictated by, nor traceable to, specific aspects of the scenarios. In the work presented here, this lack of traceability is remedied by Alexander's concept of forces.

Figure 2 depicts the high-level forces acting on a system of people and machines to accomplish a task. In general, forces emanate from the organization that causes the task to be undertaken.

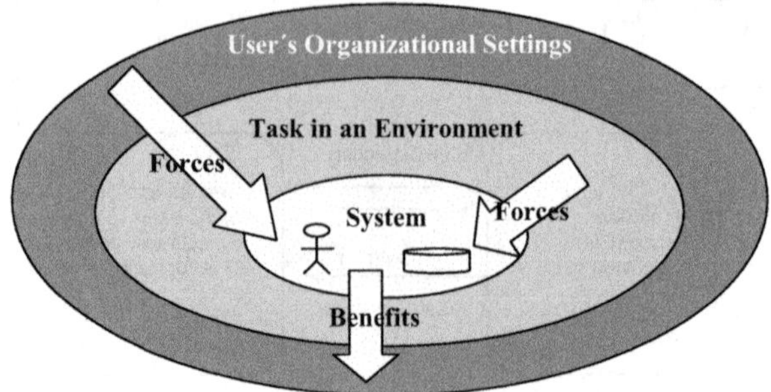

Fig. 2. Forces influencing the solution and benefits of the solution.

That is, the organization benefits from efficiency, the absence of error, creativity, and job satisfaction, to varying degrees, forcing the people to behave and the machines to be designed to provide these benefits. The costs of implementing, or procuring, software systems that provide such benefits is balanced against the value of those benefits to the organization. Although the balance is highly dependent on the specific organization and will not be discussed further, our work provides a solid foundation for determining costs, benefits, and the link between them.

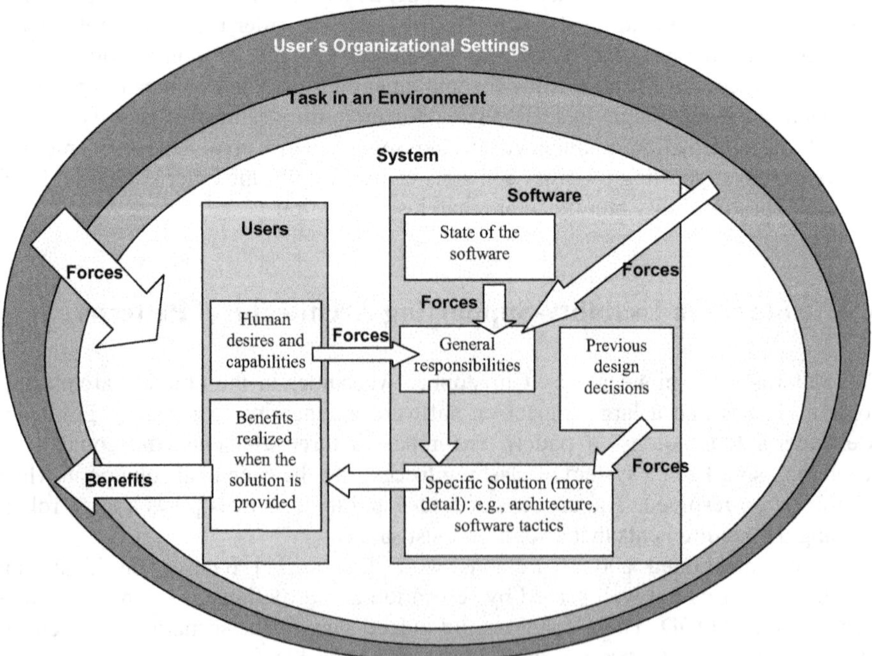

Fig. 3. Forces impacting the software architecture.

Figure 3 gives more detail about the forces acting on the software that is the object of design. In addition to the general organizational forces that put value on efficiency, the reduction of errors and the like, there are specific forces placed on the design of a particular software application, which may conflict or converge, but are eventually resolved in a design solution. These forces have several sources: the task the software is designed to accomplish and the environment in which it exists, the desires and capabilities of humans using the software, the state of the software itself, and prior design decisions made in the construction of the software in service of quality attributes other than usability (e.g., maintainability, performance, security).

The first three sources of forces, task and environment, human, and software state, combine to produce a general usability problem and a set of general responsibilities that must be satisfied by any design purporting to solve the problem. These responsibilities can serve as a checklist when evaluating an existing or proposed software design for its ability to solve a given usability problem.

Combining these general responsibilities with the forces exerted by prior design decisions produces a specific solution, that is, an assignment of responsibilities to new or existing subsystems in the software being designed. If we assume, for example, the common practice of using an overall separation-based architectural pattern for a specific design, the choice of this pattern introduces forces that affect any specific solution. In this sense, our usability-supporting architectural patterns differ from other architectural patterns in that most other patterns are presented as if they were independent of any other design decisions that have been made.

We now turn to the elements of a usability-supporting architectural pattern, illustrated with an example.

4. A Template for Usability-Supporting Architectural Patterns: Example & Process

Table 1 presents a template for a usability-supporting architectural pattern, containing the context, the problem, and both a general solution and a specific solution. This template is based on the concepts in Alexander's patterns [1], past experiences teaching architectural support for usability problems [6,11], and usability evaluation of the pattern format itself. For example, the forces are listed in columns according to their source under the **Problem** section of the template. Each row of forces is resolved by a general responsibility of the software being designed. Even though the responsibilities constitute the **General Solution**, we place them in the rows occupied by the forces that they resolve because this spatial configuration emphasizes the traceability of responsibilities back to the forces. In the **Specific Solution** we repeat the general responsibilities rather than simply pointing to them, because it is easier for the designer to read the text of the general responsibility in proximity to the prior design decisions than to continually switch between different sections of the pattern template. As with the general responsibilities, the rows in the **Specific Solution** provide a traceability lacking in our previous presentations of similar material.

Table 1. Usability-supporting architectural pattern template.

<table>
<tr><td colspan="4">Name: The name of the pattern</td></tr>
<tr><td colspan="4">Usability Context</td></tr>
<tr><td colspan="4">Situation: A brief description of the situation from the user's perspective that makes this pattern useful</td></tr>
<tr><td colspan="4">Conditions on the Situation: Any conditions on the situation constraining when the pattern is useful.</td></tr>
<tr><td colspan="4">Potential Usability Benefits: A brief description of the benefits to the user if the solution is implemented. We use the usability benefit hierarchy from [3,5] to express these benefits.</td></tr>
<tr><td colspan="3">Problem</td><td>General solution</td></tr>
<tr><td>Forces exerted by the environment and the task. Each row contains a different force</td><td>Forces exerted by human desires and capabilities. Each row contains a different force.</td><td>Forces exerted by the state of the software. Each row contains a different force.</td><td>Responsibilities of the general solution that resolve the forces in the row.</td></tr>
<tr><td colspan="4">Specific Solution</td></tr>
<tr><td>Responsibilities of general solution (repeated from the General Solution column)</td><td>Forces that come from prior design decisions</td><td>Allocation of responsibilities to specific components.</td><td>Rationale justifying how this assignment of responsibilities to specific modules satisfy the problem</td></tr>
<tr><td colspan="4">Component diagram of specific solution</td></tr>
<tr><td colspan="4">Sequence diagram of specific solution</td></tr>
<tr><td colspan="4">Deployment diagram of specific solution (if necessary)</td></tr>
</table>

4.1 Cancellation: An Example of a Usability-Supporting Architectural Pattern

Consider the example of canceling commands. Cancellation is an important usability feature, whose value is well known to UI specialists and users alike, which is often poorly supported even in modern applications. This example shows the extent to which a usability concern permeates the architecture. Space does not permit us to include a completed pattern for this example, so we will illustrate specific points with selected portions of the pattern.

Usability Context. Table 2 contains the **Name** and the **Usability Context** portions of the usability-supporting architectural pattern for canceling commands. The **Situation** briefly describes the pattern from the point of view of the user, similar to the situation in other pattern formats. However, the **Conditions** section provides additional information about when the pattern is useful in the usability context. For example, cancellation is only beneficial to users when the system has commands that run longer than a second. With faster commands, users do not get additional benefit from cancellation over simply undoing a command after it has completed. The loci of control may also appear in the **Condition** section. In our example, the cancellation may be initiated by the user or by the software itself in response to changes in the environment. The last section in the usability context is the **Potential Usability Benefits** to the user if the solution is implemented in the software. Quantifying these benefits will depend on the particular users, tasks, and organizational setting and is beyond the scope of this paper. However, the list of potential benefits and their rationale is a starting point for a cost/benefit analysis of providing the solutions in the pattern. The benefits are cast in terms of the benefit hierarchy given in [3,5] ranging from efficiency, to supporting non-routine behavior (i.e., problem-solving, creativity, or learning), to user confidence and comfort. The ability to cancel commands has the potential to benefit each of these categories.

The **Problem** and **General Solution**

Table 2. Usability context of the Cancelling Commands pattern.

Name: Cancelling Commands
Usability Context
Situation: The user issues a command then changes his or her mind, wanting to stop the operation and return the software to its pre-operation state. It doesn't matter why the user wants to stop; he or she could have made a mistake, the system could be unresponsive, or the environment could have changed.
Conditions of the Situation: A user is working in a system where the software has long-running commands, i.e., more than one second. The cancellation command can be explicitly issued by the user, or through some sensing of the environment (e.g., a child's hand in a power car window).
Potential Usability Benefits: *A. Increases individual user effectiveness* *A.1 Expedites routine performance* *A.1.2 Reduces the impact of routine user errors (slips)* by allowing users to revoke accidental commands and return to their task faster than waiting for the erroneous command to complete. *A.2 Improves non-routine performance* *A.2.1 Supports problem-solving* by allowing users to apply commands and explore without fear, because they can always abort their actions. *A.3 Reduces the impact of user errors caused by lack of knowledge (mistakes)* *A.3.2 Accommodates mistakes* by allowing users to abort commands they invoke through lack of knowledge and return to their task faster than waiting for the erroneous command to complete. *B. Reduces the impact of system errors* *B.2 Tolerates system* errors by allowing users to abort commands that aren't working properly (for example, a user cancels a download because the network is jammed). *C. Increases user confidence and comfort* by allowing users to perform without fear because they can always abort their actions.

Sections of the pattern are the heart of this paper's contribution to the research in usability and software architecture. Previous research jumped from a general scenario, like that in our **Situation** section, directly to a short list of general responsibilities and an architectural solution [2,3,5] or to detailed design solution [6] using the expertise of the authors. Considering the forces is a step forward in codifying the human-computer interaction and software engineering expertise that was tacit in the previous work. Making tacit knowledge explicit provides a rationale for design recommendation, increases the understanding of the software engineers who use these patterns to inform their design, and provides a basis for deciding to include or exclude any specific aspect of the solution.

The **Problem** is defined by the system of forces stemming from the task and environment, recurring human desires and relevant capabilities, and the state of the software itself. These forces are arranged in columns and rows, a portion of which is shown in Table 3 for Cancelling Commands. Each row of conflicting or converging forces is resolved by a responsibility of the software, presented in the rightmost column of Table 3. These responsibilities constitute a **General Solution** to the problem.

The first row in the **Problem** and **General Solution** records the major forces that motivate the general usability situation. In our example, the facts that networks and other environmental systems beyond the software are sometimes unresponsive, that humans make mistakes or change their minds but do not want to wait to get back to their tasks, and that the software itself is sometimes unresponsive dictate that the software provide a means to cancel a command. The subsequent rows list other forces that come into play to dictate more specific responsibilities of the software. Some forces are qualitative and some are quantitative. For example, the middle of Table 3 shows a quantified human capability force that produces a performance responsibility; the software must acknowledge the reception of a cancel command within 150 ms and in a manner that will be perceived by the user [2]. These forces encapsulate decades of human performance research and provide specific performance and UI design guidance in a form that is usable and understandable by software designers.

In some rows, the forces converge and the responsibility fulfills the needs of the different sources of force. For example, in the second row of Table 3, both the environment and the human are unpredictable in their need for the cancellation function. The responsibilities that derives from these needs, that the system always be listening for the cancellation request and that is always be collecting the necessary data to perform a cancellation, solve both these compatible forces. Sometimes the forces conflict, as in part of the last row of Table 3, where the user wants the command to stop but the software is unresponsive. The responsibility must then resolve these opposing forces, in this case, going outside the software being designed to the system in which it runs.

Process of Creating the Problem and General Solution. Our process of creating the entries in the **Problem** and **General Solution** columns begins by examining prior research in usability and software architecture.

Table 3. Portion of the Problem and General Solution for Cancelling Commands.

Problem			General solution
Forces exerted by the environment & task.	**Forces exerted by human desires and capabilities.**	**Forces exerted by the state of the software.**	**General responsibilities of the software.**
Networks are sometimes unresponsive. Sometimes changes in the environment require the system to terminate	Users slip or make mistakes, or explore commands and then change their minds, but do not want to wait for the command to complete.	Software is sometimes unresponsive	Must provide a means to cancel a command
No one can predict when the environment will change	No one can predict when the users will want to cancel commands		Must always listen for the cancel command or environmental changes. Must be always listening and gathering the actions related to the command being invoked.
	User needs to know that the command was received within 150 msec, or they will try again. The user can be assumed to be looking at the cancel button, if this is how they canceled the command People can see changes in color and intensity in their peripheral vision as well as in their fovea.		Must acknowledge the command within 150 msec. Acknowledgement must be appropriate to the manner in which the command was issued. For example, if the user pressed a cancel button, changing the color of the button will be seen. If the user used a keyboard shortcut, flashing the menu that contains that command could be detected in peripheral vision.

Table 3. Portion of the Problem and General Solution for Cancelling Commands (continued).

Problem				General solution
Forces exerted by the environment & task.	**Forces exerted by human desires and capabilities.**		**Forces exerted by the state of the software.**	**General responsibilities of the software.**
	User wants the command to stop	EITHER	The command itself is responsive	The command should cancel itself regardless of the state of the environment
		OR	The command itself is not responsive or has not yet been invoked	An active portion of the system must ask the infrastructure to cancel the command, or The infrastructure itself must provide a means to kill the application (e.g., task manager on Windows, force quit on MacOS) (These requirements are independent of the state of the environment.)
Collaborating processes may prevent the command from canceling promptly			The command has invoked collaborating processes	The collaborating processes must be informed of the cancellation of the invoking command (these processes have their own responsibilities that they must perform in response to being informed).

From the previously documented scenarios we can read, or infer, forces from the task and environment or human desires and capabilities, and sometimes from the state of the software itself. From previously enumerated responsibilities, we uncover tacit assumptions about the forces they are resolving. From prior solutions, additional general responsibilities can sometimes be retrieved. We list all these forces in the appropriate columns and the responsibilities that resolve them.

This preliminary table then becomes the framework for further discussion around what we call *considerations*. Considerations are recurring forces, or variations in forces, that cut across multiple scenarios. The considerations we have found to be useful involve issues of feedback to the user, time, initiative, and scope.

With any interactive system, there is always a consideration of feedback to the user. The user wants to be informed of the state of the software to make best use of their time, to know what to do next, perform sanity checks, trouble-shoot and the like. There are several types of feedback in almost every pattern: acknowledgement of the user's action, feedback on the progress of software actions, and feedback on the results of software actions. The need for each of these types of feedback is forces in the human needs and capability column. In Table 3, this consideration shows up in the third row.

The time consideration involves forward-looking, current, and backward-looking issues of time. One forward-looking consideration is the issue of persistence. Does the pattern involve any objects that must persist over time? If so, there are often issues of storing those objects, naming them, finding them later, editing them, etc. (This consideration can also be thought of as a need for authoring facilities). A current time issue is whether the pattern involves a process that will be operating concurrently with human actions. If so, how will the human's actions be synchronized at an effective time for both the software and the human? An example of a backward-looking time consideration occurs in the cancelling command pattern (not included in the portion of the pattern in Table 3). What state should the software roll back to? In most applications the answer is clearly "the state before the last command was issued." However, in systems of collaborating applications or with consumable resources, the answer becomes less clear. An extreme example of this consideration for a system-level undo facility can be found in the examination of system administrators by Brown and Patterson [7].

The initiative consideration involves which entity can control the interaction with the software being designed. In the cancelling commands pattern, initiative comes from several places. One normally thinks of a cancel command being deliberately instigated by the user. However, it is also possible that the environment can change, initiating the equivalent of a cancel command to the software. For example, the software that controls an automobile window lifter should stop the window rising if the driver presses a button (user's initiative), or if a child's hand is about to be trapped (system's initiative).

The scope consideration asks whether a problem is confined to the software being designed or concerns other aspects of the larger system. In the cancelling commands example, a larger scope is evident in the last two rows in Table 3 when considering responsibilities when the software is unresponsive and when there are collaborating processes.

Thus, the combination of mining prior research in usability and software architecture and asking the questions associated with considerations, allow the definition of the forces and responsibilities that resolve them. The general responsibilities constitute a general solution to the problem created by the forces. Some pattern advocates would eschew our process of defining responsibilities because the solution is generated, not recognized as an accepted good design used repeatedly in practice. We believe that these general responsibilities have value nonetheless because (1) they serve as requirements for any specific solution, and (2) many of the usability problems we have examined are not consistently served in practice as yet, so no widely accepted solution is available.

Specific Solution. The specific solution is derived from the general responsibilities and the forces that come from prior design decisions. Usability-supporting architectural patterns differ from other architecture patterns in that they are neither overarching nor localized. Patterns such as client-server, layers, pipe and filter, and blackboard [8] tend to dominate the architecture of the systems in which they are used. It may be that they only dominate a portion of the system but in this case, they are usually encapsulated within a defined context and dominate that context. Other patterns such as publish-subscriber, forward-receiver, and proxy [8] are local in how they relate to the remainder of the architecture. They may impose conditions on components with which they interact but these conditions do not seriously impact the actions of the components.

Usability-supporting architectural patterns are not going to be overarching. One does not design a system, for example, around the support for cancelling commands. The support for this usability feature must be fit into whatever overarching system designs decisions are made to facilitate the core functionality and other quality attributes of the system. Usability-supporting architectural patterns are also not local, by definition. They involve multiple portions of the architecture almost regardless of what the initial design decisions have been made. Cancel, for example, ranges from a requirement to listen for user input (at all times), to freeing resources, to knowing about and informing collaborators of the cancellation request. All these responsibilities involve different portions of the architecture.

When presenting a specific solution, then, there are two choices – neither completely satisfactory.

1. Present the solution independent of prior design decisions. That is, convert the general responsibilities into a set of components and assign the responsibilities to them, without regard for any setting. A specific solution in this form does not provide good guidance for architects who will come to the usability supporting architectural patterns after having made a number of overarching design decisions. For example, if the J2EE-MVC pattern is used as the overarching pattern, then a listener for the cancel command is decoupled from the presentation of feedback to indicate acknowledgement of the command. If the PAC pattern is used, then a listener would be part of the presentation and would also be responsible for feedback.
2. Present the solution in the context of assumed prior design decisions. That is, assume an overarching pattern such as J2EE-MVC or PAC and ensure that the specific solution conforms to the constraints introduced by this decision. This increases the utility of the specific solution for those who are implementing within the J2EE-MVC context but decreases the utility for those implementing within some other context.

We have tried both solutions when we have presented earlier versions of this material, without finding a completely satisfactory solution. However, common practice in interactive system development currently uses some form of separation of the interface from the functionality. Therefore demonstrating the interplay of general responsibilities with a separation-based overarching architecture is a necessity to make contact to current practice. Given the popularity of J2EE-MVC, we present our specific solution in that context.

For our cancel example, the forces caused by a prior design decision to use J2EE-MVC govern the assignment of function to the model objects, the view objects, or to the control objects (Figure 1). Any new responsibilities added by the usability problem must adhere to the typical assignments in J2EE-MVC. Thus, responsibilities that interact with the user must reside in the view, responsibilities that map user gestures to model updates or define application behavior or select views must reside in controller objects, and responsibilities that store state or respond to state queries must reside in models.

Table 4. Row of specific solution that concerns the general responsibility of always listening for the cancel command or environmental changes

Specific Solution			
Responsibilities of general solution. i.e., requirements	**Forces exerted by prior design decisions**	**Allocation of responsibilities to specific components**	**Rationale**
Must always listen for the cancel command or environmental changes.	In J2EE-MVC, user gestures are recognized by a controller J2EE-MVC is neutral about how to deal with environmental sensors	Listener component is a controller. It must • run on an independent thread from any model. • receive user gestures that are intended to invoke cancel. • receive environmental change notification that require a cancel.	Since the command being cancelled may be blocked and preempting the Listener, the Listener is assigned to a thread distinct from the one used by the command. Since J2EE-MVC is neutral with respect to environmental sensors, we chose to listen for the environmental sensors in the same controller that listens for user gestures that request cancellation (the Listener)

Table 4 shows a small portion of the **Specific Solution** for cancelling commands in J2EE-MVC, resolving the general responsibilities with the prior design decisions. For easy reading, the general responsibilities, i.e., requirements of the specific solution are repeated in the first column of the Specific Solution. In Table 4, we've chosen to illustrate the responsibility of always listening for the cancel command or environmental changes that signal the need for cancellation. This general responsibility was the first responsibility in the second row of Table 3. The next column contains those forces exerted by the prior design decisions that apply to the general responsibility in the same row. The fact that J2EE-MVC controllers recognize user gestures is one such force. That J2EE-MVC does not mention environmental sensors is listed as a force, but its inclusion simply records that J2EE-MVC does not exert a force on this point. The third column resolves these forces by further specifying the general responsibilities and allocating them to specific components in the overarching architecture. In this case, a new controller entitled the Listener is assigned the specific responsibilities that fulfil the general responsibility. The last column provides additional rational for this allocation, for example, that since J2EE-MVC does not specify a component for environmental sensors, we chose to use the same controller as that listening for user requests to cancel.

After allocating all general responsibilities, all the new components and their responsibilities, and all new responsibilities assigned to old components of the overarching architecture can be collected into a specification for implementation. For example, when the remainder of the complete **Specific Solution** table (not shown) is considered, the Listener is responsible for

- always listening for a user's request to cancel,
- always listening for external sensor's request for cancellation (if any), and
- informing the Cancellation Manager (a model) of any cancellation request.

A component diagram of our specific solution is given in Figure 4. The View, Controller and Active Command (model) and Collaborating Processes (if any) are the components associated with J2EE-MVC under normal operations, without the facility to cancel commands. The results of the analysis in the complete **Specific Solution** table (not shown) added several new components. The Listener has already been described.

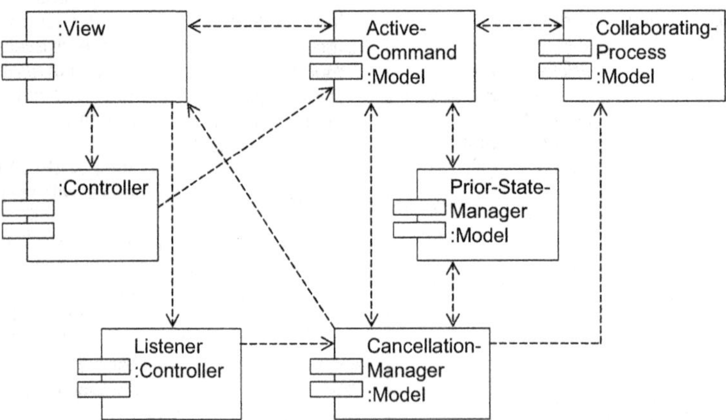

Fig. 4. Component diagram for the specific solution.

The Cancellation Manager and Prior State Manager are new models fulfilling the other general and specific responsibilities of cancelling commands. Because dynamic behaviour is important for the cancel command we also use two different sequence diagrams. The first (Figure 5) shows the sequence of normal operation with a user issuing a command to the software. This figure represents the case in which:

- The user requests a command
- The command can be cancelled

The command saved its state prior to execution using the Prior State Manager. The sequence diagram in Figure 6 represents the case in which:

- The user requests cancellation of an active command
- The current command is not blocked

- The prior state was stored
- Time of cancellation will be between 1 and 10 seconds. Change cursor shape but progress bars are not needed.
- It is not critical for the task that the cancellation be complete before another user action is taken
- All resources are properly freed by the current command.
- Original state is correctly restored.

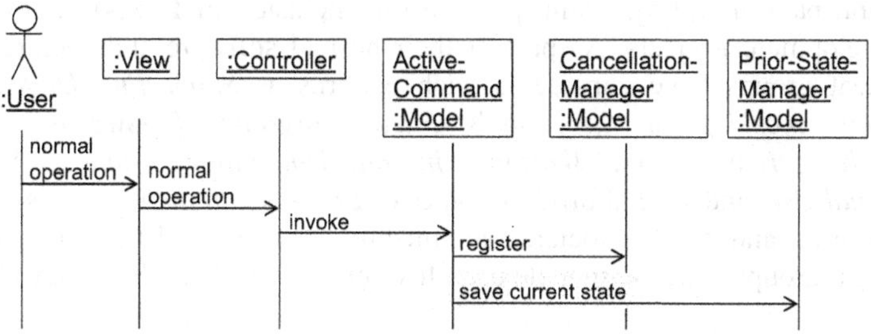

Fig. 5. Sequence diagram of normal operation, before cancel is requested.

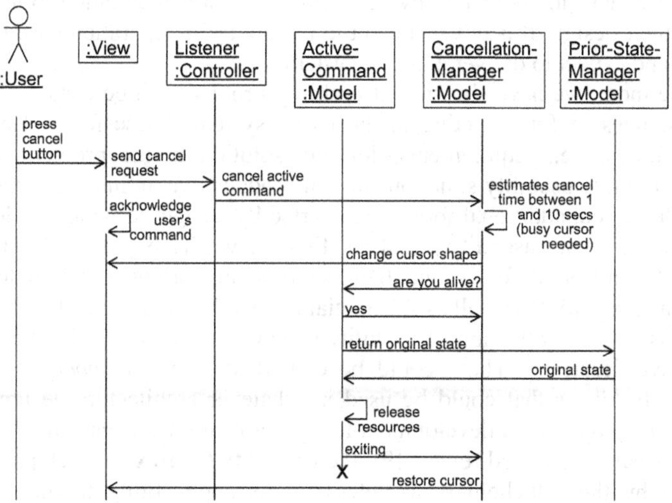

Fig. 6. Sequence diagram of canceling.

5. Experience with Usability-Supporting Architectural Patterns

We have presented the cancel example (although not this pattern of forces and their link to responsibilities) to professional audiences several times (e.g., [11]). After each presentation, audience members have told anecdotes about their experiences with implementing cancellation. One professional told us about the difficulty of adding cancel after initial implementation, confirming the utility of having a set of commonly encountered usability problems that can be considered early in design. Another professional told us that his company had included the ability to cancel from the beginning, but had not completely analyzed the necessary responsibilities and each cancellation request left 500MB of data on the disk. This anecdote confirms the utility of having a detailed checklist of general responsibilities that must be fulfilled with sufficient traceability and rationale to convince developers of their importance.

We have also applied a collection of about two dozen usability-supporting architectural patterns ([3,5], again, prior to our inclusion of forces) in several real-world development projects. As part of their normal software architecture reviews, development groups have considered such patterns as *Supporting Undo*, *Reusing Information, Working at the User's Pace, Forgotten Passwords, Operating Consistently across Views, Working in an Unfamiliar Context, Supporting International Use,* and several different types of *Feedback to the User*. Discussions of these scenarios and their associated architectural recommendations allowed these development groups to accommodate usability concerns early in the design process.

6. Conclusions

Our major conclusion is that software architects must pay attention to usability while creating their design. It is not sufficient to merely use a separation based pattern such as MVC and expect to deliver a usable system.

Furthermore, we have shown that usability problem can be considered in light of several sources of forces acting in the larger system. These forces lead to general responsibilities, i.e., requirements, for any solution to the problem. Because the solutions to these usability situations do not produce overarching patterns and yet are also not localized, additional forces are exerted by design decisions made prior to the consideration of the usability situation. Finally, we have proposed a template that captures the different forces and their sources and provides a two level solution (general and specific), as well as substantial traceability and rationale.

We visualize a collection of usability-supporting architectural patterns formatted as we have described. These could be embodied in a *Handbook of Usability for Software Architects* that could be used in whatever architecture design and review processes employed by a development team. For example, as part of an Architectural Tradeoff Analysis Method review [9], the **Usability Context** of each pattern could be examined by the stakeholders to determine its applicability to their project. The usability specialists and software architects could then work together to determine the risks associated with particular architecture decisions and whether the benefits of supporting the pattern in the context of that project exceed the costs. They could use the general responsibilities to verify that their adaptation of the specific solution satisfies all of the forces acting in their context. The raw material for the production of such a handbook is in place. About two dozen usability scenarios exist with explicit solutions, at different levels, documented by several research groups. Half a dozen of these have been augmented with forces and responsibilities using the template proposed here [4]. We believe that publication of such a handbook would make a significant contribution to improving the usability of fielded systems because the concept of forces resolved by responsibilities provides a traceability and rationale surpassing previous work.

References

1. Alexander, C., Ishikawa, S., and Silvernstein, M. *A Pattern Language*, Oxford University Press, New York, 1997.
2. Bass, L. and John, B. E. *Supporting the CANCEL Command Through Software Architecture*, CMU/SEI-2002-TN-021, Software Engineering Institute, Carnegie Mellon University, Pittsburgh, PA, 2002.
3. Bass, L. and John, B. E. "Linking Usability to Software Architecture Patterns through general scenarios", *Journal of System and Software*, 66, Elsevier, 2003, pp. 187-197.
4. Bass, L., John, B. E., Juristo, N., and Sanchez-Segura, M. Tutorial "Usability-Supporting Architectural Patterns" in *Proceedings of the 26th International Conference on Software Engineering*, IEEE Computer Society, May 23-28, 2004, Edinburgh, Scotland.
5. Bass, L., John, B. E. and Kates, J. Achieving Usability Through Software Architecture, CMU/SEI-TR-2001-005 Pittsburgh, PA: Software Engineering Institute, Carnegie Mellon University, (2001). Available for download at http://www.sei.cmu.edu/publications/documents/01.reports/01tr005.html
6. Bosch, J. and Juristo, N. Tutorial "Designing Software Architectures for Usability" in *Proceedings of the 25th International Conference on Software Engineering*, IEEE Computer Society, May 3-10, 2003, Portland, Oregon, USA.
7. Brown, A. B. and Patterson, D. A., "Undo for Operators: Building an Undoable E-mail Store" *Proceedings of the 2003 USENIX Annual Technical Conference*, San Antonio, TX, June 2003.
8. Buschmann, F., Meunier, R., Rohnert, H., Sommerlad, P., Stal, M., *Pattern-Oriented Software Architecture: A System Of Patterns*, Volume 1. John Wiley & Sons Ltd., New York, 1996.
9. Clements, P., Kazman, R., and Klein, M. *Evaluating Software Architectures: Methods and Case Studies.* Addison-Wesley, Reading. MA, 2001.
10. Gamma, E., Helm, R., Johnson, R., Vlissides, J., Design Patterns: Elements of Reusable Object-Oriented Software, Addison-Wesley, Reading, Massachusetts, 1995.
11. John, B. E. and Bass, L., Tutorial, "Avoiding "We can't change THAT!": Software Architecture and Usability" In Conference Companion of the ACM Conference on Computer-Human Interaction, 2002, 2003, 2004.
12. Sun Microsystems, Inc, "Java BluePrints, Model-View-Controller," September 2003, http://java.sun.com/blueprints/patterns/MVC-detailed.html. Copyright 2000-2003 Sun Microsystems. All rights reserved.

Discussion

[Michael Harrison] I'm not familiar with this work, so forgive the naive question. It sounds like you've got a generic notion of CANCEL and you're trying to situate that within a particular context and within a particular application. Is this correct?

> [Bonnie John] No, we're looking more at generic contingencies, conditions and forces. We're trying to say "if you look at your specific situation and these fit" then you have to take the architectural guidance into account.

[Tom Omerod] You raised the question of how you know when you're done producing one of these descriptions. For example, you've ended up with about twenty responsibilities for CANCEL alone. How do you know when you're done?

> [Bonnie John] We don't have a good answer for that question. In essence, we have to keep presenting the description to new audiences, and comparing it to new systems, and seeing if we get new insights. In the particular case of CANCEL, we've only added one responsibility in the last year so we think we may be close to done. However, the fact that there is no reliable way of telling whether you're done is quite disconcerting.

[Tom Ormerod] Maybe it would be better if you were exploring several issues in parallel, rather than just CANCEL.

> [Bonnie John] Yes, and we are. In fact we have documented six of these usability architectural issues, which is helping us to derive general patterns (as shown in the paper).

[Willem-Paul Brinkman] Does usability prescribe only one software architecture, or are only responsibilities mentioned? Because if there is only one right architectural solution, then you can simply start checking the architecture.

> [Bonnie John] No, absolutely not. This is why we particularly like having the forces and responsibilities in our descriptions --- they give insight into how to fit the solution into the rest of the system's architecture (which will necessarily vary based on many other concerns).

[Gerrit van der Veer] You are labelling parts of your solutions as patterns. This suggests that it is design knowledge that can be shared. Doesn't this imply that you need examples of each pattern, as well as counter-patterns, to provide the generic design knowledge? Is there an intention or effort to collect these (which is a huge effort)?

> [Bonnie John] Yes. We're working with Dick Gabriel at Sun, president of Hillside Group, to get better integrated with the patterns community. With the community's help we're hoping to make a collective effort to document both these kinds of patterns.

[Jurgen Ziegler] Developers may get overwhelmed with the large number of requirements, particularly since there are also many more requirements that are not usability-related. Wouldn't it help to show developers different examples of architectures that fulfil your requirements to different degrees?

> [Bonnie John] Yes, absolutely. For example, one thing we're doing is keeping track of products that don't do cancel correctly or completely, and how. We haven't documented all of these yet.

[Nick Graham] In designing an architecture you have two basic options --- either attempt to anticipate all cases, or make the architecture sufficiently resilient to change that it is possible to modify afterwards. In the first case you may end up with an architecture that's bloated by features that may never be used. In the second, you seem to be back with the original "you can't change that" problem. Where does your approach really fit in?

[Bonnie John] We use risk assessment techniques to assess which requirements are really likely to come up. Since these requirements aren't core to the system function (in some sense they're peripheral) we're hoping that with these checklists people can consider stuff like this early in the process. We're not trying to anticipate everything, but rather things that we know get left out. The kinds of things we're considering are general problems that recur frequently and that reach deep into the architecture.

[Michael Harrison] Have you looked at whether people are actually helped by the forces and responsibilities?

[Bonnie John] We've done one really in-depth project with this approach using a Mars Rover control board with NASA. They say that the architectural suggestions helped them, but now we're looking at the actual code and the user performance data that NASA collected to get a view beyond their subjective evaluation. (However, this was before we had the forces and responsibilities directly in our model.) We're also doing similar things with some of our tutorial participants. The data is sparse so far. We're conducting a controlled experiment to answer this question which we hope to report on at ICSE and/or CHI 2005.

Empirical Usability Testing in a Component-Based Environment: Improving Test Efficiency with Component-Specific Usability Measures

Willem-Paul Brinkman[1], Reinder Haakma[2], and Don G. Bouwhuis[3]

[1] Brunel University, Uxbridge, Middlesex, UB8 3PH
United Kingdom
Willem.Brinkman@Brunel.ac.uk
[2] Philips Research Laboratories Eindhoven, Prof. Holstlaan 4,
5656 AA Eindhoven, The Netherlands
Reinder.Haakma@Philips.com
[3] Technische Universiteit Eindhoven, P.O. Box 513,
5600 MB Eindhoven, The Netherlands
D.G.Bouwhuis@tue.nl

Abstract. This paper addresses the issue of usability testing in a component-based software engineering environment, specifically measuring the usability of different versions of a component in a more powerful manner than other, more holistic, usability methods. Three component-specific usability measures are presented: an objective performance measure, a perceived ease-of-use measure, and a satisfaction measure. The objective performance measure is derived from the message exchange between components recorded in a log file, whereas the other measures are obtained through a questionnaire. The power of the measures was studied in an experimental setting. Eight different prototypes of a mobile telephone were subjected to usability tests, in which 80 subjects participated. Analyses of the statistical power of these measures show that the component-specific performance measure can be more powerful than overall usability measures, which means fewer users are needed in a test.

1 Introduction

Instead of building an application from scratch, Component-Based Software Engineering (CBSE) focuses on building artefacts from ready-made or self-made components (e.g. pop-up menus, radio buttons, or more complex components such as a spell checker or an email component). Current empirical usability measures do not correspond well with this engineering approach. They do not measure the usability of the individual component, but only its impact on the overall usability (e.g. number of keystrokes, task duration, or questions about the overall ease of use and satisfaction). This indirect way of measuring the usability of a component means that many participants are needed in a usability test. We argue here that component-specific usability measures can be more effective in measuring the usability of an individual component, as they are more focused and therefore require fewer participants in a

R. Bastide, P. Palanque, and J. Roth (Eds.): EHCI-DSVIS 2004, LNCS 3425, pp. 20-37, 2005.

usability test. Several authors [9, 19] have suggested that component-specific usability testing might be feasible. They argue that a component can be regarded as an interactive system in its own right with its capacity of receiving input messages, providing users with feedback, and having its own internal state.

In this paper we present a usability testing method that can be used to compare different versions of a component on their usability. The method consists of three component-specific usability measures: an objective performance measure, a perceived ease-of-use measure, and a satisfaction measure. Before describing the testing method, the following section gives an overview of the general characteristics of component architectures on which this method can be applied. After describing the method, an experimental evaluation will be presented, in which the statistical power of the component-specific measures is examined. This section is followed by a discussion of the limitations of the method and its relationship with other empirical usability evaluation methods.

2 Component-Based Interactive Systems

The following three subsections introduce the concepts: control loop, interaction component, and layer. With these concepts it is possible to identify interactive system architectures on which the testing method can be applied, such as the Model-View-Controller (MVC) model [13], PAC (Presentation, Abstraction, Control) model [5] and in particular the CNUCE agent model [17]. The generic architecture described here is based on the ideas of the Layered Protocol Theory [19], which decomposes the user-system interaction into different layers that can be designed and analysed separately.

2.1 Control Loop

Central concepts in the Layered Protocol Theory are the control loop and the accumulation of these control loops. The concept of control loop explains how interaction between users and a system progresses. Interaction is regarded as an exchange of messages between users and the system. Users send messages to the system to change its state. The system sends messages to inform the users about its state. This forms the basis of a negative feedback loop where users compare the received system feedback with their internal mental representation of the state they want the system to be in, the so-called *reference value*. If the reference value and system feedback are not similar, the users may decide to send a message to the system in an attempt to get it in the desired state. When the system receives the users' message, it acts on it, and sends feedback to the users to inform them of the outcome, which again triggers another cycle of the control loop. Once the system is in the desired state, the need for sending messages stops. Therefore, the number of messages sent by the users presents the effort users have made to control the system as each user message indicates a cycle of the loop.

2.2 Architectural Elements

Interaction components define the elementary units of interactive systems, on which behaviour-based evaluation is possible. An *interaction component* is a unit within an application that can be represented as a finite state machine which directly, or indirectly via other components, receives signals from the user. These signals enable the user to change the state of the interaction component. Furthermore, the user must be able to perceive or to infer the state of the interaction component. Therefore, an interaction component should provide feedback. Without the possibility of perceiving the state, the users' behaviour is aimless. Next, it should have a changeable state. A minute label of a radio alarm clock button is not an interaction component on its own because users cannot change it. A behaviour-based measurement of the quality of this label can only be made as part of an interaction component responsible for the minute digits, whose state users can control.

Fig. 1. Front of a radio alarm clock.

The points where input and output of different interaction components are connected demarcate the border between layers. An interaction component operates on a higher-level layer than another interaction component, when the higher-level interaction component receives its user messages from the other interaction component.

Figure 2 illustrates how these concepts can be used to describe a part of the architecture of a radio alarm clock. The three interaction components on the lowest-level layer are responsible for the time (Clock), the selection of the radio stations (Radio Station), and the volume of the sound (Volume). These interaction components receive messages from the users and they send their feedback via the Display component or in case of the Volume component also via the Speaker. Besides sending messages to users as part of their individual control loop, the Clock and Radio Station interaction components also send messages upwards to the higher-level Radio Receiver interaction component. This component fulfils its responsibility in its control loop by sending feedback to the users via the Speak component.

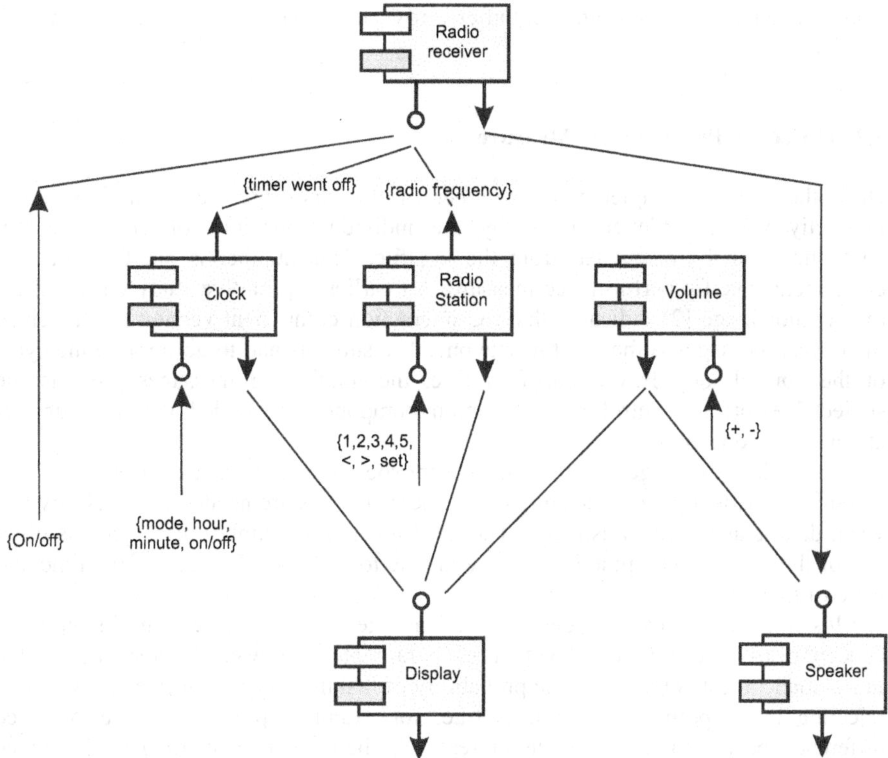

Fig. 2. Compositional structure of a radio alarm clock. The boxes represent components and the arrows the flow of the message exchange between the components.

3 Testing Method

The testing method presented here can be used to test the relative usability difference between two or more versions of a component while the other parts of the system remain the same, e.g. two similar radio alarm clocks that only differ on the implementation of the Radio Station component.

3.1 Test Procedure

The test procedure of the method roughly corresponds to the normal procedure of a usability test. Subjects are observed while they perform the same task with different versions of a system. The task is finished once subjects attain a specific goal that would require them to alter the state of the interaction component under investigation. In advance, subjects should be instructed to act as quickly as possible to accomplish the given goal. As subjects perform the task, messages sent to the interaction component are recorded in a log file. Once the subjects reach the goal, the recording stops, since new user messages sent afterwards will probably be sent with a new goal in mind.

3.2 Objective Performance Measure

Once the task is completed, the number of user messages received directly, or indirectly via lower-level layers, by the individual versions of the interaction component can be calculated from the log file. This number is put forward as a component-specific performance measure. An earlier explorative study on the affect of foreknowledge [2] indicated that the interaction component version that received the fewest messages is the most usable one. The subjects had to go through the cycle of the control loop less often. Therefore, the number of messages presents the subjects' effort to control the interaction component, provided that the subjects attained only one goal.

The main advantage of the component-specific performance measure is its potential statistical power, meaning that far less subjects are needed in a usability test when data is analysed statistically. The need for a large number of subjects is often one of the reasons why practitioners are unable to run a test because of the time and the cost involved.

Most statistical books that describe statistical testing methods explain in depth the concept of p-values but only devote a few paragraphs on power. Whereas the p-value in a statistical test is related to the probability of making a type I, or α, error (wrongly rejecting the hypothesis when it is true; for example, predicting a performance difference based on a test while in real life there is no performance difference between two versions of a component) the power of a test is related to a type II, or β, error (failing to reject the hypothesis when it is false). Consider the two distributions in the upper part of Figure 3. The shaded region to the left of the rejection boundary presents the likelihood of making a type β error. The unshaded region on the right of the boundary presents the statistical power of the test, defined as $1- \beta$. In the context of a usability test the power presents the probability of finding a difference between two versions of a component provided there is a difference. A traditional way of increasing the power is by increasing the number of subjects in a test; making the prediction of the distribution more reliable. Another way, however, is to increase the precision of the measuring; making the measure more robust against outside interfering factors, such as possible usability problems the subjects may or may not encounter with other components in the system while completing a task. For parametric statistical tests (e.g. t-test, or F-test) this means reducing the variance of the sample distribution. Reducing the variance, or in other words making the sample distribution more compact, will also reduce the p-value in a statistical test, because the contrast between the two sample groups becomes clearer.

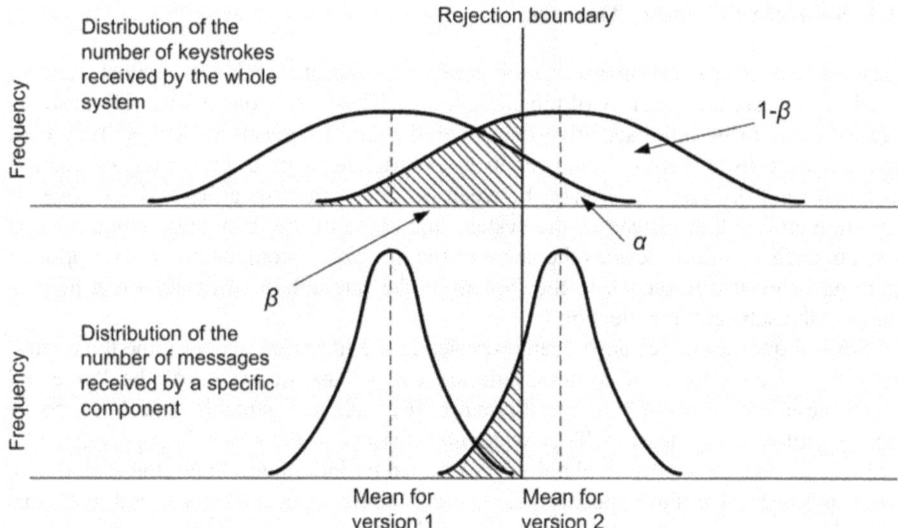

Fig. 3. Performance comparison of two systems implemented with different versions of a component. The variation in the number of keystrokes is larger than the variation in the number of user messages received by the component under investigation, because the first also includes variations caused when users interact with other components, whereas the latter only focuses on the interaction with the relevant component.

The number of user messages a component received directly, or indirectly via lower-level layers, can be a more powerful measure than an overall measure, such as the number of keystrokes, as its variance is smaller. The number of messages received by a component is less likely to be affected by problems located in other parts of the system, whereas overall measures are. In the example with the radio alarm clock, the likelihood that the Radio Station component will receive some extra messages because some subjects have a problem with understanding the Clock component is lower than the likelihood that these subjects make some additional key presses in general. The additional variance, created as subjects try to control other interaction components, is left out in the component-specific measure because of its specific focus. This variance reduction can be apparent in the analysis of lower-level interaction components, but this can apply to higher-level interaction components as well. A low-level message does not always lead to a high-level message. For example, users can still undo a wrong time setting, before the Clock component sends a < *timer went off* > message upwards. Measuring the number of high-level messages will be less affected by variations between subjects interacting with lower-level components. Therefore, the effect of replacing a high-level interaction component with another version can be more obvious in the number of high-level messages than in the number of keystrokes.

The main advantage of making a test more powerful is that fewer samples (subjects) are needed to detect a difference (if there is any) with the same reliability (p-value). Fewer samples are needed because the likelihood of a type β error is smaller. The lower part of Figure 3 illustrates this point. The shaded region left of the rejection boundary is smaller when samples are more concentrated.

3.3 Subjective Usability Measures

Besides the performance measures, the perceived usability, scaled by subjects, can be used to evaluate the usability of the components. These component-specific questions are expected to be more sensitive than overall usability questions because they help the subjects to remember their control experience with a particular interaction component [4]. The difference between a component-specific and an overall questionnaire is that instead of the system, the name of the interaction component is used in each question. Besides the name of the interaction component, a description, a picture, or even a reference in the system of the interaction component can help to support the subjects' recollection.

Several questionnaires have been proposed in the literature to determine the overall usability of an interactive system. The six ease-of-use questions of the Perceived Usefulness and Ease-of-Use questionnaire [6] seems a suitable small set for a component-specific measure. They make no reference to the system's appearance and are able to capture well-formed beliefs developed by individuals about the ease-of-use after only a brief initial exposure [8]. The component-specific satisfaction questions are taken from the Post-Study System Usability Questionnaire [15], one about how pleasant an interaction component was, and one about how much subjects liked an interaction component. Both the ease-of-use and satisfaction questions use a 7 points answer scale.

4 Experimental Evaluation of the Testing Method

An experiment was conducted to study the method and to test the statistical power of the proposed component-specific measures. The experiment compared prototypes with variations in their usability. The use of predefined usability variations had to emphasise the validity of the usability measures. By seeding *known* usability problems into the prototypes, this experimental set-up ensured that the testing method would identify actual usability problems, and limit uncertainty about whether the measuring had anything to do with usability. In this experiment, all usability variations addressed the complexity of dialogue structures that can be understood in terms of the Cognitive Complexity Theory (CCT) [12]. This theory holds that the cognitive complexity increases when users have to learn more rules.

4.1 Prototypes

A mobile telephone was chosen for the experiment because of its relatively complex system architecture. Furthermore, some of the mobile telephones' interaction components are receptive to well-known and well-documented usability problems. Three interaction components of a mobile telephone were manipulated (printed in bold type in Figure 4). The three interaction components were responsible for the way subjects could input alphabetic characters (Keypad), activate functions in the telephone (Function Selector), and send text messages (Send Text Message).

For each of these three interaction components two versions were designed. In one version of the Function Selector (FS), the menu was relatively broad but shallow, i.e. all eight options available within one stratum. In the other version, the menu was relatively narrow but deep, i.e. a binary tree of three strata. Users tend to be faster and make fewer errors in finding a target in broad menus than in deep menus [18]. In terms of CCT, the deep menu structure requires the subjects to learn more rules to make the correct choices when going through the deep menu structure. In the more usable version of the Send Text Message (STM) component, the component guided the subjects through the required steps. The less usable version left the sequence of steps up to the subjects. All these steps were options presented as icons, which forced the subjects to learn the icon-option mapping rules. Furthermore, they also had to learn in which order to choose the options.

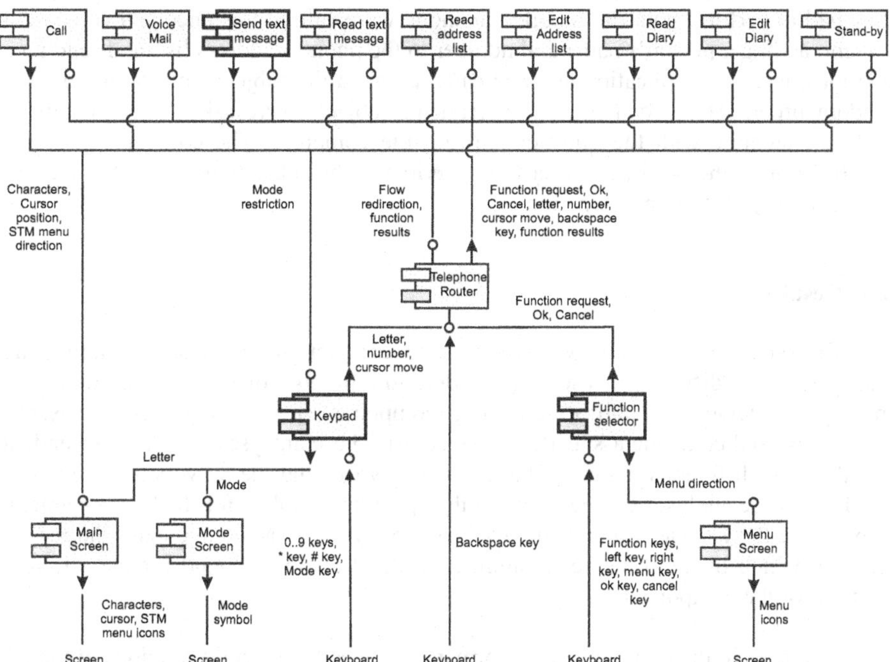

Fig. 4. The architecture of the Mobile telephones (bold interaction components were manipulated in the experiment).

Finally, to enter letters, one keypad version used the Repeated-Key method, and the other version a Modified-Model-Position method. The first is easier to use, because the subjects had to learn one simple rule [7]. It involved having the subjects press the key, containing the letter, the number of times corresponding to its ordinal position on the key (e.g. one time on the "GHI" key for "G"). The other method involved having subjects first press either "*" or "#" key, depending on whether the letter was in the left or right position on the button label and nothing when the letter was in the middle.

This was followed by a press on the key containing the letter (e.g. "*" followed by "GHI" for "G").

Combining these versions led to eight different mobile telephone prototypes. The experimental environment was programmed in Delphi 5, and included PC prototypes of the eight mobile telephones, a recording mechanism to capture the message exchange between the interaction components, and automatic procedure to administer the questionnaire.

4.2 Procedure and Subjects

All 80 participating subjects were students of Technische Universiteit Eindhoven. None of them used a mobile telephone on a daily or weekly basis[1]. The kinds of tasks they had to perform with the mobile telephone were calling to someone's voice-mail system; adding a person's name and number to the phone's address list; and sending a text message. The application automatically assigned the subjects to a prototype in a random order. At the end of the experiment, subjects were asked to evaluate the mobile telephone with the questionnaire on the computer. The computer gave the questions in a random order. After the experiment, the subjects received NLG 22.50 (roughly €10) for their participation.

4.3 Results

The first step in the analysis phase was to conduct multivariate and univariate analyses on the different measures (task duration, number of keystrokes, number of messages received, overall ease-of-use, component-specific ease-of-use, overall satisfaction and component-specific satisfaction). These analyses took as independent variables the different versions of the FS, the Keypad, and the STM component. The results of these analyses can be found in the appendix: Table 3 for the FS component, Table 4 for the Keypad component, and Table 5 for the STM component. The results show in which of the measures a significant effect could be found for the different versions of the component.

Differences in the optimal task performance existed between the versions of the FS and STM component. To compensate for these a priori differences, extra multivariate analyses were performed on the corrected[2] number of keystrokes and messages received measures for the FS and STM component. The results of the analyses can be found in the lower part of Table 3 and Table 5. Unfortunately, no direct way existed to correct the other measures. Still, the corrected keystrokes measure seems an appropriate indicator of how a corrected measure of the task duration would perform; as the time to complete a task was highly correlated (0.91) with the number of keystrokes.

---

[1] The experiment was conducted in the autumn of 2000, when a large group of students did not own or use a mobile telephone on a regular basis.

[2] Any additional number of keystrokes or number of messages received created by differences in the optimal task performance between prototypes was subtracted from these samples.

In the second step of the analysis phase, the focus was on the statistical power of the various measures. Because of the relative large sample size (80 subjects), the tests on several measures had a statistical power that approximates to 1. If the experiment were to be repeated, it is almost certain that a significant effect would be found again in these measures. Therefore, a post-hoc power analysis was conducted to calculate the likelihood that a significant difference was found if fewer subjects had participated in the experiment. Various sample sizes were entered in G*Power, a general power analysis program, with the effect size ($\eta^2/(1-\eta^2)$) obtained from Tables 3, 4 and 5.

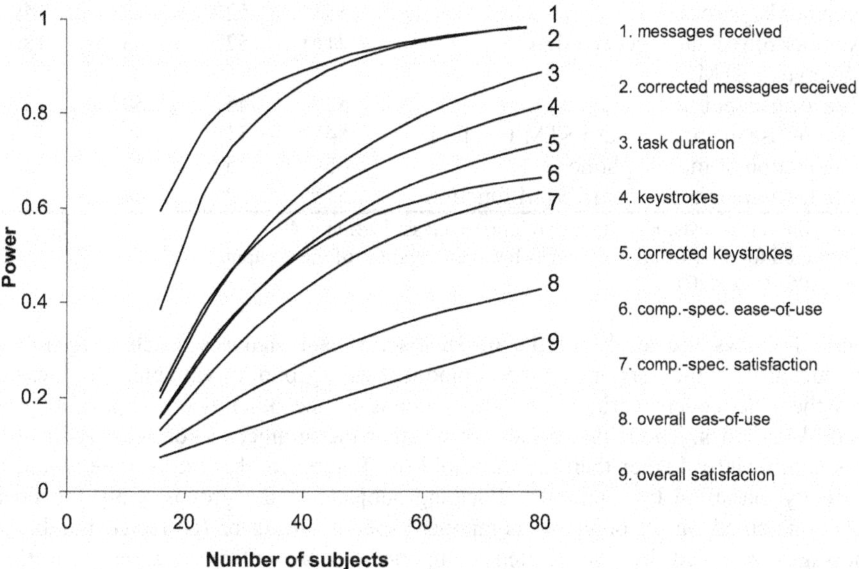

Fig. 5. Average probability that a measure finds a significant ($\alpha = 0.05$) effect for the usability difference between the two versions of FS, STM, or the Keypad components.

Figure 5 presents the statistical power of the different measures averaged over the tests of the three components. The number of messages received was more powerful than the overall objective performance measures such as task duration and the number of keystrokes. For example, if this experiment was set out to find a significant difference with a 60% chance of detecting it, using the number of messages received as a measure would require 16 subjects, whereas the task duration or the number of keystrokes would require 40 subjects —a reduction of 60%.

The effectiveness of the objective component-specific measure is also confirmed by discriminant analyses on the measures. A discriminant analysis does the opposite from what an analysis of variance does. It takes a measure and analyses how well it can predict to which prototype a subject was assigned in the experiment. For each measure per component, a discriminant analysis fitted a linear function that gave the highest number of correct classifications. The function classified the 80 subjects into two groups, one for each version of the component. Although the fitted parameters of the linear functions are less relevant in this context, the number of correct classifications shows how useful a measure is to discriminate between two versions of a component. In other words, how useful would a measure be in discriminating between low and high usability?

Table 1. Number of correctly classified subjects out of a total of 80 subjects calculated by 18 discriminant analyses. The analyses took the versions of the component as the grouping variable.

Type of Measure	Grouping Variable			Total
	FS	Keypad	STM	
Number keystrokes[a]	55**	52*	42	149
Number of messages received by FS/keypad/STM[a]	71**	52*	63**	186
Ease of use mobile phone	52*	45	50*	147
Ease of use menu/keyboard/STM function	54**	51*	40	145
Satisfaction of mobile phone	45	45	48	138
Satisfaction menu/keyboard/STM function	51*	52*	44	147

Note. Binominal tests, H_0: Number of correct classification = 40.
[a] Corrected for all a-priori differences between versions of the components.
* *p*. < .05. ** *p*. < .01

Table 1 shows the results of the of 18 discriminant analyses. Each analysis was conducted with the versions of the component as a grouping variable. The measure was the independent variable and the versions of the other two components were control variables. The table also shows whether the number of correct classification was significantly higher than the threshold of 40 subjects that on average would be correctly classified by randomly allocating subjects to the groups. Only the linear functions fitted on an objective component-specific measure (corrected number of messages received by the related component) were effective across the three components.

Table 2 shows the results of comparisons on the effectiveness, across the three components, between functions fitted on overall and component-specific measures when it comes to classifying subjects. These comparisons were done on six new variables, two for each type of measure: an overall and component-specific one. A score was assigned to these variables according to the number of times an individual subject was correctly classified. For each subject, the score ranged from zero to three: a zero for no correct classification, a one for one correct classification, a two for two correct classifications, and a three if the versions of all the three components were correctly predicted.

The analyses on the corrected number of keystrokes revealed that 62% (149/240) of the classifications for the versions were correct. This was significantly lower than the 78% correct classifications by functions fitted on the corrected number of messages received. Again, to put the percentage into perspective, note that random allocation would on average link 50% of the subjects with the correct version of the component they had interacted with. Therefore, the relative effectiveness improvement is 32% ((0.78-0.62)/(1-0.5)).

The post-hoc power analysis (Figure 5) indicated that the subjective component-specific ease-of-use and satisfaction measures were on average more powerful than the subjective overall measures. However, the comparison between the results of the discriminant analyses revealed no significant difference in the number of correct classifications. Looking at Table 1, it seems that the subjective component-specific measures were only ineffective in the case of the higher-level STM component. An unclear reference to this component in the questions might have caused this.

Table 2. Results of Wilcoxon Matched-Pairs Signed-Ranks Tests between the number of correct classification made by discriminant analyses on overall and component-specific measures.

	Correctly classified				
Type of Measure	Overall	Component-Specific	*N*	*T*	*p*
Observed performance	62%	78%	37	3	<0.001
Perceived ease-of-use	61%	60%	62	30	0.907
Perceived satisfaction	58%	61%	61	27	0.308

5 Discussion

To summarize the results, both the power analyses and the discriminant analyses seem to suggest that the objective components-specific measure was more effective than overall measures such as the number of keystrokes. The power analyses also seem to suggest that the subjective component-specific measures were more effective than their overall counterparts. However, the discriminant analyses did not reveal a difference for the subjective measures.

5.1 Limitations

The testing method assumes that the users have to spend the same amount of effort each time they send a message on the level of the interaction component. When high-level interaction components are tested, this assumption is reasonable between the two versions, because the mediating low-level interaction components are the same. However, when the lowest-level interaction components are tested, more attention should be given to this point, as the effort may not be similar. A possible way to solve this problem is by assigning individual weighting factors to the messages [3].

The total number of keystrokes could be more powerful than the component-specific measure when the usability variation of one interaction component influences the number of messages received by another interaction component. This can be caused by three factors: the user, the environment, and the system architecture. For instance, in the mobile telephones equipped with the Modified-Modal-Position method, higher-level String components embedded in the STM and the Edit Address List component (Figure 4) received unintended letters, which the subjects also had to delete. An analysis of variance on the number of backspace messages showed this measure as even more powerful than the number of messages received by the Keypad component [2].

A more practical limitation is the assumption that instrumentation code can be inserted in the software to record the message exchange, which may not always be possible. Fortunately, software tools are being developed to cope with that. For example, the iGuess tool [16] automatically inserts recording code into a Java application without any need for access to the source code.

5.2 Other Empirical Evaluation Methods

Unit Testing. Focussing on the usability of a single component is not new. One of the first usability testing papers presented at the first SIGCHI conference [1] focused on specific components of the Xerox's 8010 "Star" office workstation, such as text selection, icon recognition and the selection of graphic objects. In these kinds of so-called *unit tests*, users are asked only to perform a very limited task that requires interaction with a particular component such as selecting text. For lower-level components this is a powerful testing strategy, since it reduces the variation in the data otherwise caused by the interaction with other components. The drawback is the limited nature of these tasks, as users are not asked to perform the task in the context of a larger, everyday task, such as writing a letter. It assumes that the usability of the lower-level component will not be influenced by other components. However, factors like memory load or inconsistency can create relations between the components that influence the task performance [2]. Instead, applying component-specific usability measures, which presumably are equally powerful, means that users can be asked to perform complex tasks.

Sequential Data Analysis. Often, in sequential data analysis, only lower-level events are recorded, which are first pre-processed into more abstract events before they are analysed. However, these compound messages leave more room for discussion about the system interpretation of the lower-level messages and therefore lack a direct relation with the higher-level components. Extending the low-level messages log file with the system's state makes it possible to construct the system interpretation of lower-level into higher-level messages. Still, it would require the analysis to envision the system response to a low-level message when the system is in a particular state. An example of such an approach can be found in the work of Lecerof and Paternò [14].

Not Event-Based Usability Evaluations. Other usability evaluation methods, such as thinking-aloud, cognitive walkthrough, and heuristic evaluations may in some cases be quicker in assessing the usability of an entire user interface. However, they suffer from a substantial evaluator effect in that multiple evaluators end up with different conclusions when evaluating the same user interface [10]. Usability measures that can be applied automatically leave very little room for such an effect.

Furthermore, current usability evaluation methods have also received criticism for their ineffectiveness in finding real problems that lead to changes in a new version of a system [11]. The introduction of component-specific usability measures may help to overcome this as they lead designers unambiguously to the part that should be changed.

5.3 Exploitation of the Testing Method

In CBSE the creation and the deployment of a component are two independent processes separated over time. In both processes, designers can conduct usability tests and apply the component-specific testing method described in this paper. Identifying and dealing with usability problems in the creation process has the advantage that they do not have to be dealt with each time the component is deployed in a new application. Testing the component in the creation process may require developing a test bed as an actual application might not be available or even unknown when developing a general component library for a specific development environment.

Usability testing once the application is assembled is also needed because only then will it be possible to study the component in the context of the other components. If only *one* version of each component is considered and the aim is to compare the usability of the different components in a single application, the component-specific subjective measures can still be useful. The component-specific performance measure, however, cannot be applied directly since user effort to create messages on different layers may not be the same. A combination of adding weight factors to the messages and correcting for inefficiencies of the user's interaction with higher and lower components has been suggested [3] as a possible solution in that case.

6 Conclusions and Final Remarks

The current study confirms the possibility of testing the usability of individual components, which can be applied in a CBSE environment. The direct benefit of the method seems the statistical power of the component-specific measures. Usability testing of individual components opens the door for sets of usable and re-usable components. Applying these components will increase the chance that the final system will also be usable. However, it will not guarantee this. Components can have an impact on each other's usability [2]. More research is needed to understand how and when outside factors affect the usability of a component, and how system developers should deal with this. Furthermore, the testing method also has the potential for usability testing outside the laboratory. However, the component-specific performance measure will need to be re-examined because now the evaluator sets the users' goal, which is inappropriate in normal field tests.

References

1. Bewley, W., Roberts, T.L., Schroit, D., Verplank, W.L.: Human factors testing in the design of Xeror's 8010 "Star" Office workstation. Proceedings of CHI'83. ACM Press, New York, NY (1983) 72-77

2. Brinkman, W.-P. Is usability compositional? Doctoral dissertation. Technische Universiteit Eindhoven, The Netherlands (2003)
3. Brinkman, W.-P., Haakma, R., Bouwhuis, D.G.: Usability testing of interaction components: Taking the message exchange as a measure of usability. In Jacob, R.J.K., Limbourg, Q., Vanderdonckt, J. (eds.): Pre-Proceedings of CADUI'2004. Kluwer Academics, Dordrecht, The Netherlands (2004) 159-170
4. Coleman, W.D., Williges, R.C., Wixon, D.R.: Collecting detailed user evaluations of software interfaces. In Swezey, R.W., Post, T.J., Strother, L.B. (eds.): Proceedings of the Human Factors Society - 29th Annual Meeting. Human Factors Society, Santa Monica, CA (1985) 240-244
5. Coutaz, J.: PAC, an object oriented model for dialog design. In Bullinger, H.-J., Shackel, B. (eds.): INTERACT'87. North-Holland, Amsterdam (1987) 431-436
6. Davis, F.D.: Perceived usefulness, perceived ease of use, and user acceptance of information technology. MIS Quarterly 13 (1989) 319-340
7. Detweiler, M.C., Schumacher, M.C., Gattuso, N.: Alphabetic input on a telephone keypad. In Proceedings of the Human Factors Society 34th Annual Meeting. Human Factors Society, Santa Monica, CA (1990) 212–216
8. Doll, W.J., Hendrickson, A., Deng, X.: Using Davis's perceived usefulness and ease-of-use instruments for decision making: A confirmatory and multigroup invariance analysis. Decision Sciences 29 (1998) 839–869
9. Haakma, R.: Layered feedback in user-system interaction. Doctoral dissertation. Technische Universiteit Eindhoven, The Netherlands (1998)
10. Hertzum, M., Jacobsen, N.E.: The evaluator effect: A chilling fact about usability evaluation methods. Int. J. of Human-Computer Interaction 13 (2001) 421–443
11. John, B.E., Marks, S.J.: Tracking the effectiveness of usability evaluation methods. Behaviour and Information Technology 16 (1997) 188-202
12. Kieras, D., Polson, P.G.: An approach to the formal analysis of user complexity. Int. J. of Man-Machine Studies 22 (1985) 365-394
13. Krasner, G.E., Pope, S.T.: A cookbook for using the Model-View-Controller user interface paradigm in Smalltask-80. Journal of object-oriented programming 1 (1988) 27-49
14. Lecerof, A., Paternò, F.: Automatic support for usability evaluation. IEEE Transactions on Software Engineering 24 (1998) 863–888
15. Lewis, J.R.: IBM computer usability satisfaction questionnaires: Psychometric evaluation and instructions for use. Int. J. of Human-Computer Interaction 7 (1995) 57-78
16. McLeod, I., Evans, H., Gray, P., Mancy, R.: Instrumenting bytecode for the production of usage data. In Jacob, R.J.K., Limbourg, Q., Vanderdonckt, J. (eds.): Pre-Proceedings of CADUI'2004. Kluwer Academics, Dordrecht, The Netherlands (2004) 185-196
17. Paternò, F.: Model-based design and evaluation of interactive applications. Springer, London (2000)
18. Snowberry, K., Parkinson, S.R., Sisson, N.: Computer display menu. Ergonomics 26 (1983) 699-712
19. Taylor, M.M.: Layered protocols for computer-human dialogue. I: Principles. Int. J. of Man-Machine Studies 28 (1988) 175-218

Appendix: Results of Multivariate and Univariate Analyses of Variance

Table 3. Results of two multivariate analyses and related univariate analyses of variance with the version of the Function Selector as independent between-subjects variable.

	Mean		*df*				
Measure	Broad	Deep	Hyp.	Er.	*F*	*p*	η^2
Normal							
Joint measure	—	—	7	66	34.47	<0.001	0.80
Time in seconds	947	1394	1	72	29.56	<0.001	0.29
Number of keystrokes	461	686	1	72	37.72	<0.001	0.34
Number of messages received	67	265	1	72	155.34	<0.001	0.68
Ease of use mobile phone	5.5	4.8	1	72	11.86	0.001	0.14
Ease of use menu	5.6	4.5	1	72	22.33	<0.001	0.24
Satisfaction of mobile phone	4.4	3.8	1	72	4.25	0.043	0.06
Satisfaction of menu	4.6	3.5	1	72	15.96	<0.001	0.18
Corrected[a]							
Joint measure	—	—	2	71	60.96	<0.001	0.63
Number of keystrokes	437	602	1	72	20.27	<0.001	0.22
Number of messages received	52	190	1	72	75.36	<0.001	0.51

[a]Corrected for all a-priori differences between versions of the components.

Table 4. Results of multivariate and related univariate analyses of variance with the version of the Keypad as independent between-subjects variable.

	Mean		*df*				
Measure	RK	MMP	Hyp.	Er.	*F*	*p*	η^2
Normal							
Joint measure	—	—	7	66	4.05	0.001	0.30
Time in seconds	872	1083	1	72	9.44	0.003	0.12
Number of keystrokes	438	537	1	72	10.34	0.002	0.13
Number of messages received	233	271	1	72	13.92	<0.001	0.16
Ease of use mobile phone	5.3	5.0	1	72	1.07	0.305	0.02
Ease of use keyboard	5.6	4.9	1	72	11.13	0.001	0.13
Satisfaction of mobile phone	4.3	3.9	1	72	1.76	0.188	0.02
Satisfaction of keyboard	4.6	3.8	1	72	8.97	0.004	0.11

Note. RK: Repeat-Key, MMP: Modified-Model-Position. Analyses on corrected measures are not presented since these are practically the same.

Table 5. Results of two multivariate analyses and related univariate analyses of variance with the version of the STM component as independent between-subjects variable.

Measure	Mean		*df*		F	p	η^2
	Simple	Complex	Hyp.	Er.			
Normal							
Joint measure	—	—	7	66	18.16	<0.001	0.66
Time in seconds	523	672	1	72	8.15	0.006	0.10
Number of keystrokes	269	320	1	72	4.56	0.036	0.06
Number of messages received	12	49	1	72	74.18	<0.001	0.51
Ease of use mobile phone	5.0	5.3	1	72	1.15	0.288	0.02
Ease of use STM function	5.1	4.9	1	72	0.35	0.555	0.01
Satisfaction of mobile phone	3.9	4.2	1	72	0.93	0.339	0.01
Satisfaction of STM function	3.9	3.8	1	72	0.26	0.614	0.01
Corrected[a]							
Joint measure	—	—	2	71	20.85	<0.001	0.37
Number of keystrokes	249	289	1	72	2.30	0.134	0.03
Number of messages received	12	34	1	72	26.23	<0.001	0.27

[a]Corrected for all a-priori differences between versions of the components.

Discussion

[Claus Unger] If you have a set of component-specific measures in a system and then decide to change your architecture, how can you move the measures across?

> [Willem-Paul Brinkman] The assumption in this method is that we're only varying one component at a time. However if you want to compare components across very different architectures that's a much more difficult problem. We don't address that with our method.

[Nick Graham] The measure that you're using is the number of messages going back and forth. Wouldn't that tend to say that, for example, the vi editor is more usable than MS Notepad. For example, in vi you can use a regular expression to make many changes, whereas in Notepad you'd have to do each one manually.

> [Willem-Paul Brinkman] The measures are based on participants really performing tasks. A user who does not know vi might generate 1000 messages before they figure out how to make the change. In related areas, we're also looking at assigning different weights to different kinds of messages in the system.

[Bonnie John] A lot of usability errors seem to lie at component boundaries. Your method doesn't seem to address that.

[Willem-Paul Brinkman] If there is a component that bridges between others, then you can analyse it there. However, if the bridge is made in the user's mind then overall measures rather than component-specific measures will be better. However, if there are mismatches between components, or one of the components is occupying all the user's attention, then the method won't necessarily find these errors.

[Bonnie John] I'm not sure that the questionnaires will allow people to give you valid data. What is your feeling?

[Willem-Paul Brinkman] The questionnaires are difficult to apply, and in fact we frequently see issues with vocabulary mismatch where the users don't reliably understand which component we're talking about in the questions.

Software Architecture Analysis of Usability

Eelke Folmer, Jilles van Gurp, Jan Bosch

University of Groningen, the Netherlands
mail@eelke.com, jilles@jillesvangurp.com, Jan.Bosch@cs.rug.nl

Abstract. Studies of software engineering projects show that a large number of usability related change requests are made after its deployment. Fixing usability problems during the later stages of development often proves to be costly, since many of the necessary changes require changes to the system that cannot be easily accommodated by its software architecture. These high costs prevent developers from meeting all the usability requirements, resulting in systems with less than optimal usability. The successful development of a usable software system therefore must include creating a software architecture that supports the right level of usability. Unfortunately, no documented evidence exists of architecture level assessment techniques focusing on usability. To support software architects in creating a software architecture that supports usability, we present a scenario based assessment technique that has been successfully applied in several cases. Explicit evaluation of usability during architectural design may reduce the risk of building a system that fails to meet its usability requirements and may prevent high costs incurring adaptive maintenance activities once the system has been implemented.

1 Introduction

One of the key problems with many of today's software is that they do not meet their quality requirements very well. In addition, it often proves hard to make the necessary changes to a system to improve its quality. A reason for this is that many of the necessary changes require changes to the system that cannot be easily accommodated by the software architecture [4] The software architecture, the fundamental organization of a system embodied in its components, their relationships to each other and to the environment and the principles guiding its design and evolution [12] does not support the required level of quality.

The work in this paper is motivated by the fact that this also applies to usability. Usability is increasingly recognized as an important consideration during software development; however, many well-known software products suffer from usability issues that cannot be repaired without major changes to the software architecture of these products. This is a problem for software development because it is very expensive to ensure a particular level of usability after the system has been implemented. Studies [24,17] confirm that a significant large part of the maintenance costs of software systems is spent on dealing with usability issues. These high costs can be explained because some usability requirements will not be discovered until the software has been implemented or deployed. This is caused by the following:

R. Bastide, P. Palanque, and J. Roth (Eds.): EHCI-DSVIS 2004, LNCS 3425, pp. 38-58, 2005.

- Usability requirements are often weakly specified.
- Usability requirements engineering techniques have only a limited ability to capture all requirements.
- Usability requirements may change during development.

Discovering requirements late is a problem inherent to all software development and is something that cannot be easily solved. The real problem is that it often proves to be hard and expensive to make the necessary changes to a system to improve its usability. Reasons for why this is so hard:

- Usability is often only associated with interface design but usability does also depend on issues such as the information architecture, the interaction architecture and other quality attributes (such as efficiency and reliability) that are all determined by the software architecture. Usability should therefore also be realized at the architectural level.
- Many of the necessary usability changes to a system cannot be easily be accommodated by the software architecture. Some changes that may improve usability require a substantial degree of modification. For example changes that relate to the interactions that take place between the system and the user, such as undo to a particular function or system wide changes such as imposing a consistent look and feel in the interface.

The cost of restructuring the system during the later stages of development has proven to be an order of magnitude higher than the costs of an initial development [4]. The high costs spent on usability during maintenance can to an extent be explained by the high costs for fixing architecture-related usability issues. Because during design different tradeoffs have to be made, for example between cost and quality, these high costs may prevent developers from meeting all the usability requirements. The challenge is therefore to cost effectively usable software e.g. minimizing the costs & time that are spent on usability.

Based upon successful experiences [18] with architectural assessment of maintainability as a tool for cost effective developing maintainable software, we developed architectural analysis of usability as an important tool to cost effectively development usable software i.e. if any problems are detected at this stage, it is still possible to change the software architecture with relative cheap costs. Software architecture analysis contributes to making sure the software architecture supports usability. Software architecture analysis does not solve the problem of discovering usability requirements late. However, it contributes to an increased awareness of the limitations the software architecture may place on the level of usability that can be achieved. Explicit evaluation of software architectures regarding usability is a technique to come up with a more usable first version of a software architecture that might allow for more "usability tuning" on the detailed design level, hence, preventing some of the high costs incurring adaptive maintenance activities once the system has been implemented.

In [7] an overview is provided of usability evaluation techniques that can be used during the different stages of development, unfortunately, no documented evidence exists of architecture level assessment techniques focusing on usability. The contribution of this paper is an assessment technique that assists software architects in designing a software architecture that supports usability called SALUTA (Scenario based Architecture Level UsabiliTy Analysis).

The remainder of this paper is organized as follows. In the next section, the relationship between software architecture and usability is discussed. Section 3 discusses various approaches to software architecture analysis. Section 4 presents an overview of the main steps of SALUTA. Section 5 presents some examples from a case study for performing usability analysis in practice and discusses the validation of the method. Finally the paper is concluded in section 6.

2 Relationship Between Usability and Software Architecture

A software architecture description such as a decomposition of the system into components and relations with its environment may provide information on the support for particular quality attributes. Specific relationships between software architecture (such as - styles, -patterns etc) and quality attributes (maintainability, efficiency) have been described by several authors. [6,9,4]. For example [6] describes the architectural pattern layers and the positive effect this pattern may have on exchangeability and the negative effect it may have on efficiency.

Until recently [3,8] such relationships between usability and software architecture had not been described nor investigated. In [8] we defined a framework that expresses the relationship between usability and software architecture based on our comprehensive survey [7]. This framework is composed of an integrated set of design solutions such as usability patterns and usability properties that have a positive effect on usability but are difficult to retrofit into applications because they have architectural impact. The framework consists of the following concepts:

2.1 Usability Attributes

A number of usability attributes have been selected from literature that appear to form the most common denominator of existing notions of usability:

- Learnability - how quickly and easily users can begin to do productive work with a system that is new to them, combined with the ease of remembering the way a system must be operated.
- Efficiency of use - the number of tasks per unit time that the user can perform using the system.
- Reliability in use the error rate in using the system and the time it takes to recover from errors.
- Satisfaction - the subjective opinions of the users of the system.

2.2 Usability Properties

A number of usability properties have been selected from literature that embody the heuristics and design principles that researchers in the usability field consider to have a direct positive influence on usability. They should be considered as high-level design primitives that have a known effect on usability and most likely have architectural implications. Some examples:

- Providing Feedback - The system should provide at every (appropriate) moment feedback to the user in which case he or she is informed of what is going on, that is, what the system is doing at every moment.
- Consistency - Users should not have to wonder whether different words, situations, or actions mean the same thing. Consistency has several aspects:
  - Visual consistency: user interface elements should be consistent in aspect and structure.
  - Functional consistency: the way to perform different tasks across the system should be consistent.
  - Evolutionary consistency: in the case of a software product family, consistency over the products in the family is an important aspect.

2.3 Architecture Sensitive Usability Patterns

A number of usability patterns have been identified that should be applied during the design of a system's software architecture, rather than during the detailed design stage. This set of patterns has been identified from various cases in industry, modern software, literature surveys as well as from existing (usability) pattern collections. Some examples:

- Actions on multiple objects - Actions need to be performed on objects, and users are likely to want to perform these actions on two or more objects at one time [26].
- Multiple views - The same data and commands must be potentially presented using different human-computer interface styles for different user preferences, needs or disabilities [5].
- User profiles - The application will be used by users with differing abilities, cultures, and tastes [26].

Unlike the design patterns, architecturally sensitive patterns do not specify a specific design solution in terms of objects and classes. Instead, potential architectural implications that face developers looking to solve the problem the architecturally sensitive pattern represents are outlined. For example, to facilitate actions on multiple objects, a provision needs to be made in the architecture for objects to be grouped into composites, or for it to be possible to iterate over a set of objects performing the same action for each. Actions for multiple objects may be implemented by the composite pattern [9] or the visitor pattern [9].

(Positive) relationships have been defined between the elements of the framework that link architectural sensitive usability patterns to usability properties and attributes. These relationships have been derived from our literature survey. The usability properties in the framework may be used as requirements during design. For example, if a requirements species, "the system must provide feedback", we use the framework to identify which usability patterns may be implemented to fulfill these properties by following the arrows in Figure 1. Our assessment technique uses this framework to analyze the architecture's support for usability.

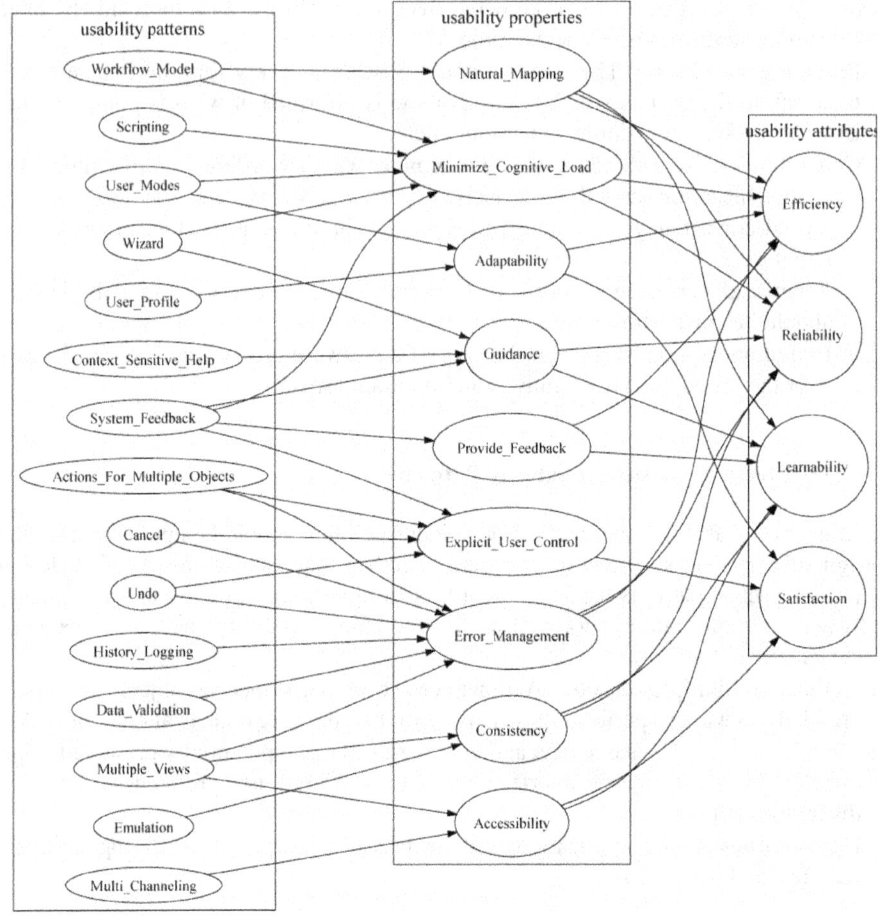

Fig. 1. Usability Framework.

3 Software Architecture Assessment

The design and use of an explicitly defined software architecture has received increasing amounts of attention during the last decade. Generally, three arguments for defining an architecture are used [2]. First, it provides an artifact that allows discussion by the stakeholders very early in the design process. Second, it allows for early assessment of quality attributes [15,4]. Finally, the design decisions captured in the software architecture can be transferred to other systems.

Our work focuses on the second aspect: early assessment of usability. Most engineering disciplines provide techniques and methods that allow one to assess and test quality attributes of the system under design. For example for maintainability assessment code metrics [20] have been developed. In [7] an overview is provided of usability evaluation techniques that can be used during software development. Some of the more popular techniques such as user testing [22], heuristic evaluation [21] and cognitive walkthroughs [27] can be used during several stages of development. Unfortunately, no documented evidence exists of architecture level assessment techniques focusing on usability. Without such techniques, architects may run the risk of designing a software architecture that fails to meet its usability requirements. To address to this problem we have defined a scenario based assessment technique (SALUTA).

The Software Architecture Analysis Method (SAAM) [14] was among the first to address the assessment of software architectures using scenarios. SAAM is stakeholder centric and does not focus on a specific quality attribute. From SAAM, ATAM [15] has evolved. ATAM also uses scenarios for identifying important quality attribute requirements for the system. Like SAAM, ATAM does not focus on a single quality attribute but rather on identifying tradeoffs between quality attributes. SALUTA can be integrated into these existing techniques.

3.1 Usability Specification

Before a software architecture can be assessed, the required usability of the system needs to be determined. Several specification styles of usability have been identified [19]. One shortcoming of these techniques [21,23,11] is that they are poorly suited for architectural assessment.

- Usability requirements are often rather weakly specified: practitioners have great difficulties specifying usability requirements and often end up stating: “the system shall be usable” [19].
- Many usability requirements are performance based specified [19]. For example, such techniques might result in statements such as “customers must be able to withdraw cash within 4 minutes” or “80% of the customers must find the system pleasant”.

Given an implemented system, such statements may be verified by observing how users interact with the system. However, during architecture assessment such a system is not yet available. Interface prototypes may be analyzed for such requirements however we want to analyze the architecture for such requirements.

A technique that is used for specifying the required quality requirements and the assessment of software architectures for these requirements are scenario profiles [18]. Scenario profiles describe the semantics of software quality attributes by means of a set of scenarios. The primary advantage of using scenarios is that scenarios represent the actual meaning of a requirement. Consequently, scenarios are much more specific and fine-grained than abstract usability requirements. The software architecture may then be evaluated for its support for the scenarios in the scenario profile. Scenario profiles and traditional usability specification techniques are not interfering; scenarios are just a more concrete instance of these usability requirements.

3.2 Usage Profiles

A usage profile represents the required usability of the system by means of a set of usage scenarios. Usability is not an intrinsic quality of the system. According to the ISO definition [13], usability depends on:

- The users - who is using the product? (system administrators, novice users)
- The tasks - what are the users trying to do with the product? (insert order, search for item X)
- The context of use - where and how is the product used? (helpdesk, training environment)

Usability may also depend on other variables, such as goals of use, etc. However in a usage scenario only the variables stated above are included. A usage scenario is defined as "an interaction (task) between users, the system in a specific context of use". A usage scenario specified in such a way does not yet specify anything about the required usability of the system. In order to do that, the usage scenario is related to the four usability attributes defined in our framework. For each usage scenario, numeric values are determined for each of these usability attributes. The numeric values are used to determine a prioritization between the usability attributes.

For some usability attributes, such as efficiency and learnability, tradeoffs have to be made. It is often impossible to design a system that has high scores on all attributes. A purpose of usability requirements is therefore to specify a necessary level for each attribute [19]. For example, if for a particular usage scenario learnability is considered to be of more importance than other usability attributes (maybe because of a requirement), then the usage scenario must reflect this difference in the priorities for the usability attributes. The analyst interprets the priority values during the analysis phase (section 4.3) to determine the level of support in the software architecture for the usage scenario.

4 SALUTA

In this section we present SALUTA (Scenario based Architecture Level UsabiliTy Analysis). SALUTA consists of the following four steps:

1. Create usage profile.
2. Describe provided usability.
3. Evaluate scenarios.
4. Interpret the results.

When performing an analysis the separation between these steps is not very strict and it is often necessary to iterate over various steps. In the next subsections, however the steps are presented as if they are performed in strict sequence.

4.1 Create Usage Profile

The steps that need to be taken for usage profile creation are the following:

1. Identify the users: rather than listing individual users, users that are representative for the use of the system should be categorized in types or groups (for example system administrators, end-users etc).
2. Identify the tasks: Instead of converting the complete functionality of the system into tasks, representative tasks are selected that highlight the important features of the system. For example, a task may be "find out where course computer vision is given".
3. Identify the contexts of use: In this step, representative contexts of use are identified. (For example. Helpdesk context or disability context.) Deciding what users, tasks and contexts of use to include requires making tradeoffs between all sorts of factors. An important consideration is that the more scenarios are evaluated the more accurate the outcome of the assessment is, but the more expensive and time consuming it is to determine attribute values for these scenarios.
4. Determine attribute values: For each valid combination of user, task and context of use, usability attributes are quantified to express the required usability of the system, based on the usability requirements specification. Defining specific indicators for attributes may assist the analyst in interpreting usability requirements as will be illustrated in the case study in section 5. To reflect the difference in priority, numeric values between one and four have been assigned to the attributes for each scenario. Other techniques such as pair wise comparison may also be used to determine a prioritization between attributes.
5. Scenario selection & weighing: Evaluating all identified scenarios may be a costly and time-consuming process. Therefore, the goal of performing an assessment is not to evaluate all scenarios but only a representative subset. Different profiles may be defined depending on the goal of the analysis. For example, if the goal is to compare two different architectures, scenarios may be selected that highlight the differences between those architectures. If the goal is to analyze the level of support for usability, scenarios may be selected that are important to the users. To express differences between usage scenarios in the usage profile, properties may be assigned to scenarios, for example: priority or probability of use within a certain time. The result of the assessment may be influenced by weighing scenarios, if some scenarios are more important than others, weighing these scenarios reflect these differences. A usage profile that is created using these steps is summarized in a table (See Table 2). Figure 2 shows the usage profile creation process.

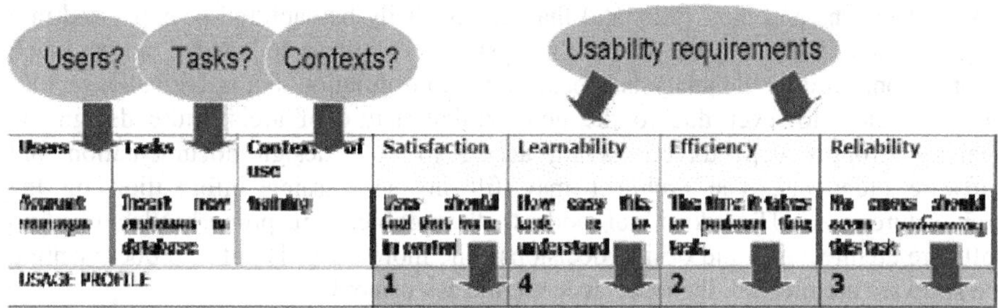

Fig. 2. Example usage profile.

This step results in a set of usage scenarios that accurately express the required usability of the system. Usage profile creation is not intended to replace existing requirements engineering techniques. Rather it is intended to transform (existing) usability requirements into something that can be used for architecture assessment. Existing techniques such as interviews, group discussions or observations [21,11,25] typically already provide information such as representative tasks, users and contexts of use that are needed to create a usage profile. Close cooperation between the analyst and the person responsible for the usability requirements (such as a usability engineer) is required. The usability engineer may fill in the missing information on the usability requirements, because usability requirements are often not explicitly defined.

4.2 Describe Provided Usability

In the second step of SALUTA, the information about the software architecture is collected. Usability analysis requires architectural information that allows the analyst to determine the support for the usage scenarios. The process of identifying the support is similar to scenario impact analysis for maintainability assessment [18] but is different, because it focuses on identifying architectural elements that may support the scenario. Two types of analysis techniques are defined:

- Usability pattern based analysis: using the list of architectural sensitive usability patterns defined in our framework the architecture's support for usability is determined by the presence of these patterns in the architecture design.
- Usability property based analysis: The software architecture can be seen as the result of a series of design decisions [10]. Reconstructing this process and assessing the effect of such individual decisions with regard to usability attributes may provide additional information about the intended quality of the system. Using the list of usability properties defined in our framework, the architecture and the design decisions that lead to this architecture are analyzed for these properties.

The quality of the assessment very much depends on the amount of evidence for patterns and property support that is extracted from the architecture. Some usability properties such as error management may be implemented using architectural patterns such as undo, cancel or data validation. However, in addition to patterns there may be additional evidence in the form of other design decisions that were motivated by usability properties. The software architecture of a system has several aspects (such as design decisions and their rationale) that cannot easily be captured or expressed in a single model. Different views on the system [16] may be needed access such information. Initially the analysis is based on the information that is available, such as diagrams etc. However due to the non explicit nature of architecture design the analysis strongly depends on having access to both design documentation and software architects. The architect may fill in the missing information on the architecture. SALUTA does not address the problem of properly documenting software architectures and design decisions. The more effort is put into documenting the software architecture the more accurate the assessment is.

4.3 Evaluate Scenarios

SALUTA's next step is to evaluate the support for each of the scenarios in the usage profile. For each scenario, it is analyzed by which usability patterns and properties, that have been identified in the previous step, it is affected. A technique we have used for identifying the provided usability in our cases is the usability framework approach. The relations defined in the framework are used to analyze how a particular pattern or property affects a specific usability attribute. For example if it has been identified that undo affects a certain scenario. Then the relationships of the undo pattern with usability are analyzed (see Figure 1) to determine the support for that particular scenario. Undo in this case may increase reliability and efficiency. This step is repeated for each pattern or property that affects the scenario. The analyst then determines the support of the usage scenario based on the acquired information. See Figure 3 for a snapshot assessment example.

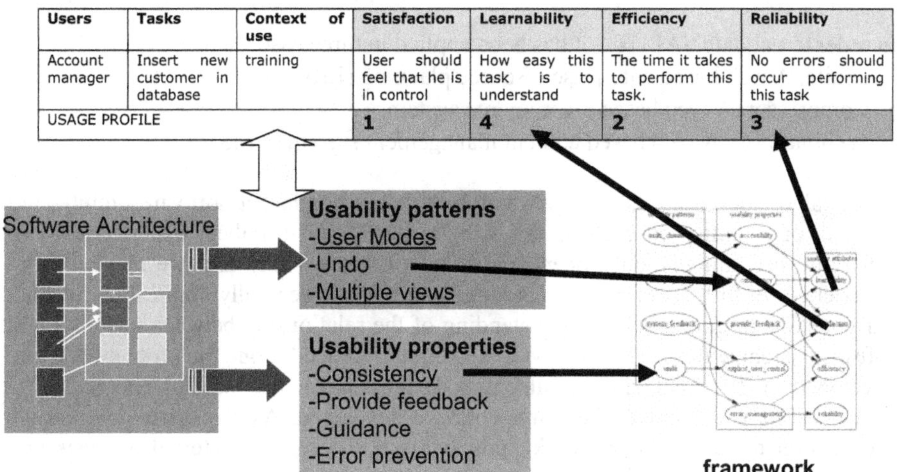

Fig. 3. Snapshot evaluation example.

For each scenario, the results of the support analysis are expressed qualitatively using quantitative measures. For example the support may be expressed on a five level scale (++, +, +/-,-,--). The outcome of the overall analysis may be a simple binary answer (supported/unsupported) or a more elaborate answer (70% supported) depending on how much information is available and how much effort is being put in creating the usage profile.

4.4 Interpret the Results

Finally, after scenario evaluation, the results need to be interpreted to draw conclusions concerning the software architecture. This interpretation depends on two factors: the goal of the analysis and the usability requirements. Based on the goal of the analysis, a certain usage profile is selected. If the goal of the analysis is to compare two or more candidate software architectures, the support for a particular usage scenario must be expressed on an ordinal scale to indicate a relation between the different candidates. (Which one has the better support?). If the analysis is sufficiently accurate the results may be quantified, however even without quantification the assessment can produce useful results. If the goal is to iteratively design an architecture, then if the architecture proves to have sufficient support for usability, the design process may be ended. Otherwise, architectural transformations need to be applied to improve usability. Qualitative information such as which scenarios are poorly supported and which usability properties or patterns have not been considered may guide the architect in applying particular transformations. The framework may then be used as an informative source for design and improvement of the architecture's support of usability.

5 Validation

In order to validate SALUTA it has been applied in three case studies:

- eSuite. A web based enterprise resource planning (ERP) system.
- Compressor. A web based e-commerce system.
- Webplatform. A web based content management system (CMS)

The goal of the case studies was twofold: first to conduct a software architecture analysis of usability on each of the three systems and to collect experiences. Our technique had initially only been applied at one case study and we needed more experiences to further refine our technique and make it generally applicable. Second, our goal was to gain a better understanding of the relationship between usability and software architecture. Our analysis technique depends on the framework we developed in [9]. Analyzing architectural designs in the case studies allowed us to further refine and validate the framework we developed. As a research method we used action research [1], we took upon our self the role of external analysts and actively participated in the analysis process and reflected on the process and the results.

These cases studies show that it is possible to use SALUTA to assess software architectures for their support of usability. Whether we have accurately predicted the architecture's support for usability is answered by comparing our analysis with the results of user tests that are conducted when the systems are implemented. These results are used to verify whether the usage profile we created actually matches the actual usage of the system and whether the results of the assessment fits results from the user tests For all three cases, the usage profile and architecture assessment phase is completed. In the case of the Webplatform, a user test has been performed recently. In this article, we limit ourselves to highlighting some examples from the Webplatform case study.

ECCOO develops software and services for one of the largest universities of the Netherlands (RuG). ECCOO has developed the Webplatform. Faculties, departments and organizations within the RuG are already present on the inter/intra/extra –net but because of the current wild growth of sites, concerning content, layout and design, the usability of the old system was quite poor. For the Webplatform usability was considered as an important design objective. Webplatform has successfully been deployed recently and the current version of the RuG website is powered by the Webplatform. As an input to the analysis of the Webplatform, we interviewed the software architect and usability engineer, examined the design documentation, and looked at the newly deployed RuG site. In the next few subsections, we will present the four SALUTA steps for the Webplatform.

5.1 Usage Profile Creation

In this step of the SALUTA, we have cooperated with the usability engineer to create the usage profile.

- Three types of users are defined in the functional requirements: end users, content administrators and CMS administrators.
- Several different tasks are specified in the functional requirements. An accurate description of what is understood for a particular task is an essential part of this step. For example, several tasks such as "create new portal medical sciences" or "create new course description" have been understood for the task "make object", because the Webplatform data structure is object based.
- No relevant contexts of use were identified for Webplatform. Issues such as bandwidth or helpdesk only affect a very small part of the user population.

The result of the first three steps is summarized in Table1.

The next step is to determine attribute values for the scenarios. This has been done by consulting the usability requirements and by discussing these for each scenario with the usability engineer. In the functional requirements of the Webplatform only 30 guidelines based on Nielsen's heuristics [21] have been specified. Fortunately, the usability engineer in our case had a good understanding of the expected required usability of the system. As an example we explain how we determined attribute values for the usage scenario: "end user performing quick search".

Table 1. Summary of selected users, tasks for Webplatform.

#	Users	Tasks	example
1	End-user	Quick search	Find course X
2	End-user	Navigate	Find employee X
3	Content Administrator	Edit object	Edit course description
4	Content Administrator	Make object	Create new course description
5	Content Administrator	Quick search	Find course X
6	Content Administrator	Navigate	Find phone number for person X
7	CMS Administrator	Edit object	Change layout of portal X
8	CMS Administrator	Make object	Create new portal medical sciences
9	CMS Administrator	Delete object	Delete teacher X
10	CMS Administrator	Quick search	Find all employees of section X
11	CMS Administrator	Navigate	Find section library

First, we formally specified with the usability engineer what should be understood for each attribute of this task. We have associated reliability with the accuracy of search results; efficiency has been associated with response time of the quick search. Then the usability requirements were consulted. A usability requirement that affects this scenario states: "every page should feature a quick search which searches the whole portal and comes up with accurate search results". In the requirements, it has not been specified that quick search should be performed quickly. However, in our discussions with the usability engineer we found that this is the most important aspect of usability for this task.

Table 2. Attribute priority table for Webplatform.

#	Users	Tasks	S	L	E	R
1	End-user	Quick search	2	1	4	3
2	End-user	Navigate	1	4	2	3
3	Content Administrator	Edit object	1	4	2	3
4	Content Administrator	Make object	1	4	2	3
5	Content Administrator	Quick search	2	1	4	3
6	Content Administrator	Navigate	1	4	2	4
7	CMS Administrator	Edit object	2	1	4	3
8	CMS Administrator	Make object	2	1	4	3
9	CMS Administrator	Delete object	2	1	4	3
10	CMS Administrator	Quick search	2	1	4	3
11	CMS Administrator	Navigate	1	2	3	4

Consequently, high values have been given to efficiency and reliability and low values to the other attributes. For each scenario, numeric values between one and four have been assigned to the usability attributes to express the difference in priority. Table 2 states the result of the quantification of the selected scenarios for Webplatform.

5.2 Architecture Description

For scenario evaluation, a list of usability patterns and a list of usability properties that have been implemented in the system are required to determine the architecture's support for usability. This information has been acquired, by analyzing the software architecture (Figure 4) consulting the functional design documentation (some specific design decisions for usability had been documented) and interviewing the software architect using the list of patterns and properties defined in our framework.

One of the reasons to develop Webplatform was that the usability of the old system was quite poor; this was mainly caused by the fact that each "entity" within the RuG (Faculties, libraries, departments) used their own layout and their own way to present information and functionality to its users which turned out to be confusing to users.

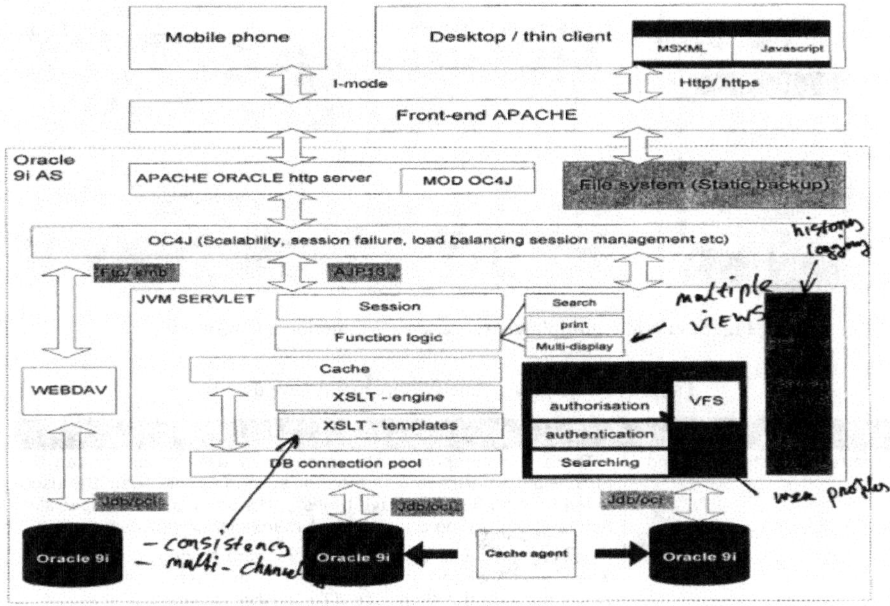

Fig. 4. Webplatform software architecture.

A specific design decision that was taken which facilitates several patterns and properties in our framework was to use the internet file system (IFS):

- Multiple views [8]: The IFS provides an interface that realizes the use of objects and relations as defined in XML. Using XML and XSLT templates the system can provide multiple views for different users and uses on the server side. CSS style sheets are used to provide different views on the client site, for example for providing a "print" layout view but also to allow each faculty their own "skin" as depicted in Figure 5.
- Consistency [8]: The use of XML/ XSLT is a means to enforce a strict separation of presentation from data. This design decision makes it easier to provide a consistent presentation of interface and function for all different objects of the same type such as portals. See for example Figure 5 where the menu layout, the menu items and the position of the quick search box is the same for the faculty of arts and the faculty of Philosophy.
- Multichanneling [8]: By providing different views & control mappings for different devices multichanneling is provided. The Webplatform can be accessed from an I-mode phone as well as from a desktop computer.

Next to the patterns and properties that are facilitated by the IFS several other patterns and properties were identified in the architecture. Sometimes even multiple instances of the same property (such as system feedback) have been identified. Some properties such as consistency have multiple aspects (visual/functional consistency). We need to analyze the architecture for its support of each element of such a property. A result of such a detailed analysis for the property accessibility and the pattern history logging is displayed in Table 3.

Fig. 5. Provide multiple views/ & Visual/Functional Consistency.

Table 3. Pattern and propetry implementation details.

[pattern]- History Logging	- There is a component that logs every user action. It can be further augmented to also monitor system events (i.e. "the user failed to login 3 consecutive times"). History logging is especially helpful for speeding up the object manipulation process. - Cookies are used to prevent users from having to login again when a connection is lost. Cookies also serve as a backup mechanism on the client site. (To retrieve lost data).
[property] - Accessibility	
• Disabilities	x
• Multi channel	Multi channeling is provided by the web server which can provide a front end to I-Mode or other devices based on specified XLST templates.
• Internationalization	- Support for Dutch / English language, each xml object has different language attribute fields. - Java support Unicode

5.3 Evaluate Scenarios

The next step is to evaluate the architecture's support for the usage scenarios in the usage profile. As an example, we analyze usage scenario #4 "content administrator makes object" from table 2. For this scenario it has been determined by which patterns and properties, that have been identified in the architecture it is affected. It is important to identify whether a scenario is affected by a pattern or property that has been implemented in the architecture because this is not always the case. The result of such an analysis is shown in a support matrix in Table 3 for two scenarios. A checkmark indicates that the scenario is affected by at least one or more patterns or properties. Some properties such as consistency have multiple aspects (visual/functional consistency). For a thorough evaluation we need to analyze each scenario for each element of such a property. The support matrix is used together with the relations in the framework to find out whether a usage profile is sufficiently supported by the architecture. The usage profile that we created shows that scenario #4 has high values for learnability (4) and reliability (3). Several patterns and properties positively contribute to the support of this scenario. For example, the property consistency and the pattern context sensitive help increases learnability as can be analyzed from Figure 1. By analyzing for each pattern and property, the effect on usability, the support for this scenario is determined. Due to the lack of formalized knowledge at the architecture level, this step is very much guided by tacit knowledge (i.e. the undocumented knowledge of experienced software architects and usability engineers). For usage scenario #4, we have concluded that the architecture provides weak support. Learnability is very important for this scenario and patterns such as a wizard or workflow modeling or different user modes to support novice users could increase the learnability of this scenario.

Table 4. Architecture support matrix.

Scenario number	Usability patterns															Usability properties								
	System Feedback	Actions for multiple obj.	Cancel	Data validation	History Logging	Scripting	Multiple views	Multi Channeling	Undo	User Modes	User Profiles	Wizard	Workflow model	Emulation	Context sensitive help	Provide feedback	Error management	Consistency	Adaptability	Guidance	Explicit user control	Natural mapping	Accessibility	Minimize cognitive load
1	✓	×	×	×	×	×	×	✓	×	×	×	×	✓	×	✓	✓	✓	✓	×	✓	×	✓	✓	×
4	✓	×	✓	✓	✓	✓	✓	✓	×	×	×	×	×	×	✓	✓	✓	✓	×	✓	✓	✓	✓	×

5.4 Interpret the Results

The result of the assessment of the Webplatform is that three scenarios are accepted, six are weakly accepted and that two scenarios are weakly rejected. The main cause for this is that we could not identify sufficient support for learnability for content administrators as was required by the usage profile. There is room for improvement; usability could be improved if provisions were made to facilitate patterns and properties that have not been considered. The usability requirement of consistency was one of the driving forces of design and our analysis shows that it has positive influence on the usability of the system. Apart from some general usability guidelines [21] stated in the functional requirements no clearly defined and verifiable usability requirements have been specified. Our conclusion concerning the assessment of the Webplatform is that the architecture provides sufficient support for the usage profile that we created. This does not necessarily guarantee that the final system will be usable since many other factors play a role in ensuring a system's usability. Our analysis shows however that these usability issues may be repaired without major changes to the software architecture thus preventing high costs incurring adaptive maintenance activities once the system has been implemented.

5.5 Validation

Whether the usage profile we created is fully representative for the required usability is open to dispute. However, the results from the user test that has recently been completed by the ECCOO is consistent with our findings. 65 test users (students, employees and graduate students) have tested 13 different portals. In the usability tests, the users had to perform specific tasks while being observed. The specific tasks that had to be performed are mostly related to the tasks navigation and quick search in our usage profile. After performing the tasks, users were interviewed about the relevance of the tasks they had to perform and the usability issues that were discovered. The main conclusions of the tests are:

- Most of the usability issues that were detected were related to navigation, structure and content. For example, users have difficulties finding particular information. Lack of hierarchy and structure is the main cause for this problem Although the architecture supports visual and functional consistency, organizations themselves are responsible for structuring their information.
- Searching does not generate accurate search results. This may be fixed by technical modifications. E.g. tuning the search function to generate more accurate search results. (This is also caused by that a lot of meta-information on the content in the system has not been provided yet).

The results of this usability tests fit the results of our analysis: the software architecture supports the right level of usability. Some usability issues came up that where not predicted during our architectural assessment. However, these do not appear to be caused by problems in the software architecture. Future usability tests will focus on analyzing the usability of the scenarios that involve content administrators. Preliminary results from these tests show that the system has a weak support for learnability as predicted from the architectural analysis.

6 Conclusions

In this paper, we have presented SALUTA, a scenario based assessment technique that assists software architects in designing a software architecture that supports usability. SALUTA consists of four major steps: First, the required usability of the system is expressed by means of a usage profile. The usage profile consists of a representative set of usage scenarios that express the required usability of the system. The following sub-steps are taken for creating a usage profile: identify the users, identify the tasks, identify the contexts of use, determine attribute values, scenario selection & weighing. In the second step, the information about the software architecture is collected using a framework that has been developed in earlier work. This framework consists of an integrated set of design solutions such as usability patterns and usability properties that have a positive effect on usability but are difficult to retrofit into applications because they have architectural impact. This framework is used to analyze the architecture for its support of usability. The next step is to evaluate the architecture's support of usage profile using the information extracted in the previous step. To do so, we perform support analysis for each of the scenarios in the set. The final step is then to interpret these results and to draw conclusions about the software architecture. The result of the assessment for example, which scenarios are poorly supported or which usability properties or patterns have not been considered, may guide the architect in applying particular transformations to improve the architecture's support of usability. We have elaborated the various steps in this paper, discussed the issues and techniques for each of the steps, and illustrated these by discussing some examples from a case study. The main contributions of this paper are:

- SALUTA is the first and currently the only technique that enables software architects to assess the level of usability supported by their architectures.
- Because usability requirements tend to change over time and may be discovered during deployment, SALUTA may assist a software architect to come up with a more usable first version of a software architecture that might allow for more "usability tuning" on the detailed design level. This prevents some of the high costs incurring adaptive maintenance activities once the system has been implemented.

Future work shall focus on finalizing the case studies, refining the usability framework and validating our claims we make. Our framework is a first step in illustrating the relationship between usability and software architecture. The list of architecturally sensitive usability patterns and properties we identified are substantial but incomplete. The framework possibly needs to be specialized for particular applications domains. Architectural assessment saves maintenance costs spent on dealing with usability issues. To raise awareness and change attitudes (especially those of the decision makers) we should clearly define and measure the business and competitive advantages of architectural assessment of usability. Preliminary experiences with these three case studies shows the results from the assessment seem reasonable and do not conflict with the user tests. The usage profile and usage scenarios are used to evaluate a software architecture, once it is there. However a much better approach would be to design the architecture based on the usage profile e.g. an attribute-based architectural design, where the SAU framework is used to suggest patterns that should be used rather than identify their absence post-hoc.

Acknowledgments

This work is sponsored by the STATUS[1] project under contract no IST-2001-32298. We would like to thank the partners in the STATUS project and ECCOO for their input and their cooperation.

---

[1] STATUS is an ESPRIT project (IST-2001-32298) financed by the European Commission in its Information Society Technologies Program. The partners are Information Highway Group (IHG), Universidad Politecnica de Madrid (UPM), University of Groningen (RUG), Imperial College of Science, Technology and Medicine (ICSTM), LOGICDIS S.A.

References

[1] C. Argyris, R. Putnam, and D. Smith, *Action Science: Concepts, methods and skills for research and intervention*, Jossey-Bass, San Francisco, 1985.
[2] L. Bass, P. Clements, and R. Kazman, *Software Architecture in Practice*, Addison Wesley Longman, Reading MA, 1998.
[3] L. Bass, J. Kates, and B. E. John, Achieving Usability through software architecture, *Technical Report* CMU/SEI-2001-TR-005, 1-3-2001.
[4] J. Bosch, *Design and use of Software Architectures: Adopting and evolving a product line approach*, Pearson Education (Addison-Wesley and ACM Press), Harlow, 2000.
[5] Brighton, *The Brighton Usability Pattern Collection.* http://www.cmis.brighton.ac.uk/research/patterns/home.html
[6] F. Buschmann, R. Meunier, H. Rohnert, P. Sommerlad, and M. Stal, *Pattern-Oriented Software Architecture: A System of Patterns*, John Wiley and Son Ltd, New York, 1996.
[7] E. Folmer and J. Bosch, *Architecting for usability; a survey*, Journal of systems and software, Elsevier, 2002, pp. 61-78.
[8] E. Folmer, J. v. Gurp, and J. Bosch, *Investigating the Relationship between Usability and Software Architecture* , Software process improvement and practice, Wiley, 2003, pp. 0-0.
[9] E. Gamma, R. Helm, R. Johnson, and J. Vlissides, *Design patterns elements of reusable object-orientated software.*, Addison -Wesley, 1995.
[10] J. v. Gurp and J. Bosch, *Design Erosion: Problems and Causes*, Journal of systems and software, Elsevier, 3-1-2002, pp. 105-119.
[11] D. Hix and H. R. Hartson, *Developing User Interfaces: Ensuring Usability Through Product and Process.*, John Wiley and Sons, 1993.
[12] IEEE, IEEE Architecture Working Group. Recommended practice for architectural description. Draft IEEE Standard P1471/D4.1, IEEE, 1998.
[13] ISO, ISO 9241-11 Ergonomic requirements for office work with visual display terminals (VDTs) -- Part 11: Guidance on usability., 1994.
[14] R. Kazman, G. Abowd, and M. Webb, SAAM: A Method for Analyzing the Properties of Software Architectures, *Proceedings of the 16th International Conference on Software Engineering*, 1994.
[15] R. Kazman, M. Klein, M. Barbacci, T. Longstaff, H. Lipson, and J. Carriere, The Architecture Tradeoff Analysis Method, *Proceedings of ICECCS'98*, 8-1-1998.
[16] P. B. Kruchten, The 4+1 View Model of Architecture, IEEE Software, 1995.
[17] T. K. Landauer, *The Trouble with Computers: Usefulness, Usability and Productivity.*, MIT Press., Cambridge, 1995.
[18] N. Lassing, P. O. Bengtsson, H. van Vliet, and J. Bosch, *Experiences with ALMA: Architecture-Level Modifiability Analysis*, Journal of systems and software, Elsevier, 2002, pp. 47-57.
[19] S. Lauesen and H. Younessi, Six styles for usability requirements, *Proceedings of REFSQ'98*, 1998.
[20] W. Li and S. Henry, *OO Metrics that Predict Maintainability*, Journal of systems and software, Elsevier, 1993, pp. 111-122.
[21] J. Nielsen, *Usability Engineering*, Academic Press, Inc, Boston, MA., 1993.
[22] J. Nielsen, *Heuristic Evaluation.*, in Usability Inspection Methods., Nielsen, J. and Mack, R. L., John Wiley and Sons, New York, NY., 1994.
[23] J. Preece, Y. Rogers, H. Sharp, D. Benyon, S. Holland, and T. Carey, *Human-Computer Interaction*, Addison Wesley, 1994.
[24] R. S. Pressman, *Software Engineering: A Practitioner's Approach*, McGraw-Hill, NY, 1992.
[25] B. Shneiderman, *Designing the User Interface: Strategies for Effective Human-Computer Interaction*, Addison-Wesley, Reading, MA, 1998.

[26] J. Tidwell, Interaction Design Patterns, *Conference on Pattern Languages of Programming 1998*, 1998.
[27] C. Wharton, J. Rieman, C. H. Lewis, and P. G. Polson, *The Cognitive Walkthrough: A practitioner's guide.*, in Usability Inspection Methods, Nielsen, Jacob and Mack, R. L., John Wiley and Sons, New York, NY., 1994.

Discussion

[Helmut Strieger] How do you know that you really have the right usage scenarios.

> [Eelke Folmer] That's always a problem. However, we think that having a first guess is better than having none at all.

[Bonnie John] In our approach we always try to have the whole design team there when we're working on things and we find that the scenarios do seem to come out in the discussion.

[Nick Graham] Can you give a comparison to the SEI approach that Bonnie discussed earlier? For example, you seem to be doing a post-facto evaluation where the SEI seems to be focusing on the front end architectural design.

> [Eelke Folmer] For now we're focusing on architectural evaluation. One concern is that on the front end we run the risk of software architects designing for usability (without support from usability experts) which we feel is not a good thing.

[Tom Omerod] How impactful and important is the process of rating and prioritising the four factors that you use in your system (learnability, efficiency of use, reliability in use, and satisfaction)?

> [Eelke Folmer] This helps us to establish which issues are most critical in a particular system. Also, we did that to get the factors into a format that we can use for the architectural analysis by mapping to the rest of the framework.

[Tom Ormerod] The fact that you're trading these things off one against the other is worrying. For example, if you were working on a birth control system to reduce unwanted teen pregnancies, you wouldn't be trading off learnability versus reliability --- they're both absolute requirements.

[Bonnie John] In our experience the prioritisation doesn't end up being a big issue, since if you're only focusing on usability the teams seem happy to look at all of them. However, it is true that in larger ATAMs (where there are many more kinds of requirements to address) we do find some issues resulting from prioritisation.

[Michael Harrison] This seems very much a top-down approach. How would you apply this in a more bottom-up, contextual design kind of approach? The interesting thing about doing it that way is you see some of the unforeseen effects of your decisions.

> [Eelke Folmer] In our approach we start from the usability requirements and don't put any constraints on where they came from. We think this is OK as it allows more of a separation of disciplines.

[Gerrit van der Veer] One of the issues you mentioned up front is that requirements tend to change. Since you are using scenarios, would it make sense to include stakeholders who have a vision of business goals --- to involve these in the analysis and in the development of scenarios regarding changeability and adaptability.

> [Eelke Folmer] I agree. However, we find that those requirements tend to get addressed more under the heading of modifiability than usability.

[Bonnie John] It looks to me that the procedure in your analysis takes the architecture and asks which patterns and properties appear in the architecture and how. However, when you're doing the scenario analysis, what happens if the scenario is supported, but not in a way that's particularly addressed by your patterns?

> [Eelke Folmer] Yes, that's an interesting issue. Ultimately it has to be a collaborative process between the usability engineer and the software architect.

Support for Task Modeling – A "Constructive" Exploration

Anke Dittmar[1], Peter Forbrig[1], Simone Heftberger[2], Chris Stary[2]

[1]University of Rostock, Department of Computer Science
A.-Einstein-Str.21, D-18051 Rostock
[ad/pforbrig]@informatik.uni-rostock.de

[2]University of Linz, Department of Business Information Systems – Communications Engineering, Freistädterstr. 315, A-4040 Linz
[Simone.Heftberger /Christian.Stary]@jku.at

Abstract. Although model-based approaches focusing on task modeling for user-interface design are well accepted among researchers, they are rarely used by industrial developers. Besides a lack of theoretical frameworks for task modeling insufficient tool support might be the reason for the low diffusion of this approach to interactive software-development processes. Thus, we explored the leading-edge tools TaOSpec, ProcessLens, and CTTE with respect to the formal representation of work tasks, and the creation of task scenarios. The results reveal that current model-based design approaches should be more conceivable by their users with respect to work tasks and their organization. This objective can be met by embedding scenario-based design elements into current tools, thus, increasing integrative tool and organizational development support.

1. Introduction

With the emergence of interactive software systems and their widespread use over the last decades, the needs of potential users have increasingly become crucial to design. Design techniques, such as model-based approaches (cf. [1], [2]) encourage designers to embed user tasks into design representations to achieve accurate interactive functionality of software systems. Such representation might be based on common representation schemes, such as XIML [3]. Other approaches, such as participatory design (cf. [4]) and scenario-based design (cf. [5]) emphasize the active participation of users during the design process to achieve user-centered systems.

Although traditional model-based design techniques do not require user participation, they reflect user perspectives on work tasks and work processes. The designers create different models and their relations to describe tasks, task domains, user characteristics etc. A variety of representations has to be used in the course of design, in order to involve all stakeholders, to discuss their interests and to capture contextual knowledge [6].

R. Bastide, P. Palanque, and J. Roth (Eds.): EHCI-DSVIS 2004, LNCS 3425, pp. 59-76, 2005.

Considering sustainable diffusion of model-based approaches to industrial software design, the latest developments (cf. [7]) do not indicate significant progress, although several task-based tools has been tested successfully from the functional perspective (cf. [8]). The user side, in particular designers and involved users accomplishing work tasks, has not been investigated thoroughly. Given the fact that scenarios of use can be created interactively from formal task specifications, scenario-based design elements might help to make task models more conceivable by users and trigger organizational developments (cf. [9]).

Consequently, we review major task-based design tools with respect to their accurate representation and capability to help users understand task-specific support capabilities based on design specifications and/or on their execution. Tools as a kind of representation of modeling concepts are intended to support task modeling activities of designers. Our review should also help developers to get more insight in applying certain representation schemes and some underlying ideas. They might recognize gaps between what they want to express and what they can describe applying a certain modeling approach. In this way, they experience a similar situation as users given a certain work task, namely when they are co-constructing an interactive application with designers.

For the sake of a structured review we first introduce a use case in Section 2. We use that case to demonstrate the capabilities of the considered task-modeling tools. For its description we use generally accepted constructs within the task modeling community. In Section 3 we briefly introduce the considered tools including their conceptual background. For each of the 3 state-of-the-art tools (TaOSpec, Process-Lens, CTTE) we demonstrate how the example introduced in Section 2 can be described formally and processed. The generated task scenarios and their interactivity are discussed in Section 4. Sophisticated model-based approaches enable to create interactive task scenarios as hands-on experience for users, and thus, trigger reflective organizational developments. Given the inputs from Section 3 and 4 we finally provide a comparative analysis of the considered approaches with respect to their capabilities in Section 5. Although differences between existing task-modeling approaches can already be identified at the conceptual level (see Section 2) besides the tool level, those differences might be required for dedicated design purposes, such as to provide hands-on experience of envisioned task scenarios, and the scope of applying representations, such as to specify workplace improvements. In Section 6 we conclude the paper stressing those benefits and proposing further constructive explorations.

2. A Sample Interactive Task

Our running example is taken from [10] (Figure 1) and specified in TaskMODL, the Task MODeling Language. In order to accomplish the task *Read email* a user has to perform the sub-tasks *Get new email* and *Manage email* in arbitrary order. Emails are managed by executing the sub-task *Manage message* iteratively. Each cycle requires a message to be read (sub-task *Read message*) and being transferred (sub-task *Transfer message*).

The concepts *Mailbox* and *Message* represent the task domain. They are specified in RML, a domain modeling language based on language and set theory. It is assumed that a Mailbox contains messages. *In* and *Out* are specific instances of *Mailbox*. Elements of the task domain are used as resources for tasks. In the graphical notation they appear within the bottom part of task nodes or at the edges between nodes (cf. [10]).

Although this example addresses a simple work task, it captures all relevant constructs and items for the purpose of studying task modeling and the propagation of those constructs to scenarios of use. We consider task modeling essential along hierarchical and sequential structures. In addition, task modeling has to capture objects of the task domain, and relations between tasks and objects (cf. [11]).

The following scenario-like description of the graphically displayed situation helps to reveal the usefulness of some other concepts for contextual task modeling.

Patty Smith works as an assistant in the small company ExampleOrg. She is responsible for receiving all inquiries and for presorting them before they are transferred to Mr. Young, the manager of ExampleOrg. In case of email messages she skims through the sender, the topic and, if necessary, she also skims through the content of a message in order to decide if it needs to be handled at all.

All members of the staff have internal mailboxes called 'Urgent' and 'Normal'. They are used to send them inquiries which need to be treated urgently or in a regular time. Everybody knows that all urgent mail messages have to be answered and that the mailbox 'Urgent' has to be empty before normal inquiries should be handled.

Mr. Young opens his mailboxes every morning and late in the afternoon to react to inquiries Patty has sent him. He forwards those messages he does not answer by himself to Paul or Peter . . .

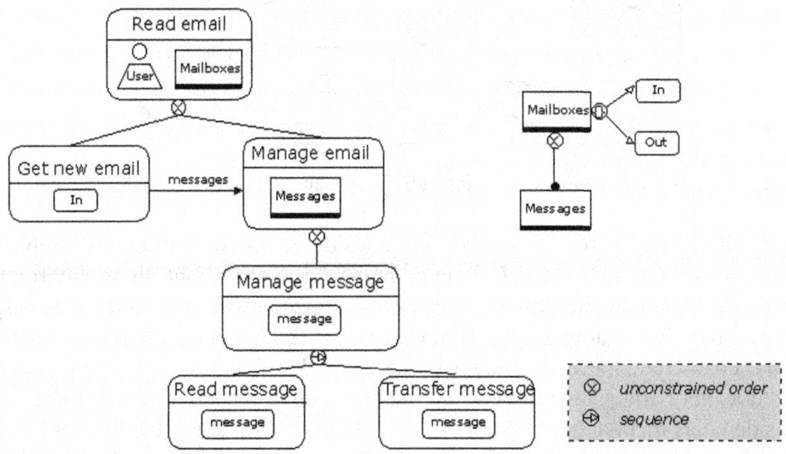

Fig. 1. Task model Read email (left side) and domain model (right side), from [10].

The scenario description enriches the graphically displayed content, since it considers human actors, their relations to tasks and their collaboration more deliberately. Hence, we will check whether and how the considered tools are able to capture those constructs applied in the example. In particular, we will analyze the use of

- tasks,
- task domains,
- actors,
- relations between tasks and actors, and
- relations between tasks and domain objects

and corresponding design support.

3. Tool Support for Creating Task Models

3.1 TaOSpec – An Executable Specification Language for Tasks and Objects

TaOSpec is a specification language that has been developed for higher-order task modelling (cf. [12]). In contrast to other task-modeling approaches in TaOSpec (sub-) models of goals, tasks, actions and (task) objects (created, deleted, used, or manipulated by actions) are structured along identical modeling principles. Models are described through cognitive elements (objects) and their mutual relations. A dedicated relation is the instance-pattern relation between objects explaining abstractions.

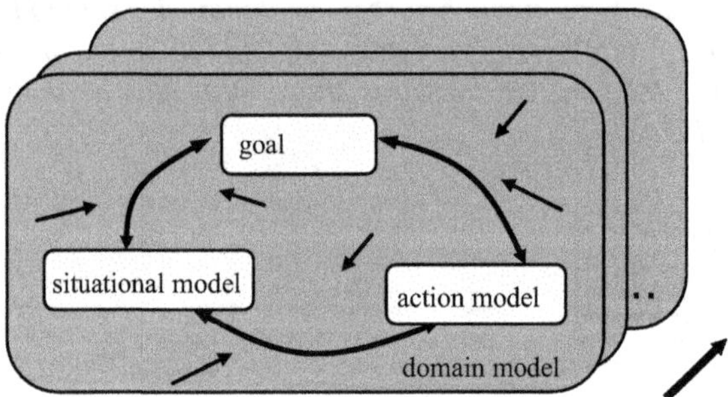

Fig. 2. Tasks as meta-actions modifying sub-models about situations, goals, and actions.

Action, *goal*, and *situational models* are considered as sub-structures within the universal model (*domain model*) human beings possess about their environment (observed world). Such sub-structures can be organized more efficiently with respect to their purpose. For example, an action is assumed to have a simple hierarchical and sequential character as already shown in the example of Figure 1, whereas goals are organized as networks, since there might be contradictions between sub-goals. Tasks are considered as meta-actions (that is to say processes) including the manipulation of sub-models capturing actual situations, goals, and actions to achieve these goals (see Figure 2).

Higher-order task models give a more comprehensive understanding of what tasks represent for humans. Since in TaOSpec there is no strict borderline between procedural and state descriptions, it is possible, for instance, to treat actions as objects of other action environments, to manipulate them with respect to certain goals, and to incorporate them as parts of other actions.

Basically, objects of the domain model are the result of basic operations on sets and sequences of symbols. However, TaOSpec supports a more elaborated structure of objects which is more convenient in order to describe pattern objects. Objects are characterized by a (finite) set of attributes (name-value pairs). We distinguish between basic and additional attributes. An object O_I is considered an instance of object O_P (called pattern object), if, at least, all names of the basic attributes of O_P also occur as attribute names in O_I, and their corresponding values are instances of the attribute values in O_P.

Furthermore, TaOSpec facilitates the description of subsets of instances of a pattern object by partial equations. On the left hand side of such an equation, the designer specifies the identifier of the subset of interest. The right hand side consists of an expression whose operands can be identifiers of other defined subsets, restrictions of attribute values and introduced additional attributes. TaOSpec offers a set of predefined state and temporal operators on these operands (like the operator or in Figure 3). For a more detailed description of TaOSpec see, e.g. [13], [14].

Fig. 3. Pattern objects *Mailbox* and *Message* specified in TaOSpec and some instances.

Figure 3 depicts the way of specifying objects. *Mailbox* and *Message* serve as pattern objects describing concrete task situations, as illustrated by some instances. Mailbox *in* contains 2 messages, all other mailboxes are empty. Message *msg1* is a member of subset *Urgent* according to its attribute *$receiver: "Anke"*. Another, more appropriate interpretation in this context, is that *msg1* is in state *Urgent*.

For describing the hierarchical and sequential character of actions pattern objects with partial equations containing temporal operators are used. Figure 4 shows the skeleton of the action structure for the running example. (For convenience, we chose CTTE-notation for temporal operators.)

```
EQU

HandleEMail(...)=                              ⊗
      GetEMail(...) >> PreSortEMail(...) >>
ManageMail(...),

PreSortEMail(...)=
    SelectInMail(...) >> SkimThroughMail(...)
    >> TransferOrDeleteMail(...),

ManageMail(...)=
    ManageUrgentMail(...) >> ManageNormalMail(...),

ManageUrgentMail(...) =
    SelectUrgentMail(...) >> ReadUrgentMail(...)
    >> (  AnswerUrgentMail(...)
      [] TransferUrgentMail(...) ),

ManageNormalMail(...) =
    SelectNormalMail(...)
    >> ReadNormalMail(...)
    >> (  AnswerNormalMail(...)
        [] DeleteNormalMail(...)
        [] TransferNormalMail(...) )
```

temporal operators:

- >> sequential op.
- ||| concurrent op.
- [] alternative op.
- * iteration

Fig. 4. Action skeleton of *HandleEMail* in TaOSpec (for explanation of mark ⊗ see Section 4)

Actions and objects of a task domain are related by assigning pre- and post conditions to actions. Such conditions are specified by sets of objects in certain states and denoted in square brackets. Figure 5 shows part of the declaration of action HandleEMail.

```
OPERATION HandleEMail
USES Mailbox,Message
DECL
HandleEMail ($in:Mailbox,$urgent:Mailbox,$normal:Mailbox,
             $out:Mailbox) [POST $in.Empty],
GetEMail($in:Mailbox),
*PreSortEMail($in:Mailbox,$urgent:Mailbox,$normal:Mailbox),
ManageMail($urgent:Mailbox,$normal:Mailbox,$out:Mailbox)
           [PRE $urgent.NonEmpty or $normal.NonEmpty],    ...
EQU ...
TransferOrDeleteMail($m,$urgent,$normal)[$m.Urgent] = ...,
TransferOrDeleteMail($m,$urgent,$normal)[$m.Trash] = ...,
TransferOrDeleteMail($m,$urgent,$normal)[$m.Normal] = ...,   ...
```

Fig. 5. Some pre- and post conditions assigned to sub-actions of *HandleEMail*.

For example, sub-action *ManageMail* can only be performed, if at least one of the mailboxes *urgent* and *normal* is not empty. It is also possible to assign different preconditions to one sub-action as shown in the specification of the sub-action *TransferOrDeleteMail*. It depends on the actual state of the mail message referred to by *$m ($m.Urgent* denotes the request that *$m* has to be in state *Urgent* etc.) which one of the three equations is selected.

TaOSpec is an executable specification language. It allows a user to animate "concrete" actions and to observe the modifications of "concrete" domain objects caused by the actions (see Section 4). For that reason a set of basic operations is implemented which corresponds to the general structure of objects in TaOSpec. There are operations to create/remove objects, to introduce/delete additional attributes to objects, and to set/get attribute values. TaOSpec supports the use of strings, integer and real numbers, Boolean values, and lists together with some basic functionality, such as string concatenation ('&'), arithmetic operations ('+', ...), and the insertion/deletion of elements to/from a list (':', 'delete') .

Figure 6 describes the effect of answering a standard message by using basic operations. After object *$m* "is changed to an answer message" it is "sent" to mailbox *$out*.

```
EQU ...
SkimThroughMail($m) = done(),

AnswerNormalMail($m,$out) =
   addAttr($m,"answer","hallo "&$m.$sender)
   >> setAttr($m,"receiver",$m.$sender)
   >> setAttr($m,"sender","ExampleOrg")
   >> setAttr($out,"messages",:($m,$out.$messages))
...
```

Fig. 6. Implementations of sub-actions using predefined operations.

In TaOSpec, we use the keyword OPERATION in specifications instead of ACTION, since delivering executable basic operations makes an action model *operational*. Finally, there is a dedicated basic operation called *done()* which has no effect at all. It can be used to leave sub-actions "unspecified" as shown for *SkimThroughMail* in Figure 6.

3.2 ProcessLens – Framework and Tool

ProcessLens supports the task- und role-sensitive development of interactive software through providing an ontology that captures the essentials of work processes (cf. [15],[16]). It incorporates task and user models into a model-based representation scheme. The unifying specification language BILA (Business Intelligence Language) is based on UML and allows to capture model-specific elements and relationships, as well as the structural and dynamic linking of executable models.

The ProcessLens approach also contains a certain design procedure that is based on the representation scheme as shown in Figure 7. The ProcessLens models relevant for task modeling are the user, task and data model:

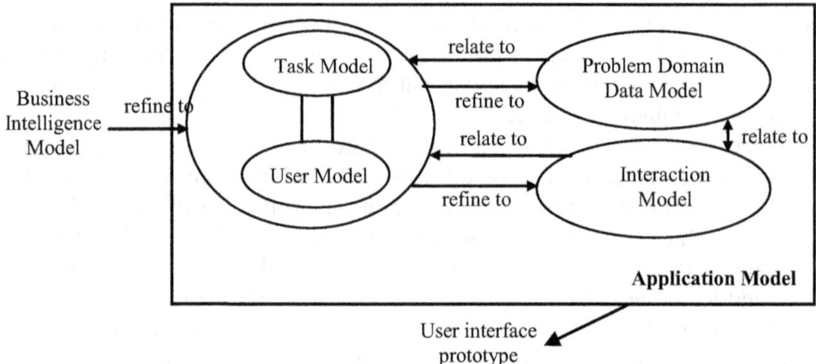

Fig. 7. The ProcessLens Model-Based Framework.

- The *user model* represents a role model by defining specific views on tasks and data (according to the functional roles of users). Typical elements of BILA used in this context are *organizational unit*, *position* and *person.*
- The *task model* comprises the decomposition of user tasks according to the economic and the social organization of work as well as the different activities that users have to perform to accomplish their tasks. Typical elements used for modeling are *task*, *activity* and *tool.*
- The (*problem domain*) *data model* describes the data required for work-task accomplishment. In contrast to traditional data modeling, in ProcessLens both aspects of data are captured: structure and behavior. A particular element of BILA is used extensively in the data model, namely *material.*

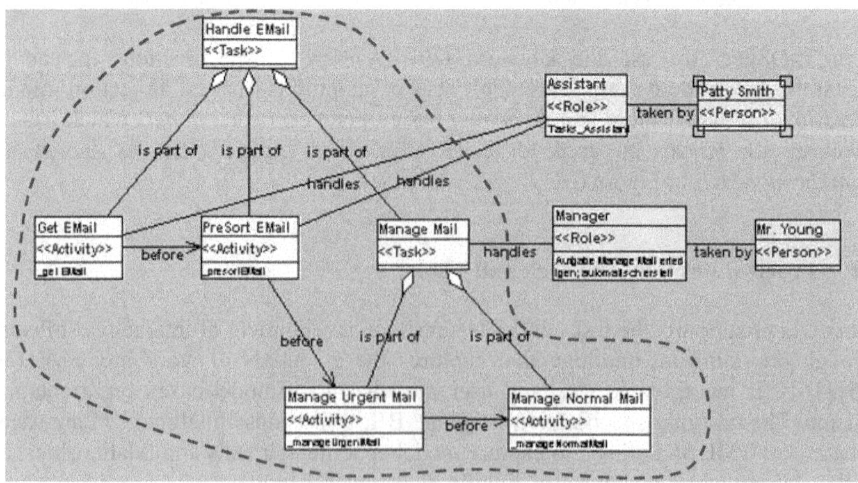

Fig. 8. An integrated structure view on tasks and users of *Handle Email.*

In ProcessLens we use UML class diagrams [17] to specify the structure of all models and their mutual relationships. A set of predefined elements and relations (some of them are mentioned above) supports the modeling activities of work processes. Figure 8 depicts the task model (encircled with a dotted line), the user model and some relations for the running example. Task domain objects (data objects) have to be added and related to the task model.

Designers or users have to specify and assign activity diagrams [18] to dedicated model elements to describe the actual accomplishment of tasks (including the manipulation of data) and role-specific behavior. If elements from different models are related (structure level) their corresponding activity diagrams have to be synchronized using a special kind of ProcessLens transition (synchronization transition at the behavior level). This dynamic linking makes the models operational and is illustrated in Figure 9, in conformance to our example.

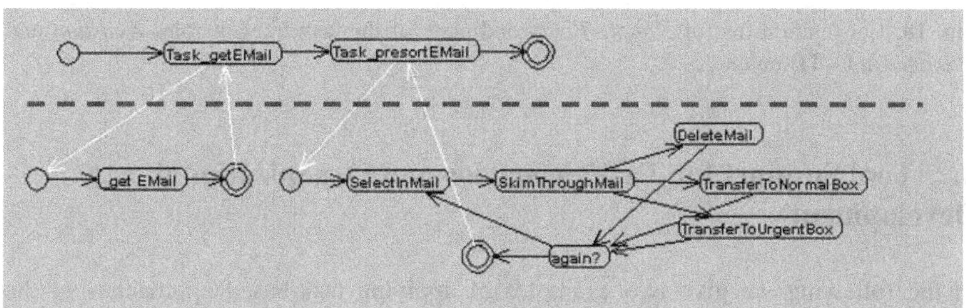

Fig. 9. Activity diagrams of the role element Assistant (above the dotted line) and of the activity elements Get EMail and PreSort EMail of the task model (left and right bottom part), including their synchronization - the white directed links denote synchronization transitions.

In order to animate an application based on its specification, several aspects need to be considered for synchronization. First, action states of activity diagrams of elements of the user model have to be synchronized with (parts of) activity diagrams assigned to elements of the task model – ProcessLens supports role-specific user-interface prototyping. Secondly, action states of activity diagrams of the task model have to be synchronized within the task model as well as with (parts of) activity diagrams of the data model. Although the way of specifying is similar, the semantics for synchronization is different: In the first case (as shown in Figure 9) the division of labor directs the synchronization, whereas in the second case the detailed design of (interactive) functionality is captured.

3.3 CTTE

CTTE is a popular task modeling tool (cf. [19],[20]). Figure 10 illustrates how we applied the tool to model the cooperation between Mr. Young and Patty Smith (see Section 2) in the roles *Manager* and *Assistant*. There are task trees for each role. Some of their nodes are mapped to leaf nodes in the cooperation tree.

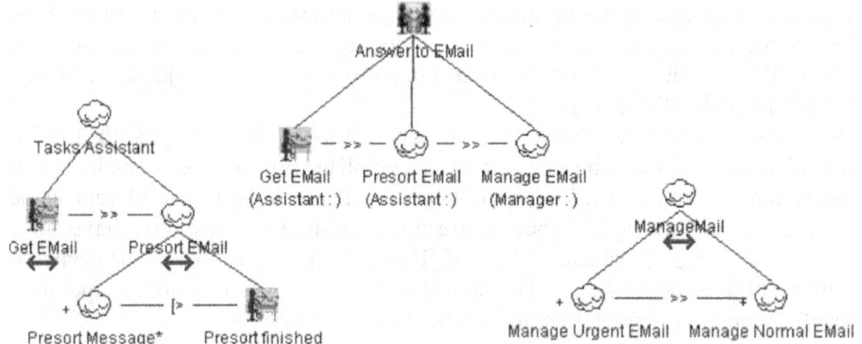

Fig. 10. Cooperation tree of *Handle Email* and parts of the task trees of roles *Assistant* and *Manager* in CTTE-notation.

4. Tool Support for Task Scenarios and Organizational Development

In the following we give two examples of applying task-based approaches in the context of scenario-based developments.

Fig. 11. A task scenario of *Handle Email* in CTTE.

Tool Support 1: Improving the Description of Existing Work Situations

"I'm not sure", said Mr. Young as we animated an execution of task 'Handle EMail' (see CTTE-model in Figure 10 and a snapshot of the animation in Figure 11). "but I think there is something wrong here. Patty works on the incoming mail messages during the whole day. So, if there are some messages in my mailboxes I don't need to wait for her in order to manage the inquiries she has already transferred to me."

Task models are abstract descriptions. Corresponding tools enable users to animate (more or less) concrete task executions interactively. One run of such an animation is referred to a task scenario in the context of this work. As indicated in the introduction, these scenarios can (and should) bridge the gap between model-based and scenario-based ideas. They do not have a narrative character like the scenarios in [5] since they are created on the basis of a formal model. In this way, they are not likely to reflect implicit goals or reveal intrinsic motivation of stakeholders. However, as the above comment of Mr. Young shows task scenarios might encourage involved stakeholders to discuss alternative task scenarios and organizational issues of work when provided with a formal task model.

```
?- animation(situation1).
actual task situation:
(1) Mailbox - {messages:[{sender:"Simone", receiver:"Anke", ...},
                         {sender:"Harry", ..., topic:"news", ...}],
              name="InBox"}
(2) Mailbox - {messages:[], name:"UrgentBox"}
(3) Mailbox - {messages:[], name:"NormalBox"}
(4) Mailbox - {messages:[], name:"OutBox"}
enabled actions:
(1) GetEMail
>: 1
----------------------------
actual task situation: ...
enabled actions:
(1) SelectInMail
(2) _PreSortEMail        /* finish cycle PreSortEMail */
>: 1
----------------------------

after performing steps SkimThroughMail and TransferOrDeleteMail[$m.Urgent]
...
----------------------------
actual task situation:
(1) Mailbox - {messages:[{sender:"Harry", ..., topic:"news", ...}],
              name:"InBox"}
(2) Mailbox - {messages:[(5)], name:"UrgentBox"}
(3) Mailbox - {messages:[], name:"NormalBox"}
(4) Mailbox - {messages:[], name:"OutBox"}
(5) Message - {sender="Simone", receiver="Anke", ... / answer:nil}
enabled actions:
(1) SelectInMail
(2) _PreSortEMail
(3) SelectUrgentMail
(4) _ManageUrgentMail
>: 3
```

Fig. 12. Parts of the task scenario < GetEMail, SelectInMail, SkimThroughMail, TransferOrDeleteMail[$m.Urgent], SelectUrgentMail, ...>.

Furthermore, task scenarios reveal the capabilities of the underlying modeling mechanisms. For instance, it is not possible to formalize the description of a task domain in CTTE although required for task modeling.

Figure 12 contains parts of a task scenario as created by interpreting the TaOSpec-model developed in Section 3.1 and modified. TaOSpec not only presents sub-tasks (sub-actions in the context of TaOSpec) to users which are executable through step-by-step animation, but also the state of each task object of the actual task situation. In addition, users can choose the initial task situation (in this case, situation1 which is illustrated in Figure 3).

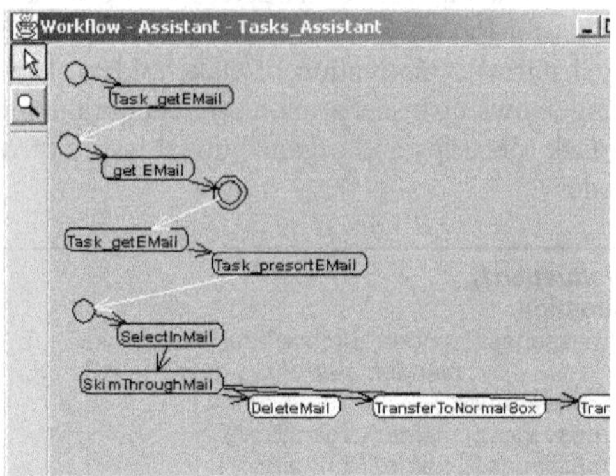

Fig. 13. A task scenario of the tasks of role *Assistant* in ProcessLens.

The integration of knowledge about tasks (actions) and domain objects in TaOSpec allows precise task descriptions. In the example, only one sequential (temporal) operator had to be changed to a concurrent one, in order to solve the problem Mr. Young had with the existing model (see □ in Figure 4). The precondition on ManageMail (see Figure 5) guarantees that this action is only enabled if there is a message for Mr. Young.

Tool Support 2: Development and Description of the Envisioned Organization of Work

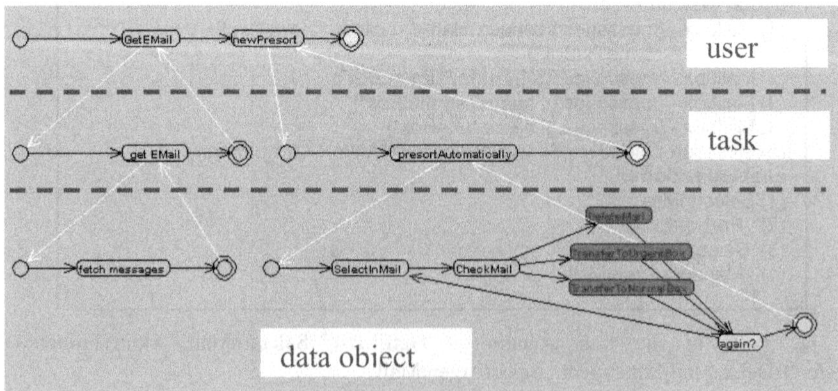

Fig. 14. Synchronization of activity diagrams belonging to the user, task, and data object level according to the envisioned task allocation.

During the creation of the task scenario shown in Figure 13 Patty Smith proposed to automate task PreSort Email (see Figure 8, Figure 9)…

Envisioning organizational developments comprises issues such as the task allocation between humans and software systems. Task modeling tools are useful for discussing such issues. In ProcessLens Patty Smith's proposal can be described and then animated by simplifying the activity diagram of the (human) activity PreSort Email (leading to a single action state _presortAutomatically) and "moving the work" to activity diagrams of the respective data objects, in this case, to the material object Mailbox In, as illustrated in Figure 14.

5. Comparative Analysis

Although each of the described tools and their conceptual foundations have been developed within the model-based tradition of design, and consequently support the representation of tasks, they focus on different aspects: While ProcessLens and CTTE mainly focus on the development of interactive systems, even allowing hands-on UI-experience in case of ProjectLens, TaOSpec targets towards explaining human activities including those in work systems. These differences are reflected through their means for describing task models and task scenarios.

Table 1. Comparative analysis

<table>
<tr><th></th><th>task</th><th>task domain</th><th>actor</th><th>task ↔ domain</th><th>task ↔ actor</th></tr>
<tr><td rowspan="2">TaOSpec</td><td>- task = meta action
- action hierarchy
- explicit temporal relations between sibling actions
- predefined operations assigned to basic actions</td><td>objects with attributes and state descriptions</td><td>one implicit actor</td><td>by pre- and post-conditions of actions</td><td>none</td></tr>
<tr><td colspan="3">- same description mechanism (objects with attributes and partial equations),
- instance-pattern relationship</td><td></td><td></td></tr>
<tr><td rowspan="2">ProcessLens</td><td>- task hierarchy
- sequential temporal relations between tasks
- activities with behavior</td><td>data objects comprising attributes and behavior spec.</td><td>organizat. units, roles, persons, incl. behavior spec.</td><td>- predefined static relations (e.g., creates)
- synchronization of corresponding behavior</td><td>predefined static relations (e.g., handles)</td></tr>
<tr><td colspan="3">class and activity diagrams to describe structure and behavior of model elements (conform to UML)</td><td></td><td></td></tr>
<tr><td>CTTE</td><td>- cooperation tree to control task trees
- explicit temporal relations between sibling tasks</td><td>informal description</td><td>roles</td><td>none</td><td>- one task tree for each role
- simple concept of coordination</td></tr>
</table>

	task scenario
TaOSpec	sequence of basic actions in a concrete task domain (a set of instances of pattern objects occurring in pre- and post conditions)
ProcessLens	- combination of user and task model: sequence of action states of activities dedicated to a task of an actor - combination of user, task, and data model: sequence of action states of corresponding user, task and data objects - no representation of concrete task domains
CTTE	- sequence of tasks of all roles involved - no representation of a task domain

It turns out that the tools offer different types of presentation of (sub-)models and their relations, with TaOSpec providing textual presentations of models and relationships, ProcessLens and CTTE providing diagrammatic notations for specification. In the concluding section, we propose an integration of different representations.

From the comparative data it also becomes evident that task models seem to be related to cooperation models and workflow descriptions. Some concepts like the cooperative trees in CTTE reflect this fact.

Finally, it can be observed that in none of the tools existing work descriptions are distinguished from envisioned ones (cf. Tool Support 2 in Section 4). A mechanism similar to task domain modeling might be used to capture the temporal scope of task descriptions.

6. Concluding Proposals

Ann Simpson and Simon Brown are responsible for describing the management of incoming inquiries by the staff of ExampleOrg. Usually, they apply the CTTE-tool to represent such task models. However, the tool ProcessLens was introduced in their company three months ago: "I'm happy that I can use activity diagrams to show how tasks are completed.", said Simon who has written a diploma thesis about object-oriented analysis. "I hate these temporal operators in CTTE. I always forget their semantics and precedence."

Ann knows Simon's problem (and his deep task trees with all the "artificial" nodes). "Sure, but I think it should be possible to describe richer temporal constraints between sibling tasks in ProcessLens. In that respect, I prefer CTTE."

6.1 Integrating Different Task Representations

When exploring the reasons for the low acceptance of model-based design approaches (cf. [8]) we have investigated three different task-modeling tools. Although these tools and their underlying theoretical or conceptual base assume similar (sub-) models representing tasks (actions), task domains, and users (actors), we could identify significant differences with respect to formal granularity and semantic expressiveness when describing these (sub-)models. For instance, CTTE does not allow formal specifications of task objects in contrast to TaOSpec. The temporal relationships between tasks are less formal defined in ProcessLens than in CTTE or in TaOSpec. For that reason much of the behavior description has to be moved to the level of activities (as the bottom part of a task hierarchy). Evidently, so far there exists no commonly agreed level of description, either for fine-grained specifications or abstract descriptions.

We know from our experience when teaching task modeling and applying corresponding tools in projects that we need both means to describe sequences of sub-tasks and means to describe states of objects of a task domain. We also have noticed that people accept the idea to assign temporal descriptions to each level of a task hierarchy (as realized in CTTE and TaOSpec) although this strategy restricts the expressiveness of temporal constraints [21]. However, many of them have similar problems as Simon Brown. For example, they introduce nodes into a CTTE-hierarchy which do not play the role of a conceptual sub-task, but rather do allow more sophisticated temporal descriptions.

In order to guide users to accurate modeling dedicated elements help that supports the (partially) separate consideration of hierarchi¬cal and sequential aspects of tasks. For example, a temporal equation can be assigned to each non-basic task T containing all direct sub-tasks of T (cf. [21]). Other representations are possible as well. In this case, temporal equations can be replaced by activity diagrams. Figure 15 shows an abstract example. (Note that ProcessLens does not allow the assignment of activity diagrams to tasks.) It can be shown that each temporal equation with temporal operators like >> (sequence), ||| (concurrency), [] (alternative), [...] (option), or * (iteration) can be transformed into a corresponding activity diagram. It is beyond the scope of this paper to give the set of transformation and simplification rules.

TaOSpec offers a hybrid notation of temporal constraints between sub-tasks and constraints on object states (in pre- and post conditions of sub-tasks). For those developers more used to activity diagrams, object flows can support such a hybrid notation.

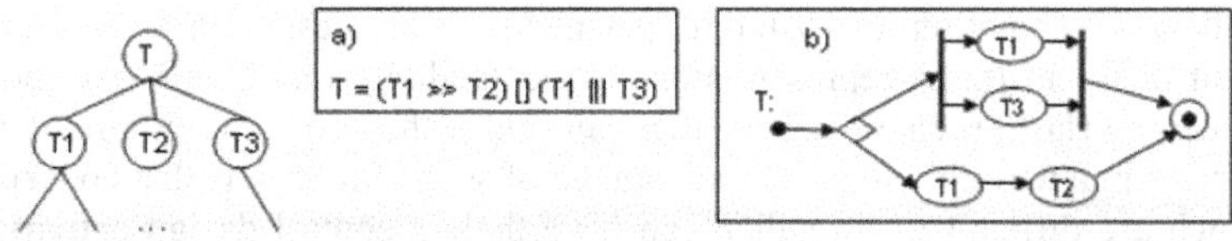

Fig. 15. Part of an abstract task hierarchy of task T (left side), a) a temporal equation assigned to T, b) a corresponding activity diagram.

In Figure 16, a mapping of an abstract fragment in TaOSpec to an activity diagram with object flows is shown. Implicit object flows in TaOSpec become explicit object flows in activity diagrams.

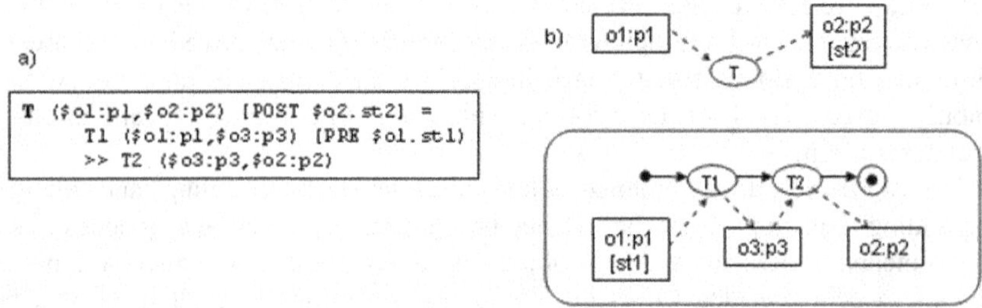

Fig. 16. Constraints on temporal relations and object states of task T: a) in TaOSpec, b) in activity diagrams with object flows.

6.2 Integrating Different Design Approaches

We suggest not only striving for modeling conventions but also for modeling tools (and the underlying frameworks) that encourage an integrated use of different design approaches. As we have demonstrated, the creation of concrete task scenarios helps to connect model-based and scenario-based ideas. However, in order to achieve that goal elaborated relations between model elements are required, in particular some instance-pattern relationship (cf. Tool Support 1 in Section 4).

An animation of task scenarios at different levels of granularity could also be useful. Existing animation or prototyping techniques could be improved so that users need not to concentrate on the correct use of animation features, but rather on the improvement of the task scenarios and the organization of work.

For each of the tools some kind of self-referential application of scenario- or model-based design ideas could lead to improvements of their user interfaces. For example, more convenient interaction techniques for changing an activity node to a task node, e.g., in ProcessLens, could be achieved through interactive temporal relations.

Overall, a combination of different perspectives on design processes and the creation of different (task) representations could facilitate tool-based task modeling besides creating (task) scenarios. The latter can bridge the gap between formal models and scenarios in a narrative form. An advantage of such a linkage is that concepts like goals which are difficult to formalize can nevertheless control design activities like the development of scenarios (which, in return, influence more formal modeling activities again).

References

1. P. Johnson, S. Wilson. A framework for task based design. Proceedings of VAMMS'93, second Czech-British Symposium, Prague. Ellis Horwood, 1993.
2. A. Puerta, E. Cheng, T. Ou, J. Min. MOBILE: User-centered interface building. Proceedings of the ACM Conf. on Human Aspects on Computing Systems CHI'99. ACM Press, pages 426-433, New York, 1999.
3. XIML: A Universal Language for User Interfaces. http://www.ximl.org.

4. E. O'Neill. User-developer cooperation in software development: building common ground and usable systems. PhD thesis. Queen Mary and Westfield College, Univ. of London, 1998.
5. M.B.Rosson, J.M.Carroll. Usability Engineering – Scenario-Based Devel¬op¬¬ment of Human-Computer Interaction. Morgan Kaufmann Publishers, 2002.
6. L. Constantine, Canonical Abstract Prototypes for Abstract Visual and Interaction Design. In [7].
7. J. Jorge, N. J. Nunes, J. F. e Cunha, editors, DSV-IS 2003 : Issues in Designing New-generation Interactive Systems Proceedings of the Tenth Workshop on the Design, Specification and Verification of Interactive Systems. Nr. LNCS volume 2844, Springer, 2003.
8. H. Trætteberg, P. Molina, N. Nunes. Making model-based UI design practical: Usable and open methods and tools. Workshop at the International Conference on Computer-Aided Design of User Interfaces, CADUI 2004, Madeira, 2004.
9. P. Forbrig, A. Dittmar. Bridging the gap between scenarios and formal models. In C. Stephanidis, Proc. of the HCI International 2003, pages 98-102, Greece, 2003.
10. H. Trætteberg. Model-based User Interface Design. PhD thesis. Norwegian University of Science and Technology - NTNU Trondheim, 2002.
11. Q. Limbourg, C. Pribeanu, J. Vanderdonckt. Towards Uniformed Task Models in a Model-Based Approach. In C. Johnson, editor, DSV-IS 2001, LNCS 2220, pages 165-182, Springer, 2001.
12. A. Dittmar, P. Forbrig. Higher-Order Task Models. In [7].
13. A. Dittmar. Ein formales Metamodell für den aufgabenbasierten Entwurf interaktiver Systeme. PhD thesis. University of Rostock, 2002.
14. M. Stoy. TaOSpec - Implementation einer aktionsorientierten Spezifikationssprache. Studienarbeit, FB Informatik, Univ. Rostock, 2003.
15. C. Stary. TADEUS: Seamless Development of Task-Based and User-Oriented Inter¬fa¬ces. IEEE Transactions on Systems, Man, and Cybernetics, Vol. 30, pp. 509-525, 2000.
16. C. Stary, S. Stoiber. Model-based Electronic Performance Support. In [7].
17. M. Fowler, S. Kendall. UML Distilled - Applying the Standard Object Modeling Language. Addison Wesley, Reading, Massachusetts, 1997.
18. G. Booch, J. Rumbaugh, I. Jacobson. The Unified Modeling Language User Guide. Addison Wesley, 1999.
19. CTTE: The ConcurTaskTree Environment. http://giove.cnuce.cnr.it/ctte.html.
20. F. Paterno, C. Mancini, S. Meniconi. ConcurTaskTrees: A notation for specifying task models. In INTERACT'97, pages 362-369, 1997.
21. A. Dittmar. More precise Descriptions of Temporal Relations within Task Models. In: Palanque, P., Paterno, F., editors, DSV-IS 2000, LNCS 1946, Springer-Verlag, pages 151-168, 2000.

Discussion

[Gerrit van der Veer] As far as I understand, it seemed that all three approaches have no concept like event or trigger. E.g. in your scenario you have an inquiry arriving, but none of these three tools can model this properly, since these all model reactive processes. In real life there should be proactive agents, showing new things arriving from the outside. This is a basic problem with all three tools--they don't model the arrival of new events.

> [Anke Dittmar, Peter Forbrig] This is not in the current analysis, but we think that all three could describe these process interruptions.

[Gerrit van der Veer] Yes, but the tools can only model where the tasks have to be waiting for something to happen.

> [Anke Dittmar, Peter Forbrig] Yes, you are right. We are not interested in modifying modelling concepts; we are just looking at what is being modelled right now. However, you could easily make this change to these tools, to allow that a message is coming from the outside and a task has to respond to it.

[Juergen Ziegler] Towards the end of your talk you showed how you can model this approach to UML activity diagrams. What are the advantages of your approach to activity diagrams or equivalent notations? In your approach you are focusing on the decompositions of tasks instead of the flow aspects. Do you have any rules, in your mapping, as to where in the decomposition you may or may not use sequential or temporal definitions?

> [Anke Dittmar, Peter Forbrig] Our specification is much richer than UML diagrams. For example, UML diagrams cannot specify interrupts. Our notation is much richer, and it can also specify new temporal relations. But it might be useful to present these ideas in UML diagrams. Also, UML (or whatever) specifications are just a means to express task modelling concepts. For example, here we use activity diagrams to represent the relation between siblings within the structure. Also, task models are very simple. For example, they only allow temporal constraints on one level of the hierarchy. So this is restricted, compared with something like Petri nets. So you cannot describe complex temporal relations with this notation.

[Michael Harrison] How do your tools help you to express non-normative behaviours, work-arounds, and errors? For example, attaching (or forgetting to attach) files within the email example.

> [Anke Dittmar, Peter Forbrig] To do this you need to modify the modeling concepts themselves, so that you can combine different task models. But that is not the topic of this talk. Perhaps we can do this in the future with something like an aspect-oriented specification.

DynaMo-AID: A Design Process and a Runtime Architecture for Dynamic Model-Based User Interface Development

Tim Clerckx, Kris Luyten, and Karin Coninx

Limburgs Universitair Centrum – Expertise Centre for Digital Media
Universitaire Campus, B-3590 Diepenbeek, Belgium
{tim.clerckx,kris.luyten,karin.coninx}@luc.ac.be

Abstract. The last few years a lot of research efforts have been spent on user interfaces for pervasive computing. This paper shows a design process and a runtime architecture, DynaMo-AID, that provide design support and a runtime architecture for context-aware user interfaces. In the process attention is focused on the specification of the tasks the user and the application will have to perform, together with other entities related to tasks, like dialog and presentation. In this paper we will show how we can model tasks, dialogs, and presentation when the designer wants to develop context-sensitive user interfaces. Besides the design process, a runtime architecture will be presented supporting context-sensitive user interfaces. Pervasive user interfaces can change during the runtime of the interactive application due to a change of context or when a service becomes available to the application. We will show that traditional models like task, environment and dialog model have to be extended to tackle these new problems. This is why we provide modeling and runtime support solutions for design and development of context-sensitive user interfaces.

keywords: model-based user interface design, pervasive user interface, context, design process, runtime architecture, task model, service.

1 Introduction

There is a continuing and growing interest in designing user interfaces for mobile computing devices and embedded systems. This evolution is driven by a very fast evolving hardware market, where mobile computing devices like Personal Digital Assitants (PDAs) and mobile phones are getting more powerful each new generation. The mobile nature of portable devices and the increasing availability of (wireless) communication with other resources require applications that can react on context changes. When we talk about context and context-aware applications, we mean applications that can adapt to environmental changes, like the change of platform, network capabilities, services that become available and disappear or even physical conditions like light intensity or temperature. In [8], Hong states there are several

R. Bastide, P. Palanque, and J. Roth (Eds.): EHCI-DSVIS 2004, LNCS 3425, pp. 77-95, 2005.

goals why context-aware computing is interesting to achieve. Advancing development of context-aware computing gives incentives to:

- increase the amount of input channels for a computer;
- gather implicit data;
- create more suitable models for the input;
- use the previous elements in useful ways.

To create consistent adaptive user interfaces (UI), UI developers should consider adaptivity in early design stages. When using the model-based approach in the design phase some problems can be identified: traditional models, like a task model and a dialog model are static and not suited to adapt to context changes. This paper shows how designers can take adaptability of the UI in consideration by extending these traditional models to support design of context-sensitive user interfaces.

In previous work [3] we have shown how a modified task notation can be used in order to design context-sensitive user interfaces for static context. Our former approach limited the influence of the context upon the different models in time. The context was sensed when the UI was deployed and started on the target device. From that moment on no context changes were taken into account. In this paper we extend this method to design and provide runtime support for user interfaces that can be affected by dynamic context changes. With dynamic context changes we do not only take into account the target platform, network properties and other environmental conditions. We also seek a way to consider how we can design a UI for a service. How to cope with this service when it becomes available to the application on the portable device of the user is an important issue and the main contribution of this paper.

According to [5], a **service** is "*a distinct part of a computer system that manages a collection of related resources and presents their functionality to users and applications*". An example of a service is a software component, running on a particular device, offering access to some functionality it provides (e.g., a surveillance camera can "export" its output video stream, zoom and focus functions). A service offers functionality that should be used in conjunction with other application logic. Arbitrary clients can connect to this service and make use of the exported functionality.

The next section shows existing Model-Based User Interface Development approaches that support context changes in different ways. In section 3 we discuss our own design process, **DynaMo-AID** (**Dyna**mic **Mo**del-b**A**sed user **I**nterface **D**evelopment), to develop context-sensitive user interfaces that support dynamic context changes. DynaMo-AID is part of the Dygimes [4] User Interface Creation Framework. Section 4 introduces a runtime architecture to support user interfaces created with the DynaMo-AID process. Afterwards a genuine case study will be shown in section 5 to illustrate the practical use of DynaMo-AID. In this paper we show how the DynaMo-AID process is supported by the appropriate design tools. Finally the paper is concluded with a discussion of the obtained results and a description of the future work.

2 Related Work

The current literature shows a growing interest in the creation of context-sensitive user interfaces. During the last few years we see more interest in defining and exploiting context information on several levels of the UI conception. The primary goal of most initiatives is to more flexibly design user interfaces, with increasing design/code reusability resulting in user interfaces that become more usable in different contexts of use.

The different levels for introducing context information can be summarized as follows. First, the task model can be made dependent on the context, as shown in [15,21]. Next, at the dialog level navigation can be dependent on the context e.g. allowing navigation to take place in a multiple-device setting where the user can take advantage of multiple devices or settings in the same time span [3,28]. Finally at the presentation level context information can be considered to choose the most appropriate widgets, as in [27,14]. Notice we consider the user model to be part of the context information. In this work we will allow to integrate context on different levels of the user interface design and creation like shown in the next sections.

Calvary et al. [2] describe a development process to create context-sensitive user interfaces. The development process consists of four steps: creation of a task-oriented specification, creation of the abstract interface, creation of the concrete interface, and finally the creation of the context-sensitive interactive system. The focus however, lays upon a mechanism for context detection and how context information can be used to adapt the UI, captured in a three-step process: (1) recognizing the current situation (2) calculating the reaction and (3) executing the reaction. In our approach we will focus on the exposure of a complete design process using extended versions of existing models, and how context reflects on these models. Furthermore we extend context by taking into account the effects of incoming and abolished services.

Mori et al. present a process [15] to design device-independent user interfaces in a model-based approach. In this approach, a high-level task model is constructed to describe tasks that can be performed on several platforms. Afterwards, the designer has to specify which tasks of the high-level description can be performed on which device. When this is done, an abstract UI will be created followed by the UI generation. In our approach we describe the differences between target platforms in one complete task model and provide the possibility to take into account other sorts of context information than platform.

In the next sections we integrate several solutions to build context-sensitive user interfaces into one process with appropriate tool support for this process. To our knowledge there is no other initiative trying to combine context-information on the different levels of model-based user interface development. The distinct parts of this process will be presented separately.

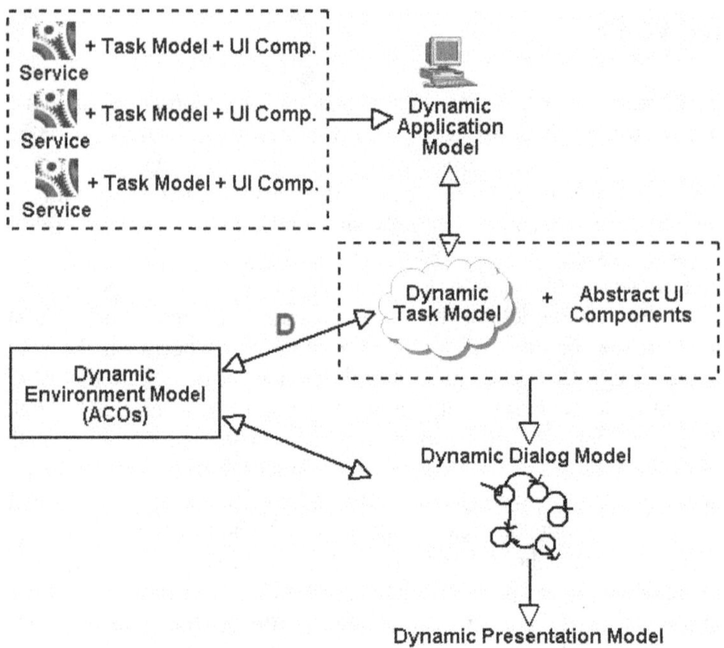

Fig. 1. The DynaMo-AID Design Process.

3 The DynaMo-AID Design Process

The main goal is to create a process that enables the user interface designer to create user interfaces for pervasive systems. Since pervasive interfaces have a strong link to the information provided by their direct environment, these interfaces should be capable to evolve according to the context changes initiated in their environment. Figure 1 gives an overview of the DynaMo-AID Design Process. In this process the designer can specify the interaction by constructing and manipulating abstract models because at design time it may be unknown for which environments (available hardware and software services, physical environment, target user,...) the UI will be rendered.

The models used in our process try to enhance the ones commonly used in Model-Based User Interface Design [20]. This is why extra attention is payed on the representation and semantics of these models: we will investigate how expressive traditional existing models are, and where they need to be extended for pervasive systems. For this purpose a "meta" model is introduced: the *Dynamic Model* is a model that can change at runtime in a way that the model can be merged with another model from the same type (e.g. attaching subtrees to an existing tree) or parts of the model can be pruned. This way the *Dynamic Model* can be seen as a dynamic extension of *Interface Model*, as introduced in [22]. The Interface Model exists out of the set of relevant abstract models (task, dialog, domain, user,...) necessary to describe the interface of a system.

In the DynaMo-AID Design Process there is a difference between the main application, for example running on a PDA or a cell phone, and services (applications that provide a service and an interface) that can be encountered during the runtime of the interactive application. Services have to be modelled separately from the design of the main application.

In summary, the DynaMo-AID Design Process consists of the following steps:

1. constructing the Dynamic Task Model for the main application (section 3.1).
2. attaching abstract descriptions to the unit tasks[1] of the Dynamic Task Model. Platform-independent high-level user interface components are connected with these leaf tasks similar as we have shown in previous work [4,13,3].
3. calculation of the *ConcurTaskTrees Forest*. This is the collection of ConcurTaskTrees describing the tasks to be performed for each common occurence of context during the runtime of the main application. For uncommon occurences of context, these tasks have to be specified as a service.
4. automatic extraction of the dialog model for each ConcurTaskTree in the ConcurTaskTree Forest.
5. construction of the atomic dialog model by the designer. This dialog model consists of the subatomic dialog models created in the previous step and contains all transitions that may occur during the runtime of the main application, triggered by an action of the user, the application or even a change of context (section 3.2).
6. linking context information to the task and dialog model through abstract context objects (section 3.3).
7. modeling the services: accomodate each service with a task tree describing the tasks user and application can perform when they are able to use the service (can be done anywhere in the process and services can be used by different applications)

This process enables us to design context-sensitive user interfaces and supports fast prototyping. It enables us to create a prototype presentation using the methodology we introduced in [4]. This will be further explained in section 3.5. This design process demands further explanation. This is why the Dynamic Models will be separately discussed in the following subsections.

3.1 Dynamic Task Model

To specify tasks we use a modified version of the ConcurTaskTree notation, introduced by Fabio Paterno [17]. This notation offers a graphical syntax, an hierarchical structure and a notation to specify the temporal relations between tasks. Four types of tasks are supported in the CTT notation: abstract tasks, interaction tasks, user tasks, and application tasks. These tasks can be specified to be executed in several iterations. Sibling tasks, appearing in the same level in the hierarchy of decomposition, can be connected by temporal operators like choice ([]), independent concurrency (|||), concurrency with information exchange (|[]|), disabling ([>) , enabling (>>), enabling with information exchange ([]>>), suspend/resume (|>) and

[1] A unit task that can not be devided in subtasks any further. In a ConcurTaskTree specification these are the leaf tasks [21]

order independency (|=|).The support for concurrent tasks is very valuable because of our envisioned target: pervasive systems where users can transparently interact with the (embedded) computing devices in their environment. Some tasks can be supported by multiple devices, thus concurrent usage of these different resources should be supported in the task design notation. In the remainder of this paper we will make extensive use of "Enabled Task Sets" (ETS). An ETS is defined in [17] as:

> *a set of tasks that are logically enabled to start their performance during the same period of time.*

To link abstract information about how a task can be performed by an actor (user or application), we attach platform-independent high-level user interface components to these leaf tasks [13,3]. This way all possible user interfaces are covered by a complete annotation of the task specification.

Several approaches that use the ConcurTaskTrees Notation [17] exist for modelling context-sensitive human-computer interaction. In [18], Paternò and Santoro show how ConcurTaskTrees can be used to model user interfaces suitable for different platforms. Pribeanu et al. [21,26] proposed several approaches to integrate a context structure in ConcurTaskTrees task models. The main difference in our approach is the support for runtime context-sensitivity introduced in the different models.

In order to make a connection with the dynamic environment model we choose the approach described in [3] where *decision nodes*, denoted by **D**, collect distinct subtrees from which one of them will be selected at runtime according to the current context of use. To link the dynamic task model with the dynamic environment model and to gather information about a suitable presentation of the UI, decision nodes are coupled to Abstract Context Objects (section 3.3). We can summarize it here as follows. The decision nodes notation enables to specify task models that describe the tasks (1) a user may have to perform in different contexts of use and (2) where tasks that are enabled by new incoming services will find there place in the task model. To obtain this, services are accompanied by a task description as a formal description for the goals that can be accomplished through their use. Figure 5 shows a decision tree where "Use ImogI" is a decision node where a distinction in tasks is made between the use of a mobile application inside or outside a certain domain.

3.2 Dynamic Dialog Model

A dialog model describes the transitions that are possible between user interface states. Although transitions usually are invoked by a user action or a call from the application core, in this case the current context is also an actor that can perform a transition.

To specify a dialog model, several notations are used: State Transition Networks [29], Dialogue Graphs [25], Window Transitions [28], Petri Nets [19],... The State Transition Network (STN) notation describes the dialog between user and application by defining states (including a start-state and possibly several finish states) of the UI and transitions between these states.

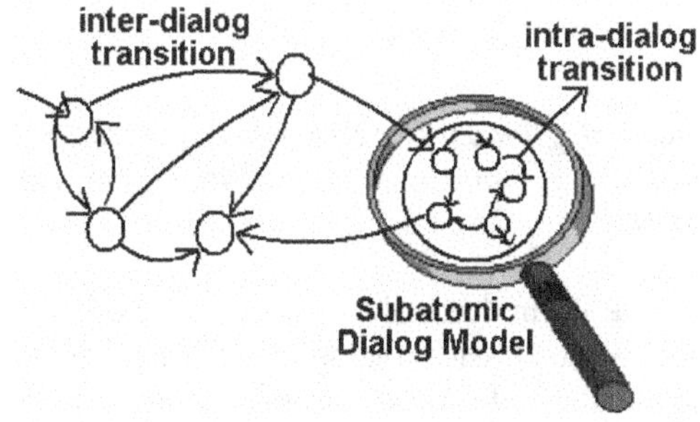

Fig. 2. Dynamic Dialog Model.

Puerta and Eisenstein [23] introduced the *mapping problem*: the problem of mapping abstract models (domain/task/data model) in model-based user interface design to more concrete models (dialog/presentation model). Limbourg, Vanderdonckt et al. [12,28] proposed several rules to derive dialog information from constrained ConcurTaskTrees task models (a parent task has exactly one child task). In [13] we have already shown it is possible to extract a dialog model automatically from a task model. We made use of the ConcurTaskTrees Notation to represent a task specification and the dialog model is structured as a STN. In this method, the states in a STN are extracted from the task specification by calculating the *enabled task sets* [17].

Because the context may change during the execution of the application, the dialog model becomes more complex. First, the dialog models can be extracted automatically from each possible ConcurTaskTree that may occur. Afterwards the designer can draw transitions, that can only be invoked by a context switch, between the dialog models. This way a dynamic dialog model is created. To express this approach, we introduce following definitions:

Definition 1 *An* ***intra-dialog transition*** *is a transition in a STN caused by the completion of a task through user interaction or by the application. Intra-dialog transitions connect enabled task sets from the same ConcurTaskTree. Transitions are triggered by the execution of a task, either by the user or by the application, and can be denoted by:* $(CTT_i, ETS_k) \xrightarrow{task} (CTT_i, ETS_l)$

Definition 2 *An* ***inter-dialog transition*** *is a transition in a STN caused by a context switch. Inter-dialog transitions connect enabled task sets from different ConcurTaskTrees of the same ConcurTaskTrees Forest and are triggered by a positive evaluation of a context condition. Inter-dialog transitions can be denoted by:* $(CTT_i, ETS_k) \xrightarrow{condition} (CTT_j, ETS_l)$

Definition 3 *A **subatomic dialog mode** is a STN containing the states and transitions from the same ConcurTaskTree. This means a subatomic dialog model is a regular STN, extracted from one ConcurTaskTree.*

Definition 4 *An **atomic dialog model** is a STN where the states are subatomic dialog models and the transitions are inter-dialog transitions between states of different subatomic dialog models.*

Figure 2 illustrates the definitions of *subatomic* and *atomic* dialog model. The subatomic dialog model is the classical dialog model where actions of user or system imply the transition to another state. When a context change occurs, this dialog model can become obsolete. As a result a transition to another subatomic dialog model takes place and an updated UI comes into play. Note that a context change can also invoke a system function instead of performing an inter-dialog transition (e.g. turning on the backlight of a PDA when entering a dark room). This explains the *invocation* arrow in figure 4 that connects dialog and application.

3.3 Dynamic Environment Model

Despite several efforts to describe context information and using it for interactive applications [2,7,24,11], it still is a challenging issue due to the lack of a standard and practical implementations.

Calvary et al. [1,2] introduce an *environment model* to be specified by designers for defining the current context of use together with the platform model. Furthermore the *evolution model* describes when a context switch takes place and defines the appropriate reaction.

Coutaz and Rey [7] define the *contextor*, a software abstraction of context data that interprets sensed information or information provided by other contextors. In this way a chain of contextors can be created to produce one logical component.

Salber et al. [24] describe a widget-based toolkit, the Context Toolkit, containing abstract widgets in order to:

- encapsulate rough context details to abstract context from implementation details (like the proxy design pattern);
- reuse widgets in different applications.

The Dynamic Environment Model (figure 3) represents context changes, and provides us with a model to react on these changes in an appropriate way. In contrast with other approaches, a service is also part of the environment in our model. Since a service offers (previously unknown) functionality that can integrate with the whole of the application, a more dynamic approach is neccessary here. This means calculated changes in the navigation through the interface should be supported. To explain the effect of the Dynamic Environment Model, some definitions are introduced here:

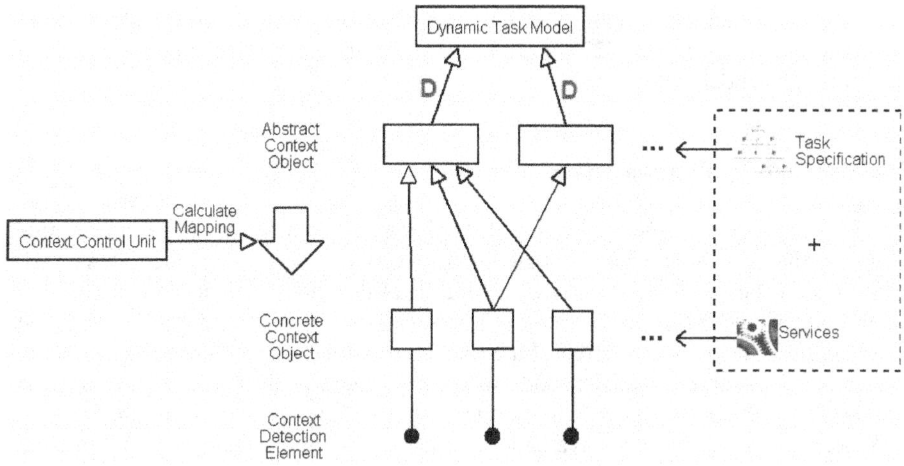

Fig. 3. Dynamic Environment Model.

Definition 5 *A* ***Concrete Context Object (CCO)*** *is an object that encapsulates entities (like low level sensors) that represent one sort of context.*

Definition 6 *An* ***Abstract Context Object (ACO)*** *is an object that can be queried about the context it represents.*

Different from the approach in [24] we separate the abstraction and encapsulation functions of a context widget. This is necessary because due to context changes, the number of available widgets can change on the abstract and concrete level. Moreover this separation allows to support context-sensitive user interfaces on the design level. First, a new service may introduce new abstract widgets (ACOs), linked to the accompanying task specification. Furthermore, a change of platform resources (e.g. moving into the reach of a wireless LAN may imply connection to a server and a printer) can give or take away access to CCOs. As a result, the mapping of an ACO to CCOs has to be repeated when the collection of ACOs or available CCOs changes.

This can be taken care of by defining mapping rules in order to select the appropriate CCOs currently available for each ACO used by the interactive application. The mapping function can be implemented by dividing CCOs into categories, and specify for each ACO the appropriate CCOs relevant to the abstract widget. The detection of context changes and the call to repeat the mapping is handled by the **Context Control Unit (CCU)** that is part of the runtime architecture (section 4).

To link the environment model to the task and dialog model, ACOs are attached to the decision nodes (section 3.1). For each subtree, a *query* is provided to denote which conditions have to be fulfilled by an ACO to select the subtree. In this way, when the atomic dialog model is constructed, the transitions can be marked with the correct ACOs and belonging queries.

Remark the analogy with abstract interaction objects (AIOs) and concrete interaction objects (CIOs) [27] used to describe user interface components in a platform independent way.

3.4 Dynamic Application Model

The functional core of the application does change when a service (dis)appears: this change influences the models. As stated before, services are accompanied with a task specification they support to provide a high-level description of the interaction that should be enabled when the service becomes available. When the designer wants the main application to update the UI at the time an unknown service becomes available, he/she has to reserve a decision node to specify where in the interaction a place is provided to interact directly with the service (e.g. the "Service"-task in figure 5).

When the service becomes available, the dialog and environment model also have to be updated. The atomic dialog model has to be extended with the new subatomic dialog models, provided by the task model attached to the service. Next, the environment model needs to be changed on two levels: (1) the new task model can provide new decision nodes. As a result new ACOs can be introduced, and these have to be mapped on the available CCOs. (2) the service can provide access new CCOs. In this case the CCU will also have to recalculate the mappings.

3.5 Presentation Model Enabled for Fast Prototyping

During the design of the different models we support direct prototyping of the UI. Our system supports the automatic generation of the UI from the different models that are specified. For this purpose we start with calculating the ETSs from the annotated task model: each ETS is a node in the dialog model. One such node represents all UI building blocks that have to be presented to complete the current ETS (section 3 showed that UI building blocks were attached to unit tasks).

The designers (and future users) can try the resulting interface during the design process. Important aspects of the UI can be tackled in the design phase: improving navigation, consistency, layout and usability in general are done in an early stage. Tool support is implemented and presented in section 6. There is only limited support for styling the UI; enhancing the graphical "aesthetic" presentation is currently not supported in our tool.

4 The DynaMo-AID Runtime Architecture

To put a designed UI into practice, a runtime architecture must exist to support the results of the design process. [6] gives an overview of several software architectures to implement interactive software. Architectures based on SEEHEIM, ARCH, SLINKY and PAC make use of a dialog controller, to control the interaction flow between the presentation of the UI and the functional core of the interactive application. Because we present a runtime architecture where tasks and environment can change during the execution of the application (sections 3.3 and 3.4), the dialog controller is assisted in making decisions about dialog changes by the task controller and the Context Control Unit.

Figure 4 shows the DynaMo-AID runtime architecture. When the application is started, first the current context will be detected, and the applicable task model will be chosen before the UI will be deployed. Then the subatomic dialog model belonging to this task model will be set active and the start state of this model will be the first dialog to be rendered in the concrete UI. The context will be sensed by scanning the information provided by posing the queries in the ACOs.

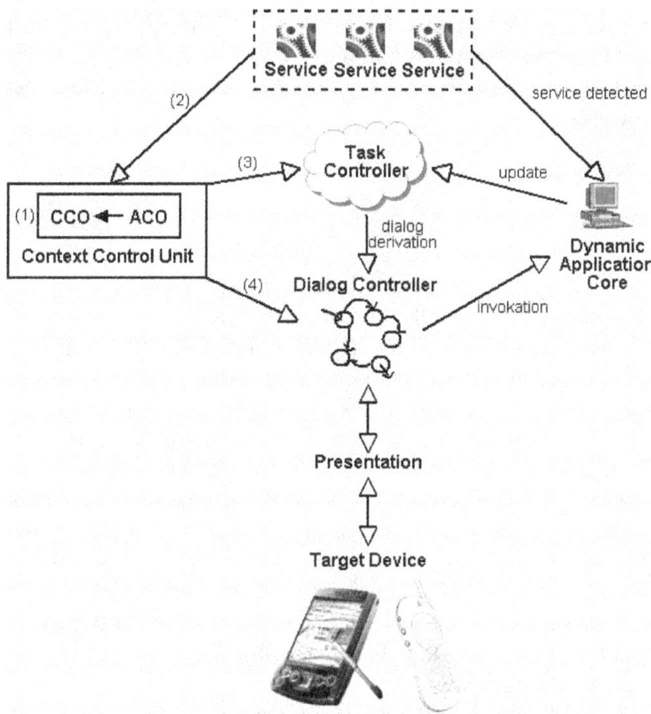

Fig. 4. The DynaMo-AID Architecture.

From now on interaction can take place and the state of the UI can change due to three actors: the user, the application and the Context Control Unit (CCU).

The user interacts with the target device to manipulate the presentation. As a result, the dialog controller will perform an intra-dialog transition and update the presentation of the UI. The second actor is the application. The application core can also manipulate the UI (e.g. displaying the results of a query after processing). Also, an incoming service extends the application core and can carry a task model containing abstract user interface components. This is why the task controller will be notified with an update to modify the dialog model. It is obvious that an abolished service also implies an update of the task as well as the dialog model. The last actor that is able to change the state of the UI is the CCU, introduced in section 3.3.

The tasks of the CCU are:

1. **detection** of context changes: a context change will be detected by the CCU when an ACO throws an event.
2. **recalculation** of mappings from CCO to ACO: a service can also be a provider of context information and this is why, in that case, the service must be reachable for the CCU to recalculate ACO to CCO mappings. When the service is abolished, the CCU will also apply the recalculation.
3. **selection** of the current context-specific task model: the CCU will inform the Task Controller of the changed ACO and the Task Controller will return the current valid context-specific task model.
4. **execution** of inter-dialog transition (together with the dialog controler): using the appropriate context-specific task model, the dialog controller will be informed to perform an inter-dialog transition.

The next section will show how the runtime architecture and the design process can be of practical use.

5 A Case Study

Within a few kilometres from our research department there is an open-air museum of 550 ha large. It contains a large collection of old Flemish houses and farms of the late 18th century, and allows the visitors to experience how life was in those days. Currently we are developing a mobile tourist guide "ImogI" for this museum, and use the methodology discussed above to create a usable context-sensitive interface for this application. The hardware setup is as follows: the visitor has a PDA with a GPS module as a touristic guidance system and museum artefacts are annotated with "virtual information" that can be sent to the guide once the tourist enters the artefacts range. The mobile guide contains a map of the museum and some information about the whereabouts of the artefacts; more detailled information is sent by the artefacts themselves (through a built-in system using bluetooth communication) to the mobile guide. This makes sure new artefacts can be placed at an arbitrary place in the museum without the guidance system becoming obsolete. The system depicted on the mobile guide is always up-to-date.

Figure 5 shows a simple ImogI task specification. On the first level of the task specification there are two context-dependencies expressed as decision nodes: the first one determines whether the user is inside or outside the domain. When the user is situated outside the museum premises, the application will act like a normal GPS navigation system. When the user moves into the open air museum, the application transforms into a mobile guide and vice versa. The other decision node allows to attach new services that become available in the direct surroundings of the PDA. The former context information is obtained by a GPS module on the PDA. We are currently implementing the latter with Bluetooth. The task specification in figure 5 can anticipate visitors leaving the actual museum boundaries to explore the facilities outside the premises. Figure 6 shows how the resulting dialog specification supporting automatic detection of the context change looks like. The dashed arrows

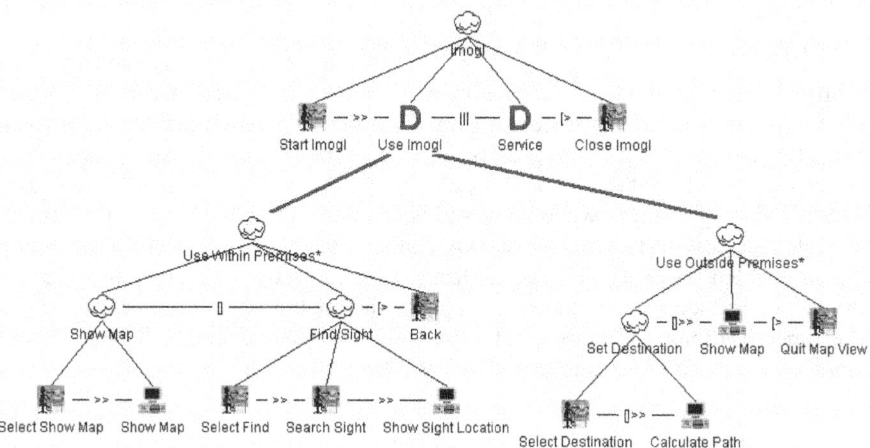

Fig. 5. ImogI Decision Tree

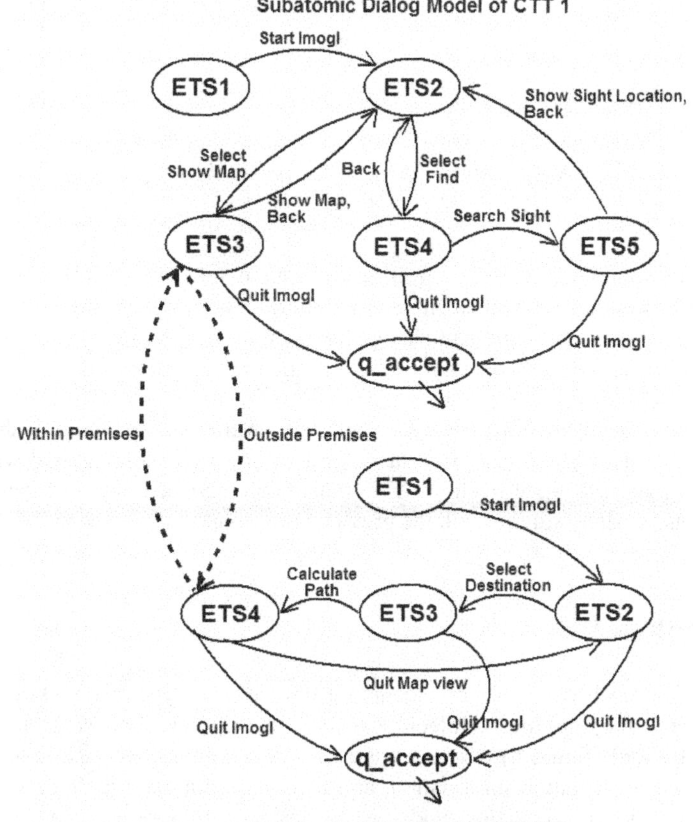

Fig. 6. ImogI Atomic Dialog Model.

$(CTT_1, ETS_3) \xrightarrow{OutsidePremises} (CTT_2, ETS_4)$
and $(CTT_2, ETS_4) \xrightarrow{InsidePremises} (CTT_1, ETS_3)$ specifiy the transition between the different dialog models. An important remark is the designer must specify between witch ETSs of the different ConcurTaskTrees inter-dialog transitions can occur. This way the designer can preserve usability when the user is performing a task existing of several subtasks. For example, the user can be confused if the user interface suddenly changes when he or she is scrolling through a map or performing some other critical task. Notice the two dialog models are the result out of two different enabled task sets. A context change influences the task groupings, and by consequence influences the navigational properties of the interface. For this reason dialog specifications are considered separately for each context change. In our example, the ETS $E(CTT_1)$ is followed by $E(CTT_2)$.

$$E(CTT_1) = \begin{cases} ETS_1 = \{Start\ ImogI\} \\ ETS_2 = \{Select\ Show\ Map, Select\ Find, Service, Back, Close\ ImogI\} \\ ETS_3 = \{Show\ Map, Service, Back, Close\ ImogI\} \\ ETS_4 = \{Search\ Sight, Service, Back, Close\ ImogI\} \\ ETS_5 = \{Show\ Sight\ Location, Service, Back, Close, ImogI\} \end{cases}$$

$$E(CTT_2) = \begin{cases} ETS_1 = \{Start\ ImogI\} \\ ETS_2 = \{Select\ Destination, Service, Close\ ImogI\} \\ ETS_3 = \{Calculate\ Path, Service, Close\ ImogI\} \\ ETS_4 = \{Show\ ImogI, Quit\ Map\ View, Service, Close\ ImogI\} \end{cases}$$

Our starting-point here is the support for dynamic extensible models to have better support for designing context-sensitive user interfaces. The case study here shows their use: the open-air museum can change the location of their information kiosks or add other artefacts without constantly updating the mobile guide. Information kiosks can communicate with the mobile guide and offer all kinds of services (photo publishing, extra information, covered wagon reservations,...). Figure 7 shows the task specification for the kiosk. This task specification will be integrated within the context-sensitive task specification. The transitions between the different dialog specifications are done similar with the previous example.

6 Tool Support

To test our approach we have implemented a limited prototype of the DynaMo-AID design process and runtime architecture using the Dygimes rendering engine. The DynaMo-AID tool (figure 8) *aids* to construct a context-sensitive task model [3], to attach abstract presentation information, and to construct atomic dialog models. The construction of the atomic dialog model by the designer supports automatic extraction of the subatomic dialog models belonging to all ConcurTaskTrees in de ConcurTaskTrees Forest.

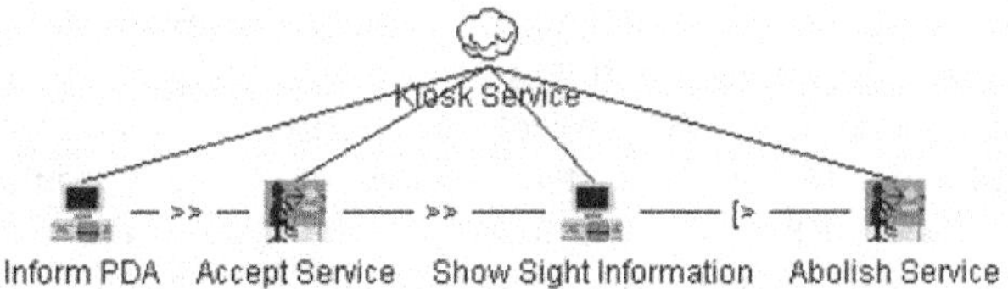

Fig. 7. Task Model attached to the Kiosk Service.

Fig. 8. The DynaMo-AID Tool.

After the modeling phase, a context-sensitive user interface prototype can be rendered. When the prototype is deployed, a control panel is shown where the user interface designer can manipulate context parameters. The designer can then see how a change of context reflects on the prototype.

7 Conclusions and Future Work

We have presented both a design process and a runtime architecture to support the creation of context-sensitive user interfaces. We believe this work can be an incentive for reconsidering the model-based user interface development approaches to enable the design of user interfaces for pervasive computing applications.

The next step is to integrate more general context specifications. At the moment our applications consider a fixed set of Abstract Context Widgets, but there is work in progress within the CoDAMoS[2] project to construct a more general context specification and integrate it in our system. Another extra feature could be to support propagating the effect of new services to the UI prototype of the main application. Another issue we whish to tackle is usability. At the moment usability is to a large extent the responsibility of the user interface designer when he/she draws the inter-dialog transitions. In this way context switches can only affect the UI where the designer wants the UI to change. To bring a change of context to the user's attention, changes with the previous dialog could be marked with colors, or a recognizable sound could tell the user a context-switch has occured.

8 Acknowledgements

Our research is partly funded by the Flemish government and European Fund for Regional Development. The CoDAMoS[2] (Context-Driven Adaptation of Mobile Services) project IWT 030320 is directly funded by the IWT (Flemish subsidy organization).

References

1. Gaëlle Calvary, Joëlle Coutaz, and David Thevenin. Embedding Plasticity in the development process of interactive systems. In *6th ERCIM Workshop "User Interfaces for All". Also in HUC (Handheld and Ubiquitous Computing) First Workshop on Resource Sensitive Mobile HCI, Conference on Handheld and Ubiquitous Computing, HU2K,* Bristol, 2000.
2. Gaëlle Calvary, Joëlle Coutaz, and David Thevenin. Supporting Context Changes for Plastic User Interfaces: A Process and a Mechanism. In *Joint Proceedings of HCI 2001 and IHM 2001. Lille, France*, pages 349-364, 2001.
3. Tim Clerckx, Kris Luyten, and Karin Coninx. Generating Context-Sensitive Multiple Device Interfaces from Design. In *Pre-Proceedings of the Fourth International Conference on Computer-Aided Design of User Interfaces CADUI'2004, 13-16 January 2004, Funchal, Isle of Madeira, Portugal*, pages 288-301, 2004.
4. Karin Coninx, Kris Luyten, Chris Vandervelpen, Jan Van den Bergh, and Bert Creemers. Dygimes: Dynamically Generating Interfaces for Mobile Computing Devices and Embedded Systems. In *Human-Computer Interaction with Mobile Devices and Services, 5th International Symposium, Mobile HCI 2003*, pages 256-270, Udine, Italy, September 8-11 2003. Springer.
5. George Coulouris, Jean Dollimore, and Tim Kindberg. *Distributed Systems: concepts and design, Third Edition.* Addison-Wesley, ISBN: 0201-61918-0, 2001.
6. Joëlle Coutaz, Software architecture modeling for user interfaces. In *Encyclopedia of Software Engineering. Wiley and sons*, 1993.

---

[2] http://www.cs.kuleuven.ac.be/cwis/research/distrinet/projects/CoDAMoS/

7. Joëlle Coutaz and Gaëtan Rey. Foundation for a Theory of Contextors. In Kolski and Vanderdonckt [10], pages 13-33. Invited Talk.
8. Jason I. Hong. The Context Fabric: An infrastructure for context-aware computing. In *CHI'02 extended abstracts on Human factors in computer systems, Minneapolis, Minnesota, USA*, pages 554-555, ACM Press, 2002.
9. Chris Johnson, editor. *Interactive Systems: Design, Specification, and Verification, 8th International Workshop, DSV-IS 2001, Glasgow, Scotland, UK, June 13-15, 2001, Revised Papers*, volume 2220 of *Lecture Notes in Computer Science*. Springer, 2001.
10. Christophe Kolski and Jean Vanderdonckt, editors. *Computer-Aided Design of User Interfaces III*, volume 3. Kluwer Academic, 2002.
11. Panu Korpipää, Jani Mätyjärvi, Juha Kela, Heikki Keränen, and Esko-Juhani Malm. Managing context information in mobile devices. *IEEE Pervasive Computing, Mobile and Ubiquitous Systems*, 2(3):42-51, July-September 2003.
12. Quentin Limbourg, Jean Vanderdonckt, and Nathalie Souchon. The Task-Dialog and Task-Presentation Mapping Problem: Some Preliminary Results. In Palanque and Paternò [16], pages 227-246.
13. Kris Luyten, Tim Clerckx, Karin Coninx, and Jean Vanderdonckt. Derivation of a Dialog Model from a Task Model by Activity Chain Extraction. In Joaquim A. Jorge, Nuno Jardim Nunes, and João Falcão e Cunha, editors, *Interactive Systems: Design, Specification, and Verification*, volume 2844 of *Lectures Notes in Computer Science*, pages 191-205. Springer, 2003.
14. Kris Luyten and Karin Coninx. An XML-based runtime user interface description language for mobile computing devices. In Johnson [9], pages 17-29.
15. Giulio Mori, Fabio Paternò, and Carmen Santoro. Tool Support for Designing Nomadic Applications. In *Proceedings of the 2003 International Conference on Intelligent User Interfaces, January 12-15, 2003, Miami, FL, USA*, pages 141-148, 2003.
16. Philippe A. Palanque and Fabio Paternò, editors. *Interactive Systems: Design, Specification, and Verification, 7th International Workshop DSV-IS, Limerick, Ireland, June 5-6, 2000, Proceedings*, volume 1946 of *Lecture Notes in Computer Science*. Springer, 2000.
17. Fabio Paternò. *Model-Based Design and Evaluation of Interactive Applications*. Springer Verlag, ISBN: 1-85233-155-0, 1999.
18. Fabio Paternò and Carmen Santoro. One model, many interfaces. In Kolski and Vanderdonckt [10], pages 143-154.
19. Carl Adam Petri. Kommunikation mit automaten, second edition. *New York: Griffiss Air Force Base, Technical Report RADC-TR-65-377, Vol.1*, 1966.
20. Paulo Pinheiro da Silva. User interface declarative models and development environments: A survey. In Palanque and Paternò [16], pages 207-226.
21. Costin Pribeanu, Quentin Limbourg, and Jean Vanderdonckt. Task Modelling for Context-Sensitive User Interfaces. In Johnson [9], pages 60-76.
22. Angel Puerta. A Model-Based Interface Development Environment. In *IEEE Software*, pages 40-47, 1997.
23. Angel Puerta and Jacob Eisenstein. Towards a general computational framework for model-based interface development systems. In *Proceedings of the 1999 International Conference on Intelligent User Interfaces, Los Angeles, CA, USA*, pages 171-178, 1999.
24. Daniel Salber, Anind K. Dey, and Gregory D. Abowd. The Context Toolkit: Aiding the Development of Context-Enabled Applications. In *Proceedings of the 1999 Conference on Human Factors in Computing Systems (CHI '99), Pittsburgh, PA, May 15-20*, pages 434-441, 1999.
25. Egbert Schlungbaum and Thomas Elwert. Dialogue Graphs – a formal and visual specification technique for dialogue modelling. In *Formal Aspects of the Human Computer Interface*, 1996.

26. Nathalie Souchon, Quentin Limbourg, and Jean Vanderdonckt. Task Modelling in Multiple contexts of Use. In Peter Forbrig, Quentin Limbourg, Bodo Urban, and Jean Vanderdonckt, editors, *Interactive Systems: Design, Specification, and Verification*, volume 2545 of *Lecture Notes in Computer Science*, pages 60-76. Springer, 2002.
27. Jean Vanderdonckt and François Bodart. Encapsulating knowledge for intelligent automatic interaction objects selection. In *ACM Conference on Human Aspects in Computing Systems InterCHI'93*, pages 424-429. Addison Wesley, 1993.
28. Jean Vanderdonckt, Quentin Limbourg, and Murielle Florins. Deriving the navigational structure of a user interface. In *Proceedings of the 9th IFIP TC 13 Int. Conference on Human-Computer Interaction Interact2003 Zürich 1-5 september 2003*, pages 455-462, 2003.
29. Anthony Wasserman. Extending State Transition Diagrams for the Specification of Human-Computer Interaction. *IEEE Transactions on Software Engineering*, 11:699-713, 1985.

Discussion

[Willem-Paul Brinkman] How do you approach the problem that the user may be confused if the interface changes because of the context? Users may not be aware that the device is able to sense the environment.

> [Tim Clerckx] This is an important issue in context-aware computing. We have tried to put this responsibility in the hands of the UI designer, to make the UI user aware. The designer can then know when a change is happening and can do something about it.

[Willem-Paul Brinkman] Do you provide any guidance to the designer as to what to do?

> [Tim Clerckx] This is difficult to do in general.

[Juergen Ziegler] I like the approach to provide different levels of abstraction. What is the range of factors that you consider: location, temporal, etc. Is there any limitation? Also, you showed that several concrete context factors can be handled in an abstract object. How do you deal with the potential combinatorial explosion of factors?

> [Tim Clerckx] Regarding the first question, we have done experiments with the hardware sensors and GPS coordinates and we can easily define other context objects. For the second question, we handle the complexity in the abstract context objects. At the moment these are ad hoc implementations to interpret the information.

[Michael Harrison] In a different context you may absorb information in a different way. It isn't clear to me how your approach would capture this kind of information.

> [Tim Clerckx] In each layer we abstract a bit of information. So these context changes can be captured.

[Michael Harrison] Yes, but in different contexts you may have different information flows. This is critical in some contextual interfaces. Is this embedded in the actions?

> [Tim Clerckx] You could encapsulate user input with a concrete context object and this could be interpreted by an abstract object.

[Bonnie John] What if the user wants to override the default task context, e.g. the user is in a museum but wants to discuss where to go for lunch. How do you reprent this in your tool?

[Tim Clerckx] If you want to do that it must be included at the task design time, where the designer explicitly allows the user to override the context and provides some user interaction for this purpose. The concrete contetx object would be a button press. The abstract context object would say to change the context and not change it back because of sensors until the user is done.

Using Task Modelling Concepts for Achieving Adaptive Workflows

Carsten Eichholz, Anke Dittmar, Peter Forbrig

University of Rostock,
Institute of Computer Science,
A.-Einstein-Str. 21,
18059 Germany
{eichholz|ad|pforbrig}@informatik.uni-rostock.de

Abstract. Business processes are usually described by abstract workflow specifications. However, existing workflow descriptions are often too restricted to reflect the true nature of work. For instance tasks might be added or deleted during execution. The presently available workflow management systems insufficiently support the desired flexibility for workflows. In this article we present an approach, how certain kinds of adaptability can be achieved on the base of task modelling combined with the principle of "Order & Supply". Task models offer means to describe the way humans perform tasks in cooperation focussing on the individual level. We show that the principles of task modelling can also be used for cooperative workflow models providing means on group level.

1. Introduction

The introduction of workflow management systems (WFMS) in companies has emerged as a major advantage to plan, control, and organise a company's business processes. Workflow processes can be modelled and executed, thus the business process is assisted by a software while it is running. Chiefly, the flow of documents through a process, but also scheduling, notification, and other communicative tasks are assisted.

Although these advantages are of great help, it is often desired to keep workflows more flexible. The definition of a business process cannot be completely foreseen at its beginning. A lot of changes and adaptations are done while the process is already running. The presently available workflow management systems do scarcely support adaptability for workflows as the following statements show: "Traditionally, workflow management systems have not been designed for dynamic environments requiring adaptive response."[1] "It is widely recognised that workflow management systems should provide flexibility. [...] However, today's workflow management systems have problems dealing with changes."[13]

This is constituted by several problems, e.g. changing workflows should be possible even during execution, but what happens with already started tasks? Are the renewed or the extended tasks in execution still consistent to old tasks that have been

R. Bastide, P. Palanque, and J. Roth (Eds.): EHCI-DSVIS 2004, LNCS 3425, pp. 96-111, 2005.

finished in the workflow? Because of these and other questions, *adaptive workflows* have become an important research area.

In this paper, we present an approach for dealing with workflow adaptability by using task models. Recent approaches in task modelling offer means to specify more flexible task models. We show that certain kinds of adaptability for workflows can be solved using task models. In section 2 we introduce the ideas behind the concepts of task analysis and workflows, and show that the similarity between them can be a basis for our approach. Section 3 gives an overview of the question of adaptation in workflows. Different aspects of adaptability are presented, mainly based on the paper of van der Aalst [13]. In the subsequent section 4, we show with our method of "Order & Supply" how certain aspects of adaptation can be solved by using task models. This method is finally illustrated in an example presented in section 5. Some related approaches concerning adaptivity in workflows are shown and compared in section 6 while in the last section some conclusions of our approach are summarised as well as some perspectives on future expectations are presented.

2. Task Models and Workflows

In this chapter we briefly characterise the two main concepts our approach is based on, namely task models and workflow specifications. Trætteberg compared workflow models and task models in [12]. He states that both "essentially describe the same domain, but at different levels". While workflows support work on the organisational and group level, task models rather consider the individual level of work. We show that the similarity between these concepts allows an implementation of certain adaptation aspects desired in workflows by use of task models.

2.1. Task Models

Task models play an important role in the model-based design of user interfaces for interactive systems. The process of interaction—the process of working with a software system—is modelled with the aim "to have a structured method for allowing designers to manage such a complexity"[7] as it emerges in user interface design. According to [7], task models can be useful for the purpose of:

- Understanding an application domain
- Recording the results of interdisciplinary discussions
- Designing new applications consistent with the user conceptual model
- Analysing and evaluating usability of an interactive system
- Supporting the user during a session
- Documenting interactive software

In addition, we propose to use task models for coordinating tasks and activities in a more general way, i.e. coordination of activities in business processes.

Tasks consist of activities that are performed to reach a goal, which can be considered as modifying a system into a desired state. Tasks are structured hierarchically (see hierarchical task analysis, HTA [2]), forming so-called task-trees. Thus, tasks can be described at different levels of abstraction and detail. Between activities exist certain dependencies defining the order of execution. Often, such dependencies are described by a set of temporal equations, using predefined temporal operators. Task models can therefore be seen as a combination of HTA and a description of temporal execution. Paternò et al. developed ConcurTaskTrees, a method for task modelling using these principles. They define temporal operators [9] like:

- T1|||T2 Interleaving (parallel execution)
- T1|=|T2 Order independency
- T1>>T2 Enabling (sequential execution)
- T1[>T2 Deactivation
- T1[]T2 Choice
- [T] Option
- T* Iteration

In the ConcurTaskTree notation, the dependencies between activities in the task tree are included into the diagrammatic notation. Unary operators are marked at a task's name (e.g. "*" at "enter terms" in **Fig. 1**) and binary operators are put between two tasks, read from left to right (e.g. "|||" between "collect terms" and "define terms").

Different types of tasks are identified: abstract tasks, user tasks, interaction tasks, and application tasks. Later extensions of this method introduce cooperative trees, where sub-tasks can be distributed to and performed by different roles/employees (cf. [8]). This allows modelling task execution not only at individual but at group level as well. **Fig. 1** shows an example for a cooperative task tree, as it can be modelled in CTTE, a tool supporting the ConcurTaskTree modelling approach.

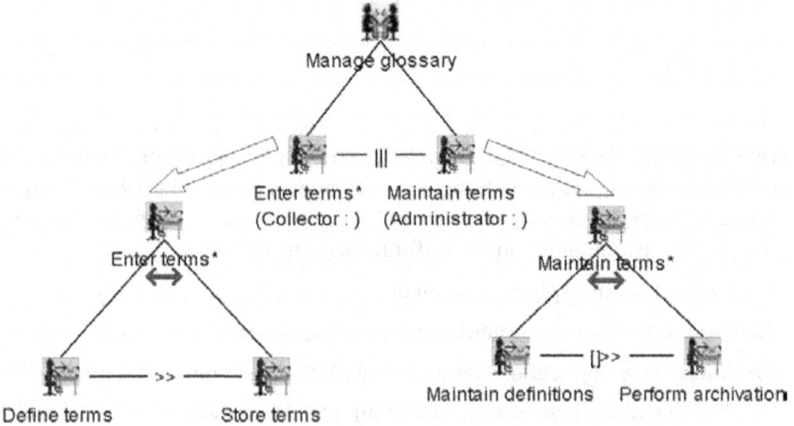

Fig. 1. Cooperative task tree for the task "manage glossary".

This example models the task of managing a glossary. The sub-tasks "enter terms" and "maintain terms" are assigned to the roles "Collector" and "Administrator" respectively. Each role is assigned a sub-task tree and performs the execution of it.

The broad arrows symbolise the distribution of work (not part of the CTT notation). The double arrows mark the sub-tasks as being part of a cooperative task. CTTE allows to animate the execution of such a cooperative model.

2.2. Workflow Models

Processes in an organisation require to be constantly reconsidered and optimised to meet the market's claims, as well as to fit new requirements in changing environment, like availability of resources etc. Workflow technology facilitates the modelling, redesign and administration of processes in an organisation.

Georgakopoulos et al. define workflow as "a collection of tasks organized to accomplish some business process" and the definition of "the order of task invocation or condition(s) under which tasks must be invoked, task synchronization, and information flow (data flow)"[5]. According to this, business processes can be described by specifying workflows. Business processes can be implemented as material processes (mainly production processes focussing on the manipulation of physical objects) or information processes (partly or fully automated transaction processes). One of the main reasons for using workflow technology in organisations is to understand business activities and thus have a means for improving customer satisfaction, increasing efficiency, and reducing costs.

Yet, it is necessary to periodically reconsider the business activities by so-called business process engineering (BPR) to fit new requirements. BPR addresses issues of customer satisfaction. It is complemented by information process reengineering (IPR) which addresses system efficiency and costs and describes the process requirements for information system functionality and human skills [5]. Conversely to the periodical reconsideration through business process reengineering, a continuous process examination, known as continuous process improvement (CPI) becomes more and more important (see [1]). As we see in the next section, workflow adaptation while the workflow is running comes with a number of difficulties.

Workflows are commonly classified in three categories: (I) *ad-hoc workflows*, with low complexity, few participants and short-term activities, (II) *administrative workflows*, with repetitive and predictable processes where the coordination of tasks may be automated, and (III) *production workflows*, which typically have a high complexity and the processes are, like in administrative workflows, repetitive and predictable (cf. [5,10,1]).

In the following, the definitions are given according to the Workflow Management Coalition (WfMC), an organisation of practitioners as well as researchers, who have provided a glossary of standardised terms of workflow technology, to have a more precise understanding of what workflow is [14]:

Workflow: The automation of a business process in whole or part, during which documents, information or tasks are passed from one participant to another for action, according to a set of procedural rules.

Business Process: A set of one or more linked procedures or activities which collectively realise a business objective or policy goal, normally within the context of an organisational structure defining functional roles and relationships.

Process Definition: The representation of a business process in a form which supports automated manipulation, such as modelling, or enactment by a workflow management system. The process definition consists of a network of activities and their relationships, criteria to indicate the start and termination of the process, and information about the individual activities, such as participants, associated IT applications and data, etc.

Workflow Management System (WFMS): A system that defines, creates and manages the execution of workflows through the use of software, running on one or more workflow engines, which is able to interpret the process definition, interact with workflow participants and, where required, invoke the use of IT tools.

Workflows represent business processes. Business processes are modelled by process definitions and executed/interpreted by a workflow management system.

As we have seen, workflow management deals with coordination as well as execution. Buhler and Vidal [1] express the idea of workflow in the aphorism workflow = activities + processes, in analogy to the view on software programs as application = calculation + coordination. Here we see activities as the de facto executable components (called coordinables in [1]) while a process (coordinator in [1]) comprises the structuring of the activities, i.e. the activities' coordination.

Buhler's and Vidal's idea of introducing flexibility in workflows is based on web services and agents. Web services are components that execute a task and deliver results. Agents are used to coordinate the provided results of web services according to a certain goal. Buhler and Vidal speak of adaptive workflow engines = web services + agents, in analogy to the previously given equations.

2.3. Business Processes Modelled as Tasks

As stated in [12], workflow models and task models address the same domain, namely, how can tasks and activities be coordinated in such a way that their execution accomplishes the business goals. The difference between these two means lies in the different levels. Workflow models mainly focus on collaborative work, while task models primarily represent the individual task execution [12]. In the following, we are using the principles of task modelling to model group activities in a more flexible way by introducing distributable sub-tasks.

In our approach we call the parts, into which a business process is structured, *tasks*. Such tasks are assigned to groups or single persons for execution. We call the assignment of a task *order*, following the notions from business perspective. According to [3], we can distinguish tasks and orders in the way, that tasks are interpreted subjectively, while an order necessarily has objective characteristics. Thus, when an order is given to a group or person, it has to be transformed into a task. Fig. 2 illustrates this relation between the notions "task" and "order".

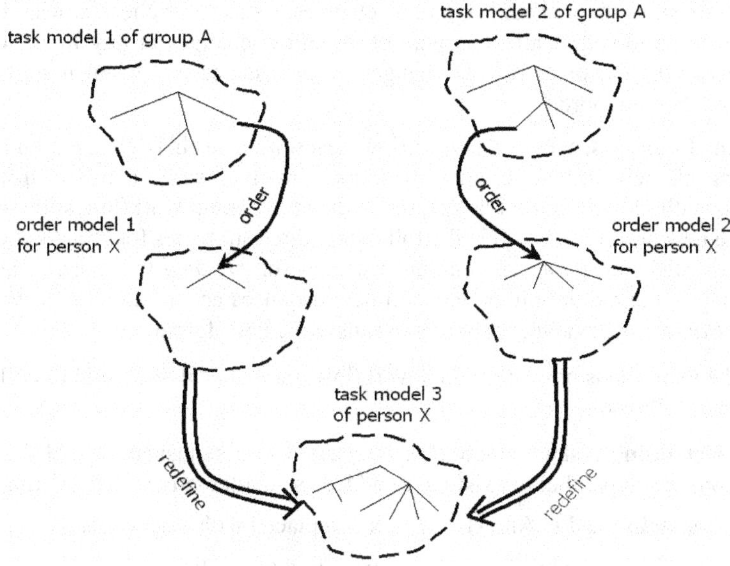

Fig. 2. Relation between task models and order models (according to [3]).

Group A planned two task models for different tasks and orders a certain person X (possibly a member of another group) with both tasks. Person X now has a set of tasks to do and has to compose his own task model from these two orders. This means, person X has to transfer the given (objective) orders into an own (subjective) task model.

In this transferring step, person X can make certain adaptations in the allowed range of the predefined structures of the orders. The following section gives a brief overview of different aspects of adaptation in connection with workflows.

3. Aspects of Adaptation

When speaking of flexibility in workflows, one can imagine several aspects of change. Van der Aalst et al. [13] made a comprehensive classification of these changes, of which we present an overview in this section.

Process definitions—our workflow specifications—are an aggregation of cases, i.e. runs through processes. Thus, a process definition is an abstraction of a concrete workflow, sometimes also called workflow schema. From this process definition, instances are created for the enactment in a WFMS. So the possible instances (or runs) can be seen as cases and the process definition comprises the description of a number of cases. Similarly, a task model comprises a set of different runs according to the task model definition.

Based on this idea, we can distinguish between two main types of change [13]:

- **ad-hoc changes,** where a change only inflicts one instance. Such a change might occur on exceptions or errors, or maybe special demands. In this case the workflow description stays untouched. For ad-hoc changes, it has to be checked what kinds of changes are allowed at all. It is possible to allow changes at any time, so-called changes *on-the-fly*, or to restrict changes in an instance just when it starts (*entry time*) and then no more.

- **structural changes,** where the workflow description itself is changed and is thus affecting all new instances. This, of course, involves some conflicts like: What happens with already started tasks?, or: Is the old running workflow still consistent with the new definition? In [13] the following, three strategies for structural changes are distinguished: *restart* all running instances, or *proceed* the existing instances according to the old definition and start new instances according to the new one, or finally *transfer* the existing instances to satisfy the new definition.

In [13] the main kinds of changes in a workflow, no matter if structural or ad-hoc, are classified as follows:

1. **Extending tasks:** A new task is inserted in a sequence, or added as being processed parallel to existing, or added as an alternative of an existing task.
2. **Replacing tasks:** An existing task is replaced with a new one.
3. **Reordering tasks:** The order of execution of existing tasks is changed.

Besides these three kinds of changes we introduce some additional kinds of change, that affect the set of possible instances of a workflow model:

4. **Selecting tasks:** Alternative and optional tasks, as defined in the task definition, can be constrained, thus the degrees of freedom, the set of possible runs, can be reduced. This means, an option may be made obligatory, or alternatives may be removed. This kind of change may be done before the actual execution and renders the task definition more precisely.
5. **Constraining:** The existing structure of task execution is further constrained by additional global rules, which means rules that may be defined over tasks in any layers of the task tree. Thus, the set of possible runs through the model is being reduced.

The latter two types of change lead us to some concrete adaptation approaches as explained in the context of different aspects of change. According to [13], the aspects of changes cover the following branches:

- **control perspective**: covers the allocation and introduction of new resources to processes.
- **system perspective**: covers the infrastructure and configuration of the WFMS.
- **task perspective**: covering the adaptation of the set of possible runs.
- **resource perspective**: Resources may influence the order, respectively the choice of tasks in a business process.
- **process perspective**: covers the adaptation of the process definition.

We understand the task perspective as a reduction of degrees of freedom in the definition of a task., mainly using the idea of *constraining* the structure (see the fifth head point of kinds of change above). This can be done by introducing additional rules (temporal equations) besides the rules for each node. These additional rules create relations using any activities, not just those of a sub-tree. This idea is already presented in [2] and illustrated there by an example.

As regards the resource perspective, exhausted resources can constrain the options and alternatives for certain tasks. We understand this perspective as a way of using resources as a means of control. Thus, assigning resources to tasks can be used as a control criteria for preferred choices and thus prioritise possible alternative task executions.

The process perspective covers the idea of extending tasks. During its execution a task is refined by adding new sub-tasks (*extending*) or determining alternatives and options (*selecting*) in the predefined structure. The selecting is done, before the execution starts. This will be the basis for our approach of Order & Supply as described in the next section.

4. Workflow Adaptation by "Order & Supply"

Since a business process cannot be completely modelled in all details in the planning phase, adaptation has to be done by different employees after the enactment of a model. An adaptation in our approach can lead to either extending a task by new sub-tasks, or making a choice for alternative or optional tasks.

Considering the execution of a complex business process, we follow the metaphor of "Order & Supply", which means, in cooperative work, an employee A wants the execution of a task done by another employee B, i.e. A *orders* B to perform the task.

Often, an order comes with some predefined task structure. We assume that tasks and orders resemble the same structural description (see also [3] for more detail). Thus, an order already might have defined some constraints for its execution (cf. **Fig. 1** above: when interpreting the sub-trees of collector and administrator as orders, then we see that their orders already have a predefined structure).

B has to redefine A's order to his own task. In this redefinition process, B can adapt the order according to the degrees of freedom that are allowed within the predefined structure. Additionally, B can order some tasks further to another employee C, who again may adapt this order to his task. Such ordering can be done recursively.

After having solved the ordered task, the employee returns his results to the employee who ordered, i.e. he supplies the results. Thus, when B completed the task, he gives the results back to employee A, thus B supplies results for A. The principle of order and supply is summarised in **Fig. 3**.

Regarding our task model, an order corresponds to passing a sub-tree of the task tree to another employee. In the following, we consider business processes as being structured like tasks. We suggest a number of steps, how the above introduced Order & Supply principle can be realised.

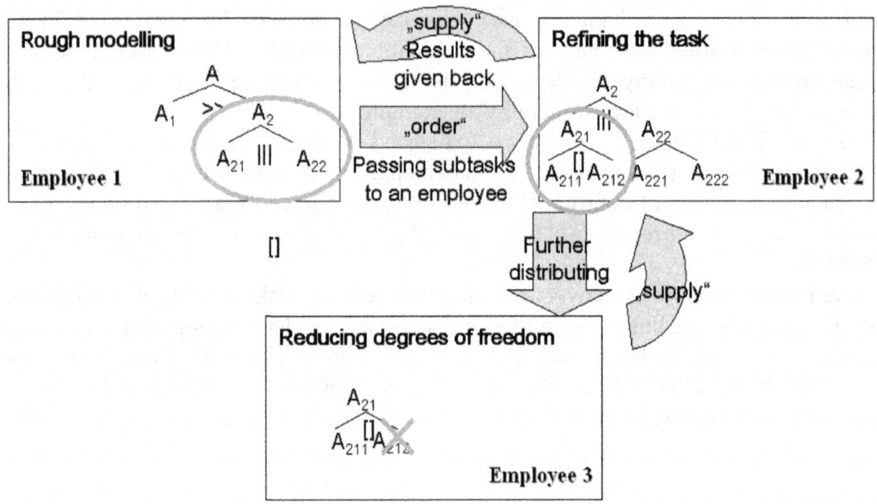

Fig. 3. The principle of Order and Supply.

Step 1. **coarse modelling**: Before a business process comes into enactment, it has to be modelled at least roughly to have a basis for the work. The main task has to be defined (this will be the root node of the corresponding task-tree) and the sub-tasks have to be determined. As described in [9] the task model is built in three phases: (i) hierarchical logical decomposition of the tasks forming a tree-like structure. (ii) identification of the temporal relationships between tasks. (iii) identification of the objects associated with each task. We neglect objects here and concentrate on the tree structure and temporal relations. After building a task model in such a way, we have a more or less coarse model.

Step 2. **distribution of tasks**: After the coarse model is built, it is being instantiated and the tasks are executed according to the defined rules. The execution of a business process, is planned by distributing it in parts which have to be performed by actors in certain roles. A role model maps the set of employees to the set of roles necessary for our business process. We call the distribution of a task to an employee *order*. When distributing an order, i.e. a sub-tree, the sub-tasks of this task may give a predefinition which can be adapted by the receiving employee as we see in the next step. Each employee has one or more tasks (task-trees) to process and each employee can further distribute parts of his task-tree(s) to other employees. The distribution should consider the workload of the employee for efficient and balanced processing. Hence, one can imagine monitoring the workload. Additionally, an employee should have the possibility to accept/deny a given order. An employee who receives a task as an order uses it as his view on the business process. All other tasks are hidden and not accessible. So any adaptation does generally not influence other tasks in the business process.

Step 3. **adaptation of task**: When an employee receives an order, he is going to adapt it when necessary. On the one hand, the adaptation of a task can happen before starting to execute the task. This comprises appending new sub-tasks, thus refining and specifying the task in more detail (according to adaptation by *extending, reordering* or also *replacing* as described in the section above). In our approach, we neglect the adaptation by reordering and replacing, rather we presuppose an intention in the given task tree, that means the employee who gives the order has put his imagination into the model that he distributes. On the other hand the task can be adapted after the enactment of the model, i.e. while executing it. This means, alternatives are chosen and options are taken or rejected (according to adaptation by *selecting*, see above). It is, of course, also imaginable to select alternatives/options before starting the execution, for example if the employee has enough information to make such a decision. All adaptations made in this step are local and in the current instance only (cf. ad-hoc change, in the above section), so we avoid problems of inconsistency.

Step 4. **execution of task**: This step means de facto performing the task during the enactment of the model. The sub-tasks are executed according to the defined temporal equations. In this phase, *selecting* is still possible, although selecting during the execution means no adaptation, rather it characterises a concrete run. Only the leaves of the task tree are actual operations that are executed. Non-leaf-nodes just serve for structuring the task. When all leaves of a node are completed, the node itself is marked as complete as well.

Step 5. **returning results**: This is the *supply* phase of the process. After the employee has completed his task tree, the results are given back to the employee, who has ordered it. This is done recursively through the whole tree until all nodes (sub-tasks) are completed and the global goal of the task tree is achieved and the business process is finished. Mainly, the results consist of certain artefacts, documents or notifications (like acceptance or denial of requests).

These steps should illustrate, how to perform the whole or parts of a business process. Steps 1 and 2 are done at the beginning of processing a workflow. Steps 3, 4, and 5, as well as step 2, when further distributing, are then performed until the task is complete. The business process in a whole can be seen as one big and complex task model in the background which is processed and adapted continuously during runtime. The participating employees only see their view on parts of the business process. To describe the global task model of the business process, one can use XML descriptions, for instance as suggested by Stavness and Schneider[11].

In the next section we show, how this method can be put into practice by illustrating the principles at the example of maintaining a web glossary.

5. An Example: Maintenance of a Web Glossary

In this section, we illustrate the above described method of Order & Supply in a simple example. Lets consider the business process of maintaining a web-based glossary. This process can be classified as a certain kind of content management.

In our example, a research group is responsible for setting up and maintaining a web glossary. Necessary tasks are: adding new notions and definitions, editing existing notions like adding a figure or a reference, or removing terms from the glossary database. These tasks are done by the members of the research group. A first rough version of the task "maintain web glossary" might be modelled as shown in **Fig. 4**.

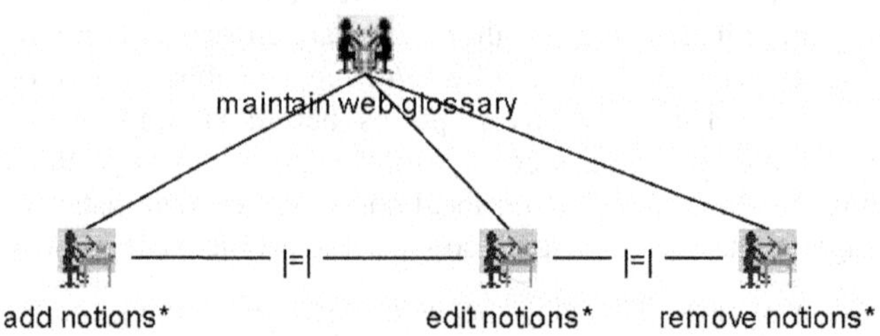

Fig. 4. Coarse model.

We can divide the maintenance in the way that each member of the group is responsible for a different subject, lets say one employee maintains notions from the area of object oriented technologies, another employee maintains notions in usability engineering, and a third employee is responsible for programming languages. In the following, lets concentrate on adding a notion to the glossary. **Fig. 5** shows, how a refinement of our first draft might look like and how we distribute tasks to employees, i.e. our experts in OO, Usability, respectively PL, thus realising ordering.

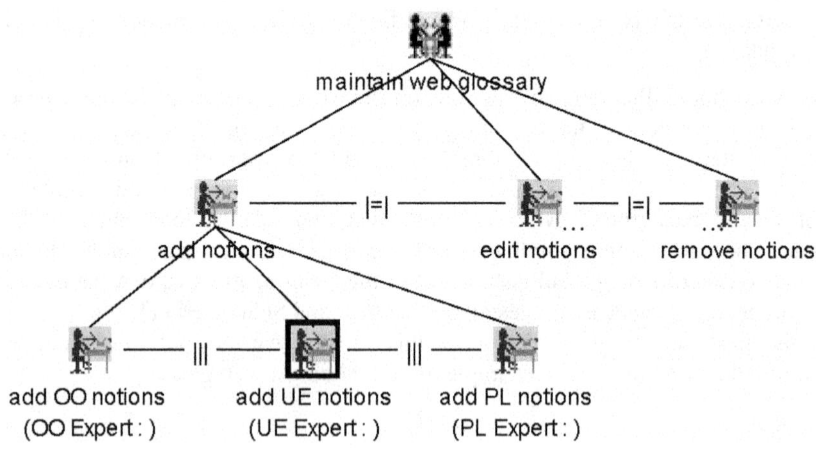

Fig. 5. Distributing sub-tasks.

Lets take a look at the activities of the OO expert. As we explained in the section before, the employees can adapt their tasks before they are executing them as well as during execution. Adding notions to a glossary might be structured by predefinition and could be as illustrated in **Fig. 6**. Hence, a definition needs the definition text, and definition reference, while figures and links are optional.

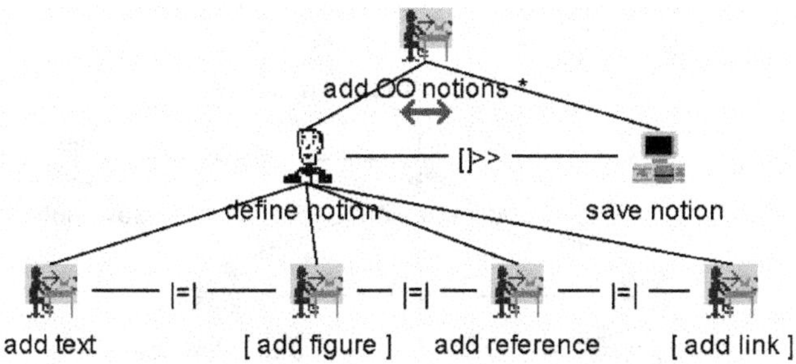

Fig. 6. Predefined sub-tree distributed to an employee.

If an employee is adding a notion, he has certain degrees of freedom. He might give an own definition text or do a research about the notion and referencing to the source (alternatives). He might add a figure to his definition text or not (option). The Employee adapts his task tree by adding further tasks and making a decision about optional tasks. **Figure 7** illustrates possible points of adaptation.

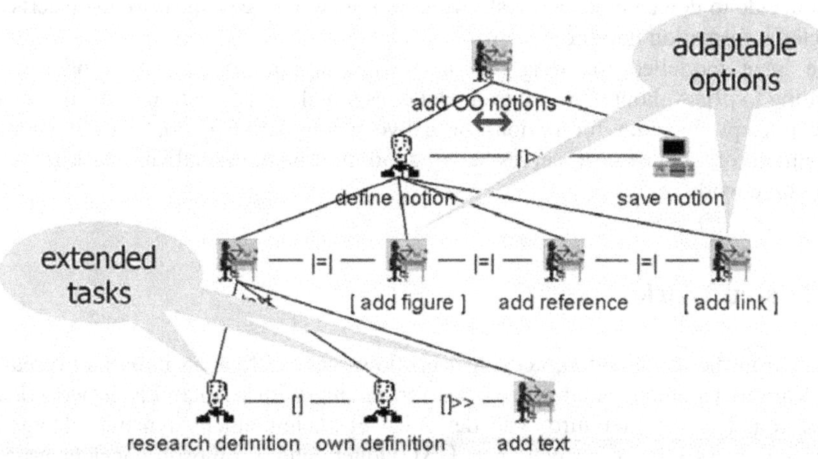

Fig. 7. Adaptation possibilities

Our employee decided to research a definition. Also, he is not adding a figure nor a link to his description. The adapted task tree of our software expert might look like in **Fig. 8**.

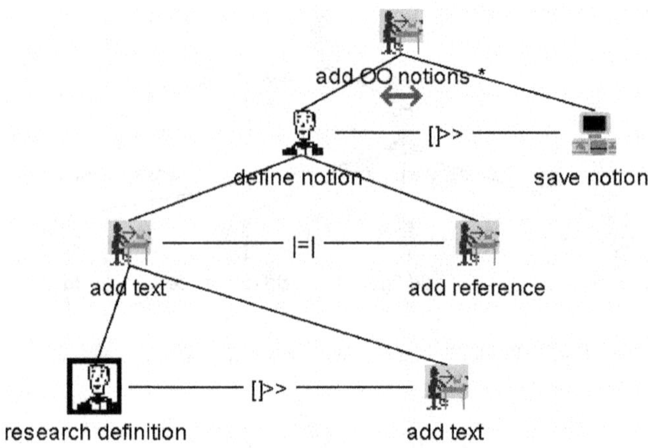

Fig. 8. Task tree after adaptation.

In this example, we have illustrated adaptation before execution starts. The employee can as well make decisions during performing his task. For instance, he might decide to delegate the sub-task "save notion" to an assistant who just inserts all collected information into the system.

We have modelled the diagrams in CTTE, an environment to model tasks according to [9]. Although the environment does not allow adaptation as we described above (except deciding for options or between alternatives), nor does it support distribution of subtasks, it serves as a good means of visualising task-trees in cooperative work.

6. Related Works

As shown in the introduction, keeping workflows adaptable is an important research area. Various techniques and approaches for dealing with adaptability in workflows can be found in the literature. Van der Aalst et al. implement dynamic change in business processes by using petri nets [13]. Odgers and Thompson consider aspect-oriented process engineering, combining techniques from the aspect-oriented programming with business process management [6]. Edmond and ter Hofstede use reflection and meta-object protocols [4]. They introduce task meta-objects for appropriate abstraction, thus allowing reasonable adaptation of a process' structure.

Furthermore, the idea of using Agents and Web Services for realising adaptation in workflows as described by Buhler and Vidal [1] is a promising topic for further enquiry. In a more general view, the subject of adaptive workflows can be seen as a new paradigm in software engineering, in terms of the new view described in [1]. This subject transcends to the area of structure dynamic systems and self organization from general systems theory.

7. Conclusions

We have seen that task models are an appropriate way of describing workflows, at least covering the group-level-oriented workflows. It comprises main aspects of workflow modelling. Using task models for describing workflows opens new ways of dealing with adaptation as we tried to show by examining the process perspective with our "Order & Supply" principle. This principle resembles the delegation in object-oriented technologies from a technical point of view. From the business perspective, "ordering" means to distribute tasks to different institutions. This may become clearer especially when tasks are distributed across a company's borders. In this context, the results of a solved *order* are *supplied* to the ordering *customer*.

We can distinguish adaptation before and while performing a task, e.g. Certain temporal relations, like option and choice allow to be processed before runtime as well as during runtime. We speak of adaptation of the workflow definition when options and alternatives are constrained before execution.

All adaptations we considered, only concern a reduction of degrees of freedom or extending tasks in a closed sub-tree. We did not inquire complete structure changes in processes. The general problem of adaptation in systems can be identified as structure-dynamic systems, a challenging area and large application field not only in the ambit of workflow modelling.

References

1. Buhler, P. A., Vidal, J. M.: Towards Adaptive Workflow Enactment Using Multiagent Systems. In Information Technology and Management Journal, 2003.
2. Dittmar, A., More Precise Descriptions of Temporal Relations within Task Models. in P. Palanque and F. Paternò (eds.), Interactive Systems: Design, Specification, Verification; LNCS 1946, pp. 151–168, Springer 2000.
3. Dittmar, A., Ein formales Metamodell für den aufgabenbasierten Entwurf interaktiver Systeme. PhD Thesis, University of Rostock, 2002.
4. Edmond, D., ter Hofstede, A. H. M.: Achieving Workflow Adaptability by Means of Reflection. In Proceedings of CSCW-98 Workshop Towards Adaptive Workflow Systems, Seattle, USA, 1998.
5. Georgakopoulos, D., Hornick, M., Sheth, A.: An Overview of Workflow Management: From Process Modeling to Workflow Automation Infrastructure. In Distributed and Parallel Databases, vol. 3, No. 2, pp. 119–153, 1995.
6. Odgers, B., Thompson, S. G.: Aspect-oriented Process Engineering (ASOPE), Workshop on AOP at European Conference on Object-oriented Programming, Lisbon, Portugal, 1999.
7. Paterno, F.: Task Models in Interactive Software Systems. In S. K. Chang (ed.), Handbook of Software Engineering & Knowledge Engineering, World Scientific Publishing, 2001.
8. Paterno, F.: Model-Based Design and Evaluation of Interactive Applications. Springer, 2000.
9. Paternò, F., Mancini, C., Meniconi, S.: ConcurTaskTrees: A Diagrammatic Notation for Specifying Task Models. In Human Computer Interaction – INTERACT'97, pp. 362–369, 1997.
10. Plesums, Ch.: An Introduction to Workflow. Workflow Handbook 2002, Workflow Management Coalition, 2002.

11. Stavness, N., Schneider, K.: Supporting Workflow in User Interface Description Languages. Workshop on Developing User Interface Description Languages, AVI2004, Gallipoli, Italy, 2004.
12. Trætteberg, H.: Modeling Work: Workflow and Task Modeling. In J. Vanderdonckt and A. Puerta (eds.), Computer-Aided Design of User Interfaces II (CADUI); Louvain-la-Neuve, Belgium, Kluwer, 1999.
13. van der Aalst, W. P. M., Basten, T., Verbeek, H. M. W., Verkoulen, P. A. C., Voorhoeve, M.: Adaptive Workflow — On the interplay between flexibility and support. In J. Filipe and J. Cordeiro (eds.), Proceedings of the first International Conference on Enterprise Information Systems, vol. 2, pp. 353–360, Setúbal Portugal, March 1999.
14. Workflow Management Coalition: Terminology & Glossary, Document Number TC-1011, 3rd version, http://www.wfmc.org/standards/docs/TC-1011_term_glossary_v3.pdf.

Discussion

[Tom Ormerod] I am interested in your claim that your adaptations can be made at the local level without running into dependency problems. For example, if I was teaching RE and someone made a change to the OO course, this would have implications. So how can local effects be accounted for?

> [Carsten Eicholz] If there is such an influence, it must be modelled explicitly, at a higher level of abstraction. A dependency would mean that we could not, in the example, have paralellism, since paralellism means that there is no dependency.

[Tom Ormerod] I'm wondering how you could slice that in a way that you can guarantee that there are no dependencies.

> [Carsten Eicholz] It depends on the expectations that you have of the model. In our study we have modeled complex independence. When there is a dependency, you cannot slice things in this way. Perhaps you could have a single lecturer who is responsible for both lectures.

[Simone Barbosa] How do you deal with an order that cancels another order that was partially executed? Would you then need to model all the other partially executed tasks?

> [Carsten Eicholz] There is nothing in our model to explicitly handle this. Perhaps one would need to specify each "canceling" workflow separately and have it selected if needed.

[Simone Barbosa] So you would have to model these as separate independent workflows?

> [Carsten Eicholz] Yes, we would need a new workflow model to do that.

[Michael Harrison] The reason for modeling workflow is so you can ask questions of the workflow. E.g. an auditor would want to know who signs off on purchases. Have you thought about how you would inspect workflows.

> [Carsten Eicholz] No, we have a straight-forward approach where the absract modelling is only done at the beginning. We don't save all of the adaptations.

We have the idea of saving such a library, where we save and preserve all these tasks for analysis, to see what can be optimized. But this is not currently included.

[Juergen Ziegler] How do you model splits and joins in this model.

[Carsten Eicholz] The splits should be clear--parallel execution. A join--in what case do we have a join?

[Juergen Ziegler] In some processes you have joins, e.g. building a car you have separate processes that have to come together.

[Carsten Eicholz] Our approach is completely different from net-based approach that is common in process modelling. We are hierarchical. So a join must be represented as the super-task of two sub-tasks. It cannot be visualized by a join as in an activity diagram.

Mixing Research Methods in HCI: Ethnography Meets Experimentation in Image Browser Design

T.C. Ormerod[1], J. Mariani[1], N.J. Morley[1], T. Rodden[2], A. Crabtree[2], J. Mathrick[2], G. Hitch[3] & K. Lewis[3]

[1] Lancaster University, Lancaster, LA1 4YD, UK
{t.ormerod; j.mariani; nicki_morley}@lancaster.ac.uk
[2] Nottingham University, Nottingham, NG8 1BB, UK
{tar; a.crabtree; jym}@cs.notts.ac.uk
[3] York University, York, YO10 5DD, UK
{g.hitch; k.lewis}@psych.york.ac.uk

Abstract. We report the specification and evaluation of a browser designed to support sharing of digital photographs. The project integrated outcomes from experiments, ethnographic observations, and single-case immersive observations to specify and evaluate browser technologies. As well as providing and evaluating new browser concepts, a key outcome of our research is a case study showing the successful integration of ethnography and experimentation, research and design methods that are often viewed as orthogonal, sometimes even mutually exclusive, in HCI.

Keywords: Ethnography, controlled experimentation, digital photographs, browser design and evaluation.

1. Introduction

1.1 Methods for Specifying Technologies

In the search for appropriate ways to specify and evaluate user-centered technologies, researchers and developers are increasingly turning away from laboratory-based controlled interventions towards more contextually-rich methods for studying user behaviours. This shift is exemplified by the emergence of ethnography as a method for informing systems design [1, 2]. Ethnography offers a non-invasive approach to observing rich social interactions around technologies in-situ. The approach facilitates the recognition of important exceptions and exemplars that inform technologies for supporting best practice, as well as revealing common patterns of activity. The shift in methods has partly been at the expense of controlled experiments that sacrifice detailed description of context and outliers in favour of factorial descriptions of user activity patterns. Indeed, proponents of ethnography [3, 4] cite limitations of experimentation as a key motivator for adopting an ethnographic stance.

Despite the advantages that accrue from ethnography, there is still a role for controlled empirical methods. Ball & Ormerod [5] point to the need for verifiability of observations to justify investments in technology, and the need for specificity and

R. Bastide, P. Palanque, and J. Roth (Eds.): EHCI-DSVIS 2004, LNCS 3425, pp. 112-128, 2005.

goal-directedness to focus upon the design imperative, as key reasons why designers need to supplement ethnographic data with controlled empirical studies. A further reason comes from the fact that people, both users and observers, are not always aware of or able to report the processes that influence their behaviour [6]. Hypothesis-driven experiments can reveal implicit influences on behaviour that affect user activities with information technologies.

Digital photography provides a domain that illustrates the relative merits of ethnographic and experimental approaches. Photographs are inherently social artifacts: the reasons for taking pictures, the uses we put them to, and the ways in which we handle, store and reveal them are guided by the context of use. To specify technologies for digital photography without conducting some form of ethnographic study risks underestimating the complex social activities that surround image handling. Yet, the ways in which individuals categorise, remember and subsequently recall information about photographs will also play a key role in determining the success of image handling technologies. Like many aspects of human cognition, these memory-based processes are not easy to observe or report.

We have previously argued [5] that ethnographic methods can and should be combined with other research techniques to properly inform user design. Other exemplars of research programmes that mix experimental and observational methods (e.g., case studies) in HCI exist [7]: This paper focuses upon mixing experimentation with an ethnographic approach to design and evaluation in HCI. In the remainder of the paper, we report empirical studies that use three research methods to inform the design of image handling technologies, and the development of a photo browser prototype that reflects the findings of these studies. The studies used *experimentation* to investigate the feasibility of interventions to reduce collaborative inhibition, *ethnography* to identify natural categories of shared encoding cue, and a detailed *case observation* to validate the feasibility of our chosen encoding approach. Evaluation of the browser again used experiments to assess the relative strengths of a prototype photo browser against a commercial alternative.

1.2 Digital Image Handling

There is a growing shift from chemical to digital photography, with mass-market and low-cost technology becoming commonplace within homes and families. As the digital camera grows in popularity, the number of images that individuals and groups store and handle can increase dramatically. An important consequence of digitalization is that photographs lose their physical availability. Physical artifacts provide retrieval cues for photographs (e.g., 'the shoe box under the bed full of wedding photographs') that are lost in digitalization [8]. From a situated perspective, methods for sharing non-digital photographs are central to how they are used. For example, traditional photograph albums serve as a constructed way of sharing information, often representing a collective familial resource. Methods for sharing images are likely to change greatly when photographs are stored on computers. Internet-based image transfer opens up new opportunities to share photographs across virtual communities, changing the nature of image communication and ownership in as yet poorly understood ways.

A number of different forms of software exist to manage digital images. Many commercial and research applications offer single-user query-based approaches to retrieval, with commands based on filename (i.e., a name of a photograph), user fields and keywords assigned by the user to photographs. Commercial browsers focus upon management of disk space for storing images (e.g., Thumbplus, Jasc). A number of research projects have also examined human-centred issues in image handling. For example, the Maryland PhotoFinder project [9] offers a browser for personal image management that supports encoding and retrieval through novel interface features for Boolean searches and visual overviews of search match results.

Other projects have focussed upon image sharing. For example, the Personal Digital Historian (PDH) is a table-based environment around which users collaborate to construct stories around a set of images [10]. One interesting feature of the PDH is the use of an image categorization scheme based around four dimensions that describe who the image pertains to, what the subject of the image is, where it was taken, and when it was taken. User selections under each dimension are combined automatically, providing an innovative solution to problems associated with constructing Boolean searches. Intuitively, the 'Who, What, Where and When' scheme captures the main episodic dimensions associated with the event portrayed by an image.

1.3 Psychological Studies of Memory

Studies of autobiographical memory suggest that 'Who, What, Where and When' dimensions play a key role in remembering. For example, Wagenaar [11] kept a diary in which he noted personal events over a period of some years. Subsequently he tested his ability to recall details of individual events by cuing himself with features such as who was involved, what happened, where and when the event took place or combinations of these cues. Among his findings were that 'when' is a poor cue and that combinations of cues are in general more effective than single cues.

There are other aspects of psychological research into human memory that might inform the development of image handling technologies. For example, a number of studies have demonstrated an effect of *collaborative inhibition*. In these studies, participants learn items individually, and subsequently recall the items either collaboratively (e.g., in pairs) or on their own. The effect is demonstrated when the total number of unique items recalled by groups is less than that recalled by nominal pairs made up of individuals recalling on their own [12]. The locus of the effect appears to be at retrieval: cues reflecting the subjective organization that one individual imposes upon information at encoding inhibit the subjective organization of a collaborating individual and so suppress their recall contribution [13]. If individuals who recall together have also encoded together, they tend to share the same subjective organization of the material, and an effect of inhibition is not found [14]. Collaboration at encoding reduces the incompatibility between cues generated by one individual and the subjective organization of the other individual. Technologies for sharing images that organize encoding and retrieval around individuals' categorisation preferences may provide precisely the conditions under which collaborative inhibition arises. The corollary to this argument is that image-sharing systems need to provide dimensions for encoding images that are common to collaborating users.

2. Experimental Manipulations to Reduce Collaborative Inhibition

The collaborative inhibition effect presents a challenge to the development of image handling technologies, since it suggests that an individual's organization of information at encoding may inhibit later retrieval of the same information by others. To address the problem, it was necessary first to find further evidence that collaborative inhibition effects can be reduced by appropriate interventions. If the effect arises because individuals impose different subjective organizations at encoding, then eliciting shared encoding categories might ameliorate the effect. Below we describe one experiment that investigated how self-determined categorization influences collaborative recall of image categories. It tested a prediction that partners who organise material similarly will show less collaborative inhibition than those who organise differently.

2.1 Method

Participants. Eighty undergraduate students from York University were paid £10 each to take part.

Design and materials. Participants were assigned to one of two groups, comprising either nominal pairs or pairs who collaborated at retrieval. Nominal pairs were made up by combining data from participants recalling alone to allow comparison with collaborating participants. Each of these groups was further divided, participants being paired with a partner who generated either the same or different categories when encoding the materials. Materials consisted of image labels of famous people (Elvis Presley, Margaret Thatcher, Britney Spears, etc.), which could be organised along various dimensions (e.g., gender, occupation, country).

Procedure. Encoding and retrieval phases were separated by approximately one week. In the encoding phase, participants sorted word sets into two self-determined categories. In the recall phase, participants recalled word sets collaboratively or alone (for nominal pairs).

2.2 Results and Discussion

Figure 1 illustrates the recall performance of each group. A two-way analysis of variance on these data showed significant effects of type of pair (nominal versus collaborating), $F(1, 36) = 37.0$, $MSe=4.11$, $p<.01$, and of coding category (same versus different), $F(1, 36) = 6.4$, $p<.01$. Most importantly, the interaction between these factors was significant, $F(1, 36) = 6.4$, $p<.01$. These results indicate that, while collaborative recall by pairs with the same encoding categories (17.3/40 items) was similar to nominal pair recall with both same and different encoding categories (19.6/40), collaborating pairs who had different encoding categories showed the effect of collaborative inhibition (14.1/40).

A second experiment examined whether the same effects are found when the dimensions for sorting are imposed externally. The stimuli comprised words that could be organised into three-member groups, either associatively (e.g., shepherd, sheep, wool) or categorically (e.g., shepherd, chef, fisherman). Participants sorted items associatively or categorically. Individual recall was unaffected by sorting associatively or categorically. Collaborating pairs who sorted items according to different criteria recalled less (29/45 items) than nominal pairs (33/45 items). In contrast, collaborators who encoded items according to the same criteria showed no inhibition (34/45 items).

These experiments suggest that methods to increase the similarity of subjective organizations that individuals bring to encoding information will enhance collaborative retrieval. A reduction in collaborative inhibition was found both with explicit presentation of organizational schemes at encoding and when individuals with self-determined schemes were paired with like-minded participants. However, the experiments leave open the question as to which category labels might suit image sharing best. It appeared, from the results of both experiments, that there is no one semantic dimension that is superior to any other in enhancing retrieval. Thus, in the next phase, we turned to ethnographic studies to investigate whether natural accounts of image sharing yield dimensions appropriate for instantiation within image handling technologies.

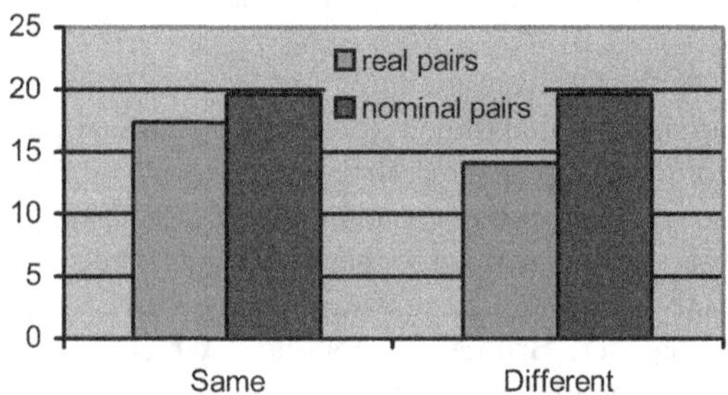

Fig. 1. Recall by collaborating and nominal pairs, sorts by partner having same or different categories.

3. Ethnographic Studies of Families and Photographs

We undertook ethnographic studies of how photographs are handled and involved in everyday activity across a number of families. The studies build upon the work of Frolich et al [8], who used home-based interview and diary-keeping methods to examine how families manage photographs. Among the important observations made by Frolich et al was the multiplicity of archiving approaches adopted (e.g., special project mini-albums), and the social nature of co-sharing of physical photographs, a process that was not easily supported by digital media. The aim of our studies was to provide a broad background for on-going experimental investigations, illustrating the different forms of interaction that surround photographs within the home. Below we offer specific examples of issues that informed the refinement of an encoding approach within the TW3 browser prototype.

Photographs differ from other forms of record because of the cultural significance of photographs within family life. Perhaps the most significant thing to note is the ways in which photographs find their way into the set of everyday activities central to our family lives. One of the most visible aspects of photograph use in the home is the symbolic and decorative role they assume. Photographs of family members in particular are displayed around the home in prominent positions. They recall people that are important to us, significant events in our lives, places that visit and memories of past times.

The framed photographs made visible in our homes provide a public display of our family lives and the episodes that make up the family history are often placed on displace for public inspection. These photographs fine their way into the everyday fabric of our home. Figure 2 exemplifies the everyday settings within which photographs are routinely placed. With one family group we studied, photographs were kept in boxes, bags, and albums according to the *significance of particular ensembles*:

1. Pictures of a family wedding were kept in simple but ornate boxes.
2. Pictures of the householder's own wedding were kept in specially made album, which in turn was kept inside a white cloth cover to protect the album.
3. Pictures of children over the years were kept in another album.
4. An ongoing project (a photographic family tree) was kept in a folder of plastic wallets inside a shopping bag underneath the cupboard 'ready to hand'.

The storage of photographs may seem haphazard, but it is possible to detect an organizing principle informing storage. Thus, wedding photos are kept in formal albums, pictures of a child over the years in a less formal, more sentimental album, pictures of another's wedding in simple decorative boxes, whereas ordinary photos are left in the packing they came in and may be thrown together in a large box, ongoing projects might be placed in a plastic bag, and so on. Each of these concrete storage arrangements reflects, for members, an order of significance such that the meaning of any particular ensemble can be seen-at-a-glance. Some orders of significance are thoroughly social; the use of special wedding albums is widespread for example, whereas others, such as storing photos of special occasions in simple but decorative boxes, are more personal and idiosyncratic.

By inference, one can interpret the arrangements of use we have observed as a physical instantiation of implicit categorization by Who, What, Where and When dimensions. However, the conceptual separators underlying these physically separate collections map onto Who, What, Where and When dimensions in interesting ways. For example, some events are clearly demarcated by all four dimensions (e.g., picture of a recent family celebration such as a Christening). Others lose one or more dimensions as organizing principles (e.g., collections of photographs of children over the years).

The majority of photographs, rather than being on public display, are brought out to be shown to visitors and friends, and in the showing to be used to explain the events surrounding then. A family member who puts the photographs away normally mediates this process. For example, in Figure 2, we see a collection of photographs (kept in a plastic carrier bag) being retrieved. Once retrieved from their normal place of storage, broad collection becomes a resource at hand to support the telling of stories.

Fig. 2. Photographs retrieved from hiding place.

Analysis of conversations shows how identifying the 'Who' of a photograph is built up from the physical manipulation of artifacts and from an emerging interactive discourse that relies on a specific family member, the mediator, to supply the recognition information, with new participants being drawn into the discourse as it unfolds. A unifying feature of the studies is the emphasis upon collaborative descriptions of images. What matters is not the taxonomic status of an image (as investigated in the experimental phase) but its situated characteristics, in terms of time, place, and involvement of people. These episodic cues are drawn upon as part of the storytelling surrounding the presentation of photographs across a grouping. This emphasis upon episodic descriptions is similar to that which is apparent in Wagenaar's [11] study of autobiographical memory.

4. Single-Case Observation of Image Encoding and Retrieval

We conducted an in-depth study of the efficacy of a category scheme for photograph collections for one individual. The aim of the study was to validate design hypotheses for image browsers, notably the usability of a Who, What, Where, and When encoding and retrieval scheme. The study addressed three questions: first, can these dimensions be used effectively, and, in particular, how efficient is encoding? Second, do the categories discriminate well among items within a personal photograph album? Third, do the dimensions provide sufficient cues at recall?

The study focused upon the photograph collection of a married couple. The male member of the couple provided access to, and an overview of, a large set of photographs collected both before and since marriage. In the encoding phase, we elicited descriptive categories from his partner for 200 photographs selected from this collection. She then sorted photographs into categories under each of the Who, What, Where, and When dimensions. A week later, the participant gave each of the photographs a title.

Results of the encoding phases showed that sorting under the scheme was meaningful to the participant. The participant spontaneously chose no more than six categories on each of the four dimensions, with some overlap of subcategory label between different dimensions. Measures of fan size (the number of photographs that received exactly the same categorical assignment under the four dimensions) varied over the photographs, reflecting marked asymmetries in the use of the coding space (see Figure 3). In essence, the majority of photographs were categorised uniquely under the four dimensions, though some instances of large sets (up to 23 photographs) received identical categorisation under all four dimensions.

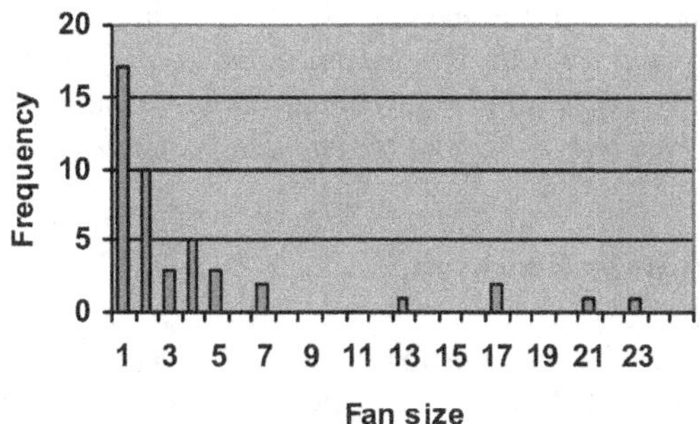

Fig. 3. Fan size during encoding phase (= no. of images encoded with same categories under Who, What, Where, and When dimensions; Frequency = instances of each fan size).

In the retrieval phase, four different procedures were used to vary retrieval cue and task (recall of photograph codes or titles versus recognition of photograph). Each procedure was evaluated using a different set of 24 photographs with varying fan sizes. Comprehensive *recall* of titles was poor (25% correct), as was recall of the codes used for each photograph (accurate recall of all 4 subcategories for only 54% of photographs). However, individual dimension recall was good (averaging 3 subcategories per photograph). Furthermore, code *recognition* was high (86% of photographs had all four codes accurately recognised). Overall the results suggest that the coding scheme was effective for recognition-based retrieval. Importantly, many of the errors in the retrieval phase were errors of commission (i.e. the participant including known photographs in her recall that were not among the 24 target items).

In summary, the case study provides some supportive evidence for a Who, What, Where and When scheme at both encoding and retrieval. The implication of the fan size results is that a browser must offer a categorization scheme that is extremely flexible, because the majority of photographs receive a unique categorisation. A two-level scheme such as that used in the case study, in which up to six categories are created under each dimension, allows 4^6 (or 4096) unique categorizations. Whether this space is sufficient to capture a large image set depends upon the extent to which images can be meaningfully categorized together. Further work is in progress to investigate the efficacy of the scheme for image sets of 1000+ that come from multiple sources (photographs from a decade of news articles).

When errors were made they were errors of commission. The implication for a browser is that if only one sorting code is incorrectly recalled, the target photograph will not be found. However, we found that if any one of the four codes was ignored, a larger but manageable set of photos was retrieved with a high probability of containing the target. This pattern suggests a two-stage browser search mechanism in which the user can enter partial cues when not all of them can be remembered, and then visually scan the resultant set of retrieved photos for the target. A further implication is that while collaborative users will share a generic 'what' where' 'when' 'who' organizational scheme, they will typically differ in the categories they use within this shared scheme. We hypothesize that limiting categorization to four key dimensions, each with six categories to be specified by the user at encoding, will maximize the degree of overlap across the subjective organizations of multiple users. Where category systems differ among users, or where the search under four dimensions fails to yield a result, the gradual removal of one of the four dimensions will increase the degree of similarity among coding schemes and allow users to recover items for which one or more of the encoding categories has been forgotten.

5. The TW3 Browser Prototype

The case study provided validation for the use of an episodic organization scheme based around Who, What, Where, and When dimensions. In principle, there are a large number of ways in which such a scheme might be delivered within a browser, and the remainder of the TW3 project is exploring how these approaches might be optimized. The first prototype embodies the scheme explicitly as a procedural encoding and retrieval task.

The prototype is implemented as a Java point-and-click interface to a MySQL database. Figure 4 illustrates the encoding interface. The TW3 browser requires users to work through categorization under four dimensions. The user can code all photographs under one dimension at a time, or code each photograph under all four dimensions in parallel. Usability tests to date suggest that users require the capability to switch between encoding modes in real time during a single encoding run. Initially they typically choose to step through categories one by one. Once categories under each dimension become stable, however, some users prefer to switch to a mode of encoding each photograph under all four dimensions at once.

The retrieval mode uses the category structure created at encoding as cues to guide photographic description under each dimension. We make no use of user-assigned descriptive titles or keywords, since the case study pointed towards the inadequacy of labeling or keyword approaches. Moreover, early file-naming studies showed that file-naming even among experts yielded little consistency [15], a finding echoed by our own results in the experiments reported above, suggesting that keyword and label approaches will not support collaborative retrieval.

Items are retrieved according to their degree of fit with the categories under Who, What, Where, and When dimensions. If the target photograph remains undetected, the user can step through the dimensions, investigating the effects of removing each dimension in turn. By expanding on the retrieved sets with one dimension missing, the user is able to see a 'best fit' selection and discover the missing picture. In this way, the scheme allows an option to use partial encoding cues that are likely to offer a close match to the target items. In this respect, our use of a Who, What, Where and When scheme differs from that of Shen et al [10], who manipulate each dimension separately. Wagenaar's [11] results suggest that additional power for retrieval might gained by allowing the user access to these dimensions in parallel, and that the systematic dropping of dimensions that are uninformative at recall can guide people to the correct target set.

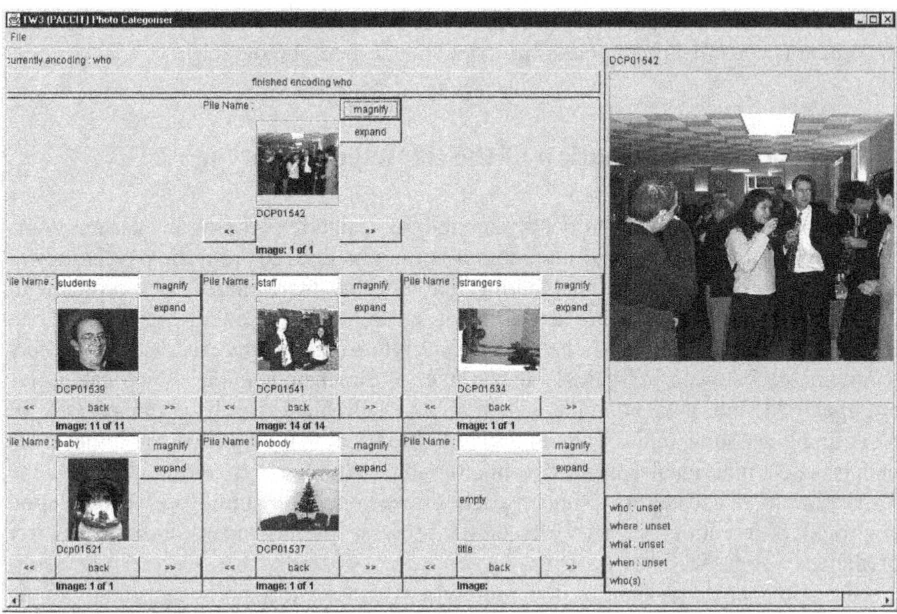

Fig. 4. The TW3 encoding tool. Photographs are presented as a stack (top center) ready for classification. The user categorizes under Who, What, Where and When dimensions in turn. The user can assign photographs to up to six categories for each dimension. Photographs can be magnified and categories expanded overview membership.

Perhaps the key difference between the TW3 prototype and other (e.g., commercially available) browsers is in the role of *constraint.* For example, other browsers tend to allow unlimited expansion of coding dimensions and categories (e.g., using a folder and sub-folder metaphor, labeling individual photographs with category tags), whereas the TW3 browser constrains encoding to four dimensions, and allows only six categories under each dimension. Also, because encoding is relatively unconstrained in other browsers, there is no restriction on the kinds of dimensions that users may use: they are just as likely to classify photographs semantically as episodically. In contrast, the Who, What, Where and When approach of the TW3 browser effectively constrains the user to an episodic category scheme. Moreover, the ways in which users retrieve photographs in other browsers is typically unconstrained: users can search for named photographs by keyword, or add and change as many label tags to photograph searches that they wish, when they wish. In contrast, to retrieve a photograph in the TW3 prototype, users must select categories under each of four dimensions. If the required photograph is not found, users are constrained to dropping one dimension at a time.

While this level of user constraint is uncommon (indeed, arguably, it is generally frowned upon) in user-centered design, we hypothesise that it might prove crucial to successful sharing of digital images. For example, constraint on encoding increases the relative likelihood and degree of overlap between different peoples' subjective organizations of photograph collections. Also, the inclusive use of all four dimensions during retrieval, followed by their systematic removal to continue to search, provide a procedural structure to guide the process of recovering from error (i.e., knowing what to do next if your first attempt does not yield the desired photograph).

6. Experimental Evaluation of the Browser Prototype

The TW3 browser prototype reflects a number of design hypotheses and assumptions. Perhaps the most fundamental assumption is the one derived from the psychological literature on collaborative remembering, namely that there might be a problem in retrieving photographs that are stored under someone else's coding categories. Then there is the issue of the Who What Where and When coding approach itself – it offers commonality between individuals at the level of dimensions under which categories are specified, but it is not clear whether this will hinder or help the process of photograph encoding and retrieval relative to browsers that do not fix the dimensions under which individuals categorise photographs. Another hypothesis concerns the restriction to six categories under each dimension. This limit was based upon empirical observation, yet its effects on browser performance cannot be easily predicted.

One approach to evaluating the prototype might be to employ an ethnographic approach, situating the browser in, say, a family context and observing over a number of weeks or months how peoples' activities around photograph handling are supported or changed by the imposition of the new technology. Indeed, we are adopting this approach in studies currently in progress on a substantially revised second prototype. However, we chose in the first instance to conduct a controlled experimental evaluation of the browser prototype, for three main reasons. First, an experimental evaluation allowed us to collect comparative data that pits our prototype against a commercially available browser, in this instance, the Adobe™ Jasc browser. Second, we were concerned that a situated evaluation of the browser might provide an unduly negative outcome for the simple reason that the TW3 browser was an early prototype with all the lack of functionality and irritations that early prototypes tend to have. In particular, we felt that users would be likely to abandon use of the browser prematurely, regardless of any merits that its key design features might bring, simply because of fixable prototype limitations. Third, we wanted to investigate whether the browser does address problems of shared encoding and retrieval using measures of search and retrieval which would simply not be observable using ethnographic methods.

The comparison between TW3 and Jasc browsers is not intended to be simply one assessing relative performance: we confidently expected the Jasc browser to outstrip our prototype on a majority of performance measures, if only because it is a properly-tested and fully-functional piece of commercial software developed for market by a team of designers, programmers, and testers. We were interested only in how the TW3 prototype compared with the Jasc browser in terms of *change* in performance, both across conditions (notably, when retrieving from ones own codes compared with retrieval using someone else's codes) and within conditions (notably, how the browsers fared in terms of recovery from failure to find photographs). In some respects, one might not expect major differences between the two browsers. In particular, the Jasc browser comes with three pre-configured tag dimensions, of

People (i.e. who), Event (i.e., what) and Place (i.e., where), with only the time-based tag missing. Where differences emerge, they must then reflect user preferences to make use of the freedom within Jasc to create their own categories and ignore system-set ones.

6.1 Method

Participants. 28 undergraduate and postgraduate students from Lancaster University were paid £10 each to take part.

Design and materials. Materials consisted of 200 photographs of members of the British royal family or places and events relating to them, gathered from a trawl of Internet media sites. Participants were assigned to one of two groups. One group used the TW3 browser to encode and retrieve photographs, the other used the Adobe Jasc browser (the free demonstration version available on the Adobe web site). For the retrieval phase of the experiment, each participant was nominally paired with another participant from the same group, matched by average encoding time. A second (within-subjects) factor in the retrieval phase was whether participants retrieved photographs using their own codes or those of their nominal pair.

Procedure. Encoding and retrieval phases were separated by approximately one week. In the encoding phase, participants were first shown all 200 photographs at a rate of 2 seconds per image. They then encoded each of the 200 photographs. For participants using the TW3 browser, they coded each photograph in a category under each of the four dimensions before proceeding to the next photograph, the categories (maximum = 6) emerging during the encoding process. For participants using the Jasc browser, they encoded each photograph by assigning either system-set or new tags (i.e., category labels). In the retrieval phase, participants retrieved 30 photographs using their own codes and 30 different photographs using their nominal pairs codes. Each photograph to be retrieved was presented on paper, and the participant's task was to find the photo in the browser by selecting categories under each dimension (TW3) or tag sets (Jasc).

6.2 Results and Discussion

The average time taken to encode each image was significantly greater with the Jasc browser (38.4s) than with the TW3 browser (20.6s), $t=7.85$, $p<.01$. The fact that encoding times were nearly twice as long with the Jasc browser is probably a function of the number and complexity of tags assigned to images compared with the limited categories used with the TW3 browser.

Table 1 shows the average number of tags/categories created under each dimension. Interestingly, tags under the Event and Place dimensions created with Jasc are comparable, quantitatively at least, with those created under What and Where with the TW3 browser. The People dimension appears to have been encoded at a much greater level of detail with Jasc than with TW3. This may result from the use of multiple overlapping tags in Jasc (e.g., "Charles", "Diana", "Charles with Diana" as separate categories), a strategy that is effectively blocked by the category limit within TW3. The 'other' dimension of Jasc is not comparable with the 'when' dimension of

TW3, since the former refers to all tags created by the user that did not fall within the system-set dimensions whereas the latter refers to the time dimension. What is clear is that users were making use of the flexibility inherent within Jasc to create many personalized coding categories.

Table 1. Mean number of tags/categories created under each dimension using Jasc/TW3 browsers at encoding.

	Who/Person	What/Event	Where/Place	When/Other
TW3	6.0	5.6	5.2	4.2
Jasc	24.2	6.2	6.9	19.3

Table 2 shows retrieval performance with the two browsers under a number of measures. A significant interaction was found between Browser and Code factors in the number of photographs retrieved at the first attempt, $F(1, 26) = 8.94$, $MSe = 5.61$, $p < .01$. The Jasc browser gave the highest level of retrievals at the first attempt, particularly with own codes. This result suggests that, as long as you find a photograph first time and you are the sole user of a collection, the Jasc browser is the better of the two.

Table 2. Mean number of photographs retrieved (N = 30) on first attempt, and overall (i.e. after dropping categories or adding extra tags), and mean time to retrieve image.

	No. found at first attempt	No. found overall	Mean retrieval time (s)
TW3 with own codes	14.4	24.4	35.5
TW3 with others codes	10.7	23.2	36.8
Jasc with own codes	18.2	23.6	40.9
Jasc with others codes	10.8	18.4	47.0

A significant interaction was also found for the number retrieved overall, $F(1, 26) = 9.87$, $MSe = 6.09$, $p < .01$. It appears that, while there is no advantage for either browser when retrieving using ones own codes, the TW3 browser leads to greater retrieval using someone else's codes. Indeed, performance is comparable with using ones own codes with the TW3 browser. Thus, the main advantage of the TW3 browser appears to be in recovering from a failed first attempt to find a photograph using someone else's codes.

A main effect of Browser was also found with retrieval times, $F(1, 26) = 5.44$, $MSe = 209.8$, $p < .05$, though the interaction between Browser and Code factors was not significant. It seems likely that the advantage for the TW3 browser is a result of different strategies for finding a photograph after a failed first attempt. With the TW3 browser, users were limited to dropping each dimension in turn in order to inspect whether the required photograph had been mis-categorised or mis-recalled under that particular dimension. With the Jasc browser, users were also able to drop tags, but a much more common strategy was to add another tag in order to combine the results from tag categories. As well as taking longer to execute, this strategy was limited in effect. While it could deal with errors of omission (photographs not classified under a particular tag dimension), it was less successful in dealing with errors of commission (i.e. photographs wrongly classified or mis-recalled under a particular tag dimension).

The results of the study confirm our key hypotheses. First, there is a detrimental effect of trying to retrieve photographs using another persons coding scheme. This result is not surprising in theoretical terms, but it has important practical implications for the design of collaborative browsers. Second, the Who, What, Where and When scheme seems to provide an efficient and effective set of dimensions and procedure around which to configure a browser. The study is, of course, limited to a particular observation and set (and size) of materials. It may be, for example, that a less favorable outcome would be found with less familiar materials (e.g., archeological shards) and with larger sets of photographs, especially when they are encoded over a longer and more fragmented time frame.

Of key importance, it appears that the two browsers are optimized for different contexts of use. The Jasc browser appears best suited to individual users maintaining photograph collections for private use, where they can code photographs in uniquely meaningful ways. In line with our hypotheses, the TW3 browser appears to be better configured to support collaborative use of photographs. While first-attempt retrieval is perhaps disappointing with the TW3 browser, recovery is as strong as with the Jasc browser using ones own codes, and more importantly, it is much better when using someone else's codes.

7. Conclusions

The design of the TW3 prototype was informed by converging results from three empirical methods that are often seen as diametrically opposed to each other. However, we argue that each can offer an essential and unique contribution to systems design. The experiments demonstrated the potential for categorization-based interventions to enhance collaborative retrieval. The brief sample from a longer ethnographic study highlights the point that photographs are routinely viewed as part of a collaborative set of activities and are used to support a broader set of social activities across the family. The case study showed how a four-dimensional scheme can offer a simple yet powerful approach to encoding and retrieving digital images. The case study also illustrates how methods used in experimental studies can be applied in more naturalistic and rich observational studies.

These ideas have come together within a set of image browsing tools that allow users to collaborate in encoding and retrieving images while supporting them in overcoming a major source of difficulty, namely errors of commission. The aim is to develop equivalents of social discourse around images for digital technologies. While researchers have explored the development of different presentation techniques for this purpose [16, 17], we are more interested in how digital photographs will be stored and retrieved as part of this process.

Experimental demonstrations of collaborative inhibition point to a phenomenon that must be addressed in all systems designed for collaborative use. The ethnographic studies provide support for an episodic approach to collaborative encoding and retrieval. The dominance of episodic discourse around photographs is consistent with results from the case study, notably the finding that recall of photographs by semantic keyword was very inefficient compared with recall by episodic category. This finding suggests that query-based approaches are of limited efficacy in managing large image sets, and do little to address problems of collaboration.

The importance of understanding contexts of use is emphasized by the results of the comparative evaluation, where it appears that the Jasc browser is optimized for individual use while the TW3 browser is better for shared use (albeit tested here in a context where users worked individually with codes produced by a nominal partner). As one encounters other contexts of use, this pattern might change. For example, it is possible that in professional contexts (e.g., commercial photo libraries), the advantages of detailed coding of individual photograph characteristics may outweigh the benefits of a restricted coding scheme.

The studies reported here show how different methods make valuable contributions to the design and evaluation of interactive systems. In planning empirical studies that inform design, there are competing pressures. The need for ecologically valid observation or real contexts of use must be balanced against the efforts required to collect data and the costs of early commitment to prototypes that can be evaluated in-situ. At the same time, there must be a recognition that no single method can provide everything a designer needs. Our mixed method approach allows both situated observation of contexts of use and also detailed assessment of the impacts of cognitive phenomena that are otherwise hard to observe and measure.

Acknowledgements

The TW3 project is supported by the ESRC/EPSRC ‘People at the Centre of Communications and IT’ initiative, L32830300198. We thank Fleur Finlay and Rachel Attfield for help with the experiments.

References

1. Hammersley, M., Atkinson, P.: Ethnography: Principles in practice. Routledge, London (1983)
2. Hughes, J.A., King, V., Rodden, T., Andersen, H.: Moving out from the control room: Ethnography in system design. In Proc. CSCW ’94, Chapel Hill, North Carolina (1994)
3. Hutchins, E.: Cognition in the wild. Cambridge, MIT Press, MA (1995)
4. Suchman, L.: Plans and situated actions: The problem of human-machine communication. CUP, Cambridge (1987)
5. Ball, L. J., Ormerod, T. C.: Putting ethnography to work: The case for a cognitive ethnography of design. Int. J. Human-Computer Studies 53 (2000) 147-168
6. Nisbett, R., Wilson, T.D.: Telling more than we can know: Verbal reports as data. Psychological Review. 84 (1977) 231-259.
7. Murphy, G.C., Walker, R.J., Baniassad, E.L.A.: Evaluating emerging software technologies: Lessons learned from assessing Aspect-Oriented programming. IEEE Trans. on Software Engineering, 25 (1999) 438-455
8. Frolich, D., Kuchinsky, A., Pering, C., Don, A., Ariss, S.: Requirements for photoware. Proc. CSCW 2002, New Orleans, ACM Press (2002) 166-175

9. Kang, H., Shneiderman, B.: Visualization methods for personal photo collections, Proc. IICME 2000, New York: IEEE Computer Society (2000)
10. Shen, C., Lesh, F., Vernier, F., Forlines, C. Frost, J.: Sharing and building digital group histories. Proc. CSCW 2002, New Orleans, ACM Press (2002) 324-333
11. Wagenaar, W. A.: My Memory: A study of autobiographical memory over six years. Cognitive Psychology, 18 (1986) 225-252
12. Weldon, M.S., Bellinger, K.D.: Collective memory: Collaborative and individual processes in remembering. J.Exp Psych: Learning, Memory & Cognition, 23 (1997) 1160-1175
13. Basden, B. H. Basden, D.R., Bryner, S., Thomas, R.L.: A comparison of group and individual remembering: Does collaboration disrupt retrieval strategies? J.Exp Psych: Learning Memory & Cognition, 23, (1997) 1176-1191
14. Finlay, F. Hitch, G., Meudell, P.: Mutual Inhibition in collaborative recall: Evidence for a retrieval-based account. J.Exp Psych: Learning Memory & Cognition 26 (2000) 1556-1567
15. Furnas, G.W., Landauer, T., Gomez, L. Dumais, S.: Statistical semantics: analysis of the potential performance of keyword systems. Bell Systems Technical Journal, 62 (1983) 1753-1806
16. Balobanovic, M. Chu, L.L., Wolff, G.J.: Storytelling with digital photographs, Proc. CHI 2000, Amsterdam, ACM Press (2000) 564-571.
17. Vernier, F., Lesh, N. Shen, C.: Visualisation techniques for circular tabletop interfaces. AVI 2002, Trento, Italy, ACM Press (2002)

Discussion

[Michael Harrison] About titles and their semantics. What does it mean to fail to get the semantics right?

> [Tom Ormerod] Both recall and recognition of photo titles were very poor. Elements of the description didn't match more than 50% of the titles.

[Bonnie John] Are a lot of your results because of specific features of the photos you used? E.g., Relatively few (hundreds not thousands). Maybe the six categories is just because there are so few, which would be different if there were a lifetime of photos. Not many that are actually photos of the same thing (e.g., the professional photographer did more of the exact same labeling, perhaps because professionals take many of the same thing, so why wouldn't there be the same label? -- and as people understand that digital cameras don't waste film, they'll take many of the same thing, too.).

> [Tom Ormerod] That's what I was trying to say on the last slide -- we don't know the exact locus of the effects we report. However, we have ongoing work with professional image colelctions where volumes are 20000 images plus. So far, results are promising.

[Hong-Mei Chen] Do you intend to generalize your research results beyond the family photo retrieval system to a general image retrieval system?

> [Tom Ormerod] Yes. We are currently exploring possibilities such as PDF file retrieval.

[Hong-Mei Chen] I think it may have some difficulties as family photos, as Bonnie pointed out, may have a lot of similar photos and the precision of retrieval may not be as critical as other applications such as document retrievals.
In addition, in your experiment, you used the British Royal family photos instead the subjects' own photos, that may affect your experimental results applicable to family photo retrievals as most people have intrinsic memories associated with their own photos.

> [Tom Ormerod] I don't really have answers to the first part of this question. However, we did an experiment looking at couples who handled their own photos, encoding either together or separately. To our surprise, we got similar effects with these personalised materials.

[Joaquim Jorge] Have you thought of methods for automatically capturing metadata ? People are not very adept at cataloguing photos and documents.

> [Tom Ormerod] Metadata can be re-used, e.g. when taking a series of photos on the same subjects. Also when temporal labels are very close the photos can "inherit" labels from others in the sequence.

[Joaquim Jorge] What about using "stories about photos" to create photo archetypes from those stories and extract content? Another possibility would be sketching descriptions for content-based retrieval?

> [Tom Ormerod] We have a different research agenda. We suspect that good browsers would do a little of both and minimize labeling problems.

"Tell Me a Story"
Issues on the Design of Document Retrieval Systems

Daniel Gonçalves, Joaquim Jorge

Computer Science Department, Instituto Superior Técnico, Av. Rovisco Pais
1049-001 Lisboa Portugal
djvg@gia.ist.utl.pt, jorgej@acm.org

Abstract. Despite the growing numbers and diversity of electronic documents, the ways in which they are cataloged and retrieved remain largely unchanged. Storing a document requires classifying it, usually into a hierarchic file system. Such classification schemes aren't easy to use, causing undue cognitive loads. The shortcomings of current approaches are mostly felt when retrieving documents. Indeed, how a document was classified often provides the main clue to its whereabouts. However, place is seldom what is most readily remembered by users. We argue that the use of narratives, whereby users 'tell the story' of a document, not only in terms of previous interactions with the computer but also relating to a wider "real world" context, will allow for a more natural and efficient retrieval of documents. In support of this, we describe a study where 60 stories about documents were collected and analyzed. The most common narrative elements were identified (time, storage and purpose), and we gained insights on the elements themselves, discovering several probable transitions. From those results, we extract important guidelines for the design of narrative-based document retrieval interfaces. Those guidelines were then validated with the help of two low-fidelity prototypes designed from experimental data. This paper presents these guidelines whilst discussing their relevance to design issues.

1 Introduction

In recent years, computer hardware has become increasingly cheap. As a consequence people tend to use computers not only at work, but also at home. Furthermore, PCs are losing their dominance and laptops or PDAs are ever more commonly used in all settings. Moreover, the advent of ubiquitous, pervasive computing will only increase the number of devices available from which documents can be handled. Because of this trend, more and more often users edit and store related documents in different locations. Thus, new tools that allow users to more easily find a specific piece of information, regardless of where they are, or to visualize the Personal Document Space (PDS) as a whole will soon become imperative. One of the major challenges of HCI in the upcoming years will revolve around these issues, as pervasive computing becomes a reality 1 2 13.

The biggest problem with current hierarchic organization schemes is that they continuously require users to classify their documents, both when they are named and

R. Bastide, P. Palanque, and J. Roth (Eds.): EHCI-DSVIS 2004, LNCS 3425, pp. 129-145, 2005.

when they are saved somewhere in the file system. Such approaches force users to fit their documents into specific categories. Also, since users know that a good classification determines their ability to later retrieve the documents, classifying ever increasing numbers of documents becomes a painful task, causing undue cognitive loads while choosing the category in which each document should be placed.

This was first recognized by Thomas Malone 12 on his groundbreaking work where two main document organization strategies were identified: *files* and *piles*. On files documents are classified according to some criteria, whereas Piles are *ad-hoc* collections of documents. The latter were shown to be more common due to the difficulties inherent to the classification task. Nowadays, similar results are found not only for documents on computers but also for other applications in which hierarchic classification has become the primary information organization strategy. Such is the case of email, where it was found 4 that most users' inboxes are often filled with large numbers of messages, given the difficulty and reluctance in classifying them into other folders. However, despite the apparent lack of classification, the same study found that the users think it easier to find email messages in the inbox than finding a document on the file system. This is because email messages are associated to useful information elements, ranging from the sender of a message to when it was sent and what messages were received at about the same time. This causes some people to overload their email tools to work as To Do lists or to maintain sets of unread documents 14. Even considering that email tools were not designed with those ends in mind, the trade-off in relation to traditional applications seems to be positive.

This shows the importance of information other than a name or classification for retrieving documents. Users more readily remember other contextual, real world, information, rather than some arbitrary classification made months or years ago. Several works try to make use of such additional information to help users retrieve their documents. One of the first was Gifford's *Semantic File Systems* 7, where properties are associated to documents, either automatically inferred (from email headers, for instance), or explicitly created by users. Documents can then be found in 'virtual-folders', whose contents are determined by queries on the defined properties. This work inspired others such as Dourish et al's *Placeless Documents* 4 and Baeza-Yates et al's *PACO* 3, where enhancements for features such as support for multiple document locations and management of shared documents can be found. Other works, such as Freeman and Gelernter's *Lifestreams* 6 recognize the importance of temporal information, presenting all documents in an ordered stream.

Although alleviating some of the problems users must face, new problems appear with those approaches. Property-based systems require users to handle (and remember) arbitrary sets of properties. Furthermore, each property is an isolated piece of information with no apparent relation to the others. Temporal-based approaches disregard other kinds of information. An integration of the several relevant information elements that could help users in finding their documents is lacking. The most natural way in which users can convey that information to someone is in the form of stories or narratives. Humans are natural-born storytellers. From early times have stories been told, first in oral tradition and later in written form. Elements in a story do not appear separately but as part of a coherent whole. The relations between those elements make the story easier to remember. An interface that takes advantage of those abilities and allows users to tell a story describing a document in order to retrieve it will allow for a more natural and efficient interaction.

The design of such an interface should take into account not only the most common and expected elements in a narrative, but also how they inter-relate. This will allow it to know what shape the stories might have, what will come up next at any given point in the narrative, and what information users might remember even if it wasn't volunteered in the first place, resulting in a dialogue that is natural, informative and not awkward. Thus, it is important to find out exactly what document-describing stories are like.

To correctly address the aforementioned challenges, we performed a set of interviews where several stories describing documents were analyzed. This allowed us to extract patterns for common narrative elements and ways in which they are used. Some recurrent story structures were found. From those, we extracted a set of guidelines that systems for narrative-based document retrieval should follow to correctly address the users' needs. Ultimately, we envision the design of a system that continuously gathers information about the users' interactions with their documents and whose narrative-based interface is able to extract vital information about the documents from the users, allowing the documents to be retrieved.

We'll start by describing how the study was conducted. Next, we'll analyze the results thus obtained. Then we will present the design guidelines, and how they were validated. Finally, we'll discuss the main conclusions and possible future work on the area.

2 Procedure

With this study, we tried to answer two main research questions: (1) in document-describing stories, *what are the most common elements?* (2): *how do they relate to form the story?* To find the answers, we conducted 20 semi-structured interviews. The volunteers were interviewed at a time and place of their choice (previously arranged), often in their own offices or other familiar environments, to set them at ease. We asked for their consent in recording the interviews.

Of the 20 subjects we interviewed, 55% were male and 45% female, with ages ranging from 24 to 56. Academic qualifications spanned all levels, from high-school to PhDs. Their professions were also fairly diversified: Computer Science Engineers, High-School Teachers, Law Students, economist, social sciences professor, etc. This accounts for the wide range of computer expertise we found, from programming skills to sporadic use of common applications (such as Microsoft Word). Overall, we feel we collected data from a diverse sample that won't unduly bias the results.

After explaining the study to the subjects, they were asked to remember specific documents from three different classes and to tell stories describing them. Those classes were: Recent Documents on which the user worked on in the past few days or weeks; Old Documents, worked on at least a year ago; and Other Documents, not created by the user. They were chosen to allow us to evaluate the effect that time might have on the nature and accuracy of the stories (regardless of their correctness, since real documents were not available to validate them), and to find if stories are remembered differently for documents not created by the users themselves, since their interaction with those documents was different. We didn't provide actual documents to be described because that would require the interviewer to have access to the subject's computer in order to choose those documents. Previous experiments 8 showed that users are reluctant to allow that kind of intrusion. Also, preliminary test interviews demonstrated computers to be distractive elements during the interviews, resulting in stories of poor quality. Furthermore, asking interviewees to remember the documents to be described better mimics the situations in which they might want to find a document in everyday life.

For each document, the interviewees were instructed to "tell the story of the document", and to recall all information they remembered about it. It was specifically recommended that information besides the one resulting from the interaction with the computer itself was important. Additional questions regarding several expected elements were posed in the course of the interview. They were asked only when the interviewees seemed at a loss of anything else to say, to see if some other information could still be elicited from them, or whenever they had started talking about some unrelated subject and we needed to make them go back to describing the document at hand. Three test interviews were conducted to tune and validate this procedure

Stories usually took five minutes to be told. Their transcripts averaged two to three plain text pages, although some users told longer stories. A typical story might start like this translated excerpt from a real interview:

Interviewer: So, now that you have thought of a document, please tell me its story…
Interviewee: It's a paper I had sent to my supervisor. We had sent it to a conference some time ago. It was rejected… meanwhile I had placed the document on my UNIX account…

3 Interview Analysis

All interviews were subjected to a Contents Analysis 15. We coded for several elements we expected to find in the stories (Table 1). New elements could be considered if required during the analysis process. As it turned out, no new elements were necessary after the initial encoding. Since the users were free to tell their stories as they chose, we're fairly confident that we considered all relevant elements.

Table 1. Story Elements.

Time	Place	Co-Authors	Purpose
Author	Subject	Other Docs.	Personal Life
World Events	Doc Exchanges	Doc Type	Tasks
Storage	Versions	Contents	Events
Name			

Contents analysis is often performed by defining a coding dictionary which contains, for each specific word or expression that might occur in the interviews, the class to which it belongs 11. In our domain such a dictionary could contain an entry stating that the occurrence of the word "hours" is a reference to a "Time" element. This approach would allow the encoding to be made automatically. However, it requires the researcher to anticipate all relevant words or expressions that might appear. This was impossible in our experiment since the subjects were free to say whatever they chose about documents previously unknown to us. Hence, no coding dictionary was used. Instead, we conducted the coding manually with the help of a set of heuristic rules that clearly define what should belong to each category, considering not only specific words or expressions but also their meanings. We coded for frequency rather than for occurrence, since frequency can give us an estimate of the relative importance of the elements in terms of the amount of information of each kind in the stories. Also, we took notice of what elements were *spontaneous* (proposed by the interviewees) and *induced* (promptly remembered by the interviewee after a question or suggestion from the interviewer). We also considered that not knowing something is different from knowing something not to have happened. An element was recorded only in the latter case. For instance, some users remembered that a document had no co-authors, while others couldn't remember if that was the case or not.

We also performed a Relational Analysis 15 to estimate how the several elements relate in the story. We considered the strength of all relationships to be the same. The direction of the relationships was given by the order in which the elements appear in the story. The signal of a relationship (whether two concepts reinforce or oppose each other) wasn't considered since it isn't relevant in this case. This allowed us to create a directed graph whose nodes are story elements, arcs represent the relationships between those elements, and arc labels contain the number of times the corresponding transition was found. No transition was considered when the destination element was induced, since in that case no real connection between the elements existed in the interviewee's mind.

4 Results

Overall, we collected and analyzed 60 different stories, 20 for each document type. We produced not only quantitative results relating to the relative frequencies of the different story elements and transitions between those elements, but also qualitatively analyzed the stories' contents. We took care to compare stories for different document kinds. Finally, we were able to infer archetypical stories about documents. Several statistical tests were used whenever relevant. In what follows, all quantitative values are statistically significant to 95% confidence. More results can be found in the experiment's technical report 9.

4.1 Story Length

We found stories to be 15.85 elements long, on average (std. dev.=5.97). The fairly large standard deviation accounts for the difference between stories relating to documents created by the user and those of others, with average lengths of 17.7 and 12.15, respectively. From this we conclude it is easier to remember information about your own documents. There is no significant correlation between story length and subject age. Although the interviewees were relatively young, this is a surprising result. Cognitive problems arise with age and some trend could already be visible. As to gender, we observed that women tend to tell longer stories than men (16.81 vs.

14.67 elements), suggesting it is easier for them to remember potentially relevant information.

4.2 Transition Numbers

Since no transition is recorded between two elements if the second is induced, the ratio between the numbers of transitions and story elements provides a good estimate of how in control of their stories the interviewees were. On average, 47% of stories were spontaneous, regardless of document type and interviewee gender. A significant but weak (0.22) correlation was found in relation to age: older users are marginally more in control of their stories, allowing for less interference from the interviewer.

4.3 Story Elements

The most common overall story elements were **Time**, **Place**, **Co-Author**, **Purpose**, **Subject**, **Other Documents**, **Exchanges**, **Type**, **Tasks**, **Storage** and **Content** (Fig. 1). Some elements appear more than once in a story, showing that users sometimes provide additional information to reinforce or clarify them. The least mentioned elements were those pertaining information about **Authors**, **Personal Events**, **World Events**, **Versions**, **Events**, and **Names**. This shows how those elements are harder to remember or considered less important by the users.

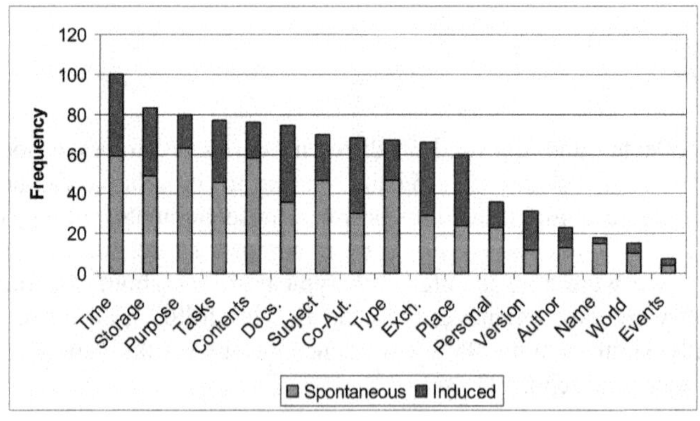

Fig. 1 – Overall Element Frequencies.

Fig. 2 shows that element frequencies for Recent and Old Documents seem to follow similar distributions. Statistically, we found significant differences only for the **Subject** element. When a document is recent, users tend to reiterate it on their narratives, since they easily remember more relevant details.

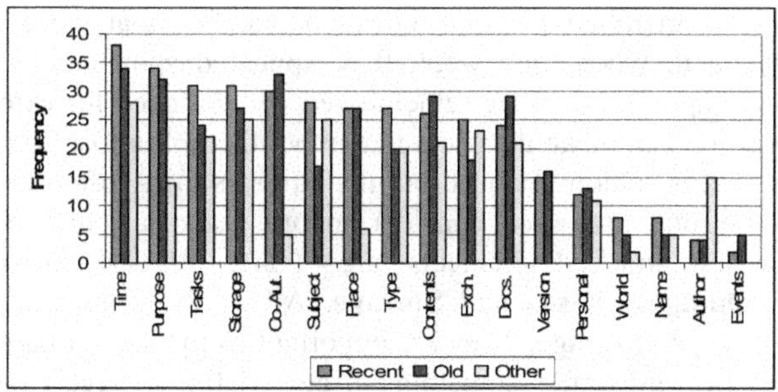

Fig. 2 – Element Frequencies by Document Kind.

Larger differences could be found among documents created by the user and those of others. The most noteworthy differences are related to the frequencies of **Place, Co-Authors**, **Purpose, Author**, and **Version**. The differences in Author and Version are easy to explain: when the user itself is the author of a document, he will take the fact for granted, and it is hard if not impossible for a person to know if a document someone else wrote had different versions. Co-Authors are also harder to remember. Only the author, if anything, is remembered. As to the Place where the document was handled, reading a document is less prone to memorable interactions than actively writing it, making it harder to remember where it happened. Finally, and regarding the document's Purpose, the reason for the difference seems once again to be the ease in which it is possible to remember what a document was for when we were its author.

We found little difference in the amount of times an element was induced, given its total number of occurrences, for the different document types. The only significant differences occurred between documents created by the users and those of others, for **Place, Co-Author** and **Version**, as was to be expected from the different element frequencies we described above.

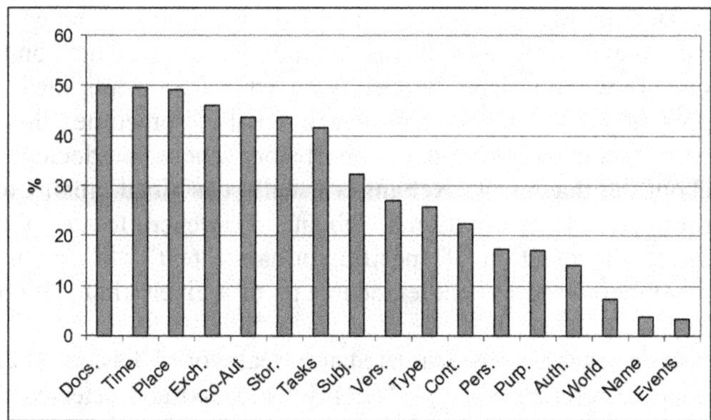

Fig. 3 – Overall Percentages of Induced Elements.

Overall (Fig. 3), we found that the less often induced elements are **Purpose**, **Author**, **Personal Events**, **World Events**, **Events** and **Name**. With the exception of Purpose, these are the least frequent element categories. Keeping in mind that induced elements are those subjects remembered after a question, the fact that these elements were rarely mentioned and, when they were, they appeared spontaneously, means that either they are so important they are remembered without need for external aid, or no amount of suggestion can make the users remember them. Purpose's case is different. It is an element that is seldom induced but that appears fairly often in the narratives. This shows it to be something users consider important and easy to remember.

The more often induced elements are **Time**, **Place**, **Co-Author**, **Other Documents**, **Exchanges**, **Tasks** and **Storage**. All of these appear fairly often in stories, at least once, on average. They are important elements, but hard to remember: mentioned often but only after something triggered the subject's memories about them. Even so, no element is, on average, induced more than 50% of its occurrences in the stories, showing that, even if it is hard to remember, there is a fair chance it might come up spontaneously after all.

The Nature of Story Elements

A closer look at the elements themselves allowed us to find exactly what form the phrases where they are described actually takes.

The level of accuracy for references to **Time** tends to vary. For Recent Documents it is fairly specific: *"(...) about one hour and a half ago (...)"*. For Old Documents it is only roughly remembered: *"(...)I delivered it around April (...)"*. In stories about Other Documents, the references to Time vary in accuracy, depending solely on how long ago the document was handled. References to **Place**, on the other hand, are very accurate (*"At home"*; *"It was updated here"*), as are those about the document's **Purpose**, which include information on where and for what the document was used: *"(...) it will be used in the school's newspaper (...)"*.

References to **Co-Authors** are seldom actual names. Often, the subjects only remember if they existed or not. The mentioned **Subjects** were of very diverse natures: *"(...) the subscription to a magazine (...)"*; *"(...) the weekly results of my work"*; *"(...) an analysis of the company's communications infrastructure"*.

The **Other Documents** that were mentioned sometimes included actual paper documents, and not electronic ones. It was common for users to mention the existence of other documents without actually specifying what documents they were talking about (but apparently knowing it themselves). Finally, sometimes the reference to another document was enough to cause a 'short story' about that document to be told. Information about the document **Exchanges** usually described email exchanges, but also other forms, such as posting it on a web site. References to a document's **Type**, included not only the mention of specific formats ("text", "image"), but also to applications commonly used to handle documents of a given kind ("Word", "Excel", "PowerPoint").

We found references to computer-related and 'real world' **Tasks**: "(…) went to the library to find some references (…)"; "(…) downloaded and selected the photos."; "(…) I printed the document (…)". References to where the document was **Stored** often mention entire computers, but also removable media and specific (unnamed) locations in a hard drive or local networks. In the case of online documents, the site is often mentioned.

As to **Content**, it was common to find mentions to specific information about the document's structure. References to specific contents were rare: *"It had a sentence* *that started by 'And to those persons that...' "; "(...) it was divided into tables (...) It had lots of graphics (...)".*

It is not always possible to remember a document's **Author,** especially for foreign, hard to pronounce names. **Personal Events** usually happened to the interviewees themselves or to someone directly related to them. Often it is something that could be found on someone's agenda, but not always: *"It was the day my car's battery went dead."; "(...) I finished it before my vacations."; "(...) my son had a serious asthma crisis (...)".*

Almost completely absent were references to **World Events**, often not directly associated to the users but directly relating to their jobs or co-workers. Only once was some important news event mentioned. Also rare were references to **Versions**, normally to state that they didn't exist. The least mentioned story element, **Events** that might have occurred when the subject was interacting with the document, often described actions done by the users and unrelated to the documents, rather than events outside their control. It seems that such incidents are unimportant and quickly forgotten: *"(...) I prepared instant soups (...)"; "Someone arrived at my home (...)".* Finally, there were some references to **Names**, either of the document files themselves or of folders where those files are stored. Sometimes, no specific names were uttered, but it was clear the user had a specific, well identified, folder in mind.

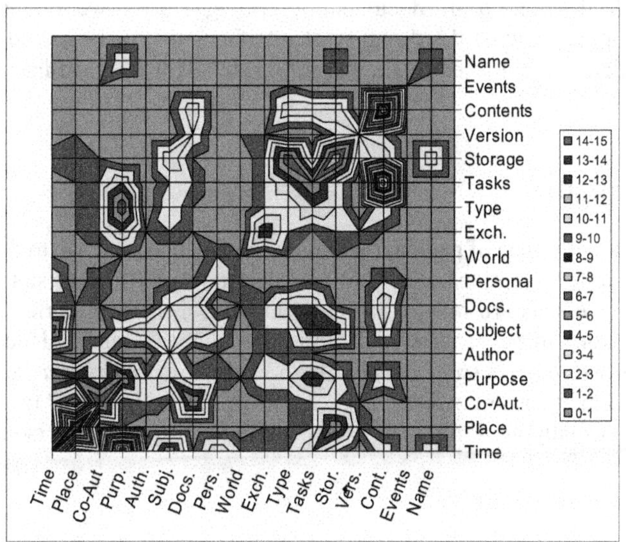

Fig. 4 – Transition Frequencies

Element Transitions

Only 36.7% of all possible transitions occurred more than once, reinforcing our assumption that there are indeed especially relevant transitions underlying the stories. The most common transitions were **Time-Purpose**, **Tasks-Content**, **Subject-Time**, **Type-Purpose**, and **Storage-Type** (Fig. 4). Reflexive transitions such as those involving **Content, Place,** and **Time,** are also common, whenever the user feels the need to refine or clarify something.

A situation could arise in which a transition between two frequently-occurring elements would itself have a high absolute frequency while happening (for instance) only 50% of the times those elements were present in a story. This could make it seem more important that a transition that occurs 100% of times among rarer elements. Normalized transition frequency values accounting for the frequencies of the involved elements were calculated and no significant bias was detected.

We calculated, for each story element, the probabilities that another of a particular kind might follow. For the most common transitions (for the others, the data is not trustworthy), we found the most probable to be **Place-Place** (0.417), **Content-Content** (0.344), **Tasks-Content** (0.316), and **Time-Purpose** (0.25). Also with a fairly high transition probability we found **Co-Author-Co-Author** (0.259), **Author-Co-Author** (0.25), **Author-Subject** (0.25), and **Place-Storage** (0.25). These probabilities are enough to build some expectations but not to have any certainties.

Finally, we found little symmetry in the transitions. For instance, the Time-Purpose transition occurs over three times as often as Purpose-Time.

5 Discussion

The thorough description of document-describing stories we obtained provides important insights on what the designer of interfaces that make use to those stories should consider. We collected those insights in the form of guidelines we will now describe.

5.1 Customization

We found little relevance of personal factors such as gender and age to the way stories are told. The only exceptions were that women tend to tell longer stories than man, and that older persons are marginally more in control of their stories than younger ones. Apart from those aspects, the stories remain the same. Hence, *little user customization will be necessary in relation to what to expect from a story*. This does not preclude other customizations, such as adapting the interface to the particular subjects users usually work on, or to better visualize a particular Personal Document Space.

5.2 Memory

We expected to find that a user's memory about a document would fade with time, allowing them to remember less information. However, except for Subject (more common for Recent documents), no significant time-related difference was found for the remaining elements, story length, or transition numbers. Likewise, no differences were recorded in the percentages of induced elements stories: nearly half of the narratives were spontaneously told by the subjects. Differences in information correctness might exist, but were not addressed by this study.

What does seem to affect the information a user can remember about documents is their origin. Stories about documents created by the user, regardless of when, are longer. Some elements such as Place or Purpose are mentioned more often, suggesting they are easier to remember. In short, *some differences in the story structures and accuracy can be expected according to the age of the document being described.* However, the biggest differences derive from the document's origin. *It is important to determine it early in the narrative, to correctly form expectations about what can be found ahead in the story.*

5.3 The Importance of Dialogues

For some story elements, a significant number of occurrences were induced by questions posed by the interviewer. Elements such as Time, Place, and Other Documents are among them. They are also some of the most frequent elements, suggesting that users consider them important and can actually remember them, if asked.

It is important to establish dialogues with users in order to obtain all information they can actually remember. Some care should be taken about thematic shifts. However, they are fairly rare and should pose no significant problem.

On the other hand, *the dialogues should not waste time and resources trying to discover certain elements*, such as Author, Personal Events, World Events, Events and Names. They are rarely mentioned but generally spontaneously, showing that if they are remembered at all, they will most likely be volunteered with no need for inducement.

5.4 Context-Dependent Information

It is common for stories to include indirect references to elements that are taken for granted by the storyteller. For instance, references to the Place where a document was produced and its Author are based on assumptions or contextual information. Often, no specific places or names are mentioned because they seem obvious to the person telling the story. This happens, for instance, if a document arrived by email and the user only has email access at work. *It is important to take the context in which the story is told into consideration, comparing it to a model of the users' world and of users themselves.*

5.5 Ambiguity

Some level of ambiguity is common in stories. For instance, references to time become more inaccurate for older documents. Something similar occurs when trying to remember names of authors or co-authors. The user can remember what the name sounded like, or that it had some co-authors, but not their actual names.

Some level of ambiguity must be tolerated by narrative-based interfaces. Techniques to automatically disambiguate stories with the help of context and user and world models are to be considered. Users themselves often try to help, providing information about the same element more than once in the same story. That willingness to help should be encouraged and used.

5.6 World and User Models

When referring to such elements as Purpose, World Events or Personal Events, a wide range of information can be conveyed. It is probably impossible to just use keywords extracted from the stories to effectively gain some insight on what document is being talked about. Trying to understand those elements just by looking at what was said is also insufficient, due to great numbers of things that would be important to understand them but are taken for granted and not explicitly mentioned. To aid in that understanding, *a model of the world around the users and of the users themselves (including typical activities, co-workers, etc.) should be used.* Important information can also be found on the user's agenda, and also in that of his friends or co-workers. Some facts from the 'wider world', such as important news could also helpful, albeit rarely.

5.7 Overall Document Structure

Users remember more easily overall document structures than actual keywords or phrases in that document. Some technique that identifies the overall structure or visual appearance of a document and can use that information to differentiate among several documents would be useful.

5.8 Events Arising During Interactions with the Document

In short, *these are not relevant*. It was extremely rare for any such events (someone entering the office, a phone call, etc) to be remembered.

5.9 Recursive Stories

When describing related documents, it is common for several information elements pertaining those documents to be told. They can constitute small recursive stories (stories within a story). *Special care should be taken to capture those elements, which provide important information, while keeping in mind they relate to a document different than the one the story is about*. Also, those stories should somehow be controlled in order to prevent the storyteller from loosing himself in them, sidetracking from the document he really wants to find.

5.10 Expected Elements and Structure

The stories we analyzed share, up to a point, similar structures. Designers of narrative-based interfaces should take advantage of those similarities. They will allow the system to know what to expect from the stories, help guide the user towards providing useful information, and collect that information.

Some story elements are more frequent than others, and should be expected more often. Several will be mentioned only if prompted by some external factor. This information is useful, helping decide if some more information should be expected (if some frequent elements weren't yet mentioned) or not. It will help decide whether it's worthy to invest some time and effort to discover more elements.

5.11 Probable Transitions

Of all possible transitions between different story elements, only 37% have some credible probability of showing up. Of those, five are to be expected fairly often. Combining this information with the probabilities of what will be the next element, given the current point in the narrative, it will be possible to build expectations of what the next element in the story will be. This will help recognize it and extract all relevant information, facilitating disambiguation.

6 Validating the Guidelines

The guidelines we just described are based solely on stories told to human interviewers. To validate them, it is necessary to verify if stories told to computers, no longer free-form but in a more structured environment, are similar to those in which the guidelines were based. We designed two low-fidelity prototypes that embody the guidelines. In both, time plays a special role, as does determining the documents' authors, allowing the use of the different expected story structures. Several story elements are suggested to the users in the order found to be the most likely in the previous study, but any of them can be referred to at any time, if the users so wish. Specialized dialogue boxes are used to enter the elements. Prototype A allows the direct manipulation of the elements, graphically represented on the interface as little boxes, and Prototype B presents those elements as natural language sentences (Fig. 5 and Fig. 6). More details on the prototypes' design can be found in the experiment's technical report 10. Ten users where asked to tell document-describing stories using Prototype A, and ten others using Prototype B. We used a Wizard-of-Oz methodology, in which the researcher simulates the workings of the prototypes.

Comparing the stories told using the prototypes to those previously collected immediately showed them to be similar. The relative frequencies and importance of the several story elements is analogous to those found for stories told to humans, as is the nature of the information. The stories were actually longer than those told to humans (20%), thus conveying more information. Prototype B was clearly better, allowing for longer stories to be told, with fewer differences to the ones in the previous study. For instance, in only 3% of stories did the users of that prototype deviate from the proposed story order, whereas this happened on 43% of the stories told using Prototype A. Also, the qualitative evaluation of the prototypes (using a questionnaire), showed that the users found Prototype A to be more confusing. We attribute the differences between the two prototypes to the fact that on Prototype B, the users were able to see the entire story as a whole, in textual form, and Prototype A dispels the illusion of telling a story by dividing the narratives into discrete elements.

This shows that, despite the validity of the guidelines (using them, we were able to come up with an interface that allows stories similar to those told to humans to be told), the judicious design of the interface is crucial for the quality of the stories.

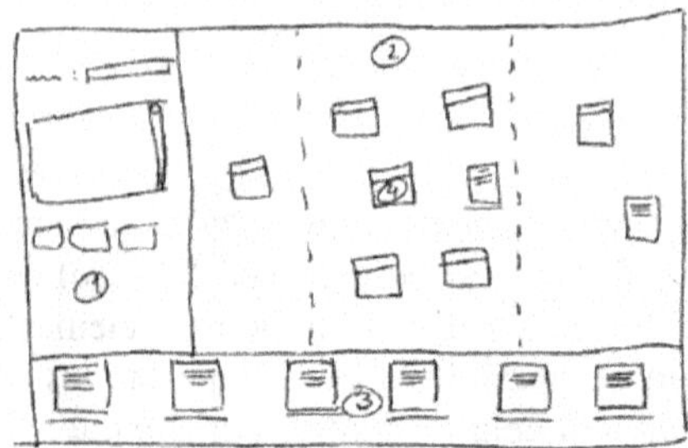

Fig. 5. Prototype A.

Fig. 6. Prototype B

7 Conclusions and Future Work

With the growing numbers of documents users must deal with on a daily basis, new techniques to help finding them are imperative. One such technique involves taking advantage of our innate ability to tell stories. We verified that stories about documents provide a wealth of information about them, helping the users to remember more details than they would otherwise, as shown by the existence of induced elements. We found that dialogues are important to allow those elements to come up. The stories shared several common properties and structure, including the most common elements. This will allow for narrative-based interfaces to build expectations on what shapes the stories might take, helping to understand and disambiguate them. In short, several important guidelines could be extracted that will allow future research in the area to be developed on a sound basis. Those guidelines were validated with the help of low-fidelity prototypes.

One factor we didn't take into account in this study and that might constitute interesting future research is to ascertain to what extent the information users tell in their stories is accurate. In the present study, when someone said that a document was written four months ago, we had no way of verifying that assertion. Such verifications would require access to the users' documents. However, such extended access leads to important privacy concerns that will have to be dealt with. This would be something better tested by resorting to a story-gathering prototype which is able to gather story details and verify their accuracy without the intervention of a human interviewer.

References

1. Abowd, G. Software Engineering Issues for Ubiquitous Computing. *Proceedings of the 21st international conference on Software engineering*, pp 75-84, ACM Press, 1999.

2. Abowd, G. and Mynatt, E. Charting Past, Present, and Future Research in Ubiquitous Computing. *ACM Transactions on Computer-Human Interaction*, 7(1), pp 29-58, ACM Press 2000.

3. Baeza-Yates, R., Jones, T. and Rawlins, G. A New Data Model: Persistent Attribute-Centric Objects, Technical Report, University of Chile, 1996

4. Bälter, O., Sidner, C.. Bifrost inbox organizer: giving users control over the inbox. In *Proceedings of the second Nordic conference on Human-computer interaction*, pages 111-118, ACM Press, 2002.

5. Dourish, P. *et al.* Extending Document Management Systems with User-Specific Active Properties. *ACM Transactions on Information Systems*, 18(2), pp 140-170, ACM Press 2000.

6. Freeman, E. and Gelernter, D. Lifestreams: A Storage Model for Personal Data, *ACM SIGMOD Record,*25(1), pp 80-86, ACM Press 1996.

7. Gifford, D., Jouvelot, P., Sheldon, M. and O'Toole, J. Semantic File Systems. *13th ACM Symposium on Principles of Programming Languages*, October 1991.

8. Gonçalves, D. and Jorge, J. An Empirical Study of Personal Document Spaces. In *Proceedings DSV-IS 2003*, Lecture Notes on Computer Science, Springer-Verlag, vol. 2844, pp. 47-60, June 2003, Funchal, Portugal.

9. Gonçalves, D. Telling Stories About Documents, Technical Report, Instituto Superior Técnico, 2003 (http://narrative.shorturl.com/files/telling_stories.zip).

10. Gonçalves, D. 'Telling Stories to Computers'. Technical Report, Instituto Superior Técnico, December 2003. http://narrative.shorturl.com/files/telling_stories_to_computers.zip.

11. Huberman, M. and Miles, M. Analyse des données qualitatives. Recueil de nouvelles méthodes. Bruxelles, De Boeck, 1991.

12. Malone, T. How do People Organize their Desks? Implications for the Design of Office Information Systems, *ACM Transactions on Office Information Systems*, 1(1), pp 99-112, ACM Press 1983.

13. Myers, B, Hudson, S and Pausch, R.. Past, present, and future of user interface software tools. *ACM Transactions on Computer-Human Interaction*, 7(1), pp 453-469, ACM Press 2000.

14. Whittaker, S., Sidner, C. Email overload exploring personal information management of email. In *Conference proceedings on Human factors in computing systems*, pages 276-283, ACM Press, 1996.

15. Yin. R. Case Study. Design and Methods. London, Sage Publications, 1989.

Discussion

[Tom Ormerod] Both approaches share an interaction mode that is fun and engaging (although they impose a task load on users). The engagement aspects of the system will possibly prove to be important. When do you want to capture that information? You said you do it a while ago, instead of when saving a document (as in MS Word). Is the delay between document production and narrative elicitation important?

> [Joaquim Jorge] It is intentional. One of our main tenets is to save people from needing to classify "too much" when working. The experiment was devised by asking people to classify instead of snooping their personal information on their personal file systems.

[Greg Phillips] When I'm searching for a document I'm highly motivated to tell my story. But using the story to search requires the presence of meta-data. As Tim Bray says: "there is no cheap meta-data". Where does your meta-data come from?

> [Joaquim Jorge] To collect the meta-data, we're assuming something like factoids (Digital Western Research Lab 1997), which automatically does it. In the near term, we want to use people's personal calendar, agendas, e-mail folders. We assume users will have these data in their computer and willing to share it if they can trust the system. It does raise some privacy issues as noted in our presentation.
>
> The purpose of this research is to find out how best to get people to tell stories, and to find out what kinds of stories they tell. In our case study, we have just evaluated what kind of interface would be good to capture such information.

[Bonnie John] About practice and research: Apple says next OSX will have full-text search of all documents, encoded when saved, so instantaneous retrieval -- are companies overtaking research?

> [Joaquim Jorge] This particular technique can be used on non-textual files, so Apple's technique will not solve all search problems.
>
> Some documents contain only non textual information (eg pictures). Full-text searches will not work on unlabeled images and movies. The proposed Views can ease search problems. But stories can be used for unlabeled content and use autobiographical information, to complement those conventional techniques.

[Michael Harrison] The narratives you have shown seem to be more autobiographical than about the documents that were stored (based on the content). Was this true?

> [Joaquim Jorge] That was one of the surprising outcomes of our experiment.

[Hong-Mei Chen] How do you do the encoding of meta data?

> [Joaquim Jorge] We have to do the encoding using personal data granered from personal information.

[Hong-Mei Chen] How do you motivate people to do the encoding when first filing the document as it will take a long time to tell the story?

[Joaquim Jorge] People found it easier to tell the story in a structured environment than telling it to a real human. Our research results showed that people are satisfied with telling the story.

[Hong-Mei Chen] Do you have problems justifying the statistical power and sample size, 20, to elicit the 17 story elements you used as guidelines in your design?

[Joaquim Jorge] We didn't have a problem with the statistical significance but the sample size is a problem. It takes a lot of effort to do the interviews. 20 was the minimum acceptable sample.

CanonSketch: A User-Centered Tool for Canonical Abstract Prototyping

Pedro F. Campos and Nuno J. Nunes

Department of Mathematics and Engineering, University of Madeira
Campus da Penteada, 9000-390 Funchal, Portugal
{pcampos,njn}@uma.pt

Abstract. In this paper, we argue that current user interface modeling tools are developed using a formalism-centric approach that does not support the needs of modern software development. In order to solve this problem we need both usable and expressive notations and tools that enable the creation of user-interface specifications that leverage the design and thought process. In this paper we present the CanonSketch tool. CanonSketch supports a new UI specification language – Canonical Abstract Prototypes (CAP) – that bridges the gap between envisioned user behavior and the concrete user interface. The tool also supports two additional and synchronized views of the UI: the Wisdom UML presentation extension and concrete HTML user interfaces. In this way the tool seamlessly supports designers while switching from high level abstract views of the UI and low-level concrete realizations.

1 Introduction

Model-based user interface design (MB-UID) has been the target of much research during the last decade. However, and despite the success obtained by user interface development tools, approaches based on models are not reaching the industrial maturity augured in the 90's [4].

In a paper presented at a recent Workshop on MB-UID [9], we argued that in order to achieve a stronger market acceptance of modeling tools, a new generation of user-centric tools would have to emerge. The existing tools are focused on the formalisms required to automatically generate the concrete user-interfaces. This legacy of formalism-centric approaches prevents the current tools from adequately supporting the thought and design tasks that developers have to accomplish in order to create usable and effective user-interfaces. Model based approaches concentrate on high-level specifications of the user-interface, thus designers loose control over the lower level details. These problems with MB-UI tools are described in [4]. In particular, those tools suffered from trying to solve the "whole problem" and thus providing a "high threshold/low ceiling" result. The threshold is related to the difficulty of learning a new system and the ceiling is related with how much can be done using the system. Thus, those tools don't concentrate on a specific part of the UI design process and are difficult to learn, while not providing significant results.

R. Bastide, P. Palanque, and J. Roth (Eds.): EHCI-DSVIS 2004, LNCS 3425, pp. 146-163, 2005.

In order to overcome these limitations, designers directly use a user-interface builder (a low threshold/low ceiling tool) that provides them with adequate and flexible support for designing the user-interface. Designers that recognize the value of modeling at higher levels of abstraction are forced to use different tools and notations to capture the user-interface specifics at different levels of abstraction – what could be considered as using many low-threshold/low ceiling tools.

Some of the requirements for such tools were also discussed in a recent workshop about usability of model-based tools [11]. Among other issues, the participants at the workshop highlighted the following requirements as paramount to promote usability in tools: traceability (switching back and forth between models, knowing which parts can be affected by changes), support for partial designs, knowledge management (for instance, a class that is selected or modified often is probably more important than classes not often changed) and smooth progression from abstract to concrete models.

In this paper we present a new tool, under development, that tries to leverage the users' previous experience with popular Interface Builder (IB) tools in order to achieve better adoption levels. Our aim is to build a developer-centric modeling tool that applies successful concepts from the most usable and accepted software tools. Instead of defining a complex semantic model and formalisms to automatically generate the user interface (UI), we start by using a simple sketch application and extending it to accommodate the required concepts and tools. The tool supports the creation and editing of Canonical Abstract Prototypes [2] and Wisdom Presentation Models [7]. It is capable of automatically generating HTML interfaces from the Canonical specification. In this initial phase, we are focusing on specifying GUI's for Web-based applications, although conceptually the tool is not restricted to this type of interface, since the languages are platform and implementation independent. However, this allows us to test the main concepts of the tool/language by focusing on a well-known interface type.

This paper is organized as follows: Section 2 relates our work to some approaches for UI design and Section 3 briefly describes the main notation our tool supports: Canonical Abstract Prototypes. Section 4 presents CanonSketch, detailing some of its user-centered features. Section 5 proposes an initial extension to the Wisdom presentation model in order to support the Canonical notation. Section 6 investigates the capability of both notations to express UI design patterns in an abstract way. Finally, Section 7 draws some conclusions on our present work and presents possible future paths to follow.

2 Prototyping and Sketching Interfaces

Rapid prototyping of interactive systems is a technique used in order to assess design ideas at an early stage of the development process. It attempts to foster the collaboration between all the stakeholders involved in the project (managers, end-users, graphic designers, coders...) and to facilitate iterative cycles of reviewing and testing.

Being a de facto standard in the development community, the UML provides a good medium to specify UIs enabling higher acceptance rates and promoting artifact interchange between modeling tools. UML class stereotypes have become a very popular alternative to structure the presentation elements of interactive systems [7]. In particular, the Wisdom notation complies with the UML standard, thus enhances communication with software developers. Another strategy, used by the DiaMODL approach, combines this with a strong linkage to concrete UI elements [10]. Other approaches are used in different areas: Hypermedia applications, such as in [13] and [14] and Cooperative System modeling [15].

Prototyping interfaces with electronic sketching tools has also proven successful in systems such as SILK [3] or DENIM [5]. Sketching is believed to be important during the early stages of prototyping, because it helps the designers' creative process: the ambiguity of sketches with uncertain types or sizes encourages the exploration of new designs without getting lost in the details, thus forcing designers to focus on important issues at this stage, such as the overall structure and flow of the interaction [3].

However, widget recognition is hard for these systems [3], since any widget recognition algorithm might be too error-prone. Also, usability tests reported that some users had trouble manipulating and entering text, and understanding how to select, group and move objects.

Calgary et al. [16] describe a framework that serves as a reference for classifying user interfaces supporting multiple targets, or multiple contexts of use in the field of context-aware computing. This framework structures the development life cycle into four levels of abstraction: task and concepts, abstract user interface, concrete user interface and final user interface [16]. These levels are structured with a relationship of reification going from an abstract level to a concrete one and a relationship of abstraction going from a concrete level to an abstract one. As we will see in this paper, maintaining a connection between these levels is well supported in CanonSketch.

Canonical Abstract Prototypes [2] were developed by Constantine and colleagues, after a growing awareness among designers regarding the conceptual gap between task models and realistic prototypes. They provide a common vocabulary for expressing visual and interaction designs without concern for details of behavior and appearance. Moreover, they fill an important gap between existing higher-level techniques, such as UML-based interaction spaces and lower-level techniques, such as concrete prototypes. This is why we chose this notation as our starting point for our modeling tool. In the following section, we briefly describe the Canonical notation.

3 Canonical Abstract Prototypes

Constantine [2] proposes a stable collection of abstract components, each specifying an interactive function, such as inputting data or displaying a notification. Following on the successful path of interface builders, these components can be selected from a palette in order to build abstract prototypes, thus fostering flexibility and modeling usability. Having a standardized set of abstract components also eases the comparison of alternative designs and enhances communication between members of the development team [2].

The symbolic notation underlying Canonical Abstract Prototypes is built from two generic, extensible[1] universal symbols or glyphs: a generic *material* or *container*, represented by a square box and a generic *tool* or *action*, represented by an arrow. Materials represent content, information, data or other UI objects manipulated or presented to the user during the course of a task. Tools represent operators, mechanisms or controls that can be used to manipulate or transform materials [2]. By combining these two classes of components, one can generate a third class of generic components, called a *hybrid* or *active material*, which represents any component with characteristics of both composing elements, such as a text entry box (a UI element presenting information that can also be edited or entered). Figure 1 shows the three basic symbols of the Canonical Abstract notation. For a more detailed look of the notation, please refer to Figure 6.

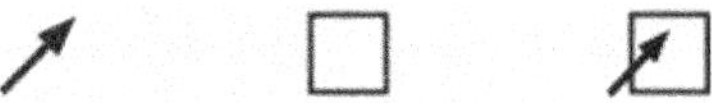

Fig. 1. The three basic symbols underlying the symbolic notation of Canonical Abstract Prototypes (from left to right): a generic abstract tool, a generic abstract material and a generic abstract hybrid, or active material (taken from [2]).

Although Canonical Abstract Prototypes lack a precise formalism and semantics required to provide tool support and automatic generation of UI, we found the notation expressive enough to generate concrete user interfaces from abstract prototypes. In the following section, we present our tool, including a proof of feasibility in which we generate HTML pages from sketches of Canonical Abstract Prototypes.

4 CanonSketch: The Tool

Different tools (business presentation applications and even sticky notes or whiteboards) can be used for creating Canonical Abstract Prototypes. However, in order to assess and benefit from all of the advantages of this notation, software tool support is ultimately needed [2].

CanonSketch aims at providing a usable and practical tool to support Canonical Abstract Prototypes. Starting with an easy to learn notation, developed from real world projects, we built a tool that provides the user a palette of abstract components that can be drawn, grouped, resized and labeled within a drawing space representing an interaction space. The tool supports all the successful features one expects to find in software nowadays, like multiple undo/redo, grid layout, tool tips or send to back/bring to front.

Our tool already supports the creation (at the syntactic level only) of Wisdom interaction spaces [6]. Our aim is to leverage developer experience of the Unified Modeling Language (UML) by designing an extension to the UML that fully supports Canonical Abstract Prototypes. Figure 2 shows a CanonSketch screenshot of the Wisdom view, where the designer is creating a Wisdom presentation model as if she

[1] Meaning all other components can be derived, or specialized, from these classes.

were sketching in a simple drawing application. Figure 3 shows a screenshot of the Canonical view: we can see that there are several palettes of tools available (e.g. for controlling font-size, coloring and grid layout) and an inspector as well as an optional ruler.

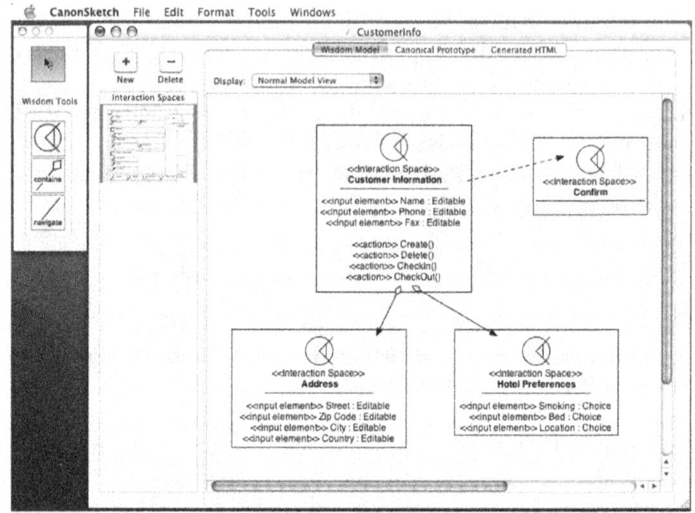

Fig. 2. CanonSketch screenshot: creating Wisdom UML presentation models.

In our path to building a usable modeling tool for UI design, we began with a different approach from the conventional way these tools are envisioned: instead of focusing on the formalisms and semantics, we began with a simple drawing application and built a modeling tool that relies on interaction idioms more closely related to Office applications, as we discuss in the following sections. Our remit here is that we intend to focus on achieving a modeling tool that is as easy to use as a drawing application.

4.1 User-Centered Features

UI tools represent an important segment of the tool market, accounting for 100 million US Dollars per-year [4]. However, there has been a gross decline on the modeling tools market revenue, according to reliable sources such as the International Data Corporation. The lack of usability present in modeling tools is believed to be responsible for this weak adoption [11].

A more developer-centered approach was followed in CanonSketch: Figure 4 shows some of the aspects we took into account. Canonical Abstract Prototypes are organized in terms of sequences of interaction spaces that appear as thumbnails of their corresponding specifications. By using this pattern, very common on business presentation applications, we aim at leveraging the existing user experience while also promoting communication and collaboration between developers and clients (who are often businessmen familiar with this pattern).

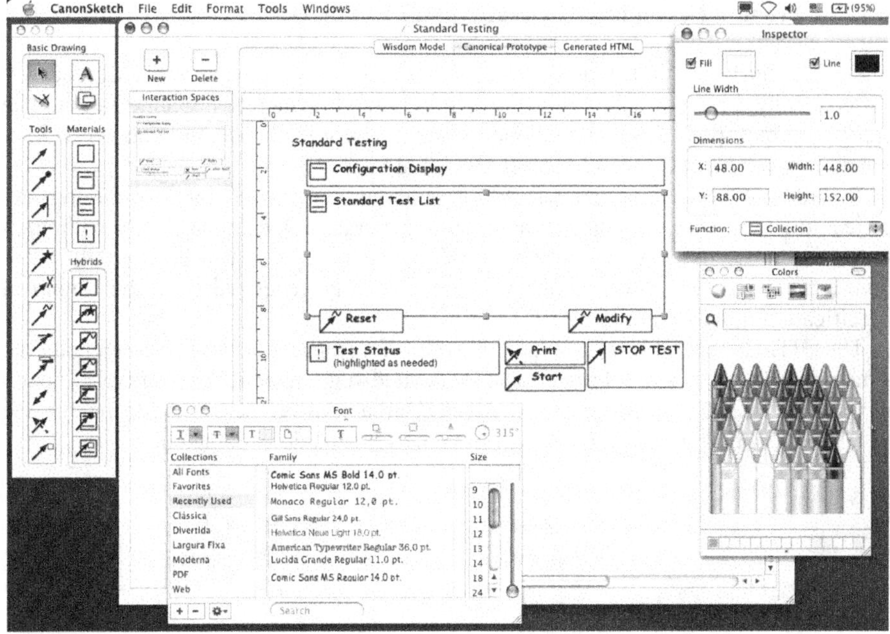

Fig. 3. CanonSketch screenshot: creating and editing Canonical Abstract Prototypes.

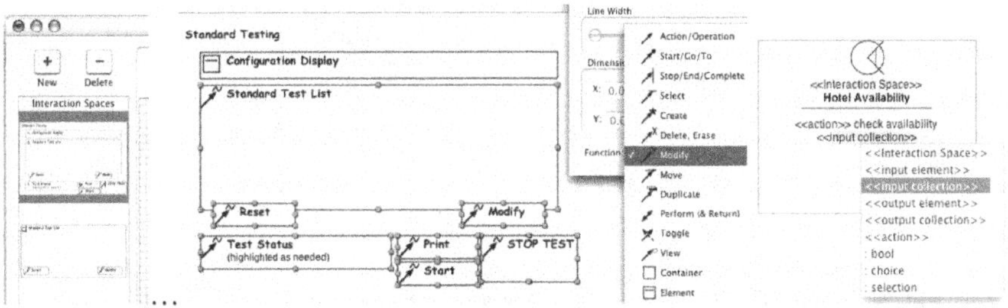

Fig. 4. Some of the developer-centered features in CanonSketch.

The center image on Figure 4 shows a selection of several canonical components to apply a transformation of their interactive function all at once. The rightmost image shows code completion for when the designer is specifying a Wisdom Interaction Space (which is a UML class stereotype representing "space" where the user can interact with the application). We believe this way of editing UML models is more usable than filling in complex forms that only update the UML view after validating everything the developer introduced.

Finally, the grid layout option may help position and resizing the components more rapidly, and the tool palettes follow the pattern of the successful Interface Builders. Tabbed-view navigation is important in order to achieve, in the future, model linkage at the various stages of the process.

4.2 A Proof of Feasibility: Generating HTML Forms

There is a third view in CanonSketch where a concrete prototype, in HTML form, is automatically generated, thus illustrating one possible concrete implementation. The concrete prototype is fully navigational, since it is rendered using an embedded, fully functional web browser, as we can see in Figure 5.

In order to verify the richness of the notation developed by Constantine and colleagues, and also to support automatic generation techniques, still without a semantic model defined, we built a proof of feasibility that can be exemplified in Figure 5. The HTML form shown was automatically generated from the canonical specification illustrated in Figure 3.

The HTML clickable prototype is useful for rapidly testing the navigational structure of the specified interface. The tool can also generate a PDF printable version of the Canonical/Wisdom models, which can act as a means to document the development process and commit to design decisions made with the client.

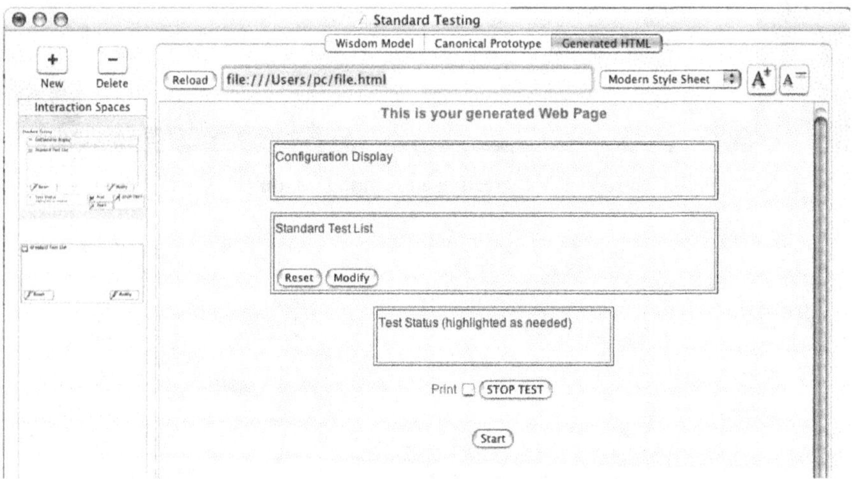

Fig. 5. Simple HTML automatically generated from the specification in Figure 2.

In the absence of a semantic model incorporated into our tool, this proof of concept already shows the potential of the notation, and achieves our goal of checking the richness of the abstract prototype notation. This is also part of our approach based on starting from a usable, simple tool and successfully add semantic mechanisms in an incremental way, rather than building a complex, formalism-centered tool.

5 Towards a Common Semantic Model

The automatic generation presented in the previous section was done at this stage without complete semantics of our intended adaptation of Canonical Abstract Prototypes. We are currently working on incrementally adding the mechanisms required to automatically generate concrete user interfaces from abstract prototypes.

From this initial proof of concept, we aim at specifying an extension to the UML 2.0 notation capable of fully supporting Canonical Abstract Prototypes. In particular, the Wisdom notation [7], which is a set of UML-compatible notations supporting efficient and effective interactive systems modeling, can be used and refined to achieve this goal.

In order to maintain synchronized Wisdom/Canonical views, a common semantic model is required. Specifying such a model will lead to a tool capable of not only supporting the design process at several stages (from early design ideas to concrete implementation) but also complementing the weaknesses of one model with the strengths of the other. The designer will be able to choose between one model view and switch back and forth while maintaining coherence between the models.

To support the modeling of presentation aspects of the UI, the Wisdom method proposes the following extensions to the UML [8]:

- «Interaction Space», a class stereotype that represents the space within the UI where the user interacts with the all the tools and containers during the course of a task or set of interrelated tasks;
- «navigate», an association stereotype between two interaction space classes denoting a user moving from one interaction space to another;
- «contains», an association stereotype between two interaction space classes denoting that the source class (container) contains the target class (contained); The contains association can only be used between interaction space classes and is unidirectional.
- «input element», an attribute stereotype denoting information received from the user, i.e., information the user can operate on;
- «output element», an attribute stereotype denoting information displayed to the user, i.e., information the user can perceive but not manipulate;
- «action», an operation stereotype denoting something the user can do in the concrete UI that causes a significant change in the internal state of the system.

Some problems identified with applying the Wisdom approach to UI patterns derive from the presentation aspects some of the patterns capture, such as size, position, or use of color [8]. Specifying a linkage between Canonical Abstract Prototypes and the Wisdom Presentation Model can help solve some of these problems, while also adding the necessary formalism to the Canonical notation.

In Figure 6, we show an initial specification of a possible connection between the Wisdom Presentation Model and Canonical Abstract Prototypes. An interaction space in Wisdom is clearly an interaction context in a Canonical Prototype.

Although not present in Figure 6, the «navigate» association can be unidirectional or bi-directional; the later usually meaning there is an implied return in the navigation. This essentially has the same meaning Constantine defines when describing the Canonical contexts' navigation map [1].

An «input element» attribute stereotype is mapped to a generic active material, unless typified. Input elements specify information the user can manipulate in order to achieve a task.

An «output element» attribute stereotype maps to an element and an «action» operation stereotype to an action/operation Canonical component.

The «contains» association stereotype is mapped to a Canonical container.

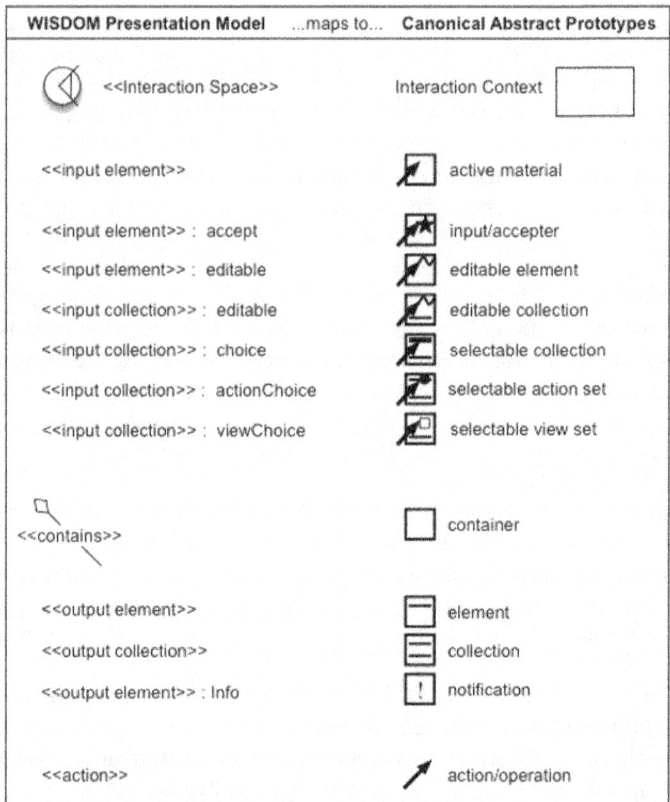

Fig. 6. Extending the Wisdom profile to support Canonical Abstract Prototypes: this figure shows the correspondence between Wisdom stereotypes and Canonical components.

We can also see from Figure 6 that one possible initial extension to the Wisdom presentation model notation to fully support Canonical Abstract Prototypes consists in adding two more attribute stereotypes:

- «input collection», an attribute stereotype denoting a set of related information elements received from the user, i.e., a set of input elements; an «input collection» can be used to select from several values in a drop-down list, or choosing one element from a table to perform any given operation;
- «output collection», an attribute stereotype denoting a set of related information elements displayed to the user, i.e., a set of output elements. Typically, an «output collection» conveys information to the user about a set of elements of the same kind, for instance a search results list or the results display from a query to a database.

By typifying these attribute stereotypes, one can map a Wisdom presentation model to all Canonical components that belong to the classes of Materials or Hybrids. For instance, an input collection typified as choice can be mapped to a selectable collection. The designer starts by specifying the general structure of the UI using a UML extension (the Wisdom notation). That specification is mapped to one or more

Canonical interaction contexts, where the designer expands and details the model in terms of size, position and interactive functions.

Figure 7 shows an example of a Wisdom Presentation Model for a Hotel Reservation System (described in and taken from [7]). Figure 8 depicts a Canonical Abstract Prototype that corresponds to the area inside the dashed rectangle in Figure 7. This mapping clearly shows the role of Wisdom interaction spaces realizing the interface architecture, and how it can be combined with the Canonical notation to help bridge the gap between abstract and concrete models of the user interface.

The capability of identifying UI patterns and expressing the solution in an abstract way independent of any particular platform or implementation is becoming more and more important, with the increase in the number of information appliances [8]. The Wisdom notation enables an abstract definition of UI patterns [8], and also complies with the UML standard. However, some problems remain for patterns expressing more concrete presentation aspects, such as size or positioning.

Having a tool that provides a common semantic model linking Canonical components to Wisdom elements can help solve some of these problems. It also adds the required formalisms for generating concrete user interfaces from Canonical specifications. We expect to incrementally build such a tool from our current version of CanonSketch.

As we will see in the next section, both notations can be used in conjunction in order to express abstract design patterns.

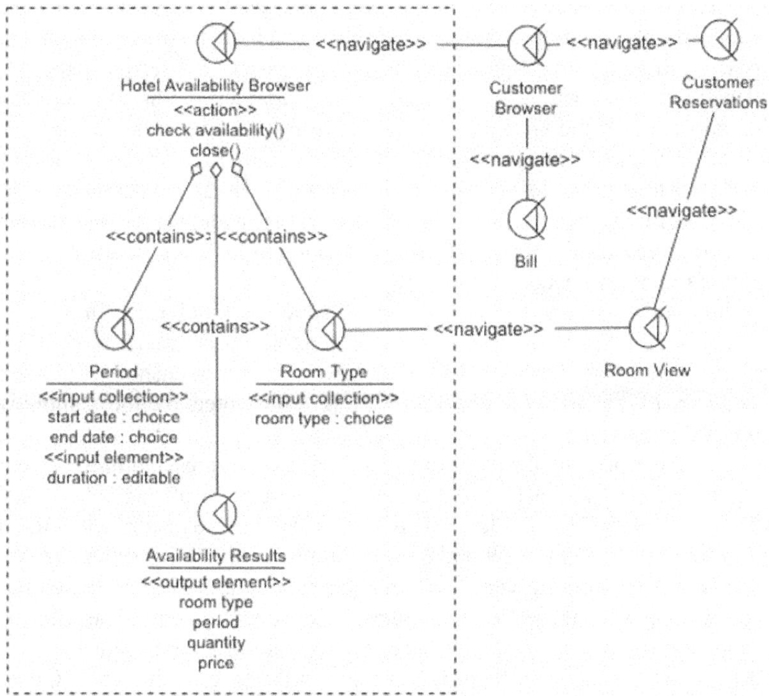

Fig. 7. A Wisdom Presentation Model for a Hotel Reservation System (described in and taken from [7]).

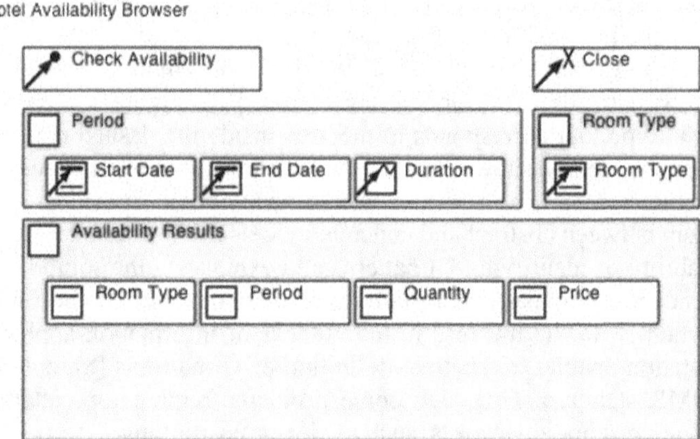

Fig. 8. A Canonical Abstract Prototype for the same Hotel Reservation System as in the area inside the dashed rectangle in Figure 7.

6 Using CanonSketch to Represent UI Patterns

Since the Canonical Abstract Notation is a way to express visual design ideas that was devised to support decision-making at a higher level of abstraction than concrete prototypes, we tried to investigate the ability to express GUI design patterns using CanonSketch. In this section, we present some examples of the Wisdom notation extension applied to some GUI patterns (taken from the Amsterdam collection [12]) and also the Canonical representation for the same patterns. As Constantine points out, "the ability to express design patterns in terms of generalized abstract models has seen little use in UI patterns". We still lack some widely accepted notation to represent commonly used solutions to some interaction tasks in an abstract way that can be applied to many design scenarios [8].

Throughout this section, all the Figures illustrate a Final User Interface (FUI) linked to a Concrete User Interface (CUI) or Abstract User Interface (CUI), in the terms defined in [16]. The FUI is represented by a screenshot of a particular implementation of the pattern, and the AUI is represented by the Canonical and Wisdom representations.

In Figure 9, we present the Wisdom and Canonical representations for the GUI Preview pattern [12]. We also present a concrete realization of this pattern (a dialog from MS PowerPoint). The problem this pattern tries to solve occurs when the user is looking for an item in a small set and tries to find the item by browsing the set. This pattern is particularly helpful when the items' content nature does not match its index (e.g. a set of images or audio files are indexed by a textual label). The solution is to provide the user with a preview of the currently selected item from the set being browsed [12]. As we can see, there is not much difference in this case. On the one hand, the Wisdom representation (on the top left), is much more compact, because it is based on the UML. But the Canonical representation has the advantage of clearly stating that the browsable list of items is placed to the left of the item preview, which conforms with the western way of reading and therefore adjusts to the task being performed: the user first selects an item, and only then he focuses on the preview. It is also evident that the Canonical notation is much closer to the concrete representation of this pattern (at the bottom of Figure 9).

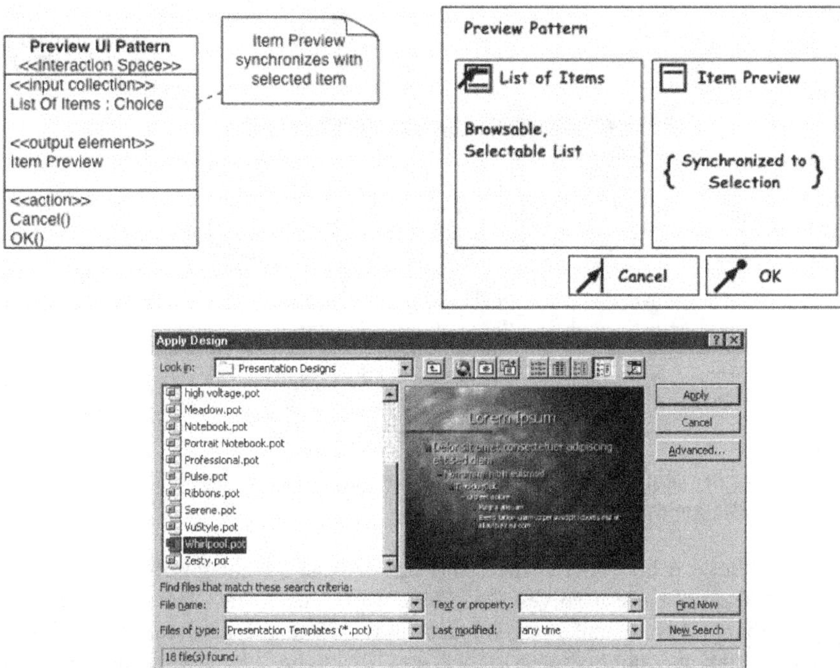

Fig. 9. A Wisdom (top left) model, a Canonical prototype (top right), both applied to the Preview Pattern. A concrete example is shown at the bottom: a dialog from MS PowerPoint.

In the following pattern, the advantages of combining both Wisdom and Canonical representations are also evident. The grid layout pattern, also from the Amsterdam collection [12], tries to solve the problem of quickly understanding information and take action depending on that information. The solution is based on arranging all objects in a grid using a minimal number of rows and columns, making the cells as large as possible [12]. The bottom of Figure 10 shows an example of a concrete GUI where this is achieved (a dialog box from Word 97). By using this pattern, screen clutter is minimal and the layout is more consistent. The top of Figure 10 shows the Wisdom representation at the left and the Canonical representation on the right.

It is clear that the Canonical notation has potential for easily expressing patterns that employ spatial, layout or positioning relationships between UI elements. Both notations have mechanisms for adding useful comments and constraints. The repetition element in the Canonical notation (represented by a triple chevron) is expressed as a one-to-many «contains» association in Wisdom.

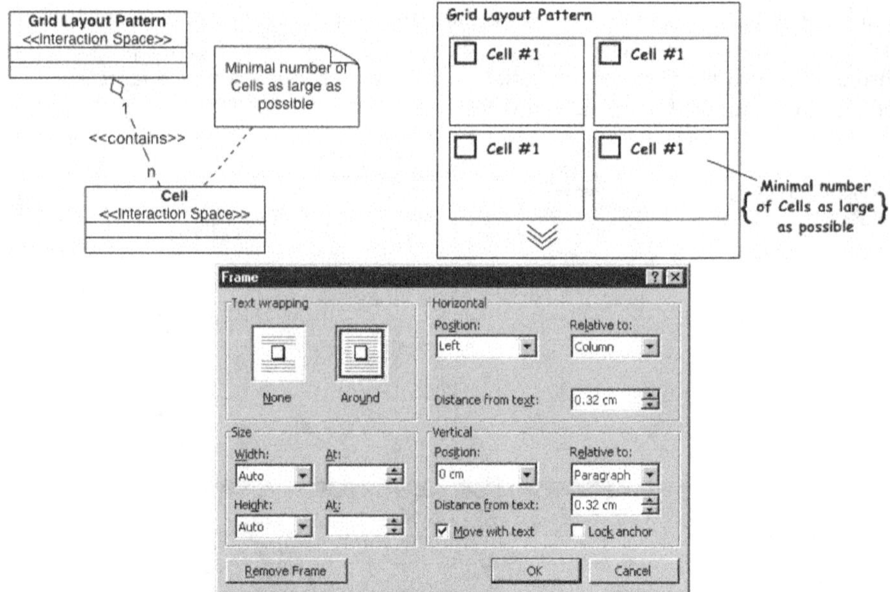

Fig. 10. The grid layout pattern: a Canonical (top left) and Wisdom (top right) representation and a concrete GUI application (bottom).

Figure 11 shows a UI pattern where one can see the advantage of Wisdom over CAP. The "Wizard" pattern solves the problem of a user that wants to achieve a single goal, but needs to make several decisions before the goal can be achieved completely, which may not be know to the user [12]. Figure 11 shows an instantiation of this pattern through a Wisdom model (top left) that has two interaction spaces: Wizard body and Wizard step. Multiple steps are denoted by the 1..* cardinality in the <<contains>> association stereotype. Abstract actions (denoted by the <<action>> operation stereotype) are associated with each interaction space denoting typical actions performed in a Wizard pattern (for instance *next*, *back*, *cancel* and *finish*) [8].

This example illustrates an advantage of Wisdom over CAP regarding the modeling of navigation relationships between the abstract interface elements. In CAP, it is not possible to model a container that allows navigation to other instances of itself (like the Wizard step in this example). Modeling a containment relationship (like a Wizard body that contains successive interaction Wizard steps) is also difficult, unless an informal annotation or comments are used.

Finally, we show yet another abstract design pattern, the Container Navigation pattern [17]. When the user needs to find an item in a collection of containers, this pattern splits a window into three panes: one for viewing a collection of containers, one for viewing a container and one for viewing individual items. Figure 12 shows a Wisdom UML model, the Canonical prototype and a concrete GUI example of this pattern (Netscape's mail/news viewer).

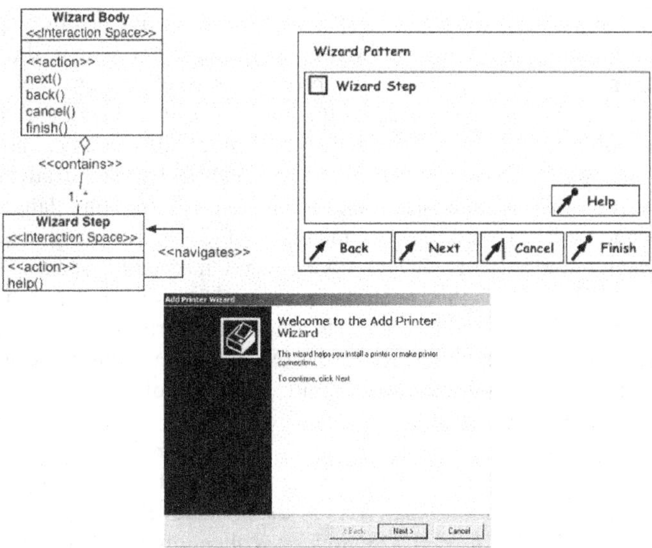

Fig. 11. The "Wizard" pattern. The top left part of the figure shows the Wisdom UML representation, which shows the navigation between "Wizard steps". The top right shows the Canonical representation and at the bottom a particular realization: the Add Printer Wizard in Windows 2000.

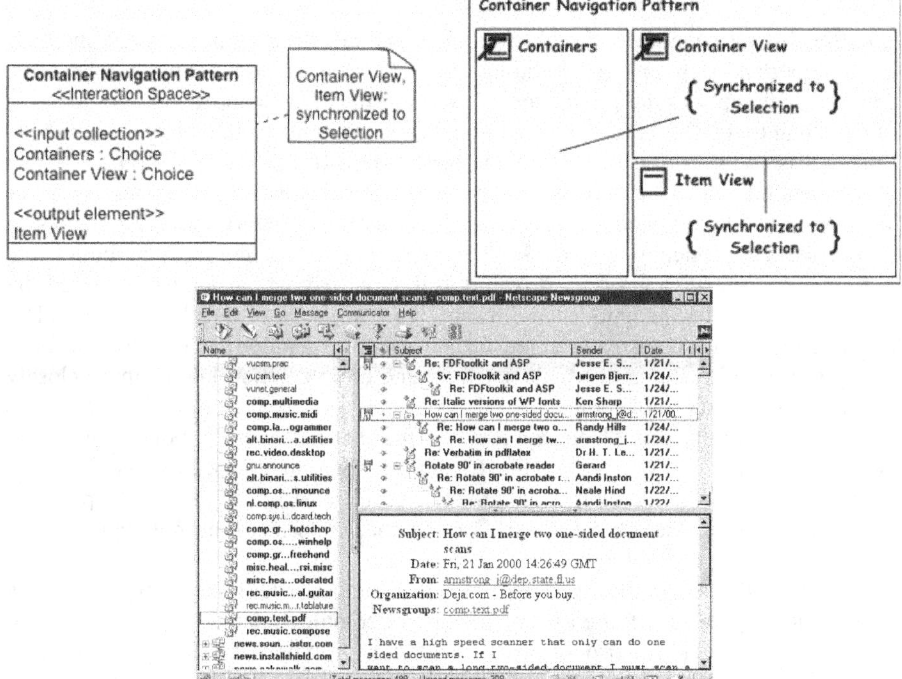

Fig. 12. The container navigation pattern: a Wisdom (top left) model, a Canonical prototype (top right) and a concrete GUI application (bottom), in this case Netscape's news reader.

In order to adequately express this UI pattern, size and relative positioning do matter. They support the user's task because the user first selects a container, then selects the item in the container and finally browses through the selected item. The information that the collection of containers occupies the left part of the screen, and that the item view is at the bottom right can only be conveyed through the Canonical notation.

To conclude, we observe that the Wisdom notation has some advantages over CAP, mainly due to its' compactness and the fact that is based on a language (UML) well understood and adopted by the majority of developers and designers. For expressing navigation patterns that involve several interaction spaces, such as the Wizard pattern [8], the Wisdom notation is more expressive and intuitive. Patterns dealing with spatial layout and size aspects are more clearly represented using CAP. The designer's mind works at several levels of abstraction, thus there is a need for languages and tools supporting those multiple levels of abstraction, while also maintaining a low learning curve.

When trying to express and compare the abstract design patterns presented in this section, we found CanonSketch to be a very useful and practical tool, because it supports two different notations that employ different levels of abstraction and also because it can easily be used to compile a collection of design patterns, thus simplifying the design's comparison and communication.

7 Conclusions and Future Work

To offer software engineers a usable, efficient and effective set of tools and methods is an important step towards building valuable, easy to use software. The same concepts that apply to the production of usable software also apply to the production of modeling tools. Our remit with CanonSketch is to achieve a modeling tool for MB-UID that is as easy to use as a drawing application. In this paper we presented the CanonSketch tool that supports the design of Canonical Abstract Prototypes as well as Wisdom Presentation Models. The CanonSketch project described here attempts to change the way modeling tools are built and envisioned. Existing tools are built using a formalism-centric approach, driven by the underlying semantics required by automatic generation techniques and not by the real needs of developers. Instead of focusing on the mechanisms required for automatic generation techniques, we focus on the successful features of usable software and on interaction idioms more closely related to Office-like applications.

One of the limitations of our approach is the fact that there is not a simple and clearly defined process of using the Canonical notation to specify interfaces for multiple devices. Although CanonSketch can clearly allow multi-platform development (Win, Mac, Palm, Web…) multimodal interfaces are not supported by this tool.

Nevertheless, even in the absence of model semantics, a tool like CanonSketch has significant value in specifying the architecture of complex interactive systems. Being able to generate HTML also means the notation is expressive enough to support automatic generation techniques and that it is possible to generate UI's for any platform based on GUI's and Forms like JavaSwing, Palm, Windows or MacOS. After this initial proof of feasibility, we presented a first specification for a UML extension based on the Wisdom notation that is a step towards a full support of Canonical Prototypes in a language that had a major impact on Software Engineering but still remains far from achieving the industrial maturity augured in the 90's, regarding UI modeling. We also showed how useful the tool can be in expressing UI patterns, and compared Wisdom UML representations of some patterns to the Canonical representations using the proposed correspondence between the two notations. We showed that patterns dealing with spatial or layout aspects could be adequately expressed in a Canonical representation, while Wisdom UML is better at modeling navigation relationships. We are currently finishing the integration of the semantic model of the UML into the tool. This will allow, among other possibilities, to export the abstract UI specification in XMI format, thus promoting artifact exchange between UML-based tools.

As for future work, it would be interesting to identify which notation designers prefer according to the development stage and the type of prototype they are busy with (low, mid or high fidelity). We also expect to refine the Wisdom notation taking advantage of the enhanced extensibility mechanism provided by UML 2.0, and add other features such as knowledge management (capturing hidden information, like the most edited classes or interaction contexts, etc.), support for changing requirements and integration with application development in order to bridge the gap between industry and academy.

References

1. Constantine, L. and Lockwood, L. A. D.: Software for use : a practical guide to the models and methods of usage-centered design, Addison Wesley, Reading, Mass, 1999.
2. Constantine, L.: Canonical Abstract Prototypes for abstract visual and interaction design. In: Jorge, J., Nunes, N. and Falcão e Cunha, J. (eds.): *Proceedings of DSV-IS'2003, 10th International Conference on Design, Specification and Verification of Interactive Systems.* Lecture Notes in Computer Science, Vol. 2844. Springer-Verlag, Berlin Heidelberg New York, 2003.
3. Landay, J. and Myers, B.: Sketching Interfaces: Toward More Human Interface Design. IEEE Computer, pages 56-64, March 2001.
4. Myers, B., Hudson, S. and Pausch, R.: Past, Present and Future of User Interface Software Tools. *ACM Transactions on Computer Human Interaction,* 7(1):3-28, March 2000.
5. Newman, M., Lin, J., Hong, J. I. and Landay, J. A.: DENIM: An Informal Web Site Design Tool Inspired by Observations of Practice. Human-Computer Interaction, 18(3):259-324, 2003.
6. Nunes, N. J.: Wisdom - A UML based architecture for interactive systems. In *Proceedings of the DSV-IS'2000,* Limerick, Ireland. Springer-Verlag.
7. Nunes, N. J.: *Object Modeling for User-Centered Development and User Interface Design: the Wisdom Approach.* PhD Thesis, University of Madeira, Funchal, Portugal, April 2001.
8. Nunes, N. J.: Representing User-Interface Patterns in UML. In *Proceedings of OOIS'03 - 9th European Conference on Object-Oriented Information Systems,* pages 142-163, Geneva, Switzerland, 2003.
9. Nunes, N. J. and Campos, P.: Towards Usable Analysis, Design and Modeling Tools. In *Proceedings of the IUI/CADUI'04 Workshop on Making model-based UI design practical: usable and open methods and tools,* Funchal, Portugal, January 2004.

10. Trætteberg, H. Dialog modelling with interactors and UML Statecharts - A hybrid approach. In *Proceedings of DSV-IS'2003, 10th International Workshop on Design, Specification and Verification of Interactive Systems*. Springer-Verlag, 2003.
11. Trætteberg, H., Molina, P. J. and Nunes, N. J. (eds.): *Proceedings of the IUI/CADUI'04 Workshop on Making model-based user interface design practical: usable and open methods and tools*, Funchal, Portugal, 2004.
12. M. van Welie and Trætteberg, H.: Interaction Patterns in User Interface. In PLoP 2000. 2000.
13. Koch, N. and Wirsing, M.: Software Engineering for Adaptive Hypermedia Systems. In Paul de Bra, editor, *Third Workshop on Adaptive Hypertext and Hypermedia, 8th International Conference on User Modelling*, July 2001.
14. Schwabe, D. and Rossi, G.: *An Object-Oriented Approach to Web-Based Application Design*, Theory and Practice of Object Systems 4 (4), 1998. Wiley & Sons, New York.
15. Garrido, J. L. and Gea, M.: A Coloured Petri Net Formalisation for a UML-Based Notation Applied to Cooperative System Modelling. In *Proceedings of DSV-IS'2003, 10th International Workshop on Design, Specification and Verification of Interactive Systems*. Springer-Verlag, 2003.
16. Calvary, G., Coutaz, J., Thevenin, D., Limbourg, Q., Bouillon, L., Vanderdonckt, J.: A Unifying Reference Framework for Multi-Target User Interfaces, Interacting with Computers, Vol. 15, No. 3, June 2003, pp. 289-308.
17. Nilsson, E. Combining compound conceptual user interface components with modeling patterns: a promising direction for model-based cross-platform user interface development. In *Proceedings of DSV-IS'2003, 10th International Workshop on Design, Specification and Verification of Interactive Systems*. Springer-Verlag, 2002.

Discussion

[Morten Harning] How does your approach cope with the Wizard pattern with respect to enabling/diabling availability of "next" and "previous" buttons, e.g. showing that "previous" should not be part of the first step and "next" should not be part of the last?

> [Pedro Campos] We can not show that kind of information in a formal way, but we can add informal notes as used in the previous examples where a note describes that the preview is synchronized with the selected item.

[Morton Harning] Does that not mean that <<navigates>> is just a high-level note?

> [Pedro Campos] Yes, there is no free lunch!

[Greg Phillips] In Constantine`s method, the development of Canonical Abstract Prototypes is typically done in parallel with context maps. Does your tool support context maps?

> [Pedro Campos] Yes, in the sense that the Wisdom "navigates" relation represents navigation. This is shown in the prototype side by separate slides.

[Greg Phillips] A component then; maybe part of an answer to Morten's question is that the wizard pattern isn't a single interaction context, as you've shown, but rather a collection of related concepts. My other question is that in showing the correspondence between Wisdom and C.A.P. you only shared a single "action" type where Constantine provides a rich set of actions.

[Pedro Campos] Yes, that's on purpose. We find that in UML/Wisdom it only makes sense to show general "actions". Then, when the user moves to the C.A.P. view they specialize the actions into selection, cancellation, or whatever. This is part of the general theme of moving from abstract to concrete.

[Michael Harrison] How are you evaluating the tool?

[Pedro Campos] Currently informal but there is a plan to evaluate in more detail.

[Bonnie John] Are you using your tool to design your tool?

[Pedro Campos] Yes to some extent - I used it to design the tool's website.

Finding Iteration Patterns in Dynamic Web Page Authoring

José A. Macías and Pablo Castells

E.P.S. Universidad Autónoma de Madrid
Ctra. de Colmenar, km. 15
28049 – Madrid – Spain
+ 34 91 497 22{41, 84}
{j.macias, pablo.castells}@uam.es
http://www.ii.uam.es/~{jamacias, castells}

Abstract. Most of the current WWW is made up of dynamic pages. The development of dynamic pages is a difficult and costly endeavour, out-of-reach for most users, experts, and content producers. We have developed a set of techniques to support the edition of dynamic web pages in a WYSIWYG environment. In this paper we focus on specific techniques for inferring changes to page generation procedures from users actions on examples of the pages generated by these procedures. More specifically, we propose techniques for detecting iteration patterns in users' behavior in web page editing tasks involving page structures like lists, tables and other iterative HTML constructs. Such patterns are used in our authoring tool, DESK, where a specialized assistant, DESK-A, detects iteration patterns and generates, using Programming by Example, a programmatic representation of the user's actions. Iteration patterns help obtain a more detailed characterization of users' intent, based on user monitoring techniques, that is put in relation to application knowledge automatically extracted by our system from HTML pages. DESK-A relieves end-users from having to learn programming and specification languages for editing dynamic-generated web pages.

1 Introduction

Since its emergence in the early 90's, the WWW has become not only an information system of unprecedented size, but a universal platform for the deployment of services and applications, to which more and more activity and businesses have been shifting for more than a decade. The user interfaces of web applications are supported by a combination of server-side and client-side technologies, such as CGIs, servlets, JSP/ASP, XML/XSLT, JavaScript, Flash, or Java applets, to name a few. For most applications, client-side GUI facilities are not enough or, as in the case of applets, have unsolved portability problems. Architectural characteristics of web systems typically bring about an inherent need for not only creating web pages that contain interactive interface components, but for generating the pages dynamically on servers or intermediate web nodes. Moreover, using as simple client-side technologies (i.e. client-side requirements) as possible is usually the preferred approach for businesses

R. Bastide, P. Palanque, and J. Roth (Eds.): EHCI-DSVIS 2004, LNCS 3425, pp. 164-178, 2005.

for which reaching the widest audience possible is a critical concern. As a matter of fact, dynamic pages make up the vast majority of the current web ([23] gave an estimate of 80% in year 2000).

With dynamic web pages, user interfaces can be generated whose contents, structure, and layout are made up on the fly depending on application data or state, user input, user characteristics, and any contextual condition that the system is able to represent. However the development of dynamic pages is a quite complex task that requires advanced programming skills. The proliferation of tools and technologies like the ones mentioned above require advanced technical knowledge that domain experts, content producers, graphic designers or even average programmers usually lack. Development environments have been provided for these technologies that help manage projects and provide code browsing and debugging facilities, but one still has to edit and understand the code. As a consequence, web applications are expensive to develop and often have poor quality, which is currently an important hurdle for the development of the web.

The research we present here is an effort to leverage these problems by developing Programming By Example (PBE) techniques [5, 9, 16] to allow regular users, with minimum technical skills, to edit dynamic web pages. Our work can be situated in the End-User Development (EUD) area [19], concerned with enabling a non-expert user to deal with a software artifact in order to modify it easily. Many WYSIWYG tools are available today for the construction of static HTML pages, but is it not clear how procedural constructs, like the ones needed for creating dynamic web pages, can be defined within the WYSIWYG principle. Our proposal consists of letting the user edit the product of the page generation procedures, i.e. one or more examples of the type of dynamic pages that will be generated at runtime, and build a system that is able to generalize the actions of the user on the examples, and modify the page generation procedure accordingly.

We have worked our proposal through the development of a purely WYSIWYG authoring tool, DESK [10, 11, 12], which supports the customization of page generation procedures in an editing environment that looks like an HTML editor from the author point of view. With DESK, users edit dynamic pages produced by an automatic page generation system; DESK keeps track of all user's actions on edited documents, finds a semantic meaning to the editing actions, and carries the changes to the page generation system. A differential aspect of our approach with respect to previous PBE techniques is the explicit use of an application-domain model, based on ontologies, to help characterise the user's actions in relation to system objects and interface components. Semantic relationships between application objects underlying HTML constructs are used by DESK to trace back the inverse path from generated pages up to the generation procedure.

In this paper we focus on the inference mechanisms by which DESK infers the user's intent, by means of data models and characterizations of user actions. A particularly interesting and complex problem to make sense of the user's actions is when the user manipulates complex layout structures made of tables, lists, trees, or combinations thereof. The need for these layout primitives is unavoidable in any but most trivial HTML pages and, when it comes to dynamic pages, they are often used in correspondence to application information structures. A specialized assistant, DESK-A, attempts to find out *iteration patterns* in the user behavior when s/he handles these structures, in order to infer the user's intent and provide with assistance in addressing complex high-level tasks. An iteration pattern involves –and provides a means to correlate– a layout structure, application information structures, and a likely structure in user's actions. How to correctly identify and find the relation between these three parts of the equation is a problem addressed by the work presented here.

This paper is organized as follows: Section 2 describes how our system deals with iteration patterns as well as the metrology used for extracting and classifying different types of patterns. Additionally, an specific case of use will be presented and deployed throughout the paper in order to show how DESK-A works and finds out iteration patterns from user actions. Section 3 describes related work on EUD and PBE systems that mostly exploit user monitoring techniques. Finally, in Section 4, some conclusion will be provided.

2 Iteration Patterns

Iteration patterns can be though of as a generalization of common user actions that can appear more than once, so that they can be used to apply similar behavior on future interaction. Iteration patterns help be able for the system to suggest the user to achieve cumbersome tasks on her behalf.

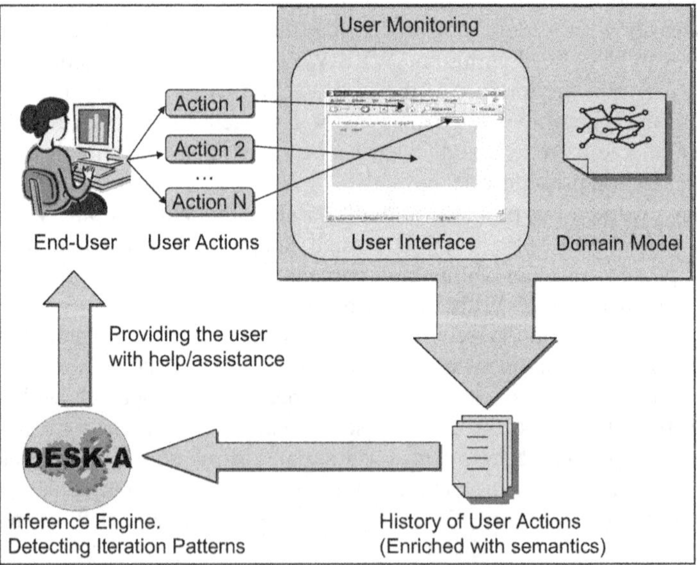

Fig. 1. Our approach. The end-user interacts with the system that extracts information from her actions. A domain model is in turn used to create a detailed history of user actions enriched with semantics from the domain model. Finally DESK processes all this information to detect high-level tasks on the monitoring model, in order to provide the end-user with assistance at the interaction.

In order to address iteration patterns, our approach needs the system to record the user's actions by building a specialized *monitoring model*. The monitoring model can be regarded as a built-in low-level task model, where all the actions the user achieves on the web interface are stored and enriched with add-on implicit information about the interface itself. This way, one of the advantages in using a monitoring model is that a semantic history of user actions can be built in real time. Therefore in our approach the system analyses and manages such history to find iteration patterns.

Fig. 1 shows how the system tracks the user's actions and then uses domain information to generate a semantic history. Such history is in turn added on with references of the interface's components as well as with internal annotations. The system also detects and models presentation structures like tables and selection lists. An inference engine (i.e. DESK-A) processes the history of user actions and detects iteration patterns than can be applied to assist the user. Finally the system provides the end-user with help and performs task as a user's surrogate.

2.1 Detecting Iteration Patterns

Detecting iteration patterns consists of analyzing the history of user actions (i.e. the monitoring model) to find out meaningful information about the user's high level tasks. To carry out this challenge, the system implements a set of heuristics for finding relationships between the user's actions and the interface's presentation elements (i.e. widgets) than are being manipulating by the end-user in the interaction.

The system detects linear relationships between the geometry features of the widgets and, basically, divides interaction patterns into two different categories: *regular pattern* and *non-regular patterns*.

Regular patterns are meant to be iteration sequences on certain widget attributes that define linear relationships between the widget's features (such as table columns and rows, selection list items and so on), whereas non-regular patterns are meant to be iteration sequences without regular relationships (i.e. no linear relationships can be found out) between widget attributes, and they have to be tackled apart.

Regular Patterns

Regular patterns are detected and processed by means of specialized heuristics called *Iteration Patterns Algorithms* (hereafter IP Algorithms). IP Algorithms are a set of algorithms specialized in studying widgets geometry and extracting specific properties about them. Such properties will help find suitable iteration masks for copying elements automatically from one widget into another, holding the same domain model properties and mappings.

Fig. 2 shows two snapshots of DESK environment where a transformation of widgets takes place. This example will be used throughout the paper to put into context the algorithms for dealing with iteration patterns. That figure depicts how the user is attempting to copy elements from a selection list into a table previously created. After a couple of intents, DESK asks the user for confirmation to transform the selection list into a table, and finally the tool accomplishes the transformation. Therefore, it results in removing the list and replacing it by a table which has the same number of items and internal domain model mappings.

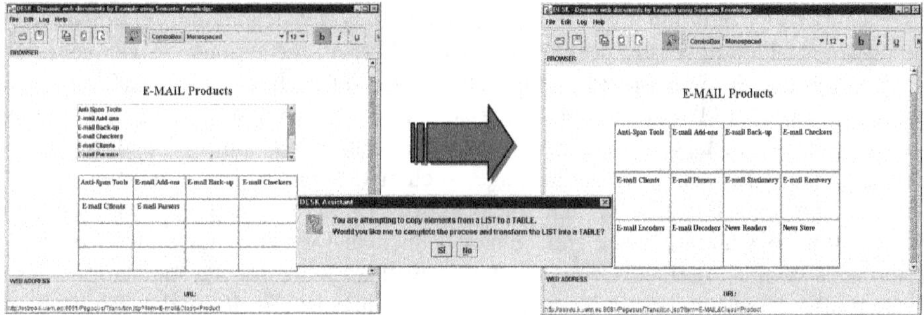

Fig. 2. Two snapshots from DESK. The scenario depicts an automatic transformation from a selection list into a table. The system detects the user's intent while s/he copies elements from a selection list into a table (left window), so the system suggests her (central message box) to convert the whole list into a table automatically (right window after the end-user has accepted the suggestion)

There are several IP Algorithms that can are applied depending on the type of the widget the system deals with. A sample code of one of these algorithms (inspired in Fig. 2) for managing transformation of tables and selection lists is as follows:

```
IP_Algorithm (Widget W1, W2, Set TG) {
  ColumnSequence        = A.getColumnSequence(W2);
  RowSequence           = A.getRowSequence(W2);
  ElemIndexSequence     = A.getElementIndexSequence(W1);
  ColJumpSet            = ColSequence.getColJumpSet();
  RowJumpSet            = RowSequence.getRowJumpSet();
  ColShiftSet           = BuildColShiftSet(ColumnSequence,
                          ColJumpSet,RowJumpSet);
  RowShiftSet           = BuildRowShiftSet(RowSequence,
                          ColJumpSet,RowJumpSet);
  Iterator              = BuildIterator(W2.getBounds(),
                          TG, ColShiftSet, RowShiftSet,
                            ElemIndexSequence);
  ...
  While (Iterator.hasNext()) {
     i = Iterator.getNexti(i);
     j = Iterator.getNextj(j);
     k = Iterator.getNextk(k);
     W2.setElementAt(i,j,W1.getElementAt(k));
  }
}
```

`W1` represents the source widget (i.e. a selection list) and `W2` is the destination one (i.e. a table). `TG` contains information about the widget's properties (i.e. number of fixed columns and rows). `A` is a set that stores information about actions that concern the process of copying elements from one widget into another. This set is very useful in order to obtain common properties about the widget's manipulation sequence (for example, the column insertion sequence of elements into a table), as well as to obtain an abstract model about the widgets are being manipulated by the user throughout the interaction. Properties stored in `A` can be accessed by means of specialized methods:

- `A.getSize(Widget)`
- `A.getElementIndexSequence (Widget)`
- `A.getColumnSequence(Widget)`
- `A.getRowSequence (Widget)`
- `A.getElementAt(Widget,i[,j])`
- `A.getID(Widget)`
- `A.getClassName(Widget)`
- `A.getObjectName(Widget)`
- `A.getExistsRelation(Widget1,Widget2)`

The main goal of above operators is to provide the inference engine with information about the widget (and its properties), such as the size of a given widget, the insertion sequence of elements (index, column and row), the class and the object's names as they appear in the domain model, and the existing relationships between the source widget and the destination one. Therefore it is be able for the engine to build-in an iteration mask (`Iterator`) which provides with a mechanism for copying automatically elements from the source widget to the destination one, and adapting the properties of the destination widgets as the original one appears in the underlying models of the interface.

Fig. 3 depicts an example (based on Fig. 2) as the result of executing the above algorithm for copying elements from the selection list into the table. As shown in this figure, `ColumnSequence` and `RowSequence` sets store the insertion sequence achieved at each user step on the table. On the other hand, `ElemIndexSequence` stores the followed-up sequence of item selection on the selection list. Furthermore, the IP Algorithm calculates the column (`ColJumpSet`) and the row (`RowJumpSet`) jump's sets by processing `A`. The algorithm also detects whether the insertion is carrying out either on rows or columns by comparing both jump sets. This way, if `RowJumpSet` is greater (in size) than `ColJumpSet`, the insertion is achieved by iterating the rows, if not the insertion is achieved by iterating the columns. Otherwise, if both sets have the same size, special considerations has to be taken since there is a straight linear relationship between row and column on the insertion sequence. Next an increment mask is calculated for columns (`ColShiftSet`) and rows (`RowShiftSet`) by using an operator, namely $\Delta_{Average}$ defined in equation (1).

$$\Delta_{Average}(x_1,x_2,x_3,\ldots,x_n)=\begin{cases}\dfrac{(x_2-x_1)+(x_3-x_2)+\ldots+(x_n-x_{n-1})}{n-1}, & n>1\\ 0, & n\leq 1\end{cases}=\begin{cases}\dfrac{x_n-x_1}{n-1}\\ 0,\end{cases} \quad (1)$$

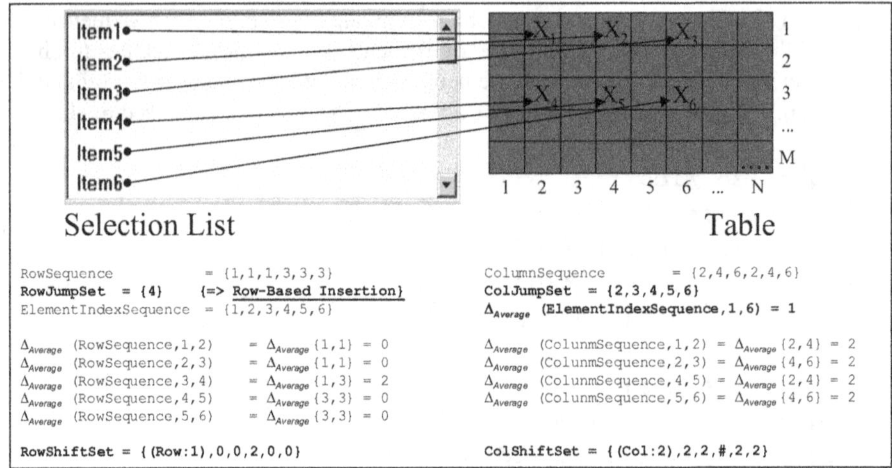

Fig. 3. Execution of an IP Algorithm for a table and a selection list. Before transforming the selection list intro a table, the system generates specific sets that store information concerning the rows and columns involved as well as the jump sequence's sets. Finally, a couple of iteration masks are calculated for both column and row, those intended to create an automatic iteration process for carrying out the transformation among widgets

Equation (1) represents an operator that calculates the average sequence of jumps. The operator is applied to obtain a couple of masks (`ColShiftSet` and `RowShiftSet` sets) which include the increments used in the loop for column and row jumps. Initial positions are also considered at loop starting (`Col:2` and `Row:1`), resulting in this case as follows: increasing 2 columns for the first time, jumping then two more rows (# in `RowShifSet` and 2 in `ColShiftSet`), next jumping 2 columns, and finally repeating the sequence all over again.

All these sets are finally used to create the iteration index to iterate though the widgets and to easily complete the iteration sequence previously calculated.

Fig. 4 shows examples of similar transformation processes, where different cases of tables with different types of insertion sequences are depicted. Those result in different values for each set depending on widget geometry. As shown, the algorithm can face correctly a great deal of cases where cut-in columns and rows are detected as a part of the iteration mask, using `&` symbol for row-based jumps and # one for colum-based jumps. Fig. 4 also shows a case where the iteration pattern is defined as an identity function (i.e. the same number of row jumps than column ones), finely detected by DESK-A as well.

Non-regular Patterns

Unfortunately it is not always able to create an iteration pattern that best fits a sequence started by the user. Actually, when the system is not able to find out linear relationships in iterative sequences on widget geometry then had-hoc or specific-purpose iteration patterns have to be considered.

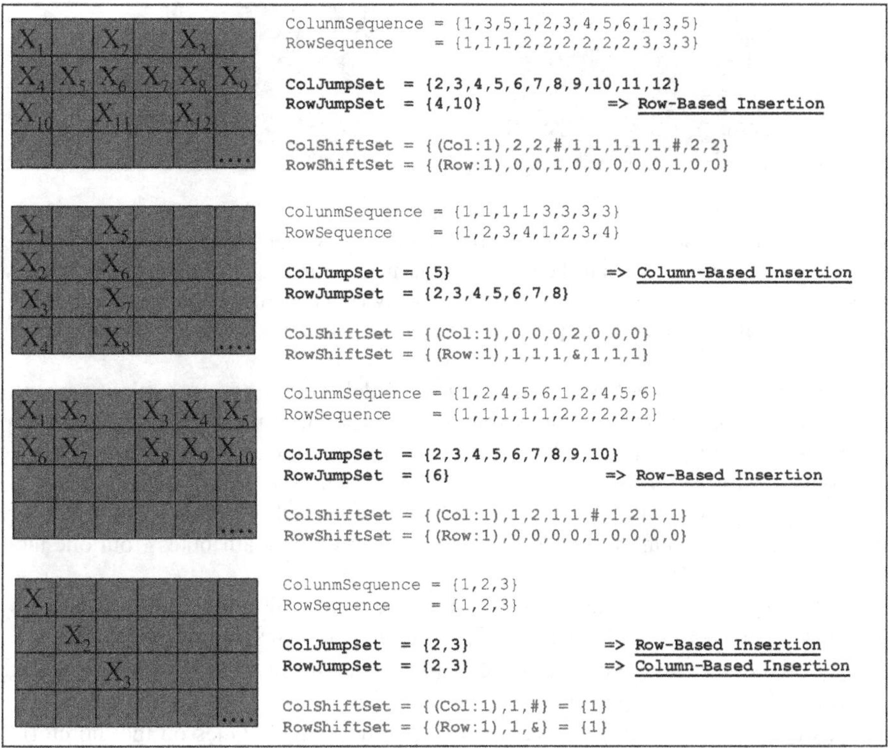

ColunmSequence = {1,3,5,1,2,3,4,5,6,1,3,5}
RowSequence = {1,1,1,2,2,2,2,2,2,3,3,3}
ColJumpSet = {2,3,4,5,6,7,8,9,10,11,12}
RowJumpSet = {4,10} => Row-Based Insertion
ColShiftSet = {(Col:1),2,2,#,1,1,1,1,1,#,2,2}
RowShiftSet = {(Row:1),0,0,1,0,0,0,0,0,1,0,0}
ColunmSequence = {1,1,1,1,3,3,3,3}
RowSequence = {1,2,3,4,1,2,3,4}
ColJumpSet = {5} => Column-Based Insertion
RowJumpSet = {2,3,4,5,6,7,8}
ColShiftSet = {(Col:1),0,0,0,2,0,0,0}
RowShiftSet = {(Row:1),1,1,1,&,1,1,1}
ColunmSequence = {1,2,4,5,6,1,2,4,5,6}
RowSequence = {1,1,1,1,1,2,2,2,2,2}
ColJumpSet = {2,3,4,5,6,7,8,9,10}
RowJumpSet = {6} => Row-Based Insertion
ColShiftSet = {(Col:1),1,2,1,1,#,1,2,1,1}
RowShiftSet = {(Row:1),0,0,0,0,1,0,0,0,0}
ColunmSequence = {1,2,3}
RowSequence = {1,2,3}
ColJumpSet = {2,3} => Row-Based Insertion
RowJumpSet = {2,3} => Column-Based Insertion
ColShiftSet = {(Col:1),1,#} = {1}
RowShiftSet = {(Row:1),1,&} = {1}

Fig. 4. Some examples of iteration patterns. These examples are generated using IP Algorithms, as it depicted in Fig. 3. So that Figure shows the iteration patterns for copying elements to the table as well as the sets generated for achieving the final transformation among the selection list and the table.

The system faces the challenge of non-regular patterns by allowing the user to create a pool of pre-defined iteration patterns. Therefore s/he can customize the design and tell the system how to resolve the iteration in order to accomplish the transformation successfully. The pool of non-regular patterns can be included in the engine configuration, specifying the behavior for how the assistant (i.e. DESK-A) has to deal with each type of widget.

Fig. 5 shows an example of two iteration patterns that can be defined in the non-regular part of the DESK-A configuration file (see Section 2.2). This example reflects non-regular patterns where linear relationships are hard to find out, since there is not a straight relationship among the widget's attributes (i.e. column and row insertion sequences), so that IP Algorithms cannot be applied directly.

2.2 DESK-A

DESK-A (DESK-Agent) is a specialized inference assistant for finding out high level tasks (i.e. changes) related to the user's actions. DESK-A is based on the idea of the *Information Agent* [1] focused on *wrappers* paradigm [8, 16]. By contrast, in our

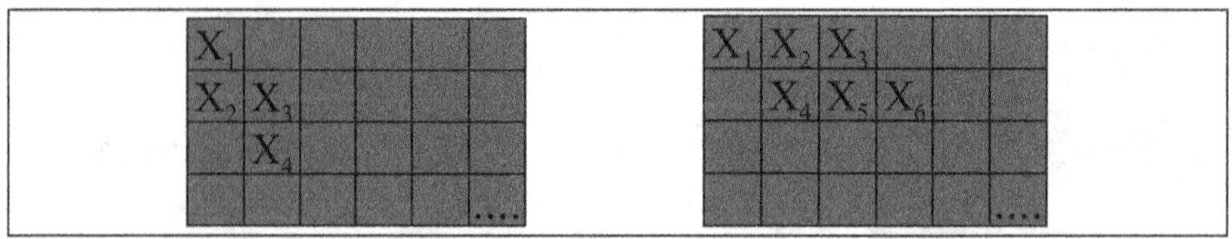

Fig. 5. Two examples of non-regular iteration patterns detected while copying elements from a selection list into a table. Here the relationship between rows and columns is not easy to find out since non linear sequences make IP Algorithms unlikely to deal with those cases. Anyway, those kinds of patterns are not usual to find in mostly common practice, so that a customized pool of predefined patterns is enough in order for the system to tackle non-regular patterns.

approach the agent searches the monitoring model, which has an explicit semantic representation of the user's actions, rather than searching the HTML code directly. Therefore it is able for DESK-A to activate more complex heuristics [13] in order to find out transformation of presentation widgets, such as transforming a combo box into a table or transforming a table into a selection list. DESK-A can also infer more complex intents such as sorting a selection list and copying attributes from one table cell into another [13].

DESK-Agent detects and manages both regular and non-regular patterns by monitoring the user input. Basically, DESK-Agent comprises three main states:

- pre-activation: where the agent checks up the monitoring model for detecting high level tasks. This depends on the configuration set.
- activation: where the agent searches for specific widget values on the monitoring model once is pre-activated. Here, DESK-A analyzes in-depth the history of user actions and makes up different models for each widget involved in the interaction.
- execution: where the agent executes the transformations taking into account the values found at the activation step.

DESK-Agent searches the monitoring model for primitives that better fit the requirements defined at its configuration. The agent can be set-up by defining a configuration file at client-side. That configuration reflects the agent's behavior:

```
<TransformationHint>
  ...
  <widget type="List" changeTo="Table">
    <Condition action="Creation"
               widget="Table"  />
    <Condition action="PasteFragment"
               from="Table" to="List" />
    <Non_Regular_Pattern_Pool>
      <Pattern  col_sequence="1,1,2,2"
                row_sequence="1,2,2,3"
                elem_sequence="1,2,3,4">
        <Resolve i="from 1 to List.getSize(); i++1"
                 next_col_sequence="col[i],col[i]"
                next_row_sequence="row[i],row[i+1]"
                next_elm_sequence="elm[i]" />
      </Pattern>
```

```
        <Pattern col_sequence="1,2,3,2,3,4"
                 row_sequence="1,1,1,2,2,2"
                   elm_sequence="1,2,3,4,5,6">
          <Resolve
                  next_col_sequence="3,4,5,4,5,6,..."
                  next_row_sequence="3,3,3,4,4,4,..."
                  next_elm_sequence="7,8,9,10,11,..." />
        </Pattern>
       ...
     </Non_Regular_Pattern_Pool>
   </widget>
   ...
</TransformationHint>
```

The above code is a fragment of the DESK-A configuration, where `<TransformationHint>` elements are pre-activation directives the agent will check for arranging transformations between both widgets (`<widget>`), in that case a selection list (`type="List"`) and a table (`changeTo="Table"`). Furthermore, DESK-A checks the creation status (`action="Creation"`) of the table, as reflected in `<Condition>` elements, and analyses the copy sequence of elements (`action="PasteFragment"`) from the table into the selection list, making up dependences between the two widgets.

When all these prerequisites are satisfied, the agent executes transformation heuristics for detecting iteration patterns (see IP Algorithms at regular patterns Section) by selecting meaningful information from the monitoring model. Finally, the process results in transforming the widgets and keeping the same structure that holds the source widget by firstly asking the user for confirmation.

DESK-Agent also deals with non-regular patterns by allowing the user to create a pool of pre-defined iteration pattern (`<Pattern>` element inside `<Non_Regular_Pattern_Pool>`, at agent configuration code). This way DESK-A completes and resolves (`<Resolve>` element) the iteration sequence in order to accomplish the transformation successfully. Non-regular patterns are represented by using an indexed-construction, defining a for-like loop to iterate trough columns, rows and selection list items (`<Resolve i="from 1 to List.getSize(); i++1"`). Furthermore DESK-A allows a numerical representation of iteration sets (`<Resolve next_col_sequence = "3,4,5,4,5,6,..."`) for column, row and item indexes. This kind of specification becomes more natural and easy-to-understand for non-expert users.

3 Related Work

One of the main limitations of early PBD systems that monitor actions [5] is that they are too literal. Some of these systems replay a sequence of actions at the keystroke and mouse-click level, without taking any account of context or attempting any kind of generalization. By contrast, later works are based on recording the user's actions at a more abstract level and making explicit attempts to generalize them. However, they have been demonstrated only in special, non-standard, often tailor-made software environments (see [9]).

Our approach aims at providing PBD techniques for domain-independent web-based interfaces, focused on dealing with high level tasks where different domains have been proposed in order to evaluate the level of trust of the tool. DESK-A is comparable to *Predictive Interfaces* [6] and *Learning Information Agents* [1] approaches, where the system observes the user while she interacts with the environment. These approaches assist the user by predicting and suggesting some commands to carry out tasks automatically.

Eager [5] is one of the most famous PBD attempts to bring together PBD and Predictive Interfaces. Eager is a Macintosh-based assistant which detects consecutive occurrences of a repetitive task, thus Eager proposes the user to complete the loop automatically. The loop is inferred by observing the user's actions. Eager needs the user to enter two consecutive tasks. This becomes a limitation since occurrences do not have to appear consecutive.

Familiar [22] overcomes some Eager's limitations but it also does not address the previous mentioned problem. Other works, like APE and SMARTEdit (both described in [9]) attempt to solve this difficulty by using *machine-learning* mechanisms in order to learn efficiently and rapidly when to make a suggestion and which sequence of actions to suggest to the user.

DESK-A analyses the monitoring model, regardless of the number and the sequence of user actions, and finds meaningful high-level information about the user's intents. DESK-A does not need to learn about the user's behavior and operates in-real time, without the necessity of *machine-learning* algorithms. As well as Familiar, DESK-A is domain-independent, but in DESK-A the domain information is used in order to enhance the inference process.

Some Lieberman's earlier work like Mondrian (described in [5]) was based on AppleScript to monitor the user and control applications, but it does not exploit its domain independence and high-level application knowledge. Similarly, in TELS [17] the system takes into account the user's actions, inferring iteration patters for addressing loops and conditions. TELS enables the end-user to meet the inference process, by asking for her opinion. In DESK-A, the system avoids the user from having to make assumptions of the inference mechanism, the PBE-based inference process is being as transparent as possible.

The use of data models was already present in PBE systems like Peridot [16] and HandsOn [3]. In a very simple form, Peridot enables the user to create a list of sample data to construct lists of user interface widgets. The data model in Peridot consists of lists of primitive data types. In HandsOn, the interface designer can manipulate explicit examples of application data at design-time to build custom dynamic displays that depend on application data at run-time. Our view in this regard is that it is interesting to lift these restrictions and support richer information structures. To this end, DESK-A uses ontology-based domain information for user intent characterization.

Concerning EUD related work, there has been interesting approaches during last two years. WebRevenge [20] makes the reverse path of a web page. WebRevenge generates a CCTT (ConCurTaskTrees, see [21]) based task model by analyzing the interaction as well as the web interface elements: tags and links. WebRevenge works together with TERESA [15], an abstract authoring tool for modeling applications from CCTT based task models. TERESA makes the straight engineering and WebRevenge the reserve one, in order to carry through an approach that allows for migration to different platforms. By contrast DESK is intended to assist the user while s/he interacts with the system rather than using it as a multi-modal generation system. DESK also takes into account user interaction and, in addition, an ontological data model as well as information extracted from the interaction. DESK uses a low-level task model rather than a CCTT based task model, where interface objects, domain information and user actions are embedded to enrich the semantic of the monitoring model.

Another interesting work also closely tied to EUD paradigm is LAPIS [14]. LAPIS is a web scraper that allows for rendering high conceptual level information by means of a pattern library using a simple web browser. LAPIS parsers the HTML and transforms tag and link level elements into conceptual representations that help end-user understand web information easily. As well as LAPIS, DESK parsers HTML and characterizes information from the page by using a data model. By contrast DESK enables the user to authoring the web page, so the user's actions are taking into account and analyzed as an important step of the process.

Personal Wizards [2] is also a great contribution to EUD as a PBE-based system. This approach tracks user actions and records interaction from an expert. The system generates a wizard in order to guide a non-expert user throughout the application. Personal Wizards are intended to help users configure Windows based applications easily.

4 Conclusions

We have presented an approach for inferring the user's intents in a WYSIWYG web-based authoring environment. Our approach is based on PBE strategies such as monitoring the user during the interaction. In addition our system features data models for enriching the user's actions with semantics. We have also reported on a model-based representation of user actions for detecting and processing iteration patterns.

Our authoring environment, DESK, features a specialized assistant, namely DESK-Agent detects the user's high level tasks throughout the interaction and executes heuristics to achieve transformations on presentation widgets for automating iterative tasks. DESK-A checks up on pre-activation condition and searches the monitoring model for obtaining meaningful information about widget characteristics. Therefore IP Algorithms exploit widget models to build an iterator for moving elements from one widget to another. This automates a great deal of transformation processes and provides the user with assistance to complete iterative tasks on her behalf. Furthermore, DESK-A can deal with non-regular patterns by defining a pool. This information is part of the agent configuration and can be set-up by the user. This allows to build more sophisticated patterns for automatically DESK-A to address.

The main idea of DESK-A is to provide with an assistant to help end-user carry out different, somehow hard to achieve, kind of actions in editing web pages. However, this mechanism can be extended for increasing productivity in user interaction by means of providing non-expert user with continuous assistance in her daily solving activities with computer applications as well as generating programming code without the necessity of learning programming or specification languages. This challenge can be carried through by exploiting the monitoring and semantic detection strategies. The main goal is to assist the user in a great deal of different scenarios, such as classical interface builders and toolkits, authoring tools for generating model-based user interfaces and, in general terms, programming environments. To this purpose, the abstract mechanism of pattern detection can be extended and new IP Algorithms can be created, in order for other kind of user intents to be detected by the system regardless of the domain and the interface used.

In general terms, DESK works according to EUD paradigm. The authoring tool helps end-user modify a web page generated by a previous application. This way the system generates a programmatic model of user actions as a high-level knowledge representation in order to finally modify the generation procedure of the web page. The end-user is continuously assisted while s/he interacts with the authoring tool. DESK ensures the *Gentle Slope of Complexity* [8] where expressiveness and complexity of use are balanced by the means of the WYSIWYG environment; low abstract representation imply low rate of expressiveness but also easy of use.

As DESK-A is based on an ontology-driven domain model [4], it works regardless of the domain applied. Several scenarios such as educational, travel and e-shopping have been used in order to evaluate the efficiency of the system. In [13] there is an experience carried out with end-users in order to evaluate the usability of DESK as an authoring tool. Although the comments of the results are out of the scope of this paper, the main outcomes of the experience pointed out the high satisfaction rate of the user with respect to the tool. This is due to the similarity that the users perceive with respect to ordinary web editing and browsing tools, but by contrasts with some add-on mechanisms that allow for editing dynamic web pages and assisting the user in accomplishing cumbersome tasks.

Acknowledgements

The work reported in this paper is being supported by the Spanish Ministry of Science and Technology (MCyT), project number TIC2002-1948.

References

1. Bauer, M., Dengler, D. and Paul, G. Instructible Information Agents for Web Mining. In Proceedings of the International Conference on Intelligent User Interfaces (January 9-12, pp. 21-28, New Orleans, USA, 2000).
2. Bergman, L., Lau, T., Castelli, V. and Oblinger, D.: Personal Wizards: collaborative end-user programming. *In Proceedings of the End User Development Workshop at CHI'2003 Conference* (Ft. Lauderdale, Florida, USA. April 5-10).
3. Castells, P. and Szekely, P. Presentation Models by Example. En: Duke, D.J., Puerta A. (eds.). Design, Specification and Verification of Interactive Systems. Springer-Verlag, pp. 100-116, 1999.

4. Castells, P. and Macías, J.A.: Context-Sensitive User Interface Support for Ontology-Based Web Applications. Poster Session of the 1st. International Semantic Web Conference (ISWC'02), Sardinia, Italia; June 9-12th, 2002.
5. Cypher A. (ed.).: Watch What I Do: Programming by Demonstration. The MIT Press, 1993.
6. Darragh, J. J. and Written, I.H.: Adaptive predictive text generation and the reactive keyboard. Interacting with Computers 3, no. 1:27-50, 1991.
7. Hurst, Matthew Francis: The Interpretation of Tables in Texts. *PhD. Thesis*. University of Edinburgh, 2000.
8. Klann, M.: End-User Development Roadmap. *In Proceedings of the End User Development Workshop at CHI'2003 Conference* (Ft. Lauderdale, Florida, USA. April 5-10).
9. Lieberman, H. (ed): Your Wish is my Command. Programming By Example. Morgan Kaufmann Publishers. Academic Press, USA. 2001.
10. Macías, J.A. and Castells, P. Dynamic Web Page Authoring by Example Using Ontology-Based Domain Knowledge. In *Proceedings of the International Conference on Intelligent User Interfaces (IUI'03)* (Miami, Florida, USA. January 12-15).
11. Macias, J.A. and Castells, P. Using Domain Models for Data Characterization in PBE. *In Proceedings of the End User Development Workshop at CHI'2003 Conference* (Ft. Lauderdale, Florida, USA. April 5-10).
12. Macías, J.A.; Castells, P.: DESK-H: building meaningful histories in an editor of dynamic web pages. In Proceedings of the 11th Internacional Conference on Human-Computer Interaction (HCII). Creta, Grece, June 23-27, 2003.
13. Macías, J.A.: Authoring Dynamic Web Pages by Ontologies and Programming by Demonstration Techniques. PhD. Thesis. Departamento de Ingeniería Informática. Escuela Politécnica Superior. Universidad Autónoma de Madrid. September, 2003. http://www.ii.uam.es/~jamacias/tesis/thesis.html.
14. Miller, Rober C.: End User Programming for Web Users. *In Proceedings of the End User Development Workshop at CHI'2003 Conference* (Ft. Lauderdale, Florida, USA. April 5-10).
15. Mori, G., Paternò, F. and Santoro, C.: CTTE: Support for Developing and Analysing Task Models for Interactive System Design. IEEE Transactions in Sotware Engineering. IEEE Press. Vol. 28, No.8, pp. 797-813, August 2002.
16. Myers, B. A. Creating User Interfaces by Demonstration. Academic Press, San Diego, 1988.
17. Mo, D.H.; Witten, I.H.: Learning text editing tasks from examples: A Procedural approach. Behaviour & Information Technology, Vol. 11, No. 1, pp. 32-45, 1992.
18. Muslea, I. Extraction Patterns for Information Extraction Tasks: A Survey. In *Proceedings of AAAI Workshop on Machine Learning for Information Extraction* (Orlando, Florida, July, 1999).
19. Network of Excellence on End-User Development. http://giove.cnuce.cnr.it/EUD-NET.
20. Paganelli, L., Paternò, F.: Automatic Reconstruction of the Underlying Interaction Design of Web Applications. Proceedings of the SEKE Conference, pp. 439-445. ACM Press, Ischia, 2002.
21. Paternò, F.: Model-Based Design and Evaluation of Interactive Applications. Springer Verlag, 2001.
22. Paynter, G.W.; Witten, I.H.: Automating Iteration with Programming by Demonstration: Learning the User's Task. Proccedings of the IJCAIWorkshop on Learning about Users, 16th International Joint Conference on Artificial Intelligence. Stockholm, Sweden, 1999.
23. Sahuguet, A.; Azavant, F.: building Intelligent Web Applications Using Lightweight Wrappers. Data and Knowledge Engineering, 2000.
24. Shneiderman, B.: Leonardo's Laptop. The MIT Press, 2003.

Discussion

[Morton Harning] Your motivation for this work is a wish for simplifying the design of dynamic web-pages ... How does what you have shown help here? Are you not only improving editing of static pages? Hence, this is more about helping avoid monotonous task in any text editor ... not programming by example?

[José Macías] Definitely this is a help in order for the end-user to modify dynamic web pages. You are modifying the final version of a dynamically generated page; this will be interpreted into change of the presentation model. The system infers the mappings and makes the changes automatically. So that Programming by Example takes place.

[Morton Harning] When I present information in a table it is most often highly structured data. Hence, the structure will be already in the domain model. Do you use that kind of information in the algorithm or is it only a question of changing simple layout rules?

[José Macías] We do use knowledge of sequences in the domain model. In other words, the model-based information of the interface is represented in such a model. Our system deals with this semantic information and infers high-level changes the user wants to accomplish by means of just analyzing the low-level actions s/he carries out.

[Michael Harrison]: Why distinguish between regular and non-regular patterns?

[José Macías] These are simply linear algorithms, that can be applied when the insert/copy/paste sequence is linear. Non-linear patterns have to be defined in a separated pool as they cannot be detected by linear algorithms (see some examples of linear and non-linear cases in the paper).

[Bonnie E. John] Have you done an analysis of the types of dynamic web pages that are in existence and the frequencies of those types? What percentage of the space does your tool cover?

[José Macías] We believe that we can handle 100% of what dynamic web pages in existence today as long as theses pages can be represented using our model-based approach. We have all the expressibility necessary and all the algorithms in place to handle what we have seen in existence on the web today.

[Michael Harrison] 95% uptake of use - what does this mean in practice?

[José Macías] This is the hit rate of DESK in inferring high-level changes to Dynamic Web Pages from low-level actions the user achieves. Since it is hard to follow the reverse path (from the final generated web page to the underlying models), some ambiguity can appear and has to be dealt (see paper in detail).

Very-High-Fidelity Prototyping for Both Presentation and Dialogue Parts of Multimodal Interactive Systems

David Navarre, Pierre Dragicevic, Philippe Palanque, Rémi Bastide & Amélie Schyn

LIIHS-IRIT, Université Paul Sabatier, F-31062 Toulouse Cedex, France
{dragice, navarre, palanque, bastide, schyn}@irit.fr
http://liihs.irit.fr/{navarre, dragice, palanque, bastide, schyn}

Abstract. This paper presents a tool suite (made up of two previously unrelated approaches) for the engineering of multimodal Post-WIMP Interactive Systems. The first element of this integration is ICoM (a data-flow model dedicated to low-level input modelling) and its environment ICoN which allows for editing and simulating ICoM models. The other element is ICOs (a formal description technique mainly dedicated to dialogue modelling) and its environment PetShop which allows for editing, simulating and verifying ICOs models. This paper shows how these two approaches have been integrated and how they support multimodal interactive systems engineering. We show on a classical rubber banding case study how these tools can be used for prototyping interactive systems. We also present in details how the changes in the interaction techniques impact the models at various levels of the software architecture.

Keywords. Interactive Systems Engineering, Multimodal interaction, Prototyping, CASE tools, Formal methods, formal description techniques; Post-WIMP.

Introduction

According to the recurring desire of increasing the bandwidth between the interactive system and the users more sophisticated interaction techniques called Post-WIMP have been proposed. However, the current contribution from the research community to the construction of such interactive systems remains at the level of working prototypes showing the feasibility and making empirical evaluation possible.

Recent contributions in the field of model-based approaches have been explicitly addressing this issue of coping with new interaction techniques. The aim of the work presented in this paper is to describe an approach (that is able to go beyond prototyping post-WIMP interaction techniques) fully integrated within interactive systems development. To this end we have integrated work done on low-level input management [7] with work on formal description techniques of dialogue models [3, 16].

Several notations have already proposed for dealing with post WIMP interaction techniques and for different kinds of applications. Data-flow-based notations such as Wizz'Ed [10] or ICon [7] have been proposed for dealing with low-level flow of

R. Bastide, P. Palanque, and J. Roth (Eds.): EHCI-DSVIS 2004, LNCS 3425, pp. 179-199, 2005.

events produced directly by input devices. This notion of flow has also been addressed with other notations where classical event and status based behaviours have been enhanced with continuous modelling such continuous Petri nets as in Marigold [18] or Hynets [17]. Higher-level models of this kind of interaction techniques have also been addressed using state-based notations as with basic Petri nets in [13] or with high-level Petri nets [16]. Early work in the field of multimodal interaction techniques has also addressed the aspects of fusion of modalities and a comparison of these work can be found in [6].

The paper is structured as follows. Section 2 presents the Input Configuration approach that is dedicated to low-level input handling in post-WIMP interactive systems. Section 3 recalls the Interactive Cooperative Objects formalism and its environment PetShop. In these sections, the two model-based approaches are exemplified on the same simple case study of the rubber banding interaction technique. Section 4 details a generic framework for the integration of these two approaches. Section 5 introduces a line drawing application exploiting the rubber banding interaction technique previously presented. The aim of this small case study is to show that the model-based approaches that we propose can deal completely with non standard interface components and innovative interaction techniques. This section presents also how to modify that case study to allow for multimodal (two handed) interaction. For space reasons, only such multimodal interaction technique is presented here while several others (including voice and gesture) have been dealt with in a similar way and presented at the conference.

Input-Configurations Modelling and Prototyping

ICON (Input Configurator) is a tool for designing input-adaptable interactive applications, i.e., applications that can be controlled with a wide variety of alternative input devices and techniques. ICON provides an interactive editor for the ICOM (Input Configuration Model) graphical notation. In this section, we give a brief overview of the ICOM notation and the ICON visual prototyping environment. More details on the notation and its associated tools can be found in [7, 8, 9].

Overview of the ICOM Notation

The ICOM (Input Configuration Model) notation describes low-level input handling using interconnected modules, with reactive data-flow semantics. In this section, we briefly describe the main features and concepts behind ICOM.

Input Configurations

Devices and slots. ICOM's main building blocks are *devices*, which are a broad generalization of input devices: ICOM devices can produce output values, but can also receive input values. Fig. 1 shows on the left the graphical representation of a device. A device has typed channels called *input slots* and *output slots*, each type having a distinct graphical representation (e.g., circle for Booleans, triangle for integers). Slots can be hierarchically grouped to form structured types, as shown on Fig. 1.

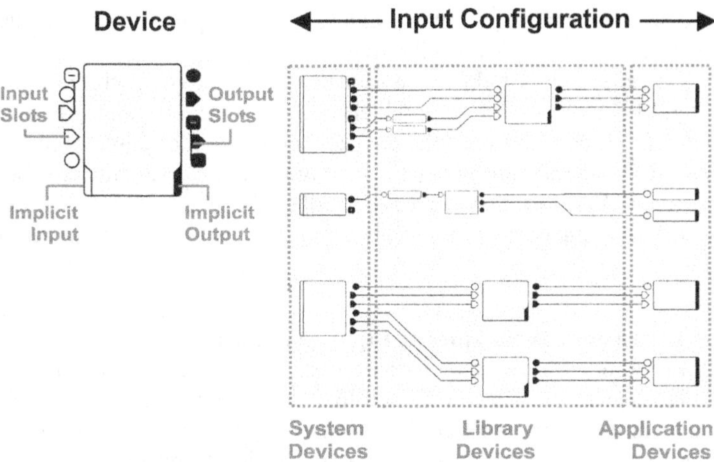

Fig. 1. Elements of the ICoM notation.

Implicit I/O. Whereas the basic behaviour of an ICoM device is processing input values into output values, alternative behaviour is shown on the device by the presence of "notches" (see Fig. 1). Non-deterministic devices are described as having *implicit input*, i.e.,additional source of information not fully described by its set of input slots. Example of such devices include devices which are producing data on their own (physical input devices), or asynchronous devices which are temporally non-deterministic. Similarly, devices having *implicit output* produce alternative effects in addition to simply putting values on the output slots. Examples are devices that manipulate application objects, or devices producing graphical or sound feedback.

Connections. An input slot of a device can be linked to one or several compatible output slots of other devices by *connections*, which are represented by wires. ICON's execution model forbids multiple connections on the same input slot, as well as connections that generate cyclic dependencies.

Types of devices. There are three main categories of devices: *System devices* describe system resources such as input peripherals; *Library devices* are system-independent utility devices such as processing devices and adapters; *Application devices* are devices that control a specific application.

Input configurations. An *input configuration* is defined by a set of system and application devices, as well as a set of library devices and connections which map the system devices to the application devices.

ICON is modular, and subparts of an input configuration can be encapsulated into compound devices. For example, an input device and a feedback device can be connected then grouped to form a compound device having both external input and external output.

ICoM's Execution Model

Whereas the contract of a device is to update its output slots every time it is asked to, ICoM's execution model describes which devices must be triggered and when, and how values are propagated to other devices. The propagation mechanism used, described in [9], is very simple and effective.

ICoM's execution model follows the semantics of reactive synchronous languages such as Esterel [5] or Lustre [12], in which information propagation is conceptually instantaneous. In *reactive* systems, the environment (e.g., the source of input signals) is the master of the interaction, as opposed to conversational systems in which clients wait to be served. As a result, the way we handle input is closer from device drivers, which are reactive, than from event-driven mechanisms, which are intrinsically conversational.

Describing Interaction Techniques as Input Configurations

From ICoM's point of view, interaction techniques are transformation flows with feedback. Fig. 2 gives an example of scrolling through a document, and shows the feedback loop through implicit I/O. The Mouse device receives implicit input from the user, the Cursor device produces immediate feedback towards this user, and the Scrollbar tells the application to update its document view.

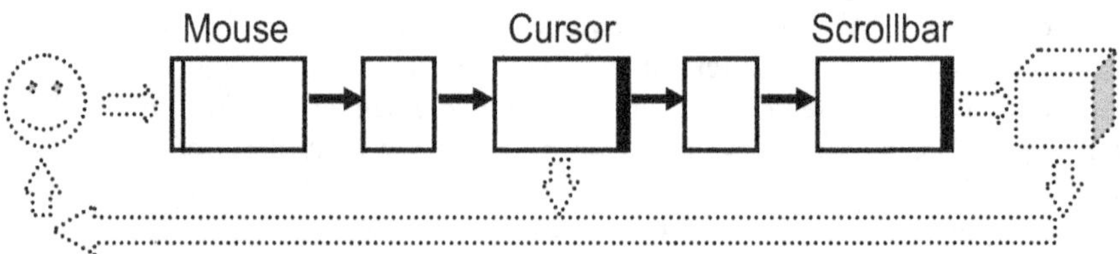

Fig. 2. Feedback flow while scrolling through a document

The ICon Environment

The ICon (Input Configurator) Input Toolkit contains an extensible set of system devices and library devices for building input configurations. It provides a reactive machine for executing them, as well as a graphical editor for rapid prototyping. ICon is written in Java, and uses native libraries for managing input devices. In this section, we briefly describe the main features of ICon.

ICon Devices

System devices. ICon's system devices provide a low-level view of standard and alternative input devices. Under Microsoft Windows operating systems, ICon currently supports multiple mice, graphical tablets, gaming devices and 3D isometric controllers, speech and gesture recognition, and MIDI controllers. System output devices are also available, such as Midi devices for playing music on soundcards, or speech synthesis devices.

Library devices. The ICon toolkit has a set of built-in utility devices including mathematical and boolean operators, signal processing devices, type and domain adapters, and devices for conditional control and dispatch. It also provides a set of graphical feedback devices such as cursors and semi-transparent components, which support overlay animation on top of Swing frames.

Toolkit devices. ICON provides a set of "Swing devices" for controlling existing Java applications that have no knowledge of ICON. One device allows generic control of any Swing widget by sending them mouse and keyboard events, whereas a set of widget-specific devices allow moving scrollbars programmatically or sending strings and caret commands to text components. Event dispatching strategies such as picking and focus are also encapsulated into individual devices.

Application devices. Developers can enhance controllability of their application by implementing devices that are specific to their application. Writing an application device is quite straightforward, and mainly requires declaring a set of input slots and implementing an "update" method which is automatically called each time an input slot has received a signal [9].

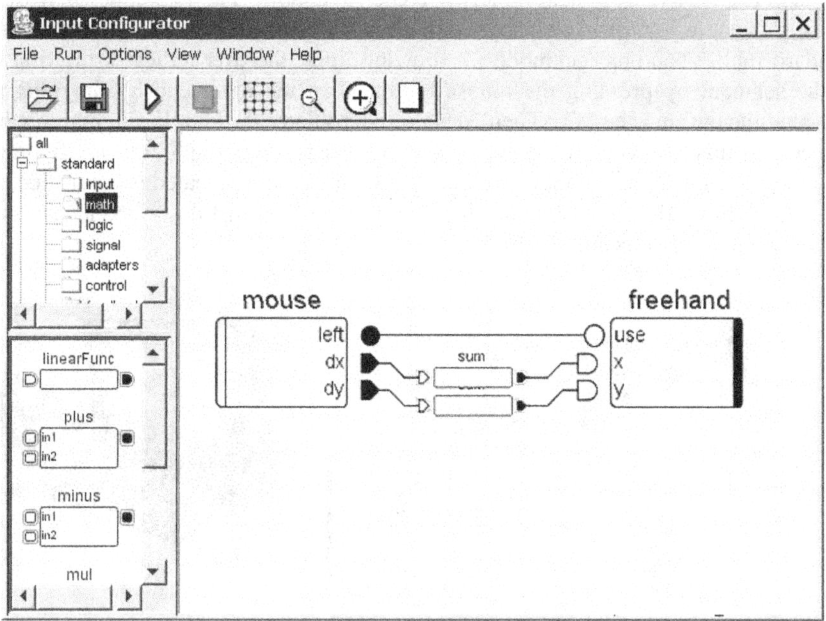

Fig. 3. A screenshot of the Input Editor.

The Input Editor

ICON configurations can be built or modified by direct manipulation through a graphical editor. An early prototype of this editor has been described in [7]. In this contribution, the authors showed how the behavior of a standard mouse/keyboard configuration could be easily changed using the editor and its dedicated interaction techniques. In [9], we also give a subset of interaction techniques that can be described with our graphical notation and directly built using ICON.

The Fig. 3 shows a screenshot of the Input Editor window. Library devices and available system and application devices are listed on the left pane, and organized in folders just like a file system. Clicking on a folder (top left pane) displays the devices it contains (bottom left pane). Those devices are dragged on the editing pane to be used. The minimalist input configuration shown on the editing pane of the Figure 7 describes how a freehand tool from a drawing application called ICONDraw [7] is controlled using the mouse. The "sum" devices convert relative (delta) positional values sent by the low-level mouse into absolute values.

The toolbar on the top of the window contains two buttons for executing and stopping the input configuration. Execution is fast and does not need compilation, thus allowing easy testing and refinement of input configurations.

One Simple Example: One-Handed and Two-Handed Rubber Banding

ICON's graphical editor allows the application designer to quickly build and test input configurations that make use of alternative sets of physical input devices, or modify existing configurations to adapt to enriched or impoverished input. Fig. 4 illustrates how a conventional technique can be changed into a Post-WIMP technique when a new input device (a graphical tablet) becomes available. The left upper part of the Fig. 4 shows the part of ICONDraw's default input configuration which describes the standard rubber-banding technique for drawing lines: the user indicates the first end of the segment by pressing the mouse button, then the other end by dragging and releasing the button. The "firstThen" device encapsulates the simple automaton which implements this behavior. As shown on the lower part of the Fig. 4, this configuration has then been simplified so that each end of a segment being created is controlled by a separate pointing device. By doing this, the designer has just described a very basic bimanual interaction technique (Figure 8 on the right).

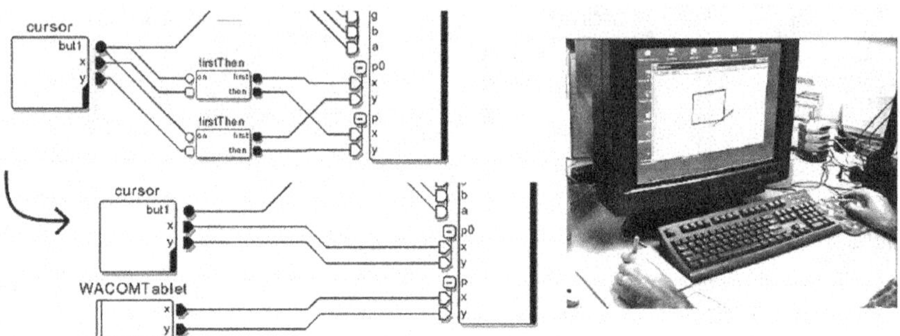

Fig. 4. A conventional line drawing technique, modified to make use of a second pointing device.

Dialogue Modelling and Prototyping

This section recalls the main features of the ICO formalism, which we use to model the case study. We encourage the interested reader should look at [2, 3] for a complete presentation of the formal description technique.

Overview of the ICO Formalism

The Interactive Cooperative Objects (ICOs) formalism is a formal description technique dedicated to the specification of interactive systems [3]. It uses concepts borrowed from the object-oriented approach to describe the structural or static aspects of systems, and uses high-level Petri nets [11] to describe their dynamic or behavioural aspects.

Petri Nets is a graphical formalism made up of four components: the state variables (called place, depicted as ellipses), states changing operators (called transitions, depicted as rectangles), arcs, and tokens. Tokens are hold by places; arcs link transitions to places and places to transitions. The current state of a system is fully defined by the marking of the net (i.e., both the distribution and the value of the tokens in the places). For a state change to occur a transition must be fired. A transition is fireable if and only if each of its input places holds at least one token. When the transition is fired, one token is removed from each input place and a token is deposited in each output place.

ICOs are dedicated to the modelling and the implementation of event-driven interfaces, using several communicating objects to model the system, where both behaviour of objects and communication protocol between objects are described by Petri nets. The formalism made up with both the description technique for the communicating objects and the communication protocol is called the Cooperative Objects formalism (CO and its extension to CORBA COCE [4]).

In the ICO formalism, an object is an entity featuring four components:

Cooperative Object (CO): a cooperative object models the behaviour of an ICO. It states how the object reacts to external stimuli according to its inner state. This behaviour, called the Object Control Structure (ObCS) is described by means of high-level Petri net. A CO offers two kinds of services to its environment. The first one, described with CORBA-IDL [15], concerns the *services* (in the programming language terminology) offered to other objects in the environment. The second one, called *user services*, provides a description of the elementary actions offered to a user, but for which availability depends on the internal state of the cooperative object (this state is represented by the distribution and the value of the tokens (called marking) in the places of the ObCS).

Presentation part: the Presentation of an object states its external appearance. This Presentation is a structured set of widgets organized in a set of windows. Each widget may be a way to interact with the interactive system (user → system interaction) and/or a way to display information from this interactive system (system → user interaction).

Activation function: the user → system interaction (inputs) only takes place through widgets. Each user action on a widget may trigger one of the ICO's user services. The relation between user services and widgets is fully stated by theactivation function that associates to each couple (widget, user action) the user service to be triggered.

Rendering function: the system → user interaction (outputs) aims at presenting to the user the state changes that occurs in the system. The rendering function maintains the consistency between the internal state of the system and its external appearance by reflecting system states changes.

ICO are used to provide a formal description of the dynamic behaviour of an interactive application. An ICO specification fully describes the potential interactions that users may have with the application. The specification encompasses both the "input" aspects of the interaction (i.e., how user actions impact on the inner state of the application, and which actions are enabled at any given time) and its "output" aspects (i.e., when and how the application displays information relevant to the user). Time-out transitions are specials transitions that do not belong to the categories above. They are associated with a timer that automatically triggers the transition when a dedicated amount of time has elapsed. When included in a system model such transition is considered as a system transition. They can also be included in a user model representing spontaneous user's activity.

An ICO specification is fully executable, which gives the possibility to prototype and test an application before it is fully implemented [14]. The specification can also be validated using analysis and proof tools developed within the Petri nets community and extended in order to take into account the specificities of the Petri net dialect used in the ICO formal description technique.

ICO Models for a Rubber Banding Interaction Technique

The *rubber banding* is a very classical interaction technique used in most graphical tools. It allows a user to draw a line (or a shape) based on the "drag and drop" interaction technique, where, while dragging, a temporary line is drawn, called ghost. We present here, through this classical example, the four parts of an ICO specification: the behaviour, the presentation part and the link between them stated by the activation and the rendering function.

1. **Behaviour (ObCS).** The behaviour of the rubber banding application is represented by its ObCS shown in Fig. 5. Initially, the application is in an idle state. When the mouse button is pressed, it starts the drawing of a ghost that is updated while moving the mouse pointer (dragging). When the mouse button is released, the definitive line is drawn, and the application returns in its idle state.

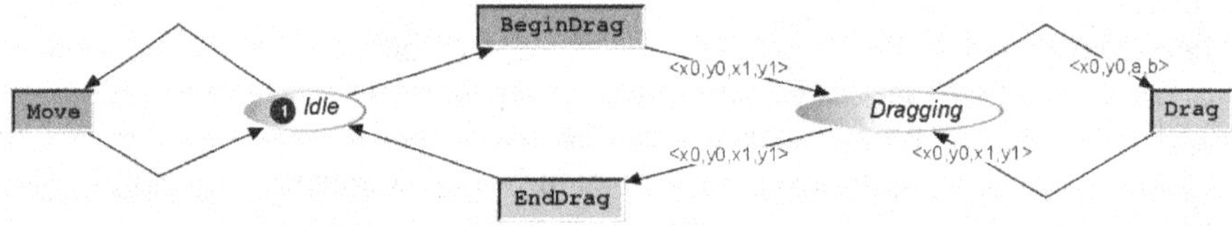

Fig. 5. Behaviour of the rubber banding interaction technique

2. **Presentation part.** The presentation part described the external presentation part of the drawing line application. We describe hereafter (Fig. 6) a set of basic rendering methods that characterise the DrawablePanel. This set of methods is used to produce rendering by the rendering function (see the point 3).
3. **Rendering Function.** The rendering function describes how state changes impact the presentation part of the application. As state changes are linked to token movements, rendering items may be linked to either place or transition. Figure 7 describes the rendering function for the rubber banding application. The first line, for instance, shows that when a token enters the place Dragging, the corresponding rendering is to draw a ghost between the coordinates brought by the token.

```
Class DrawableJPanel
    Rendering methods {
        drawGhost(int x0, int y0, int x1, int y1) {
            //Draw a dashed line between point (x0, y0)
            //and point (x1, y1).
        }
        eraseGhost(int x0, int y0, int x1, int y1) {
            //Erase the dashed line drawn between
            // point (x0, y0) and point (x1, y1).
        }
        drawLine(int x0, int y0, int x1, int y1) {
            //Draw a line between point (x0, y0)
            //and point (x1, y1).
        }
    }
}
```

Fig. 6. Overview of the widget implied in the rubber banding application.

ObCS element		Rendering method
Name	Feature	
Place Dragging	Token <x0, y0, x1, y1> Entered	drawGhost(x0, y0, x1, y1)
	Token <x0, y0, x1, y1> Removed	eraseGhost(x0, y0, x1, y1)
Transition EndDrag	Fired with <x0, y0, x1, y1>	drawLine(x0, y0, x1, y1)

Fig. 7. Rendering function of the rubber banding application.

4. **Activation Function.** The activation function (shown by Fig. 8) relates the events produced by a widget to the transitions of the ObCS. Thus if the transition is fireable and the event is produced (by a corresponding user action on the widget) then the transition is fired (and its action is executed).

Widget	Event	Service
Panel	Move	Move
Panel	MouseDown <x, y>	BeginDrag
Panel	MouseDrag <x, y>	Drag
Panel	MouseReleased <x, y>	EndDrag

Fig. 8. Activation function of the rubber banding application

Overview of PetShop Environment

In this section we present precisely how PetShop environment supports the design process of interactive systems. Some screen shots are included in order to show what is currently available.

ObCS Editor

Our approach is supported by a tool call PetShop which includes a distributed implementation of high-level Petri net interpreter written in Java. All the components of the ObCS can be directly built using PetShop. PetShop also automatically generates an Object Petri net from the IDL description [11]. The edition of the Object Petri net is done graphically using a palette of tools. The left part of the toolbar is used for generic functions such as load, save, cut copy and paste. The right hand side of the toolbar drives the execution of the specification.

Edition of the Presentation

Currently, PetShop is linked to JBuilder environment for the creation of the presentation part of the ICOs. Thus creation of widgets is done by means of JBuilder interface builder. However, we have not yet created a visual tool for editing the rendering and the activation function that still have to be typed-in in Java.

Execution Environment

A well-known advantage of Petri nets is their executability. This is highly beneficial to our approach, since as soon as a behavioural specification is provided in term of ObCS, this specification can be executed to provide additional insights on the possible evolutions of the system.

Fig. 20 shows the execution of the specification of the line drawing application in Petshop. The ICO specification is embedded at run time according to the interpreted execution of the ICO. At run time user can both look at the specification and the running application. They are in two different windows overlapping as in Fig. 20. The window Line Drawing Application corresponds to the execution of the window with the ICO model underneath. In this window we can see the set of transition that are currently fireable (represented in dark grey and the other ones in light grey). This is automatically calculated from the current marking of the Object Petri net. Each time the user acts in the Line Drawing Application windows, the event is passed on to the interpreter. If the corresponding transition is fireable then the interpreter fires it, performs its action (if any), changes the marking of the input and output places and performs the rendering associated (if any).

Coupling Input Configurations and Dialogue

This section presents how the two approaches have been effectively integrated. We show first how this coupling takes place at the model level (ICoM and ICOs) and then at the environment level (ICON and PetShop).

Models Coupling: ICoM and ICOs

Whereas ICO's activation function lists the couples *Widget* × *Event* and the user services they trigger, ICoM describes how each event is produced. For space reasons we only present here a simplified integration between ICO and ICoM models.

In an ICO specification, the *Widget x Event* represents the higher level event triggered by a widget translating the classical input events it receives. A widget thus behaves as a transducer that converts lower level events into higher level events, called widget events.

A simple way to couple ICoM and ICO is to extend standard widgets in order to represent them as output devices in ICoM model. Thus the ICoM model describes the events needed by the widgets. These ICoM output devices are then connected to ICoM Input devices through links and via other bricks. The resulting ICoM configuration represents how user actions on the input devices feed the widget with the correct events.

For instance, the previous section describes the rubber-banding application, specified with ICO. The activation function (see Figure 7) shows the events produced by our DrawableJPanel widget (MouseMove, MouseDragged …), but does not make explicit the input device(s) used. Even if, in this example, the use of a simple mouse seems natural, we want to be able to deal with other input devices (such as graphical tablet, joystick, motion capture …). The DrawableJPanel needs three information ((x, y) coordinates and a dragging trigger) to produce the relevant higher level events. The corresponding ICoM device is presented by Fig. 9.

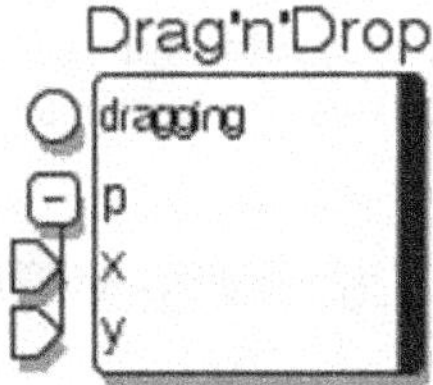

Fig. 9. ICoM output device representing inputs needed by the DrawableJPanel

Fig. 10 represents an ICoM configuration providing modelling the transformation of low level events on the mouse to transformed events in the output device.

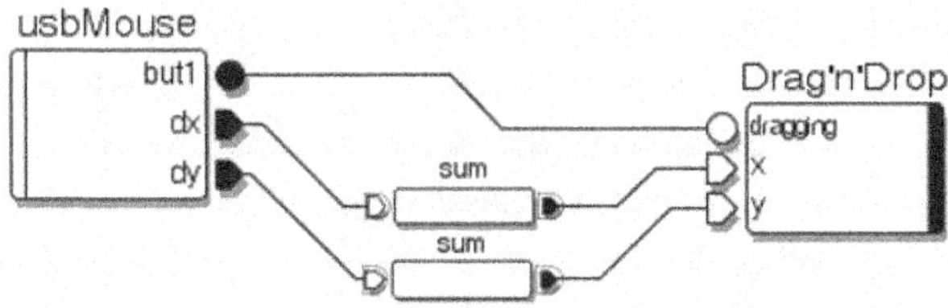

Fig. 10. ICoM model for DrawableJPanel

Systems Coupling: ICON and PetShop

In order to implement the link presented at the level of models in previous section, we need to make an application running within Petshop visible to ICON. This means that the set of widgets composing the presentation part, the activation and rendering functions and the dialogue part must register output devices as described above.

Initially, these applications are launched from the PetShop environment. While running, an input configuration can be deactivated using the Alt-C keystroke. This is essential as ICON allows redefining input handling at a very low-level, which can possibly hang all the system. For similar reasons, input configurations can be edited while paused but not while running. In contrast, the edition and simulation of the ICO model within Petshop is fully dynamic.

Case Study of a Two Handed Line Drawing Application

In order to present the tool suite that we have developed for the engineering and very-high prototyping of multimodal interactive systems, this section presents the use of this tool suite on a case study. We first present the case study offering standard interaction technique and show how this case study can be easily extended in order to be manipulated by means of various input devices and thus using multimodal interaction techniques.

The Line Drawing Application

This application (shown on Fig. 11) allows a user to handle a line, defined by two points. Modification of the line uses a rubber banding-like interaction technique for each point.

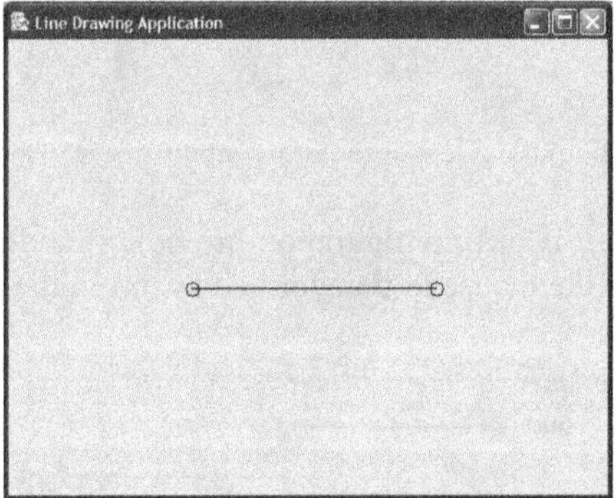

Fig. 11. The line drawing application

Application Specification

Behaviour (ObCS). The ICO model in Fig. 12 describes the behaviour of the rubber banding interaction technique. Initially, the application is in an idle state. When the mouse button is pressed on the left point (resp. right point), it starts the drawing of a ghost (a dashed line). While moving the mouse pointer (dragging) the dashed-line is updated. When the mouse button is released, the definitive line is drawn, and the application returns in its idle state. With respect to the rubber banding interaction technique presented in Fig. 5 the model is duplicated here as two rubber banding are available at a time (one for each end of the line).

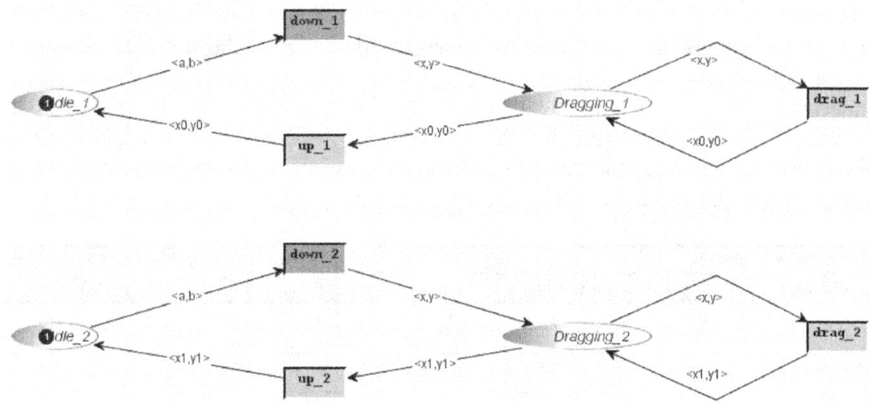

Fig. 12. Behaviour of the line drawing application.

Presentation part. The presentation part describes the external presentation part of the application. We describe hereafter (Fig. 13) a set of basic rendering methods that characterise the LineDrawingJPanel. This set of methods is used to produce rendering by the rendering function described in next section.

```
Class LineDrawingJPanel
    Rendering methods {
        drawGhost1(int x, int y) {
            //Draw a dashed line between point (x, y)
            //and the second point of the line.
        }
        eraseGhost1(int x, int y) {
            //erase the dashed line between point (x, y)
            //and the second point of the line.
        }
        drawLine1(int x, int y) {
            //Draw a line between point (x, y)
            //and the second point of the line.
        }
        drawGhost2(int x, int y) {
            //Draw a dashed line between point (x, y)
            //and the first point of the line.
        }
        eraseGhost2(int x, int y) {
            //erase the dashed line between point (x, y)
            //and the first point of the line.
        }
        drawLine2(int x, int y) {
            //Draw a line between point (x, y)
            //and the first point of the line.
        }
    }
}
```

Fig. 13. Overview of the widgets employed in the line drawing application.

Rendering Function. The rendering function describes how state changes in the Petri net describing the behaviour of the application impact the presentation part of the application. As state changes are linked to token moving from places to places, rendering items may be linked to either place or transition. Fig. 14 describes the rendering function for the drawing line application. The first line, for instance, shows that when a token enters the place Dragging, the corresponding rendering is to draw a ghost between the coordinates brought by the token.

ObCS element		Rendering method
Name	Feature	
Place Dragging_1	Token <x, y> Entered	drawGhost1(x, y)
	Token <x, y> Removed	eraseGhost1(x, y)
Transition Up_1	Fired with <x, y>	drawLine1(x, y)
Place Dragging_2	Token <x, y> Entered	drawGhost2(x, y)
	Token <x, y> Removed	eraseGhost2(x, y)
Transition Up_2	Fired with <x, y>	drawLine2(x, y)

Fig. 14. Rendering function of the line drawing application.

Activation Function. The activation function (shown by Fig. 15) relates the events produced by a widget to the transitions of the ObCS. Thus if the transition is fireable and the event is produced (by a corresponding user action on the widget) then the transition is fired (and its action is executed). The events produced are linked to one of the two points of the line. MouseDown1, MouseDrag1 and MouseReleased1 represents classical drag'n'drop events that occurs related to the first point. The three others events are linked to the second point.

Widget	Event	Service
LineDrawingJPanel	MouseDown1 <x, y>	Down_1
LineDrawingJPanel	MouseDrag1 <x, y>	Drag_1
LineDrawingJPanel	MouseReleased1 <x, y>	Up_1
LineDrawingJPanel	MouseDown2 <x, y>	Down_2
LineDrawingJPanel	MouseDrag2 <x, y>	Drag_2
LineDrawingJPanel	MouseReleased2 <x, y>	Up_2

Fig. 15. Activation function of the line drawing application

Interface Between the ICO Specification and ICoM

As stated in section 4, the widget part is extended into an ICoM output device. Fig. 16 shows the ICoM model that represents the inputs needed by the line drawing application.

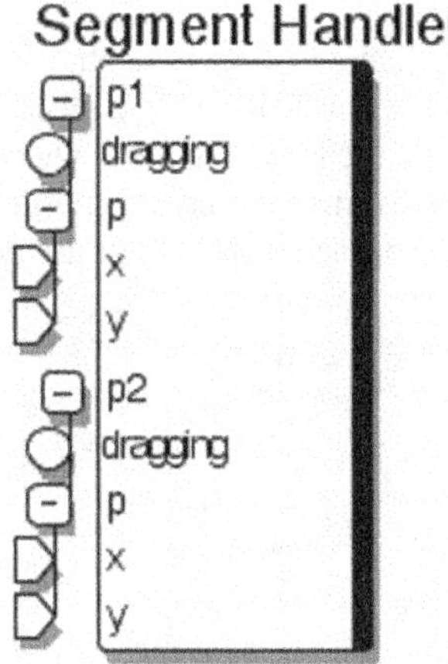

Fig. 16. ICoM device representing inputs needed by the LineDrawingJPanel of the ICO specification

Input Configuration of the Conventional Line Drawing Application

The input configuration of the line drawing application describes how it is manipulated with a mouse. Fig. 17 shows this configuration: Mouse moves are transformed to coordinates (sum components) then used to animate a mouse cursor on top of the application frame (cursor component). In addition to the coordinates, the cursor propagates also the state of the left mouse button to the rest of the configuration. *Shortcuts*, represented by grey vertical lines, are used to display the *same* cursor device at different places of the configuration (this means that the same cursor can manipulate both ends of the line).

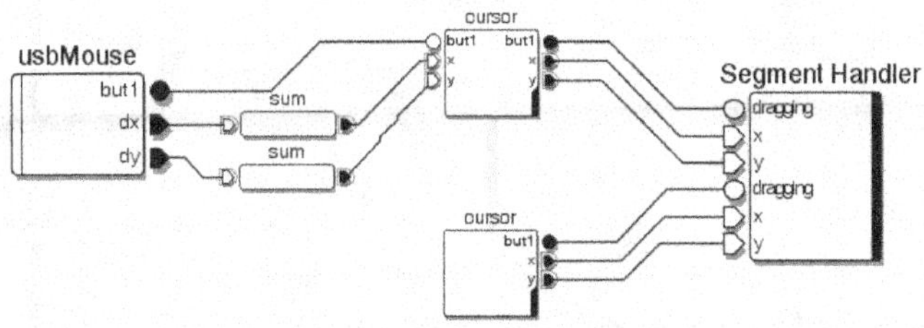

Fig. 17. Input configuration of the conventional (i.e. monomodal) line drawing application

The two copies of the cursor device thus provide the LineDrawingJPanel (of the ICO specification) with the correct parameters (i.e. x and y coordinates and the dragging state).

Two Handed Line Drawing Application

This section presents a modification of the case study in order to allow for two handed interaction on the line drawing application. The point is not here to discuss about the usability of such interaction technique but to show the impact of changing the behaviour of the application from monomodal interaction technique to a multimodal one and how the integrated approach proposed in this paper can deal with it.

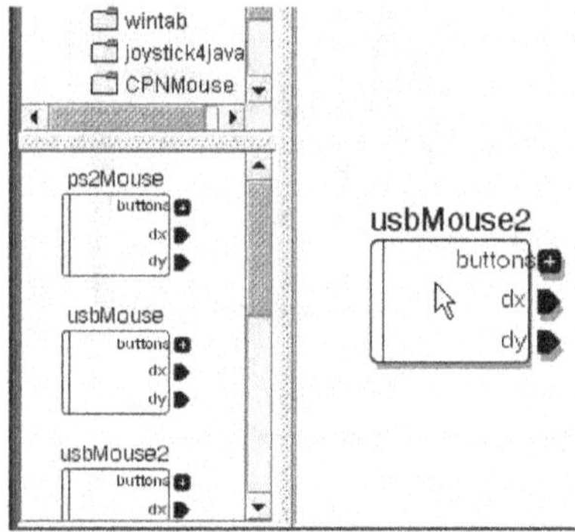

Fig. 18. A screenshot of ICON's editor with all available (connected) mice showing on the left pane (2 USB mice and a PS2 Mouse)

We describe a scenario in which the default input configuration is modified to handle two mice. In this scenario, each mouse moves a dedicated pointer but both pointers are used in the same way to control each extremity of the line. This allows both symmetric bimanual interaction and two-user collaborative interaction with the line.

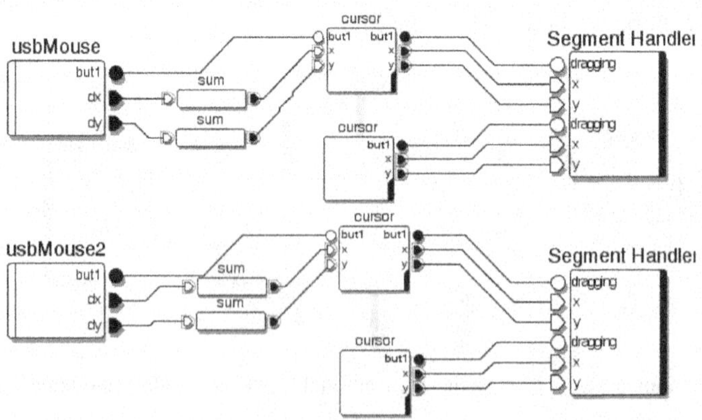

Fig. 19. Input configuration of the two-handed line drawing application

When launched, ICON's editor also shows on the left pane all currently connected mice as *individual devices*, including PS/2, serial and USB mice (see Fig. 18). The user just has to identify the mice he wants to use (USB mice are sorted according to the HUB port they are connected to) and drag them in the edition pane. Note that other pointing devices such as graphical tablets can also be used, or even emulated with devices such as keyboard or voice recognition.

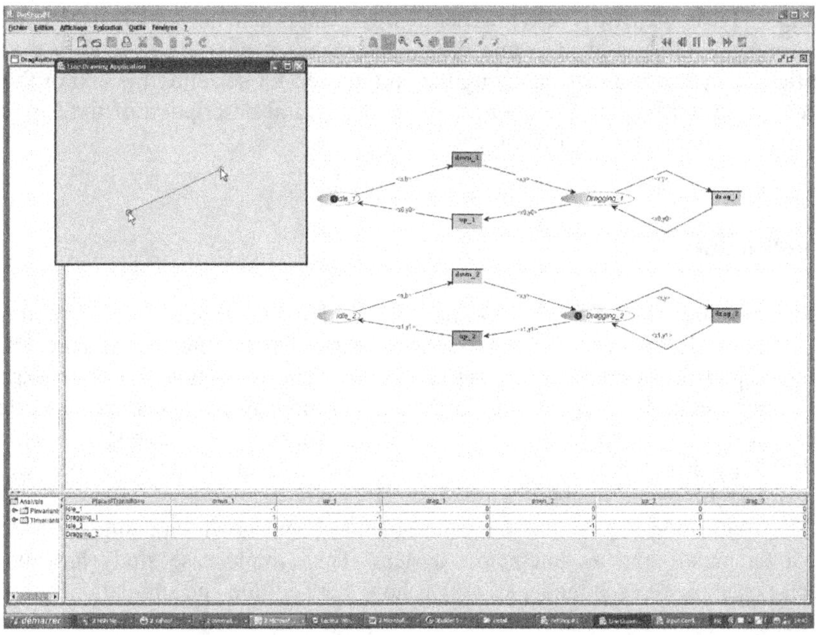

Fig. 20. Executing the two-handed drawing line application within PetShop

As both pointers share the same behaviour, the configuration described in Fig. 17 only has to be duplicated and mouse devices replaced. Lastly, two instances of this compound device are instantiated and connected to two separate USB mice, as shown on Fig. 19.

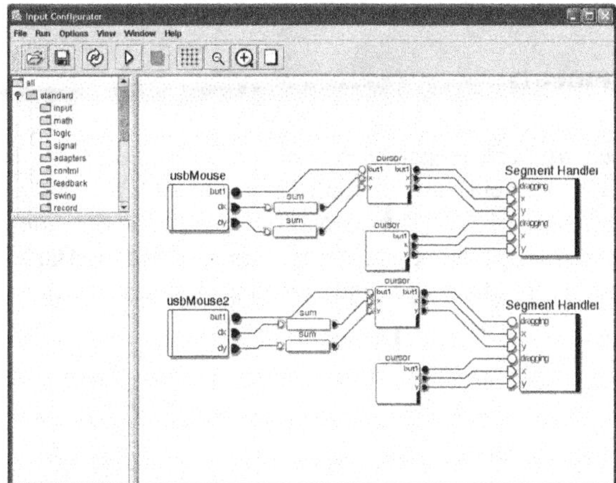

Fig. 21. Executing the two-handed drawing line application within ICON

When the configuration is edited, it may be executed. Fig. 20 shows the execution of the two-handed line drawing application within PetShop. Due to the locality principle of Petri nets (the firing of a transition only has impact on its input and output places) there is no change to make from the model in Fig. 12 to make the application usable in a multimodal way.

Fig. 21 shows ICoN environment. It is important to understand that both environments are use at the same time. This makes it possible to modify the input configuration (for instance changing the button used for selecting the end of the line) by changing the lines in the configuration. Behavioral description of the application can also be changed using PetShop.

Conclusion

This paper has presented a tool suite dedicated to the engineering of multimodal interactive systems. The ICOs formalism deals with the functional core and the dialogue part of multimodal interactive systems. The ICoN notation deals explicitly with input devices and input configurations. As these two models are supported by dedicated edition, simulation and execution environments, we have shown how very high fidelity prototyping can be performed and its related impact at various levels of the Arch architectural model.

The application of the notations and tools has been shown on a simple case study i.e. a bimanual drawing interactive system. This simple case study has shown a precise example of each model as well as how there edition and simulation.

This work belongs to a more ambitious projects (see acknowledgement section) dedicated to the engineering of multimodal interactive systems for safety critical applications including military aircraft cockpits and satellite ground stations. The aim of this work is not only to provide notations and tools for building multimodal interactive systems but also to support verification and validation in order to support certifications activities that are a critical phase in the development process of interactive safety critical applications.

Acknowledgements

The work presented here is partly funded by French defence agency (Direction Générale pour l'Armement) under contract n° 00.70.624.00.470.75.96 and by the French Space Agency CNES (Centre National d'Etudes Spatiales) under the R&T action n°CC201*02. Special thanks are due to Didier Bazalgette for precise information about the field of command and control systems in military applications.

References

1. L. Bass, R. Little, R. Pellegrino, S. Reed, R. Seacord, S. Sheppard & M. R. Szezur. (1991) The Arch Model: Seeheim Revisited. *User Interface Developpers' Workshop*. Version 1.0.
2. R. Bastide & P. Palanque. (1995) A Petri-Net Based Environment for the Design of Event-Driven Interfaces . *16th International Conference on Applications and Theory of Petri Nets, ICATPN'95*, Torino, Italy, 66-83. Giorgio De Michelis, and Michel Diaz, Volume editors. Lecture Notes in Computer Science, no. 935. Springer.
3. R. Bastide, P. Palanque, Le Duc H., and Muńoz J. Integrating Rendering Specifications into a Formalism for the Design of Interactive Systems. Proceedings of the 5th Eurographics workshop on Design, Specification and Verification of Interactive systems DSV-IS'98 . 1998. Springer Verlag
4. R. Bastide, O. Sy, P. Palanque, and D. Navarre. Formal specification of CORBA services: experience and lessons learned. ACM Conference on Object-Oriented Programming, Systems, Languages, and Applications (OOPSLA'2000); Minneapolis, Minnesota USA. ACM Press; 2000: 105-117. ACM SIGPLAN Notices. v. 35 (10)).
5. G. Berry. (1999) The Esterel v5 language primer. Technical report, april 1999. http://www-sop.inria.fr/meije/esterel/doc/main-papers.html.
6. J. Coutaz, Paterno F. , Faconti G. , and Nigay L. A Comparison of Approaches for Specifying MultiModal Interactive Systems. Proceedings of the ERCIM Workshop on Multimodal Human-Computer Interaction. 165-174. 1993.
7. P. Dragicevic & J-D. Fekete. (2001) Input Device Selection and Interaction Configuration with ICON. Proceedings of IHM-HCI 2001, Blandford, A.; Vanderdonckt, J.; Gray, P., (Eds.): People and Computers XV - Interaction without Frontiers, Lille, France, Springer Verlag, pp. 543-448.
8. P. Dragicevic & J-D. Fekete. (2002) ICON: Input Device Selection and Interaction Configuration. Companion proceedings of UIST'02, 15th Annual Symposium on User Interface Software and Technology, Paris, October 2002.
9. P. Dragicevic & J-D. Fekete. (2004) ICON: Towards High Input Adaptability of Interactive Applications. Internal Report 04/01/INFO, Ecole des Mines de Nantes. Nantes, France.
10. O. Esteban, S. Chatty, and P. Palanque. Whizz'Ed: a visual environment for building highly interactive interfaces. Proceedings of the Interact'95 conference, 121-126. 1995.
11. H. J. Genrich. Predicate/Transition Nets, in K. Jensen and G. Rozenberg (Eds.), High-Level Petri Nets: Theory and Application. Springer Verlag, Berlin, pp. 3-43.
12. N. Halbwachs, P. Caspi, P. Raymond, D. Pilaud. (1991) The synchronous data-flow programming language LUSTRE. In Proceedings of the IEEE, volume 79, September 1991.
13. Hinckley, K., Czerwinski, M., Sinclair, M., Interaction and Modeling Techniques for Desktop Two-Handed Input, ACM UIST'98 Symposium on User Interface Software & Technology, pp. 49-58.
14. D. Navarre, P. Palanque, R. Bastide & O. Sy. Structuring Interactive Systems Specifications for Executability and Prototypability. 7th Eurographics Workshop on Design, Specification and Verification of Interactive Systems, DSV-IS'2000, Limerick, Ireland, 2000, Lecture notes in Computer Science n° 1946.
15. OMG. The Common Object Request Broker: Architecture and Specification. CORBA IIOP 2.2 /98-02-01, Framingham, MA (1998).

16. P. Palanque & A. Schyn. A Model-Based Approach for Engineering Multimodal Interactive Systems in INTERACT 2003, IFIP TC 13 conference on Human Computer Interaction.
17. R. Wieting 1996. Hybrid High-Level Nets . Page 848 855Proceedings of the 1996 Winter Simulation Conference. ACM Press.
18. J.S. Willans & Harrison M. D. Prototyping pre-implementation designs of virtual environment behaviour. 8th IFIP Working conference on engineering for human-computer interaction (EHCI'01) 2001. LNCS, Springer Verlag.

Discussion

[Rick Kazman] The context of this is safety critical systems. Two properties to address are reliability and performance. How do you guarantee that in the model you are presenting that these properties are there and, given that the model is compositional, that the properties are preserved?

> [Philippe Palanque] The intention is not to embed PetShop in an aircraft. The model is intended to be a specification and a high-fidelity prototype. So we produce a specification and a running example. On the aeroplane, for example, it was necessary to have response within 20ms. This is met with our system. We hope to provide a set of tests as well to allow the developers to be sure that they have met the requirements. We are working on this now.

[Bonnie John] In the spirit of the grand challenge of the "UI crash test dummy", have you thought of attaching this to a cognitive modeling architecture such as ACT-R (which has its own model of human-like concurrency and human-scale timing?)

> [Philippe Palanque] We work at a low level. So we use Fitts' Law for example, to tell us that the average time for a user to respond will be some value. Petri Nets allow time to be attributed to arcs and specification of the size of buttons, which allow this kind of analysis.

[Michael Harrison] Petri nets have a lot of "good" baggage allowing you to prove many properties of systems. You presented this tool primarily as a rapid prototyping environment. Have you taken advantage of the properties of Petri nets for analysis?

> [Philippe Palanque] There is a tradeoff in designing Petri nets for evaluation vs prototyping. In the past we've worked on the modelling approach, but now we're looking at expressiveness. We have performed analyses such as invariant checking.

[Michael Harrison] Do you feel this is a good way of specifying this kind of system?

> [Philippe Palanque] We have a contract with the French certification authority. They have no idea of how to certify a cockpit. Now several people at Thalès are using our tools to work on this.

[Willem-Paul Brinkman] Synchronization over feedback is also important as well as synchronization of inputs. Do you handle this?

> [Philippe Palanque] Our approach can handle the specification of the entire system. We have seen this in practice. For example, in the A380, they have a

server (X Windows). There is feedback indicating that the server has not yet received feedback from the application, during which the pilot must wait.

[Grigori Evreinov] There was no clear definition of multi-modal. What is the difference between multi-modal and multi-channel interaction? E.g., if you can manipulate with two mice, it's two channel manipulation. If you have speech fused with mouse motion, it's multi-modal. Content should not be fused in head of the user.

[Philippe Palanque] You are right. The example was multi-channel interaction. The point was to show the integration of multiple devices. For multi-modal, we can have models of two mice, which are fused via a single model at the logical interaction level. This is perfectly possible with PetShop. For example, using two fingers on a touch-sensitive display.

USIXML: A Language Supporting Multi-path Development of User Interfaces

Quentin Limbourg[1], Jean Vanderdonckt[1], Benjamin Michotte[1], Laurent Bouillon[1], Víctor López-Jaquero[1 2]

[1] Université catholique de Louvain, School of Management (IAG), ISYS-BCHI
Place des Doyens, 1 – B-1348 Louvain-la-Neuve, Belgium
{limbourg,vanderdonckt,michotte,bouillon,lopez}@isys.ucl.ac.be
http://www.isys.ucl.ac.be/bchi

[2] Laboratory of User Interaction and Software Engineering (LoUISE)
University of Castilla-La Mancha, Albacete, Spain
victor@info-ab.uclm.es

Abstract. USer Interface eXtensible Markup Language (USIXML) consists in a User Interface Description Language (UIDL) allowing designers to apply a multi-path development of user interfaces. In this development paradigm, a user interface can be specified and produced at and from different, and possibly multiple, levels of abstraction while maintaining the mappings between these levels if required. Thus, the development process can be initiated from any level of abstraction and proceed towards obtaining one or many final user interfaces for various contexts of use at other levels of abstraction. In this way, the model-to-model transformation, which is the cornerstone of Model-Driven Architecture (MDA), can be supported in multiple configurations, based on composition of three basic transformation types: abstraction, reification, and translation.

Keywords: context-sensitive user interface, development processes, modality independence, model-driven architecture, model-to-model transformation, multi-path development, rendering independence, user interface description language.

1 Introduction

Due to the rapid changes of today's organisations and their business, many information systems departments face the problem of quickly adapting the user interface (UI) of their interactive applications to these changes. These changes include, but are not limited to: task redefinition [4], task reallocation among workers [4], support of new computing platforms [10], migration from stationary platforms to mobile computing [17], evolution of users with more demands, increasing need for more usable UIs, transfer of tasks from one user to another one [7], redefinition of the organisation structure, adaptation to dynamic environments [16], changes in the language, redesign due to obsolescence [3], evolution of the domain model [1]. All these changes change to some extent the context of use, which is hereby referred to as

R. Bastide, P. Palanque, and J. Roth (Eds.): EHCI-DSVIS 2004, LNCS 3425, pp. 200-220, 2005.

the complete environment where final users have to carry out their interactive tasks to fulfil the roles they are playing in their organisations.

To address the challenges posed by these changes, the development processes used in these organisations are not always considered appropriate, as they do not reflect the implication of any change throughout the complete development life cycle. As a matter of fact, organisations react to changes in very different ways in their UI development processes. For instance, one organisation starts by recovering existing input/output screens, by redrawing them and by completing the functional core when the new UI is validated by the customer (*bottom-up approach*). Another organisation prefers modifying the domain model (e.g., a UML class diagram [12]) and the task model [20] to be mapped further to screen design (*top-down approach*). A third one tends to apply in parallel all the required adaptations where they occur (*wide spreading approach*). A fourth one relies on an intermediate model and proceeds simultaneously to the task and domain models, and the final UI (*middle-out approach*) [15]. The UI development process has also been empirically observed as an ill-defined, incomplete, and incremental process [24] that is not well supported by rigid development methods and tools. Such methods and tools usually force developers to act in a way that remains peculiar to the method. The tool does not allow for more flexibility. For instance, SEGUIA [25] only supports a single fixed UI development path [11].

The variety of the approaches adopted in organisations and the rigidity of existing solutions provide ample motivations for a UI development paradigm that is flexible enough to accommodate multiple development paths and design situations while staying precise enough to manipulate information required for UI development. To overcome these shortcomings, the development paradigm of ***multi-path UI development*** is introduced that is characterised by the following principles:

- *Expressiveness of UI*: any UI is expressed depending on the context of use thanks to a suite of models [20] analysable, editable, and manipulable by a software [21].
- *Central storage of models*: each model is stored in a model repository where all UI models are expressed according to the same UI Description Language (UIDL).
- *Transformational approach*: each model stored in the model repository may be subject to one or many transformations supporting various development steps.
- *Multiple development path*: development steps can be combined together to form developments path that are compatible with the organisation's constraints, conventions, and context of use. For example, a series of transformations should be applied to progressively move from a task model to a dialog model, to recover a domain model from a presentation model, to derive a presentation model from both the task and domain models.
- *Flexible development approaches*: development approaches (e.g., top-down, bottom-up, wide spreading, and middle-out) are supported by flexibly following alternate development path and enabling designers to freely shift between these paths depending on the changes imposed by the organization [15].

The remainder of this paper is structured as follows: Section 2 reports on some significant pieces of work that are partially related to multi-path UI development. Section 3 introduces the reference representations used throughout this paper to address the principles of expressiveness and central storage of models based on USer Interface eXtensible Markup Language (USIXML). Section 4 shows how a transformational approach is represented and implemented thanks to graph grammars and graph transformations applied on models expressed in USIXML and stored in a model repository. Three basic transformation types (i.e., abstraction, reification, and translation) are exemplified. Section 6 exposes the tool support proposed around USIXML. Section 7 concludes by reporting on the main benefits and difficulties encountered so far with multi-path UI development.

2 Related Work

The multi-path UI development, as defined in Section 1, is at the intersection of two mainstreams of research and development: on the one hand, UI modelling and design of multi-platform UIs represent significant advances in Human-Computer Interaction (HCI) and on the other hand, program transformation that is considered promising in Software Engineering (SE) as a mean to bridge the gap between abstract description of software artefacts and their implementation [4,23].

Teallach tool and method [11] exploit three models: a task model, a domain model as a class diagram, and a presentation model both at logical and physical levels. Teallach enables designers to start building a UI from any model and maps concepts from different models one to each other (e.g., map a widget to a domain concept, or map a task onto a domain concept). Teallach also provides rules to derive model elements using information contained in another model.

XWEB [25] produces UIs for several devices starting from a multi-modal description of the abstract UI. This system operates on specific XWEB servers and browsers tuned to the interactive capacities of particular platforms, which communicate thanks to an appropriate XTP protocol. MORE [10] produces applications that are platform independent by relying on Platform Independent Application (PIA). A PIA can be created either by a design tool or by abstracting a concrete UI by a generalization process done by reverse engineering [17] the UI code.

UIML consists of a UIDL supporting the development of UIs for multiple computing platforms by introducing a description that is platform-independent to be further expanded with peers once a target platform has been chosen [2]. The TIDE tool [2] transforms a basic task model into a final UI. XIML [21] is a more general UIDL than UIML as it can specify any type of model, any model element, and relationships between them. Although some predefined models and relationships exist, one can expand the existing set to fit a particular context of use. XIML has been used in MANNA for platform adaptation [9], and in VAQUITA and Envir3D [5] to support re-engineering [7] of web sites by applying a series of model transformations. SeescoaXML [21] is the base UIDL exploited in the SEESCOA project to support the production of UIs for multiple platforms and the run-time migration of the full UI across these platforms.

TERESA (Transformation Environment for inteRactivE Systems representAtions) [17] produces different UIs for multiple computing platforms by refining a general task model for the different platforms. Then, various presentation and dialogue techniques are used to map the refinenements into XHTML code adapted for each platform, such as Web, PocketPC, and mobile phones. TERESA exploits TERESAXML, a UIDL that supports several types of transformations such as: task model into presentation task sets, task model into abstract UI, abstract UI to concrete UI, and generation of the final UI. In [26], a very interesting example of a platform modulator [9] is provided that maps a hierarchical task model to a presentation model explicitly taking into account platform characteristics such as screen resolution.

The above pieces of work all represent an instance with some degree of coverage and restrictions of the multi-path UI development. Regarding the *UI expressiveness* for multiple contexts of use, XTP of XWeb, UIML, XIML, TERESAXML and SeescoaXML are UIDLs that address the basic requirements of UI modelling and expressivity. XIML is probably the most expressive one as a new model, element or relationship can be defined internally. Yet, there is no systematic support of these relationships until they are covered by specific software. Regarding the *transformational approach*, Seescoa, Teallach, TERESA and TIDE include some transformation mechanism to map a model onto another one, but the logics and the definition of transformation rules are completely hard coded with little or no control by designers. In addition, the definition of these representations is not independent of the transformation engine. Regarding multiple development path, only Teallach explicitly addresses the problem, as models can be mapped one onto another according to different ways. Other typically apply top-down (e.g., TIDE), bottom-up (e.g., VAQUITA), middle-out (e.g., MIDAS [15]), but none of them support all development approaches.

To satisfy the requirements subsumed by the four principles, *Graph Transformation* (GT) [22] will be applied because substantive experience shows applicability in numerous fields of science (e.g., biology, operational research) and, notably, to computer science (e.g., model checking, parallel computing, software engineering). GTs are operated in two steps: expressing abstract concepts in the form of a graph structure and defining operations producing relevant transformations on the graph structure. Sucrow [23] used GT techniques to formally describe UI dialog with dialog states (the appearance of a UI at a particular moment in time) and dialog transitions (transformations of dialog states). An interesting edge typology is proposed to describe dialog states, emphasises, widget hierarchy, semantic feedback, and relationships with the functional core of the application. To support "a continuous specification process of graphical UIs", two models are defined in the development process: abstract and concrete. GTs map one model into another, and vice versa, thus leading to reversibility. Furthermore, elements such as dialog patterns, style guides, and metaphors are used to automate abstract to concrete transition. However, conceptual coverage and fundamental aspects of this work remains silent: presented concepts remain at the model level without going to any final UI and there is no description of the meta-level or of the instance level. To structure the models involved in the UI development process and to characterise the model transformations to be expressed through GT techniques, a reference framework is now introduced.

3 The Reference Framework Used for Multi-path UI Development

Multi-path UI development is based on the Cameleon Reference Framework [6], which defines UI development steps for multi-context interactive applications. Its simplified version, reproduced in Fig. 1, structures development processes for two contexts of use into four development steps (each development step being able to manipulate any specific artefact of interest as a model or a UI representation) [5,6]:

1. *Final UI* (FUI): is the operational UI i.e. any UI running on a particular computing platform either by interpretation (e.g., through a Web browser) or by execution (e.g., after compilation of code in an interactive development environment).
2. *Concrete UI* (CUI): concretises an abstract UI for a given context of use into Concrete Interaction Objects (CIOs) [25] so as to define widgets layout and interface navigation. It abstracts a FUI into a UI definition that is independent of any computing platform. Although a CUI makes explicit the final Look & Feel of a FUI, it is still a mock-up that runs only within a particular environment. A CUI can also be considered as a reification of an AUI at the upper level and an abstraction of the FUI with respect to the platform.
3. *Abstract UI* (AUI): defines interaction spaces (or presentation units) by grouping subtasks according to various criteria (e.g., task model structural patterns, cognitive load analysis, semantic relationships identification), a navigation scheme between the interaction spaces and selects Abstract Interaction Objects (AIOs) [25] for each concept so that they are independent of any modality. An AUI abstracts a CUI into a UI definition that is independent of any modality of interaction (e.g., graphical interaction, vocal interaction, speech synthesis and recognition, video-based interaction, virtual, augmented or mixed reality). An AUI can also be considered as a canonical expression of the rendering of the domain concepts and tasks in a way that is independent from any modality of interaction. For example, in ARTStudio [5], an AUI is a collection of related workspaces. The relations between the workspaces are inferred from the task relationships expressed at the upper level (task and concepts). An AUI is considered as an abstraction of a CUI with respect to modality.
4. *Task & Concepts* (T&C): describe the various tasks to be carried out and the domain-oriented concepts as they are required by these tasks to be performed. These objects are considered as instances of classes representing the concepts manipulated.

This framework exhibits three types of *basic transformation types*: (1,2) *Abstraction* (respectively, *Reification*) is a process of elicitation of artefacts that are more abstract (respectively, concrete) than the artefacts that serve as input to this process. Abstraction is the opposite of reification. (3) *Translation* is a process that elicits artefacts intended for a particular context of use from artefacts of a similar development step but aimed at a different context of use. With respect to this framework, *multi-path UI development* refers to a UI engineering method and tool that enables a designer to (1) start a development activity from any entry point of the reference framework (Fig. 1), (2) get substantial support in the performance of

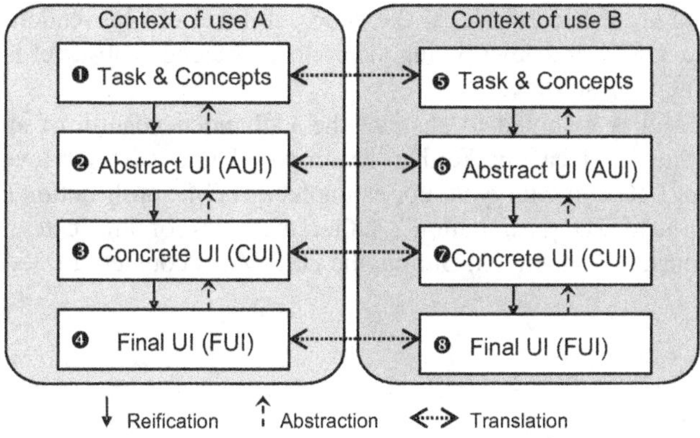

Fig. 1. The Cameleon Reference Framework.

all basic transformation types and their combinations of Fig. 1. To enable such a development, the two most important requirements gathered from observations are:

1. A language that enables the expression and the manipulation (e.g., creation, modification, deletion) of the model at each development steps and for each context of use. For this purpose, USIXML is introduced and defined (http://www.usixml.org). It is out of the scope of this paper to provide an extensive discussion on the content of USIXML. USIXML is composed of approximately 150 concepts enabling the expression of different levels of abstraction as introduced in Fig. 1.
2. A mechanism to express design knowledge that would provide a substantial support to the designer in the realisation of transformations. For this purpose, a GT technique is introduced and defined based on USIXML.

4 Graph Transformation Specification with USIXML

Graph transformation techniques were chosen to formalize USIXML, the language designed to support multi-path UI development, because it is (1) **Visual**: every element within a GT based language has a graphical syntax; (2) **Formal**: GT is based on a sound mathematical formalism (algebraic definition of graphs and category theory) and enables verifying formal properties on represented artefacts; (3) **Seamless**: it allows representing manipulated artefacts and rules within a single formalism. Furthermore, the formalism applies equally to all levels of abstraction of USIXML (Fig. 2). USIXML model collection is structured according to the four basic levels of abstraction defined in the Cameleon Reference Framework that is intended to express the UI development life cycle for context-sensitive interactive applications. Fig. 2 illustrates more concretely the type of concepts populating each level of Cameleon reference framework:

- At the FUI level, the rendering materialises how a particular UI coded in one language (markup, programming or declarative) is rendered depending on the UI toolkit, the window manager and the presentation manager. For example, a push button programmed in HTML at the code sub-level can be rendered differently, here on MacOS X and Java Swing. Therefore, the code sub-level is materialised onto the rendering sub-level.

- The CUI level is assumed to abstract the FUI independently of any computing platform, this level can be further decomposed into two sub-levels: platform-independent CIO and CIO type. For example, a HTML push-button belongs to the type "Graphical 2D push button". Other members of this category include a Windows push button and XmButton, the OSF/Motif counterpart.
-

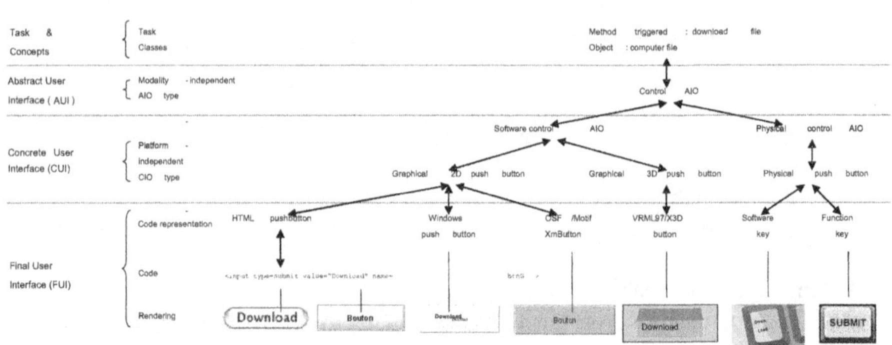

Fig. 2. Example of transformations in USIXML.

- Since the AUI level is assumed to abstract the CUI independently of any modality of interaction, this level can be further decomposed into two sub-levels: modality-independent AIO and AIO type. For example, a software control (whether in 2D or in 3D) and a physical control (e.g., a physical button on a control panel or a function key) both belong to the category of control AIO.
- At the T&C level, a task of a certain type (here, download a file) is specified that naturally leads to AIO for controlling the downloading.

Thanks to the four abstraction levels, it is possible to establish mappings between instances and objects found at the different levels and to develop transformations that find abstractions or reifications or combinations. For example, if a Graphical User Interface (GUI) needs to be virtualised, a series of abstractions is applied until the sub-level "Software control AIO" sub-level is reached. Then, a series of reifications can be applied to come back to the FUI level to find out another object satisfying the same constraints, but in 3D. If the GUI needs to be transformed for a UI for augmented reality for instance, the next sub-level can be reached with an additional abstraction and so forth. The combinations of the transformations allow establishing development path. Here, some first examples are given of multi-path UI development. To face multi-path development of UIs in general, USIXML is equipped with a collection of basic UI models (i.e., domain model, task model, AUI model, CUI model, context model and mapping model) (Fig. 4) and a so-called transformation model *(Fig. 3) [13]. Beyond the AUI and CUI models that reflect the AUI and CUI levels, the other UI models are defined as follows:*

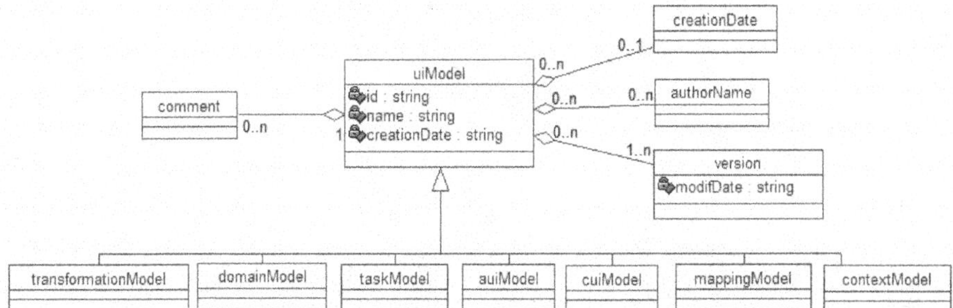

Fig. 3. USIXML Model Collection.

- **uiModel**: is the topmost superclass containing common features shared by all component models of a UI. A uiModel may consist of a list of component model in any order and any number, such as task model, a domain model, an abstract UI model, a concrete UI model, mapping model, and context model. A user interface model needs not include one of each model component. Moreover, there may be more than one of a particular kind of model component.
- **taskModel** (Inherits from: uiModel): is a model describing the interactive task as viewed by the end user interacting with the system. A task model represents a decomposition of tasks into sub-tasks linked with task relationships. Therefore, the decomposition relationship is the privileged relationship to express this hierarchy, while temporal relationships express the temporal constraints between sub-tasks of a same parent task. A task model is here expressed according to the ConcurTaskTree notation [20].
- **domainModel** (Inherits from: uiModel): is a description of the classes of objects manipulated by a user while interacting with a system [12].
- **mappingModel** (Inherits from: uiModel): is a model containing a series of related mappings (i.e, a declaration of an inter-model relationship) between models or elements of models. A mapping model serves to gather a set of inter-model relationships that are semantically related.
- **contextModel** (Inherits from: uiModel): is a model describing the three aspects of a context of use in which a end user is carrying out an interactive task with a specific computing platform in a given surrounding environment. Consequently, a context model consists of a user model, a platform model, and an environment model.

Transformations are specified using transformation systems. Transformation systems rely on the theory of graph grammars [22]. We first explain what a transformation system is and then illustrate how they may be used to specify UI model transformations. The proposed formalism to represent model-to-model transformation in USIXML is graph transformations. This formalism has been discussed in [13,14]. USIXML has been designed with an underlying graph structure. Consequently any graph transformation rule can be applied to a USIXML specification. Graph transformations have been shown convenient and efficient for our present purpose in [19].

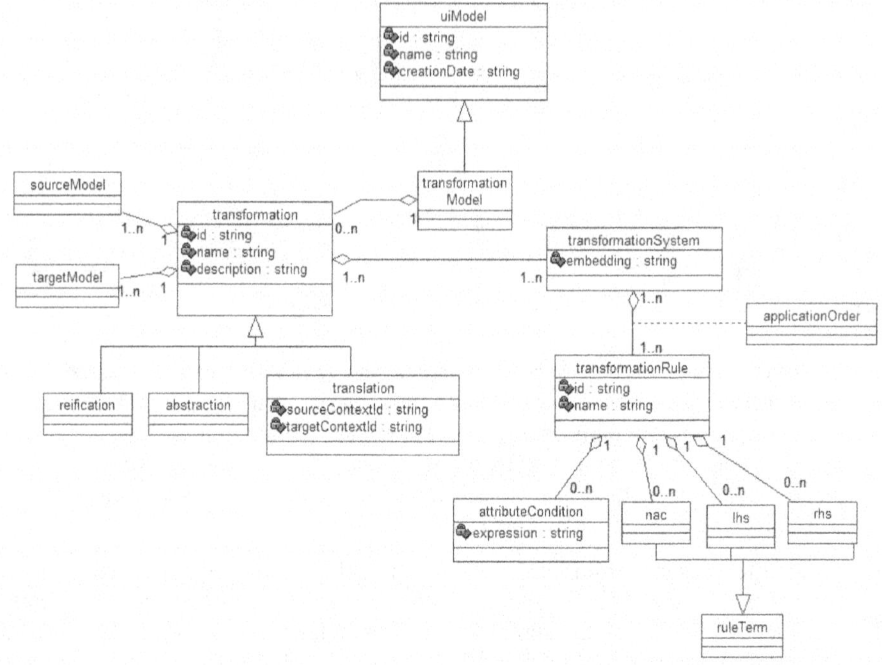

Fig. 4. Transformation model as defined in USIXML.

A transformation system is composed of several transformation rules. Technically, a rule is a graph rewriting rule equipped with negative application conditions and attribute conditions [19].

Fig. 5 illustrates how a transformation system applies to a USIXML specification: let G be a USIXML specification (represented as a graph), when 1) a Left Hand Side (LHS) matches into G and 2) a Negative Application Condition (NAC) does not matches into G (note that several NAC may be associated with a single rule) 3) the LHS is replaced by a Right Hand Side (RHS). G is resultantly transformed into G, a resultant USIXML specification. All elements of G not covered by the match are considered as unchanged. All elements contained in the LHS and not contained in the RHS are considered as deleted (i.e., rules have destructive power). To add more expressive power to transformation rules, variables may be associated to attributes within a LHS. Theses variables are initialized in the LHS and their value can be used to assign an attribute in the expression of the RHS (e.g., LHS : button.name:=x, RHS : task.name:=x). An expression may also be defined to compare a variable declared in the LHS with a constant or with another variable. This mechanism is called 'attribute condition'.

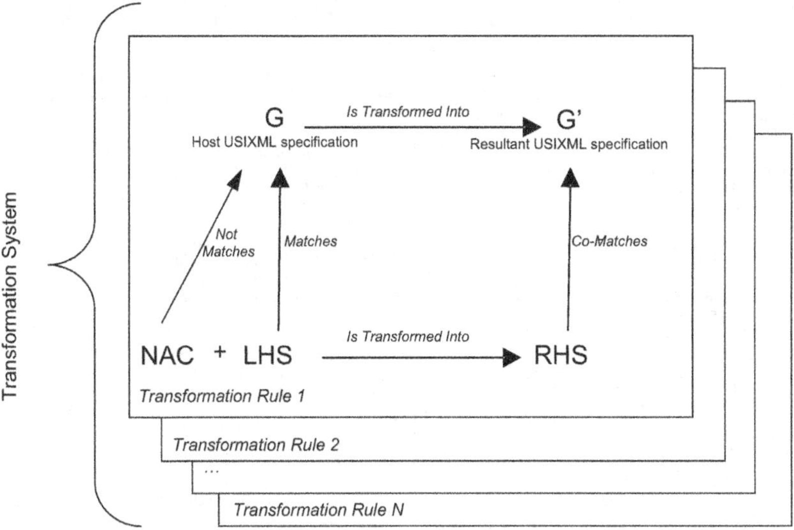

Fig. 5. Transformation system in USIXML.

We detail hereafter a simplified scenario illustrating the three basic types of transformation (thus inducing different path) mentioned in Section 3.

Step 1 (Abstraction): a designer reverse engineers an HTML page with Rutabaga [3] in order to obtain a CUI model. Transformation 1 (Fig. 6) is an abstraction that takes a button at the concrete level and abstracts it away into an abstract interaction object. The LHS selects every button and the method they activate and create a corresponding abstract interaction object equipped with a control facet mapped onto the method triggered by its corresponding concrete interaction object. Some behavioural specification is preserved at the abstract level. Note that behaviour specification in USIXML is also done with graph transformations rules. It is out of the scope of this paper to explicit this mechanism. This is why rule 1 in transformation 1, in its LHS, embeds a fragment of a transformation system specification. This may seem confusing at first sight but is very powerful at the end i.e., we dispose of a mechanism transforming a UI behavioural specification into another one! In the RHS, one also see that a relationship *isAbstractedInto* has been created. This relationship ensures traceability of rule application and helps in maintaining coherence among different levels of abstraction.

Step 2 (Reification): the designer decides to add, by hand, to the abstract level a navigation facet to every abstract interaction object that has a control facet. From this new abstract specification, Transformation 2 (Fig. 7) reifies every abstract interaction object into image components (i.e., a type of concrete interaction object). By default, the control facet is activated when an event "*onMouseOver*" is triggered, and the navigation facet is activated when the *imageComponent* is double-clicked. This rule may of course be customized by the designer to reflect his own preferences or needs.

Transformation 1: abstraction

```
...
<abstraction id="AB1" name =
"AbstractButtonWithControl" description = "this
translation abstracts buttons into an AIO with an
activation facet"

<transformationSystem id = "TR2" name="Transfo2"...>
<transformationRule id = "rule1" name "abstractsBut">

<lhs>
    <button ruleSpecificID="1" mapID="2">
        <behavior>
        <action>
        <transformationSystem>
        <transformationRule>
        <rhs>
        <method ruleSpecificID="3"
                    mapID ="4" name="X" />
        <isTriggeredBy isFired="true">
        <source sourceId="1">
        <target targetId="3">
        </isTriggeredBy>
        </rhs>
        </transformationRule>
        </transformationSystem>
        </action>
        </behaviour>
    </button>
</lhs>

<rhs>
    <abstractIndividualComponent ruleSpecificId="5">
        <control activatedMethod="X">
    </abstractIndividualComponent>

    <isAbstractedInto>
        <source sourceId="2"/>
        <target targetId="5"/>
    <isAbstractedInto>

    <button ruleSpecificId="1" mapID="2">
        <behavior>
        <transformationSystem>
        <transformationRule>
        <rhs>
        <method ruleSpecificID="3" mapID ="4"/>
        <isTriggeredBy isFired="true">
        <source sourceId="1">
        <target targetId="3">
        </isTriggeredBy>
        </rhs>
        </transformationRule>
        </transformationSystem>
        </behaviour>
    </button>
</rhs>
...
<nac.../>

</transformationRule>
</transformationSystem>
</abstraction>
...
```

Fig. 6. Transformation 1.

Transformation 2: reification

```
...
<reification id="Reif1" name = "ReifiesAioImgCtlrNav"
 description = " reifies a control AIO into an image
Component with corresponding behavior template"

    <transformationSystem id = "TRE1" name="TR2"...>
    <transformationRule id = "rule44" name
"ReiFControl44">

<lhs>
    <abstractIndividualComponent mapID="1">
    <control activatedMethod="X"/>
    <navigation target="Y"/>
    </abstractIndividualComponent>
<lhs>
<rhs>
    <imageComponent ruleSpecificID="2">
        <behavior>
        <event type="doubleClick"/>
        <action>
        <transformationSystem>
        <transformationRule>
        <lhs/>
        <rhs>
        <method ruleSpecificID="3" name="X"/>
        <isTriggeredBy isFired="true">
        <source sourceId="2">
        <target targetId="3">
        </isTriggeredBy>
        </rhs>
        </transformationRule>
        </transformationSystem>
        </behaviour>
        <behavior>
        <event type="onMouseOver(self)"/>
        <action>
        <transformationSystem>
        <transformationRule>
        <lhs/>
        <rhs>
        <graphicalContainer id="Y" visible="true"/>
        </rhs>
        </transformationRule>
        </transformationSystem>
        </behaviour>
    </imageComponent>

    <isReifiedInto>
        <source sourceId="1"/>
        <target targetId="2"/>
    </isReifiedInto>

    <abstractIndividualComponent mapID="1">
        <control activatedMethod="X">
    </abstractIndividualComponent>
</rhs>
<nac.../>
    <transformationRule>
    </transformationSystem>
    </reification>
    ...
```

Fig. 7. Transformation 2.

Step3 (Translation): to adapt a UI to a new type of display/browser that has the characteristic to be tall and narrow. The designer decides then to apply Transformation 3 (Fig. 8) to her CUI model. This transformation is made of a rule that selects all boxes (basic layout structure at the CUI level) and sets these boxes type to "*vertical*". All widgets contained in this box are then glued to the left of the box (again in the idea of minimizing the width of the resulting UI). Note the presence of a negative application condition (too long to show in previous examples) that ensures that rule 1 in transformation 3 is not applied to an already formatted box.

Fig. 8 shows a simple example of translation specified with USIXML. This rule of the rule selects all boxes (basic layout structure at the CUI level), sets these boxes to "vertical". All widgets contained in this box are then glued to the left of the box (again in the idea of minimizing the width of the resulting UI). A negative application condition ensures that a rule is not applied to an already formatted box.

Transformation 3: translation

```
...
<translation id="TL1" name="squeezeDisplay"
description= "this translations vertically aligns all widgets of a
container">
<sourceModel type="cui"/>
<targetModel type="cui"/>
<transformationSystem id="TR1" name="Transfo1"...>
<transformationRule id="rule1" name="squeeze1">

<lhs>
<box mapID="1">
<graphicalIndividualComponent mapId="2" />
</box>
</lhs>

<rhs>
<box mapID="1" type="vertical">
<graphicalIndividualComponent mapId="2" glueHorizontal="left"/>
</box>
</rhs>

<nac>
```

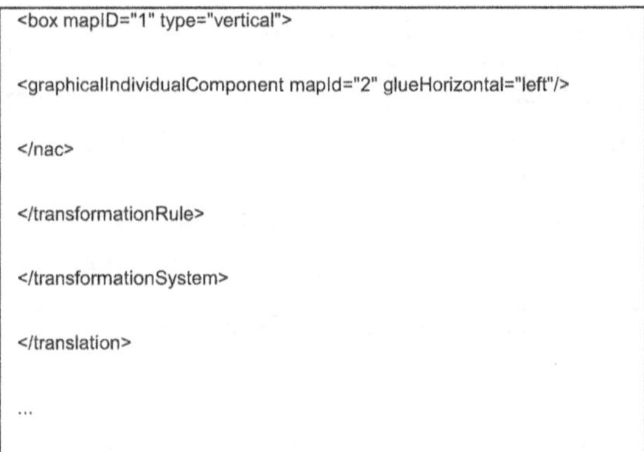

```
<box mapID="1" type="vertical">

<graphicalIndividualComponent mapId="2" glueHorizontal="left"/>

</nac>

</transformationRule>

</transformationSystem>

</translation>

...
```

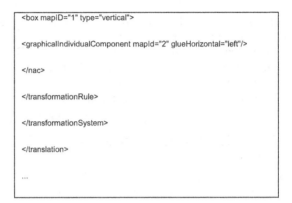

Fig. 8. Transformation 3.

Alternatively to textual representation, transformation rules are easily expressed in a graphical syntax. Fig. 9 shows a graphical equivalent for the rule contained in Fig. 8. A general purpose tool for graph transformation called AGG (Attributed Graph Grammars) was used to specify this example. There is no proof that states the superiority of graphical formalism over textual ones, but at least USIXML designer can choose between both.

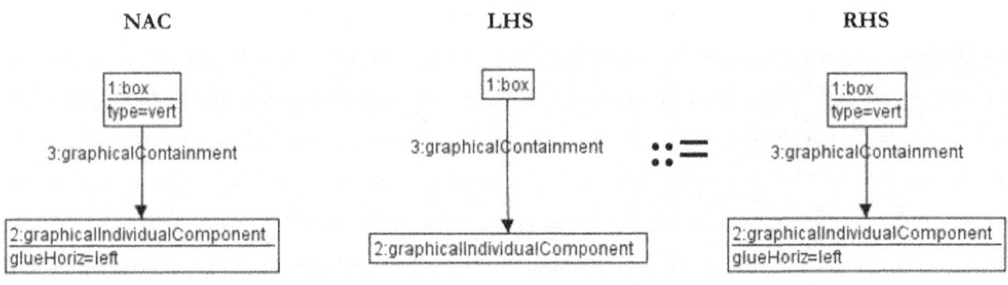

Fig. 9. Graphical representation of the transformation.

Traceability (and as a side-effect reversibility) of model transformation is enabled thanks to a set of 'so-called' *interModelMappings* (e.g., *isAbstractedInto*, *IsReifiedInto*, *isTranslatedInto*) allowing a relation between model elements belonging to different models. Thus, it is possible to keep a trace of the application of rules i.e., when a new element is created a mapping indicates of what element it is an abstraction, a reification, a translation, etc. Another advantage of using these mappings is to support multi-path development is that they explicitly connect the various levels of our framework and realizes an seamless integration of the different models used to describe the system. Knowing the mappings of a model increases dramatically the understanding of the underlying structure of a UI. It enables to answer, at no cost, to question like: what task an interaction object enables?, what domain object attributes are updated by what interaction object? Which interaction object triggers what method?

5 Tool Support

Tool support is provided for several of the levels shown in Fig. 2.

- **Reverse engineering of UI code**: a specific tool, called *Rutabaga* [3], automatically reverse engineers the presentation model of an existing HTML Web page at both the CUI and AUI levels, with or without intra-model, inter-model mappings. This tool allows developers to recuperate an existing UI so as to incorporate it again in the development process. In this case, a re-engineering can be obtained by combining two abstractions, one translation, and two reifications. This is particularly useful for evolution of legacy systems.
- **Model edition**: as editing a new UI in USIXML directly can be considered as a tedious task, a specific editor called *GrafiXML* has been developed to face the development of USIXML models. Being at first hand a textual language, an *ad hoc* USIXML editor was created. In this editor, the designer can draw in direct manipulation any graphical UI by directly placing CIOs and editing their properties in the Composer, which are instantly reflected in the UI design (Fig. 10). At any time, the designer may want to see the corresponding USIXML specifications (Fig. 11) and edit it. Selecting a USIXML tag automatically displays possible values for this tag in a contextual menu. When the tag or the elements are modified, those changes are propagated to the graphical representation. In this way, a bidirectional mapping is maintained between a UI and its USIXML specification: each time a part is modified, the other one is updated accordingly.

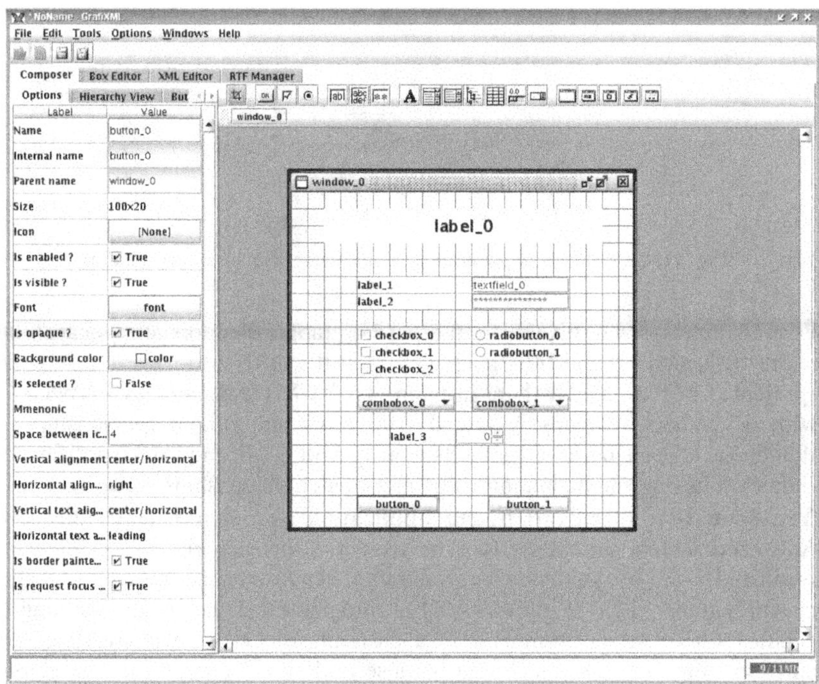

Fig. 10. Graphical Editing of a UI in GrafiXML.

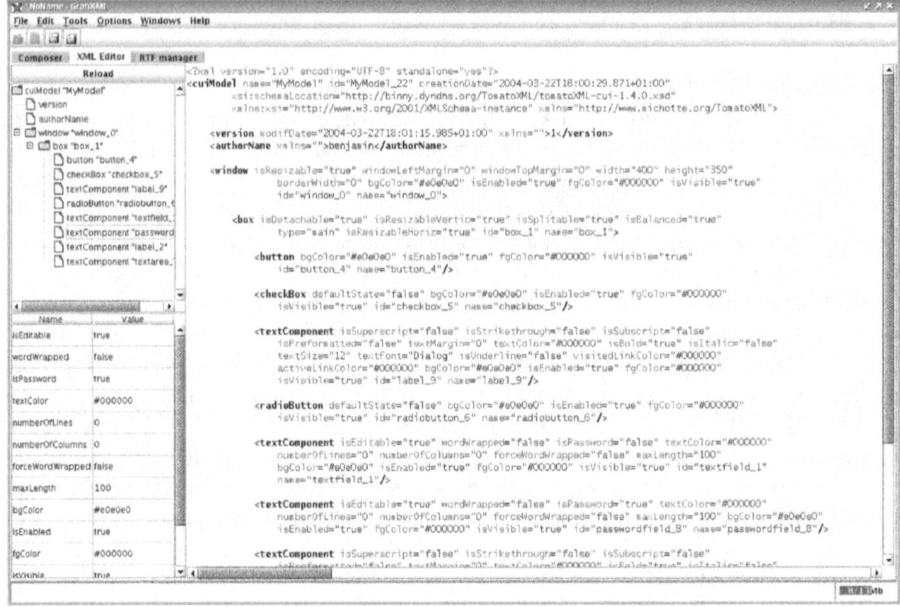

Fig. 11. USIXML equivalent of a UI edited in GrafiXML.

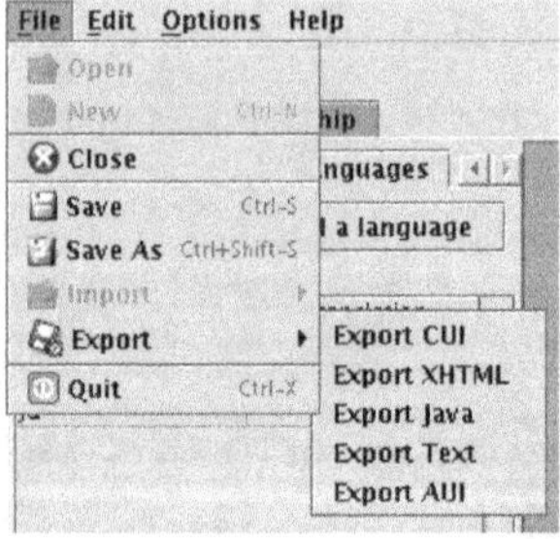

Fig. 12. Capabilities to generate a UI at different levels of abstraction.

What distinguishes GrafiXML from other UI graphical editors are its capabilities to directly generate USIXML specifications at the different levels of abstractions represented in Fig. 2: FUI (here in plain text, in XHTML and Java AWT), CUI (with or without relationships), and AUI (with or without relationships). In addition, a UI can be saved simultaneously with CUI and AUI specifications, while establishing and maintaining the inter-model relationships between.

- **Transformation specification and application:** an environment called AGG (Attributed Graph Grammars tool) is used for this experiment. AGG can be considered as a genuine programming environment based on graph transformations [12]. It provides 1) a programming language enabling the specification of graph grammars 2) a customizable interpreter enabling graph transformations. AGG was chosen because it allows the graphical expression of directed, typed and attributed graphs (for expressing specifications and rules). It has a powerful library containing notably algorithms for graph transformation [14], critical pair analysis, consistency checking, positive and negative application condition enforcement. AGG user interface is described in Fig. 13. Frame 1 is the grammar explorer. Fig. 13 Frames 2, 3 and 4 enable to specify sub-graphs composing a production: a negative application (frame 2), a left hand side (frame 3) and a right hand side (frame 4). The host graph on which a production will be applied is represented in Frame 5.

- **A tool for transformation application:** several Application Programming Interfaces are available to perform model-to-model transformations (e.g., DMOF at http://www.dstc.edu.au/Products/CORBA/M-OF/ or Univers@lis at http://universalis. elibel.tm.fr/site/). We tested AGG API as this API proposes to transform models with as graph transformations. This scenario is described in Fig. 14. An initial model along with a set of rules are transmitted to a Application Programming Interface that performs appropriate model transformations and provide a resulting model that can be edited.

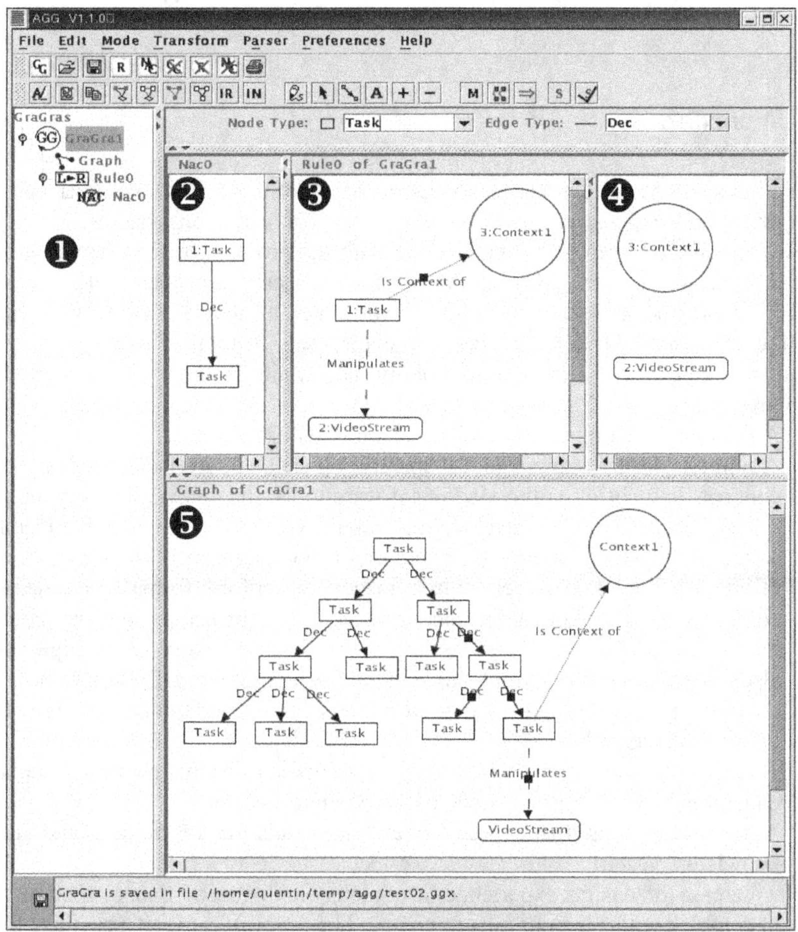

Fig. 13. AGG user interface.

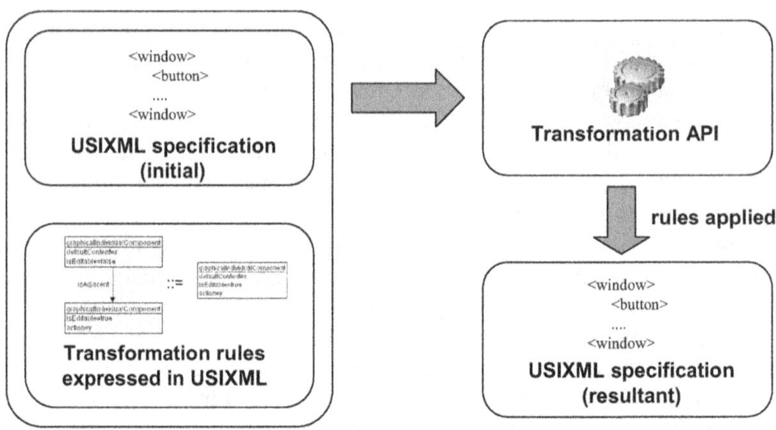

Fig. 14. Development process based on transformation application.

6 Conclusion

Information systems are subject to a constant pressure toward change. UIs represent an important and expensive software component of information systems. Multi-path UI development has been proposed to cope with the problem of UI adaptation to an evolving context of use. Multi-path UI development has been defined as an engineering method and tool that allows a designer to start a UI development by several entry points in the development cycle, and from this entry point get a substantial support to build a high quality UI. Main features of multi-path UI development are:

1. A flexible development process based on transformations.
2. A unique formal language to specify UI related artefacts. So far, these concepts have been hard coded in software tools, thus preventing anyone from reusing, redefining or exchanging them. USIXML provides a mean to overcome these shortcomings. The core of this language is composed of a set of integrated models expressed in a formal and uniform format, governed by a common meta-model definition, graphically expressible and a modular, modifiable and extensible repository of executable design knowledge that is also represented with a graphical syntax. Furthermore, a definition of an XML notation supporting the exchange of models and executable design knowledge has been presented.
3. A transformational approach based on systematic rules that guarantee semantic equivalence when applied, some of them being reversible.
4. A tool supporting the expression and manipulation of models and design knowledge visually.

With increase of design experience, a copious catalogue of transformation rules can be assembled into meaningful grammars. The level of support provided to the accomplishment of design steps varies from one transition to another. Indeed, some transitions are better known than others. For instance, the reification between physical and logical UI can be supported by hundreds of rules namely by widget selection rules. On the contrary, rules that enable the translation of a task model from a desktop PC to a handheld PC are, for now, understudied. Some transitions are intrinsically harder to support (e.g., abstraction transitions). For instance, retrieving a task model from the physical UI is not a trivial problem.

Acknowledgements

The authors would like to thank Cameleon partners who contributed to V1.2 of USIXML: Lionel Balme, Gaëlle Calvary, Cristina Chesta, Alexandre Demeure, Joëlle Coutaz, Jean-Thierry Lechein, Fabio Paternò, Stéphane Raymond, Carmen Santoro, and Youri Vanden Berghe. This paper is related to USIXML V1.4, an extension of USIXML V1.2 with dialog model, more inter-model mappings, a context model made up of user, platform, and environment, and the concrete user interface level. Laurent Bouillon is supported by Cameleon research project (http://giove.cnuce.cnr.it/cameleon.html) under the umbrella of the European Fifth Framework Programme (FP5-2000-IST2). Benjamin Michotte is supported by the SIMILAR network of excellence (http://www.similar.cc), the European research task force creating human-machine interfaces similar to human-human communication of the European Sixth Framework Programme (FP6-2002-IST1-507609).

References

1. Agrawal, A., Karsai, G., Ledeczi, K.: An End-to-end Domain-Driven Software Development Framework. In: Companion of the 18th Annual ACM SIGPLAN Conference on Object-oriented Programming Systems, Languages, and Applications OOPSLA'2003 (Anaheim, October 26-30, 2003). ACM Press, New York (2003) 8–15
2. Ali, M.F., Pérez-Quiñones M.A., Abrams M.: Building Multi-Platform User Interfaces with UIML. In: Seffah, A., Javahery, H. (eds.): Multiple User Interfaces: Engineering and Application Framework. John Wiley and Sons, New York (2003)
3. Bouillon, L., Vanderdonckt, J., Chow, K.C.: Flexible Re-engineering of Web Sites. In: Proc. of 8th ACM Int. Conf. on Intelligent User Interfaces IUI'2004 (Funchal, January 13-16, 2004). ACM Press, New York (2004) 132–139
4. Brown J.: Exploring Human-Computer Interaction and Software Engineering Methodologies for the Creation of Interactive Software. SIGCHI Bulletin 29,1 (1997) 32–35
5. Calvary, G., Coutaz, J., Thevenin, D.: A Unifying Reference Framework for the Development of Plastic User Interfaces. In: Little, M.R., Nigay, L. (eds.): Proc. of IFIP WG2.7 (13.2) Working Conference EHCI'2001 (Toronto, May 11-13, 2001). Lecture Notes in Computer Science, Vol. 2254. Springer-Verlag, Berlin (2001) 173–192
6. Calvary, G., Coutaz, J., Thevenin, D., Limbourg, Q., Bouillon, L., Vanderdonckt, J.: A Unifying Reference Framework for Multi-Target User Interfaces. Interacting with Computers 15,3 (2003) 289–308
7. Chikofsky, E.J., Cross, J.H.: Reverse Engineering and Design Recovery: A Taxonomy. IEEE Software 1,7 (1990) 13–17

8. Constantine, L.: Canonical Abstract Prototypes for Abstract Visual and Interaction Design. In: Jorge, J., Nunes, N.J., Falcão e Cunha, J. (eds.), Proc. of 10th Int. Workshop on Design, Specification, and Verification of Interactive Systems DSVIS'2003 (Funchal, June 4-6, 2003). Lecture Notes in Computer Science, Vol. 2844. Springer-Verlag, Berlin (2003) 1–9
9. Eisenstein, J., Vanderdonckt, J., Puerta, A.: Model-Based User-Interface Development Techniques for Mobile Computing. In: Lester, J. (ed.), Proc. of 5th ACM Int. Conf. on Intelligent User Interfaces IUI'2001 (Santa Fe, January 14-17, 2001). ACM Press, New York (2001) 69–76
10. Gaeremynck, Y., Bergman, L.D., Lau, T.: MORE for Less: Model Recovery from Visual Interfaces for Multi-Device Application Design. In: Proc. of 7th ACM Int. Conf. on Intelligent User Interfaces IUI'2003 (Miami, January 12-15, 2003). ACM Press, New York (2003) 69–76
11. Griffiths, T., Barclay, P.J., Paton, N.W., McKirdy, J., Kennedy, J., Gray, P.D., Cooper, R., Goble, C.A., da Silva, P.P.: Teallach: A Model-Based User Interface Development Environment for Object Databases. Interacting with Computers 14, 1 (December 2001) 31–68
12. Larman, C.: Applying UML and Patterns: An Introduction to Object-Oriented Analysis and Design and the Unified Process. Prentice Hall, Englewood Cliffs (2001)
13. Limbourg, Q., Vanderdonckt, J., Michotte, B., Bouillon, B.: TomatoXML, a General Purpose XML Compliant User Interface Description Language, TomatoXML V1.2.0. Working Paper n°105. Institut d'Administration et de Gestion (IAG), Louvain-la-Neuve (19 February 2004).
14. Limbourg, Q., Vanderdonckt, J.: Transformational Development of User Interfaces with Graph Transformations. In: Jacob, R., Limbourg, Q., Vanderdonckt, J. (eds.): Proc. of 5th Int. Conf. on Computer-Aided Design of User Interfaces CADUI'2004 (Madeira, January 14-16, 2004). Kluwer Academics Pub., Dordrecht (2004)
15. Luo, P.: A Human-Computer Collaboration Paradgim for Bridging Besign Conceptualization and Implementation. In: F. Paternò (ed.): Interactive Systems: Design, Specification, and Verification, Proc. of the 1st Eurographics Workshop on Design, Specification, and Verification of Interactive Systems DSV-IS'94 (Bocca di Magra, June 8-10, 1994). Springer-Verlag, Berlin (1995) 129–147
16. Luyten, K., Van Laerhoven, T., Coninx, K., Van Reeth, F.: Runtime Transformations for Modal Independent User Interface Migration. Interacting with Computers 15,3 (2003) 329–347
17. Mori, G., Paternò, F., Santoro, C.: Tool Support for Designing Nomadic Applications. In: Proc. of 7th ACM Int. Conf. on Intelligent User Interfaces IUI'2003 (Miami, January 12-15, 2003). ACM Press, New York (2003)141–148
18. Olsen, D.R., Jefferies, S., Nielsen, T., Moyes, W., Fredrickson, P.: Cross Modal Interaction using XWEB. In: Proc. of the 13th Annual ACM Symposium on User Interface Software and Technology UIST'2000 (San Diego, November 5-8, 2000). ACM Press, New York (2000) 191–200
19. Partsch, H., Steinbruggen, R.: Program Transformation Systems. ACM Computing Surveys 15,3 (September 1983), 199–236
20. Paternò, F. Model-Based Design and Evaluation of Interactive Applications. Springer-Verlag, Berlin (2000)
21. Puerta, A., Eisenstein, J.: Developing a Multiple User Interface Representation Framework for Industry. In: Seffah, A., Javahery, H. (eds.): Multiple User Interfaces: Engineering and Application Framework. John Wiley and Sons, New York (2003)
22. Rozenberg, G. (ed.). Handbook of Graph Grammars and Computing by Graph Transformation. World Scientific, Singapore (1997)
23. Sucrow, B.: On Integrating Software-Ergonomic Aspects in the Specification Process of Graphical User Interfaces. Transactions of the SDPS Journal of Integrated Design & Process Science. Society for Design & Process Science 2,2 (June 1998) 32–42

24. Sumner, T., Bonnardel, N., Kallak, B.H.: The Cognitive Ergonomics of Knowledge-Based Design Support Systems PAPERS: Intelligent Support. In: Proceedings of ACM Conference on Human Factors in Computing Systems CHI'97 (Atlanta, April 1997). ACM Press, New York (1997) 83–90
25. Vanderdonckt, J., Berquin, P.: Towards a Very Large Model-Based Approach for User Interface Development. In: Paton, N.W., Griffiths, T. (eds.): Proc. of 1st IEEE Int. Workshop on User Interfaces to Data Intensive Systems UIDIS'99 (Edinburgh, September 5-6, 1999). IEEE Computer Society Press, Los Alamitos (1999) 76–85
26. Wong, C., Chu, H.H., Katagiri, M.A., Single-Authoring Technique for Building Device-Independent Presentations. In: Proc. of W3C Workshop on Device Independent Authoring Techniques (St. Leon-Rot, 15-26 September 2002), accessible at http://www.w3.org/2002/07/DIAT/posn/docomo.pdf

Discussion

[Stephen Gilroy] USIXML is an instantiation of your particular graph. Do you think USIXML has sufficient expressiveness to represent all the aspects of your graph?

> [Victor Jaquero] Yes USIXML is a raw transcript from our graph structure to an XML-like syntax. USIXML has been designed to overcome the intrinsic tree-like structure of XML languages. Like other language (e.g., GXL), USIXML allows to define a real graph structure with nodes and edges. So, as soon as a concept is defined in our conceptual graphs it is transposable into USIXML.

[Stephen Gilroy] Is USIXML extensible?

> [Victor Jaquero] At the model level USIXML allows to define any kind of model. In this sense it is possible to instantiate new context models, new domain models,...At meta-model level USIXML offers a modular structure which clearly segregates the models it describes (these models being integrated with inter-model relationships). Consequently, integrating new models in USIXML is facilitated. The model and its concept is simply declared along with the relationships that integrates this newcomer with existing models. Rules exploiting this new model can be defined afterward. Another point of extensibility is inside existing models themselves. In the concrete user interface models for instance node types relevant to different modalities (e.g., 2-D graphic and vocal) are clearly differentiated in separated sub-trees. The introduction of a new modality, for instance, would consist in introducing a new sub-tree into the node classification.

[Peter Forbrig] Is the idea to transform the model interactively, or is there a set of pre-defined rules?

> [Victor Jaquero] There is an editor for rules (AGG) that allows them to be created for the particular application, as well as re-using existing rules (these rules have been defined for our case studies).

[Michael Harrison] So are the rules applied interactively, or does the system specify how to apply them?

[Victor Jaquero] The application of the rules may depend on different types of scenarios, they can be applied blindly (with no user control), or step by step with undo facilities. TransformiXML GUI enables also to define alternate transformation systems for a same development step, it is also possible modify the application order of rules populating a transformation system.

A Novel Dialog Model for the Design of Multimodal User Interfaces

Robbie Schaefer, Steffen Bleul, Wolfgang Mueller

Paderborn University, Fuerstenallee 11,
33102 Paderborn, Germany
robbie@c-lab.de, bleul@upb.de, wolfgang@c-lab.de

Abstract. Variation in different mobile devices with different capabilities and interaction modalities as well as changing user context in nomadic applications, poses huge challenges to the design of user interfaces. To avoid multiple designs for each device or modality, it is almost a must to employ a model-based approach. In this short paper, we present a new dialog model for multimodal interaction together with an advanced control model, which can either be used for direct modeling by an interface designer or in conjunction with higher level models.

1 Introduction and Related Work

Most natural human computer interaction can be achieved by providing the right user interface for the right situation, which also implies selecting an adequate device together with one or several interaction modalities. For this approach, any available input or output device with their respective modalities can be used, which requires a framework to synchronize the interaction as, e.g., presented with W3Cs Multimodal Interaction Framework [1].

These environments can be considered to be highly dynamical with the consequence that just providing platform specific UIs is not sufficient to support all possible kinds of devices and modalities. Therefore, we propose a model based approach to develop UIs that can be provided and adapted on the fly.

As we have identified the necessity to work with UI modeling (see also. [2]), we present MIPIM (Multimodal Interface Presentation and Interaction Model), a new dialog model for the design of multimodal User Interfaces. MIPIM concerns lower levels in contrast to high level approaches as task modeling, e.g. given in [2]. Mainly covered are UI specification and control modeling that allow easy modifications of the UIs during the development cycles and support automated UI adaptations.

2 Dialog Model

Our dialog model provides three components for interaction, dialog flow, and presentation. Since our model aims for multimodality, user interaction is received by

R. Bastide, P. Palanque, and J. Roth (Eds.): EHCI-DSVIS 2004, LNCS 3425, pp. 221-223, 2005.

the *multimodal interaction* component. This component accepts input in different modalities and triggers the behavior resolver, which in turn starts generating the resulting UI that will be presented by the *multimodal interface presentation* component for the activated modalities. The dialog flow specification plays a central part. On a first glance it resembles the model, UIML [3] is based on, with a separation between structure and style and the specification of the dialog behavior. However, the specification of the dialog behavior takes a different approach and is based on DSN concepts [4].

DSN allows bundling several local states of a UI and performing a multi state transition through the definition of variables and events together with rules that map events to a new set of states in one pass.

The second important property of this new dialog model is the support of generic widgets that are modality agnostic by providing most basic operations, as described in [5], along with a presentation of the architecture and an according XML-based modeling language. The *multimodal presentation* component is used to map the generic widgets to widgets in a specific modality, while the interaction component does a reverse mapping of these widgets and by that allowing the use of virtually any device or modality for interaction.

3 Conclusion and Future Work

We have presented the MIPIM dialog model, which provides the theoretical background of the framework we presented in [5]. At the moment, we have built a prototype implementation for mobile phones, which demonstrates the efficiency in which our dialog model works on limited devices. In near future, we explore further how to establish real multi device interaction. The foundation is already laid in the control model. Furthermore we plan to integrate our work in larger environments with respective mappings.

References

1. Larson, J.A.., Raman, D.R.(eds.): Multimodal Interaction Framework. W3C Note (2003)
2. Paternò, F., Santoro, C.: One model, many interfaces. In: Proceedings Forth International Conference on Computer Aided Design of User Interfaces, Kluwer Academic (2002)
3. Abrams, M., Phanouriou, C., Batongbacal, A.L., Williams, S.M., Shuster, J.E.: UIML: an appliance-independent xml user interface language. In Computer Networks 31, Elsevier Science (1999)
4. Curry, M.B., Monk, A.F.: Dialogue modeling of graphical user interfaces with a production system. In Behaviour and Information Technology, Vol. 14, No. 1, pp 41-55 (1995)
5. Mueller, W., Schaefer, R., Bleul, S.: Interactive Multimodal User Interfaces for Mobile Devices. In: Proc. 37th Hawaii International Conference on System Sciences (2004).

Discussion

[Remi Bastide] I wonder if there is a significant difference in expressiveness between DSN and UML Statecharts.

[Robbie Schaefer] Statecharts are very powerful and can express many things that DSN cannot. But DSN is more convenient to use.

[Michael Harrison] DSN appear to be an enconding of StateCharts.

[Remi Bastide] Statecharts avoid the combinatorial explosion of finite state machines.

[Robbie Schaefer] I will have to examine that.

Navigation Patterns – Pattern Systems Based on Structural Mappings

Jürgen Ziegler, Markus Specker

University Duisburg-Essen, Germany
ziegler@informatik.uni-duisburg.de
specker@informatik.uni-duisburg.de

The use of design patterns as a methodical approach to codifying and communicating design knowledge and best practice solutions has become popular in software engineering and, more recently, also in the field of human computer interaction (e.g. [Tidwell, 1999], [Borchers, 2001], [Lyardet et al., 1999] and [van Duyne et al., 2002]). Existing HCI pattern collections, however, often appear rather unsystematic and arbitrarily composed, lacking the quality of a coherent pattern language that some authors have demanded. To address this problem, we propose a stronger conceptual integration of the notions *design pattern* and *design space*. Design spaces allow to explore potential design solutions along the values of one or more defined dimensions. We aim at systematizing design patterns by allocating (or deriving) them in (or from) design spaces. This approach allows to not only categorize existing patterns, but also to derive new patterns (which may subsequently be analyzed for their usability).

The design space with associated patterns we propose here, is aimed at describing user navigation in interactive systems. The central idea is that a navigation pattern is defined by the mapping from the structure of the content to be shown and navigated, to the actual navigation structure offered by the user interface. This notion corresponds to the well-known model-view concept and assumes that each content structure type (essentially sets, lists, hierarchies and networks) can, in principle, be mapped to all types of navigation structures (see Fig. 1). Three major cases can be distinguished for this mapping:

In the *isomorphic* case, both the content structure and the navigation structure are identical. This is the case, for instance, when mapping a hierarchical content structure to a tree widget, which supports hierarchical access to the content nodes. While this case is straightforward and probably the easiest for the user in terms of transparency, there are two important other cases that may be used for a variety of reasons such as screen space limitation, visual search etc. In the *structure loss* case, complex content structures are mapped to simpler navigation structures by leaving out dependency information (example see Fig. 2 top). Conversely, there is the case of *structure gain*, where simple content structures, such as sets of information objects, can be accessed through more complex navigation structures (such as a tree) which are created interactively 'on the fly' based on some attribute or characteristic of the content (see Fig. 2 bottom). As an example, a flat list of emails can be grouped hierarchically by sender and subject. Although this dynamically created navigation tree may look identical to a 'real' hierarchy, there are important differences in the underlying

R. Bastide, P. Palanque, and J. Roth (Eds.): EHCI-DSVIS 2004, LNCS 3425, pp. 224-227, 2005.

semantics and the operations the user can perform. Rearranging nodes in the case of grouped emails, for instance, is not meaningful.

The pattern categories presented are elementary and can be combined in a variety of ways for designing navigation in real user interfaces. We believe that this approach allows a more grounded and systematic exploration and evaluation of navigational patterns. Future work is planned to investigate usability characteristics of these patterns to associate suitable usability metrics with each pattern.

Navigation structure / Content structure	Set	List	Hierarchy	Net
Set	panel with objects (e.g. as icons or thumbnails)	objects interactively sorted by some attributes	multi-level grouping of set elements (based e.g. on value of some attribute)	-/?
List	panel with ordered objects (e.g. as icons or thumbnails)	menu list, index	multi-level grouping of list items (based e.g. on value of some attribute)	-/?
Hierarchy	-/?	single menu per level, 'bread crumbs' list	tree view with expand/collapse functions. menu with multiple levels visible,	tree with auto-generated cross-links
Net	-/?	list of traversed nodes	tree view showing spanning tree	graph representation of network

Structure gain

Structure loss

Fig. 1. Design space for navigation patterns ('-/?' : no meaningful patterns known). Several concrete patterns can exist in each category.

Home > Mitgliedervorteile > Europa > Frankreich

- SW-Technologies
  - Agents
    - Berners-Lee, T.; Hendler, J. & Lassila, O. 2001 The Semantic Web
    - Maybury, M. & Wahlster, W. 1998 Readings in Intelligent User Interfaces
  - Graphen
  - Groupware
  - Knowledge Processing
    - Berners-Lee, T.; Hendler, J. & Lassila, O. 2001 The Semantic Web
  - User Interface Systems & Tools
    - Dourish, P.; Edwards, W.K.; Lamarca, A. & Salisbury, M. 1999 Presto: An Experimental Architecture for F
    - Boies,S. J. ; Ukelson,J. P. & Gould, J. D. 1993 Using ITS to Create an Insurance Industry
    - Adolf,Jurine 1989 An expert system for the selection of inpu
    - Donald D. Cowan & Carlos J.P. Lucena 1995 Abstract Data Views: An Interface Specific
    - H.J. Bullinger (Ed.) 1994 IAO - Forum: Neue Software-Technologien
    - Tißen,A. 1991 A Case-Based Architecture for a Doaloque

Fig. 2. *Top*: example for the mapping from *hierarchy* to *list* ('bread crumbs' pattern, only one path into a hierarchy is visible). *Bottom*: mapping from *list* to *hierarchy* by multi-level grouping of emails.

References

[Borchers, 2001] Borchers, J.:A Pattern Approach to Interaction Design. Chichester, USA, John Wiley & Sons, (2001).

[Lyardet et al., 1999] Lyardet, F., Rossi, G., Schwabe, D. : Discovering Patterns in the WWW. Multimedia Tools and Applications, 8, 293-308.

[Tidwell, 1999] Tidwell, J.: Common Ground: A Pattern Language for Human Computer Interface Design. – http://www.mit.edu/~jtidwell/common_ground.html

[van Duyne et al., 2002] van Duyne, B., Landay, J.A., Hong, J.I.: The Design of Sites: Patterns, Principles, and Processes for Crafting a Customer-Centered Web Experience, Boston USA: Addison-Wesley, (2002).

Discussion

[Gerit van der Veer] I like the approach of building a design space and then populating it. This is the opposite of what we did, where we started from user problems and started categorizing based on problems seen by users. You are right that this approach will not lead to solutions, but this helps understand the design space.

> [Jürgen Ziegler] The use of design spaces here gives a lot of insight. But there may be patterns that are more valuable expressed from the user's point of view, particularly if it represents best practices or years of experience. The two approaches should come together.

[Bonnie John] I like this stuff. What is navigational about this space? it looks like representation of structured information. Navigation is about getting from one place to another.

> [Jürgen Ziegler] Essentially you need means of getting from one place to another. The patterns provide the access instruments to the content.

[Bonnie John] But someone could use an expandable tree view, expand everything and simply scroll over it. There is missing some way of capturing the interaction component.

> [Jürgen Ziegler] Yes, this is primarily structural. There needs to be some way of showing how they are used and composed.

[Bonnie John] And how they are useful.

> [Jürgen Ziegler] We would like to come up with usability characteristics. Is it better to have a single expanding tree or multiple expanding trees? For what purposes is each best appropriate.

[Bonnie John] There was some stuff you listed that doesn't appear in the design space. E.g., drawings with a lot of detail.

> [Jürgen Ziegler] Yes, there is room for further distinctions, like if you have a large map.

[Bonnie John] I'm trying to fit in some of the examples you had, like the detailed view in the wired view, used to navigate in a CAD system.

[Jürgen Ziegler] It depends on what the interactor is being used for. Is it a hierarchical collection of documents? It is still important to know that the underlying thing is hierarical. I think it fits into the scheme.

[Morten Borup Harning] I have a problem with what you call the structure gain. I think that content-wise, what is there is not what you would call content. E.g., if you have a simple list of things, you need to add information to do that. Otherwise, the added information will be random, which moves the content over to the other side.

[Jürgen Ziegler] That's an issue for discussion. I was thinking of explicit structural representations, like in the mail or task sorting example, the information must be there showing where the items are categorized. One might argue that it's difficult to build up a structure from nothing, and that is true. Some information must be used to build the structure even if it was not there in the first place.

[Morten Borup Harning] I would argue from the point of view of the pattern, it makes no difference if the structure was initially there or not.

[Jürgen Ziegler] But there may be impacts on the interface. For example, can we allow drag and drop between clusters? This is a surface operation that may not be encoded in the underlying data structure.

Spatial Control of Interactive Surfaces in an Augmented Environment

Stanislaw Borkowski, Julien Letessier, and James L. Crowley

Project PRIMA, Lab. GRAVIR-IMAG
INRIA Rhône-Alpes, 655, ave de l'Europe
38330 Montbonnot, France
{Stan.Borkowski, Julien.Letessier, James.Crowley}@inrialpes.fr

Abstract. New display technologies will enable designers to use every surface as a support for interaction with information technology. In this article, we describe techniques and tools for enabling efficient man-machine interaction in computer augmented multi-surface environments. We focus on explicit interaction, in which the user decides when and where to interact with the system. We present three interaction techniques using simple actuators: fingers, a laser pointer, and a rectangular piece of cardboard. We describe a graphical control interface constructed from an automatically generated and maintained environment model. We implement both the automatic model acquisition and the interaction techniques using a Steerable Camera-Projector (SCP) system.

1 Introduction

Surfaces dominate the physical world. Every object is confined in space by its surface. Surfaces are pervasive and play a predominant role in human perception of the environment. We believe that augmenting surfaces with information technology will act as an interaction modality easily adopted for a variety of tasks. In this article, we make a step towards making this a reality.

Current display technologies are based on planar surfaces [8, 17, 23]. Displays are usually treated as access points to a common information space, where users manipulate vast amounts of information with a common set of controls. Given recent developments in low-cost display technologies, the available interaction surface will continue to grow, forcing the migration of interfaces from a single, centralized screen to many, space-distributed interactive surfaces. New interaction tools that accommodate multiple distributed interaction surfaces will be required.

In this article, we address the problem of spatial control of an interactive display surface within an office or similar environment. In our approach, the user can choose any planar surface as a physical support for interaction. We use a steerable assembly composed of a camera and video projector to augment surfaces with interactive capabilities. We exploit our projection-based augmentation to attain three goals: *(a)* modelling the geometry of the environment by using it as a source of information, *(b)* creation of interactive surfaces anywhere in the scene, and *(c)* realisation of novel interaction techniques through augmentation of a handheld display surface.

R. Bastide, P. Palanque, and J. Roth (Eds.): EHCI-DSVIS 2004, LNCS 3425, pp. 228-244, 2005.

In the following sections, we present the technical infrastructure for experimentation with multiple interactive surfaces in an office environment (Sections 3 and 4). We then discuss spatial control of application interfaces in Section 5. In Sections 6, 7 and 8 we describe three applications that enable explicit control of interface location. We illustrate interaction techniques with a single interaction surface controlled in a multi-surface environment, but we emphasize that they can be easily extended to the control of multiple independent interfaces controlled within a common space.

2 Camera-Projector Systems

Camera-projector systems are increasingly used in augmented environment systems [11, 13, 21]. Projecting images is a simple way of augmenting everyday objects and allows alteration of their appearance or function. Associating a video projector with a video camera offers an inexpensive means of making projected images interactive. However, standard video-projectors have small projection area which limits their flexibility in creating interaction spaces. We can achieve some steerability on a rigidly mounted projector by moving sub windows within the cone of projection [22], but extending or moving the display surface requires increasing the angle range of the projector beam. This requires adding more projectors, an expensive endeavor. An alternative is to use a steerable projector [2, 12]. This approach is becoming more attractive, due to a trend towards increasingly small and inexpensive video projectors.

Projection is an ecological (non-intrusive) way of augmenting the environment. Projection does not change the augmented object itself, only its appearance. Augmentation can be used to supplement the functionality of objects. In [12], ordinary artefacts such as walls, shelves, and cups are transformed into informative surfaces, but the original functionality of the objects does not change. The objects become physical supports for virtual functionalities. An example of object enhancement is presented in [1], where users can interact with both physical and virtual ink on a projection-augmented whiteboard.

While vision and projection-based interfaces meet most of the ergonomic requirements of HCI, they suffer from lack of robustness due to clutter and insufficiently developed methods for text input. People naturally avoid obstructing projected images, so occlusion is not a problem when camera and projector share the same viewpoint. As for the issue of text input on projected steerable interfaces, currently available projected keyboards like the Canesta Projection Keyboard [16] rely on hardware configuration, which excludes their use on arbitrary surfaces. Resolving this issue is important for development of projection-based interfaces, but it is outside the scope of this work.

3 The Steerable Camera-Projector System

In our experiments, we use a Steerable Projector-Camera (SCP) assembly (Figure 1). It enables us to experiment with multiple interactive surfaces in an office environment.

Fig. 1. The Steerable Camera-Projector pair.

The Steerable Camera-Projector (SCP) platform is a device that gives a video-projector and its associated camera two mechanical degrees of freedom, pan and tilt. Note that the projector-camera pair is mounted in such a way that the projected beam overlaps with the camera view. Association of the camera and projector creates a powerful actuator-sensor pair enabling observation of users' actions within the camera field of view. Endowed with the ability to modify the scene using projected light, projector-camera systems can be exploited as sensors (Section 5.2).

4 Experimental Laboratory Environment

The experiments described below are performed in our Augmented Meeting Environment (AME). The AME is an ordinary office equipped with ability to sense and act. The sensing infrastructure includes five steerable cameras, a fixed wide angle camera, and a microphone array. The wide angle camera has a field of view that covers the entire room. Steerable cameras are installed in each of the four corners of the room. A fifth steerable camera is centrally mounted in the room as part of the steerable camera-projector system (SCP).

Within the AME, we can define several surfaces suitable for supporting projected interfaces. Some of these are marked by white boundaries in Figure 2. These regions were detected by the SCP during an automatic off-line environmental model building phase described below (Section 5.2). Surfaces marked with dashed boundaries can be optionally calibrated and included in the generated environment model using the device described in Section 8.

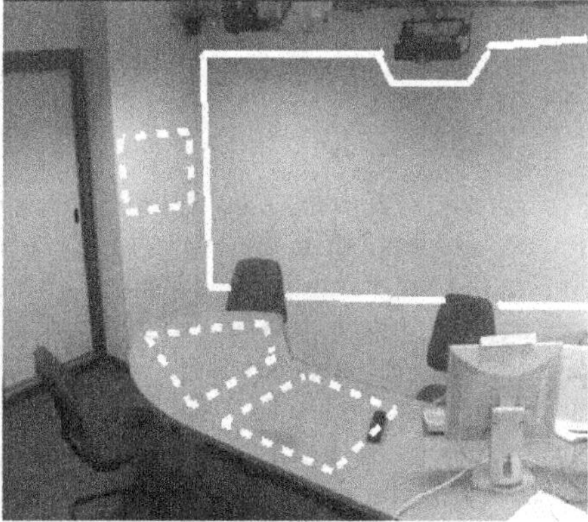

Fig. 2. Planar surfaces in the environment.

5 Spatial Control of Displays

Interaction combines action and perception. In an environment where users may interact with a multitude of services and input/output (IO) devices, both perception and interaction can be complex. We present a sample scenario in Section 5.1 and describe our approach to automatic environment model acquisition in Section 5.2, but first we discuss the relative merits of our approach to interaction within an augmented environment.

Explicit vs. Implicit. Over the last few years, several research groups have experimented with environments augmented with multiple display surfaces using various devices such as flat screens, whiteboards, video-projectors and steerable video-projectors [3, 8, 11, 13, 21, 23]. Most of these groups focuse on the integration of technical infrastructure into a coherent automated system, treating the problem of new methods for spatial control of interfaces as a secondary issue. Typically, the classic paradigm of drag and drop is used to manipulate application interfaces on a set of wall displays and table display [8]. In such systems, discontinuities in the transition between displays disrupt interaction and make direct adaptation of drag and drop difficult.

An alternative is to liberate the user by letting the system take control of interface location. In [11], the steerable display is automatically redirected to the surface most appropriate for the user. Assuming a sufficient environment model, the interface follows the user by jumping from one surface to another. However, this solution has disadvantages. For one, it requires continuous update of the environment model. More importantly, the system has to infer if the user wants to be followed or not. Such a degree of understanding of human activity is beyond the state of the art.

The authors in [3] combine automatic and explicit control. By default, the interface follows its owner in the augmented room. The user can also choose a display from a list. However, their approach assumes that the user is able to correctly identify the listed devices. Moreover, the method of passing back and forth from automatic to manual control mode is not clearly defined. In this work, we focus on developing interaction techniques that enable users to explicitly control the interface position in space.

Ecological vs. Emmbedded. In ubiquitous computing, panoply of small interconnected devices embedded in the environment or worn by the user are assumed to facilitate continuous and intuitive access to virtual information spaces and services. Many researchers follow this approach and investigate new interaction types based on sensors embedded in artifacts or worn by users [14, 18, 19]. Although embedding electronic devices leads to a number of efficient interface designs, in many circumstances it is unwise to assume that everyone will be equipped with the necessary technology. Moreover, as shown in [1, 3], one can obtain pervasive interfaces by embedding computational infrastructure in the environment instead. Our approach is to create new interaction modes and devices by augmenting the functionality of mundane artifacts without modifying their primary structure.

User-centric vs. Sensor-centric. Coutaz *et al.* [7] highlight the duality of interactive systems. We apply this duality to the analysis of environment models, extending our understanding of the perceived physical space. When building an environment model, the system typically generates a sensor-centric representation of the scene, but this abstraction is not necessarily comprehensible for the human actor. A common understanding of the environment requires translation of the model into a user-centric representation. Such an approach is presented in [3], where the authors introduce an interface for controlling lights in a room. Lamps are shown graphically on a 2D map of the environment, and the user chooses from the map which light to dim or to brighten. The problem is that modeling the real-world environment in order to generate and maintain a human-comprehensible representation of the space is a difficult and expensive task. Moreover, from the user's perspective, the physical location of the controlled devices is not as important as the effect of changing a device's state. Rather than showing the user a symbolic representation of the world, we enrich the sensor-centric model with contextual cues that facilitate mapping from an abstract model to the physical environment.

In summary, we impose the following constraints on multi-surface systems:

1. Users have control of the spatial distribution of applications when they have direct or actuator-mediated access to its interface.
2. Users can control the system both "as they come" without specific tools, and with the use of control devices.
3. The mapping between the symbolic representation of the controller interface and the real world is understandable by an unexperienced user, provided sufficient contextual cues.
4. The underlying sensor-centric model of the environment is generated and updated automatically.

In the following section, we illustrate our expectations of a multi-surface interaction system with a scenario.

5.1 Scenario

John, a professor in a research laboratory, is in his office preparing slides for a project meeting. As the project partners arrive, John hurryly moves the presentation he just finished to a large wall-mounted screen in the meeting room, choosing it from a list of available displays. The list contains almost twenty possible locations in his office and in the meeting room. John has no trouble making his selection because the name of each surface is beside its image as it appears in the scene.

During the meeting, John uses a wide screen to present slides about software architecture. John uses an ordinary laser-pointer to highlight important elements in the slide. The slides are also projected onto a whiteboard so that John can make notes directly on them by drawing on the white board with an ink pen. On command he can record his notations in a new slide that combines his notations with the projected material. At one point, John sees that there is not enough free space on the white board, so he decides to move the projected slide to free some space for notes. He "double-blinks" the laser-pointer on the image, so that the image follows the laser dot.

While the project participants discuss the problem at hand, it becomes apparent that it is useful to split the meeting in three sub-workgroups. John takes one of the groups to his office. From the display list, John chooses the largest surface in his office. He sends the slide to this surface. A second group gathers around the desk in the meeting room. John sends the relevant slide from the wide screen to the desk with the use of a laser-pointer. The third smaller group decides to work in the back of the meeting room. Since there is no display, they take a cardboard onto which they transfer their application interface. They continue their work by interacting directly with the interface projected on the portable screen.

5.2 Environment Modeling and Image Rectification

In our approach to human-computer interaction, it is critical that the system is aware of its working space in order to provide appropriate feedback to the user. The graphical user interfaces enabling explicit control of the display location (Sections 6 and 7) are generated based on the environment model. They contain information facilitating mapping of the virtual sensor-centric model to the physical space.

Although 3D environment models have many advantages for applications involving the use of steerable interfaces, they are difficult to create and maintain. One often makes the simplifying assumption that they exist beforehand and do not change over time [3, 11]. Instead, we propose automatic acquisition of a 2D environment model. The model consists of two layers: *(a)* a labelled 2D map of the environment in the SCP's spherical coordinate system and *(b)* a database containing the acquired characteristics for each detected planar surface. Our environment model directly reflects the available sensor capabilities of our AME.

To acquire the model of the environment, we exploit the SCP's ability to modify the environment by projecting and controlling images in the scene. Model acquisition consists of two phases: first, planar surfaces are detected and labelled with unique identifiers, and second, an image of each planar surface is captured and stored in the model database. In the second phase, the system projects a sample image on each planar surface detected in the environment model and takes a shot of the scene with the camera that has the projected image in its field of view. The images show the available interaction surfaces together with their surroundings. They are used later-on to provide users with contextual information which facilitates the mapping between the sensor-centric environment model and the physical world.

In order to customize the system, users should have the ability to supplement or replace the images in the model database with other data structures (e.g. text labels or video sequences). Using an interaction tool described in Section 8, the model is updated each time a new planar surface is defined in the environment.

Detection of planar surfaces. Most existing methods for projector-screen geometry acquisition provide a 3D model of the screen [5, 25]. However, such methods require the use of a calibrated projector-camera pair separated by a significant base distance. Thus, they are not suitable for our laboratory. In our system, we employ a variation of the method described in [2]. We use a steerable projector and a distant non-calibrated video camera to detect and estimate orientation of planar surfaces in the scene.The orientation of a surface with respect to the beamer is used to calculate a pre-warp that is applied to the projected image. The pre-warp compensates for oblique projective deformations caused by the non-orthogonality of the projector's optical axis relative to the screen surface. Note that the pre-warped image uses only a subset of the available pixels. When images are projected at extreme angles, the effective resolution can drop to a fraction of the projector's nominal resolution. This implies the need for an interface layout adaptation mechanism, that takes into account readability of the interface at a given projector-screen configuration. Adaptation of interfaces is a vast research problem and is not treated in this work.

6 Listing the Available Resources

In this section, we present a menu-like automatically generated interface enabling a user to choose the location of the display or application interface.

Pop-up and scroll-down menus are known in desktop-based interfaces for at least twenty years. Since planar surfaces in the environment can be seen as potential resources, it is natural to use a menu as a means for choosing a location for the interface.

Together with the projected image as application interface, we project an interactive button that is sensitive to touch-like movements of the user's fingertip. When the user touches the button, a list of available screen locations appears (Figure 3).

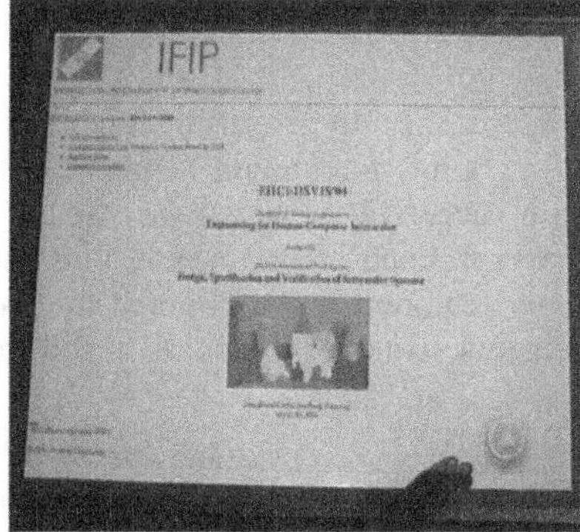

Fig. 3. Interacting with a list of displays (envisionment).

As mentioned in Section 5, we enhance the controller interface with cues that help map the interface elements to the physical world. Therefore, we present each list item as an image taken by one of the cameras installed in the room. We automatically generate the list based on images taken during the off-line model building process (Section 5.2). The images show the available interaction surfaces together with their surroundings. The user chooses a new location for the interface by passing a finger over a corresponding image. Note that one of the images shows a white cardboard, which is an interaction tool described in Section 8. In order to avoid accidental selection, we include a "confirm" button. The user cancels the interaction with the controller application by touching the initialization button again. The list also disappears if there is no interaction for a fixed period of time.

One can easily extend our image-based approach for providing contextual cues from interface control to general control of visual-output devices. For example, instead of showing a map of controllable lamps in a room, we can display a series of short sequences showing the corresponding parts of the room under changing light settings. This allows the user to visualize the effects of interaction with the system before actual execution.

6.1 Vision-Based Touch Detection

Using vision as an user-input device for a projected interface is an elegant solution because *(a)* it allows for direct manipulation, i.e. no intermediary pointing device is used, and *(b)* it is ecological – no intrusive user equipment is required, and bare-hand interaction is possible. This approach has been validated by a number of research projects, for instance the DigitalDesk [24], the Magic Table [1] or the Tele-Graffiti application [20].

Existing vision-based interactive systems track the acting member (finger, hand, or head) and produce actions (visual feedback and/or system side effects) based on recognized gestures. One drawback is that a tracking system can only detect apparition, movement and disparition events, but no "action" event comparable to the mouse-click in conventional user interfaces, because a finger tap cannot be detected by a vision system alone [24]. In vision-based UIs, triggering a UI feature (e.g. a button widget) is usually performed by holding (or "dwelling") the actuator (e.g. over the widget) [1, 20].

Various authors have tried different approaches to finger tracking, such as correlation tracking, model-based contour tracking, foreground segmentation and shape filtering, etc. While many of these are successful in constrained setups, they perform poorly for a projected UI or in unconstrained environments. Furthermore, they are computationally expensive. Since our requirements are limited to detecting fingers dwelling over button-style UI elements, we don't require a full-fledged tracker.

Approach. We implement an appearance-based method based on monitoring the perceived luminance over UI widgets. Consider the two areas depicted in Figure 4.

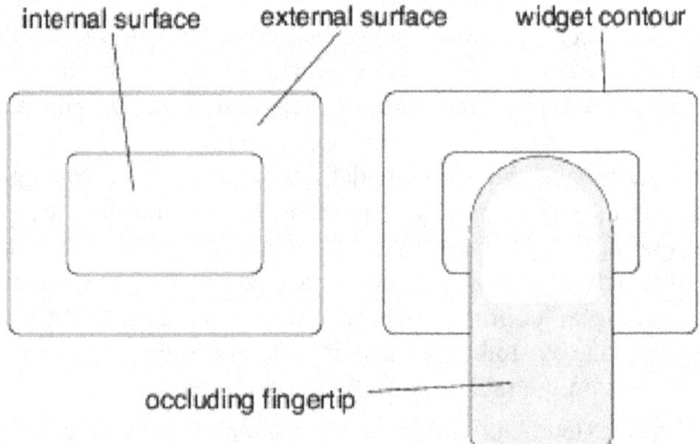

Fig. 4. Surfaces defined to detect touch-like gestures over a widget.

The inner region is assumed to roughly be of the same size as a finger. We denote $L_o(t)$ and $L_i(t)$ to be the average luminance over the outer and inner surface at time t, and

$$\Delta L(t) := |L_o(t) - L_i(t)|$$

Assuming that the observed widget has a reasonably uniform luminance, ΔL is close to zero at rest, and is high when a finger hovers over the widget. We define the threshold θ to be twice the median value of $\Delta L(t)$ over time when the widget is not occluded. Given the measured values of $\Delta L(t)$, the system generates the event e_0 (or e_1), at each discrete timestep t when $\Delta L(t)<\theta$ (or $\geq\theta$). These events are fed into a simple state machine that generates a *Touch* event after a dwell delay τ (Figure 5).

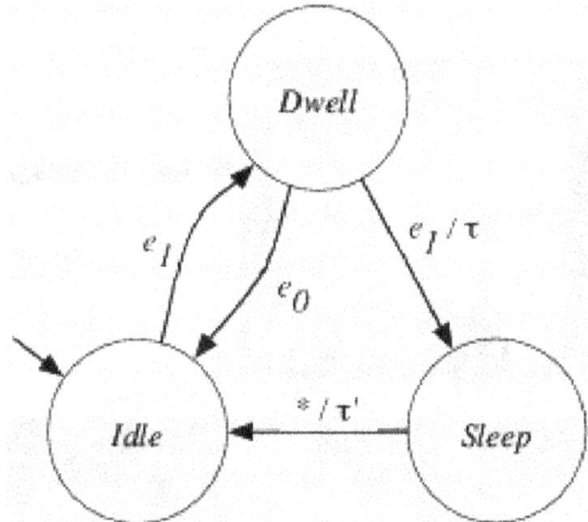

Fig. 5. The finite state machine used to process widget events.

We define two delays: τ to prevent false alarms (the *Dwell* → *Sleep* transition is only triggered after this delay), and τ' to avoid unwanted repetitive triggering (the *Sleep* → *Idle* transition is only triggered after this delay). A *Touch* event is issued whenever entering the *Sleep* state. τ and τ' are chosen equal to 200 ms. This technique achieves robustness against full occlusion of the UI component (e.g. by the user's hand or arm), since such occlusions cause ΔL to remain under the chosen threshold.

Experimental results. Our relatively simple approach provides good results because it is robust to changes in lighting conditions (it is a memory-less process), and occlusions (due to the dynamic nature of event generation and area-based filtering). Furthermore, it is implemented as a real-time process (it runs at camera frequency with less than 50 ms latency), although its cost scales linearly with the number of widgets to monitor.

An example application implemented with our "Sensitive Widgets" approach is shown in Figure 6. The minimal user interface consists of four projected buttons that can be "pressed" i.e. partially occluded with one or more fingers, to navigate through a slideshow.

Using this prototype, we confirm that our approach is robust to arbitrary changes in lighting conditions (the interface remains active during the changes) and full occlusion of widgets.

Integration. We integrate "Sensitive widgets" into a Tk application in an object oriented fashion: they are created and behave as usual Tk widgets. The implementation completely hides the underlying vision process, and provides activation (*Click*) events without uncertainty.

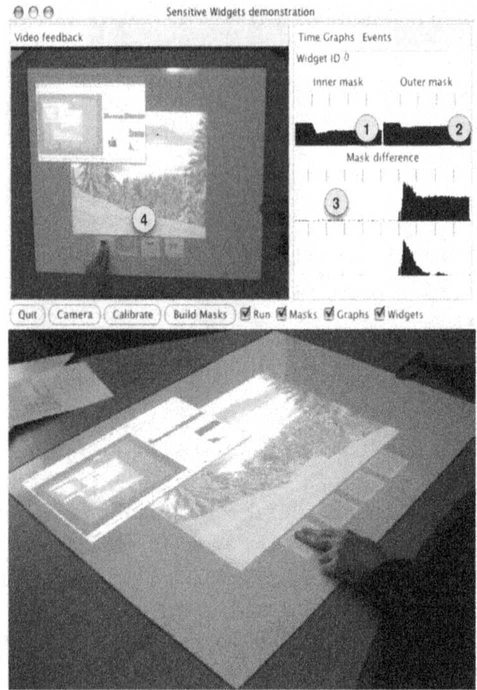

Fig. 6. The "Sensitive Widgets" demonstration interface. *Left:* The graphs exhibit the evolution of a variable in time: *(1)* $L_i(t)$; *(2)* $L_o(t)$; *(3)* $\Delta L(t)$. Notice the high value of ΔL while the user occludes the first widget. The video feedback *(4)* also displays the widget masks as transparent overlays. *Right:* The application interface as seen by the user (the control panel wasn't hidden), in unconstrained lighting conditions (here, natural light).

7 Laser-Based Control

Having a large display or several display locations demands methods to enable interaction from a distance. Since pointing with a laser is intuitive, many researchers have investigated how to use laser-pointers to interact with computers [4, 9]. Most of them try to translate laser-pointer movements to events similar to those generated by a mouse. According to Myers *et al.* [10], pointing at small objects with a laser is much slower than with standard pointing devices, and less precise compared to physical pointing. On the other hand, pointing with a hand or finger has a very limited range. Standard pointing devices like the mouse or trackball provide interaction techniques that are suitable for a single screen setup, even if the screen is large, but they cannot by adapted to multiple display environments with complex geometry. Hand pointing from a distance provides interesting results [6], but the pointing resolution is too low to be usable, and stereoscopic vision is required.

In our system, we use laser-based interaction exclusively to redirect the beamer (SCP) from one surface to another. This corresponds to moving an application interface to a different location in the scene. Users are free to use their laser pointers in a natural fashion. They can point at anything in the room, including the projected images. The system does not respond unless a user makes an explicit sign.

In our application, interaction is activated with a double sequence of switching the laser on and off while pointing to roughly the same spot on the projected image. If after this sign the laser point appears on the screen and does not move for a short time, the control interface is projected. During the laser point dwell delay we estimate hand jitter in order to scale the controller interface appropriately, as explained below.

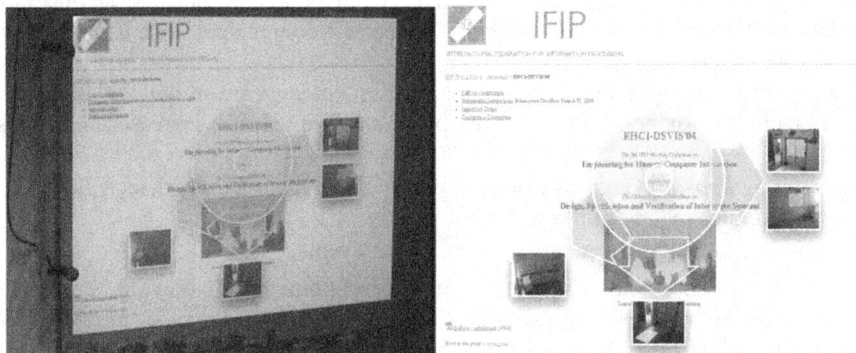

Fig. 7. Laser-based control interface (envisonment)

The interface shown in Figure 7 is a semi-transparent disc with arrows and thumbnail images. The arrows point to physical locations of the available displays in the environment. Similar to the menu-like controller application, the images placed at the end of each arrow are taken from the environment model. They present each display surface as it appears in the scene. The size of the images is a function of the measured laser point jitter. So is the size of the small internal disc representing the dead-zone, in which the laser dot can stay without reaction of the system. The controller interface is semi-transparent in order to avoid breaking users' interaction with the application, in case of a false initialization.

In order to avoid unwanted system reaction, the interface is not active when it appears. To activate it, the user has to explicitly place and keep the laser dot for a short time in any of the GUI's elements (arrow, image or disc). As the user moves the laser point within the yellow outer disc, the system starts to move the interface following the laser point with the center of the disc. This movement is limited to the area of the current display surface. Interface movement is slow for proper user control. When the laser goes outside the yellow disc or enters an arrow, movement halts. The user can then place the laser dot in the image of choice. As the laser point enters an image, the application interface immediately moves across the room to the corresponding surface. The controller interface does not appear on the newly chosen display unless it is again activated. At any time during the interaction process, the user can cancel the interaction by simply switching off the laser pointer.

7.1 Laser Tracking with a Camera

Several authors have investigated interaction from a distance using a laser pointer [4, 9,10].

Once we achieve geometric calibration of the camera and projector fields of view, detection and tracking the laser pointer dot is a trivial vision problem. Since laser light has a high intensity, a laser spot is the only visible blob on an image captured with a low-gain camera. The detection is then obtained by thresholding the intensity image and determining the barycentre of the connected component. Robustness against false alarms can be achieved by filtering out connected components that have aberrant areas.

As for other tracking systems, the output is a flow of *appear*, *motion* and *disappear* events with corresponding image-space positions. We achieve increased robustness by:

- generating *appear* events only once the dot has been consistently detected over several frames (e.g. 5 frames at 30Hz);
- similarly delaying the generation of *disappear* events.

We are not concerned by varying lighting conditions and shadowing because the camera is set to low gain. Occlusion, on the other hand, is an issue because an object passing through the laser beam causes erratic detections, which should be filtered out.

The overall simplicity of the vision process allows it to be implemented at camera rate (ca. 50Hz) with low latency (ca. 10ms processing time). Thus, it fulfils closed-loop human-computer interaction constraints.

8 A Novel User-Interface: The PDS

Exploiting robust vision-based tracking of an ordinary cardboard using an SCP unit [2] enables the use of a Portable Display Surface (PDS). We use the SCP to maintain a projected image onto the hand-held screen (PDS), automatically correcting for 3D translations and rotations of the screen.

We extend the concept of the PDS by integrating it in our AME system. As described in the example scenario (Section 5.1), the PDS can be used as a portable physical support for a projected interface. This mode of use is a variation of the "pick and drop" paradigm introduced in [15]. From the system point of view, the only difference between a planar surface in the environment and the PDS is its mobility and the image-correction matrix, so we can project the same interactive-widget-based interface on both static and portable surfaces. In practice, we have to take in account the limits of the image resolution available on the PDS surface.

The portability of this device creates two additional roles for the PDS in the AME system. It can serve as a means for explicit control of the display location and as a tool enabling the user to extend the environment model to surfaces which are not detected during the offline model acquisition procedure. Actually, the two modes are closely coupled and the extension of the environment model is transparent for the user.

To initialize the PDS, the user has to choose the corresponding item in the GUIs described in previous sections. Then, the SCP projects a rectangular region into which the user has to put the cardboard screen. If no rectangular object appears in this region within a fixed delay, the system falls back to its previous state. When the PDS is detected in the projected initialization region, the system transfers the display to the PDS and starts the tracking algorithm. The user can then move in the environment with the interface projected on the PDS. To stop the tracking algorithm, the user touches the "Freeze" widget projected on the PDS. The location of the PDS together with the corresponding pre-warp matrix is thus added to the environment model as new screen surface. This mechanism allows the system to dynamically update the model.

9 Conclusions

The emergence of spatially low-constrained working environments calls for new interaction concepts. This paper illustrates the issue of spatial control of a display in a multiple interactive-surface environment. We use steerable camera-projector assembly to display an interface and to move it in the scene. The projector-camera pair is also used as an actuator-sensor system enabling automatic construction of a sensor-centric environment model. We present three applications enabling convenient control of the display location in the environment. The applications are based on interactions using simple actuators: fingers, a laser pointer and a hand-held cardboard.

We impose a strong relation between the controller application interface and the physical world. The graphical interfaces are derived from the environment model, allowing the user to map the interface elements to the corresponding real-world objects. Our next development step is to couple controller applications with standard operating systems infrastructure.

Acknowledgments

This work has been partially funded by the European project FAME (IST-2000-28323), the FGnet working group (IST-2000-26434), and the RNTL/Proact ContAct project.

References

1. F. Bérard. The magic table: Computer-vision based augmentation of a whiteboard for creative meetings. In *Proceedings of the ICCV Workshop on Projector-Camera Systems*. IEEE Computer Society Press, 2003.
2. S. Borkowski, O. Riff, and J. L. Crowley. Projecting rectified images in an augmented environment. In *Proceedings of the ICCV Workshop on Projector-Camera Systems*. IEEE Computer Society Press, 2003.
3. B. Brumitt, B. Meyers, J. Krumm, A. Kern, and S. Shafer. Easyliving: Technologies for intelligent environments. In *Proceedings of Handheld and Ubiquitous Computing*, September 2000.

4. J. Davis and X. Chen. Lumipoint: Multi-user laser-based interaction on large tiled displays. *Displays*, 23(5), 2002.
5. R. Raskar et al. iLamps: Geometrically aware and self-configuring projectors. In *Appears ACM SIGGRAPH 2003 Conference Proceedings.*
6. Yi-Ping Hungy, Yao-Strong Yangz, Yong-Sheng Cheny, Ing-Bor Hsiehz, and Chiou-Shann Fuhz. Free-hand pointer by use of an active stereo vision system. In *Proceedings of the 14th International Conference on Pattern Recognition (ICPR'98)*, volume 2, pages 1244–1246, August 1998.
7. J.Coutaz, C.Lachenal, and S. Dupuy-Chessa. Ontology for multi-surface interaction. In *Proceedings of the ninth International Conference on Human-Computer Interaction (Interact'2003)*, 2003.
8. B. Johanson, G. Hutchins, T. Winograd, and M. Stone. Pointright: Experience with flexible input redirection in interactive workspaces. *Proceedings of UIST-2002*, 2002.
9. D. R. Olsen Jr and T. Nielsen. Laser pointer interaction. In *ACM CHI'2001 Conference Proceedings: Human Factors in Computing Systems. Seattle, WA*, 2001.
10. B. A. Meyers, R. Bhatnagar, J. Nichols, C.H. Peck, D. Kong, R. Miller, and A.C. Long. Interacting at a distance: measuring the performance of laser pointers and other devices. In *Proceedings of the SIGCHI conference on Human factors in computing systems: Changing our world, changing ourselves.* ACM Press New York, NY, USA, April 2002.
11. G. Pingali, C. Pinhanez, A. Levas, R. Kjeldsen, M. Podlaseck, H. Chen, and N. Sukaviriya. Steerable interfaces for pervasive computing spaces. In *Proceedings of IEEE International Conference on Pervasive Computing and Communications - PerCom'03*, March 2003.
12. C. Pinhanez. The everywhere displays projector: A device to create ubiquitous graphical interfaces. In *Proceedings of Ubiquitous Computing 2001 Conference*, September 2001.
13. R. Raskar, G. Welch, M. Cutts, A. Lake, L. Stesin, and H. Fuchs. The office of the future: A unified approach to image-based modeling and spatially immersive displays. In *Proceedings of the ACM SIGGRAPH'98 Conference.*
14. J. Rekimoto. Multiple-computer user interfaces: "beyond the desktop" direct manipulation environments. In *ACM CHI2000 Video Proceedings*, 2000.
15. J. Rekimoto and M. Saitoh. Augmented surfaces: A spatially continuous workspace for hybrid computing environments. In *Proceedings of CHI'99, pp.378-385*, 1999.
16. Helena Roeber, John Bacus, and Carlo Tomasi. Typing in thin air: the canesta projection keyboard - a new method of interaction with electronic devices. In *CHI '03 extended abstracts on Human factors in computing systems*, pages 712–713. ACM Press, 2003.
17. N. A. Streitz, J. Geißler, T. Holmer, S. Konomi, C. Müller-Tomfelde, W. Reischl, P. Rexroth, P. Seitz, and R. Steinmetz. i-land: An interactive landscape for creativitiy and innovation. *ACM Conference on Human Factors in Computing Systems*, 1999.
18. N. A. Streitz, C. Röcker, Th. Prante, R. Stenzel, and D. van Alphen. Situated interaction with ambient information: Facilitating awareness and communication in ubiquitous work environments. In *Tenth International Conference on Human-Computer Interaction*, June 2003.
19. Zs. Szalavári and M. Gervautz. The personal interaction panel - a two-handed interface for augmented reality. In *Proceedings of EUROGRAPHICS'97, Budapest, Hungary*, September 1997.
20. N. Takao, J. Shi, , and S. Baker. Tele-graffiti: A camera-projector based remote sketching system with hand-based user interface and automatic session summarization. *International Journal of Computer Vision*, 53(2):115–133, July 2003.
21. J. Underkofflerand B. Ullmer and H. Ishii. Emancipated pixels: Real-world graphics in the luminous room. In *Proceedings of ACM SIGGRAPH*, pages 385–392, 1999.
22. F. Vernier, N. Lesh, and C. Shen. Visualization techniques for circular tabletop interfaces. In *Advanced Visual Interfaces*, 2002.

23. S.A. Voida, E.D. Mynatt, B. MacIntyre, and G. Corso. Integrating virtual and physical context to support knowledge workers. In *Proceedings of Pervasive Computing Conference*. IEEE Computer Society Press, 2002.
24. P. Wellner. The digitaldesk calculator: Tactile manipulation on a desk top display. In *ACM Symposium on User Interface Software and Technology*, pages 27–33, 1991.
25. R. Yang and G. Welch. Automatic and continuous projector display surface calibration using every-day imagery. In *CECG'01*.

Discussion

[Joaquim Jorge] Could you give some details on the finger tracking. Do you use color information?

> [Stanislaw Borkowski] We do not track fingers, but detect their presence over projected buttons. The detection is based on measurements of the perceived luminance over a widget. Our projected widgets are robust to accidental full-occlusions and change of ambient light conditions. However, since we do not use any background model, our widgets work less reliably if they are projected on surfaces with color intensity that is similar to the color of user's fingers.

[Nick Graham] You said you want to perform user studies to validate your approach. What is the hypothesis you wish to validate?

> [Stanislaw Borkowski] What we would like to validate is our claim that a sensor-centric environment model enhanced with contextual cues is easier to interpret by humans than a symbolic representation of the environment (such as a 2D map).

[Fabio Paterno] Why don't you use hand pointing instead of laser pointing for display control?

> [Stanislaw Borkowski] There are two reasons: First, laser pointing is more precise, which is important for fine tuning the display position. Second, is the issue of privacy. Using hand pointing requires constant observation of the user, and I am not sure whether everyone would feel comfortable with that.

[Fabio] there are so many cameras!

> [Stanislaw Borkowski] Yes, but when using our system the user is not necessary aware of presence of those cameras. In contrary, using hand-pointing interaction user would have to make some kind of a "waving" sign to one of the cameras to initialize the interaction.

[Rick Kazman] Your interaction is relatively impoverished. Have you considered integrating voice command to give richer interaction possibilities?

> [Stanislaw Borkowski] Not really, because we would encounter the problem of how to verbally explain to the system our requests.

[Rick Kazman] I was thinking more of using voice to augment the interaction, to pass you into specific modes for example, or to enable multimodal interaction (e.g. "put that there").

[Stanislaw Borkowski] Yes, that is a good idea. We should look into it. Right now we need to add a button to the interface which might obscure part of the interface. So in that case voice could be useful.

[Michael Harrison] What would be a good application for this type of system?

[Stanislaw Borkowski] An example could be a project-meeting, which has to split into to working subgroups. They could send a copy of their presentation on which they work to another surface. This surface could be even in a different room. Another application could be for a collaborative document editing. In this situation users could pass the UI between each other and thus pass the leadership of the group. This could help to structure the work of the group.

[Philippe Palanque] Do you have an interaction technique for setting the focus of the video projector?

[Stanislaw Borkowski] The focus should be set automatically, so there is no need for such interaction. We plan to feed the focus lens of the projector to the auto-focus of the camera mounted on the SCP.

[Helmut Stiegler] You don't need perfectly planar surfaces. The surface becomes "planer" by "augmentation".

[Stanislaw Borkowski] That is true, but it would become more complicated to implement the same features on non-planar interfaces. The problem of projection on non-planar surfaces is that the appearance of the projected image depends on the point of view.

[Eric Schol] How is ambiguity solved in touching multiple projected buttons at the same time? Such situation appears when you reach to a button that is farther from the user than some other buttons.

[Stanislaw Borkowski] The accidental occlusion of buttons that are close to the user is not a problem since our widgets "react" only on partial occlusion.

[Pierre Dragicevic] Did you think about using color information during model acquisition phase? This might be useful for choosing the support-surface for the screen, only from surfaces that are light-colored. You could also use such information to correct colors of the projected image.

[Stanislaw Borkowski] Yes, of course I though about it. This is an important feature of surfaces, since the color of the surface on which we project can influence the appearance of the projection. At this stage of development we did not really addressed this issue yet.

[Joerg Roth] Usually users press buttons quickly with a certain force. Your system requires a finger to reside in the button area for a certain time. Get users used to this different kind of interacting with a button?

[Stanislaw Borkowski] To answer your question I would have to perform user studies on this subject. From my experience and the experience of my colleagues who tried our system, using projected buttons is quite natural and easy. We did not encounter problems with using projected buttons.

Manipulating Vibro-Tactile Sequences on Mobile PC

Grigori Evreinov, Tatiana Evreinova, and Roope Raisamo

TAUCHI Computer-Human Interaction Unit
Department of Computer Sciences
FIN-33014 University of Tampere, Finland
+358 3 215 8549
{grse, e_tg, rr}@cs.uta.fi

Abstract. Tactile memory is the crucial factor in coding and transfer of the semantic information through a single vibrator. While some simulators can produce strong vibro-tactile sensations, discrimination of several tactile patterns can remain quite poor. Currently used actuators, such as shaking motor, have also technological and methodological restrictions. We designed a vibro-tactile pen and software to create tactons and semantic sequences of vibro-tactile patterns on mobile devices (iPAQ pocket PC). We proposed special games and techniques to simplify learning and manipulating vibro-tactile patterns. The technique for manipulating vibro-tactile sequences is based on gesture recognition and spatial-temporal mapping for imaging vibro-tactile signals. After training, the tactons could be used as awareness cues or the system of non-verbal communication signals.

1 Introduction

Many researchers suppose that the dynamic range for the tactile analyzer is narrow in comparison to visual and auditory ones. This fact is explained by the complex interactions between vibro-tactile stimuli, which are in spatial-temporary affinity. This has resulted in a fairly conservative approach to the design of the tactile display techniques. However, some physiological studies [1] have shown that a number of possible "descriptions" (states) of an afferent flow during stimulation of the tactile receptors tend to have a greater amount of the definite levels than it was previously observed, that is more than 125. The restrictions of the human touch mostly depend on imaging techniques used, that is, spatial-temporal mapping and parameters of the input signals. As opposed to static spatial coding such as Braille or tactile diagrams, tactile memory is the crucial factor affecting perception of the dynamical signals similar to Vibratese language [7], [9].

Many different kinds of devices with embedded vibro-tactile actuators have appeared during the last two years. There is a stable interest to use vibration in games including small-size wearable devices like personal digital assistants and phones [2], [3], [14]. The combination of small size and low weight, low power consumption and noise, and human ability to feel vibration when the hearing and vision occupied by other tasks or have some lacks, makes vibration actuators ideal for mobile applications [4], [10].

R. Bastide, P. Palanque, and J. Roth (Eds.): EHCI-DSVIS 2004, LNCS 3425, pp. 245-252, 2005.

On the other hand, the absence of the tactile markers makes almost impossible for visually impaired users interaction with touchscreen. Visual imaging is dominant for touchscreen and requires a definite size of virtual buttons or widgets to directly manipulate them by the finger. Among recent projects, it is necessary to mention the works of Nashel and Razzaque [11], Fukumoto and Sugimura [6] and Poupyrev et al [12]. The authors propose using different kinds of the small actuators such as piezoceramic bending motor [6], [12] or shaking motor [11] attached to a touch panel or mounted on PDA.

If the actuator is placed just under the touch panel, the vibration should be sensed directly at the fingertip. However, fingertip interaction has a limited contact duration, as the finger occupies an essential space for imaging. In a case of blind finger manipulations, a gesture technique becomes more efficient than absolute pointing when making use of the specific layout of software buttons. A small touch space and irregular spreading of vibration across touchscreen require another solution. If the actuator is placed on the backside of the mobile device, vibration could be sensed at the palm holding the unit. In this case, the mass of the PDA is crucial and impacts onto spectrum of playback signals [4], [6].

From time to time vibro-tactile feedback has been added to a pen input device [13]. We have also implemented several prototypes of the pen having embedded shaking motor and the solenoid-type actuator. However, shaking motor has a better ratio of the torque to power consumption in a range of 3 – 500 Hz than a solenoid-type actuator. The vibro-tactile pen certainly has the following benefits:

- the contact with the fingers is permanent and has more touch surface, as a rule, two fingertips tightly coupled to the pen;
- the pen has smaller weight and vibration is easily spread along this unit, it provides the user with a reliable feeling of different frequencies;
- the construction of the pen is flexible and admits installation of several actuators which have a local power source;
- the connection to mobile unit can be provided through a serial port or Bluetooth, that is, the main unit does not require any modification.

Finally, finger grasping provides a better precision compared with hand grasping [5]. Based on vibro-tactile pen we developed a special technique for imaging and intuitive interacting through vibration patterns. Simple games allow to facilitate learning or usability testing of the system of the tactons that might be used like awareness cues or non-verbal communication signals.

2 Vibro-Tactile Pen

The prototype of vibro-tactile pen consists of a miniature DC motor with a stopped rotor (shaking motor), electronic switch (NDS9959 MOSFET) and battery having the voltage of 3 V. It is possible to use internal battery of iPAQ, as an effective current can be restricted to 300 mA at 6 V. Both the general view and some internal design features of the pen are shown in Fig. 1.

There are only two control commands to start and stop the motor rotation. Therefore, to shape an appropriate vibration pattern, we need to combine the pulses of the current and the pauses with definite duration. Duration of the pulses can slightly change the power of the mechanical moment (a torque). The frequency will mostly be determined by duration of the pauses.

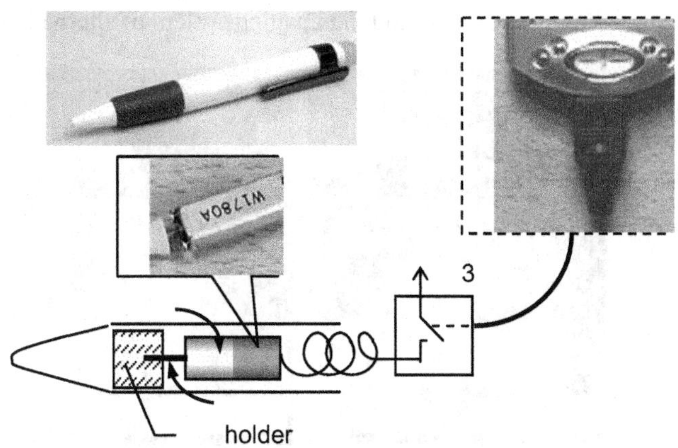

Fig. 1. Vibro-tactile pen: general view and schematics.

We used the cradle connector of Compaq iPAQ pocket PC which supports RS-232 and USB input/output signals. In particularly, DTR or/and RTS signals can be used to realize the motor control.

The software to create vibro-tactile patterns was written in Microsoft eMbedded Visual Basic 3.0. This program allows shaping some number of vibro-tactile patterns. Each of the tactons is composed of two sequential serial bursts with different frequency of the pulses. Such a technique based on contrast presentation of two well-differentiated stimuli of the same modality facilitates shaping the perceptual imprint of the vibro-tactile pattern. The number of bursts could be increased, but duration of the tacton shall be reasonable and shall not exceed 2 s. Durations of the pulses and pauses are setting in milliseconds. Number of pulses determines the duration of each burst. Thus, if the pattern consists of 10 pulses having frequency of 47.6 Hz (1+20 ms) and 10 pulses having frequency of 11.8 Hz, (5+80 ms) vibro-tactile pattern has the length of 1060 ms. All patterns are stored in the resource file "TPattern.txt" that can be loaded by the game or another application having special procedures to decode the description into output signals of the serial port according the script.

3 Method for Learning Vibro-Tactile Signals

Fingertip sensitivity is extremely important for some categories of physically challenged people such as the profoundly deaf, hard-of-hearing people and people who have low vision. We can find diverse advises how to increase skin sensitivity. For instance, Stephen Hampton in "Secrets of Lock Picking" [8] described a special procedure and the exercises to develop a delicate touch.

Sometimes, only sensitivity is not enough to remember and recognize vibration patterns and their combinations, especially when the number of the tactons is more than five. While high skin sensitivity can produce strong sensation, the discrimination of several tactile stimuli can remain quite poor. The duration of remembering tactile pattern depends on many factors which would include personal experience, making of the individual perceptive strategy, and the imaging system of alternative signals [7].

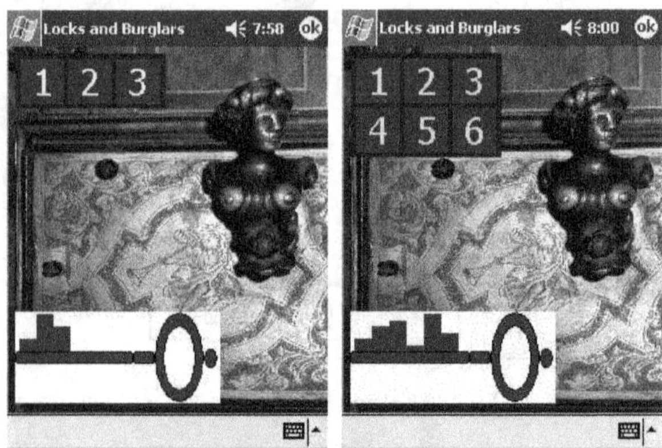

Fig. 2. Three levels of the game "Locks and Burglars".

We propose special games and techniques to facilitate learning and manipulation by vibration patterns. The static scripts have own dynamics and provoke the player to make an individual strategy and mobilize perceptive skills. Let us consider a version of the game for the users having a normal vision.

The goal of the "Burglar" is to investigate and memorize the lock prototype to open it as fast as possible. There are three levels of difficulty and two phases of the game on each level. In the "training" mode (the first phase), the player can touch the lock as many times as s/he needs. After remembering tactons and their position, the player starts the game. By clicking on the label "Start", which is visible in training phase, the game starts and the key will appear (Fig. 2). The player has the key in hand and can touch it as many times as s/he needs. That is a chance to check the memory.

After player found known tactons and could suppose in which position of the lock button s/he had detected these vibrations before, it is possible to click once the lock button. If the vibration pattern of the button coincides with corresponding tacton of the key piece, the lock will have a yellow shine. In a wrong case, a shine will be red. Repeated pressing of the corresponding position is also being considered as an error.

There is a restricted number of errors on the each level of the game: single, four and six allowed errors. We assumed that 15 s per tacton is enough to pass the third level therefore the game time was restricted to 2.5 minutes. That conditions a selection of the strategy and improves learnability. After the player did not admit the errors at all the levels, the group of tactons could be replaced. Different groups comprising nine tactons allow learning whole vibro-tactile alphabet (27 tokens) sequentially.

All the data, times and number of repetitions per tacton, in training phase and during the game are automatically collected and stored in a log file. Thus, we can estimate which of the patterns are more difficult to remember and if these tactons are equally hard for all the players, their structure could be changed.

Graphic features for imaging, such as numbering or positioning (central, corners) lock buttons, different heights of the key pieces, and "binary construction" of the tactons, each tacton being composed of the two serial bursts of the pulses, should facilitate remembering spatial-temporal relations of the complex signals in the proposed system.

Another approach was developed to support blind interaction with tactile patterns, as the attentional competition between modalities often disturbs or suppresses weak differences of the tactile stimuli. The technique for blind interaction has several features. Screenshot of the game for non-visual interaction is shown in Fig. 3. There are four absolute positions for the buttons "Repeat", "Start" and two buttons are controlling the number of the tactons and the amount of the tactons within a playback sequence. Speech remarks support each change of the button state.

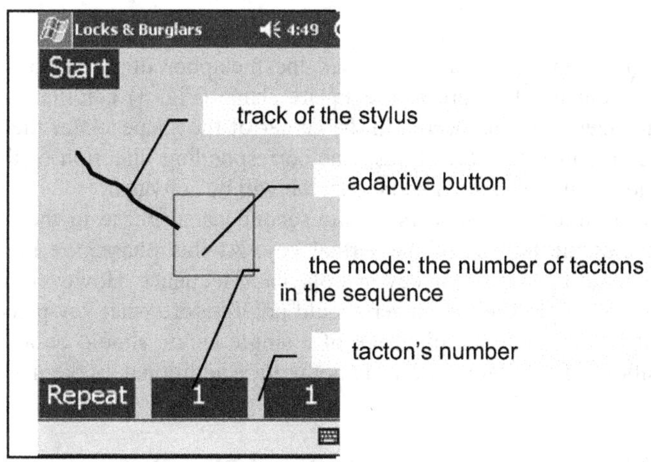

Fig. 3. The version of the game for blind player.

When blindfolded player should investigate and memorize the lock, s/he can make gestures along eight directions each time when it is necessary to activate the lock button or mark once the tacton by gesture and press down the button "Repeat" as many times as needed. The middle button switches the mode of repetition. Three or all the tactons can be played starting from the first, the fourth or the seventh position pointed by the last gesture.

Spatial-temporal mapping for vibro-tactile imaging is shown in Fig. 4. Playback duration for the groups consisting of 3, 6 or 9 tactons can reach 3.5 s, 7.2 s or 11 s including earcon to mark the end of the sequence. This parameter is important and could be improved when stronger tactile feedback could be provided with actuator attached to the stylus directly under the finger. In practice, only the sequence consisting of three tactons facilitates recognizing and remembering a sequence of the tactile patterns.

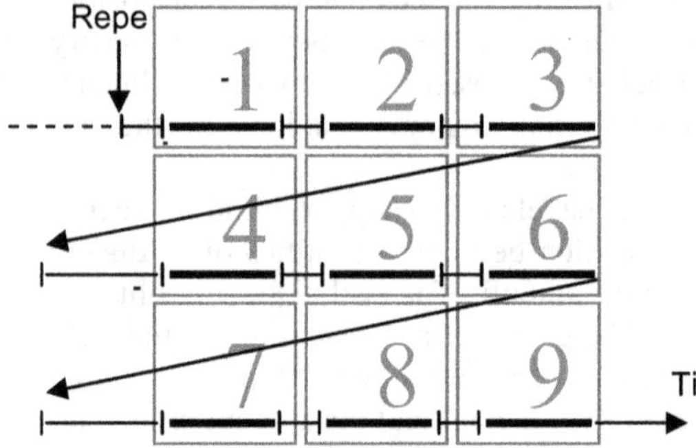

Fig. 4. Spatial-temporal mapping for vibro-tactile imaging: T_1 = 60 ms, T_2 = 1100 ms, T_3 = 300 ms.

To recognize gestures we used the metaphor of the adaptive button. When the player touches the screen, the square shape (Fig. 3) automatically changes position and finger or stylus occurs in the center of the shape. After the motion was realized (sliding and lifting the stylus), the corresponding direction or the button position of the lock will be counted and the tacton will be activated.

The button that appears on the second game phase in the bottom right position activates the tactons of the virtual key. At this phase, the middle button switches number of tactons of the key in a playback sequence. However, to select the button of the lock by gesture the player should point before what key piece s/he wishes to use. That is, the mode for playback of a single tacton should be activated. The absolute positions of software buttons do not require additional markers.

4 Evaluation of the Method and Pilot Results

The preliminary evaluation with able-bodied staff and students took place in the Department of Computer Sciences University of Tampere. The data were captured using the version of the game "Locks and Burglars" for deaf players. The data were collected concerning 190 trials in a total, of 18 players (Table 1). Despite of the fact, that the tactons have had low vibration frequencies of 47.6 Hz and 11.8 Hz, we cannot exclude an acoustic effect, as the players had a normal hearing. Therefore, we can just summarize general considerations regarding the difficulties in which game resulted and overall average results.

Table 1. The preliminary average results.

Level (tactons)	Trials	Selection time per tacton	Total selection time	Repeats per tacton	Err, %
1 (3)	48	3.8 s	12.4 s	4-7	7.7
2 (6)	123	3.4 s	16.8 s	3-13	13.3
3 (9)	19	1.7-11 s	47.3 s	4-35	55.6

The first level of the game is simple as memorizing of 2 out of 3 patterns is enough to complete the task. The selection time (decision-making and pointing the lock button after receiving tactile feedback in corresponding piece of the key) in this level did not exceed 3.8 s per tacton or 12.4 s to find matching of 3 tactons. The number of the repetitions to memorize 3 patterns was low, about 4 - 7 repetitions per tacton. The error rate (Err) was 7.7%. The error rate was counted as follows:

$$Err = \frac{[wrong\_selections]}{[trials] \times [tactons]} \times 100\% \; . \tag{2}$$

The second level of the game (memorizing six tactons) was also not very difficult. An average time of the selection per tacton was about 3.4 s and 16.8 s in a total to find matching of six tactons. The number of the repetitions to memorize six patterns was varied from 3 to 13 repetitions per tacton. However, the error rate increased up to 13.3%, it is also possible due to the allowed number of errors (4).

The third level (nine tactons for memorizing) was too difficult and only three of 19 trials had finished by the win. The average time of the selection has been changed from 1.7 s up to 11 s per tacton and reached 47.3 s to find matching of nine tactons. While a selection time was about 30% of the entire time of the game, decision-making occupied much more time and players lost a case mostly due to limited time. The number of repetitions to memorize nine patterns in training phase varied significantly, from 4 up to 35 repetitions per tacton. Thus, we can conclude that nine tactons require of a special strategy to facilitate memorizing. However, the playback mode of the groups of vibro-tactile patterns was not used in the tested version. The error rate was too high (55.6%) due to the allowed number of errors (6) and, probably, because of the small tactile experience of the players.

The blind version of the game was briefly evaluated and showed a good potential to play and manipulate by vibro-tactile patterns even in the case when audio feedback was absent. That is, the proposed approach and the tools implemented provide the basis for learning and reading of the complex semantic sequences composed of six and more vibro-tactile patterns.

5 Conclusion

We designed a vibro-tactile pen and software intended to create tactons and semantic sequences consisting of the vibro-tactile patterns on mobile devices (iPAQ pocket PC). Tactile memory is the major restriction for designing a vibro-tactile alphabet for the hearing impaired people. We proposed special games and techniques to facilitate learning of the vibro-tactile patterns and manipulating by them. Spatial-temporal mapping for imaging vibro-tactile signals has a potential for future development and detailed investigation of the human perception of the long semantic sequences composed of tactons. After training, the tactons can be used as a system of non-verbal communication signals.

Acknowledgments

This work was financially supported by the Academy of Finland (grant 200761), and by the Nordic Development Centre for Rehabilitation Technology (NUH).

References

1. Antonets, V.A., Zeveke, A.V., Malysheva, G.I.: Possibility of synthesis of an additional sensory channel in a man-machine system. Sensory Systems, 6(4), (1992) 100-102
2. Blind Games Software Development Project. http://www.cs.unc.edu/Research/assist/et/projects/blind_games/
3. Cell Phones and PDAs. http://www.immersion.com/consumer_electronics/
4. Chang, A., O'Modhrain, S., Jacob, R., Gunther, E., Ishii, H.: ComTouch: Design of a Vibrotactile Communication Device. In: Proceedings of DIS02, ACM (2002) 312-320
5. Cutkosky, M.R., Howe, R.D.: Human Grasp Choice and Robotic Grasp Analysis. In S.T. Venkataraman and T. Iberall (Eds.), Dextrous Robot Hands, Springer-Verlag, New York (1990), 5 –31
6. Fukumoto, M. and Sugimura, T.: Active Click: Tactile Feedback for Touch Panels. In: Proceedings of CHI 2001, Interactive Posters, ACM (2001) 121-122
7. Geldard, F.: Adventures in tactile literacy. American Psychologist, 12 (1957) 115-124
8. Hampton, S.: Secrets of Lock Picking. Paladin Press, 1987
9. Hong Z. Tan and Pentland, A.: Tactual Displays for Sensory Substitution and Wearable Computers. In: Woodrow, B. and Caudell, Th. (eds), Fundamentals of Wearable Computers and Augmented Reality, Mahwah, Lawrence Erlbaum Associates (2001) 579-598
10. Michitaka Hirose and Tomohiro Amemiya: Wearable Finger-Braille Interface for Navigation of Deaf-Blind in Ubiquitous Barrier-Free Space. In: Proceedings of the HCI International 2003, Lawrence Erlbaum Associates, V4, (2003) 1417-1421
11. Nashel, A. and Razzaque, S.: Tactile Virtual Buttons for Mobile Devices. In: Proceedings of CHI 2003, ACM (2003) 854-855
12. Poupyrev, I., Maruyama, S. and Rekimoto, J.: Ambient Touch: Designing Tactile Interfaces for Handheld Devices. In: Proceedings of UIST 2002, ACM (2002) 51-60
13. Tactylus tm http://viswiz.imk.fraunhofer.de/~kruijff/research.html
14. Vibration Fuser for the Sony Ericsson P800. http://support.appforge.com/

Discussion

[Fabio Paterno] I think that in the example you showed for blind users a solution based on screen readers would be easier than the one you presented based on vibro-tactile techniques.

> [Grigori Evreinov] A screen reader solution would not be useful for deaf and blind-deaf users.

[Eric Schol] Did you investigate the use of force-feedback joystick ?

> [Grigori Evreinov] Yes, among many other devices ; like force-feedback mouse, etc. But main goal of the research was the application (game), not the device

Formalising an Understanding of User-System Misfits

Ann Blandford[1], Thomas R.G. Green[2] and Iain Connell[1]

[1] UCL Interaction Centre, University College London, Remax House, 31-32 Alfred Place London WC1E 7DP, U.K.
{A.Blandford,I.Connell}@ucl.ac.uk
http://www.uclic.ucl.ac.uk/annb/
[2] University of Leeds, U.K.

Abstract. Many of the difficulties users experience when working with interactive systems arise from misfits between the user's conceptualisation of the domain and device with which they are working and the conceptualisation implemented within those systems. We report an analytical technique called CASSM (Concept-based Analysis for Surface and Structural Misfits) in which such misfits can be formally represented to assist in understanding, describing and reasoning about them. CASSM draws on the framework of Cognitive Dimensions (CDs) in which many types of misfit were classified and presented descriptively, with illustrative examples. CASSM allows precise definitions of many of the CDs, expressed in terms of entities, attributes, actions and relationships. These definitions have been implemented in Cassata, a tool for automated analysis of misfits, which we introduce and describe in some detail.

1 Introduction

Two kinds of approach have dominated traditional work in usability of interactive systems: *heuristic* (or *checklist-based*) approaches giving a swift assessment of look-and-feel (usually independent of the tasks the system is designed to support), such as Heuristic Evaluation [17]; and *procedure-based* approaches for assessing the difficulty of each step of typical user tasks, such as Cognitive Walkthrough [20].

We present a technique based on a third approach, the analysis of *conceptual misfits* between the way the user thinks and the representation implemented within the system. Such misfits pertain to the concepts and relationships the user is manipulating in their work. Some misfits are surface-level – for example, users may work with concepts that are not directly represented within the system; conversely, users may be required to discover and utilise system concepts that are irrelevant to their conceptual models. Other misfits are structural, emerging only when the user manipulates the structure of some representation and finds that changes that are conceptually simple are, in practice, difficult to achieve.

We outline an approach to usability evaluation called Concept-based Analysis of Surface and Structural Misfits (CASSM), and present Cassata, a prototype analysis tool that supports the analyst in identifying misfits. As will become apparent, in CASSM structural misfits are not analysed directly in terms of the procedures that users follow to make a change, as might happen using a procedural approach; instead,

R. Bastide, P. Palanque, and J. Roth (Eds.): EHCI-DSVIS 2004, LNCS 3425, pp. 253-270, 2005.

CASSM identifies which elements of a structure are and are not accessible to a user and amenable to direct modification, thereby deriving warnings of potential misfits.

1.1 Misfits and Their Analysis

Many approaches to usability evaluation, including work in the previously-mentioned traditions of heuristic and procedure-based analysis, have generated lists of specific user problems with a given design, but have failed to impose any structure on the lists. Each user difficulty that is spotted is a thing in itself. From one occurrence we learn nothing about how to predict further occurrences, nor how to improve design practice.

CASSM builds on the approach known as the 'Cognitive Dimensions of Notations' framework (CDs) [3,4,14,15], in which some important classes of structural misfits have been articulated and described. For example, 'viscosity' describes the 'degree of resistance to small changes': in a viscous system, something is more difficult to change than it should be – a single conceptual action demands several device actions. An example would be adding a new figure near the beginning of a document then having to increment all subsequent figure numbers and within-text references to those numbers: some word processing applications explicitly support this activity but most do not, making it very repetitive. Viscosity may be a serious impediment to the user's task or it may be irrelevant to that task, if for instance the user is searching for a target but not trying to make a change; the CDs framework therefore distinguishes types of user activity and offers a conjecture as to how each dimension affects each activity.

The Cognitive Dimensions framework as originally created [12] was intended to promote quick, broad-brush evaluation, giving non-specialists a usability evaluation technique that was based on cognitive analysis yet required no expertise from the analyst. It relied purely on definition by example. To a degree this was successful. The idea of viscosity is intuitively appealing; examples can illustrate the idea; and a vocabulary of such ideas can be used to support discourse and reasoning about features of a design, with a view to improving that design [3]. However, despite the development of a CDs tutorial [14], and a questionnaire-based evaluation tool [2], potential users have found that they need to learn too many concepts and that those concepts are not defined closely enough to avoid disagreement over the final analysis.

More than one attempt has been made to sharpen the definitions of CDs [11,19] but those attempts have lost the feel of quick, broad-brush evaluation, making them unappealing to the intended user, the non-specialist analyst.

In this paper, we show that several CDs and related user–system misfits can be represented reasonably faithfully in a form that better preserves the original quick-and-dirty appeal of CDs. With these definitions, not only are the misfit notions clarified, but it becomes possible for potential misfit occurrences to be automatically identified within Cassata, the tool that we shall describe below.

It must be kept in mind throughout that our form of analysis can only describe *potential* user problems. Whether a particular misfit causes real difficulties will depend on circumstances that are not described here.

2 CASSM and Cassata: A Brief Introduction

CASSM is a usability evaluation technique that focuses on the misfits between user and device. It was formerly known as Ontological Sketch Modelling (OSM [10]), because the approach involves constructing a partial (Sketchy) representation (Model) of the essential elements (Ontology) of a user–system interaction; the name has recently been changed to reflect a shift of focus towards the two types of misfits rather than the ontology representation.

CASSM developed from our earlier work on Entity Relationship Modelling of Information Artifacts (ERMIA [11]) and Programmable User Modelling (PUM [8]). It has also been informed by the work of others on what could broadly be termed misfit analysis, such as Moran's External Task Internal Task (ETIT) analysis [16] and Payne's Yoked State Spaces [18]. The basis of CASSM is to compare the concepts that users are working with (identified by an appropriate data gathering technique such as interviews, think-aloud protocols or Contextual Inquiry [1]) with the concepts implemented within the system and interface (identified by reference to sources such as system documentation or an existing implementation). Conceptual analysis involves identifying the concepts users are working with, drawing out commonalities across similar users (see for example [7]) to create the profile of a typical user of a particular type,; the analyst can then assess the quality of fit between user and system. As analysis proceeds, the analyst will start to distinguish between entities and attributes (as defined below), and to consider what actions the user can take to change the state of the system. Finally, for a thorough analysis, various relationships between concepts are enumerated to identify structural misfits. Each of these stages of misfit analysis is discussed in more detail below.

To support analysis, a demonstrator tool called Cassata is under development. Screen shots included in this paper are taken from version 2.1 of the tool. (Version 3 can be downloaded from the project web page [9].) The tool has provided a focus for developing the precise definitions of misfits included in this paper, and also a means of testing those definitions against a repertoire of examples that have previously been discussed informally.

Figure 1 shows the Cassata window for a partial description of a word processor document. For clarity, the picture is cropped from the right. This particular description is discussed in more detail in section 4.1; here we simply outline its main features.

It is a description of a set of figures (pictures or diagrams) in a document, which consists of one or more individual figures. For the user, there is the important idea that the figures should be sequentially numbered – so the *number-sequence* is important, and is an attribute of the *set-of-figs*. Each *figure* has an attribute which is its particular *number*, and changing a figure number changes the overall sequence of figure numbers.

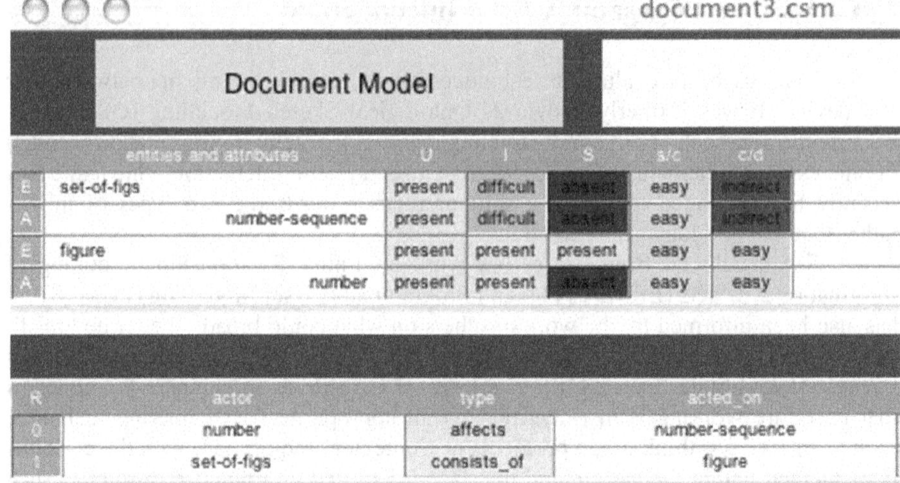

document3.csm

Document Model

	entities and attributes	U	I	S	s/c	c/d
E	set-of-figs	present	difficult	absent	easy	indirect
A	number-sequence	present	difficult	absent	easy	indirect
E	figure	present	present	present	easy	easy
A	number	present	present	absent	easy	easy

R	actor	type	acted_on
0	number	affects	number-sequence
1	set-of-figs	consists_of	figure

Fig. 1. Cassata data table for a partial description of a document. The upper table describes concepts (i.e. entities and their attributes); the lower describes relationships between those concepts.

The top half of the window shows information about concepts (entities such as *figure* and attributes such as *number*): for each concept, three columns show whether it is present, difficult or absent for the user, interface and system respectively; the next two columns show how easy it is to set or change the value of an attribute, or to create or delete an entity; the final column is a notes area in which the analyst can add comments. To take the first row as an example: the `set-of-figs` is a conceptual entity that is meaningful to the user, is not clearly represented at the interface ('difficult') and absent from the underlying system model. It is easy to create a set of figures, (because this happens automatically as the user adds figures) but harder to delete it (done indirectly because that requires deleting *all* the individual figures).

The bottom half of the window shows information about relationships (such as *affects* and *consists_of*) between concepts. In this particular case, the two lines of input state that changing any *number* (of a *figure*) affects the *number-sequence* (of the *set-of-figs*) and that a *set-of-figs* consists of (many) *figures*.

Having briefly presented the background to CASSM and Cassata, we now focus in more detail on the definitions of various kinds of misfits.

3 Surface Misfits

Surface misfits are those that become apparent without considering the details of structural representations within the system and how those representations are changed. Within 'surface', there are three levels of misfit: just identifying system and user concepts, with little reference to the interface between the two (section 3.1); more detailed analysis in terms of how well each concept is represented by the user, interface and system (section 3.2); and analysis in terms of what actions are needed to change the system, and whether there are problems with actions (section 3.3).

3.1 Level 1: Misfits Between the User and the System

Misfits between user and system are probably the most important surface-level misfits. There are three important cases: user concepts that are not represented within the system; system concepts that are inaccessible to the user; and situations where a user concept and a system concept are similar but not identical.

User concepts that are not represented within the system cannot be directly manipulated by the user. The *set-of-figs* discussed above is an example of such a concept. Other examples are using a field in an electronic form to code information for which that form was not actually designed, or keeping paper notes alongside an electronic system to capture information that the system does not accept.

Unrepresented concepts are often the most costly form of misfit; they may force users to introduce workarounds, as users are unable to express exactly what they need to, and must therefore use the system in a way it was not designed for. They sometimes result in structural misfits such as viscosity, as described below.

System concepts that are not immediately available to the user need to be learned. At a trivial level, these might include strictly device-related concepts like scroll-bars, which may be simple to use but nevertheless need to be learnt. A slightly more complex example is the apparatus of layers, channels and masks found in many graphics applications – these can cause substantial user difficulties, particularly for novice users.

For users, these misfits may involve no more than learning a new concept, or they may require the users' constant attention to the state of something that has little significance to them, such as the amount of free memory.

User- and system concepts that are similar but non-identical, and which are often referred to by the same terms, can cause more serious difficulties. One example in the domain of diaries is the idea of a 'meeting'. When a user talks about a meeting, they usually mean a pre-arranged gathering of particular individuals at an agreed location with a particular broad purpose (and perhaps a detailed agenda). Within some shared diary systems, a meeting has a much more precise definition, referring to an event about which only other users of the same shared diary system can be kept fully informed, and which has a precise start time and precise finishing time, and possibly a precise location. The difference between these concepts is small but significant [5].

Another example, within the domain of ambulance dispatch, is the difference between a *call* and an *incident*. A particular system we studied processed information strictly in terms of calls, whereas staff dealt with incidents (about which there may be one or many calls); this was difficult to detect initially because the staff referred to them as 'calls' [7], but the failure of the system to integrate information about difference calls added substantially to staff workload as they processed the more complex incidents.

These misfits may cause difficulties because the user has to constantly map their natural understanding of the concept onto the one represented within the system, which may have a subtly different set of attributes.

3.2 Level 2: Adding Interface Considerations

The second level starts to draw out issues concerning the interface between user and system. For each of user, interface and system, a concept may be *present*, *difficult* or *absent*.

In all cases, *present* means clearly represented and *absent* means not represented. We assume that underlying system concepts are either present or absent, whereas for the user or at the interface there are concepts that are present but *difficult* in some way.

For users, *difficult* concepts are most commonly ones that are implicit– ideas they are aware of if asked but not ones they expect to work with. An example would be the end time of a meeting in the diary system mentioned above: if one looks at people's paper diaries, one finds that many engagements have start times (though these are often flagged as approximate – e.g. '2ish') but few have end times, whereas electronic diaries require every event to have an end time. This forces users to make explicit information that they might not choose to. Another source of difficulty might be that the user *has to learn* the concept.

Similarly, there are various reasons why a concept may be represented at the interface but in a way that makes it difficult to work with. Difficulties that interface objects may present include:

- *Disguised*: represented, but hard to interpret;
- *Delayed*: represented, but not available to the user until some time later in the interaction;
- *Hidden*: represented, but the user has to perform an explicit action to reveal the state of the entity or attribute; or
- *Undiscoverable*: represented only to the user who has good system knowledge, but unlikely to be discovered by most users.

Which of these apply in any particular case – i.e. why the interface object might cause user difficulties – is a further level of detail that can be annotated by the analyst; for the sake of simplicity, this additional level of detail is not explicitly represented within Cassata.

At the simplest level, anything that is *difficult* or *absent* represents a misfit that might cause user difficulties. As discussed above, concepts that are difficult or absent for the user are ones that need to be learnt and worked with; how much difficulty these actually pose will depend on the interface representation. Conversely, concepts that are present for the user but absent from the underlying system will force the user to find work-arounds. In addition, as discussed above, poor interface representations are a further source of difficulty that is not considered at level 1.

3.3 Level 3: Considering Actions

At levels 1 and 2, we have referred to 'concepts' without it being necessary to distinguish between them. For deeper analysis, it becomes necessary to distinguish between entities and attributes. A description in terms of entities and attributes is illustrated in the screen-shot from the Cassata tool shown in Figure 1 (above). There, we used the terms 'entity' and 'attribute' without precisely defining them.

An *entity* is a concept that can be created or deleted, or that has attributes which the analyst wants to enumerate. In figure 1, entities are shown in the left-hand column, left-justified. Note also the 'E' in the left margin.

An *attribute* is a property of an entity. In Figure 1, attributes are shown right-justified in the left-hand column. Note also the 'A' in the left margin. Attributes can be set ('**S**/C') or changed ('**C**/D').

For economy of space, the same columns are used to define how easy it is to create ('S/**C**') or delete ('C/**D**') entities. Each of these actions can be described as follows:

- *Easy*: no user difficulties.
- *Hard*: difficult for some reason (e.g. undiscoverable action, moded action, delayed effect of action). For example, it is possible to select a sentence in MS Word by pressing the control key ('apple' key on a Mac) and clicking anywhere in the sentence; few users are aware of this.
- *Indirect*: effect has to be achieved by changing something else in the system; for example, as discussed above, it is not possible to directly change the sequence of figure numbers.
- *Cant*: something that cannot be changed, that the analyst thinks might cause subsequent user difficulties.
- *Fixed*: something that cannot be changed, that is not, in fact, problematic; for example, an entity may be listed simply because it has important attributes that need to be enumerated or analysed.
- *BySys*: this denotes aspects of the system that may be changed, but not by the user (this may include by other agents – e.g. over a network, or simply other people). Many of these cases are not actually problems, and it is up to the analyst to consider implications.

Just as describing concepts as 'present', 'absent' or 'difficult' helps to highlight some conceptual difficulties, so describing actions in terms of 'easy', 'hard' , indirect', 'cant', 'fixed' and 'bySys' highlights conceptual difficulties in changing the state of the system.

3.4 Surface-Level Misfits and Their Cognitive Dimensions

We turn now to the use of CASSM to articulate part of the Cognitive Dimensions framework introduced above, starting with surface-level misfits – notably abstraction level and visibility.

Abstraction level: devices may be classed as imposing the use of abstractions ('abstraction-hungry' in Green's terminology), rejecting the use of abstractions ('abstraction-hating'), or allowing but not imposing abstractions ('abstraction-neutral'); further, the abstractions themselves may be domain-based or device-based. CASSM can express these distinctions reasonably well and can therefore detect some of the misfits, among them:

- domain abstractions that are part of the user's conceptual but are not implemented within the device;
- device abstractions imposed upon the user.

Imposed device abstractions have to be learnt in order to work effectively with the device, such as style sheets or graphics masks, and are therefore easy or difficult to learn according to how well they are represented at the interface (as discussed above).

Visibility: the user's ability to view components readily when required, preferably in juxtaposition to allow comparison between components. CASSM cannot at present express either inter-item juxtaposability nor the number of search steps required to bring a required item to view ('navigability') but captures the essence of visibility by designating those concepts that are hidden, disguised, delayed or undiscoverable as 'difficult' in the interface representation.

4 Structural Misfits: Taking Account of Relationships

As discussed above, structural misfits refer to the structure of information, and how the user can change that structure. Here, we present the structural misfits of which we are currently aware. These are a subset of Green's Cognitive Dimensions [3]. It is worth noting that structural misfits only apply to systems where the system state can be changed in a meaningful way by the user. Thus, systems such as web sites or vending machines do not generally suffer from structural misfits. However, systems such as drawing programs, word processors, music composition systems and design tools are prone to these misfits.

Another point to note is that although structural misfits are much finer-grained than the bolder surface-level misfits discussed above, they can be immense sources of user frustration and inefficiency.

Structural misfits depend on relationships that hold within the data. Five kinds of relationships are currently defined within Cassata. These are: *consists_of*, *device_constraint*, *goal_constraint*, *affects*, and *maps_onto*. As for entities and attributes, it is possible (though not always necessary) to state how well these relationships are represented at the interface, to the user, or in the underlying system.

Consists_of takes two arguments, which we call Actor and ActedOn, which are both concepts. This means that the first consists_of the second: chapter consists_of paragraphs; set-of-paragraphs consists_of paragraphs (e.g. sharing a paragraph style); etc.

Device_constraint also takes two arguments, both concepts. The value of Actor constrains the possible values of ActedOn. For example, considering drawing a map on the back of an envelope, the starting_position (for drawing) constrains the location of a particular instruction. An easier example is that the field-width for a data entry field constrains the item-width for any items to be put in that field.

Goal_constraint takes only one argument (ActedOn), which is the concept on which there is some domain-based constraint. For example, when writing a conference paper such as this one, it is common to have a limit on the length of a document.

Affects is concerned with side-effects: that changing the value of one concept will also change the value of another. For example, changing the number of words in a document will change its length.

Maps_onto is a simple way of expressing the idea that two concepts are very similar but not quite identical. These are most commonly a domain-relevant concept and a device-relevant one. For example, a (user) meeting maps_onto a (diary-entry) meeting but, depending on the form of the diary, the two meeting types may have importantly different attributes.

We now consider three important classes of structural misfits: viscosity (section 4.1), premature commitment (section 4.2) and hidden dependencies (section 4.3). In what follows, we take A to be an entity of interest with an attribute P, and B to be some other entity with attribute Q. these are defined in the top window by juxtaposition (i.e. attributes always appear immediately below the entity to which they pertain).

4.1 Viscosity

As discussed above, "viscosity" captures the idea that a system is difficult to change in some way. Green [13] distinguished two types of viscosity, repetition and knock-on, which can be defined as follows.

1) Repetition viscosity occurs when a single action within the user's conceptual model requires many, repetitive device actions.

Changing attribute P of entity A, A(P), needs many actions if:

```
A(P) is not directly modifiable
B(Q) affects A(P)
B(Q) is modifiable
A consists-of B
```

For example, as discussed above (section 2), we get repetition viscosity on figure numbers in a document because whenever a figure is added, deleted or moved, a range of figures need to be re-numbered one by one. Stated more formally:

```
set-of-figs(number-sequence) is not directly modifiable
figure(number) affects set-of-figs(number-sequence)
figure(number) is modifiable
set-of-figs consists-of figure
```

Figure 2 shows the basic requirements on a model for it to exhibit Repetition Viscosity. Note in particular the use of 'indirect' to denote something that can be changed, but not directly. Figure 3 shows the output when this particular model is assessed by Cassata.

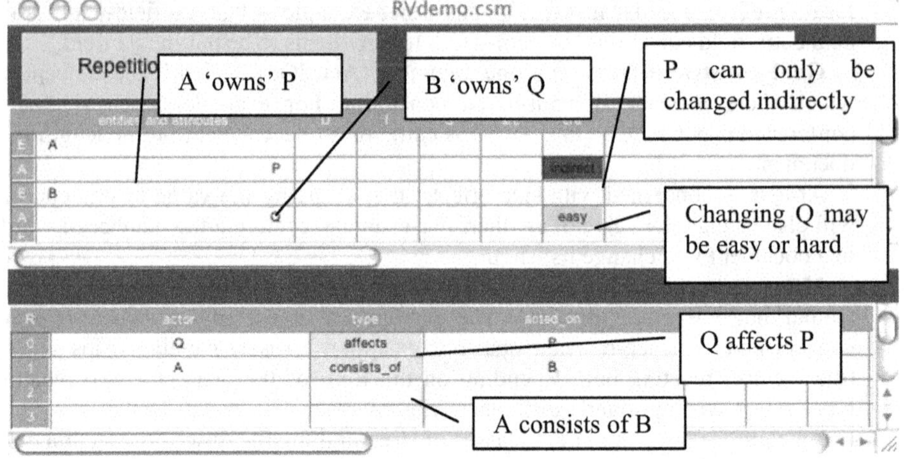

Fig. 2. Repetition Viscosity.

```
Repetition Viscosity Check ---- Repetition Viscosity Model

  attribute "Q" affects "P"
  entity "A" consists_of "B"
 "A " owns "P"
 "P " is not directly modifiable
 "B " owns "Q"
 "Q " is directly modifiable

possible case of repetition viscosity:
to change "P" user may have to change all instances of "Q"
```

Fig. 3. Output from Repetition Viscosity analysis in Cassata.

2) Knock-on viscosity: changing one attribute may lead to the need to adjust other things to restore the internal consistency. (In North America, a better-known phrase for the same concept appears to be 'domino effect'.)

Changing A(P) has possible knock-on if:

```
A(P) is modifiable
modifying A(P) affects B(Q)
there is a domain constraint on B(Q)
```

Timetables and schedules typically contain high knock-on viscosity; if one item is re-scheduled, many others may have to be changed as well.

Figure 4 shows the conditions for a model to exhibit Knock-on Viscosity. Figure 5 shows the output when this model is assessed by Cassata.

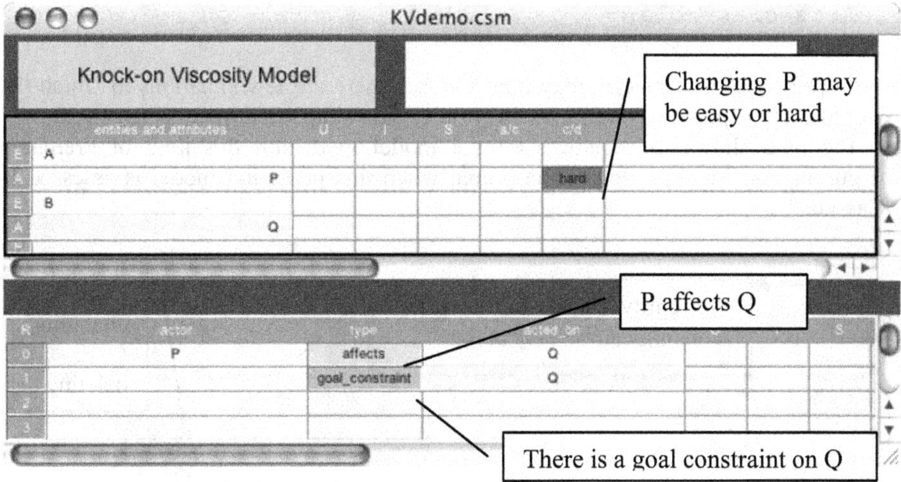

Fig. 4. Knock-on Viscosity.

Knock-on Viscosity Check ---- Knock-on Viscosity Model

attribute "P" affects "Q"
there is a goal_constraint on "Q"
"P " is directly modifiable

possible case of knock-on viscosity
modifying "P" may violate a domain constraint for "Q"

Fig. 5. Output from Knock-on Viscosity analysis in Cassata.

4.2 Premature Commitment

Informally, premature commitment occurs when the user has to provide information to the system earlier than they would wish or are prepared for. We have several sets of conditions that alert to possible premature commitment.

1) Non-modifiability premature commitment: As discussed above (under actions), if an attribute cannot be changed after it has been set then the system possibly demands premature commitment:

```
A(P) is settable
A(P) is not modifiable
```

Some painting tools exhibit this type of premature commitment: that the width and colour of a line cannot be changed once it has been set.

Extending this to entities, we may get potential non-modifiability premature commitment if entities can be created but not subsequently deleted:

```
A is creatable
A is not deletable
```

In principle the converse may hold too, but there are few situations in which that would class as premature commitment (rather than simply an irreversible action).

Figure 6 shows the conditions for a model to exhibit this kind of Premature Commitment. Figure 7 shows the output when this particular model is assessed by Cassata.

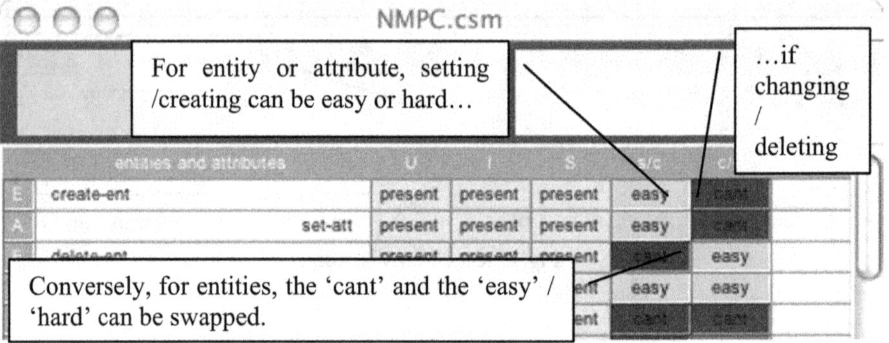

Fig. 6. Non-modifiability Premature Commitment.

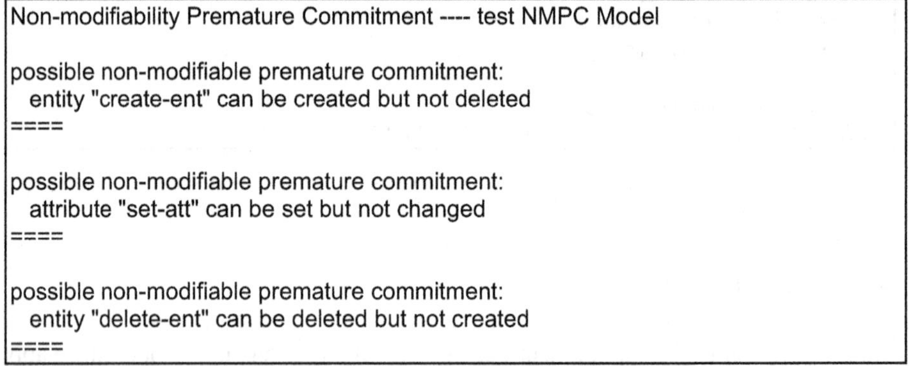

Non-modifiability Premature Commitment ---- test NMPC Model

possible non-modifiable premature commitment:
entity "create-ent" can be created but not deleted
====

possible non-modifiable premature commitment:
attribute "set-att" can be set but not changed
====

possible non-modifiable premature commitment:
entity "delete-ent" can be deleted but not created
====

Fig. 7. Output from Non-modifiability PC analysis in Cassata.

2) Abstraction-based premature commitment: If a user has to define an abstraction in order to avoid repetition viscosity, and that abstraction has to be defined in advance, then the system potentially creates abstraction-based premature commitment. Frequently that abstraction will be a simple grouping. A common example of potentially premature commitment to abstractions is the defining of paragraph styles before starting to create a technical document. The purpose is to avoid repetition viscosity by allowing all paragraphs of one type to be reformatted in one action, but the problem is to foresee the required definitions. A more technical example would be the creation of a class hierarchy in object-oriented programming.

The conventional analysis in the Cognitive Dimensions framework is to treat the abstraction management components of the system as a separate sub-device, which may have its own properties of viscosity, hidden dependencies, etc [4]. In CASSM we take a simplified approach such that this type of premature commitment is highlighted if:

```
A consists-of B
A(P) is directly modifiable
A(P) affects B(Q)
```

The paragraph styles case would be represented thus:

```
Paragraph has attribute style
Set-of-paragraphs has attribute style-description
Set-of-paragraphs consists-of paragraph
Style-description is directly modifiable
Changing style-description causes style to change
```

Figure 8 shows the basic requirements on a model for it to exhibit Abstraction-based Premature Commitment. Figure 9 shows the output when this particular model is assessed by Cassata.

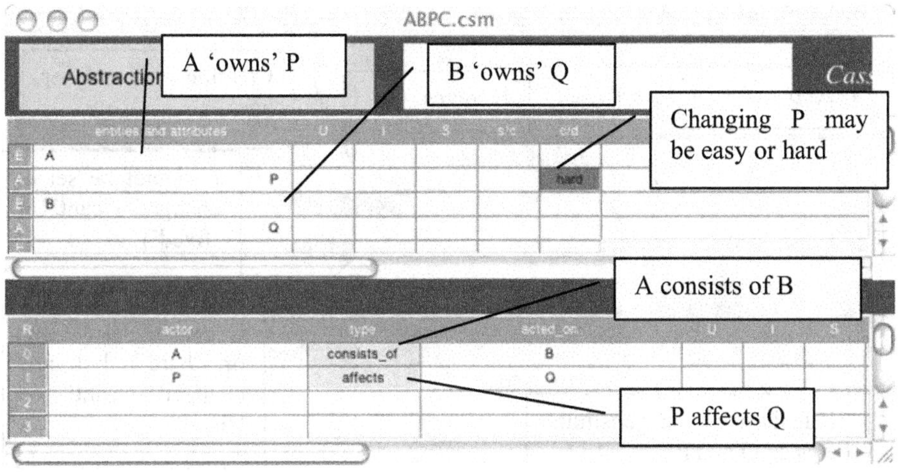

Fig. 8. Abstraction-based premature commitment.

```
Abstract-based Premature Commitment Check ---- Abstraction-based PC Model

  attribute "P" affects "Q"
  entity "A" consists_of "B"
 "A " owns "P"
 "P " is directly modifiable
 "B " owns "Q"

possible case of abstract-based premature commitment:
need to create an abstraction "A" to change all instances of "Q"
```

Fig. 9. Output from Abstraction-based PC analysis in Cassata.

3) Device-constraint premature commitment: Here, setting an attribute of one entity constrains the way that new instances of another entity can be created:

```
B(Q) is settable
A(P) is not settable
There is a device constraint between B(Q) and A(P)
It is possible to add more As
```

As mentioned above (when defining *device constraint*), one example of this is drawing a map on the back of an envelope; another is that of setting the field width in a data structure when the size of all items to be entered in that field is not known (here, “>=” is an example of a device constraint):

```
field(width) is settable
item(width) is not settable
field(width)>=item(width)
more items can be added
```

Figure 10 shows the basic requirements on a model for it to exhibit Device-constraint Premature Commitment. Figure 11 shows the output when this particular model is assessed by Cassata.

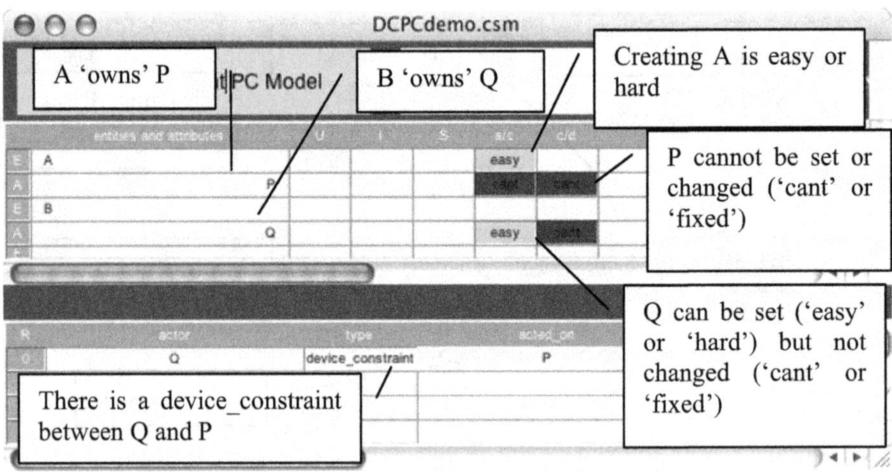

Fig. 10. Device-constraint premature commitment.

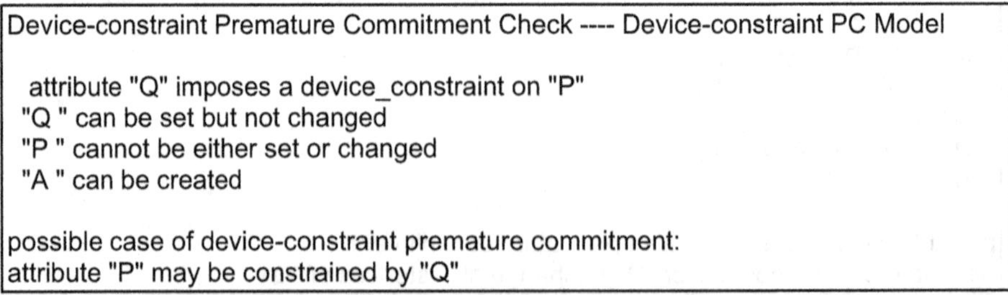

Device-constraint Premature Commitment Check ---- Device-constraint PC Model

attribute "Q" imposes a device_constraint on "P"
"Q " can be set but not changed
"P " cannot be either set or changed
"A " can be created

possible case of device-constraint premature commitment:
attribute "P" may be constrained by "Q"

Fig. 11. Output from Device-constraint PC analysis in Cassata.

4.3 Hidden Dependencies

A hidden dependency occurs when important links between concepts are not visible (or otherwise readily available to the user). Spreadsheets contain many hidden dependencies, so that changing a value or formula somewhere in a sheet can have unanticipated knock-on effects elsewhere in the sheet. Similarly, changing a style in MS Word can have unexpected knock-on effects on other styles through the style hierarchy. This is formalised simply:

```
Changing C affects D
The relationship is not visible
```

Here, C and D are concepts (entities or attributes). They may even be the same concept. For example, in the word processor because the concept 'style definition' denotes an aggregate of styles formed into a hierarchy, changing any one definition potentially changes other definitions that refer to it, so we have the reflexive relationship:

```
Changing style-definition affects style-definition
The relationship is not visible
```

Figure 12 shows the basic requirements on a model for it to exhibit Hidden Dependencies. Figure 13 shows the output when this particular model is assessed by Cassata.

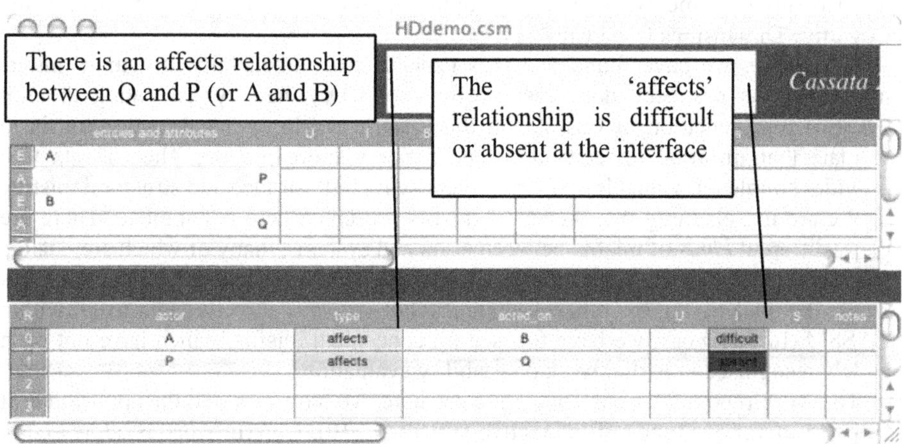

Fig. 12. Hidden Dependencies.

5 Conclusions

In this paper, we have presented a particular approach to assessing the usability of an interactive system based on the idea of 'quality of fit' between user and system. In particular, we have used the ontology of CASSM (considering entities, attributes, actions and a set of defined relationship types, and properties of each of these) to de-

```
Hidden Dependencies Check ---- Hidden Dependencies Model

 "A" affects "B"

possible case of hidden dependency:
there may be hidden dependency between "A" and "B"
====
 "P" affects "Q"

possible case of hidden dependency:
there may be hidden dependency between "P" and "Q"
```

Fig. 13. Output from Hidden Dependencies analysis in Cassata.

liver precise definitions of various kinds of surface and structural misfits. The structural misfits are all based on Green's [12] Cognitive Dimensions. Some of the surface misfits can also be identified as CDs, but most are not, and all have been independently derived from the basic CASSM ontology.

The prototype Cassata tool allows CASSM-based descriptions of systems to be created quickly and with a minimum of special concepts. When a CASSM description has been entered into Cassata, potential occurrences of both surface and structural misfits can be automatically identified, thereby alerting analysts to possible usability problems. With the help of Cassata we have preserved the original quick-to-do feel of the Cognitive Dimensions analysis, unlike previous efforts at formalising the Cognitive Dimensions framework [11,19].

In practice, we have found that it is usually easier to identify structural misfits informally (as has been done historically with CDs) than by generating the full CASSM representation in Cassata; in this case, the role of the formalisation is to validate that informal understanding and make it more precise. The Cassata tool provides simple but valuable support in identifying both surface and structural misfits.

We are not claiming that the set of misfits presented here is complete. There are many different *kinds* of misfits between users and systems, many of which are outside the scope of CASSM – for example, inconsistencies in procedures for similar tasks would be picked up by other techniques but are not directly addressed within CASSM. In this work, we have focused on conceptual misfits, which have not been widely recognised in earlier work on usability evaluation.

The work reported here is ongoing; elsewhere, we have reported the application of CASSM to various kinds of interactive systems [7,10]. Current work is addressed at refining the Cassata prototype, extending the set of structural misfits and scoping CASSM by comparison with other usability evaluation techniques (e.g. [6]). We believe that this work makes an important contribution to the overall repertoire of evaluation approaches for interactive systems.

Acknowledgements

This work is supported by EPSRC grant GR/R39108.

References

1. Beyer, H., Holtzblatt, K.: *Contextual Design*. San Francisco : Morgan Kaufmann. (1998).
2. Blackwell, A.F., Green, T.R.G.: A Cognitive Dimensions questionnaire optimised for users. In A.F. Blackwell & E. Bilotta (Eds.) *Proceedings of the Twelfth Annual Meeting of the Psychology of Programming Interest Group* (2000).137-152.
3. Blackwell, A., Green, T. R. G.: Notational systems – the Cognitive Dimensions of Notations framework. In J. Carroll (ed.), *HCI Models, Theories and Frameworks*, Morgan Kaufmann. (2003) 103-134.
4. Blackwell, A., Hewson, R., Green, T. R. G.: The design of notational systems for cognitive tasks. E. Hollnagel (ed.) In E. Hollnagel (Ed.), *Handbook of Cognitive Task Design*. Mahwah, N.J.: Lawrence Erlbaum. (2003) 525-545.
5. Blandford, A. E., Green, T. R. G.: Group and individual time management tools: what you get is not what you need. *Personal and Ubiquitous Computing*. Vol 5 No 4. (2001) 213–230.
6. Blandford, A., Keith, S., Connell, I., Edwards, H.: Analytical usability evaluation for Digital Libraries: a case study. In *Proc. ACM/IEEE Joint Conference on Digital Libraries*. (2004) 27-36.
7. Blandford, A. E., Wong, B. L. W., Connell, I. W., Green, T. R. G.: Multiple viewpoints on computer supported team work: a case study on ambulance dispatch. In X. Faulkner, J. Finlay & F. Détienne (eds), *Proc. HCI 2002 (People and Computers XVI)*, Springer (2002) 139-156.
8. Blandford, A. E., Young, R. M.: Specifying user knowledge for the design of interactive systems. *Software Engineering Journal*. 11.6, (1996) 323-333.
9. CASSM: Project web site www.uclic.ucl.ac.uk/annb/CASSM.html
10. Connell, I., Green, T., Blandford, A.: Ontological Sketch Models: highlighting user-system misfits. In E. O'Neill, P. Palanque & P. Johnson (Eds.) *People and Computers XVII, Proc. HCI'03*. Springer. (2003) 163-178.
11. Green, T. R. G., Benyon, D.: The skull beneath the skin: entity-relationship models of information artifacts. *International Journal of Human-Computer Studies*, 44 (1996) 801-828
12. Green, T. R. G.: Cognitive dimensions of notations. In A. Sutcliffe and L. Macaulay (Eds.) *People and Computers V*. Cambridge University Press. (1989) 443-460
13. Green, T.R.G.: The cognitive dimension of viscosity - a sticky problem for HCI. In D. Diaper and B. Shackel (Eds.) *INTERACT '90*. Elsevier. (1990)
14. Green, T. R. G., Blackwell, A. F.: Cognitive dimensions of information artefacts: a tutorial. http://www.cl.cam.ac.uk/~afb21/CognitiveDimensions/CDtutorial.pdf (1998)
15. Green, T. R. G., Petre, M.: Usability analysis of visual programming environments: a 'cognitive dimensions' framework. *J. Visual Languages and Computing*, 7, (1996) 131-174.
16. Moran, T. P.: Getting into a system: external-internal task mapping analysis, in A. Janda (ed.), *Human Factors in Computing Systems*, (1983) pp.45-49.
17. Nielsen, J.: Heuristic evaluation. In J. Nielsen & R. Mack (Eds.), *Usability Inspection Methods*, New York: John Wiley (1994) 25-62.
18. Payne, S. J., Squibb, H. R., Howes, A.: The nature of device models: the yoked state space hypothesis, and some experiments with text editors. *Human-Computer Interaction*, 5. (1990) 415-444.
19. Roast, C., Khazaei, B., Siddiqi, J.: Formal comparison of program modification. In *IEEE Symposium on Visual Languages*, IEEE Computer Society (2000). 165-171.
20. Wharton, C., Rieman, J., Lewis, C., Polson, P.: The cognitive walkthrough method: A practitioner's guide. In J. Nielsen & R. Mack (Eds.), *Usability Inspection Methods*. New York: John Wiley (1994) 105-140.

Discussion

[Willem-Paul Brinkman] In the case of misfits, the evaluator has to come up with an idea of what concepts/ideas users are using, and whether or not they map on the concepts of the system (system model/image). However, how does the evaluator check, if his/her ideas/concepts map with ideas/concepts the users have?

> [Ann Blandford] You present your finding to the users, and ask them whether they agree with having/using these concepts. At the moment this seems the best and most practical way.

[Jürgen Ziegler] How do dimensions like 'viscosity' relate to other, more established usability measures like 'effectiveness'?

> [Ann Blandford] Effectiveness might be a higher level concept, viscosity addresses sub aspects.

[Tom Ormerod] The distinction between concepts and tasks is interesting, though examples seemed to be about the tasks. Is CASSM about discovering concepts?

> [Ann Blandford] With the figure-numbering example, it is about making explicit an issue that is implicit, so yes

[Tom Ormerod] What would CASSM offer to the easier example of the problem of understanding the layers concept?

> [Ann Blandford] It suggests a search for ways to represent the layers explicitly at the interface.

Supporting a Shared Understanding of Communication-Oriented Concerns in Human-Computer Interaction: A Lexicon-Based Approach

Simone Diniz Junqueira Barbosa[1], Milene Selbach Silveira[2], Maíra Greco de Paula[1], Karin Koogan Breitman[1]

[1]Departamento de Informática, PUC-Rio
Marquês de São Vicente, 225 / 4º andar RDC
Gávea, Rio de Janeiro, RJ, Brazil, 22453-900
simone@inf.puc-rio.br, mgreco@inf.puc-rio.br, karin@les.inf.puc-rio.br

[2] Faculdade de Informática, PUCRS
Av.Ipiranga, 6681, Prédio 30, Bloco 4
Porto Alegre, RS, Brazil, 90619-900
milene@inf.pucrs.br

Abstract. This paper discusses the role of an enhanced extended lexicon as a shared communicative artifact during software design. We describe how it may act as an interlingua that captures the shared understanding of both stakeholders and designers. We argue for the need to address communicative concerns among design team members, as well as from designers to users through the user interface. We thus extend an existing lexicon language (LEL) to address communication-oriented concerns that user interface designers need to take into account when representing their solution to end users. We propose that the enhanced LEL may be used as a valuable resource in model-based design, in modeling the help system, and in engineering the user interface elements and widgets.

Keywords: communication-centered design, model-based design of human-computer interaction, semiotic engineering, language extended lexicon

1 Introduction

In this paper, we describe a lexicon-based representation to express domain and application concepts during the design process. We propose that, by doing so, designers, users and other stakeholders may have a shared understanding of the application, detailing its relevant concepts and their relationships. We have argued elsewhere that we need representations that will make possible a more balanced participation of stakeholders and team players from different interdisciplinary background during design [3]. This paper will focus on the communicative concerns that (esp. interaction) designers must deal with throughout the design process. We follow Preece et al.'s definition of interaction design: "designing interactive products

R. Bastide, P. Palanque, and J. Roth (Eds.): EHCI-DSVIS 2004, LNCS 3425, pp. 271-288, 2005.

to support people in their everyday and working lives" [26, p.6]. This definition is in accordance with Mullet & Sano's perspective that human-computer interaction (HCI) is "concerned most directly with the user's experience of a form in the context of a specific task or problem, as opposed to its functional or aesthetic qualities in isolation" [20, p.1]. Within HCI, semiotic engineering [9,10] has emerged as a semiotics-based theory [11,24] that describes and explains HCI phenomena, adopting primarily a media perspective on the use of computer artifacts [16].

Scenarios have been used as the primary representation to foster communication among team members and stakeholders [6]. We propose that an enriched lexicon can complement scenarios by representing together the different perspectives of each sign, which are typically scattered in many scenarios. This lexicon can be used to establish a common vocabulary throughout various design stages. By doing so, we believe it would be easier to build the design models taking both the lexicon and the scenarios as a starting point. In particular, such a lexicon can be used to derive three important kinds of resources: the user interface signs, which users should understand and learn to manipulate to make the most of their interaction with application [9,10]; the help content [29, 30]; and ontologies [13, 14], which can be employed in user, dialog and task modeling, especially in adaptive user interfaces [22] and the semantic web [4].

2 Semiotic Engineering and Communication-Centered Design

Semiotic Engineering focuses on the engineering of signs that convey what HCI designers and users have in mind and what effect they want to cause in the world of things, practices, ideas and experiences [9,10]. The interface signs constitute a message sent from designers to users, representing the designers' solution to what they believe is the users' problems, what they have interpreted as being the users' needs and preferences, what the answer for these needs is and how they implemented their vision as an interactive system. In particular, semiotic engineering proposes a change of focus from *producing* to *introducing* design artifacts to users [10].

Our work builds on semiotic engineering by attempting to ensure that domain concepts are well represented and understood by every team member[1] before proceeding to later design stages. We need to promote the shared understanding among the team members (for instance, by representing domain concepts and their interrelationships), and to allow designers to represent communication-centered concerns developed for improving designer-to-user communication during interaction [9,10]. Our basic assumption is that, in order to increase the chances of engineering adequate signs at the user interface to convey the designers' vision and thus properly introduce the design artifact, we need to first establish this vision and communicate it effectively among team members themselves, always from a user's point of view (Fig. 1).

[1] By "team members" we mean the stakeholders (clients and users) and the designers (members of the development team from various disciplines, such as software engineering, human-computer interaction, graphics design, linguistics, psychology and so on).

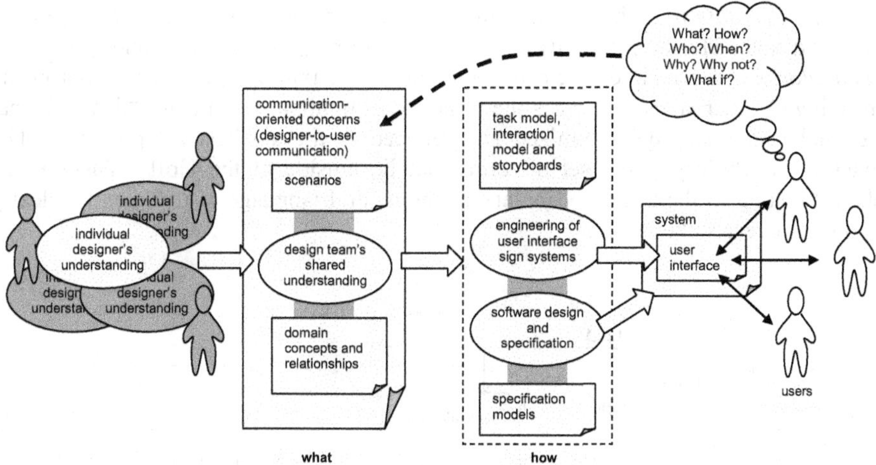

Fig. 1. Communication-centered design.

The communication-oriented concerns we will address in this paper are derived from studies about users' frequent doubts [1,28], as indicated by the dashed arrow in Fig. 1. These concerns will be described in section 4.

If designers are unable to convey their vision to each other and to every stakeholder, they will hardly succeed in conveying it to users (through carefully designing the user interface). If, on the other hand, they succeed in promoting designer-designer communication via communication artifacts, they will be better equipped to communicate with users through the user interface, i.e., to engineer the user interface sign systems. This way, we aim to take one step towards a communication-centered approach to interactive software design and development.

3 The Language Extended Lexicon (LEL)

As a starting point to building our communication artifacts, we take on the requirements engineering work of the Language Extended Lexicon (LEL) [18]. The LEL is a representation of the signs in the language of the application domain. LEL is anchored on the idea that one must first "understand the *language* of the problem, without worrying about understanding the *problem*" [18]. Researchers in different areas have pointed out the strong relationship between culture and language. In semiotics, in particular, the works of Eco and Danesi pay special attention to the web of language, culture and social environments [8,11]. In software design, the strength of using language to promote a shared understanding of the problem design domain and also of the solution accounts for the success of scenario-based approaches in various design stages [6].

To capture the language of the application domain and represent it in a Universe of Discourse (UofD), each term in LEL has two types of description: (i) *notion*, the denotation of the term or phrase; and (ii) *impact*, extra information about the context at hand[2]. In addition, each lexicon term is classified in four categories: object, subject, verb and state. The strong points in LEL are the principles of *closure* and of *minimal vocabulary*. The principle of closure attempts to "maximize the use of signs in the meaning of other signs", whereas the principle of minimal vocabulary "demands that external vocabulary be minimized and reduced to the smallest set possible". The external vocabulary is the set of terms that lie outside of the UofD. These terms should belong to the basic vocabulary of the natural language in use, i.e., be clearly known to every stakeholder.

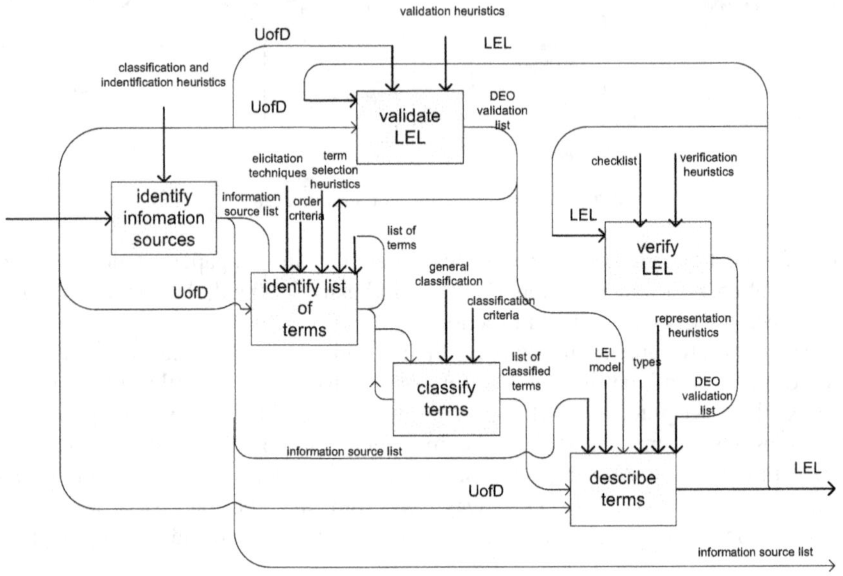

Fig. 2. Lexicon construction process [17].

Kaplan and co-authors describe in detail the process of constructing a LEL representation [17]. It comprises six steps, as depicted in Fig. 2. First one needs to identify the main information sources of the UofD, such as people and documents. Then, one must identify a list of relevant terms to be included in the UofD. By observing how people work and interviewing them, as well as by reading the documents and inspecting the artifacts they generate or use, a candidate list of terms is generated. Each term is then classified into object, subject, verb or state. The fourth step is to describe the meaning of each term —define its notion and impact—, being careful so as to respect the the principles of closure and minimal vocabulary. This step typically unveils additional terms to be included in the lexicon, and which undergo a similar process. In the last two steps, the lexicon is verified by inspection and

[2] LEL authors state that the impact, formerly known as behavioral description, describes the "*connotation*, that is., and additional meaning of a word" [18]. From a semiotic point of view, however, the use of the term *connotation* in this sense is not accurate, and thus will not be used in this paper.

validated by the stakeholders. As with scenarios, the lexicon is written in natural language, which makes it easy for non-experts to understand, question, and validate. The lexicon is also represented as a hypertext, which makes it easy to navigate between any two related terms.

In the context of the semantic web, there is a growing need to represent the semantics of the applications [4]. The need is fully met by the LEL, which provides both the meaning and relationships among its terms. However, the fact that the LEL is coded in natural language format prevents is from being automated by machines. Ontologies, in our understanding, are the formalization of the concepts captured by the LEL in a machine processable language, e.g., DAML+Oil or OWL [15, 19]. Readers who are interested in deriving formal ontologies may refer to [5], which describes how to derive a machine-processable ontological representation from the lexicon.

We argue that the quality of the resulting lexicon depends highly on the experience and domain knowledge of its builders. Moreover, in following a semiotic engineering approach to HCI, we would like the meaning descriptions to reflect the designers' assumptions about the users' knowledge and expectations of the domain and application. As we will see in the next sections, these assumptions may be captured in the form of answers to questions related to the users' most frequent doubts. In this context, this paper proposes to extend LEL to enhance its capacity as a communicative artifact among team members, and as a concrete resource for model-based design of interactive artifacts.

It is important to note that we do not suggest to use LEL in isolation. Instead, we propose to use it to complement scenarios [6]. Scenarios give all stakeholders an understanding of the domain and of the application being designed, in a contextualized manner. However, we felt the need to centralize the definitions of goals, tasks, agents and objects, because if they are scattered throughout scenarios, problems of inconsistency and incompleteness may prevent designers to build an adequate conceptual model of the domain (and later of the solution). This would make it harder to engineer the signs that will be conveyed to users through the user interface. Designers need both the contextualization of the scenarios and the different perspectives that LEL gathers together for each sign.

4 Communication-Oriented Concerns in Model-Based Interaction Design

Although LEL is a useful tool for representing domain concepts and their interrelationships, we want to shift the focus to communication-oriented concerns involved in user-system interaction. These concerns were explored in previous work on communicability evaluation [25] and help systems design [29]. In this section, we outline the communication-oriented concerns that, we believe, need to be represented throughout the design process.

Traditional model-based approaches to user interface design are rooted in cognitive theories or ergonomic approaches, which focus on the human interacting with the system image [21]. Our work is based on semiotic engineering [9], which takes on a communicative perspective to HCI, viewing the user interface as a metamessage sent from designers to users. This message is created in such a way as to be capable of exchanging messages with users, i.e., allowing human-system interaction. In semiotic engineering, the high-level message sent from the designer to users can be paraphrased as follows [9]:

> *"Here is my understanding of who you [users] are, what I've learned you want or need to do, in which preferred ways, and why. This is the system that I have therefore designed for you, and this is the way you can or should use it to fulfill a range of purposes that fall within this [my] vision."*

Because semiotic engineering brings to the picture designers themselves as communicators, we need to provide tools to better support them in this communicative process, ultimately via the user interface. One way to accomplish this is by investigating communication problems users experience when interacting with an application. These problems may be expressed by their frequent doubts and needs for instructions and information, i.e. help content. In the literature about help systems, we find that users would like to receive answers to their most frequent doubts, as summarized in Table 1 [1,28].

Table 1. Taxonomy of users' frequent doubts.

Types of Questions	Sample Questions
Informative	*What kinds of things can I do with this program?*
Descriptive	*What is this? What does this do?*
Procedural	*How do I do this?*
Interpretive	*What is happening now? Why did it happen? What does this mean?*
Navigational	*Where am I? Where have I come from? Where can I go to?*
Choice	*What can I do now?*
Guidance	*What should I do now?*
History	*What have I done?*
Motivational	*Why should I use this program? How will I benefit from using it?*
Investigative	*What else should I know? Did I miss anything?*

We propose that the questions related to the users' most frequent doubts be explicitly addressed throughout the various design stages, starting from requirements elicitation (and the construction of the LEL). Our ultimate goal is to provide designers with a comprehensive understanding of the domain and of the effects of their design decisions on the final product (i.e. the user interface), as viewed from a user's point-of-view. By using these potential user questions, we help designers to reflect while they make important design decisions, engaging in reflection-in-action [27]. At the same time, we would want to encourage the representation of these design decisions, thus building the design rationale of the envisaged application.

From the users' point-of-view, we make use of communicability and help utterances that allow users to better express their doubts during interaction [29] (Table 2). By anticipating users' doubts during design, the team members will be better equipped to deal with the users' communicative needs, either by designing applications that avoid interaction breakdowns altogether, or by giving users better chances for circumventing them [31].

Table 2. Communication-oriented utterances related to users' doubts during interaction breakdowns.

Original Communicability Utterances	(Additional) Help Utterances
What's this?	How do I do this? (Is there another way to do this?)
What now? (What can I do? What should I do? Where can I go?)	What is this for? (Why should I do this?)
What happened?	Whom/What does this affect?
Why doesn't it (work)?	On whom/what does this depend?
Oops!	Who can do this?
Where is *it*?	Where was I?
Where am I?	
I can't do it.	

An answer to the "What's this?" communicability utterance can be easily found in the *notion* part of each LEL term. For other utterances, however, the answers are not so straightforward, and depend highly on how meaning is described as an *impact* in LEL. In the next section, we describe how LEL definitions may include key elements needed in our design approach.

5 Enhancing LEL to Provide a Communicative Artifact for Design Team Members

In the previous sections, we have argued for the importance of providing a common vocabulary to promote the stakeholders' shared understanding of the domain using the LEL, and how relevant design decisions should be addressed and represented from a communication-oriented standpoint while building the design models. In this section, we explore how these two approaches may be coupled, i.e., how the answers to important design decisions can be recorded as part of the LEL, making it easier to take advantage of them in later design and specification stages.

Taking into consideration the communication-oriented concerns described in the previous section, we propose to enhance the LEL to incorporate the various communicative dimensions related to each concept or relationship. By doing so, we aim not only to create consensus among team members, but also to provide solid grounds for engineering the user interface sign systems that will minimize the effects of interaction breakdowns.

To show how our approach can be put to practical use, we briefly describe a case study we've developed: a system for managing conference submissions and reviews. Before building LEL, we felt the need for some guidance in identifying the first relevant signs. Inspired by traditional HCI work, we decided to start by building scenarios describing some of the users' roles, goals and tasks (Fig. 3). From the users' roles, we identified candidate roles (subjects in LEL), and from the goals and tasks we extracted a first set of verbs and objects.

Scenario 1. PC chair assigns submissions to reviewers. *The* ***deadline*** *for the ABC 2004* ***conference*** *has arrived, and Mark, the* **PC chair**, *needs now to start the* ***reviewing*** *process. First he* **assigns** *the* **submissions** *to the* **reviewers**, *based on the* ***maximum number of submissions*** *each* **reviewer** *has determined, as well as on the expertise level of each* **reviewer** *with respect to the****conference topics****. He would like to have at least 3* **reviews** *of each* ***submission****. To avoid having problems of fewer* **reviews**, *he decides to* **assign** *each* **submission** *to at least 4* **reviewers**. *[...] One month later, Mark* **receives** *the* **reviews** *and must now* **decide** *upon the* **acceptance** *or* **rejection** *of each* ***submission****. Since there are a few* **borderline submissions**, *whose* **grades** *do not make clear whether it should be accepted or rejected, he decides to* ***examine*** *the* ***distribution of submissions per conference topic****. In doing so, he decides, from among* **submissions** *with similar* **ratings**, *those that will* **ensure** *some* ***diversity*** *in the* **conference program**. *However, this is not enough to* **decide** *about the* **acceptance** *of all* **submissions**, *and thus he* **assigns** *the remaining cases to additional* **reviewers**, *asking them for a quick* **response**.

Scenario 2. Reviewer judges submissions. *John, an HCI* ***expert***, ***accepts*** *Mark* ***invitation*** *to become a* ***reviewer*** *for ABC 2004. He tells Mark that he will only be able to* ***review*** *3* **submissions**, *though. To help Mark with the* ***submissions assignment***, *he* **chooses** *from among the* **conference topics** *those he wishes to* ***review***, *i.e., in which he is an expert and interested. [...] He* ***receives*** *4* ***submissions*** *(one more than he'd asked for), but decides to* ***review*** *them all. He carefully* **reads** *every* **submission**, *and* **grades** *them according to the* ***form*** *Mark gave him, with the* **criteria** *of:* ***originality***, ***relevance*** *to ABC 2004,* ***technical quality***, *and* ***readability***. *For the* **submissions** *that he* **judged** *acceptable, he* ***makes*** *some* ***comments*** *that he thinks will help* ***authors*** *to* ***prepare*** *the* ***final version***. *For the* **submission** *he thinks must be* ***rejected***, *his* ***comments*** *suggest* ***improvements*** *in the* **work** *itself, for future* **submissions**.

Fig. 3. Sample scenarios, describing user roles, the corresponding goals and tasks, and highlighting the candidate LEL signs in boldface.

By coupling LEL's basic elements — object, subject, verb and state— with communicability utterances, we allow design team members to thoroughly represent and understand the domain concepts from a user's point-of-view. At later design stages, designers may also use it to reflect on how the application should support users' tasks in this domain [27]. For each pair <element, utterance>, we suggest the identification of key elements that are needed to respond to the corresponding utterance. These questions work with LEL in a way analogous to the systematic questioning of scenarios proposed in [7]. Tha major difference is that the questions we use are grounded on users' most frequent doubts.

In the following, we relate the possible kinds of answers to each pair <element,utterance>, as well as the elements designers should try to include in their phrasing in order to provide such answers (Tables 3 to 6).

Table 3. Communicative utterances and suggested content for the description of LEL subjects.

subject	elements included in the sign meaning	comm. utterances
basic notion	1. what goals the subject {may | must | must not} achieve;	*What's this?* *What's this for?*
impact	2. which goal(s), task(s) and action(s) are available; 3. what task sequences (are assumed that) the subject will prefer for each goal	*How do I do this? Why should I do this? What now? (What can I do?)*
	4. breakdowns that hinder the performance of an action or task, or the achievement of a goal	*What happened?*

Table 4. Communicative utterances and suggested content for the description of LEL objects.

object	elements included in the sign meaning	comm. utterances
basic notion	5. object type, with respect to a generalization/specialization hierarchy of object-signs; 6. object composition, with respect to a partonomy of object-signs and a set of attribute-signs	*What's this?*
impact	7. which goal(s) {produce | destroy | modify | require} the object; 8. which task(s) or action(s) {produce | destroy | modify | require } the object, and why (associated with which goal)	*What's this for?*
	9. which subject(s) {may | must | must not} { create | destroy | modify | view } the object	*Who can do this?*

Table 5. Communicative utterances and suggested content for the description of LEL verbs.

verb	elements included in the sign meaning	comm. utterances
basic notion	10. subtasks or subordinate atomic actions; 11. what objects are {produced | destroyed | modified | required}	*What's this?*

	12. subjects who {may | must | must not} achieve the goal; 13. subjects who {may | must | must not} perform the action or task	*Who can do this? (I can't do it.)*
	14. associated user goal(s); 15. reasons for choosing this task or action over another that achieves the same goal(s)	*What's this for? Why should I do this?*
	16. task or action sequences available for achieving the goal	*How do I do this? Is there another way to do this?*
impact	17. possible outcomes of the action; 18. for outcomes that may represent a breakdown, actions for circumventing it	*What happened?*
	19. subjects affected by the achievement of the goal or performance of the task or action; 20. the possible resulting status of the objects after the goal, task or action	*Whom/What does this affect?*
	21. preconditions for performing the action or task, or for achieving the goal; 22. subjects that restrict the achievement of the goal or performance of the task or action; 23. the necessary status of the objects before the goal, task or action	*On whom/what does this depend? (I can't do it.)*
	24. task sequence(s) necessary to reverse the action	*Oops!*

Table 6. Communicative utterances and suggested content for the description of LEL status.

status	elements included in the sign meaning	comm. utterances
basic notion	25. objects or subjects to which this status corresponds	*What's this?*
	26. tasks or actions that change this status	*What's this for?*
	27. how this status can be reached (through which task(s) or action(s))	*How do I do this?*
impact	28. explanation on how the current state was (or may have been) reached; 29. corrective measures to allow the user to reverse the effects of the task or action	*Oops!*
	30. how to change the status to achieve a goal; 31. for status that may represent a breakdown, suggested actions for circumventing it	*What now? (I can't do it)*
	32. how the status was reached	*What happened? Where was I?*

In these tables, we have extended the LEL to include some of the communication-oriented utterances, but we have maintained the independence of the technological solution. To answer the remaining utterances (*Where is it?, Where am I?, Where was I?*, and *Why doesn't it?*), it is necessary to provide more detail with respect to the interactive solution. The level of detail represented in LEL, in our view, should reflect the design decisions that have been made at each design stage.

While modeling the tasks or designing the interaction, it should be possible to answer the following questions (Table 7):

Table 7. Descriptions of LEL elements to be completed during interaction design.

Subject

LEL	elements included in the sign meaning	comm. utterances
impact	33. at each interaction step, the current "position" relative to a goal	*Where am I?*
	34. at each interaction step, the previous step; 35. how to go back to the previous step	*Where was I?*

At a later stage, while designing the user interface, it should be possible to answer the following questions:

Table 8. Descriptions of LEL elements to be completed during user interface design.

Object

LEL	elements included in the sign meaning	comm. utterances
impact	36. widget that corresponds to the object; 37. location of the widget at the user interface	*Where is it?*

Verb

LEL	elements included in the sign meaning	comm. utterances
impact	38. the kind of feedback issued after triggering the action; 39. the associated goal(s) to detect mismatches between users' goals and user interface elements	*Why doesn't it?*

Many of the responses associated to the pairs <element, utterance> are interrelated. The hypertextual nature of LEL makes it easier for team members to traverse from one concept to related questions in another concept, using the utterances as a navigation aid [18]. This mechanism is analogous to the layering technique used in the minimalist approach [12] and to the help access mechanisms proposed in [29,30].

Table 9 presents a sample of the enriched LEL for the conference management system described in the aforementioned scenarios.

Table 9. Sample of the enriched LEL for the conference management system[3].

Object: Submission

LEL	elements included in the sign meaning	comm. utterances
basic notion	40. A document describing a research work that is submitted by an author to be considered for publication in the conference. 41. Is reviewed with respect to quality. 42. May be accepted or rejected.	*What's this?*
impact	43. PC chair must assign submissions to adequate reviewers. 44. PC chair must decide about acceptance of borderline submissions, either by assigning submissions to additional reviewers or by checking for diversity of submissions with respect to conference topics. 45. Reviewer tells PC chair how many submissions he'd be willing to review, so that he doesn't receive too many submissions. **46.** Reviewer grades submissions to review. **47.** PC chair ranks submissions according to reviews.	*What's this for?* *Who can do this?*

Subject: Reviewer

LEL	elements included in the sign meaning	comm. utterances
basic notion	48. Expert in some of the conference topics. 49. Responsible for reviewing submissions.	*What's this?* *What's this for?*
impact	50. May set number of desired submissions to review. 51. May define expertise and expectations with respect to keywords/topics, to review only submission for which you are an expert. 52. Must grades and comment submissions according to their quality.	*What can I do?*
	53. May need to decline an assignment due to conflict of interest or lack of knowledge.	*What happened?*

[3] For reasons of clarity, these tables do not show the hypertext links. As in the original LEL, if any LEL sign A is found in the meaning of the current sign B, A would be marked as hypertext link to the LEL definition of A.

Verb : Review (submission) [4]		
LEL	**elements included in the sign meaning**	**comm. utterances**
basic notion	54. To evaluate the quality of the submission.	*What's this?*
	55. To comment on the content of the submission to guide authors in preparing the final version, if the submission is acceptable, or a future submission, if it is unacceptable.	*What's this for?*
impact	56. Reviewers must review the submissions assigned to him. 57. Own authors and interested parties must not review the submission. 58. Non-experts should not review the submission. 59. No one may review a submission not assigned to him.	*Who can do this?* *(I can't do it.)*
	60. To help the PC chair in deciding on the acceptance or rejection of submissions.	*What's this for?* *Why should I do this?*
	61. There must be grades to the following criteria: originality, relevance to conference, technical quality, and readability.	*How do I do this?* *Is there another way to do this?*
	62. The PC chair decisions about acceptance or rejection depend on the reviews. 63. A review may be completed and sent in time, or may be late or missing.	*Whom/What does this affect?*
	64. The PC chair is responsible for assigning submissions for reviewers to review.	*On whom/what does this depend? (I can't do it.)*
	65. If the reviewer makes a mistake in the review, he needs to be able to modify or destroy it.	*Oops!*

By exploring the answers to the questions related to each LEL element from the users' standpoint, designers not only move towards achieving a shared understanding of the domain and how the application should support the users, but also are able to envisage the consequences of their design decision with respect to the user's future interactive exchanges with the application. Also, by doing so designers are developing a large portion of the help content for the final product *pari passu* the design decisions [30]. We believe this may facilitate not only the application evolution, but also the generation of user interfaces for multiple platforms and devices.

[4] A verb in LEL typically corresponds to a goal, task or action, but we define it in terms of the objects it manipulates.

From the responses to the communication-oriented questions, designers may then proceed to modeling the application. Fig. 4 illustrates a possible schema for modeling the designers' concerns [29] as related to the communication-oriented questions.

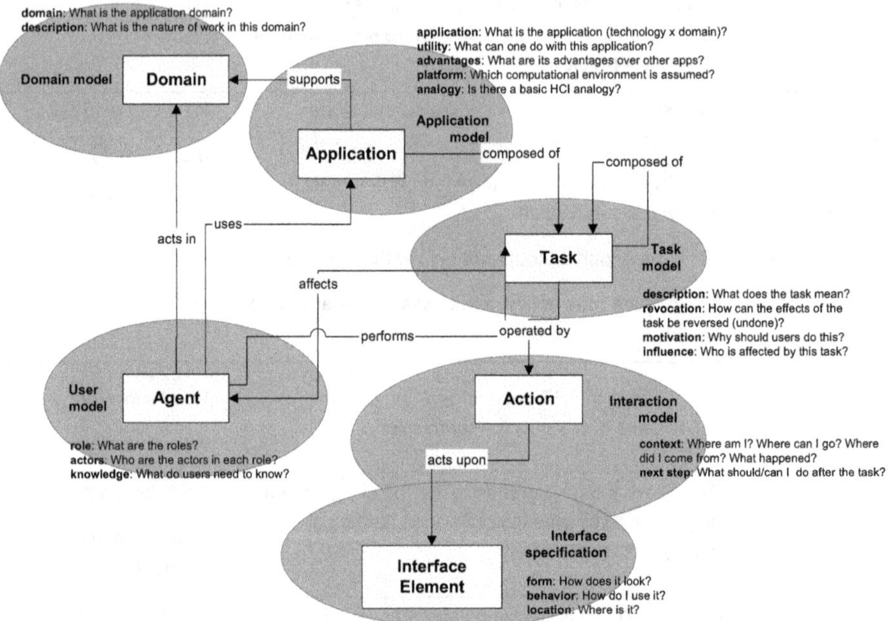

Fig. 4. Schema for representing information in model-based design of human-computer interaction.

From a first version of this schema, HCI designers may then proceed into detailed interaction modeling [2,3] and storyboarding, whereas software designers have resources to specify the system's functional aspects.

6 Concluding Remarks

In this paper, we have described a communication-oriented design approach that brings together a technique for eliciting requirements and a design method driven by users' frequent doubts. Our goal was twofold: to create a shared understanding of the domain and how the application should support users in that domain, and to provide resources (and possible the underlying design rationale) for designing the interaction and engineering the user interface signs.

We illustrated the proposed approach by briefly describing some aspects of a case study system for conference submission and reviewing. During the case study, we noticed at least two important benefits of the proposed approach. First, the communication-oriented utterances, coupled with the elements to be included in the sign meaning (described in the tables at the previous section), helped designers inspect LEL, uncovering additional signs and refining previously-defined meanings of existing signs. Second, by explicitly representing the communicative concerns associated with each domain concept, design team members succeeded in forming a comprehensive vision of the domain and the application, and could thus envisage alternative technological solutions at the users' workplace. The case study described in this paper is still underway, and we plan to evaluate the communicability of the resulting application, and also a usability inspection to compare it with an existing application of a similar kind.

To gather stronger evidence about the advantages of this approach, we are currently developing multiple case studies, in the following domains: web content publication and location-based instant messaging in mobile devices. One of the issues we want to explore is whether the LEL structure or its classification should be changed to better accommodate the communicative concerns and the evolution of each concept's definition during different design stages, to capture the underlying design rationale and to provide different levels of focus and detail to address the relevant design concerns at each moment. The reason for investigating whether LEL structure should be changed is that, in our case study, at times we were tempted to structure LEL's descriptions according to users' goals and tasks, as in common HCI practice. Also, we felt that some elements do not fit well into LEL's classification, such as "expertise" or "submission deadline". We intend to analyze in the future whether modifiers and constraints should also receive a first-class status in LEL and thus be considered relevant signs with their own set of communication-oriented questions. For now, we have treated them as generic signs, for which the only associated question is "What's this?".

As future work, we intend to elaborate a set of guidelines for deriving communication-oriented interaction models [2] and for engineering user interface signs [9] from the enhanced LEL. In addition, we want to investigate the benefits of adopting the approach described in this paper in the design of an adaptive system, by deriving formal ontologies and explicitly incorporating to these systems the users' beliefs, goals, and plans.

Acknowledgments

Simone D. J. Barbosa, Maíra Greco de Paula and Karin Breitman would like to thank CNPq for providing financial support to this work. Simone D.J. Barbosa, Milene Selbach Silveira and Maíra Greco de Paula thank their colleagues at the Semiotic Engineering Research Group at PUC-Rio for many discussions that have contributed to this work.

References

1. Baecker, R.M. et al. (1995). *Readings in Human-Computer Interaction: toward the year 2000*. San Francisco: Morgan Kaufmann Publishers, Inc.

2. Barbosa, S.D.J.; de Souza, C.S. ; Paula, M.G. (2003) "The Semiotic Engineering Use of Models for Supporting Reflection-In-Action". *Proceedings of HCI International 2003*. Crete, Greece.

3. Barbosa, S.D.J; Paula, M.G. (2004) "Adopting a Communication-Centered Design Approach to Support Interdisciplinary Design Teams". *Bridging the Gaps II: Bridging the Gaps Between Software Engineering and Human-Computer Interaction*, ICSE 2004 workshop, Edinburgh, Scotland.

4. Berners-Lee, T.; Hendler, J.; Lassila, O. (2001) "The Semantic Web", Scientific American, May 2001. Available online at: http://www.scientificamerican.com/article.cfm?articleID=00048144-10D2-1C70-84A9809EC588EF21&catID=2

5. Breitman, K. and Leite, J. (2003) Ontology as a Requirement Engineering Product .In: *11th IEEE International Requirements Engineering Conference.* Monterey Bay, California, USA, pp. 309-319.

6. Carroll, J.M. (ed., 1995) *Scenario-based Design: Envisioning Work and Technology in System Development.* New York, NY. John Wiley and Sons.

7. Carroll, J.M.; Mack, R.L.; Robertson, S.P.; Rosson, M.B. (1994) "Binding Objects to Scenarios of Use", *International Journal of Human-Computer Studies* **41**:243-276. Academic Press.

8. Danesi, M., Perron, P. (1999) *Analyzing Cultures: An Introduction and Handbook*, Indiana University Press.

9. de Souza, C.S. (in press) *The Semiotic Engineering of Human-Computer Interaction.* The MIT Press.

10. de Souza, C.S. (in press) Semiotic engineering: switching the HCI perspective from producing to introducing high-quality interactive software artifacts. *Interacting with Computers* **16**-6. Forthcoming.

11. Eco; U. (1979) *A theory of Semiotics*, Bloomington, IN: Indiana University Press.

12. Farkas, D.K. (1998) "Layering as a Safety Net for Mini-malist Documentation". In J.M. Carroll (ed.) *Minimalism Beyond the Nurnberg Funnel.* The MIT Press, Cambridge.

13. Fensel, D. (2001) Ontologies: a silver bullet for knowledge management and electronic commerce, Springer.

14. Gruber, T.R.(1993) "A translation approach to portable ontology specifications", *Knowledge Acquisition*, 5 (2): 199-220

15. Hendler, J.; McGuiness, D. (2000) "The DARPA agent Markup Language", *IEEE Intelligent Systems*, 16 (6), 2000. pp.67-73.

16. Kammersgaard, J. (1988) "Four different perspectives on Human-Computer Interaction", International Journal of Man-Machine Studies 28:343-362, Academic Press.

17. Kaplan, G.; Hadad, G.; Doorn, J.; Leite, J.C.S.P. (2000) "Inspección del Lexico Extendido del Lenguaje". *Proceedings of the Workshop de Engenharia de Requisitos, WER'00.* Rio de Janeiro, Brasil.

18. Leite, J.C.S.P.; Franco, A.P.M, (1992) "A Strategy for Conceptual Model Acquisiton". *Proceedings of the IEEE International Symposium on Requirements Engineering*, IEEE Computer Society Press, Pags. 243-246, San Diego.

19. McGuiness, D.; Harmelen, F. (2003) *OWL Web Ontology Overview*, W3C Working Draft 31 March 2003.

20. Mullet, K., and Sano, D. (1995) *Designing Visual Interfaces: Communication-Oriented Techniques*, SunSoft Press, Mountain View, CA.

21. Norman, D. e Draper, S. (eds., 1986) *User Centered System Design*. Hillsdale, NJ. Lawrence Erlbaum.

22. Oppermann, R. (1994) *Adaptive user support : ergonomic design of manually and automatically adaptable software*. Hillsdale, N.J. : Lawrence Erlbaum Associates.

23. Paternò, F. (2000) *Model-Based Design and Evaluation of Interactive Applications*, London, Springer-Verlag.

24. Peirce, C.S. (1931-55) *Collected Papers*. Cambridge, Ma. Harvard University Press. (excerpted in Buchler, Justus, ed., Philosophical Writings of Peirce, New York: Dover, 1955).

25. Prates,R.O., de Souza, C.S., Barbosa, S.D.J. (2000) "A Method for Evaluating the Communicability of User Interfaces". *ACM Interactions*, 31–38, Jan-Feb 2000.

26. Preece, J., Rogers, Y., and Sharp, H. (2002) *Interaction design: beyond human-computer interaction*, John Wiley & Sons, New York, NY.

27. Schön, D. (1983) *The Reflective Practitioner: How Professionals Think in Action*, New York, Basic Books.

28. Sellen, A.; Nicol, A. (1990). Building User-Centered On-line Help. In Laurel, B. *The Art of Human-Computer Interface Design*. Reading: Addison-Wesley.

29. Silveira, M.S.; Barbosa, S.D.J.; de Souza, C.S. (2001) Augmenting the Affordance of Online Help Content. *Proceedings of IHM-HCI 2001*, Lille, Springer-Verlag.

30. Silveira, M.S.; Barbosa, S.D.J.; de Souza, C.S. (2004) Model-based design of online help systems. Proceedings of CADUI 2004.

31. Winograd, T. and Flores, F. (1986) Understanding Computers and Cognition: A New Foundation for Design, Addison-Wesley, Reading, MA.

Discussion

[Fabio Paternò] There is a tool that takes scenario and associates with objects and with tasks. Do you think that your method can be supported by a tool able to derive more structured information?

> [Simone D.J. Barbosa] The current approach is merely oriented for a designer analysis. We are not thinking about tool support.

[Philippe Palanque] Where does your taxonomy, presented at the beginning of the talk, comes from?

> [Simone D.J. Barbosa] This comes from work on help systems

[Philippe Palanque] So it does not come from a semiotic engineering analysis?

> [Simone D.J. Barbosa] No, but Semiotic Engineering would be useful to build this kind of taxonomy

[Ann Blandford] You said there is no such thing as a typical user. How do you deal with the usability across users?

> [Simone D.J. Barbosa] What we are reasoning about is what is expected of users and how those expectations are communicated to them.

A Seamless Development Process of Adaptive User Interfaces Explicitly Based on Usability Properties

Víctor López-Jaquero[†‡], Francisco Montero[†‡], José P. Molina[†‡], P. González[†], A. Fernández-Caballero[†]

[†] Laboratory on User Interaction & Software Engineering (LoUISE)
University of Castilla-La Mancha, 02071 Albacete, Spain
{victor|fmontero|jpmolina|pgonzalez|caballer}@info-ab.uclm.es

[‡] Belgian Laboratory of Computer-Human Interaction (BCHI)
Université Catholique de Louvain, 1348 Louvain-la-Neuve, Belgium
{lopez|montero|molina}@isys.ucl.ac.be

Abstract. This work is aimed at the specification of usable adaptive user interfaces. A model-based method is used, which have been proved useful to address this task. The specification created is described in terms of abstract interaction objects, which are translated into concrete interaction objects for each particular platform. An adaptive engine is also proposed to improve the usability at runtime by means of a multi-agent system.

A Seamless Process for Adaptation Development

Currently different interaction paradigms are emerging due to several factors, such as ubiquitous access to information, the consideration of different user expertise levels, accessibility criteria or the wide range of interaction devices with specific capabilities (screen size, memory size, computing power, etc). In this paper a method is introduced for the specification of user interfaces of highly interactive systems with the capability of self-adapting to the changes in the context-of-use.

To fill the gap between model-based user interface development approaches and adaptive user interface frameworks, we propose enriching the usual model-based user interface development, to include, in a seamless manner, the development of the adaptation facilities required for adaptive user interfaces development. We propose a method for the development of adaptive user interfaces called *AL-BASIT* (Adaptive Model-Based User Interface Method), which extends usual model-based user interface development methods to support the development of adaptive user interfaces in a seamless way. Our proposal starts with requirements analysis to identify the tasks that will drive the design. Also user, physical environment and platform characteristics are collected to complete requirements analysis. In requirements analysis, use cases are used to identify the tasks and to establish a comprehensible channel of communication with the user, using an artefact understandable by the user and the designer. This stage is completed gathering the required data from the potential context-of-use for the application (user, platform and environment models). Analysis stage in aimed at the transformation of the requirements into a specification easier to handle, and usually in a more compact format. It also brings requirements

R. Bastide, P. Palanque, and J. Roth (Eds.): EHCI-DSVIS 2004, LNCS 3425, pp. 289-291, 2005.

analysis data closer to designer language. In our approach, we are using UML class diagrams to describe the domain model. To support human role multiplicity, we match each possible role a user can assume when using the user interface with the tasks they can perform. After analysis stage, design phase take place using the proposed tool. The design is based on the description of the identified tasks and their relationships with the domain elements they make use of. The task model is enriched describing the events to change from one task/action to another with the canonical abstract user interface tools [1]. From this data, an abstract user interface is generated which is independent of both modality and platform. Then, a translation is made to a concrete user interface (CUI) expressed in USIXML (http://www.usixml.org) user interface description language. The coordination between the CUI elements, the application functional core and the final running code is performed by means of connectors, as described in [2][3] This specification is adapted at runtime using a transformational approach. The adaptation engine reasons about the possible adaptation and preserves different usability properties according to the usability trade-off specified in terms of I* specification technique [4].

Conclusions

In this paper we have introduced a method for the development of adaptive user interfaces. It improves the usability of the system by adapting the user interface to the context-of-use at runtime. Thus, the user interface is adapted according to the changes in the context-of-use. For the design of adaptation engine, a multi-agent system is used. The goals of the agents in the multi-agent system are guided by the adaptation trade-off specified by the designer at design time using a goal-driven requirements notation: I*.

Acknowledgements

We gratefully acknowledge the support of the spanish PBC-03-003 grant and the SIMILAR network of excellence (http://www. similar.cc).

References

1. Constantine, L. *Canonical Abstract Prototypes for Abstract Visual and Interaction Design*. Proceedings of DSV-IS. Springer Verlag, LNCS 2844, 2003.
2. Lopez-Jaquero, V., Montero, F., Fernandez-Caballero, A. Lozano, M.D. *Towards Adaptive User Interface Generation: One Step Closer To People*. 5th International Conference on Enterprise Information Systems, ICEIS 2003. Angers, France, 2003.
3. Lopez-Jaquero, V., Montero, F., Molina, J.P., Fernandez-Caballero, A., Gonzalez, P. *Model-Based Design of Adaptive User Interfaces through Connectors*. DSV-IS 2003. Springer Verlag, LNCS 2844, 2003.
4. Yu, E. Towards Modelling and Reasoning Support for Early-Phase Requirements Engineering' Proceedings of the 3rd IEEE Int. Symp. on Requirements Engineering (RE'97) Jan. 6-8, 1997, Washington D.C., USA. pp. 226-235.

Discussion

[Fabio Paternò] How do you specify the adaptive behavior of your system?

[Victor Lopez-Jaquero] We use agents that exploit the specified rules selecting the more appropriate rules according to the current context of use. These agents include in their decision-making mechanism the XML specification of the UI.

[Willem-Paul Brinkman] You mention that you want to conduct user tests to evaluate your ideas. How do you envision you will do that?

[Victor Lopez-Jaquero] Conducting a series of small experiments to study each individual issue separately.

[Willem-Paul Brinkman] This can become a very extensive task. Would you consider a case study instead?

[Victor Lopez-Jaquero] We are considering a case study, of course, but you can just validate a small set of issues at a time, because otherwise, interdependecies can make evaluating the result an imposible task.

[Philippe Palanque] On one of your slides you said that you augmented CTT. Could you please tell us more about this augmentation?

[Victor Lopez-Jaquero] We mainly added (canonical) actions to the transitions between the tasks in the task model to allow the specification of the dialogue.

More Principled Design of Pervasive Computing Systems

Simon Dobson[1] and Paddy Nixon[2]

[1] Department of Computer Science, Trinity College, Dublin IE
simon.dobson@cs.tcd.ie

[2] Department of Information and System Sciences, University of Strathclyde, Glasgow UK
paddy@cis.strath.ac.uk

Abstract. Pervasive computing systems are interactive systems in the large, whose behaviour must adapt to the user's changing tasks and environment using different interface modalities and devices. Since the system adapts to its changing environment, it is vital that there are close links between the structure of the environment and the corresponding structured behavioural changes. We conjecture that predictability in pervasive computing arises from having a close, structured and easily-grasped relationship between the context and the behavioural change that context engenders. In current systems this relationship is not explicitly articulated but instead exists implicitly in the system's reaction to events. Our aim is to capture the relationship in a way that can be used to both *analyse* pervasive computing systems and aid their *design*. Moreover, some applications will have a wide range of behaviours; others will vary less, or more subtly. The point is not so much **what a system does** as how what it does **varies with context**. In this paper we address the principles and semantics that underpin truly pervasive systems.

1 Introduction

Pervasive computing involves building interactive systems that react to a wide variety of non-standard user cues. Unlike a traditional system whose behaviour may be proved correct in an environmentally-neutral state space, a pervasive system's behaviour is intended to change along with its environments. Examples include location-based services, business workflows and healthcare support, gaming, and composite access control policies.

Building pervasive computing systems currently revolves around one of two paradigms: (a) *event-handling systems*, where behaviour is specified in terms of reactions to events; and (b) *model-based systems*, in which rules are applied over a shared context model. The former leads to fragmented application logic which is difficult to reason about (in the formal and informal senses); the latter leaves a large number of rules whose interactions must be analysed, a situation known to be quite fragile. In addition, the majority of these approaches are premised on snapshot views of the environmental state.

A truly pervasive system requires the ability to reason about behaviours beyond their construction, both individually and in composition with other behaviours. This is rendered almost impossible when a system's reaction to context is articulated only as

R. Bastide, P. Palanque, and J. Roth (Eds.): EHCI-DSVIS 2004, LNCS 3425, pp. 292-305, 2005.

code, is scattered across the entire application, and presents largely arbitrary functional changes.

From a user perspective the design of pervasive computing systems is almost completely about interaction design. It is vitally important that users can (in the forward direction) predict when and how pervasive systems will adapt, and (in the reverse direction) can perceive why a particular adaptation has occurred. The hypothesis for our current work is that **predictability in pervasive computing arises from having a close, structured and easily-grasped relationship between the context and the behavioural change that context engenders**. In current systems this relationship is not explicitly articulated but instead exists implicitly in the system's reaction to events. Our aim is to capture the relationship in a way that can be used to both *analyse* pervasive computing systems and aid their *design*.

In this paper we describe our rationale for taking a more principled approach to the design of context-aware pervasive computing systems and outline a system that encourages such an approach, focusing on its impact on interaction. Section 2 presents a brief overview of pervasive computing, focusing on the difficulties in composing applications predictably. Section 3 explores pervasive computing from first principles to articulate the underlying motivations and factors influencing system behaviour. Section 4 describes a more principled design approach base on these factors and how they impact the interface functionality of systems, while section 5 concludes with some open questions for the future.

2 Pervasive Computing

Pervasive computing can broadly be defined as *calm* technology that delivers the correct service to the correct user, at the correct place and time, and in the correct format for the environment[1]. Context, viewed alongside this definition, is all the information necessary to make a useful decision in the face of real-world complexity. More specifically, context is central to the development of several related trends in computing: the increasing pervasiveness of computational devices in the environment, the mobility of users, the connectivity of mobile users' portable devices and the availability to applications of relevant information about the situation of use, especially that based on data from physical sensors.

2.1 Context

Historically, the use of *context* grew from roots in linguistics [2]. The term was first extended from implying inference from surrounding text to mean a framework for communication based on shared experience [3]. The importance of a symbolic structure for understanding was embraced in other fields such as [4,5,6] and subsequently developed from a purely syntactic or symbolic basis to incorporate elements of action, interaction and perception.

[7] divides context into two broad classes: *primary* context is derived directly from sensors or information sources, while *secondary* context is inferred in some sense from the primary context. A typical example is when GPS co-ordinates (primary

context) are converted into a named space (secondary context) through a look-up process (inference).

More recently, in the setting of pervasive computing, **context awareness** was at first defined by example, with an emphasis on location, identity and spatial relationships [8,9]. This has since been elaborated to incorporate more general elements of the environment or situation. Such definitions are, however, difficult to apply operationally and modern definitions [10] generalize the term to cover "any information that can be used to characterize situation". Current work in the field addresses issues including:

- developing new technologies and infrastructure elements, such as sensors, middleware, communication infrastructures to support the capture, storage, management and use of context.
- increasing our understanding of form, structure and representation of context;
- increasing our understanding of the societal impact of these new technologies and approaches and directing their application;

A more detailed retrospective of the academic history of context can be found in [10,11].

For this paper we conjecture that as we move away from the *define by example* notions of context there is an increasing demand to establish the foundational models for context. For pervasive computing systems there remains two fundamental problems. Firstly, the centrality of context to the progress in the field of pervasive computing demands new views on the theoretical underpinnings of context. For example there is no widely accepted operational theory or formal definition of context. There is also an immediate problem of providing to application developers ways in which they can describe the context needs of their applications in manner that is orthogonal to the application or business logic of the application. The programming primitives, frameworks, and tools are still in their infancy.

3 The Semantics of a Context-Aware System

3.1 What *Is* Context?

By **context** we mean the environment in which an application is executing. This might include the identity of a user, their location, the locations of other users, the device they are using, the information, task workflows they are involved in, their goals, strategies and so forth.

The intention of making a system context-aware is to allow the detailed behaviour of the application to adapt to context while keeping the overall behaviour constant: a messaging application always delivers messages, but may deliver messages differently in different contexts. Interface modality [12] may not be purely a device issue: a system might adapt its mode of interaction on the same device for different circumstances (such as going from vision to voice on a handheld), or might choose to switch devices while maintaining the same interaction style (such as making use of a wall screens instead of a PDA for form input).

Context is not monolithic: a given context may be composed of a number of different facets. Moreover the facets available may change between different executions of a context-aware application, for example when a new location system is installed. This implies that context-aware systems have defaults for "missing" contextual parameters, and that there is some mechanism for making new parameters "useful" to a wide range of applications. We do not, for example, want a context-aware system to be tied to a particular kind of location system, but want the location systems available at run-time to be leveraged to their fullest extent. This is essential for incremental, open deployment.

3.2 Behaviour

As stated above, the *gross* behaviour of an application should remain the same - sorting algorithms remain sorting algorithms in whatever context they execute. However, the *detailed* behaviour may change with context - the sorting criteria, for example - and it is this detail, and the way **behaviour varies**, that we are seeking to capture when talking about the semantics of context-aware systems.

One way to view this is as follows. Behaviour can be captured as a function from inputs to outputs, with some of the inputs being captured during execution. Context provides additional inputs describing the environment in which the function is being evaluated. Two invocations of the same function with the same (external) inputs may result in different behaviours because of changes in context.

We can therefore regard contextual variation as changing the contextual inputs to an underlying "ordinary" function. In what follows, when we refer to "behaviour" and "behavioural change'"we mean this change in parameterisation rather than an explicit change in (the code of) the function being provided. (There is no loss of generality here as the parameter might encode a function description being passed to a universal evaluator.) From an implementation perspective this makes explicit the context on which the function's detailed behaviour depends.

3.3 Design

While much of the research on pervasive computing has its roots in the programming language and distributed systems communities, the chief design task is clearly one of interfacing - creating systems that are usable as part of a larger real-world activity. Moreover, the design task is both multimodal and dynamic.

Some pervasive computing systems will be unimodal, using a single device and interaction structure. However it is widely accepted that many will be multimodal, utilising a range of different devices across the lifetime of the interaction. This includes multiple users with different constraints.

If we consider the ability to deploy context-aware applications into a shared space, we must also deal with the interactions between these applications. This may involve negative aspects such as sharing device capabilities between applications, prioritising different (and possibly conflicting) decisions. However, there are also significant potentially positive aspects including the case where one application provides context for another that might not otherwise have been obtainable.

3.4 Behaviour Variation

Some applications will have a wide range of behaviours; others will vary less, or more subtly. The point is not so much **what a system does** as how what it does **varies with context**.

Much of computer science has been devoted to the notion of *correctness* - that is, to ensuring that a system has a single behaviour, and that this is the behaviour the user wants. Context-aware systems attack the underlying assumption of a single behaviour that can be articulated, replacing it with the view that behaviour *should* change in different circumstances.

Arbitrary behavioural changes would be incomprehensible to users, and would make systems completely unusable. However, single behaviour is equally unattractive in that it prevents a system adapting to context. There is therefore a spectrum in the behavioural variation we are willing to accept (figure 1). In building a pervasive computing system we are looking for the "sweet spot" between adaptability and comprehensibility. However, this still leaves the issue of deciding *how* behaviour should change and *when* changes should occur.

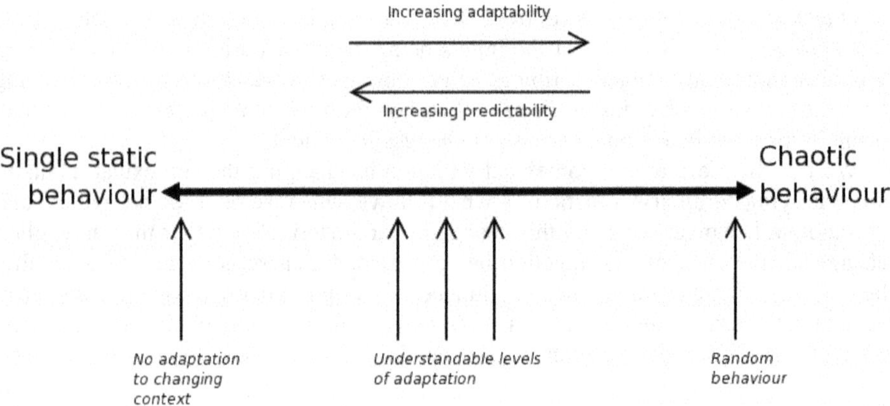

Fig. 1. The spectrum of behavioural variation.

An adaptive system adapts *to* something, and presumably adaptation happens when that something changes. Actually this turns out to be a little simplistic - adaptation may happen before or after a change - but the principle is valid. Since we are discussing context-aware systems, we can reasonably expect a system to adapt to changes in its context.

However, not all changes in context are significant or simple. A location-based service's behaviour will not typically be different at *every* different location, so not all location cues cause changes. Similarly location may not in itself be enough to define the system's behaviour without contributions from other aspects of context.

3.5 Describing the Semantics

We might regard context as having a "shape" over which the system operates. The shape is multidimensional, defined by the various contextual parameters. The shape will also have identifiable "significant" points or areas that will have meaning to the user of the application, being perceived either as points where behaviour could (or should) change, or as areas in which behaviour could (or should) remain the same.

Not only do the significant points in the context define *when* behaviour can change, for a given application they will in many cases essentially define *what* new behaviour will be selected. To take a concrete example of a service providing tourist information, we expect the information being served both to change as we move and to remain relevant to the location we are in. The interface's adaptive behaviour of the system must therefore be closely related to the external world if that adaptation is to be intuitive.

This leads to our defining observation about developing a semantics for context-aware pervasive computing: in order for a pervasive computing system to be predictable to users, **the relationship between context and behaviour must be two-way and (largely) symmetric**. An application's behavioural variation should emerge "naturally" from the context that causes it to adapt, and that variation mandates that certain structures be visible in the model of context being used. It might only adapt to large-grained changes, placing it at the static end of figure 1; alternatively it may adapt to fine-grained changes, placing it at the dynamic end. The point is that the application's position in the spectrum is not selected *a priori* but emerges naturally from the shape of its context. If a context has a fine-grained structure it will support a highly adaptable application; conversely a highly adaptive application needs fine-grained context.

An *application*, in this view, consists of four elements:

1. A baseline behaviour parameterised by a context
2. The context space with its significant points and shapes defined
3. The behavioural space with its own structures
4. A mapping matching changes in context to corresponding changes in behaviour

The first element is a standard program with adaptation hooks, and perhaps significant control structures for concurrency control and consistency maintenance. The third element describes the parameters used to control the program's adaptation. The second element describes the context expected by the application and the points at which this context forces or precludes adaptation. The fourth element describes the way in which the context adapts the program, matching significant changes in context to changes in behaviour.

The issue of correctness reappears in another guise: instead of ensuring that a single behaviour is *implemented* correctly (and that the correct behaviour is implemented), we now need also to ensure that the behaviour *varies* correctly. The problem is not as bad as it might appear, however: if the underlying function is correct then the behaviour will be correct in *some* sense for each possible contextual parameter. The issue is one of the *appropriateness* of selecting a detailed behaviour in particular circumstances.

3.6 Towards More Principled Design

Making a function context-dependent essentially adds extra parameters to its definition. However, adding extra parameters in principle allows these additional degrees of freedom to affect the function's behaviour in arbitrary ways - a situation that is probably more general than is consistent with predictable variation. The challenge, then, is to provide additional parameters in such a way that their impact on the function's behaviour is constrained to be predictable, and follows (in some sense) the structure of the context.

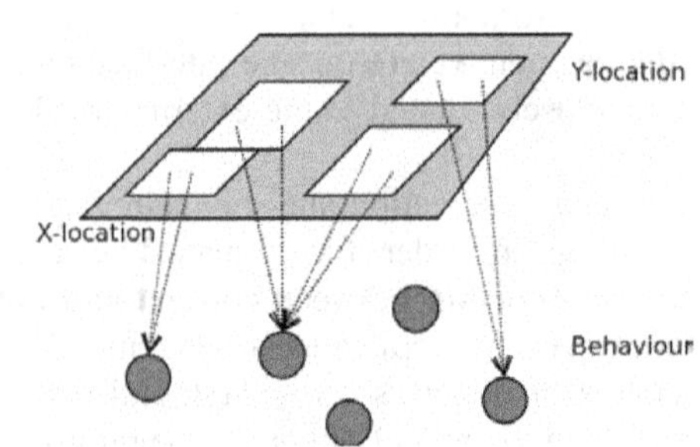

(a) Location-dependent behaviour

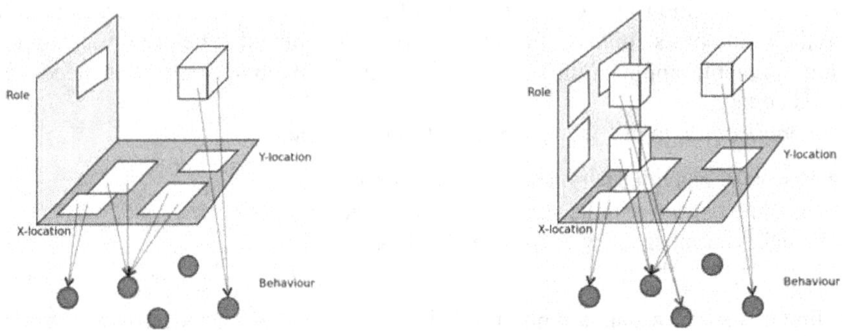

(b) Adding role (c) Different roles in the same location

Fig. 2. Context dependence as parameter selection.

The essence of this problem is shown in figure 2. Figure 2(a) shows a function whose behaviour (the lower circles) depends on the location in which it is executed (the plane). Different regions of the plane map to the same behaviour, so the function observed by the user will be the same as they move within this region. Change in behaviour will only be observed when they move between regions.

Adding a extra contextual parameter, such as the person's role, adds another dimension to the behavioural space[1]. The behaviour may not vary in some locations

[1] Of course role is usually more complicated than this diagram suggests, but it will suffice for the purposes of illustration.

for a change in role (figure 2(b)); alternatively there may be a change for some roles in some locations (figure 2(c)).

We claimed above that behaviour should only change "on cue" from context. This suggests that the change in role needs to be clear in the interface.

From a design perspective, it would also be attractive for the changed behaviour to depend structurally on the role and location: rather than making the change arbitrary, it should emerge naturally from the parameter space. This has three major advantages:

1. It simplifies the development of the adaptive controls by placing all adaptation functions in a single sub-system
2. It simplifies the development of the adaptive components by making the parameter space clearly defined and explicitly articulated
3. It provides a "closed form" of the system's context-aware behaviour for analysis

4 A Mathematical Model of Principled Design

The discussion above leads us to consider a model in which primary context conditions and constrains secondary context and behaviour. Formalising this notion leads to a semantics of context-aware systems.

We have adopted category theory as our semantic framework, for three reasons:

1. it is naturally extensible, so we can deal with an extensible collection of contextual parameters;
2. many of the well-known categorical structures suggest, at least intuitively, that they may be useful in structuring context awareness; and
3. our eventual goal is to develop programming abstractions for pervasive computing systems, and category theory's extensive use in language semantics may make this step easier.

However, our presentation here requires no understanding of the detailed mathematics of category theory: we focus here on the structural features of the approach and how it impacts the design and analysis of interface functionality. We refer the interested reader to [13] for a fuller treatment.

4.1 Modelling Primary and Secondary Context

A **category** is a generalisation of the familiar approach of sets and functions between them. A category consists of a collection of **objects** and **arrows** between them. The most familiar category is the category of sets whose objects are sets and whose arrows are total functions between them. The arrows are constrained to be compositional and associative, and each object has an identity arrow.

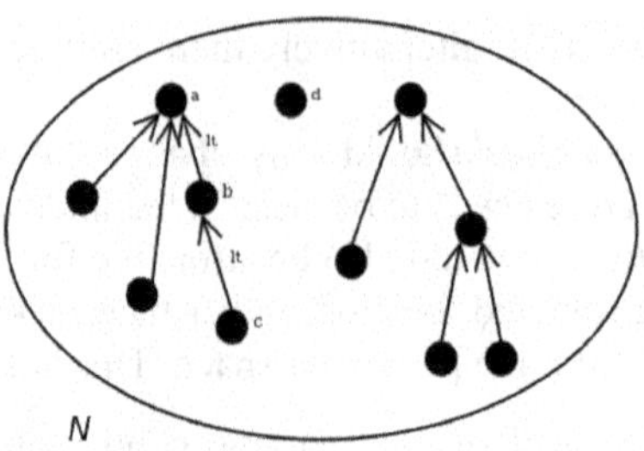

Fig. 3. Pointed structure within an object.

To each individual contextual parameter we assign an object in the category (*e.g.* a set) denoting the values the parameter can take. In a location system based on individual named spaces, for example, the "location" parameter would be represented by an object *N* whose points (elements in the case of a set) are the space names.
In many cases the elements of a parameter are themselves structured. A typical example (which occurs repeatedly) is a parameter structured as a partial order, pointed set or lattice, where each element can be "included" in at most one other (figure 3). For named spaces there is an arrow from the parameter object to itself, taking each space to its containing space or to itself if it is a "top" space. By repeatedly applying this operation we can navigate from a space up its container hierarchy. In figure 3 this means that the inclusion morphism *lt* takes space *c* to space *b*, space *b* to space *a*, and spaces *a* and *d* to themselves (we have omitted these arrows for clarity).

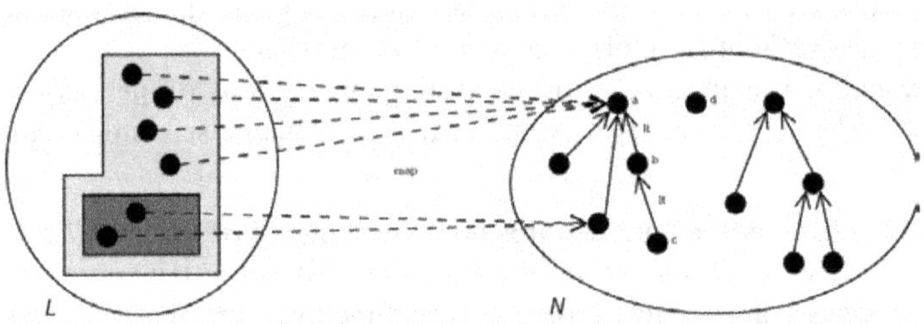

Fig. 4. Deriving secondary context.

Named spaces are probably secondary context, derived from a lower-level location system such as GPS. GPS can be modelled as an object *L* of GPS co-ordinate pairs. An obvious contextual constraint is the mapping between a GPS location and the named space containing it. We can represent this as an arrow *map:* $L \rightarrow N$ capturing the "map" (figure 4). It is important to realise that this is a *semantic* characterisation of what would implementationally be a lookup operation, the details which can be abstracted in the analysis.

Figure 4 makes clear the structural relationship between the two parameters; A region of *L* maps to an element of *N* in such a way that elements of the containing region in *L* must map to an element of *N* containing the original element. *map* is constrained to reflect the structure of one object in another, and it is this correspondence that preserves meaning in the interface.

4.2 Context as Behaviour

Current context-aware systems are not uniform, in the sense that much of a system's behaviour is conditioned by information not held in a single context model. For the purposes of analysis it is simpler to regard context in the wider sense as the sole arbiter of behaviour: the system is functional with respect to its context. (We regard this as a sound implementation strategy too.)

The easiest way to accomplish this to include the "real" parameters to the external behaviour in the context. For a simple example, consider a wireless document system which delivers a set of documents depending on the user's location. The corpus of documents being managed can be represented as a contextual parameter (object) D whose elements are possible sub-sets of documents being served related by set inclusion.

We may now define an arrow *serve:* $N \rightarrow D$ which selects the set of documents to be served by the document system in each location. Although this arrow does not define behaviour in the normal sense of describing exactly what will happen, it *does* describe how the parameter passed to that behaviour will vary. We may therefore to some extent treat D as a proxy for the behaviour of the system and study how this "behaviour" changes with context.

4.3 Analysing the Structure of Behaviour

Even in this simple model there are a number of questions we may ask of the system. Key to these is an understanding of the way in which *different* contexts select the *same* behaviour. Using figure 4 as an example, there are a number of points in L that map to the same element of N. This is captured by the categorical notion of a **fibre**: given an element a of N the fibre of *map* lying over a is the sub-object of L that maps to a under *map*. Similarly the fibres of *serve* above represent the spaces in which the system will serve the same set of documents.

The significance of fibres is that they capture both those contexts in which the system will behave the same and the points at which that behaviour changes.

4.4 Compound Context and Behaviour

One of the advantages of category theory is that it has several strong notions of composition that can be used to create complex concepts by construction. A good example of this is the use of products of context and behaviour.

If C and D are contexts (objects) we can create a product context $C \times D$ whose elements are ordered pairs of elements from C and D respectively. Moreover there is an arrow between an element (i, x) and (j, y) if there is an arrow on C from i to j and an arrow on D from x to y.

Such products represent the compound state of the system: If we take N and another context P of people's identities, the compound context $P \times N$ represents a person in a named space. We can use this product contexts to contextualise behaviour in the normal way, by specifying an arrow *serve':* $P \times N \rightarrow D$ defining how the documents available vary with identity and place. The risk here is that such behaviour will be arbitrary, in that there is no necessary relationship between the way behaviour changes with identity and the way behaviour changes with identity *and* location. In many cases we may wish to ensure that such a relationship is preserved.

If we have arrows *serveto:* $P \rightarrow D$ and *servein:* $N \rightarrow D$ we can model this by *constructing* the arrow *serve'* from the two more elementary arrows, in such a way that *serve'* preserves some of their features. For example, we might constrain *serve'* so that it always serves a set of documents that includes the set identified by *serveto* – location context may *broaden* the behaviour but always maintains the behaviour of *serveto* as a "core". Conversely we might force *serve'* to never serve a larger set of documents than permitted by *serveto* – the underlying arrow specifies the "extent" of the behaviour. A third possibility is that location "adds nothing" to the behaviour, when *serve* defines the same behaviour as *serveto*. Similar arguments apply to *servein*.

These constructions allow us to potentially specify the constraints on complex behaviours in terms of simpler behaviours. This is important both for tackling the complexity of the system and ensuring its consistency. A user of *serve'* that preserves *serveto* as a core, for example, will be able to form a mental model in which (a) they can rely on a certain minimum behaviour everywhere, and (b) their location may add significant new documents. This consistency is vital to the usability of the system, and can be made a direct consequence of its categorical model.

Similar techniques can be used when contextualising a product context, where (for example) two behaviours B_1 and B_2 are combined to form a compound behaviour $B_1 \times B_2$ that specifies two aspects of the system independently. Again, composition of underlying arrows can be used to constrain the way in which behaviour varies.

4.5 Composition and Conflict Analysis

Pervasive computing almost implies dynamic composition, in that we expect mobile systems to be carried around by users and to "discover" resources as they move. This brings positive and negative possibilities: new capabilities may become available very easily, but systems may interact in undesired ways. A major challenge for analysis is to detect such conflicts.

In certain simple cases we can both detect conflicts and identify "safe" zones when two systems are composed. Suppose we have two systems with the same context and behaviour, described by two arrows $f,g : C \rightarrow D$: for the wireless document server these might be the public and private document servers. If we run both systems together, we may ask whether they will both serve the same document set for a given user and location. A categorical construction called an **equaliser** captures the sub-object C' of C in which f and g behave the same. If we can ensure that the system will remain in this region C', the systems may be composed safely; if it strays outside then the two systems diverge. Another possibility is to force g (for example) to serve as a core or extent of f.

In both cases the composition of systems is captured cleanly within the categorical model, and can be analysed using standard techniques. This may in turn lead to improved implementation techniques.

4.6 Designing "Graspable" Systems

Systems analysis, while important, is in many ways less interesting than systems design: we want to develop pervasive computing systems that are *usable and predictable by design*, using a model that both aids in this process and in the analysis of the results.

The fibre structure of arrows provides a powerful technique for designing systems as well as analysing them. Suppose we want to design our wireless document server so that it serves a set d_1 of documents in those places in the vicinity of a place n_1, and another set d_2 in the vicinity of n_2. If we constructed this system from scratch we would need to ensure that it responded to location events in the correct manner - an arduous testing process.

However, we can observe that the system behaves the same within a fibre - changes in context that remain within a fibre do not affect the behaviour. We need only ensure that all the places around n_1 lie in the fibre of d_1 to be convinced that the system will behave as required.

From a user perspective, in order to be predictable a change in behaviour must be accompanied by a perceptible change in the context that "makes sense" for the application at hand. Changes in behaviour occur when context moves between fibres. If we ensure that these changes correspond to external contextual cues that will convey the need for behavioural change to the user, then the user will be able to develop an appropriate mental model of the way in which the behaviour changes in response to context. The cues in the outside world are reflected exactly in the fibre structure of the model.

We claimed in section 4 that, in order for a pervasive computing system to be comprehensible, the relationship between context and behaviour needed to be largely symmetrical. It is this matching of fibre structure to external cues that captures this symmetry, either constructively (for design) or analytically (for analysis).

Although the matching of cues to fibre transitions is application-dependent and generally external to the model, it is sometimes possible to capture the cues within the structure of the category. If, for example, we can identify the context points at which behaviour should change, we can often identify the "internal" points where it should remain the same, corresponding to the fibre over the desired behaviour. These regions - sub-objects of the overall context - can have their behaviour described individually, with the "full" behaviour coming by composition in a way that will detect many conflicts automatically. This means that a user-centred design that identifies the adaptation points in the environment can be used directly to construct a mathematical description of the system being constructed, carrying usability concerns directly into the system model.

5 Conclusion

We have motivated using a more principled approach to the design and development of context-aware pervasive computing systems, and presented a formal approach that captures some of the essential driving forces in a natural and compositional way. We have shown how certain aspects of usability and predictability in the requirements for a pervasive computing system can be given a formal realisation within a system model suitable for use as a basis for analysis and design.

Perhaps more than any other potentially mainstream technology, pervasive computing requires that we take an automated approach to system composition and variation - the alternative would constrain deployment to constellations of devices and information sources that could be described *a priori*. This in turn means that we need to be able to state very precisely the way in which system behaviour varies. This is the point at which our work diverges from that in the ambient calculus[14] or bigraphs[15] - two very prominent and influential formal treatments of mobile systems - in that we sacrifice the precise characterisation of system behaviour in favour of broad-brush analysis. We also do not privilege location, regarding it as just one of the possible contextual parameters to be studied.

The obvious counter in this formulation is that the baseline behaviour needs to encapsulate all possible adaptations, which are then selected by context. While this is correct to an extent, we should differentiate between the abstract semantic model of a context-aware application and its concrete realisation. One would not necessarily pass context as a parameter to a function: it might be preferable to allow the function to access a shared context model, and provide some templated mechanism for this model to affect its behaviour. There are, however, serious engineering problems to be overcome in developing a programming model under this model.

Although we have not investigated it in this paper, a design approach such as we propose needs to be backed by an engineering methodology. In particular we have largely elided the way in which a designer would decide on the correct formulation for context and behaviour, or check that his choices relate correctly to the users' perceptions of the system. While traditional analysis and design methods can help address these problems, there is also a need to deploy detailed usability evaluations - possibly modified for pervasive computing - to inform the feedback loop. This is a subject that is outside our expertise but that we would be keen to explore further.

It seems unlikely that the techniques described are sufficient to address the full range of context-aware behaviours, so there is a major open question in the applicability of the techniques to real-world applications - something we are investigating at present. We are also addressing the limitation of the model to "immediate" context, where only the current situation (and not the past or possible future) affect behaviour. However, we believe that "closed form" expressions of context awareness are a key enabler for building the next generation of complex pervasive computing systems.

References

1. Weiser, M..The computer for the 21st century. Scientific American (1991)
2. Winograd, T. Architecture for context. Human Computer Interaction **16** (1994) 85-90
3. Minsky, M. A Framework for Representing Knowledge. In The Psychology of Computer Vision. McGraw Hill (1975)
4. Brooks, R. A robust layered control system for a mobile robot. IEEE Journal of Robotics and Automation **2** (1986)
5. A.Draper, B., Collins, R.T., Brolio, J., Hansen, A.R., Riseman, E.M. The schema system. International Journal of Computer Vision **2** (1989)

6. Bajcsy, R. Active perception. Proceedings of the IEEE **1** (1988) 996-1006
7. Salber, D., Dey, A., Abowd, G. The Context Toolkit: aiding the development of context-enabled applications. In Proceedings of the ACM Conference on Computer-Human Interaction, CHI'99. (1999) 434-441
8. Ward, A., Jones, A., Hopper, A. A new location technique for the active office. IEEE Personal Comunications **4** (1997) 42-27
9. Rodden, T., K.Cheverest, Davies, K., Dix, A. Exploiting context in HCI design for mobile systems. In Workshop on Human Computer Interaction with Mobile Devices. (1998)
10. Dey, A. Understanding and using context. Personal and Ubiquitous Computing **5** (2001) 4-7
11. Crowley, L., Coutaz, J., Rey, G., Reignier, P. Perceptual components for context aware computing. In Proceedings of Ubicomp 2002. (2002)
12. Calvary, G., Coutaz, J., Thevenin, D. A unifying reference framework for the development of plastic user interfaces. In Proceedings of EHCI'01. Volume 2254 of Lecture Notes in Computer Science., Springer Verlag (2001)
13. Dobson, S., Nixon, P. Towards a semantics of pervasive computing (just the category theory). Technical report, Department of Computer Science, Trinity College Dublin (To appear)
14. Cardelli, L., Gordon, A. Mobile ambients. In Nivat, M., ed. Foundations of software science and computational structures. Volume 1378 of LNCS. Springer Verlag (1998)
15. Jensen, O.H., Milner, R. Bigraphs and mobile processes. Technical Report UCAM-CL-TR-570, University of Cambridge Computer Laboratory (2003)

Discussion

[Nick Graham] This is a semantic framework that is instantiated over a specific application. This seems to require the modeller to anticipate the possible contexts or compositions that may arise.

> [Simon Dobson] This is less a problem than with other approaches. In effect, we can define compositions without having to specify what kinds of things are being composed. This is sufficiently rich to allow interesting analyses.
> There are a small set of composition operators that seem to recur frequently: although we have to select which operator to use when we encounter a new contextual parameter, we often don't need to know its details to do something meaningful.

[Helmut Stiegler] Category theory is all about commutative diagrams. You did not show any such examples, in which you can apply such diagrams. Do you have some ?

> [Simon Dobson] Yes, we have them used. I suppressed them here on purpose. You will be able to find them in a technical report.

[Gerrit van Der Veer] How do the notions of "conflict" and "problem" relate to the framework ?

> [Simon Dobson] These notions are not automatically specified, but have to be stated explicitly in order to reason about them.

Towards a New Generation of Widgets for Supporting Software Plasticity: The "Comet"

Gaëlle Calvary, Joëlle Coutaz, Olfa Dâassi, Lionel Balme, Alexandre Demeure

CLIPS-IMAG,
BP 53, 38041 Grenoble Cedex 9, France
{Gaelle.Calvary, Joelle.Coutaz}@imag.fr

Abstract. This paper addresses software adaptation to context of use. It goes one step further than our early work on plasticity [5]. Here, we propose a revision of the notion of software plasticity that we apply at the widget level in terms of comets. Plasticity is defined as the ability of an interactive system to withstand variations of context of use while preserving quality in use where quality in use refers to the ISO definition. Plasticity is not limited to the UI components of an interactive system, nor to a single platform: adaptation to context of use may also impact the functional core, it may have an effect on the nature of the connectors, and it may draw upon the existence of multiple platforms in the vicinity to migrate all or portions of the interactive system. A new reference framework that structures the development process of plastic interactive systems is presented to cover these issues. The framework is then applied at the granularity of widgets to provide the notion of a comet. A comet is an introspective widget that is able to self-adapt to some context of use, or that can be adapted by a tier-component to the context of use, or that can be dynamically discarded (versus recruited) when it is unable (versus able) to cover the current context of use. To do so, a comet publishes the quality in use it guarantees, the user tasks and the domain concepts that it is able to support, as well as the extent to which it supports adaptation.

1 Introduction

Mobility coupled with the development of a wide variety of access devices has engendered new requirements for HCI such as the ability of interactive systems to run in different contexts of use. By context of use we mean a triple <user, platform, environment> where the user denotes the archetypal person who is intended to use the interactive system; the platform refers to the hardware and software devices available for sustaining the user interaction; the environment describes the physical and social conditions where the interaction takes place. To master the diversity of contexts of use in an economical and ergonomic way, the *plasticity* property has been introduced [31]. Basically, plasticity refers to the adaptation to context of use that preserves the user's needs and abilities. For example, FlexClock [15] is a clock that expands or shrinks its user interface (UI) when the user resizes the window (Fig. 1). The time remains readable during and after the adaptation.

R. Bastide, P. Palanque, and J. Roth (Eds.): EHCI-DSVIS 2004, LNCS 3425, pp. 306-324, 2005.

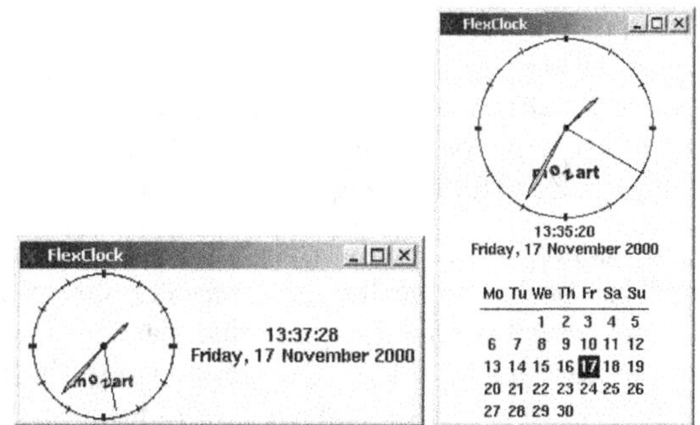

Fig. 1. FlexClock, an example of adaptation to the platform.

When applied at the widget level, the plasticity property gives rise to a new generation of widgets: the *comets* (COntext of use Mouldable widgETs). As a simple example, a set of radio buttons that shrinks into a combo box is a comet (Fig. 2).

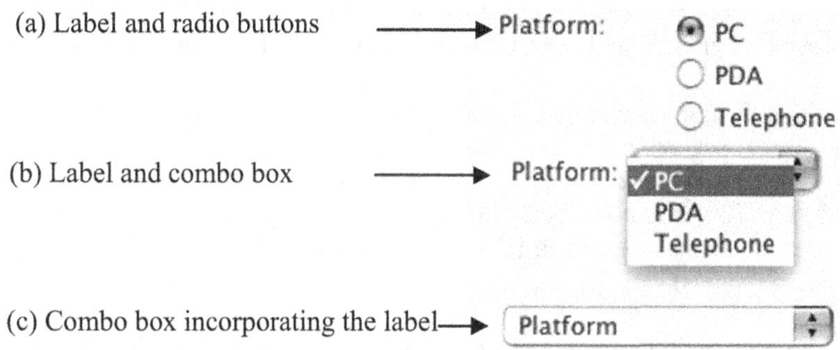

Fig. 2. Three graphical mockups supporting the same task "selecting one option among a set of options" through a) a label and radio buttons; b) a label and a combo box; c) a combo box incorporating the label. The example concerns the specification of the target platform (PC, PDA, telephone) for a centralized UI.

This paper presents our notion of comets. First we present new advances in plasticity to provide sound foundations for their elaboration. Then we focus on the comets per se considering both the design and run time perspective.

2 Foundations for Comets: Advances in Plasticity

This section focuses on the lessons learned from experience that directly underpin the notion of comets. First, we propose a new definition for plasticity, then we examine the property from both a user and a system centered perspective.

2.1 A New Definition of Plasticity

Plasticity was previously defined as "the capacity of a user interface to withstand variations of context of use while preserving usability" [31]. Based on our experience, we have identified three reasons for revising the definition:

- In reality, plasticity is not limited to the UI components but may also impact the functional core. This occurs typically with services discovery. For example, because Bob has moved and is now in a place that makes a new service available, this service now appears on his PDA. The desktop is reshuffled (or tuned) to incorporate this new service and support an opportunistic interaction. Thus, the scope of the definition must be enlarged: plasticity must refer to the capacity of an *interactive system*, and not only to its UI, to adapt to the context of use;
- The current definition focuses on the preservation of usability only. As a result, utility is implicit. To make explicit the possibility to specify requirements concerning the preservation of functional (and not only non functional) properties (e.g., task accomplishment), the scope of the definition must be enlarged. To do so, we refer to *quality in use* instead of just usability. As defined by ISO [18], quality in use is based on internal and external properties (Fig. 3) including usability (Fig. 4);
- The definition is not operational enough. Due to ISO, the definition is now reinforced by a set of reference *characteristics* (factors), *sub-characteristics* (criteria) (Fig. 4) and metrics [19]. The framework QUIM (Quality in Use Integrated Map) [29] also contributes in this area by relating data, metrics, criteria and factors. A sound basis exists in HCI for usability ([1] [17] or more specifically [32] for dialog models).

Based on this new definition, an interactive system is said to be "plastic for a set of properties and a set of contexts of use" if it is able to guarantee these properties whilst adapting to cover another context of use.

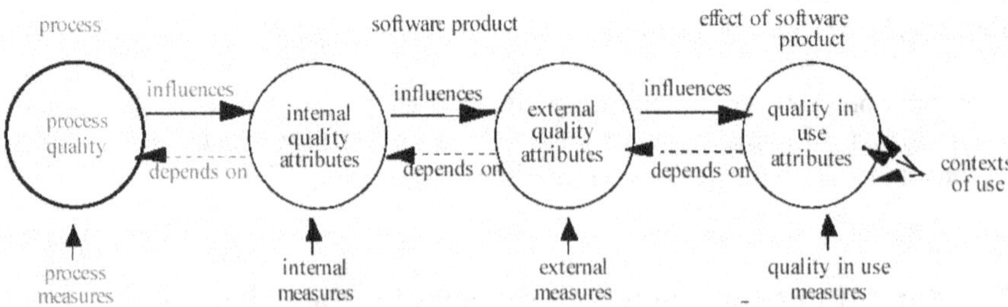

Fig. 3. Relationships between quality in use and internal and external qualities. Extracted from [18].

The properties are selected during the specification phase among the set of characteristics and sub-characteristics elicited by ISO (Fig. 4). Thus, plasticity is not an absolute property: it is specified and evaluated against a set of relevant properties (e.g., the latency and stability of the interactive system with regard to the "efficiency" characteristic, "time behavior" sub-characteristic).

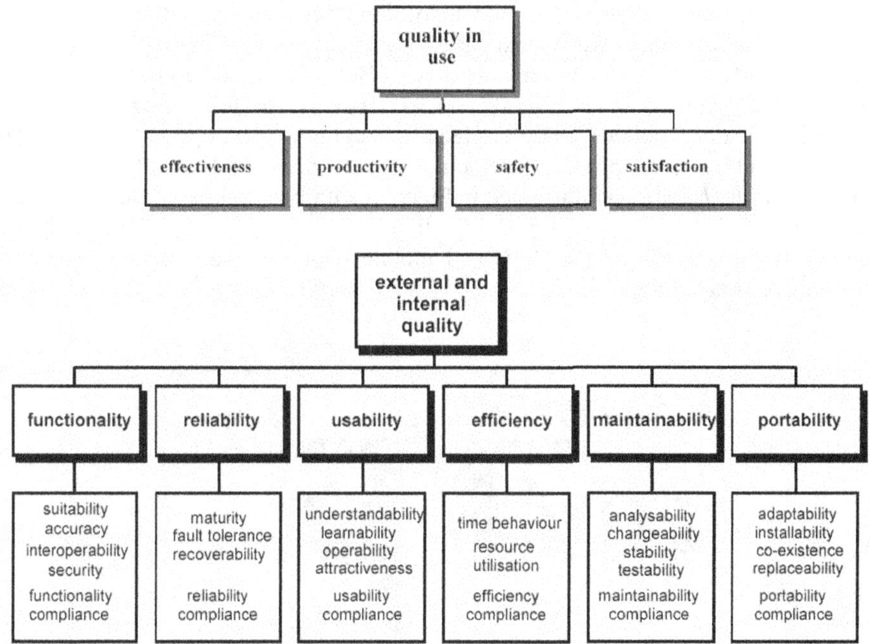

Fig. 4. Quality models for quality in use and internal and external qualities. These ISO models provide a sound basis for specifying and evaluating the extent to which an interactive system is supposed to be plastic. Extracted from [18].

The next section presents how to *plastify* an interactive system from a user centered perspective.

2.2 Plasticity from a User Centered Perspective

Whilst plasticity has always been addressed from a centralized perspective [5] (the UI was locally tuned as in FlexClock [15]), it is now obvious that ubiquitous computing favors the distribution of the interactive system among a set of platforms. As a result, two means are now available for adapting:

- Recasting the interactive system: this consists in reshuffling the UI, the functional core or the connector between both of these parts locally without modifying its distribution across the different platforms. Figure 1 provides an example of recasting;
- Redistributing the interactive system: it consists in migrating all (total migration) or part of (partial migration) the interactive system across the different platforms. Partial migration has been introduced by Rekimoto's painter metaphor [27] [4] and is now a major issue in HCI.

In ubiquitous computing, the notion of platform is no longer limited to an *elementary platform*, i.e., a set of physical and software resources that function together to form a working computational unit [7]. The notion of platform must definitely be seen as a *cluster*, i.e., a composition of elementary platforms that appear and disappear dynamically. For example, when Alice arrives in Bob's vicinity, her laptop extends the existing cluster composed of Bob's laptop, the PDA and the mobile phone. Bob's current interactive system can partially or fully migrate to Alice's laptop. Typically, to obtain a larger screen, it could be a good option to "bump" [16] the two laptops and split the interactive system between both of them (partial migration) (the *bumping* is illustrated in Figure 5 with two desktops). But when Bob's laptop battery is getting low, a full migration to Alice's laptop seems to be the best option as the screens of the PDA and mobile phone are too small to support a comfortable interaction.

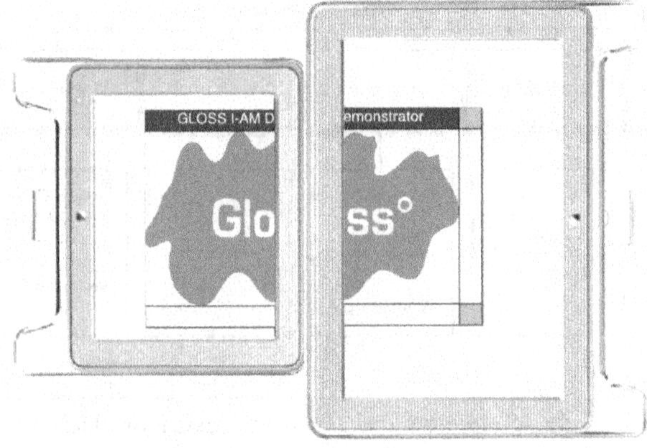

Fig. 5. A partial migration enabled by a top-to-top composition of the screens. Extracted from [9].

The granularity for distribution may vary from the application level to the pixel level [7]:

- At the *application level*, the user interface is fully replicated on the platforms of the target cluster. If the cluster is heterogeneous (e.g., is comprised of a mixture of PC's and PDA's), then each platform runs a specific targeted user interface. All of these user interfaces, however, simultaneously share the same functional core;
- At the *workspace level*, the user interface components that can migrate between platforms are workspaces. A workspace is an interaction space. It groups together a collection of interactors that support the execution of a set of logically connected tasks. In graphical user interfaces, a workspace is mapped onto the notions of windows and panels. The painter metaphor presented in Rekimoto's pick and drop [27] [4] is an example of a distribution at the workspace level: the palettes of tools are presented on a PDA whereas the drawing area is mapped onto an electronic white board. Going one-step further, the tools palette (possibly the drawing area) can migrate at run time between the PDA and the electronic board;
- At the *domain concept level*, the user interface components that can be distributed between platforms are physical interactors. Here, physical interactors allow users to manipulate domain concepts. In Rekimoto's augmented surfaces, domain concepts, such as tables and chairs, can be distributed between laptops and horizontal and vertical surfaces. As for Built-IT [26], the topology of the rendering

surfaces matters: objects are represented as 3D graphic interactors on laptops, whereas 2D rendering is used for objects placed on a horizontal surface;
- At the *pixel level*, any user interface component can be partitioned across multiple platforms. For example, in I-LAND [30], a window may simultaneously lie over two contiguous white boards (it is the same case in Figure 5 with two desktops). When the cluster is heterogeneous, designers need to consider multiple sources of disruption. For example, how to represent a window whose content lies across a white board and a PDA? From a user's perspective, is this desirable?

Migration may happen on the fly at run time or between sessions:

- *On the fly migration* requires that the state of the functional core is saved as well as that of the user interface. The state of the user interface may be saved at multiple levels of granularity: with regard to the functional decomposition promoted by Arch [3], when saved at the Dialogue Component level, the user can pursue the job from the beginning of the current task; when saved at the Logical Presentation or at the Physical Presentation levels, the user is able to carry on the current task at the physical action level, that is, at the exact point within the current task. There is no discontinuity;
- *Migration between sessions* implies that the user has to quit, then restart the application from the saved state of the functional core. In this case, the interaction process is heavily interrupted.

Recasting and redistribution are two means for adaptation. They may be processed in a complementary way. A full migration between heterogeneous platforms will typically require a recasting for fitting to a smaller screen. Conversely, when the user enlarges a window, a partial migration may be a good option to get a larger interaction surface by using a nearby platform. The next section addresses plasticity from a system's perspective.

2.3 Plasticity from a System Centered Perspective

The CAMELEON reference framework for plasticity [7] provides a general tool for reasoning about adaptation. It covers both recasting and redistribution. It is intended to serve as a reference instrument to help designers and developers to structure the development process of plastic interactive systems covering both the design time and run time.

The design phase follows a model-based approach [25] (Fig. 6). A UI is produced for a set of *initial models* according to a *reification process*:
- The initial models are specified manually by the developer. They set the applicative domain of the interactive system (concepts, tasks), the predicted contexts of use (user, platform, environment), the expected quality of service (a set of requirements related to quality in use and external/internal qualities) and the adaptation to be applied within as well as outside the current context of use (evolution, transition). The domain models are taken from the literature. Emerging works initiated by [12] [28] deal with the definition and modeling of context of use. The *Quality Models* can be expressed with regard to the ISO models presented

in section 2.1. The *Evolution Model* specifies the reaction to be performed when the context of use changes. The *Transition Model* denotes the particular *Transition User Interface* to be used during the adaptation process. A transition UI allows the user to evaluate the evolution of the adaptation process. In Pick and Drop [27], the virtual yellow lines projected on the tables are examples of transition UIs. All of these initial models may be referenced along the development process from the domain specification level to the running interactive system;
- The design process is a three-step process that successively reifies the initial models into the final running UI. It starts at the concepts and tasks level to produce the *Abstract User Interface* (Abstract UI). An abstract UI is a collection of related workspaces called *interaction spaces*. The relations between the interaction spaces are inferred from the task relations expressed in the task model. Similarly, connectedness between concepts and tasks is inferred from the concepts and tasks model. An abstract UI is reified into a *Concrete User Interface* (Concrete UI). A concrete UI turns an abstract UI into an interactor-dependent expression. Although a concrete UI makes explicit the final look and feel of the *Final User Interface* (Final UI), it is still a mockup that runs only within the development environment. The Final UI generated from a concrete UI is expressed in source code, such as Java and HTML. It can then be interpreted or compiled as a pre-computed user interface and plugged into a run-time infrastructure that supports dynamic adaptation to multiple targets.

At any level of reification:
- References can be made to the context of use. We identify four degrees of dependencies: whether a model makes hypothesis about the context of use; a modality; the availability of interactors; or the renderer used for the final UI. From a software engineering perspective, delaying the dependencies until the later stages of the reification process, results in a wider domain for multi-targeting. Ideally, dependencies to the context of use, to modalities and to interactors are associated with the concrete UI level (Fig. 7 a). In practice, the task model is very often context of use and modality dependent (Fig. 7b). As figure 7 shows, a set of four sliders (or stickers) can be used to locate the dependencies in the reification process. The movement of the stickers is limited by the closeness of their neighbour (e.g., in Figure 7b, the interactor sticker has a wide scope for movement between the concepts and tasks level and the final UI level, respectively corresponding to the position of the modality and renderer stickers);
- References can be made to the quality properties that have guided the design of the UI at this level of reification (cf. arrows denoted as "reference" in Figure 6);
- A series of abstractions and/or reifications can be performed to target another level of reification;
- A series of translations can be performed to target another context of use.

Reifications and translations may be performed automatically from specifications, or manually by human experts. Because the automatic generation of user interfaces has not found wide acceptance in the past [23], the reference framework makes possible manual reifications, abstractions and translations (Fig. 6).

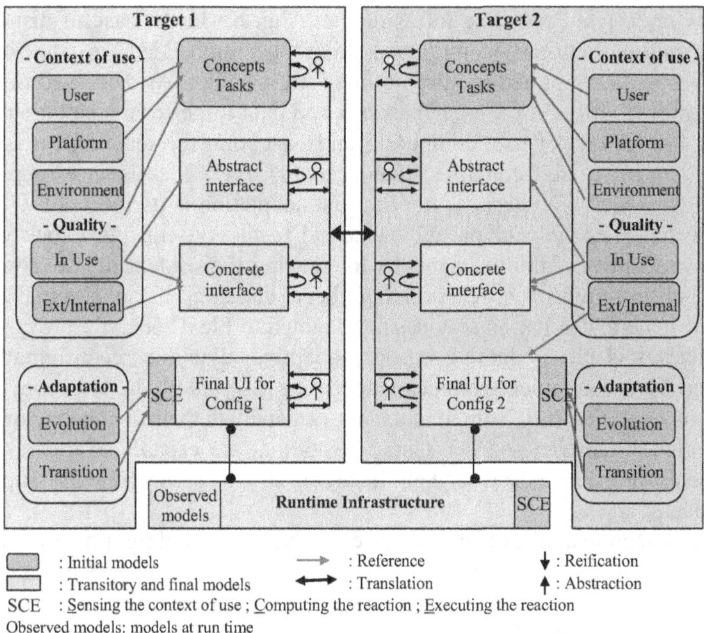

Fig. 6. The Reference Framework for supporting plastic user interfaces. The picture shows the process when applied to two distinct targets. This version is adapted from [7] where the quality models defined in 2.1 are now made explicit. Whilst reifications abstractions and translations are exhaustively made explicit, only examples of references are provided. In the example, the reference to the evolution and transition models is made at the latest stage (the final UIs).

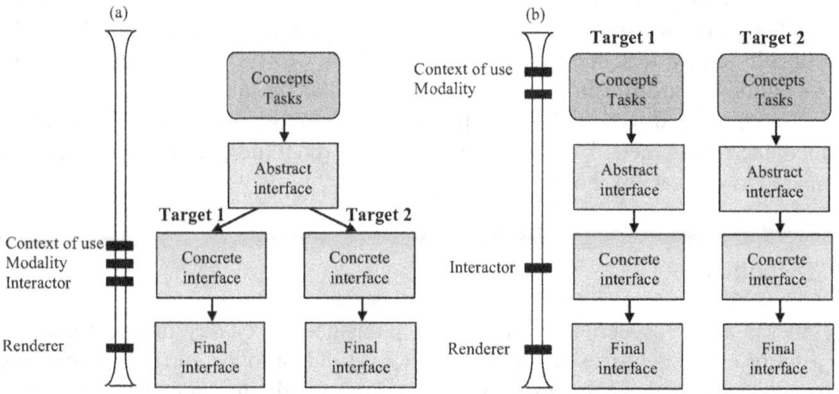

Fig. 7. Two instanciations of the design reference framework. The dependencies to the context of use, modalities, interactors and renderer are localized through stickers that constraint each other in their movement.

As for any evolutive phenomenon, the adaptation at run time is structured as a three-step process: sensing the context of use (S), computing a reaction (C), and executing the reaction (E) [6]. Any of these steps may be undertaken by the final UIs and/or an underlying run time infrastructure (Fig. 6). In the case of distributed UIs, communication between components may be embedded in the components themselves and/or supplied by the runtime infrastructure. As discussed in [24], when the system includes all of the mechanisms and data to perform adaptation on its own (sensing the context of use, computing and executing the reaction), it is said to be *close-adaptive*, i.e., self-contained (autonomous). FlexClock is an example of close-adaptive UI. *Open-adaptiveness* implies that adaptation is performed by mechanisms and data that are totally or partially external to the system. FlexClock would have been open-adaptive if the mechanisms for sensing the context of use, computing the reaction or executing the reaction had been gathered in an external component providing general adaptation services not devoted to FlexClock.

Whether it is close-adaptive or open-adaptive, dynamic reconfiguration is best supported by a component-connector approach [24] [11] [14]. Components that are capable of reflection (i.e., components that can analyze their own behavior and adapt) support close-adaptiveness [21]. Components that are capable of introspection (i.e., components that can describe their behavior to other components) support open-adaptiveness.

The next section applies these advances to the design and run time of comets.

3 The Notion of Comet

This section relies on the hypothesis that adaptation makes sense at the granularity of a widget. The validity of this hypothesis has not been proven yet, but is grounded in practice: refining an abstract UI into a concrete UI is an experimental composition of widgets with regard to their implicit functional (versus non functional) equivalence or complementarity. Basically, no toolkit makes explicit the functional equivalence of widgets (e.g., the fact that the three versions of Figure 2 are functionally but not non functionally equivalent: they support the same task of selecting one option among a set of options, but differ in many ways, in particular, in their pixels cost). Based on these statement and hypothesis, this paper introduces the notion of comet. It is first defined then examined from both a design and run time perspective. It is finally compared to the state of the art.

3.1 Definition

A comet is an introspective interactor that publishes the quality in use it guarantees for a set of contexts of use. It is able to either self-adapt to the current context of use, or be adapted by a tier-component. It can be dynamically discarded (versus recruited) when it is unable (versus able) to cover the current context of use.

The next section presents a taxonomy and a model of comets from a design perspective.

3.2 The Comet from the Design Perspective

Based on the definition of comets and the advances in plasticity (section 2.3), we identify three types of comets (Fig. 8):

- *Introspective comets* refer to the most basic kind of comets, i.e. interactors that publish their functional and non functional properties (Fig. 9). The functional properties can include adaptation abilities (e.g., sensing the context of use, computing and/or executing the reaction), or be limited to the applicative domain (e.g., selecting one option among a set of options). For instance, the "combo box" comet (Figure 2) does not have to include the adaptation mechanisms for switching from one *form* to another one. It just has to export what it is able to do (i.e., single selection, the task it supports) and at which cost (e.g., footprint, interaction trajectory) to be called a comet;
- *Polymorphic comets* are introspective comets that embed (and publish because of their introspection) multiple versions of at least one of their components. The polymorphism may rise at the functional core level (i.e., the comet embeds a set of algorithms for performing the user task; the algorithms may vary in terms of precision, CPU cost, etc.), at the connector level between the functional core and the UI components (e.g., file sharing versus sockets), or at the UI level (e.g., functional core adaptor, dialog controller, logical or physical presentations with regard to Arch [3]). A comet incorporating the three versions of Figure 2 for selecting one option among a set of options would illustrate the polymorphism at the physical level. Polymorphism provides potential alternatives in case of a change in the context of use. For instance, Figure 2c is more appropriate than Figure 2a for small windows. The mechanism for switching from one *form* to another one may be embedded in the comet itself and/or supplied by a tier-component (e.g. the runtime infrastructure – see section 2.3);
- *Self-adaptive (*or *close-adaptive) comets* are comets that are able to self-adapt to the context of use in a full autonomous way. They embed mechanisms for sensing the context of use, computing and executing the reaction. The reaction may be based on polymorphism in case of polymorphic comets.

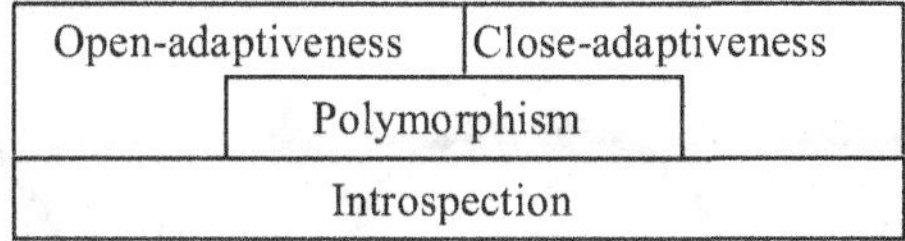

Fig. 8. A taxonomy of comets.

Introspection is the keystone capability of the comet. The properties that are published can be ranked against two criteria (Fig. 9): the type of the property (functional versus non functional) and the type of the service (domain versus adaptation). Examples of properties are provided in Figure 9. Recent research focuses on the notion of *continuity of interaction* [13]. The granularity of distribution and state recovery presented in section 2.2 belong to this area.

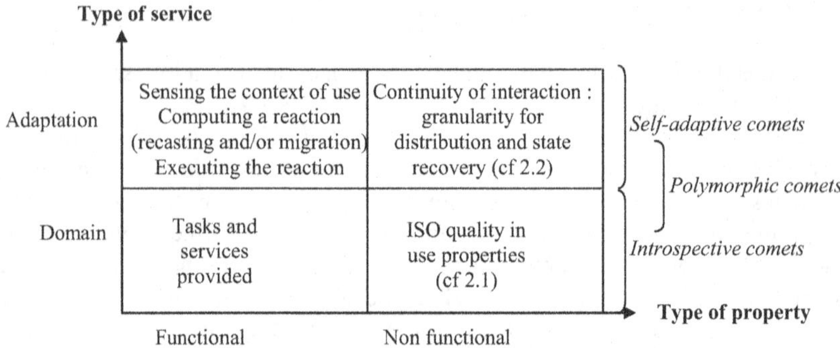

Fig. 9. A taxonomy of properties for structuring introspection.

Based on the nature of the domain task, a difference can be made between general comets that support basic tasks (i.e., those that are supported by classical widgets such as radio buttons, labels, input fields or sliders) and specific comets that support specific tasks. For instance, *PlasticClock* may be seen as a specific comet that simultaneously makes observable the time at two locations, Paris and New York (Figure 10). PlasticClock is polymorphic and self-adaptive. Its adaptation relies on two kinds of polymorphism, thus extending FlexClock:

- Polymorphism of abstraction: PlasticClock is able to compute the times in both an absolute and a relative way. The absolute version consists in getting the two times on web sites. Conversely, the relative way requests one time only and computes the second one according to the delay;
- Polymorphism of presentation: as shown in Figure 10, PlasticClock is able to switch from a large presentation format putting the two times side by side, to a more compact one gathering the two times on a same clock. Two hands (hours and minutes) are devoted to Paris. The third one points out the hours in New York (the minutes are the same). Allen's relations [2] provide an interesting framework for comparing these two presentations from a non functional perspective.

(a) A large presentation

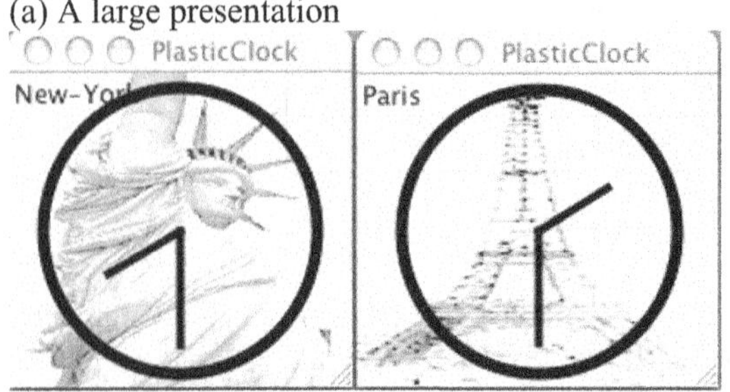

(b) A compact presentation

Fig. 10. PlasticClock.

The specific comets raise the question of the threshold between a comet and an interactive system. Should PlasticClock be considered as a comet or an interactive system? To our understanding, the response is grounded in software engineering: it depends on the expected level of reusability. As a result, comets can be designed as interactive systems. Figure 11 provides an UML class diagram obtained by applying both the reference framework and the taxonomy of comets for modeling a comet:

– A comet may be defined at four levels of abstraction. The most abstract one, called abstraction, is mandatory. This level may serve as starting point for producing abstract, concrete and final interaction objects (AIO, CIO, FIO) through a series of reifications and/or abstractions;

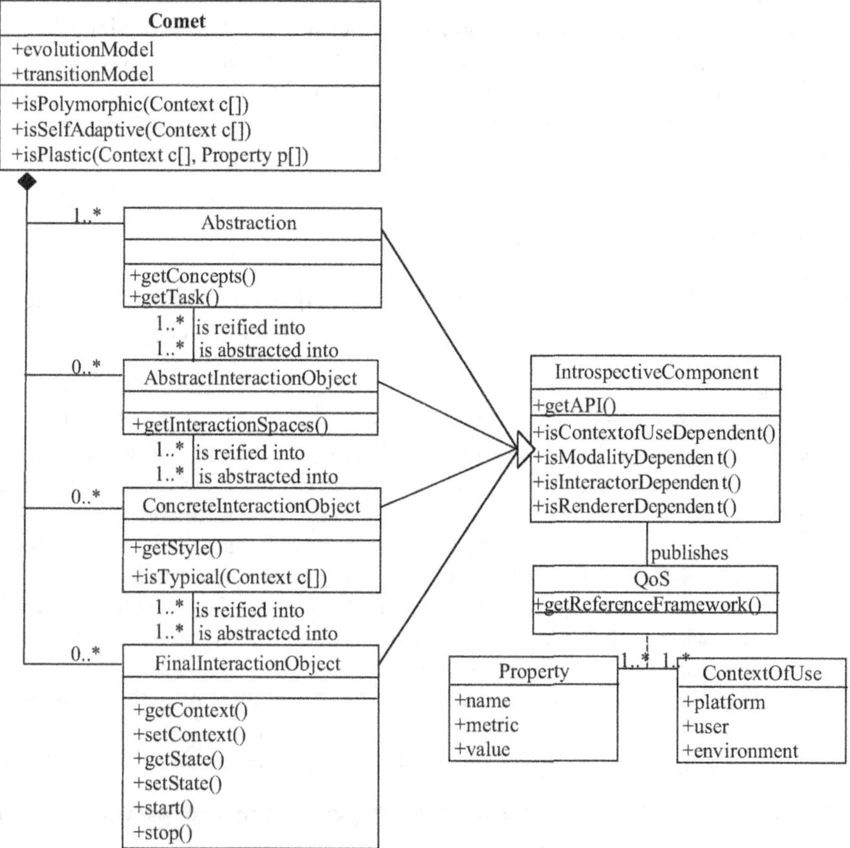

Fig. 11. A comet modeling taking benefit from both the reference framework and the taxonomy of comets.

The next section deals with the comets at run time.

– At any level of reification, comets are introspective, i.e., aware of and capable of publishing their dependencies and quality of service (QoS). The dependencies are expressed in terms of context of use, modality, interactor and renderer. The quality of service denotes the quality in use the comet guarantees on a set of contexts of use. It is expressed according to a reference framework (e.g. ISO) by a set of properties. In a more general way, introspective components publish their API;

- Specific information and/or services are provided at each level of reification. At the abstraction level, they are related to the concepts and task the comet supports; at the AIO level, the structure of the comet in terms of interaction spaces; at the CIO level, the style of the comet (e.g., the style "button") and its typicality for the given purpose (e.g., whether it is or not typical to use radio buttons for specifying the platform – Figure 2a); at the final level, the effective context of use and the interaction state of the comet. Managing the interaction state (i.e., maintaining, saving and restoring the state of the comet) is necessary for performing adaptation in a continuous way;
- The comets may embed an evolution and a transition model for driving adaptation. The comet publishes its polymorphism and self-adaptiveness capabilities for a set of contexts of use. Going one step further, it directly publishes its plasticity property for a set of properties P and a set of contexts of use C. It is plastic if any property of P is preserved for any context of C.

3.3 The Comet from the Run Time Perspective

This section addresses the execution of comets. It elicits a set of strategies and policies for deploying plasticity. It proposes a software architecture model for supporting adaptation.

We identify four classes of strategies:

- Adaptation by *polymorphism*. This strategy preserves the comet but changes its *form*. The change may be performed at any level of reification according to the three following cardinalities, 1-1, 1-N, N-1 depending on the fact that the original form is replaced by another one (cardinality 1-1), by N forms (cardinality 1-N) or that N forms, including the original form, are aggregated into an unique one (cardinality N-1). For instance, in Figure 2, when the comet switches from a to b, it performs a 1-1 polymorphism: the radio buttons are replaced with a combo box. When it switches from b to c, it performs a 2-1 polymorphism (respectively switching from c to b is a 1-2 polymorphism);
- Adaptation by *substitution*. Conversely to the adaptation by polymorphism, this strategy does not preserve the comet. Rather, it is replaced by another one (cardinality 1-1) or N comets (cardinality 1-N) or is aggregated with neighbor comets (cardinality N-1);
- Adaptation by *recruiting* consists in adding comets to the interactive system. This strategy supports, for instance, a temporary need for redundancy [1];
- Adaptation by *discarding* is the opposite strategy to the recruiting strategy. Comets may be suppressed because the tasks they support no longer make sense.

At run time, the strategies may be chosen according to the evolution model of the comet. The selected strategy is performed according to a policy. The policies depend on the autonomy of the comets for processing adaptation. We identify three types of policies:

- An *external non-concerted policy* consists in fully subcontracting the adaptation. Everything is performed externally by a tier-component (e.g. another comet or the runtime infrastructure) without any contribution of the comet. This policy is suitable for comets which are unable to deal with adaptation. In practice, this is an

easy way for guarantying the global ergonomic consistency of the interactive system. In this case, adaptation may be centralized in a dedicated agent (the tier-component);
- Conversely, the *internal non-concerted policy* consists in achieving adaptation in a fully autonomous way. Everything is performed inside the comet, without cooperating with the rest of the interactive system. The open issue is how to maintain the global ergonomic consistency of the interactive system;
- Intermediary policies, said *concerted policies*, depend on an agreement between the comet and tier-components. An *optimistic* version consists in applying the decision before it is validated by peers, whilst in a *pessimistic* version the comet waits for an authorization before applying its decision. The optimistic version is less time consuming but requires an undo procedure to cancel a finally rejected decision.

In practice, the policy decision will be chosen against criteria such as performance (c.f. the efficiency characteristic, time behavior sub-characteristic in section 2.1). The software architecture model Compact (COntext of use Mouldable PAC for plasticity) has been designed to take into account such an issue.

Compact is a specialization of the PAC (Presentation Abstraction Control) [8] model for plasticity. PAC is an agent-based software architecture model that identifies three recurrent facets in any component of an interactive system: an abstraction, a presentation and a control that assures the coherence and communication between the abstraction and the presentation facets. According to the "separation of concerns" principle promoted by software engineering, Compact splits up each facet of the PAC model in two slices, thus isolating a logical part from physical implementations in each facet (Fig. 12):

- Abstraction: as with the functional core adaptor in Arch, the logical abstraction acts as an API for the physical abstraction. It provides a framework for implementing the mechanisms to switch between physical abstractions (i.e., the functional core(s) of the comet; they may be multiple in case of polymorphism at this level). It is in charge of maintaining the current state of the comet;
- Presentation: in a symmetric way, as with the presentation component in Arch, the logical presentation acts as an API for the physical presentation part. It provides a framework for implementing the mechanisms to switch between presentations (they are multiple in case of polymorphism at this level);
- Control: the logical part of the control assumes its typical role of coherence and communication between the logical abstraction and the logical presentation. The physical part, called "Plastic" (Fig. 12), is responsible for (a) receiving and/or sensing and/or transmitting the context of use whether the comet embeds or not any sensors (i.e., the Sensing step of the Reference Framework), (b) receiving and/or computing and/or transmitting the reaction to apply in case of changes of context of use (i.e., the Computation step of the Reference Framework), and (c) eventually performing the reaction (i.e., the Execution step of the Reference Framework). The reaction may consist of switching between physical abstractions and/or presentations. The computation is based on a set of pairs composed of compatible physical abstractions and presentations. At any point in time, one or many physical abstractions and/or presentations may be executed. Conversely, logical parts are only instanciated once per comet.

As in PAC, an interactive system is a collection of Compact agents. Specific canals of communication can be established between the plastic parts of the controls to propagate information in a more efficient way and/or to control ergonomic consistency in a more centralized way. Compact is currently under implementation as discussed in the conclusion. The next section analyses the notion of comet with regard to the state of the art.

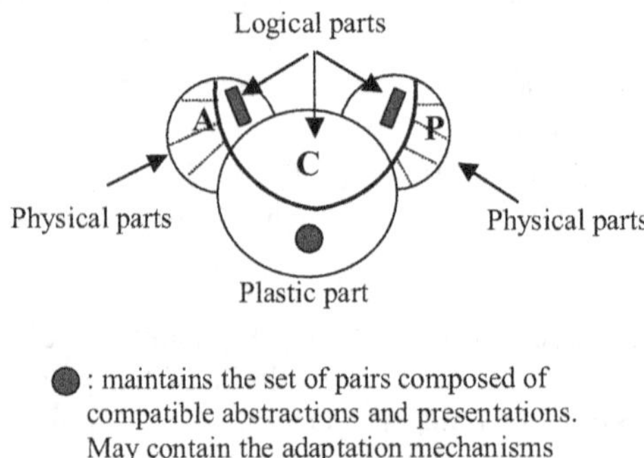

Fig. 12. The Compact software architecture model, a version of the PAC model (Presentation, Abstraction, Control) specifically mold for plasticity.

3.4 Comets and the State of the Art

Plasticity is a recent property that has mostly been addressed at the granularity of interactive systems. The widget level has rarely been considered. We note that most of these works focus on the software architecture modeling. Based on the identification of two levels of abstraction (AIOs and CIOs) [33], they propose conceptual and implementational frameworks for supporting adaptation [22] [20] [10]. But adaptation is limited to the presentation level [20] [10]. They do not cover adaptations ranging from the dialog controller to the functional core.

We now have to go further in the implementation. We keep in mind the issue of legacy systems [20] and the need for integrating multimodality as a means for adaptation [10].

4 Conclusion and Perspectives

Based on a set of recent advances in plasticity, this paper introduces a new generation of widgets: the notion of comets. A comet is an interactor mold for adaptation: it can self-adapt to some context of use, or be adapted by a tier-component, or be dynamically discarded (versus recruited) when it is unable (versus able) to cover the current context of use. To do so, a comet publishes the quality in use it guarantees, the user tasks and domain concepts it is able to support, as well as the extent to which it supports adaptation. The reasoning relies on a scientific hypothesis which is as yet unvalidated: the fact that adaptation makes sense at the widget level. The idea is to promote task-driven toolkits where widgets that support the same tasks and concepts are aggregated into a unique polymorphic comet. Such a toolkit, called "Plasturgy studio" is currently under implementation. For the moment, it focuses on the basic graphical tasks: specification (free specification through text fields, specification by selection of one or many elements such as radio buttons, lists, spinners, sliders, check boxes, menus, combo boxes), activation (button, menu, list) and navigation (button, link, scroll). This first toolkit will provide feedback about both the hypothesis and the appropriate granularity for widgets. If successful, the toolkit will be extended to take into account multimodality as a means for adaptation.

Acknowledgment

This work is being supported by the European commission funded CAMELEON R&D project IST-2000-30104. The authors would like particularly to thank Jean Vanderdonckt and Quentin Limbourg, members of the project. Many thanks to Julie Dugdale for checking the paper.

References

1. Abowd, G.D., Coutaz, J., Nigay, L.: Structuring the Space of Interactive System Properties, Engineering for Human-Computer Interaction, Larson J. & Unger C. (eds), Elsevier Science Publishers B.V. (North-Holland), IFIP (1992) 113-126
2. Allen, J.: Maintaining Knowledge about Temporal Intervals, Journal Communication of the ACM 26(11), November (1983). 832-843
3. Arch: "A Metamodel for the Runtime Architecture of An Interactive System", The UIMS Developers Workshop, SIGCHI Bulletin, 24(1), ACM Press (1992)
4. Ayatsuka, Y., Matsushita, N. Rekimoto, J.: Hyperpalette: a hybrid Computing Environment for Small Computing Devices. In: CHI2000 Extended Abstracts, ACM Publ. (2000) 53–53
5. Calvary, G., Coutaz, J., Thevenin, D.: A Unifying Reference Framework for the Development of Plastic User Interfaces, Proceedings of 8th IFIP International Conference on Engineering for Human-Computer Interaction EHCI'2001 (Toronto, 11-13 May 2001), R. Little and L. Nigay (eds.), Lecture Notes in Computer Science, Vol. 2254, Springer-Verlag, Berlin (2001) 173-192
6. Calvary, G., Coutaz, J., Thevenin, D.: Supporting Context Changes for Plastic User Interfaces : a Process and a Mechanism, in "People and Computers XV – Interaction without Frontiers", Joint Proceedings of AFIHM-BCS Conference on Human-Computer Interaction IHM-HCI'2001 (Lille, 10-14 September 2001), A. Blandford, J. Vanderdonckt, and Ph. Gray (eds.), Vol. I, Springer-Verlag, London (2001) 349-363
7. Calvary, G., Coutaz, J., Thevenin, D., Bouillon, L., Florins, M., Limbourg, Q., Souchon, N., Vanderdonckt, J., Marucci, L., Paternò, F., Santoro, C.: The CAMELEON Reference Framework, Deliverable D1.1, September 3th (2002)
8. Coutaz, J.: PAC, an Object Oriented Model for Dialog Design, In Interact'87, (1987) 431-436

9. Coutaz, J. Lachenal, C., Barralon, N., Rey, G.: Initial Design of Interaction Techniques Using Multiple Interaction Surfaces, Deliverable D18 of the European GLOSS (Global Smart Spaces) project, 27/10/2003
10. Crease, M., Gray, P.D. & Brewster, S.A.: A Toolkit of Mechanism and Context Independent Widgets. In procs of the Design, Specification, and Verification of Interactive Systems workshop, DSVIS'00, (2000) 121-133
11. De Palma, N., Bellisard, L., Riveill, M. : Dynamic Reconfiguration of Agent-Based Applications . Third European Research Seminar on Advances in Distributed Systems (ERSADS'99), Madeira Island (Portugal), (1999)
12. Dey, A.K., Abowd, G.D.: Towards a Better Understanding of Context and Context-Awareness, Proceedings of the CHI 2000 Workshop on The What, Who, Where, When, and How of Context-Awareness, The Hague, Netherlands, April 1-6, (2000)
13. Florins, M., Vanderdonckt, J.: Graceful degradation of User Interfaces as a Design Method for Multiplatform Systems, In IUI'94, 2004 International Conference on Intelligent User Interfaces, Funchal, Madeira, Portugal, January 13-16, (2004) 140-147
14. Garlan, D., Schmerl, B., Chang, J.: Using Gauges for Architectural-Based Monitoring and Adaptation. Working Conf. on Complex and Dynamic Systems Architecture, Australia, Dec. (2001)
15. Grolaux, D., Van Roy, P., Vanderdonckt, J.: QTk: An Integrated Model-Based Approach to Designing Executable User Interfaces, in PreProc. of 8th Int. Workshop on Design, Specification, Verification of Interactive Systems DSV-IS'2001 (Glasgow, June 13-15, 2001), Ch. Johnson (ed.), GIST Tech. Report G-2001-1, Dept. of Comp. Sci., Univ. of Glasgow, Scotland, (2001) 77-91. Accessible at http://www.dcs.gla.ac.uk/~johnson/papers/dsvis_2001/grolaux
16. Hinckleyss, K.: Distributed and Local Sensing Techniques for Face-to-Face Collaboration, In ICMI'03, Fifth International Conference on Multimodal Interfaces, Vancouver, British Columbia, Canada, November 5-7, (2003) 81-84
17. IFIP BOOK: Design Principles for Interactive Software, Gram C. and Cockton G. (eds), Chapman & Hall, (1996)
18. ISO/IEC CD 25000.2 Software and Systems Engineering – Software product quality requirements and evaluation (SquaRE) – Guide to SquaRE, 2003-01-13 (2003)
19. ISO/IEC 25021 Software and System Engineering – Software Product Quality Requirements and Evaluation (SquaRE) – Measurement, 2003-02-03
20. Jabarin, B., Graham, T.C.N.: Architectures for Widget-Level Plasticity, in Proceedings of DSV-IS (2003) 124-138
21. Marangozova, V., Boyer, F.: Using reflective features to support mobile users. Workshop on Reflection and meta-level architectures, Nice, Juin, (2002)
22. Markopulos, P.: A compositional model for the formal specification of user interface software. Submitted for the degree of Doctor of Philosophy, March (1997)
23. Myers, B., Hudson, S., Pausch, R.: Past, Present, Future of User Interface Tools. Transactions on Computer-Human Interaction, ACM, 7(1), March (2000), 3–28
24. Oreizy, P., Tay lor, R., et al.: An Architecture-Based Approach to Self-Adaptive Software. In IEEE Intelligent Systems, May-June, (1999) 54-62
25. Pinheiro da Silva, P.: User Interface Declarative Models and Development Environments: A Survey, in Proc. of 7th Int. Workshop on Design, Specification, Verification of Interactive Systems DSV-IS'2000 (Limerick, June 5-6, 2000), F. Paternò & Ph. Palanque (éds.), Lecture Notes in Comp. Sci., Vol. 1946, Springer-Verlag, Berlin, (2000) 207-226
26. Rauterberg, M. et al.: BUILT-IT: A Planning Tool for Consruction and Design. In Proc. Of the ACM Conf. In Human Factors in Computing Systems (CHI98) Conference Companion, (1998) 177-178
27. Rekimoto, J.: Pick and Drop: A Direct Manipulation Technique for Multiple Computer Environments. In Proc. of UIST97, ACM Press, (1997) 31-39

28. Salber, D., Abowd, Gregory D.: The Design and Use of a Generic Context Server, In the Proceedings of the Perceptual User Interfaces Workshop (PUI '98), San Francisco, CA, November 5-6, (1998) 63-66
29. Seffah, A., Kececi, N., Donyaee, M.: QUIM: A Framework for Quantifying Usability Metrics in Software Quality Models, APAQS Second Asia-Pacific Conference on Quality Software, December, Hong-Kong (2001) 10-11
30. Streitz, N. et al.: I-LAND: An interactive landscape for creativity and innovation. In Proc. of the ACM Conf. On Human Factors in Computing Systems (CHI99), Pittsburgh, May 15-20, (1999) 120-127
31. Thevenin, D., Coutaz, J.: Plasticity of User Interfaces: Framework and Research Agenda. In: Proc. Interact99, Edinburgh, A. Sasse & C. Johnson Eds, IFIP IOS Press Publ., (1999) 110–117
32. Van Welie, M., van der Veer, G.C., Eliëns, A.: Usability Properties in Dialog Models: In: 6th International Eurographics Workshop on Design Specification and Verification of Interactive Systems DSV-IS99, Braga, Portugal, 2-4 June (1999) 238-253
33. Vanderdonckt, J., Bodart, F.: Encapsulating knowledge for intelligent automatic interaction objects selection, In Ashlund, S., Mullet, K., Henderson, A., Hollnagel, E., White, T. (Eds), Proceedings of the ACM Conference on Human Factors in Computing Systems InterCHI'93, Amsterdam, ACM Press, New-York, 24-29 April, (1993) 424-429

Discussion

[Tom Ormerod] How much of the value of comet actually comes from the metaphor used at the interface ?

> [Gaëlle Calvary] The notion of comet is primary driven by the user task. In PlasticClock, when the screen size is enlarged, the date becomes observable because this task has been recognized as relevant for the user. It has been modeled in the task model. Conversely, if space is tight, then interaction is strictly reduced to the main tasks. So, the notion of comet is primary driven by functional aspects. Non functional properties are considered for selecting the most appropriate form. We will, for example, favor such or such metaphor. The problem is when no solution fits both functional and non functional requirements. Trade-offs are unavoidable. They are driven by strategies. This balance between functional and non functional properties is an interesting issue.

[Tom Ormerod] So, metaphor does not drive the design of the comet - the specification of tasks determines the appropriate metaphor.

> [Gaëlle Calvary] Yes. Of course, if the metaphor conveys an implicit task, then the task can be made explicit in a dedicated comet and the metaphor registered as possible presentation.

[Philippe Palanque] In the example of the plastic clock some tasks are not available anymore in the bigger clock such as provide the user with the precise time in Paris including minutes and seconds. Does Comet provide some help for checking such constraints ?

[Gaëlle Calvary] First point, PlasticClock is just a demonstrator of plasticity. It has not been implemented as a collection of comets. Then, in practice, a comet is created if it is promising in terms of reusability. So, it is finely analyzed from a user-centered perspective in terms of accuracy, etc. Its adaptation rules are discussed with final users. Then, at run time, tradeoffs are performed to achieve an optimum. It can be global to the interactive system, or local to a comet. As a result, mismatches may appear between local and global interests. Strategies have to deal with such issues. So, in summary, a comet is designed in a local consistent way. But, when involved in an interactive system, adaptation must be solved in a global way.

[Jurjen Ziegler] Did you address some high-level adaptation strategies such as substituting agents by others in the run-time architecture ?

[Gaëlle Calvary] Yes. We have elicited a functional decomposition of the runtime infrastructure that includes a component retriever and a configurator. The retriever is in charge of finding a component (or agent) in a repository that is then deployed by the configurator. Adaptation may be done at several levels of abstraction. Components may be retrieved at different levels of abstraction. Producing tools may be required to reify components that are not executable. Yet, adaptation is specified by rules. We are studying the appropriateness of Bayesian networks.

[Bonnie John] (to both Gaëlle and Simon Dobson) You are both offering different ways to think about the problem of contextual-aware systems. How do you evaluate whether your approach is a promising way to go forward ?

[Gaëlle Calvary] Our approach is strongly coupled with software engineering. The validation lies in the cost/benefit ratio. Does a library of comets improve the productivity of engineers and/or the quality of service of the interactive system? We have to go further in the implementation to answer the question.

[Simon Dobson] We have nothing to say about what adaptations are made. What we deal with are the situations in which adaptations should occur, and we can inform whatever mechanism is used to actually perform the adaptation. In terms of evaluation, our work should be evaluated as an aid to expression for designers and programmers: does it simplify the way in which adaptation occurs, does it improve analysis and the ability to develop correct systems. "Correct" remains an external notion depending on the application being considered.

[Grigori Evreinov] For efficient adaptation and visualization of spatial events and/or widgets the right metaphor is very important. To validate the metaphor itself it could be interesting to apply the proposed approach for adapting temporal events, objects and widgets, that is, under time-pressure condition a spatial arrangement could be present more effectively.

[Gaëlle Calvary] Yes, we have to investigate time. Bayesian networks could be an option.

Using Interaction Style to Match the Ubiquitous User Interface to the Device-to-Hand

Stephen W. Gilroy and Michael D. Harrison[1]

Dependability Interdisciplinary Research Collaboration,
Department of Computer Science, University of York, York YO10 5DD, UK.
steveg@cs.york.ac.uk

Abstract. Ubiquitous computing requires a multitude of devices to have access to the same services. Abstract specifications of user interfaces are designed to separate the definition of a user interface from that of the underlying service. This paper proposes the incorporation of interaction style into this type of specification. By selecting an appropriate interaction style, an interface can be better matched to the device being used. Specifications that are based upon three different styles have been developed, together with a prototype Style-Based Interaction System (SIS) that utilises these specifications to provide concrete user interfaces for a device. An example weather query service is described, including specifications of user interfaces for this service that use the three different styles as well as example concrete user interfaces that SIS can produce.

1. Introduction

The increasing availability of personalized and ubiquitous technologies leads to the possibility that whatever the device-to-hand is, it becomes the way to access services and systems. Therefore, interfaces to services must be designed for a variety of different types of device from desktop systems to handheld or otherwise portable devices. Different styles of interaction often suit different devices most effectively. While the appearance of ubiquitous devices has brought forth a proliferation of innovative interactive techniques, the broad categories and aspects of style as, for example, identified by Newman and Lamming [1] can still be applied. While a *key-modal* interface may be appropriate for a mobile telephone, with its limited screen and restricted keypad, a *direct manipulation* (DM) interface may be appropriate for a device based around touch / pen interactive techniques, such as current models of palmtop or tablet PCs. Typically in such situations a different low-level interface will have to be designed separately for each device. It is possible that several interaction styles may have to be supported for different users or parts of the system on the same device. As new technologies evolve to meet the demands of ubiquitous computing additional styles will emerge.

[1]Mailing address: Informatics Research Institute, University of Newcastle upon Tyne, NE1 7RU, UK. michael.harrison@ncl.ac.uk

R. Bastide, P. Palanque, and J. Roth (Eds.): EHCI-DSVIS 2004, LNCS 3425, pp. 325-345, 2005.

Style-specific design considerations normally take the form of guidelines, heuristics or ad-hoc rationalizations by designers [2]. Designs to support many devices may be facilitated by incorporating interaction style explicitly into an implementation. In this paper we demonstrate that incorporating style-level descriptions into a model of a user interface can give more flexibility than forcing a single user interface model on a heterogeneous selection of devices. This paper is concerned with an approach in which interaction with a service is bound to the features of the platform through a mediating style description. The aim is to support an interface that is appropriate given the technological constraints or opportunities afforded by the platform. In section 2 the approach to the style-based interaction system is contrasted with other approaches to platform independent service provision. In section 3 the interaction style approach is described in more detail. In section 4 an implementation of a style-based system and the specifications that drive it are described. In section 5 an example of a weather system is used to illustrate the idea. In section 6 the approach is discussed again in relation to other similar approaches and in section 7 the paper draws conclusions.

2. Modelling the Ubiquitous User Interface

Separating the user interface from application functionality [3] is a key theme in the delivery of interactive applications to multiple platforms. This is achieved by abstracting the interaction with a user interface from its presentation on a specific device. Model-based user interface development [4] provides useful tools to cleanly separate the parts of an application. However, its potential for easing cross-platform user interface development is less apparent when platforms differ in their support for styles.

The rise of ubiquitous computing and the proliferation of user appliances of widely differing capabilities and limitations have given new impetus to the need for cross-platform interface design. A provider of ubiquitous services typically wishes to target different users who may use devices of different capabilities, or a user or set of users who wish to migrate their use of services across several different devices.

Separation of application functionality and delivery via abstractly defined interfaces can be addressed in this broader context by the use of *service frameworks* [5] that organize and aggregate software functionality and data, and facilitate universal access to it. *Universal user interfaces* will provide interaction with services on a variety of devices, tailoring the interface to suit the device.

2.1 Service Frameworks

A service framework enables application functions to be delivered to devices whatever and wherever the devices are. The Web is an example of a framework for the delivery of many similar services through Hyper-Text Markup Language (HTML) files provided by web servers. Web services are delivered via Universal Resource Locators (URLs) that identify a particular service (usually requesting a single page of information). A user therefore makes the required service explicit by entering a URL into the browser manually, through a bookmark, or via a hyperlink. Other frameworks, e.g., XWeb [6], use similar approaches to existing web services and provide better support for diverse interaction.

2.2 Universal Interface Specification

An application's behaviour can be defined independently of platform, through the use of services. However, a mechanism is required to map that behavior to the specific interface components of a device. Model-based approaches map abstractions of interaction objects onto platform-specific implementations. The interactive components of the interface, for example a text box for inputting text or a drop-down list for making a choice, are abstracted and encapsulated in terms of a relatively small set of "interactors" [7]. Other approaches utilize several levels of abstraction that may include low-level "widgets", as well as more abstract components such as "group" or "choice". The sets of widgets available on different platforms may not intersect in terms of detail but as long as the abstraction can be fulfilled by a widget that *is* available on a particular platform then a concrete interface can be rendered.

2.3 Problems of Abstract User Interface Models

Abstract interface models [6, 8-12] are problematic when abstraction is such that there is no convenient implementation of the low-level interaction objects on a particular platform. A model must be defined to either restrict the set of objects to ones that are common across all platforms, or provide a wider set of objects to cover the variation in platform. In the former case, the interface becomes the "lowest common denominator" of all target platform capabilities, and is unsuitable if a new platform has interaction objects that do not exist in the available set. In the latter case, abstract objects are a union of available platforms. This gives rise to the two-fold problem of an ever-expanding library, or "toolkit", of widgets and an overly complicated mapping scheme to select the correct widgets for a platform.

Presenting a user interface for a UIML [11,12] specification on a specific platform involves more than selecting an appropriate widget representation. An interface structure that is defined *canonically* may fit one platform but not another. It is then necessary to have different specifications for cross platform structure variations, or alternatively a generic structure specification, which may be overridden when mapping the parts of the interface to actual platform elements. This defeats some of the point of a single structure definition. UIML also assumes a one-to-one mapping of parts to toolkit implementations. If a part in one interface implementation is needed it is added to the canonical definition of parts, even if it is not mapped to a particular platform.

XWeb [6], on the other hand, provides a higher-level formal specification of semantic interaction than a simple widget mapping. However, it still suffers from the "structure" problems of UIML in that it uses "grouping" interactors that arrange other interactors in a hierarchical structure, incorporating a canonical XView. An XView defines which elements of a data tree are manipulated by each interactor. While XWeb allows designers to reuse a view specification across clients with no extra effort, designs have to combine the interactors into views that are suitable for all platforms. The designer can therefore either design one set of views that maps to all client devices, or create a different set of views for different client types, losing the advantage of a single specification. Even if this is done, a new client with new interactor implementations might have usability problems with existing views, a problem encountered when speech widgets were implemented in an XWeb client [6].

3. A Model of Interaction Style

A model that incorporates interaction style makes it possible to vary the structure or interface semantics applied across devices. User interface descriptions are defined on a per-style basis and a target device selects the description that best maps onto its capabilities. Hence, if a form-fill interaction style is most appropriate for the device in the context of a particular application then that style is bound to the application and mapped to the interactive components of the device. For another target device a dialogue style might be more appropriate and in this case, the same application software would be bound with this different style.

The number of styles supported in the model should be finite and small, to allow a designer to target the maximum number of devices with the minimum amount of effort. It should also be possible to add a completely new style by creating additional definitions for existing interfaces. Although a designer does not have to support all styles, compatibility will be lost if devices do not support the styles chosen.

Two distinguishing features of a style are the manner in which they guide the user to the desired task or function and how they gather required input from the user. There may be semantic relationships that are shared across styles but which manifest themselves in different ways.

The style-based interaction system described in section 4 incorporates support for three styles: form-fill, dialogue and menu. Although these three are considered "classic" styles that can be applied to desktop systems, they also apply equally to other kinds of device. The services provided may be targeted at both desktop and mobile devices. Form-fill would map onto a web-style interface on desktop type systems, dialogue for voice-based telephone systems and menu for mobile phones or embedded devices.

3.1 Form-Fill Style

Forms are two-dimensional rather than one-dimensional, so navigation is important. The organization of a form on the display of the device requires a logical structure so that it can be decomposed to suit different display capabilities [13].

Form elements have different interaction requirements. Simple elements just require text entry while complex elements involve groups of choices or data of a particular format and may be mandatory or optional. The relation between elements might mean that two elements are mutually exclusive, or that filling in an element makes other elements or form sections mandatory. In addition, the elements that are filled in might affect what actions are available with the form data.

When the form is filled in, an action must be chosen to process the information. This is usually done by special commands, or buttons. An action might specify a certain set of form elements from which it processes information or the action invoked by a command might depend on the value of certain form elements. Validation of elements could occur before processing or feedback given if the processing finds invalid information.

A typical example of a form-fill style is the web-based form illustrated in figure 1(a).

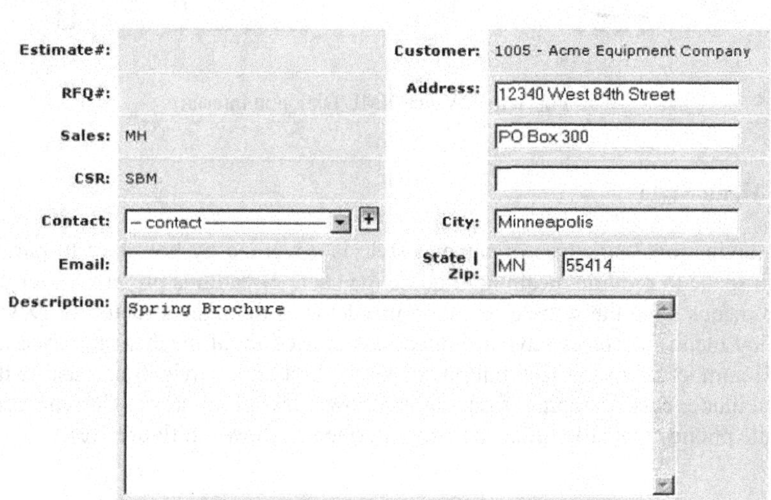

Fig. 1(a). A Web-based Form Interface.

3.2 Dialogue Style

The key feature of this style is the structure of the dialogue with the user. As questions are posed, the user's answer determines the next question asked and that answer may be a piece of data that is gathered. A state-chart notation is useful in describing this interface. Each state is a mode of the interface, and the transitions between states are the available choices. On entering a state the appropriate prompt is displayed. Input and output in a question/answer interface is one-dimensional so, while it is limited in terms of interaction, it can be supported by devices without complex graphical capabilities and the conversational nature of interaction facilitates the use of speech. VoiceXML systems (figure 1(b)) are an example of a dialogue style of interface.

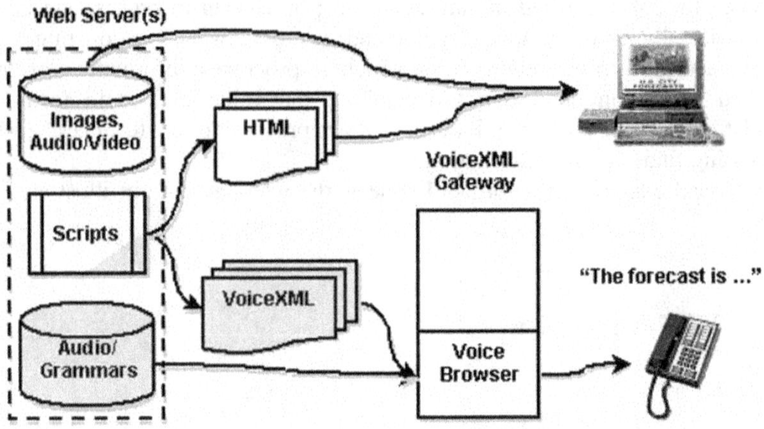

Fig. 1(b) A Voice XML Dialogue Interface.

3.3 Menu Style

The navigational structure of a menu style is governed by how best to partition the menu space to provide meaning to guide the user. Breadth is preferred over depth, as deep menus have the same orientation problems as dialogue structures. Devices that employ menu interfaces have a limited, customised input mechanism based around a small number of specialized buttons or keys. Input and navigation must be designed to facilitate easy mapping from an unknown layout of keys. Current generation mobile phones typically utilize a menu interface as shown in figure 1(c).

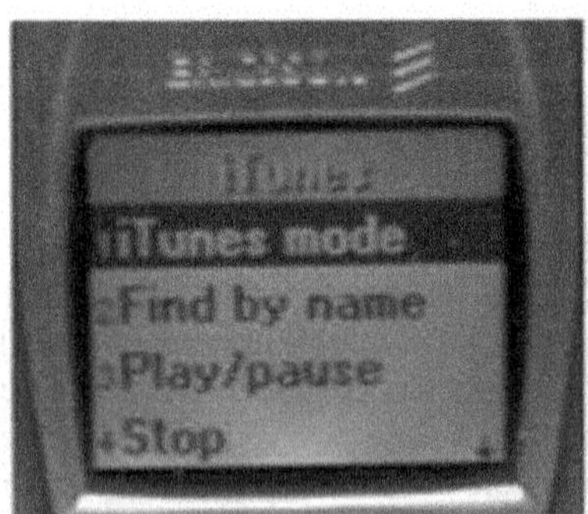

Fig. 1(c) A Mobile Phone Menu Interface.

4. Style-Base Interaction System (SIS) Framework

A prototype application framework supports interfaces using a variety of styles as outlined in section 3. The components of the framework are shown in figure 2. The framework consists of a runtime system that is configured by a set of eXtensible Mark-up Language (XML) specifications describing the service and style-based user interfaces of an application.

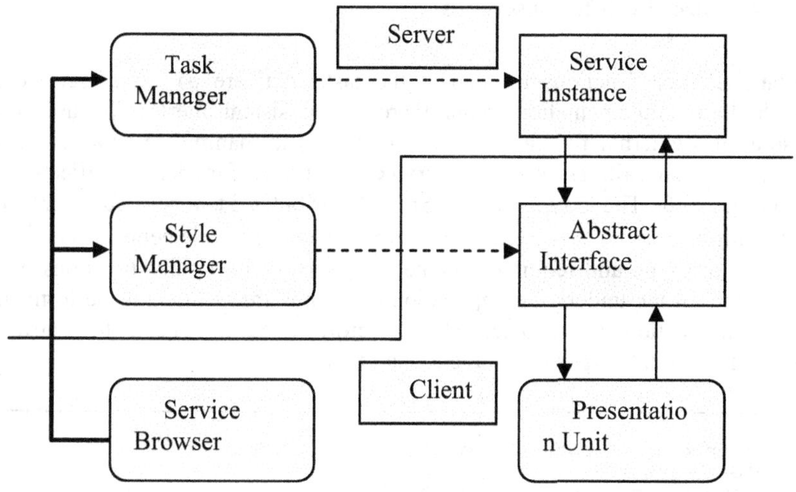

Fig. 2. SIS Framework.

SIS consists of both components that reside on a client appliance and those that can be managed on a remote server. Within a running ubiquitous application, this distinction is transparent. SIS is designed to switch easily between different style instantiations running on a single service instantiation. A user may thus migrate between different appliances without losing saved task-level information. It is feasible to swap a running style between different instances of the same service or two different services that both support the set of tasks required by the style definition.

The three components that deal with the initialization and management of an application are the *Service Browser* on the client, a *Style Manager* to look after styles and a *Task Manager* to look after the tasks required by services. Managers exist as separately running entities, possibly residing on remote servers, with their own resources and are configured using XML specifications of task and style. They use this configuration to generate the run-time components of the interface: *Service Instances* and an *Abstract Interface* for each style. Device specific *Presentation Units* provide concrete interface instantiations on each client. A weather service application is used to illustrate the approach.

4.1 Task Definition Using Service Specifications

The XML specification of a service defines its tasks, required function and data storage. A task manager generates run-time instantiations of services called service instances from these specifications. A service instance provides the data storage for its component tasks and a list of all the tasks in the service. Task instantiations are shared between services that use them, and are maintained by the task manager. When a service instance needs a task, it calls the task using the manager that created it. Tasks are identified by a namespace scheme[2] to avoid clashes between tasks of the same name utilized by different services.

Functions. Service functions implement the tasks that are part of a service and "wrap" the logic implementation so that there is a consistent interface for use in SIS. SIS also allows external functions (utility functions) to manipulate data before it is used in a function call. An example service and utility function specification are shown in figure 3. The `class` and `method` attributes identify a function's Java implementation. The `<return>` and `<parameter>` elements identify the function's return type and required parameters respectively. Utility functions do not affect the state of the underlying application logic, but are assumed to perform some repeatable translation upon data. SIS therefore does not need to know the implementation of data types to be able to manipulate them.

```
<function class="WeatherService" method="getWeather"
name="GetWeather">
    <return type="weather">weatherData</return>
<parameter type="string">cityName</parameter>
</function>

<utility name="postalToCity" class="PostUtil"
method="postalToCity">
     <return type="alpha">cityName</return>
     <parameter type="string">postalCode</parameter>
</utility>
```

Fig. 3. Function Definitions: A Service Specification XML Fragment.

Tasks. A single task within a service represents the lowest level of interaction with an application that is understandable to the user. Tasks describe a flat pool of possible functions and define how they are invoked. Task parameters can be provided either by user input or by a stored value. In the case where a needed parameter is a stored value that is not initialized, that task can be defined as unavailable.

Each task can call on at most one service function to guarantee atomicity of tasks and avoid problems of sub-task ordering. The provision of utility functions is meant to encourage data representation issues to be separated from logic. Hence, logically

[2] A *namespace* is a unique identifier that labels a group of related items. Different groups can then use the same identifiers internally to label different items.

similar tasks may use the same underlying service function and use utility functions to manipulate the data they provide to that function.

An example task specification fragment is shown in figure 4. Note the definition of the mapping of input from the user (`<variable>` elements) to parameters of the service function (`<parameter>` elements). This mapping technique is described below.

```
<task name="Get City Weather" taskFunction="Get Weather">
    <variable type="simple">cityName</variable>
    <parameter type="alpha"
               source="task"
               store="lastCity">cityName</parameter>
</task>
```

Fig. 4. Task Definition: A Service Specification XML Fragment.

Mapping Tasks onto Functions. The data passed from tasks to their underlying function are defined in terms of input *variables* and function *parameters*. These are represented in task definitions by `<variable>` and `<parameter>` element tags. The types of parameters defined in the task exactly match the input parameters of the underlying service function. However, there need not be the same number of task parameters as variables. The manipulation of a variable to provide a parameter value is defined with the `<parameter>` element tag. It identifies the variable to be used, what mapping to perform and whether to store the generated parameter value for later use.

The default mapping, if no mapping is explicitly defined (as in figure 4), is no manipulation at all. Data is output as a parameter exactly as it is received as a variable.

```
<parameter                                                    type="alpha"
            source="task"
            mapping="utility"
            store="lastCity"
            name="postalToCity">
<parameter                                                    type="alpha"
            source="task">postalCode</parameter>
</parameter>
```

Fig. 5. Utility Mapping in a Task Parameter: A Service Specification XML Fragment.

A *utility mapping* (see figure 5) assigns a utility function to transform the data of a variable that defines a mapping from postcodes to city names. The `name` attribute identifies the utility function to use, and the nested `<parameter>` element tags describe the mapping for the utility function's parameters.

Extract mappings take an element of a record type and return one of the items within the record as specified in the parameter. (Figure 6 shows extraction of an ID value from an account record.)

```
<parameter type="alpha"
           source="task"
           mapping="extract">account
accID</parameter>
```

Fig. 6. Extract Mapping in a Task Parameter: A Service Specification XML Fragment.

Keeping Track of State. A task-based service keeps track of persistent state at a task level separately from any provision made by underlying logic. State therefore can be shared between tasks directly without the underlying logic. It is possible to support stateless implementations of the logic (such as with raw HyperText Transfer Protocol (HTTP) based systems). A task parameter can define a mapping from a state variable instead of a task variable. In figure 7, a state variable keeps track of the name of a city for which weather is requested and a task uses the name to give an update of that request.

```
<state>   <variable   type="string">lastCity</variable>   </state>
...
<task    name="Update   Weather"    taskFunction="Get    Weather">
    <parameter   type="alpha"   source="store">lastCity</parameter>
</task>
```

Fig. 7. State Definition and Use in a Task Parameter: A Service Specification XML Fragment.

4.2 Interaction Style Specification

The key feature of the SIS approach is how tasks are implemented on different platforms. Each platform supports a set of presentation objects. Between the tasks and the presentation, each presentation style supports its own abstract user interface elements that gather input and display output to the user. These elements have their own distinctive way of navigating available tasks. No explicit layout or presentational information is contained in a style description; rather it is the semantic relationship between interface components that is described. It is the job of the presentation unit to resolve these relationships into an appropriate presentation.

Style instances are generated in the SIS client in order to facilitate fast user response. Therefore, events generated by presentation implementations are dealt with by style-specific, presentation-independent, objects that reside locally. The style manager generates each style instance from scratch locally on each client in order to customize a client's access to a common service.

Three styles are currently implemented but aim to provide a foundation for a potentially larger set.

4.2.1. Form-Fill Style

The style definition for a forms-based style involves: *field* elements for gathering user input, *actions* that can be invoked and a mapping from actions and fields to underlying tasks.

A field element is an abstract interactor that allows the user to enter a value to be used in a task, for example text entry, password entry, single choice, multiple choice, date entry, range entry and currency entry. Questions about whether a single choice entry would be represented by a drop-down list, radio buttons or some other selection method are deferred to platform implementation and depend on the actual data being selected and the layout constraints of the presentation. An example of a simple text field element and a single choice element are given in figure 8. The definition gives the type of the field element and the type of its value.

```
<field name="postalText" type="text"/>

-------------------------

<field name="accountChoice" type="choice" value="AccountType">
      <n-selection>1</n-selection>
      <selection-values source="utility">Get Accounts</selection-
values>
</field>
```

Fig. 8. Form-fill Style Specification: Example text field and single choice field element definitions.

Each style provides mechanisms for processing the data to produce an appropriate representation. Providers of services may specify functions that perform representational transformations. For example, in the form-fill style an output processor defines a set of items that can be extracted from a data type (see figure 9). Several output processors can be defined to work on the same types and used for different purposes.

```
<processor              name="weatherOut"              type="text">
     <input                 class="WeatherData">weatherData</input>
     <converter                                class="WeatherData">
        <item>
           <source>weatherData</source>
           <method>getWeatherText</method>
        </item>
     </converter>
</processor>
```

Fig. 9. Form-fill Style Specification: An example output definition.

A form is built out of fragments that map a set of fields to the inputs of a particular task. A fragment's task is only invoked if the requirements of the fields of that fragment are satisfied. A fragment also specifies an output processor that can extract information from the output of the task.

```
<form_fragment                                          name="cityForm">
     <task>Get                     City                   Weather</task>
     <input                            req="mandatory">cityText</input>
     <output                             type="text">weatherOut</output>
</form_fragment>
```

Fig. 10. Form-fill Style Specification: An example form fragment definition.

This definition (figure 10) outlines a hierarchy of actions that may be invoked by a user and associates with each action a set of form fragments that are evaluated when that action is invoked. Typically an action would be invoked by the user pressing a submit button to indicate completion of the form ready for processing. An action is a semantic unit within the form. Trees of actions, together with form fragments allow a presentation to compose a form representation. The presentation decides whether fields are presented on several "pages" or on a single "page" and use different buttons to invoke different actions.

4.2.2. Dialogue Style

Dialogue style definitions are described by a set of grammars of input token combinations. Dialogue structures make use of these grammars to move between elements of the dialogue. A grammar used in a transition between states is called a *match set* and contains a list of match items that can be matched by a series of tokens in input. For example in figure 12 `<matchitem>` contains a main `<token>` whose contents must match the next input token and optionally a list of match items that can be matched after that token. Items are evaluated in list order. As soon as an item matches, no more items in a list are evaluated. An item only matches if its main token matches *and* one of its sub items matches. That a possibility is optional is supported by a special `<lambda>` match item that is matched if no other items in a list are matched.

```
<matchset                                               name="CityMatch">
     <matchitem>
       <token>city</token>
       <matchitem>
       <token>name</token>
       </matchitem>
       <lambda/>
     </matchitem>
</matchset>
```

Fig. 11. Dialogue Style Specification: An example match set definition fragment.

The dialogue structure is a tree of states that has special task-invoking states as the leaf nodes in the tree (see figure 12). States are defined with `<dialogue-state>` element tags and contain possibly conditional prompts that are displayed if the dialogue stops at that state. A `transition` attribute identifies match sets or stored variables that a user's input must match. After a task is invoked, the dialog restarts at the root of the tree.

```
<dialogue-state>
      <prompt source="GetWeatherPrompt"/>
      <prompt source="GetUpdatePrompt">
       <condition task="Update Weather">
          <name>available</name>
          <value>true</value>
       </condition>
      </prompt>
       <dialogue-state transition="CityMatch">
           <prompt source="CityInput"/>
           <dialogue-state transition="$CITYVAR">
              <prompt source="CityWeather"/>
           </dialogue-state>
       </dialogue-state>
...
</dialogue-state>
```

Fig. 12. Dialogue Style Specification: An example dialogue tree definition fragment.

Task invocations are defined in special states that define the underlying task to be invoked, which dialogue variables to use, and the response to be generated with the output (figure 13).

```
<response name="weatherResponse" class="WeatherData">
   <output type="text">
     <method>getWeatherText</method>
   </output>
</response>
<task-state name="PostWeather">
   <task>Get Postal Weather</task>
   <parameter>$POSTVAR</parameter>
   <response>weatherResponse</response>
</task-state>
```

Fig. 13. Dialogue Style Specification: An example task state definition fragment.

Prompts can be either predefined questions or the response from a task invocation. Responses can also be shared between task instances. User variable input is transferred to the task states by use of a set of defined variables. The name of these variables can be used in place of a grammar match set in a transition between states.

4.2.3. Menu Style

A menu-based interface is specified by a tree of menu items (see figure 14). Each node representing an item has a label and an optional description of a task invocation. Only the leaves of the tree can have task invocations. Details of the task are wrapped into the menu item specification, with the name of the task and an output data extraction defined as usual, together with a list of inputs. Inputs can have a label to be displayed to the user when entering that input.

```
<menu-item>
    <label>Weather              by              PostCode</label>
    <task>Get               Postal              Weather</task>
    <input                                      type="string">
        <name>postalCode</name>
        <label>Enter             postal             code</label>
    </input>
    <output      class="WeatherData"      method="getWeatherText"/>
</menu-item>
```

Fig. 14. Menu Style Specification: An example menu item definition.

This current version is limited to descriptions of simple menus, but as an aim of the specifications is to simplify interface definition for simple interfaces, the descriptions are also simple. It is envisioned that the specification will be extended to cope with more complicated menu semantics and user input.

4.3 Presentation

Presentation units run on the client device and prescribe a concrete user interface for style definitions. Each style will have a presentation unit tailored for it that runs on a particular device. A client presentation unit utilizes a reference to a remote service instance and the appropriate style instance. They give access to the internal object representations of tasks and the elements of styles. When a task is to be invoked, it passes the appropriate data to the service instance.

Current implemented presentation units use simple techniques to deal with physical layout and representational issues. An expansion of the presentation component in the future might include dealing with details of physical layout in an abstract way.

5. Creating Interfaces with Styles

An example weather service together with definitions of the three different styles of interfaces described above, and their rendering by presentation units is now described. The service provides a single function that returns a textual description of the weather for a given location supplied as a string.

5.1 The AnyWeather Service

The weather query service is described by a XML task specification for the service shown in figure 15. Three separate tasks perform the service:

1. Request the weather for a city by name ("`Get City Weather`")
2. Request the weather for a city by postcode ("`Get Postal Weather`")
3. Refresh the last weather request ("`Update Weather`")

Requesting the weather for a city by name utilizes the underlying service function "`Weather Service`" directly, while a post-code based request requires the use of an external utility function, "`postalToCity`", to convert postcodes to city names.

The "`Update Weather`" task utilizes a state store object to keep track of the last city for which weather was requested.

```
<service location="http://www-
users.cs.york.ac.uk/~steveg/weather/">
<function class="WeatherService" method="getWeather" name="Get
Weather">
<return type="weather">weatherData</return>
<parameter type="string">cityName</parameter>
</function>
   <utility name="postalToCity" class="PostUtil"
method="postalToCity">
       <return type="alpha">cityName</return>
       <parameter type="string">postalCode</parameter>
   </utility>
   <state>
      <variable type="string">lastCity</variable>
   </state>
<task name="Get City Weather" taskFunction="Get Weather">
<variable type="simple">cityName</variable>
        <parameter type="alpha"
                   source="task"
                   store="lastCity">cityName</parameter>
</task>
<task name="Get Postal Weather" taskFunction="Get Weather">
<variable type="simple">postalCode</variable>
        <parameter type="alpha"
                   source="task"
                   mapping="utility"
                   store="lastCity"
                   name="postalToCity">
<parameter type="alpha" source="task">postalCode</parameter>
</parameter>
</task>
     <task name="Update Weather" taskFunction="Get Weather">
         <parameter type="alpha"
source="store">lastCity</parameter>
     </task>
</service>
```

Fig. 15. AnyWeather task specification.

5.2 Form-Fill Interface

The specification of the form-fill style for the AnyWeather service is shown in figure 16. Two fields are defined, one to enter city names ("`cityText`") and one to enter postcodes ("`postalText`"). A processor ("`weatherOut`") extracts the description of the weather from a `WeatherData` output object. Three form fragments, for each of the three tasks, use the defined processor for output and the two fields as inputs. The `<sub-form>` definitions match the form fragments to an action and a single display.

```
<style type="form"
       location="http://www.users.cs.york.ac.uk/~steveg/weather">
    <field name="cityText" type="text" />
    <field name="postalText" type="text" />
    <processor name="weatherOut" type="text">
        <input class="WeatherData">weatherData</input>
        <converter class="WeatherData">
           <item>
              <source>weatherData</source>
              <method>getWeatherText</method>
           </item>
        </converter>
    </processor>
    <form_fragment name="cityForm">
         <task>Get City Weather</task>
         <input requirement="mandatory">cityText</input>
         <output type="text">weatherOut</output>
    </form_fragment>
     ...
    <form>
        <display type="text">weatherDisplay</display>
        <action-set>
            <action-set name="getWeather">
               <action name="getCity"/>
               <action name="getPostal"/>
            </action-set>
            <action name="updateWeather"/>
        </action-set>
        <sub-form>
           <fragment>cityForm</fragment>
           <action>getCity</action>
           <display>weatherDisplay</display
        </sub-form>
...
    </form>
</style>
```

Fig. 16. AnyWeather form-fill style specification.

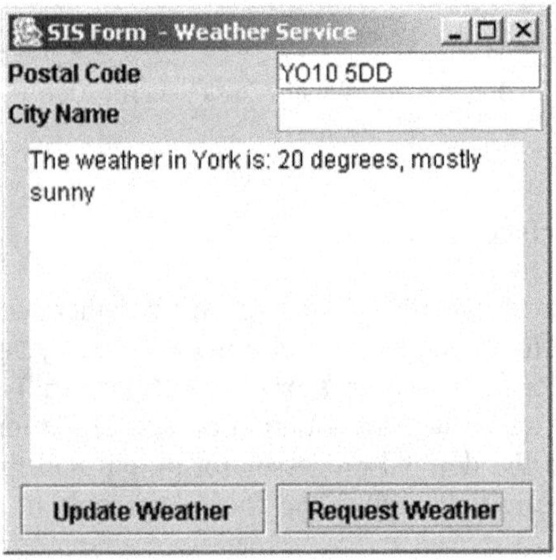

Fig. 17. Weather Service form-fill interface.

The form-fill presentation unit renders the form components on a single screen with two buttons representing the first sub-level of the action tree (see figure 17). The interface uses the requirements of the form fragments to evaluate which of the two user input tasks to invoke when the "Get Weather" button is pressed. The interface is told that "City Name" is mandatory for the "Get City Weather" task, but not required for the "Get Postal Weather" task, so if a city name is entered it can assume that the city task is required, and the button will invoke that task. In addition all non-required fields of that task will be disabled to help indicate which task has been chosen

```
<style type="dialogue">
<question name="GetWeatherPrompt">...</question>
<question name="GetUpdatePrompt">...</question>
<question name="CityInput">...</question>
<question name="PostInput">...</question>
<response name="weatherResponse" class="WeatherData">
     <output type="text"><method>getWeatherText</method></output>
</response>
<task-state name="PostWeather">
     <task>Get Postal Weather</task>
     <parameter>$POSTVAR</parameter>
     <response>weatherResponse</response>
</task-state>
...
<matchset name="PostMatch">
    <matchitem>
       <token>postcode</token>
    </matchitem>
    <matchitem>
       <token>postal</token>
      <matchitem>
         <token>code</token>
      </matchitem>
      <lambda/>
    </matchitem>
</matchset>
...
<dialogue-state>
   <prompt source="GetWeatherPrompt"/>
   <prompt source="GetUpdatePrompt">
     <condition task="Update Weather">
            <name>available</name>
             <value>true</value>
     </condition>
   </prompt>
    ...
   <dialogue-state transition="PostMatch">
        <prompt source="PostInput"/>
        <dialogue-state transition="$POSTVAR">
            <prompt source="PostWeather"/>
        </dialogue-state>
   </dialogue-state>
    ...
</dialogue-state>
</style>
```

Fig. 18. AnyWeather dialogue style specification.

5.3 Dialogue Interface

The specification of the dialog style for the AnyWeather service is shown in figure 18. Prompts are defined for the initial dialog state and for requesting user input. A response extracts the weather description from a WeatherData object in much the same way as for the form-fill style. A task state for each of the available tasks is assigned a response and an appropriate variable. Three match set grammars let a user enter a variety of phrases to select each of the tasks. For instance, a user can enter "postcode", "postal code" or just "postal" to access the `Get Postal Weather` task. A dialogue with three paths leads to the three tasks. The paths to the user input tasks have two states, one of which prompts the user to enter the appropriate input if it is not already in the token string. The update task doesn't require user input so only requires one state transition to reach it. The presentation unit for the dialogue renders the interface shown in figure 19.

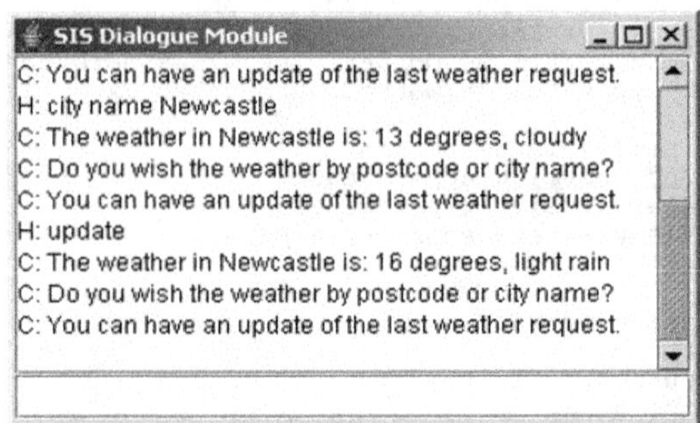

Fig. 19. Weather Service dialogue interface.

```
<style type="menu"
       location="http://www-users.cs.york.ac.uk/~steveg/weather">
       <menu>
          <title>Weather Service Menu</title>
          <menu-item>
             <label>Weather by City</label>
             <task>Get City Weather</task>
             <input type="string">
                <name>cityName</name>
                <label>Enter a city name</label>
             </input>
             <output class="WeatherData" method="getWeatherText"/>
          </menu-item>
          <menu-item>
             <label>Weather by PostCode</label>
             <task>Get Postal Weather</task>
             <input type="string">
                 <name>postalCode</name>
                 <label>Enter postal code</label>
             </input>
             <output class="WeatherData" method="getWeatherText"/>
          </menu-item>
          <menu-item>
              <label>Update Weather</label>
              <task>Update Weather</task>
              <output class="WeatherData"
method="getWeatherText"/>
          </menu-item>
       </menu>
```

Fig. 20. AnyWeather menu style specification.

5.4 Menu Interface

The specification for the menu style of interface for AnyWeather is shown in figure 20. All three tasks are available from the main menu, one item per task. The two tasks requiring user input have inputs fields rendered as separate entry screens in a menu presentation implementation as shown in figure 21.

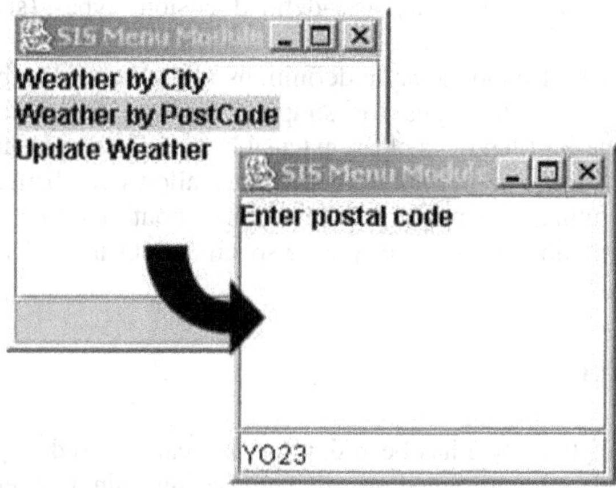

Fig. 21. Weather Service menu interface.

6. Discussion

The specifications in SIS separate the specification of the functionality of a ubiquitous application from the specification of its interface and provide a selection of different styles of interface so that an interface can more closely match the capabilities and limitations of a device. Both achievements are consistent with the original requirements of User Interface Management Systems (UIMS). Having a clean separation of function and interface has particular advantages when providing a selection of interface descriptions. It is clearly less important when providing a single "canonical" interface as in the case of XWeb and UIML (as discussed in section 2.3) or a UIMS vision based around a single type of device.

SIS achieves this separation by making the abstraction of functionality very simple. Any semantic relationships between the tasks must occur at the style level. In the AnyWeather service the relationship of tasks in the form-fill style (figure 16) is different from the dialogue style (figure 18), and this would be the case however systematically the layering was achieved.

Style specifications do not dictate how a presentation unit displays the information conveyed in the style. Presentation units on different devices display a style in different ways to fit that device even though the style definition is the same on each device. Applications can therefore use native applications on devices by having a presentation unit that renders interfaces in a way that is consistent with them. For instance a presentation unit could choose to display the AnyWeather form-fill actions as three separate buttons, rather than two, or indeed display the three sub-forms on different screens.

Although AnyWeather is designed to be simple to illustrate the basic ideas, more features can be added to each of the different styles. A further application of these features demonstrating SIS is based around an internet banking scenario. In this case more complex data types need to be supported, and this requires development of a richer type system. List and record types can be implemented to help support more complex applications as well as user-defined custom types (similar to those in XWeb).

The relative size of dialogue style definitions might be said to be in conflict with the requirements for definitions for simple interfaces to be simple themselves. However, the benefit of having a clear, extensible specification means that the parsing engine of the system can be much simpler and allows for better integration with simple tools. In future, size might be alleviated without affecting the parsing engine by using transformations from more concise specifications into the current versions.

7. Conclusion

A model of interaction style has been devised that can be used to provide a range of possible interfaces to be presented on a device. Basing a single interface specification on simple (yet still abstract) concepts can work, but is limited if target devices are too diverse in their interactive capabilities. Conversely, tying the specification too closely to the capabilities of any one device leads to the situation of having a different specification for each device. Having a finite set of styles specifications can be complex enough to make fuller use of devices capabilities yet different and flexible enough to work on a wide range of devices. Interaction styles have potential to be viable for defining interfaces for ubiquitous interactive systems on many devices. Additional applications will provide the impetus for expanding the features of SIS, and demonstrate its potential and flexibility.

References

1. Newman, W., Lamming, M: Interactive System Design. Addison-Wesley (1995) 293—322
2. Shneiderman, B: Designing the User Interface, 3rd edition. Addison Wesley Longman (1998) 71-74
3. Edmonds, E.: The emergence of the separable user interface. In Edmonds, E., ed.: The Separable User Interface. Academic Press (1992) 5-18
4. Vanderdonckt, J.: Current trends in computer-aided design of user interfaces. In Vanderdonckt, J., ed.: Computer-Aided Design of User Interfaces Proc.of CADUI '96. Namur University Press (1996) xiii-xix
5. Abowd, G., Schilit, B.N.: Ubiquitous computing: The impact on future interaction paradigms and HCI research. In: CHI97 Extended Abstracts. (1997)
6. Olsen, D.R., Jefferies, S., Nielsen, S.T., Moyes, W., Fredrickson, P.: Cross-modal interaction using XWeb. UIST 2000. (2000) 191-200

7. Myers, B.A.: A new model for handling input. ACM Transactions on Information Systems (TOIS) **8** (1990) 289-320
8. Ponnekanti, S.R., et~al.: ICrafter: A service framework for ubiquitous computing environments. In: Proceedings of Ubicomp 2001. LNCS 2201 (2001) 56-75
9. Eisenstein, J., Vanderdonckt, J., Puerta, A.: Applying model-based techniques to the development of UIs for mobile computers. In: IUI01:2001 International Conference on Intelligent User Interfaces. (2001) 69—76
10. Muller, A., Forbrig, P., Cap, C.H.: Model-based user interface design using markup concepts. In: DSV-IS. Volume 2220 of Lecture Notes in Computer Science, Springer (2001) 16-27
11. Phanouriou, C.: UIML: A Device-Independent User Interface Markup Language. PhD thesis, Virginia Tech (2000)
12. Abrams, M., Phanouriou, C., Batongbacal, A., Williams, S.: UIML: an appliance-independent XML user interface language. In: Computer Networks. Volume 31. (1999) 1695-1708
13. Turau, V.: A framework for automatic generation of web-based data entry applications based 0on XML. In: ACM Symposium on Applied Computing (SAC 2002). (2002)

Discussion

[Gerrit van Deer Veer] You did not mention/elaborate interaction styles “direct manipulation” nor “command language”. DM requires complex representation of n-dimensional interaction space and n-degrees of freedom user act to, command language seem completely upprite(?). Also, in envisioning scenarios of companies like Philips, NTT, Sun (“starfire”) these styles are mixed.

> [Stephen Gilroy] We did not elaborate DM: it’s very complex. We considered mixed styles (?). their analysis / Specification would be separate/unconnected.

[Ann Blanford] Walk-up-and-use isn’t just device or just context – it’s a tuple of device, context, user, task(s). i.e. There are combinations that work together and often that don’t. Can these combinations make style selections simpler ?

> [Stephen Gilroy] Yes.

[Kevin Schneider] Within your categorization of interaction styles, are there different styles for each device ? For example, would there be a different interaction style for filling in a form on a PC versus filling in a form on a PDA.

> [Stephen Gilroy] No, it would be the same style. The device would handle the different presentations.

Supporting Flexible Development of Multi-device Interfaces

Francesco Correani, Giulio Mori, Fabio Paternò

ISTI-CNR
56124 Pisa, Italy
{francesco.correani, giulio.mori, fabio.paterno}@isti.cnr.it
http://giove.isti.cnr.it

Abstract. Tools based on the use of multiple abstraction levels have shown to be a useful solution for developing multi-device interfaces. To obtain general solutions in this area it is important to provide flexible environments with multiple entry points and support for redesigning existing interfaces for different platforms. In general, a one-shot approach can be too limiting. This paper shows how it is possible to support a flexible development cycle with entry points at various abstraction levels and the ability to change the underlying design at intermediate stages. It also shows how redesign from desktop to mobile platforms can be obtained. Such features have recently been implemented in a new version of the TERESA tool.

1 Introduction

Model-based approaches [10, 13] have long been considered for providing support to user interface design and development. Recently, such approaches have received further attention because of the challenges raised by multi-device environments [1, 4, 6, 13]. The use of tools based on logical abstractions enables adapting the interfaces under development to the characteristics of the target devices. This can simplify the work of designers who do not have to address a proliferation of devices and related implementation details.

The potential logical descriptions to consider are well identified, and their distinctions are clear [3]: task models represent the logical activities to perform in order to reach users' goals; object models describe the objects that should be manipulated during task performance; abstract user interfaces provide a modality independent description of the user interface in terms of main components and logical interactors; concrete user interfaces provide a platform-dependent description identifying the concrete interaction techniques adopted, and lastly the user interface implements all the foregoing.

Various approaches have benefited from this logical framework, and tools supporting it have started to appear. In particular, there are tools that implement a forward engineering approach, which take an abstract description and generate more refined ones until the implementation is obtained; or tools supporting reverse engineering approaches, which instead take an implementation and aim to obtain a

R. Bastide, P. Palanque, and J. Roth (Eds.): EHCI-DSVIS 2004, LNCS 3425, pp. 346-362, 2005.

corresponding logical description. Examples of forward engineering tools are Mobi-D [13] and TERESA [6]. They both start with task models and are able to support user interface generation, though by applying different rules and additional models. TERESA is the tool for the design of multi-device interfaces developed in the EU IST CAMELEON project. It introduces the additional possibility of adapting the transformation process to the platform considered. A platform is a set of devices that share a similar set of interaction resources. Another example of tool for forward engineering is ARTstudio [4], which also starts with the task model and supports the editing of abstract and concrete user interface, but, contrary to TERESA, it generates Java code instead of Web pages and is not publicly available. Examples of different support for reverse engineering are Vaquita [2] and WebRevEnge [8]. The first one provides the possibility of rebuilding the concrete description of Web pages, whereas the latter reconstructs the task model corresponding to the Web site considered. In both cases one limitation is the lack of support for the reverse engineering of Web sites implemented using dynamic pages.

The needs and background of software developers and designers can vary considerably, and there is a need for more flexible tools able to support various transformations in the logical framework mentioned. To this end, we have designed and implemented a new version of the TERESA tool, aiming to provide new possibilities with respect to the original version [6]. In particular, the new version that is presented in this paper supports multiple entry points in the development process and the redesign of a user interface for a different platform.

In the paper we first recall the basic design criteria of the original version of the TERESA tool and then we dedicate one section to describing how multiple entry points can be supported and one for the transformation for redesign from desktop to mobile. We then show examples of applications of such new features and, lastly, we draw some conclusions and indications for future work.

2 The Initial TERESA Environment

The TERESA tool was originally designed to support the development of multi-device interfaces starting with the description of the corresponding task model. In order to facilitate such a development process the main functionality of the CTTE tool [7], supporting editing, analysis, and interactive simulation of task models, have been integrated into the new tool. So, once designers have obtained a satisfying task model, they can immediately change mode and use it to start the generation process. The tool provides automatic transformation of the task model into an abstract user interface structured into presentations. For each presentation, the tool identifies the associated logical interactors [11] and provides declarative indications of how such interactors should be composed. This is obtained through composition operators that have been defined taking into account the type of communication effects that designers aim to achieve when they create a presentation [8].

The composition operators identified are:

- Grouping (G): indicates a set of interface elements logically connected to each other;
- Relation (R): highlights a one-to-many relation among some elements, one element has some effects on a set of elements;
- Ordering (O): some kind of ordering among a set of elements can be highlighted;
- Hierarchy (H): different levels of importance can be defined among a set of elements.

In addition, navigation through the presentations is defined taking into account the temporal relations specified among tasks. The abstract user interface description can then be refined into a concrete user interface description, whereby a specific implementation technique and a set of attributes are identified for each interactor and composition operator, after which the user interface implementation can be generated. Currently, the tool supports implementations in XHTML, XHTML mobile device, and VoiceXML (one version for multimodal user interfaces in X+V and one version for graphical direct manipulation interfaces are under development).

3 Support for Flexible Forward Engineering

Interface design is complex. Often, as designers go through the various steps in order to develop suitable solutions for the current abstraction level, they would like to reconsider some of the choices made earlier in an iterative process. Furthermore, the actual results of automatic transformations may not be precisely those expected and thus would need to be refined. Lastly, the need to provide relevant support to a flexible methodology requires the ability to offer different entry points.

The original version of the TERESA tool provided a concrete solution to the issue of supporting development of multi-device interfaces through various levels of automation. However, when designers selected the completely automatic solution sometimes it happened that what they get was rather different from what they wanted (Figure 1 shows an example [12]). Thus, there was a need for providing designers with better support for tailoring the transformations to their needs.

Once a suitable description of the abstract user interface has been obtained from a given task model, it is important that its properties be adjusted to increase usability for the generated presentations. Designers may also decide to start defining the abstract interface from scratch, bypassing the task modelling phase.

In order to deal with all these issues we decided to extend TERESA functionalities by adding new features, in particular, enabling changes, even radical ones, in the properties of abstract user interface elements and the ability to develop an abstract user interface from scratch.

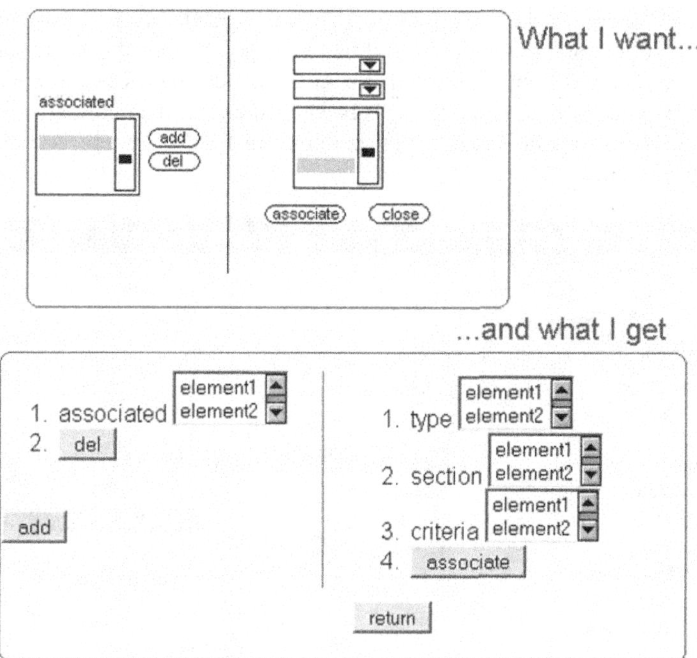

Fig. 1. Example of mismatch between designer's goals and result of automatic generation.

Once an abstract user interface has been created, there are various levels of modifications that can be possible:

- *Modifying the structure of a presentation without changing the associated interactors*. This can be performed in different ways: moving the orders of the interactors within a composition operator, changing, adding or removing composition operators;
- *Modifying the association between interactors and presentations without changing existing interactors*. This can be performed by merging or splitting existing presentations or moving one interactor from one presentation to another.
- *Modifying the set of available interactors*, this means changing the type of interactors, adding or removing interactors (this can be done by either working on single interactors or adding or removing groups of interactors or entire presentations).

In order to avoid confusing designers the editing features have to be explicitly enabled. Then, to ease the use of these functionalities, a number of features have been introduced. The type of an interactor is explicitly represented through an icon (as are the task categories in the task model) and modifications to the interactors order within a presentation can be performed through a drag and drop function. The result of a completely automatic transformation from the task model to the abstract user interface is a set of presentations (which are listed on the left side of the control panel, see Figure 2) and the related connections defining navigation through them. When one presentation is selected then its logical structure in terms of interactors and composition operators is shown in the central part. Designers can select either composition operators or interactors and the corresponding attributes are shown in the bottom part. The position of an interactor in the presentation can be moved through drag and drop interactions. If editing has been enabled it is also possible to change the type of operators and interactors. For example, in Figure 2 there is a change of a Grouping operator.

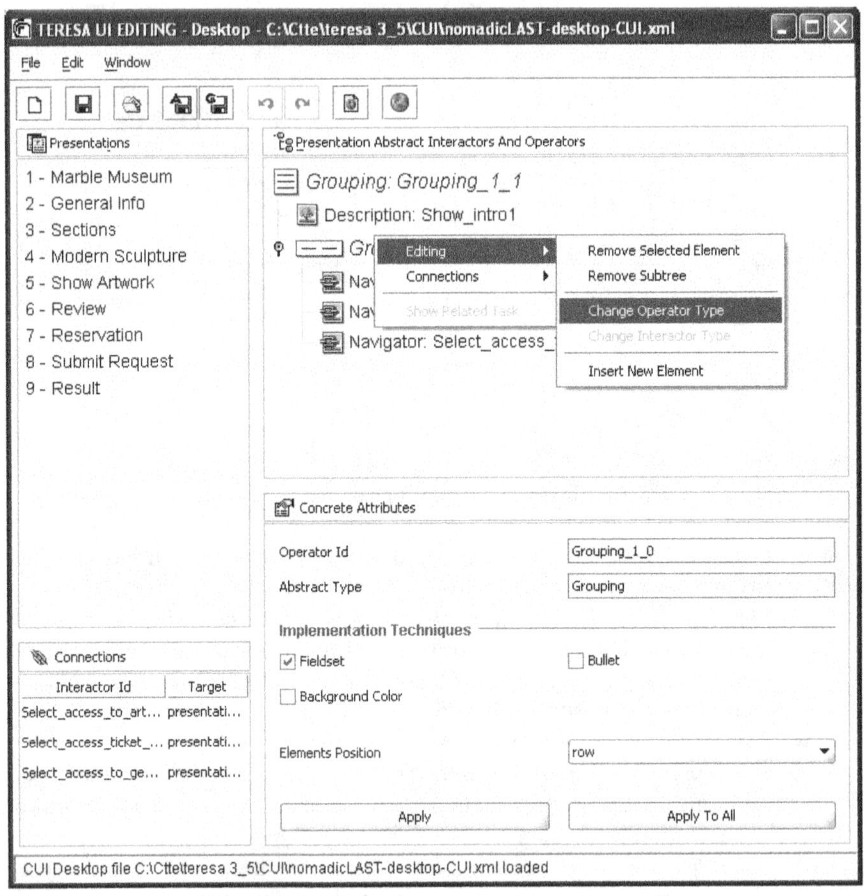

Fig. 2. Example of change of composition operator.

The editor of the abstract user interface (see Figure 3) provides designers with a view on various aspects that can be modified. One panel indicates the list of presentations defined so far. The logical structure of the currently selected presentation is shown as well. It can be represented either showing the logical structure in a tree-like manner or through the list of the elements composing it. The concrete aspects of the currently selected interactor are displayed in a separate panel. For example, in the figure a navigator interactor has been selected and its identifier, type, concrete implementation (in this case through a graphical link) and related attributes (in this case the image) are shown in the associated panel. Even the navigation through the various presentations is represented and can be edited: it is defined by a list of connections, each one defined by the interactor that triggers the change and the target presentation. The tool also provides the possibility of showing the corresponding XML-based specification and the logs of the designer interactions with the tool.

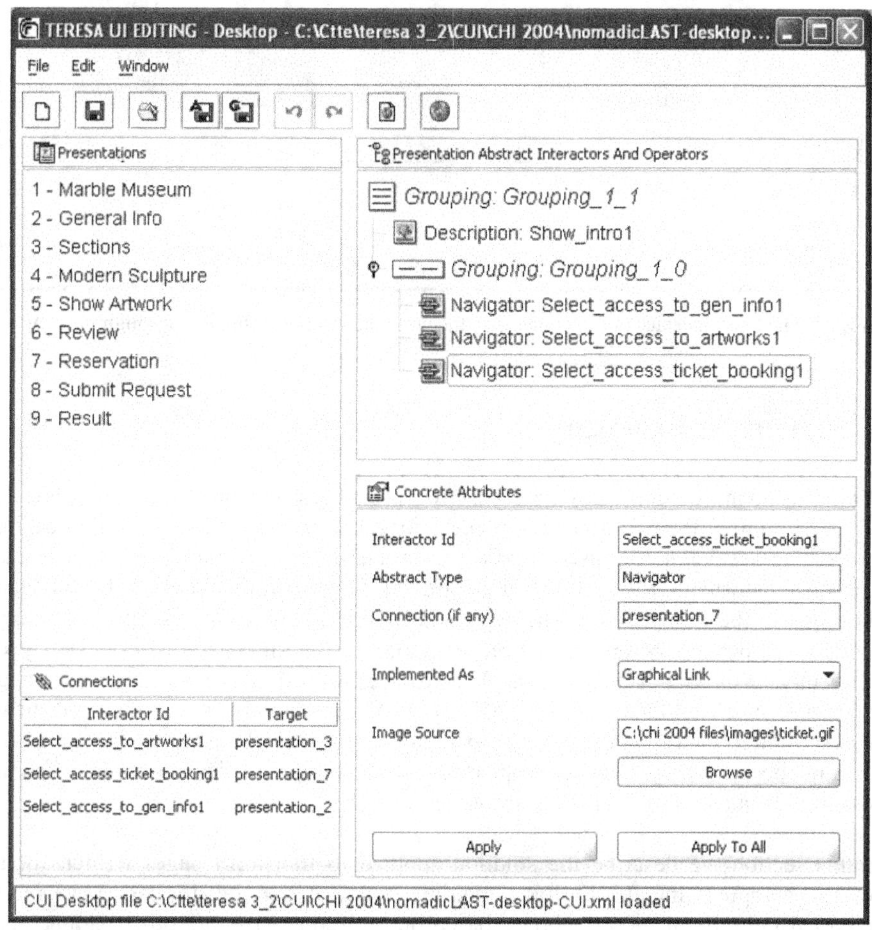

Fig. 3. Tool support for editing the abstract and the concrete user interface.

Lastly, a preview of the associated interface can be provided in order to allow designers to get a more precise idea of the resulting interface. Figure 4 shows the interface corresponding to the abstract/concrete presentation in Figure 3. Three navigator interactors are implemented through graphical links to other points in the application, and are grouped on the same row. In turn, this group is included in an additional group arranged vertically together with a description element that is implemented through images and text.

Fig. 4. The user interface corresponding to the concrete interface obtained through preview.

4 Support for Redesign

Nowadays many devices provide access to Web pages: computers, mobile phones, PDAs, etc. Often there is a need for redesigning the user interface of an application for desktop systems into a user interface for a mobile device. Some authors call this type of transformation graceful degradation [5]. One main difference between such platforms is the dimension of the screen (a mobile phone cannot support as many widgets as a desktop computer in a presentation), so the same page will be displayed differently or through a different number of pages on different devices. Transcoding techniques (such as those from HTML to WML) are usually based on syntactical analysis and transformations, thus producing results which are poor in terms of usability because they tend to propose the same design in devices with different possibilities in terms of interaction resources.

In this section we describe the solution adopted to transform pages written for a desktop computer into pages for a mobile phone. In our transformation we have classified the type of mobile phones based on the screen size and other parameters, which determine the number of widgets that can be supported in a presentation. We thus group such devices into three categories: large, medium or small. In the transformation we consider that a Web page for a specific device can display a limited number of interactors [11] that depends on the type of platform. Obviously, the number of interactors supported in a desktop presentation will be greater than the number of interactors contained in a mobile phone presentation, so a desktop Web presentation will be divided into many mobile phone presentations to still support interactions with all the original interactors.

In our transformation we consider the user interface at the concrete level. This provides us with some semantic information that can be useful for identifying meaningful ways to split the desktop presentations along with the user interface state information (the actual implemented elements, such as labels, images, ...). We also consider some information from the abstract level (see Figure 5): in particular the abstract level indicates what type of interactors and composition operators are in the presentation analysed. The redesign module analyses such inputs and generates an abstract and concrete description for the mobile device from which it is possible to automatically obtain the corresponding user interfaces. The redesign module also decides how abstract interactors and composition operators should be implemented in the target mobile platform. Thus, settings and attributes should change consequently depending on the platform. For example, a grouping operator can be represented by a field set in a desktop page but not in a page for a small mobile phone.

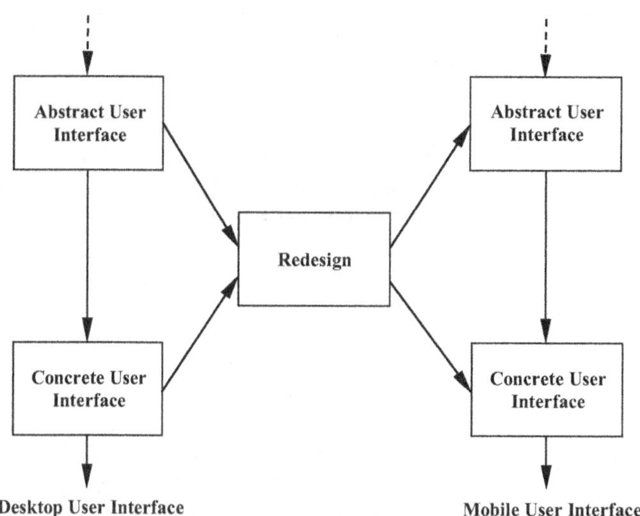

Fig. 5. The architecture of the redesign feature in TERESA.

In order to automatically redesign a desktop presentation for a mobile presentation we need to consider the limits of the available resources and semantic information. If we only consider the physical limitations we could divide large pages into small pages which are not meaningful. To avoid this, we also consider the composition operators indicated in the presentation specification. To this end, the algorithm tries to maintain groups of interactors (that are composed through some operator) for each page, thus preserving the communication goals of the designer. However, this is not always possible because of the limitations of the target platform. In this case, the algorithm aims to equally distribute the interactors into presentations of the mobile device. For example if the number of interactors supported for a large mobile presentation is six, and a desktop presentation contains a *Grouping* with eight interactors, this can be transformed into two mobile presentations, each one containing respectively a Grouping of four interactors. Since the composition operators capture semantic relations that designers want to communicate to users, this seems to be a good criterion for identifying the elements that are logically related and should be in the same presentation. In addition, the splitting of the pages requires a change in the navigation structure with the need of additional navigator interactors that allow the access to the newly created pages. The transformation also considers the possibility of modifying some interface elements. For example, the images are either resized or removed if there is no room for them in the resulting interfaces.

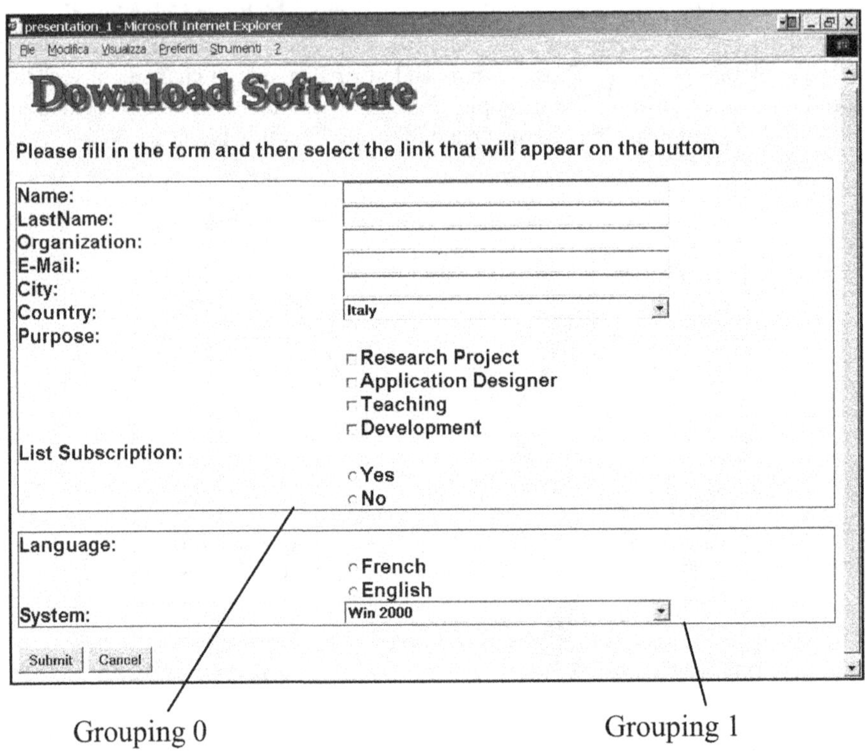

Fig. 6. Example of desktop Web user interface.

In order to explain the transformation we can consider a specific example of a desktop Web site and see how one of its pages (Figure 6) can be transformed using our method. The automatic transformation starts with the XML specification of the Concrete Desktop User Interface and creates the corresponding DOM tree-structure. The concrete user interface contains *interactors* (such as text, image, text_edit, single_choice, multiple_choice, control, etc) and *composition operators* (grouping, ordering, hierarchy or relation) which define how to structure them. A composition operator can contain other interactors and also other composition operators. Figure 7 represents the tree-structure of the XML file for the *desktop_ Download* presentation shown in Figure 6.

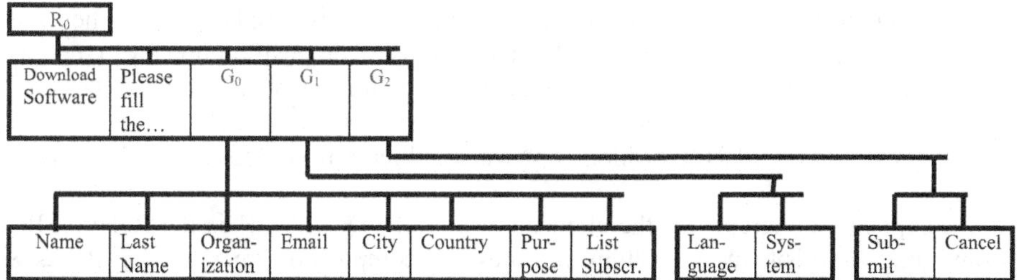

Fig. 7. Tree-structure of XML file for the "desktop_Download" *presentation.*

The resulting structure contains the following elements:

- composition operator R_0 , contains 2 interactors ("Download Software", "Please fill the form...") and 3 groupings (G_0, G_1, G_2);
- composition operator G_0 , contains 8 interactors (Name, Lastname, Organization, Email, City, Country, Purpose, List Subscription);
- composition operator G_1 , contains 2 interactors (Language, System);
- composition operator G_2, contains 2 interactors (Submit,Cancel);

The *relation* operator involves all the elements of the page: the elementary description interactor "Download Software", the elementary text interactor "Please fill in the form..." and the elements made up of the three aforementioned grouping operators. In general, the relation operator identifies a relation between the last element and all the other elements involved in the operator. In this case, the last element is represented by the composition operator G_2 which groups the "Submit" and "Cancel" buttons. In Figure 7 we can see the names of the interactors used in the *desktop_Download* presentation. There are also two *grouping* operators (G_0 and G_1) representing the two fieldsets in the user interface in Figure 6 and a grouping operator (G_2) involving the two buttons "Submit" and "Cancel".

Overall, this desktop presentation contains 14 interactors, which are too many for a mobile phone presentation. We assume that a presentation for a large mobile phone (such as a smartphone) can contain a maximum number of six interactors. Our transformation divides the "desktop_Download" presentation of the example into four presentations for mobile devices. Considering the tree structure of the XML specification of the Concrete User Interface in Figure 7, the algorithm makes a depth first visit starting with the root, and generates the mobile presentations by inserting elements contained in each level until the maximum number of widgets supported by the target platform is reached.
The algorithm substitutes each composition operator (in the example G_0 and G_1) that cannot fit in the presentation with a link pointing to a mobile presentation containing their first elements. In this case the two links point to the *mobile_Download2* and *mobile_Download4* presentations, which contain the first elements of G_0 (i.e., "Name") and the first elements of G_1 (i.e., "Language"), respectively.

So looking at the example, the algorithm begins to insert elements in the first "*mobile_Download1*" presentation and when it finds a composition operator (such as G_0), it starts to generate a new mobile presentation with its elements; so we obtain:

mobile_download1 = {**R(**"Download Software", "Please fill the form…", G_0, ….**)**}

The composition operator for the elements in mobile_Download1 is the Relation R_0. Continuing the visit, the algorithm explores the composition operator G_0. It has 8 elements but they cannot fit in a single new presentation. Thus, two presentations are created and the algorithm distributes the elements equally between them. We obtain:

mobile_Download2 = {**G(**Name, Lastname, Organization, Email**)**}
mobile_Download3 = {**G(**City, Country, Purpose, List Subscription**)**}

The composition operator for these two mobile presentations is grouping because the elements are part of G_0. The depth first visit of the tree continues and reaches G_1. It inserts a corresponding link in the mobile_Download1 presentation, which points to the new generated mobile_Download4 presentation where it inserts the elements of G_1.

Finally, we obtain:

mobile_Download1 = { **R(**"Download Software", "Please fill the form…", G_0, G_1, G_2**)** }
mobile_Download2 = {**G(**Name, Lastname, Organization, Email**)**}
mobile_Download3 = {**G(**City, Country, Purpose,List Subscription**)**}
mobile_Download4 = {**G(**Language, System**)**}

The entire last element of a Relation should be in the same presentation containing the elements composed by a Relation composition operator because it is the element that defines the association with the others elements. When the last element is another composition of elements (such as G_2), it is inserted into the presentation completely.

Thus, mobile_Download1 presentation becomes:

mobile_Download1 = { **R(**"Download Software", "Please fill the form…", "Form – part 1", "Form – Part 2", **G(**Submit,Cancel**))** }

Figure 8 shows the resulting presentations for the mobile device.

4.1 Connections

The XML specifications of concrete and abstract interfaces also contain tags for connections (*elementary_connections* or *complex_connections*). An *elementary_ connection* permits moving from one presentation to another and is triggered by a single interactor. A *complex_connection* is triggered when a Boolean condition related to multiple interactors is satisfied.

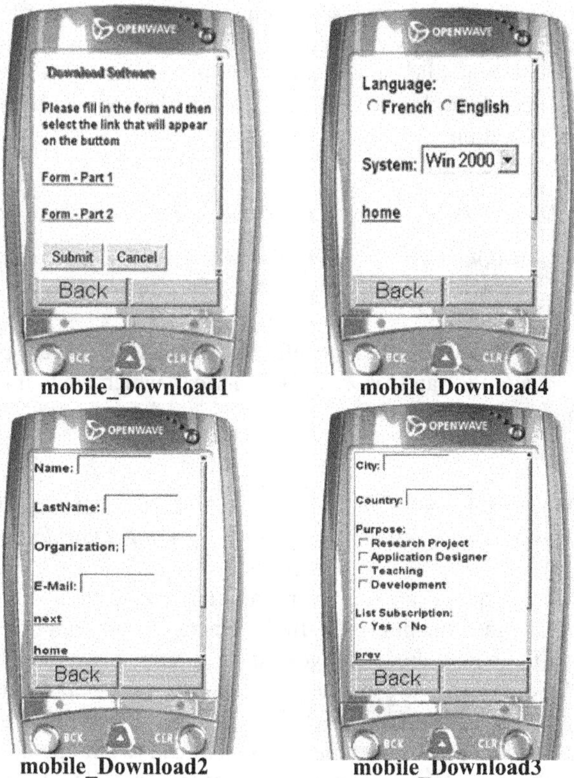

Fig. 8. Result of example desktop page transformed into four mobile pages.

The transformation creates the following connections among the presentations for the mobile phone:

- original connections of desktop presentations are associated to the mobile presentations that contain the interactor triggering the transition. In the example the connection associated with the "Submit" button is associated with the *mobile_Download1* presentation. The destination for each of these connections is the first mobile presentation obtained from the splitting of the original desktop destination presentations;
- composition operators that are substituted by a link introduce new connections to presentations containing the first interactor associated with the composition operators. In the example, we have two new links "Form - Part 1" and "Form – Part 2" which support access to the pages associated with the first interactor of G_0 and the first interactor of G_1 respectively:

mobile_Download1 ===== Form – Part 1 ======> mobile_Download2

mobile_Download1 ==== Form – Part 2 ======> mobile_Download4

- when a set of interactors composed through a specific operator has been split into multiple presentations we need to introduce new connections to navigate through the new mobile presentations. In the example *previous* and *next* links have been introduced automatically by the tool and we obtain the following connections:

  mobile_Download2 ===== *next* ======> *mobile_Download3*

  mobile_Download3 ===== *prev* ======> *mobile_Download2*

  the connections above, are useful to navigate between presentations "*mobile_Download2*" and "*mobile_Download3*" which contain the results of the splitting of the G_0 elements.

  mobile_Download2 ===== *home* ======> *mobile_Download1*
  mobile_Download4 ===== *home* ======> *mobile_Download1*

  the connections above are the corresponding connections for going back from presentations containing the first elements to presentations containing the links to the newly created pages. In the example, we have the "Form – Part 1" link, which is contained in "*mobile_Download1*" presentation. Likewise, we have the "Form – Part 2" link contained in "*mobile_Download1*" presentation. Thus, we need two home links that allow going back to mobile_Downolad1 from mobile_Download2 and mobile_Download4.

- complex desktop connections may need to be split into elementary connections if the associated interactors are included in different mobile presentations (in the example of Figure 6 there are no complex connections).

4.2 Other Considerations

Our transformation addresses a number of further issues. Attributes for desktop presentations must be adapted to mobile presentations. For example, the maximum dimension for a font used in a desktop presentation different from the maximum for a mobile device, and consequently large fonts are resized. The transformation of desktop presentations containing images produces mobile presentations also containing images only if the target mobile devices support them. Because of the dimension of mobile screens, original desktop images need to be resized for the specific mobile device. In our classification, images are only supported by large and medium mobile phones.

In consideration of the screen size of most common models of mobile phones currently on the market, we have calculated two distinct average screen dimensions: one for large models and another for medium size. From these two average screen dimensions (in pixels), we have deduced the reasonable max dimensions for an image in a presentation for both large and medium devices. The transformed images for mobile devices maintain the same aspect ratio as those of the original desktop interface. In *mobile_Download1* presentation we have an example of resize of image "Download Software".

Interactors often do not have the same weight (in terms of screen consumption) and this has consequences on presentations. From this viewpoint, *single_selection* and *multiple_selection* interactors can be critical depending on their cardinality. For example, a single_selection composed of 100 choices can be represented on a desktop page through a list, but this is not suitable for a mobile page because users should scroll a lots of items on a device with a small screen. A possible solution could be dividing 100 choices in 10 subgroups in alphabetical order (a-c, d-f,.. ...w-z) and each subgroup is connected to another page containing a pull-down menu only composed of the limited number of choices associated with that subgroup and not of all the original 100 choices. For example, the menu for selection of a Country present in desktop presentation can be transformed as shown in Figure 9.

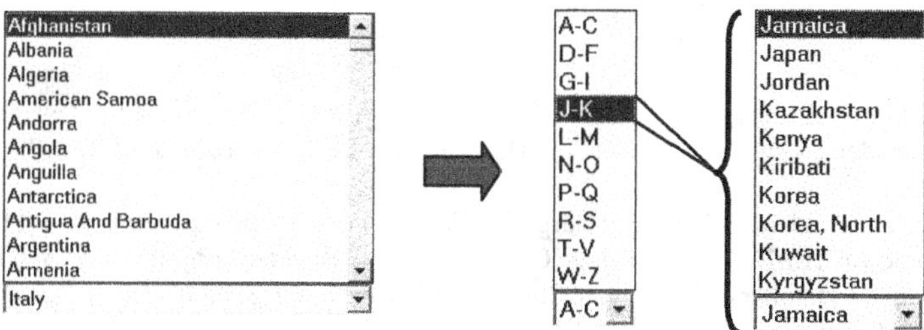

Fig. 9. Transformation of a single selection interactor for desktop system into one interactor for mobile presentations.

In the previous example of Figure 8 another simple solution has been applied, substituting the country pull-down menu of *desktop_Download* presentation with a text edit in the *mobile_Download3* presentation.

In general, the problem of redesigning and transforming a set of presentations from a platform to another is not easy and often involves many complex aspects related to user interface design.

5 Conclusions and Future Work

We have presented an approach to flexible multi-user interface design. The approach is supported by the new version of the TERESA tool, which is publicly available at http://giove.isti.cnr.it/teresa.html.

It provides designers with multiple entry points to the design process (which can be the task, abstract, or concrete user interface level) in order to change the results of automatic transformations from the task to the lower levels, and support redesign for different platforms. This last feature has also been considered in the CAMELEON project where the Vaquita tool has been used for reverse engineering of the design of a desktop Web interface. Its results are then input into the TERESA tool for redesigning for a mobile platform.

Future work will be dedicated to integrating natural interaction techniques in this environment in order to allow even people with little programming experience to easily use it in the design of multi-device interfaces. We also plan to add a feature in TERESA so that when a description at a lower level is modified, then such modifications are reflected into the description at the upper levels.

Acknowledgments

This work has been supported by the CAMELEON EU IST Project (http://giove.isti.cnr.it/cameleon.html). We also thank our colleagues in the project for useful discussions.

References

1. Abrams, M., Phanouriou, C., Batongbacal, A., Williams, S., Shuster, J. UIML: An Appliance-Independent XML User Interface Language, Proceedings of the 8th WWW conference, 1999.
2. Bouillon, L., Vanderdonckt, J., Retargeting Web Pages to other Computing Platforms, Proceedings of IEEE 9th Working Conference on Reverse Engineering WCRE'2002 (Richmond, 29 October-1 November 2002), IEEE Computer Society Press, Los Alamitos, 2002, pp. 339-348.
3. Calvary, G. Coutaz, J. Thevenin, D. Limbourg, Q. Bouillon, L. Vanderdonckt, J., "A Unifying Reference Framework for Multi-target User interfaces", Interacting with Computers Vol. 15/3, Pages 289-308, Elsevier.
4. G. Calvary, J. Coutaz, D. Thevenin. A Unifying Reference Framework for the Development of Plastic User Interfaces. IFIP WG2.7 (13.2) Working Conference, EHCI01,Toronto, May 2001, Springer Verlag Publ., LNCS 2254, M. Reed Little, L. Nigay Eds, pp.173-192.
5. Florins M., Vanderdonckt J., Graceful degradation of user interfaces as a design method for multiplatform systems, Proceedings ACM IUI'04, Funchal, ACM Press.
6. G. Mori, F. Paternò, C. Santoro, Design and Development of Multi-Device User Interfaces through Multiple Logical Descriptions, IEEE Transactions on Software Engineering, August 2004, Vol.30, N.8, pp.507-520, IEEE Press.
7. G. Mori, F. Paternò, C. Santoro, "CTTE: Support for Developing and Analysing Task Models for Interactive System Design", IEEE Transactions on Software Engineering, pp. 797-813, August 2002 (Vol. 28, No. 8), IEEE Press.
8. Mullet, K., Sano, D., *Designing Visual Interfaces*. Prentice Hall, 1995.
9. Paganelli, L., Paternò, F. A Tool for Creating Design Models from Web Site Code, International Journal of Software Engineering and Knowledge Engineering, World Scientific Publishing 13(2), pp. 169-189 (2003).
10. Paternò, F., Model-Based Design and Evaluation of Interactive Application. Springer Verlag, ISBN 1-85233-155-0, 1999.
11. Paternò, F., Leonardi, A. A Semantics-based Approach to the Design and Implementation of Interaction Objects, Computer Graphics Forum, Blackwell Publisher, Vol.13, N.3, pp.195-204, 1994.

12. Pribeanu C., Personal Communication, 2004.
13. Puerta, A., Eisenstein, J., Towards a General Computational Framework for Model-based Interface Development Systems, Proceedings ACM IUI'99, pp.171-178.
14. Puerta, A., Eisenstein, XIML: A Common Representation for Interaction Data, Proceedings ACM IUI'01, pp.214-215.

Discussion

[Stephen Gilroy] How do you deal with mis-match between interactor support on desktop and mobile platforms?

> [Fabio Paternò] The tool implements design criteria that take into account the features of the target platforms when it generates the corresponding concrete user interface. The next trasformation generates the final implementation in a language that depends on the platform. For example, it can generate XHTML for a desktop interface or XHTML Mobile Profile for a mobile interface. In case we want to support further implementation languages, such as WML, we only need to add a transformation from the concrete description for mobile devices to such implementation language. This transformation has to take into account the specific features of the new implementation language considered but it is easy to implement it because there is little distance in terms of levels of abstractions between the concrete description and the implementation language.

[José Macías] If I understand well, Teresa does the forward engineering and WebRevEnge does the reverse engineering one. Have you thought of combining both tools to obtain the whole cycle?

> [Fabio Paternò] Yes, this is the natural evolution of this research, and we think it will be very interesting to have a single tool able to suppport various levels of forward and reverse engineering.

[José Macias] How can you get the task model from an HTML page in WebRevEnge?

> [Fabio Paternò] We have analysed the most usual tasks of web applications and then we have built a tool that it is able to analyze the HTML code and identify first the corresponding basic tasks, next the tasks that are semantically related and consequently can be considered sub-task of a common higher level task, and then the temporal relations among tasks supported in one page or across multiple pages. Following this type of approach we have identified a good number of rules that are supported by the WebRevEnge tool, which is publicly available and documented in a journal publication.

[Jürgen Ziegler] Can the tool decide when a model is too complex to map to a mobile device?

> [Fabio Paternò] Not automatically; one needs to go back to the task model in order to identify tasks not suitable for a mobile device.

[Jürgen Ziegler] Can you create alternative presentations for mobile phones instead of those used on desktops?

> [Fabio Paternò] The tool generates new presentations for mobile devices according to the rules described in the paper. To this end the content for the desktop version is used and, in some cases, transformed. Future work will be dedicated to make more flexible the content transformation.

[Robbie Schaefer] Regarding the page splitting algorithm: Do you see a danger that user interfaces are generated which are processed in the wrong order by the user? What about a sequential approach?

> [Fabio Paternò] Our transformation provides results in which users have some flexibility in the choice of the order to follow when accessing the mobile pages. Users may be reluctant to process long sequences of pages on mobile phones. User evaluation has to show whether our design decision is the most appropriate.

The Software Design Board: A Tool Supporting Workstyle Transitions in Collaborative Software Design

James Wu and T.C.N Graham

School of Computing, Queen's University
Kingston, Ontario, CANADA
{wuj,graham}@cs.queensu.ca

Abstract. Software design is a team activity, and designing effective tools to support collaborative software design is a challenging task. Designers work together in a variety of different styles, and move frequently between these styles throughout the course of their work. As a result, software design tools need to support a variety of collaborative styles, and support fluid movement between these styles. This paper presents the Software Design Board, a prototype collaborative design tool supporting a variety of styles of collaboration, and facilitating transitions between them. The design of Software Design Board was motivated by empirical research demonstrating the importance of such support in collaborative software design, as well as activity analysis identifying the lack of support in existing tools for different styles of collaboration and transitions between them.

1 Introduction

The design of large, complex software systems is a team activity. A study by DeMarco and Lister found that developers working on large projects spend up to 70% of their time collaborating with others [6], while Jones found that team activities account for 85% of costs in large scale development projects [18]. This degree of interactivity between team members has necessitated the development of tools that can support collaboration within the software design process.

Designing effective collaborative design tools is a challenging task. In addition to technical and implementation issues associated with concurrent and/or distributed work, designers are hampered by a lack of data on how groups work together in software design. Collaborative applications are too often developed based on the individual experience of the designer, rather than on detailed study of the target user group and target tasks. This can result in tools that are neither useful nor usable. Even when user-centred design techniques are applied, the results are often tailored to the needs of single users, without sufficient support for collaborative work [10].

To better support collaborative work, software design tools need to support a variety of *workstyles* for collaborative interaction, as well as support fluid transitions between these workstyles. A workstyle is a characterization of the style of interaction employed by a group of collaborators, or supported by an interactive tool [36]. For example, co-located collaborators working at a whiteboard are engaged in an entirely

R. Bastide, P. Palanque, and J. Roth (Eds.): EHCI-DSVIS 2004, LNCS 3425, pp. 363-382, 2005.

different workstyle than distributed collaborators asynchronously sharing a document stored in a repository. In earlier work, we have shown that members of collaborative groups interact with each other through a variety of workstyles, and move frequently between different workstyles throughout the course of their interactions [37].

In this paper, we present a prototype collaborative software design tool, the Software Design Board. Software Design Board supports a variety of workstyles appropriate to the early stages of software development, and facilitates transitions between them. The functional requirements of the tool are informed by studies of existing design tools and by results of empirical research into collaborative software design activities. In presenting Software Design Board, we begin with a brief examination of related tools in the domain. As Software Design Board is primarily intended for use with an electronic whiteboard, these related tools are those that support software design through the use of informal media. Next, we present the empirical research that motivated the importance of supporting transitions in workstyle in collaborative design. We then introduce a model for characterizing styles of collaborative work, and show how this model is used to identify mismatches between collaborative activities and existing tool support. Finally, we introduce the Software Design Board and show how it supports a variety of important workstyles and workstyle transitions.

2 Tools Supporting Collaborative Software Design Through Informal Media

People often carry out design work using informal media such as paper or whiteboards [20]. Particularly in the early stages of design, informal media are appropriate as they allow design diagrams to be quickly and fluidly sketched [34]. Computational analogues of such informal media include electronic whiteboards, data tablets and stylus input for computers. Tools supporting interaction with informal media attempt to extend the free form, fluid interaction afforded by physical informal media to these computational counterparts.

The main advantage of informal media tools is that they support a natural working style without imposing significant cognitive overhead on the user through heavyweight interaction mechanisms. They allow users to use the tool transparently, without having to think about the tool itself. The drawback of many of these tools is the limited, or non-existent, support for movement towards more formal, structured work. This lack of support may limit development as a design evolves and begins to require more formal treatment. Also, many of these tools are intended to be general-purpose, and lack features that may be useful in the early stages of software design.

We identify three subcategories of these tools. In each, we consider an archetype tool that is typical of the subcategory, and identify other similar tools.

- *Informal CASE Tools:* These are software design tools that support interaction through informal media. Ideogramic UML [15] is a commercial tool that evolved from the Knight research project [5]. IdeogramicUML is intended to support the "agile" use of UML [1], meaning effective and lightweight use of UML. It supports a wide variety of interaction devices, including PCs, tablets, Tablet PCs and electronic whiteboards. This tool supports gesture based

modeling in UML, as well as free hand diagramming with no gestural interpretation. Furthermore, IdeogramicUML only supports co-located collaboration using electronic whiteboards, and requires additional tool support to be used by distributed teams. Other similar tools include UML Recognizer [21] and Tahuti [13].
- *Enhanced Electronic Whiteboards:* These are electronic whiteboard applications that attempt to replicate and extend the functionality of physical whiteboards using electronic whiteboards such as a Smartboard [28]. Flatland [24] is an augmented whiteboard application designed to support informal office work. Flatland provides various stylus-appropriate techniques for interaction and space management on an electronic whiteboard. Furthermore, it provides the ability to apply different behaviors to define application semantics. Flatland allows different segments on the board to respond differently to stylus input based on the applied semantics. However, it does not specifically support design tasks, but is intended to support for informal work in an office environment and as such can be appropriate in early software design tasks. Furthermore, Flatland does not support distributed collaboration, but only facilitates teamwork in a co-located setting. Other similar tools include Tivoli [25], Dolphin [30], and MagicBoard [4].
- *Shared Drawing Tools:* These tools support collaborative sketching or drawing tasks such as often found in early design work [31, 16] without providing support for any specific notation. ClearBoard [16] is a shared drawing program that allows two remote users to simultaneously draw in a shared space while providing awareness information such as hand gestures and gaze. It is based on the metaphor of 'talking through, and drawing on, a big transparent glass board' [16]. Clearboard also provides additional functionality such as simple stroke manipulations, recording of working results, as well as the ability to integrate generic files into the drawing space. Other similar tools include Commune [3], GroupSketch [11], and VideoWhiteboard [32].

Tools supporting interaction through informal media support collaboration in software design by facilitating unstructured interaction in a way appropriate to the early, creative design stages. They support an informal style of work that allows users to interact naturally and to use the tool transparently without imposing unnecessary overhead. Informal media tools support a small group of designers, and rely on social protocol to mediate group interaction. They typically produce informal artifacts of unbound semantics and free-form syntax. Most importantly for our purposes, informal media tools are typically independent of synchronicity or location, i.e. they support synchronous and asynchronous, as well as distributed and co-located interactions. This means they can support transitions in workstyle between synchronous/asynchronous and co-located and distributed styles of interaction.

3 Importance of Workstyles in Collaborative Software Design

We now present the empirical research that motivated the importance of supporting transitions in workstyle in collaborative design. We have performed extensive empirical studies into the nature of collaboration in software design [37]. We followed 5 development groups at a large software company over a 6-week period. Our research illustrated that not only is significant time spent collaborating within the design process, but also significant time and effort is spent in transitions between different collaborative styles of work. For example, team members may move frequently between asynchronous and synchronous workstyles, or between co-located and distributed workstyles, throughout the course of a single workday. These observations highlight the need for collaborative design tools that provide support for performing transitions between the various activities and working styles in which designers engage. Although some existing tools facilitate transitions in software designers' workstyles [7, 21, 12], most provide only basic communication facilities. More importantly, existing support for workstyle transitions is not commensurate with the frequency with which designers change between collaborative work styles [37, 38].

During our study, team members were observed to be highly interactive, spending on average more than two hours per day on communication tasks. Communication was predominantly face to face or via telephone or email. Also, team members often changed various aspects of their interaction such as location, synchronicity or modality of communication. These results provide evidence regarding the importance of collaboration and communication in software design, and motivate the need to support these activities in software design tools.

We also found that developers change locations frequently in order to collaborate, showing that on average, developers collaborated in more than 6 locations per day. According to interviews, this was due to a strong preference to work face-to-face. Many designers felt it was simpler, quicker and generally more efficient to use standard communication, including meeting face-to-face, than to establish remote interaction though tools. This often meant that people would walk up and down multiple flights of stairs numerous times each day to meet in person rather than use a telephone or another collaboration tool. These changes in location further indicate the frequency of workstyle transitions in collaborative software design.

Designers were also observed to frequently change the way in which they communicate, and to carry on multiple, simultaneous threads of collaboration. We found that it is typical for designers to attend a face-to-face meeting on a topic, then follow up with email, ask a supplementary question by telephone, follow up with more email, and so forth. Within individual threads of collaboration, we observed that designers change the mechanism by which they communicate more than once per day on average. These changes often involve a change in synchronicity (e.g. a change from telephone to email involves a change from synchronous to asynchronous interaction). Moreover, developers on average carried out more than three simultaneous threaded interactions in the course of a single day. All of these changes, between communication modalities, synchronicity and collaboration groups, reflect transitions in workstyle.

The results of this study have clear implications for the design of tools supporting team-based software design in large companies. These results show the importance of flexibility with respect to how a tool supports collaboration. Changes in physical location, synchronicity and communication modality are frequent, and tools should be designed to support such changes. Current tools do not sufficiently support such changes, if at all. In most existing tools, changes in synchronicity and location require a change in modality (e.g. from face-to-face to telephone) as well, imposing additional overhead on designers that choose to use them. More information on these empirical results can be found in the full study [37].

4 Understanding Workstyles

The *Workstyle Model* [36] allows us to characterize styles of collaborative work, either those employed by a group or supported by a tool. We can use these characterizations to identify mismatches between common activities and available tool support. These mismatches highlight areas where additional tool support is needed within a domain. Workstyle modeling complements task modeling [8] with supplemental information about how people communicate and coordinate their activities, and about the nature of the artifact to be produced. We have applied this model to the evaluation of how software designers collaborate, the forms of collaboration a wide variety of software design tools support, and to the design of the Software Design Board application itself. The development of the model itself was informed by the empirical study, presented in the previous section, as well as by informal laboratory studies of tools and designers.

In order to understand the relevance of workstyle analysis, consider the task of creating a design in some formal diagrammatic notation. A task model can identify the activities involved in creating such a design: drawing and labeling nodes, connecting them with relations, editing and reformatting diagram elements, and so forth. This model of design activities might lead to the development of a tool similar to Rational Rose [26] permitting mouse-based structural editing of design diagrams. However, in addition to the tasks that need to be performed, it is important to understand the users' preferred workstyle before committing to a design. Designers may be working in a brainstorming style, or may be recording precise documentation from which a system is to be built. A brainstorming workstyle is well supported by a whiteboard, which provides sufficient space for small groups to work, and supports a fluid style of interaction where multiple designers may interact with the design artifact in parallel. Alternatively, recording of precise documentation is well supported by a traditional Computer-Aided Software Engineering (CASE) tool. It is important to note that, though both tools support the activities identified in the task model, they do so in different ways that are appropriate to entirely different styles of work. The workstyle model helps in the analysis of peoples' goals and tasks by helping to understand their preferred style of work.

The *Workstyle* model characterizes a working style as an eight dimensional space that addresses the style of collaboration and communication between designers and the properties of the artifacts that are created during the collaboration. The functionality of collaborative design tools can be plotted in this space to specify the set of workstyles that they can support. It then becomes possible to compare designers' preferred workstyles to those supported by available tools and to identify potential task/tool mismatches. These mismatches can be used to guide the design of new tools that are more appropriate to particular design activities. Figure 1 depicts a graphical representation of the axes of Workstyle Model on which workstyle analyses are plotted

4.1 Dimensions Describing Collaboration Style

The first four dimensions of the model describe the nature of the collaboration in which a group is engaged, or that can be supported by a tool. They are defined as follows:

- *Location:* The location axis refers to the distribution of the people involved in the collaboration. As people become more geographically distributed, supporting some collaborative workstyles becomes increasingly difficult [27].
- *Synchronicity:* The synchronicity axis describes the temporal nature of the collaboration. People may work together at the same time (*synchronously*) or at different times (*asynchronously*).
- *Group Size:* The group size axis captures the number of people involved in the collaboration. Support for larger groups typically comes at the expense of intimacy in the interaction between collaborators.
- *Coordination:* This axis describes how users' activities are coordinated, whether by the choice of tools they are using or through the adoption of some coordination model [22].

4.2 Dimensions Describing Artifact Style

The remaining four dimensions describe the nature of the artifacts produced by the group, or able to be produced by a tool. They are defined as follows:

- *Syntactic Correctness*: The artifact being produced may be required to follow a precise syntax. This requirement may inhibit progress in early stages of design by forcing initially abstract designs to conform to a predetermined syntax [20, 35].
- *Semantic Correctness:* An artifact is considered to be semantically *sound* if its meaning is unambiguous and free of contradiction. The production of semantically sound artifacts facilitates automated analysis and evolution.
- *Archivability:* Archivability represents the difficulty of saving an artifact so that it can be used at a later time. For example, word processing documents have high archivability, as they can be saved to disk and retrieved later.
- *Modifiability:* This axis represents the ease with which an artifact can be modified. For example, small modifications to a whiteboard drawing are simply performed by erasing and redrawing.

4.3 Applying the Workstyle Model

The Workstyle Model can be applied to assess tools and/or the interaction style of users. The model can be used to evaluate the support provided by individual tools for various working styles, or applied to users to evaluate their working styles while accomplishing various tasks with preferred tools. To do so, values for each property are plotted on a two-dimensional representation of the model, as seen in Figure 1. A single workstyle is represented as a point in an eight dimensional space, while a range of workstyles is represented as a region in this space. Support for a single value in a particular property is indicated by a line intersecting the related axis, while a region over the axis represents support for a range of values in that property. So a plot that consists of a single line with no expanded areas can represent a tool or set of tools that supports a single, rigid workstyle. Similarly, if applied to users, the plot may represent a particular style of work used to accomplish some particular task. Conversely, a plot that covers an area of the graph may represent a tool or set of tools that supports a range of workstyles and transitions between them. Similarly, if applied to users, it may represent a change in the style of interaction that has occurred over a period of time. Once plotted, differences in the workstyles supported by various tools become visually apparent. These plots can be compared to workstyle plots of users accomplishing the tasks supported by those tools in their preferred manner. Mismatches between these plots identify tools that are not providing sufficient usability for their supported tasks. More detail and examples of applying the Workstyle Model can be found in [36, 38].

4.3.1 Workstyle Example – UML Design Tools

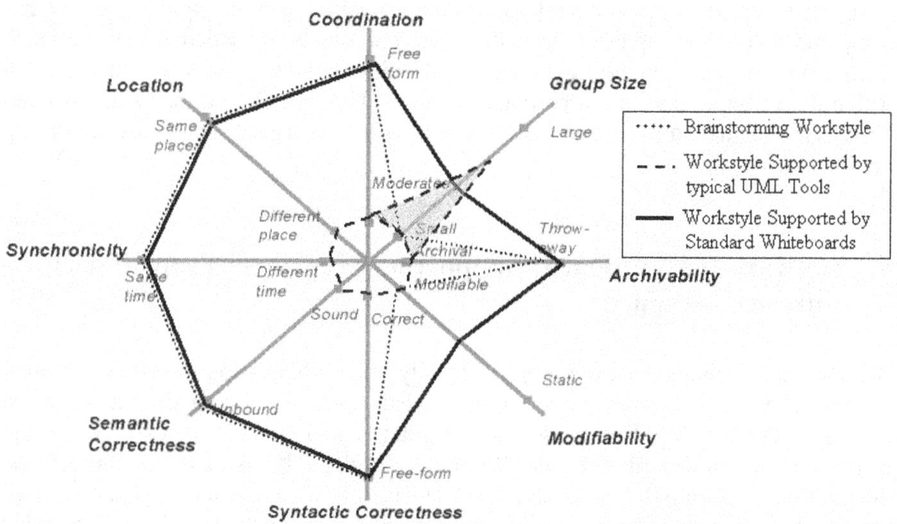

Fig. 1. A Workstyle comparison between UML tools and standard whiteboards in support for typical brainstorming activities.

It is useful to consider the workstyle supported by popular UML design tools such as Rational Rose [26]. Design tools such as these are a good fit with workstyles where little real-time communication with other designers is required, and where the goal is to create precise, archival designs. However, these design tools provide poor support for the early stages of design, such as brainstorming. During these phases, designers spend significant time on communications tasks.

The inappropriateness of UML design tools for early stages of design can be clearly shown by examining the brainstorming workstyle. As shown in Figure 1, brainstorming is typically carried out by small groups working face to face, using free-form coordination and social protocols to determine who gets to speak or write next. In brainstorming, designers do not wish to be distracted by requirements to be syntactically correct, or even semantically sound [2, 31]. Modifiability is important as early designs evolve rapidly, and archivability is important to allow early designs to be migrated to more formal designs.

Figure 1 clearly shows that while UML design tools may support the core tasks of the early stages of design, they do not support the workstyle of early design (brainstorming). The emphasis on asynchronous, moderated work with strong emphasis on syntactic correctness and semantic soundness is incompatible with the free-form brainstorming workstyle. A better match to the workstyle of early design is the workstyle supported by standard whiteboards. These tools support small groups of co-located users working synchronously, and rely upon social protocol to mediate user interaction. They impose no requirements on syntax, nor do they interpret any semantic meaning from the input.. The main incompatibility of these tools to the brainstorming workstyle is the limited ability to easily archive artifacts created on the board.

In this example, we have seen how workstyle analysis can be applied to a tool and compared to the workstyle of the collaborative activities in which it may be used. Such comparisons can highlight incompatibilities between a tool and the way in which it will be used within a particular context. Through this mechanism, tools can be selected for use in particular contexts to provide better usability to users carrying out their tasks.

5 Software Design Board: Supporting Workstyle Transitions in Software Design

Based on the findings from our empirical study into collaboration in software design, as well as workstyle analyses revealing inadequacies of existing design tools, we developed the Software Design Board to facilitate transitions between some common working styles as described by the Workstyle Model. This is achieved through the integration of informal media and flexible collaboration mechanisms, as well as support for migration between different software tools, devices and collaborative contexts. These facilities are intended to support fluid transitions between the some of the different styles of work in which designers are frequently engaged, specifically synchronous/asynchronous and/or co-located/distributed collaboration, and more generally, formal/informal interactions.

5.1 Functional Requirements

The functional requirements for the Software Design Board evolved from workstyle analyses of existing tools and of developers in the early stages of software design. For example, workstyle analyses of existing tools for collaborative software design revealed that each support only a single or limited set of collaborative workstyles. Furthermore, the empirical studies described in Section 3 revealed a variety of behavioral patterns in which developers frequently engage. Most importantly, the study found that team members regularly changed the nature of their interactions with each other in terms of synchronicity, location and modality. The results have specific implications on tool design; tools should be designed to support these frequent changes in workstyle.

All of these findings reveal some open problems in the area of tool support for collaborative software design, and motivated the functional requirements driving the design of Software Design Board. Specifically, the following are aspects of collaborative design that are poorly supported in existing tools:

- *Unsupported Workstyles:* Workstyle analyses of existing tools revealed that some workstyles are not supported by any individual class of tools. For example, large groups of synchronous collaborators, whether distributed or co-located, are not well supported by any available tool. This may be a result of hardware restrictions, or the limited applicability of such workstyles in practice. Additionally, no existing tools allow free-form interaction while supporting the creation of syntactically and semantically refined artifacts. Even informal CASE tools such as IdeogramicUML [15] employ a gesture-based syntax that places restrictions on free-form interaction.
    - **Functional Requirement 1**: Support the freehand creation of syntactically correct UML diagrams.
- *Lack of Support for Workstyle Evolution:* Workstyle analysis of existing tools revealed that individual tools only support a single or limited set of workstyles, and provide little or no support for movement between workstyles. However, our empirical investigations found that designers frequently move between synchronous/asynchronous and collocated/distributed styles of interaction. Additionally, transitions between workstyles often involve changes between interaction devices. For example, moving from an informal to a more formal workstyle may involve switching from an electronic whiteboard to a PC. Available tools do not sufficiently support migration between devices.
    - **Functional Requirement 2**: Support transitions between synchronous and asynchronous styles of collaboration.
    - **Functional Requirement 3:** Support transitions between collocated and distributed styles of collaboration.
    - **Functional Requirement 4**: Support transitions between physical devices.
- *Lack of Support for Multiple Collaborative Contexts:* In addition to frequently changing their collaborative workstyle, the results of the study presented in Section 3 show that individual designers also switch amongst a number of concurrent collaborative contexts. This means that they frequently move between multiple interactions with different groups. For example, a given designer may be participating in a number of concurrent projects or tasks, and may frequently switch their focus from one project to another. Furthermore, designers may participate concurrently in multiple collaborative contexts.
    - **Functional Requirement 5**: Support transitions between collaborative contexts.
- *Limited of Support for Integration of Existing Applications:* Current meta-tools that support sharing of existing applications, such as Netmeeting [23], impose

significant restrictions on collaboration that can be inappropriate to many of the important workstyles found identified during the empirical study. Mechanisms for integrating existing tools into a variety of collaborative workstyles would allow designers to collaborate on wide variety of tasks without giving up their preferred tools for accomplishing those tasks.

- **Functional Requirement 6**: Support integration of existing applications into all supported workstyles.

5.2 Overview of the Software Design Board

The Software Design Board (SDB) is a shared whiteboard application with additional functionality that supports collaborative software design. As seen in Figure 2, user interaction with this tool is similar to a typical interaction with a standard whiteboard.

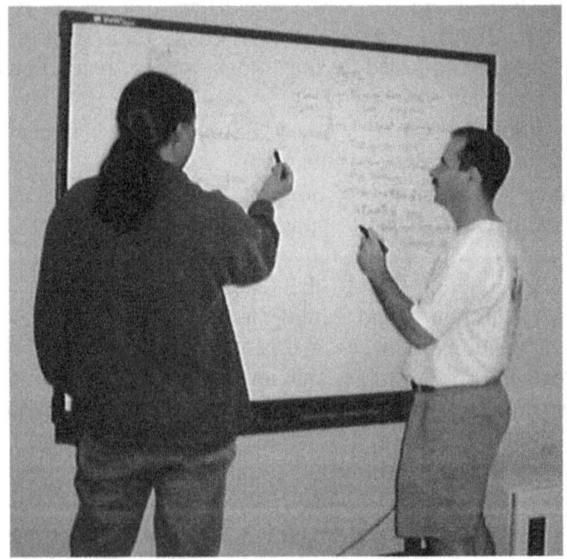

Fig. 2. Using Software Design Board.

Typical sessions using the tool via different devices are depicted in Figure 3. When used on a PC, the interface supports drawing using a typical structured drawing tool. Functionality is accessed through typical drop-down menus. When used on an electronic whiteboard or tablet PC, the user interface supports unstructured pen input of stroke information for freehand data such as diagrams, annotations, notes and lists.

This feature is in partial support of Functional Requirement 1 (*Support the freehand creation of syntactically correct UML diagrams*). Unstructured stylus-based input also provides the basis for lightweight user interaction with the tool. Furthermore, an integrated structure recognizer [9] supports automated translation of freehand diagrams into a more structured format appropriate for interpretation as UML or any other box-and-arrow notation. This functionality is similar to other tools [5, 21]. An example of this recognition functionality applied to a simple diagram is depicted in Figure 4.

In addition, objects can be placed on the board in and amongst the free hand data. These objects can include design documents or diagrams that may be browsed and annotated, or external programs that can execute other functionality. For example, a design document may be embedded into some area of the board allowing it to be communally browsed and annotated within the context of the other data on the board. This document is opened and displayed within the tool with which it was created, and all of that tool's functionality is accessible through the SDB's interface. This functionality supports Functional Requirement 6 (*Support integration of existing applications into all supported workstyles*). A typical session with an embedded design artifact is depicted in Figure 5.

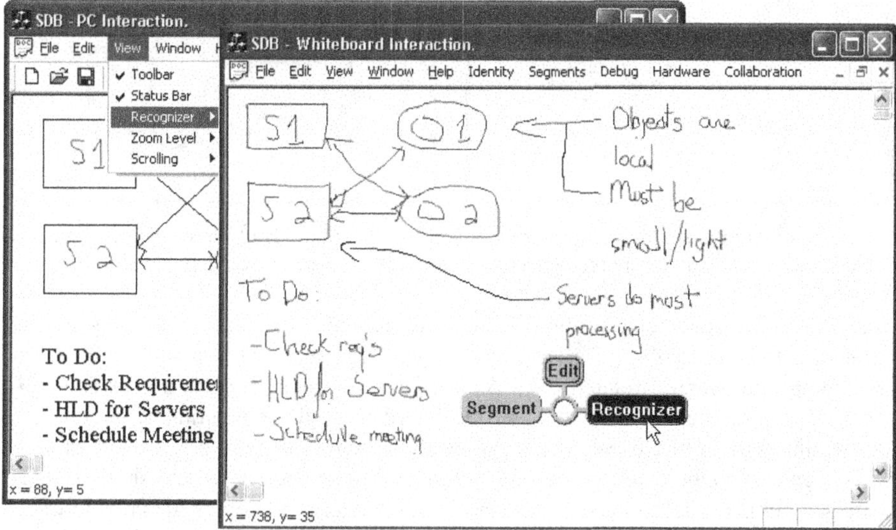

Fig. 3. Typical single-user sessions in Software Design Board. A PC user manipulates structured drawing elements and text, and interacts through drop-down menus. A whiteboard user draws free hand, and interacts through pie menus and gesture-based commands.

In order to support collaboration, the tool integrates communication and sharing mechanisms. For example, gesture transmission is supported within the context of synchronously shared whiteboard space. Voice communication mechanisms are planned, but not yet implemented. Additionally, any OLE-based communication tool can be integrated into the whiteboard space.

These communication objects are embedded and manipulated directly within the context of the board, and are maintained with the rest of the data on the board. For example, external applications such as web browsers or media streams may be embedded in the board space and used for communication. These communication mechanisms support Functional Requirement 2 (*Support transitions between synchronous and asynchronous styles of collaboration*) and Functional Requirement 3 (*Support transitions between co-located and distributed styles of collaboration*) by allowing the simultaneous use of functionality supporting all of these styles of interaction within a single application.

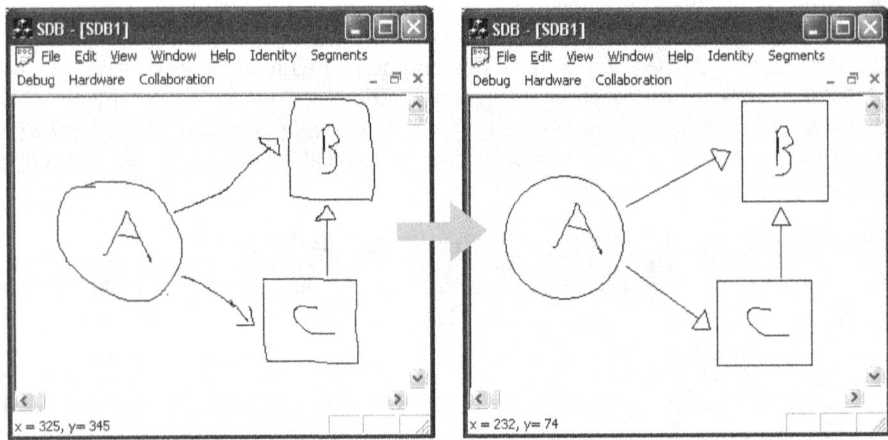

Fig. 4: Applying the syntax recognizer to a freehand diagram. Hand drawn elements such as circles, squares and arrows are recognized and converted into structured drawing elements.

The whiteboard space can be divided into any number of *segments*. These segments allow data to be shared in different ways. Generally, a segment is an area in the board containing contextually related data. As with a regular whiteboard, a user explicitly specifies the segmentation of data in the board through delineating strokes, e.g. a surrounding box or circle. Segments can be shared with others to allow users of other SDB clients to connect and synchronously interact with each other and share data. To share segments asynchronously, another client connects and copies the content of the segment to his/her local client. This data can then be manipulated without affecting the data in the original segment. Diverging copies of segments may be manually or automatically reconciled, if possible. When shared synchronously, data in a shared segment is viewed in decoupled WYSIWIS [29] fashion. Furthermore, at any time a user can change the way in which segments are shared. Synchronously shared segments can be easily detached and shared asynchronously, and vice versa. Gesture information is automatically transmitted between synchronously shared segments via telepointers. This functionality also supports Functional Requirement 2 (*Support transitions between synchronous and asynchronous styles of collaboration*) and Functional Requirement 3 (*Support transitions between co-located and distributed styles of collaboration*), by providing the mechanism by which users can freely and fluidly move between (synchronously or asynchronously) shared and private data.

Furthermore, on any SDB client, different segments may be shared concurrently and in different ways, between different groups. This functionality supports Functional Requirement 5 (*Support transitions between collaborative contexts*), by allowing users to move freely between different collaborative interactions contained within each segment. A typical session involving segment sharing is depicted in Figure 6.

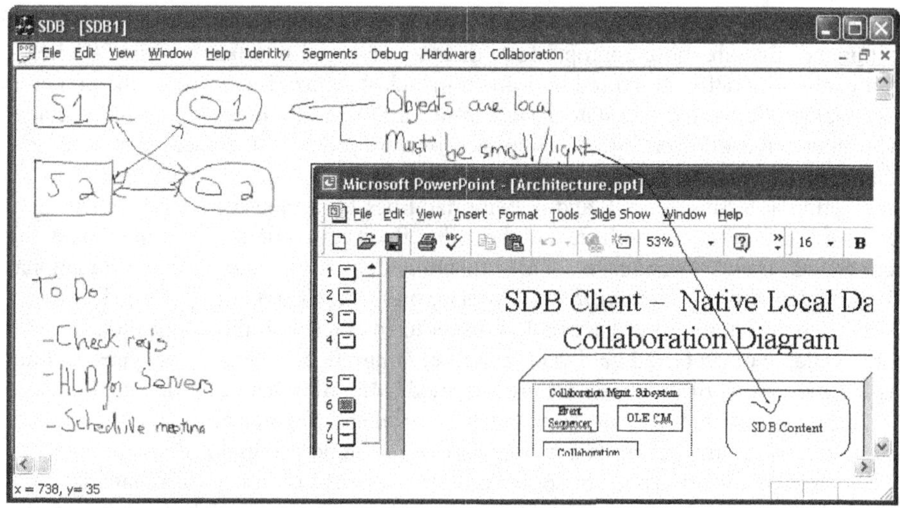

Fig. 5. A design document embedded in a Software Design Board session.

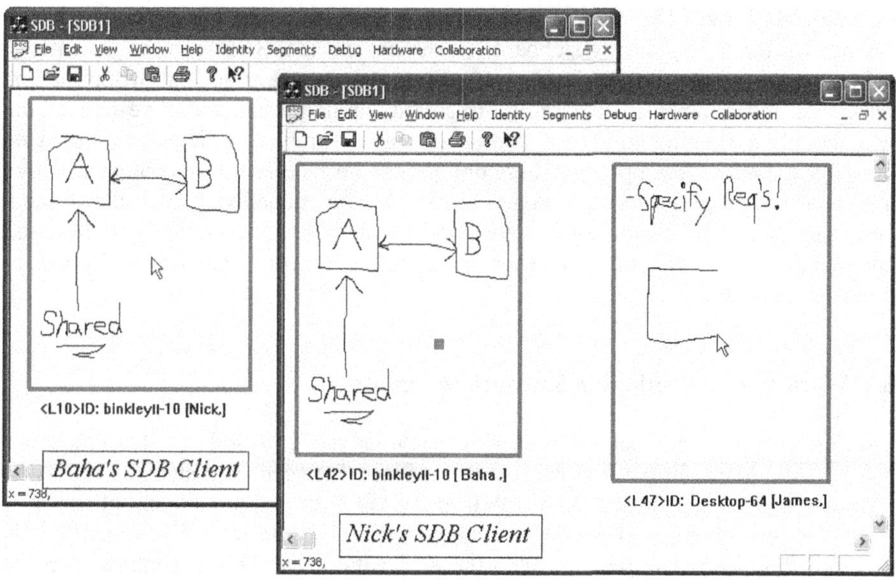

Fig. 6. The segment with ID binkley||-10 is shared between Baha and Nick. Baha's mouse pointer appears as a telepointer on Nick's client. Nick is concurrently sharing a different segment, with ID Desktop-64, with James.

Software Design Board implements a plastic interface [33] that can be used on different hardware devices. While the main platform for this application is an electronic whiteboard, it can also be accessed from a PC with or without an associated tablet. Widget-level plasticity supports appropriate interaction through each type of device [17]. For example, whiteboard users can use pie-menus and gesture based commands that are more appropriate to their stylus-based interfaces, while PC clients can use traditionally structured pull-down menus systems. There is also the potential to develop clients that facilitate access from a PDA or any other appropriate device. The interaction allowed by each interface is appropriate to the specific device. For example, interaction through a PDA would be greatly limited as compared to an interaction at a SmartBoard, and drawing facilities on a mouse-based PC client may be more structured than those on the SmartBoard, in order to accommodate the associated input mechanism. This functionality is in support of Functional Requirement 4 (*Support transitions between physical devices*).

Device appropriate interfaces allow users to interact with the application through any available or preferred hardware, and freely migrate between device types, as long as the limitations of the hardware are accepted. Migration between tools and devices is further supported by the segmentation of data. Segmentation facilitates data plasticity, wherein types of data within a segment can be manipulated appropriately in the context of a given device or application. If a segment is known to contain data of a particular type, then it can be interpreted or formatted appropriately for any specific device or tool. For example, if a segment is known to contain a UML diagram, then it can be interpreted and migrated via XML into an appropriate UML-based CASE tool.

In addition to the functionality described above, a variety of additional features are integrated into the user interface to facilitate interaction with the Software Design Board. Unlike a regular whiteboard, a session in the SDB can be essentially unbounded in size. To facilitate navigation, the interface to the workspace is scrollable and zoomable. If a more structured input mechanism is desired at the whiteboard, a floating keyboard and/or structured drawing palette can be made available through menu options. These options can be accessed from context sensitive and device appropriate menu systems. Finally, all functionality is available through both context sensitive pull-down menus and pie-menus that facilitate gesture-based commands. This allows advanced users to use the tool more effectively by bypassing the menu structure.

5.3 Workstyle Transitions in Software Design Board

We now consider some simple scenarios that illustrate how Software Design Board can be used to perform some common transitions between workstyles. This is not intended as a set of instructions for performing the indicated transition, but rather as examples of how such transitions are supported within the tool. Additionally, it is intended to demonstrate the ease with these transitions can be performed within the tool.

- ***Distribution Transitions***: A group of co-located collaborators works together around an electronic whiteboard (a co-located workstyle). They want to share their work with a remotely located group. They draw a box around their current work in order to define a segment, and use a simple gesture command to share that segment with the remote group. The availability of the remote group is indicated via the context-sensitive pie menus [14, 19] that structure the gesture. At the remote site, a change in the entry structure of the menu system indicates the availability of a newly shared segment. The remote group creates a local segment in their workspace, and uses a similar gesture to attach their segment to that which was newly shared with them. Synchronized copies of the original data now appear in both group's segments, and telepointers appear to provide a sense of awareness of the actions of each group to the other. The two groups now collaborate in this distributed workstyle.

- ***Synchronicity Transitions:*** A group of users interacts synchronously with data contained in a shared segment (a synchronous workstyle). Each user performs updates that are immediately reflected in every other user's view of the data. They decide to work separately so that each user may concentrate on a particular aspect of the data. Each user detaches his/her segment from the shared session, and is left with a local copy of the data to which asynchronous updates can be performed. Now each user interacts with the data in their local copy (an asynchronous workstyle).
- ***Device Transitions***: A user is drawing a design on an electronic whiteboard. Using the piemenu structure and gesture commands, he invokes the recognizer and converts the freehand design to a structured drawing. He then creates a shared segment containing the diagram on the whiteboard. He moves to his PC and starts the Software Design Board client. Using the traditional pull-down menu structure, he creates a segment, attaches it to the shared segment he previously created at the whiteboard. He continues to work on that diagram from the PC, manipulating the structured elements in a manner appropriate for mouse-based interaction.
- ***Context Transitions***: A user maintains two different shared segments in his Software Design Board workspace. Each segment is shared between a different group of colleagues with whom he collaborates, and therefore each segment maintains completely different data (each maintains a different work context). Through the course of the day he scrolls the workspace back and forth between those segments in order to interact with the different groups as required.
- ***Syntax Transitions***: A group of co-located users are brainstorming and free hand drawing a design on a whiteboard. Eventually, the drawing becomes too large and convoluted to easily manipulate in this manner. Some elements consume a disproportionate amount of board space; others overlap due to the freeform development of the diagram. The designers want to move the work into a structured drawing editor to clean up the drawing and continue work. They use a gesture command to select all relevant drawing elements, then another gesture to invoke the syntax recognizer. The drawing is automatically converted to discrete, structured drawing elements such as boxes, circles and arrows. A third gesture is used to invoke a 'Send To…' command, which causes the newly structured elements to be opened within a structured drawing editor. The group now restructures their drawing, and continues to work.
- ***Semantic Transitions***: A group of users has completed a freehand design diagram on a whiteboard. The users invoke the syntax recognizer to structure their drawing, as described above. Next, they use a gesture command to reselect all drawing elements, and another gesture to invoke the UML semantic interpreter. The structured drawing is automatically interpreted as a simplified UML class diagram– boxes are converted to classes, open arrows as generalizations, closed arrows as aggregations. A third gesture is used to invoke a 'Send To…' command,

which causes the newly structured elements to be opened within a UML editor for further manipulation.

5.4 Current Status of the Implementation

The Software Design Board application is currently a functional research prototype. Most of the functionality described in the previous sections exists, either wholly or partially, though some core functionality remains to be implemented. Functionality for moving, resizing and copying freehand elements still remains to be implemented, and structured drawing functionality and other PC-based interaction techniques are less developed. Distributed, synchronous sharing is currently limited to drawing data; synchronous application sharing functionality is only partially implemented and not yet functional. The functionality for implementing syntax transitions is not fully implemented. An XML DTD has been developed to describe these recognized free-hand diagrams, and standalone code for writing and reading these XML documents exists. However, this code has not yet been integrated with the Software Design Board application. Finally, only limited work has been done toward supporting semantic transitions, i.e. applying a semantic interpretation to the syntactic structure of the drawing described by the XML document. This work has been limited by the limited implementation supporting syntax transitions. As the functionality evolves to more completely support the syntax transition, so too will the functionality supporting the semantic transition.

6 Conclusions

In this paper, we have introduced a prototype collaborative software design tool, the Software Design Board. Software Design Board supports a variety of workstyles important in the early stages of software development, and facilitates transitions between them. The functional requirements for the tool evolved from workstyle analysis of existing design tools and from results of empirical research into collaborative software design activities.

The need to support workstyle transitions in tools for collaborative software design stems from the fact that designers switch amongst numerous collaborative styles throughout the course of the their work. Many factors influence the style in which they may choose to work (their *workstyle*), including the task at hand, availability of tools, distribution of collaborators, and personal preferences. These influences change frequently, thus designers often migrate between workstyles in response to such changes. Unfortunately, there are obstacles to such transitions. These may include having to recreate work artifacts in the format of a new tool, interruption of the flow of work, or physical relocation. Such obstacles may prove sufficiently burdensome that designers choose to continue to work in a style that is inappropriate for their current context. These obstacles exist because the variety of workstyles and workstyle transitions in which designers engage are not well supported by most existing design tools. Most of these tools are designed to support a single or limited set of workstyles, and their architectures are generally not capable of handling the dynamic changes in workstyle that are typical of collaborative design.

Software Design Board was developed to address some of these shortcomings and to support designers in some of the common workstyles and transitions in workstyle in which they frequently engage. Specifically, Software Design Board supports designers working synchronously/asynchronously, distributed/collocated and more generally, formally/informally. It supports the creation of syntactically bound or free-from artifacts, can be used through a variety of physical devices, and facilitates collaboration in multiple, concurrent contexts.

References

1. AgileAlliance, http://www.agilealliance.org
2. Bly, S., A. (1988). "A Use of Drawing Surfaces in Different Collaborative Settings". Conference on Computer-Supported Cooperative Work, Portland, OR.
3. Bly, S.,A. and S. Minneman (1990). "Commune: A Shared Drawing Surface." SIGOIS Bulletin: 184-192.
4. Crowley, J., Coutaz, J., Berard, F. (2000). "Things that See." Communications of the ACM **43**(3): 54-64.
5. Damm, C. H., Hansen, K. M., Thomsen, M. (2000). "Tool Support for Object-Oriented Cooperative Design: Gesture-Based Modelling on an Electronic Whiteboard". Proceedings of Conference on Human Factors and Computing Systems. The Hague, Netherlands.
6. DeMarco, T. and T. Lister (1987). Peopleware. New York, Dorset House.
7. Dewan, P. Choudary, R. (1991). "Flexible user interface coupling in collaborative systems". CHI ' 91, New Orleans, LA, ACM.
8. Diaper, D. (1989) Task analysis for human computer interaction, Ellis Horwood,.
9. Fonseca, M.,J., Pimentel, C., and Jorge, J., A. (2002). "CALI: An Online Scribble Recognizer for Calligraphic Interfaces", Proceedings of the 2002 AAAI Spring Symposium - Sketch Understanding. Palo Alto, USA. pp51-58
10. Francik, E., Rudman, S. E., Cooper, D., and Levine, S. (1991). Putting innovation to work: adoption strategies for multimedia communication systems. *Communications of the ACM*, 34(12), pp. 52-64.
11. Greenberg, S. and R. Bohnet (1991). "GroupSketch: A Multi-user Sketchpad for Geographically Distributed Small Groups". Proceedings of Graphics Interface, pp 207-215.
12. Grundy, J. C., Mugridge, W.B, Hosking, J.G., Apperley, M. (1998). "Tool Integration, Collaboration and User Interaction Issues in Component-based Software Architectures". TOOLS '98, Melbourne, Australia, IEEE.
13. Hammond, T. and R. C. Davis (2002). "Tahuiti: A Geometrical Sketch Recognition System for UML Class Diagrams". Sketch Symposium, Stanford University, Palo Alto, CA.
14. Hopkins, D. (1991) "The Design and Implementation of Pie Menus", Dr. Dobb's Journal, CMP Media. December 1991.
15. Ideogramic – IdeogramicUML, http://www.ideogramic.com
16. Ishii, H. and M. Kobayashi (1992). "ClearBoard: A seamless medium for shared drawing and conversation with eye contact". Conference on Human Factors in Computing Systems, Monterey, CA, ACM.
17. Jabarin, B., and Graham, T.C.N. (2003) "Architectures for Widget-Level Plasticity", Proceedings of DSV-IS 2003 Portugal, June 11-13. pp. 124-238
18. Jones, T. C. (1986). Programming Productivity. New York, McGraw-Hill.

19. Kurtenbach, G. and Buxton, W. (1991) "Issues in Combining Marking and Direct Manipulation Techniques" In Proceedings of ACM UIST'91. pp. 137--144.
20. Landay, J. A. and B. A. Myers (1995). "Interactive Sketching for Early Stages of Design". CHI '95, Denver, CO, ACM Press.
21. Lank, E., Thorley, J.S., Chen, S.J. (2000). "An Interactive System for Recognizing Hand Drawn UML Diagrams". CASCON2000, Toronto, ON.
22. Malone, T. W. and K. Crowston (1990). "What is coordination theory and how can it help design cooperative work systems?". Proceedings of Conference on Computer-Supported Cooperative Work. ACM Press. pp. 357-370
23. Microsoft Corp. – Netmeeting, http://www.microsoft.com
24. Mynatt, E. D., Igarashi, T., Edwards, W.K. LaMarca, A. (1999). "Flatland : New Dimensions in Office Whiteboards". CHI '99, Pittsburgh, PA, ACM.
25. Pederson, E. R., McCall, K., Moran, T.P., Halasz, F. G. (1993). "Tivoli: An Electronic Whiteboard for Informal Workgroup Meetings". INTERCHI '93. Amsterdam, Netherlands. April.
26. Rational Corp. – Rose, http://www.rational.com
27. Seaman, C.B. and Basili, V.R. (1997) "Communication and Organization in Software Development: An Empirical Study". IBM Systems Journal 36(4).
28. SMART Technologies, Inc. – SMARTBoard, http://www.smarttech.com
29. Stefik, M., Bobrow, D.G., Foster, G., Lanning, S., and Tatar, D. (1987) "WYSIWIS revised: early experiences with multiuser interfaces", ACM Transactions on Office Information Systems, 5(2), pp.147-167
30. Streitz, N. A., J. Geißler, Haake, J. M., Hol, J. (1994). "DOLPHIN: integrated meeting support across local and remote desktop environments and LiveBoards". Conference on Computer Supported Cooperative Work, Chapel Hill. NC.
31. Tang, J., C. (1991). "Findings from Observational Studies of Collaborative Work." International Journal of Man-Machine Studies. 34(2), pp. 143-160
32. Tang, J. C. and S. Minneman (1991). "VideoWhiteboard: Video Shadows to Support Remote Collaboration". Conference on Human Factors and Computing Systems, New Orleans, LA.
33. Thevenin, D., and Coutaz, J., (1999). "Plasticity of User Interfaces: Framework and Research Agenda" Proceedings of Interact '99 Edinburgh, Scotland. pp 110-117.
34. Wang, W., Dorohonceanu, B., Marsic, I. (1999). "Design of the DISCIPLE Synchronous Collaboration Framework". Internet, Multimedia Systems and Applications, Nassau, Bahamas, IASTED Press.
35. Wong, Y.Y. (1992) "Rough and ready prototypes: Lessons from graphic design". Short Talks Proceedings of CHI '92: Human Factors in Computing Systems, pp. 83-84, Monterey, CA,
36. Wu, J., Graham, T.C.N, Everitt, K., Blostein, D. and Lank, E. (2002) "Modeling Style of Work as an Aid to the Design and Evaluation of Interactive Systems". Proceedings of CADUI'02. Valenciennes, France.
37. Wu, J., Graham, T.C.N., Smith, P. (2003) "A Study of Collaboration in Software Design" ISESE 2003, Rome, IT. Sept 29-Oct 1.
38. Wu, J. (2003) "Tools for Collaborative Software Design" Queen's University, School of Computing. Technical Report 2003-462, Queen's University, Kingston, Ontario, Canada, January 2003.

Discussion

[Philippe Palanque] As you use the work style axes as a mean for evaluating the adequacy between tool and a work style do you not need more detailed information for each axes?

> [Nick Graham] All the axes are continuous and we use them more as an informational tool - we worked on making the axes more precise but we did not find it to be more useful.

[Jürgen Ziegler?] Are the dimensions independent or are there interrelationships between eg. modifiability and degree of semantic correctness?

> [Nick Graham] I think we can come up with examples for each pair of axes where you could be at either extreme and if you think of each pair of axes that the extremes are presented as cross products of all four possible positions, then we can come up with examples of all four positions for all the axis pairs, so we are quite confident that axes are orthogonal.

[Grigori Evreinov] Did you think of using parallel coordinate systems?

> [Nick Graham] No, that would be interesting; do you think that would be better?

[Grigori Evreinov] Yes, we have Information Visualization Research Group in our Department (http://www.cs.uta.fi/~hs/iv/) and the parallel coordinates system is presented on their site, so you can try it! or ask about the author Harry Siirtola

> [Nick Graham] That would be interesting!

[Jörg Roth] Your work style model reminds me of the Denver model from 1996 (they have 2 diagrams with 5 axes each instead of your 8)?

> [Nick Graham] There are similar in the sense that they are both related to groupware and presented as "quiviant diagrams". Beyond that the axes are actually very different to my recollection! I have compared to the Denver model, but to give you a proper answer I would have to look at the Denver model again, because I cannot remember the axes exactly!

[Michael Harrison] One of the interesting things about collaborative work is that, just like we have had this conference I will go away to a room and do some work and maybe have some ideas and produce some notes. Next time we have a collaborative meeting I may want to fold that back in to the collaboration and I was not sure how that kind of continuity could be achieved. This characterises different collaborative models whereas that is not essentially a collaboration model, but it is essential to the process of collaboration.

> [Nick Graham] That would be considered a tool transition, so one tool is pen and paper and the other your designed word software. We are very interested in that, so one approach is to say it would be wonderful if you had electronic paper that you had been scrip ling on and that could be imported right in to the tool, a poor mans approach to that would be to scan it, a really poor mans approach would be to sit and type it in. So those are examples of how

transitions can be easy or hard. The whole goal is certainly to find ways of making the transition easier so that people are more likely to do them.

[Hong-Mei Chen, University of Hawaii] The Work style model you presented here seems to be domain-specific to software design in your empirical case studies and not applicable to other kind of collaborative work. For instance, some brain storming tasks (as studied in Group Decision Support Systems - GDSS) consider important factors such as social cues and anonymity to be important.

> [Nick Graham] I agree with you that there are many other axes that we could put in and we have actually studied it in IFIP WG 2.7/13.4 and discussed the kind of transitions that would come up, e.g. with respect to privacy. An example could be a situation where you start out in a context where privacy is not important to you and the all of a sudden you are asked to enter your credit card information and privacy becomes very important to you. This just to say, that these are also important issues and we do not claim to have solved every issue in the world. We have used this model in other domain, but will not make any claims that this is applicable to any domain and maybe we will come back next year with the 40 dimensions version!

[Rick Kazman] How do you deal with multiple updates to a single document when people work asynchronously but they want to merge their work?

> [Nick Graham] We do not support merging in general since it is a difficult problem, but we do support merging of the whiteboard freehand drawings. Merging MS Word documents alone is big problem in it self!

[Rick Kazman] Are you aware of any general solution to the multiple merge problems?

> [Nick Graham] No, all the solutions I have seen are point solutions often commercial, such as for MS Word, but no good general solutions.

Supporting Group Awareness in Distributed Software Development

Carl Gutwin, Kevin Schneider, David Paquette, and Reagan Penner

Department of Computer Science, University of Saskatchewan
Computer Science Department, University of Saskatchewan
57 Campus Drive, Saskatoon, SK
Canada, S7N 5A9
gutwin,kas,dnp972,rpenner @usask.ca

Abstract. Collaborative software development presents a variety of coordination and communication problems, particularly when teams are geographically distributed. One reason for these problems is the difficulty of staying aware of others – keeping track of information about who is working on the project, who is active, and what tasks people have been working on. Current software development environments do not show much information about people, and developers often must use text-based tools to determine what is happening in the group. We have built a system that assists distributed developers in maintaining awareness of others. ProjectWatcher observes fine-grained user edits and presents that information visually on a representation of a project's artifacts. The system displays general awareness information and also provides a resource for more detailed questions about others' activities.

1. Introduction

Software projects are most often carried out in a collaborative fashion. The complexities of software and the interdependencies between modules mean that these projects present collaborators with several coordination and communication problems. When development teams are geographically distributed, these problems often become much more serious [2,10,11,14]. Even though projects are often organized to try and make modules independent of one another, dependencies cannot be totally removed [14]. As a result, situations can arise where team members duplicate work, overwrite changes, make incorrect assumptions about another person's intentions, or write code that adversely affects another part of the project [10].

These problems occur because of a lack of awareness about what is happening in other parts of the project. Most development tools and environments do not make it easy to maintain awareness of others' activities [10]. Current tools are focused around the artifacts of collaboration rather than people's activities (e.g., the files in a repository rather than the actions people have taken with them). An artifact-based approach is clearly necessary for certain types of work, but without better information about people, smooth collaboration becomes difficult. Awareness is a design concept that holds promise for significantly improving the usability of collaborative software development tools.

R. Bastide, P. Palanque, and J. Roth (Eds.): EHCI-DSVIS 2004, LNCS 3425, pp. 383-397, 2005.

We have built a system called ProjectWatcher that provides people with awareness information about others on the development team. The system is designed around our observations of the awareness requirements in several distributed software projects. We found that developers first maintain a general awareness of who is who and who is doing what on a project; and second, they actively look for information about people when they are going to work more closely with them. However, developers often have to use text-based sources to get that information.

ProjectWatcher observes and records fine-grained information about user edits and provides visualizations of who is active on a project, what artifacts they have been working on, and where in the project they have been working. This information about others' activities can help to improve coordination between developers and reduce some of the problems seen in distributed development.

In this paper, we introduce ProjectWatcher and describe its design and implementation. We first give an overview of the issues affecting collaboration in software development, and then discuss group awareness in more detail and the awareness requirements of a distributed development project. We then describe the two main parts of ProjectWatcher: a fact mining component that gathers developer activity information, and a visualization component that overlays activity data onto a representation of project artifacts.

2. Background

Although collaboration is an important research area of software engineering – where teams are common and where good communication and coordination are essential for success – little work has been done on group awareness in software development. Similarly, although awareness has received attention in the Computer-Supported Cooperative Work (CSCW) community, this knowledge has not been considered extensively in development settings. We believe that awareness is a design concept that holds promise for significantly improving the usability of collaborative software development tools. In the next sections, we review issues of collaboration in distributed software development, the basics of group awareness, and the awareness requirements that we have determined from observations of open source projects.

2.1 Collaboration Issues in Software Development

Collaboration support has always been a part of distributed development – teams have long used version control, email, chat groups, code reviews, and internal documentation to coordinate activities and distribute information – but these solutions generally either represent the project at a very coarse granularity (e.g., CVS), require considerable time and effort (e.g., reading documentation), or depend on people's current availability (e.g., IRC).

Researchers in software engineering and CSCW have found a number of problems that still occur in group projects and distributed software development. They found that it is difficult to:

- determine when two people are making changes to the same artifacts [14];
- communicate with others across timezones and work schedules [11];
- find partners for closer collaboration or assistance on particular issues [20];
- determine who has expertise or knowledge about the different parts of the project [24];
- benefit from the opportunistic and unplanned contact that occurs when developers are co-located, since there is little visibility of others' activities [10].

As Herbsleb and Grinter [10] state, lack of awareness – "the inability to share the same environment and to see what is happening at the other site" (p. 67) is one of the major factors in these problems.

2.2 Group Awareness

In many group work situations, awareness of others provides information that is critical for smooth and effective collaboration. Group awareness is the understanding of who is working with you, what they are doing, and how your own actions interact with theirs [5]. Group awareness is useful for coordinating actions, managing coupling, discussing tasks, anticipating others' actions, and finding help [8]. The complexity and interdependency of software systems suggests that group awareness should be necessary for collaborative software development. Knowledge of developer activities, both past and present, has obvious value for project management, but developers also use this information for many other purposes – purposes that assist the overall cohesion and effectiveness of the team. For example, knowing the specific files and objects that another person has been working on can give a good indication of their higher-level tasks and intentions; knowing who has worked most often or most recently on a particular piece of code indicates who to talk to before starting further changes; and knowing who is currently active can provide opportunities for real-time assistance and collaboration.

In co-located situations, three mechanisms help people to maintain awareness: *explicit communication*, where people tell each other about their activities; *consequential communication* [22], in which watching another person work provides information as to their activities and plans; and *feedthrough* [4], where observation of changes to project artifacts indicates who has been doing what. Of these mechanisms, explicit communication is the most flexible, and previous research has looked at the ways that groups communicate over distance, through email, text chat, and instant messaging (e.g., [18,23]). However, since intentional communication of awareness information also requires the most additional effort, many awareness systems attempt to support implicit mechanisms as well as communication. General approaches include providing visible embodiments of participants and visual representations of actions that allow people to watch each other work, and overview visualizations of artifacts that show feedthrough information.

Although group awareness is often taken for granted in face-to-face work, it is difficult to maintain in distributed settings. This is particularly true in software development: other than access to the shared code repository, development environments and tools provide almost no information about people on the project. Although communication tools such as email lists and chat systems help to keep people informed on some projects, these text-based awareness mechanisms require considerable effort, and are not well integrated with information about the artifacts of the project. As a result, coordination problems are common in distributed settings, and collaboration suffers. A few research systems do show awareness information (e.g., TUKAN [21] or Augur [7]), but it is not clear that these tools really provide the awareness information that is needed by developers. As discussed in the next section, we based our tools and techniques on findings from a study of three distributed open-source projects.

3. Awareness Requirements in Distributed Development

Open-source software development projects are a good source of information about distributed development, since they are almost always collaborative and widely dispersed (in many cases, developers never meet face-to-face). To find out what the awareness requirements are for these long-running real-world projects, we interviewed several developers, read project communication, and looked at project artifacts from three open source projects [9]. We found that distributed developers do need to maintain awareness of one another, and that they maintain both a general awareness of the entire team and more detailed knowledge of people that they plan to work with. However, developers maintain their awareness primarily through text-based communication – particularly mailing lists and chat systems.

The three open source projects we looked at are NetBSD (www.netbsd.org), Apache httpd (www.apache.org), and Subversion (www.tigris.org/subversion). We chose these projects because they are distributed, they are at least medium-sized in terms of both the code and the development team, and they all produce a product that is widely used, indicating that they have successfully managed to coordinate development.

An initial issue that we looked at was whether distributed projects can successfully isolate different software modules from one another such that awareness and coordination requirements become insignificant. There are two ways that dependencies can be reduced – by reducing the number of developers, or by partitioning the code. However, in the three projects we looked at, neither of these factors removed awareness requirements. There were at least fourteen core developers who contributed regularly to each project, and although there was general understanding that people work in 'home' areas, there were no official sanctions that prevented any developer from contributing to any part of the code. On Apache and Subversion in particular, development of a particular module was almost always spread across several developers.

The next issue studied was what types of awareness the developers maintained. We found two types: general awareness and more specific knowledge. First, developers maintain a broad awareness of who are the main people working on their project, and what their areas of expertise are. This information came from three sources: the project mailing list, where people can see who posts and what the topics of discussion are; the chat server, which provides similar information but in real time; and the CVS commits (sent out by email), which allowed developers to stay up-to-date both on changes to the project and the activities of different people. Second, when a developer wishes to do work in a particular area, they must gain more detailed knowledge about who are the people with experience in that part of the code. We found that people use a variety of sources to gather this information, including project documentation, the records in the source code repository, bug tracking systems, and other people. Further details on this study can be found in [9].

Even though these open-source projects do successfully manage their coordination, our interviews also identified some problems with the way awareness is maintained. Two problems that we consider further in this paper involve watching CVS commits, and maintaining overall awareness about project members and their activities. Although the 'CVS-commit' mailing list provides the only information that is actually based on the project artifacts, several developers said that they do not follow them because they are too time-consuming to read. Developers also suggested that some of the information sources they use often go out of date, and that understanding the relationships between people and activities was often difficult. One developer stated that new members of the project in particular could benefit from tools that provided more information than what was currently available.

4. Project Watcher

We have developed an awareness system called ProjectWatcher to address some of the awareness issues that we have seen in distributed development projects. ProjectWatcher gathers information about project artifacts and developer's actions with those artifacts, and visualizes this awareness information either as a stand-alone tool or as a plugin inside the Eclipse IDE. ProjectWatcher consists of two main parts – the mining component, and the awareness visualizations.

4.1 Mining Component

The mining component analyzes a project's source code to produce facts for use by the ProjectWatcher visualization displays. To gather developer activity information at a finer grain size than repository commits, a shadow CVS repository is maintained (see Figure 1). User edits are auto-committed to the shadow repository as developers edit source code files (e.g., on every save of the file). With each auto-commit a new version of the file is stored in the shadow repository. The mining component analyzes the auto-committed versions against each other and the versions in the shared CVS repository to obtain user edit information that can be understood in terms of the project's software architecture.

The mining component is composed of two fact extractors: the software architecture fact extractor and the user edit fact extractor. The software architecture fact extractor is run against the software repository to obtain entity/relationship facts. Entity facts extracted include: *package*, *class* and *method* facts. Relationship facts extracted include: *calls*, *contains*, *imports*, *implements* and *extends* relationships. The software architecture facts are used by the visualization system to present the software structure. The user edit fact extractor is run against the shadow repository to obtain information about the methods a developer is changing. The user edit facts are used by the visualization to present developer activity information.

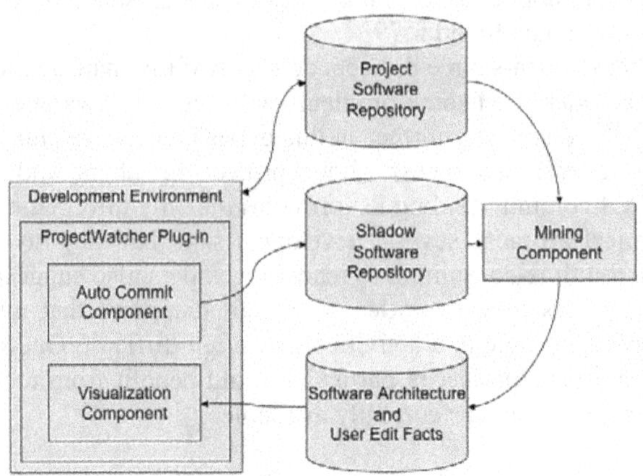

Fig. 1: User edit fact extraction.

The software architecture fact extractor is implemented in two stages and may either be run on the shadow repository or on the shared software repository (see Figure 2). The first stage, the *base fact extractor* uniquely names the entities in the source code and extracts the facts of interest. This process is accomplished with a TXL [15] program using syntactic pattern matching [3]. The second stage, the *reference analyzer*, resolves references between software architecture entities.

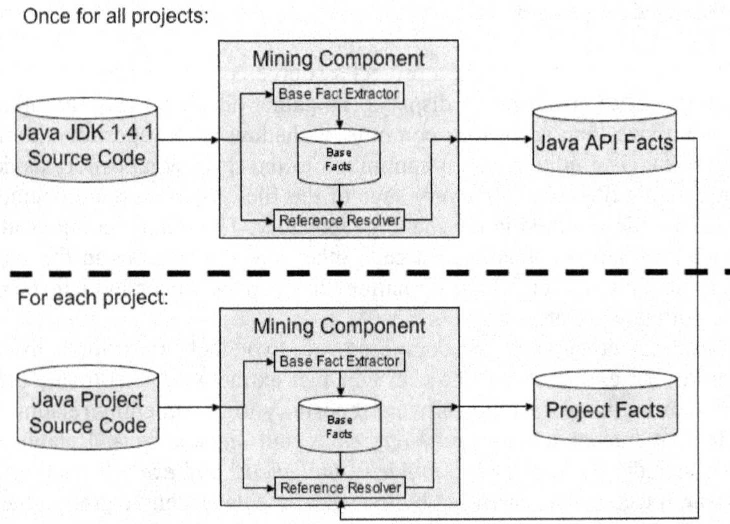

Fig. 2: Software architecture fact extraction from Java projects

The reference analyzer extracts scope facts from the project source code and integrates them with the facts extracted in stage one. Next, the method call facts are analyzed to determine which package and class the method that was called belongs to. This process involves resolving the types of variables and return types of methods that are passed as arguments to method calls. The types of all the arguments are identified. Then scope, package, class, and method facts are analyzed to determine which package and class the method belongs to. To resolve calls to the Java library, the full Java API is first processed by the ProjectWatcher mining component (this is only done once for all projects).

The user edit fact extractor (Figure 3) is implemented in three stages and is run against two versions of the project source code. The first stage splits the files into separate class and method snippets. The second stage compares and matches revisions of the code snippets. Initially, methods are matched based on their names. If a method match is not found at the method name level, methods are compared based on the percentage of lines of code that match between all methods. If a method's name is changed, a match based on percentage of similarity is still found between the two versions. When no match is found for a method from an earlier revision, the method is identified as having been added. When no match is found for a method from a later revision, the method is identified as having been removed. Facts about method additions and method removals are stored in the user edit factbase. Once the methods from each revision have been matched, a line diff is performed on each pair of methods. The diff algorithm gives us information about what lines have been added and removed from a method, and this information is stored in the user edit factbase.

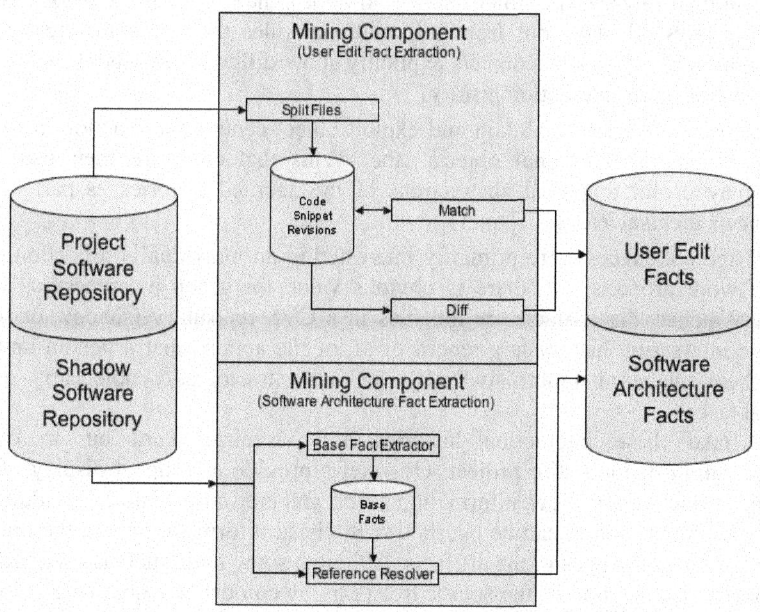

Fig. 3: User edit fact extraction.

The complete factbase contains uniquely identified facts indicating all packages, classes, methods, variables, and relationships for a Java project and all user edits. These facts are used by the visualization component to show activity and proximity information. The time and space needed for fact extraction and factbase storage depends on the size of the code; for example, the Java Development Kit 1.4.1 contains 202 package facts, 5,530 class facts, 47,962 method facts, and 106,926 method call facts

4.2 Visualization of Activity and Commits

ProjectWatcher's activity awareness display visualizes team members' past and current activities on project artifacts (see Figures 4 and 5). The goals of this display are:

- to give collaborators an overview of who works on the project
- to provide a general sense of who works in what areas
- to allow changes (i.e., commits) to be tracked without much effort
- to provide more detail when the user wants to look more closely.

The display uses the ideas of edit wear, interaction histories, and overviews. *Edit wear* is a concept introduced by Hill and colleagues [13]. Their overall motivation is the question of how computation can be used to improve "the reflective conversation with work materials" (p. 3), and the observation that most computational artifacts do not show any traces of the ways that they have been used, unlike objects in the real world. Starting with this idea of 'object wear,' their research proposes an 'informational physics' in which the visual appearance of an object arises not from everyday physical laws, but from informational rules that are semantically useful. Their notion of physics has objects explicitly show different aspects of their use over time – that is, their interaction history:

> The basic idea is to maintain and exploit object-centered interaction histories: record on computational objects…the events that comprise their use…and display useful graphical abstractions of the accrued histories as part of the objects themselves." ([13], p. 3)

Hill and colleagues were primarily interested in an individual's reflection on their use of work artifacts, but there is obvious value for group awareness as well. In ProjectWatcher, the artifacts are the files in a CVS repository (shadow or regular), and the interaction history is a record of all of the actions that a person undertakes with them (gathered unobtrusively by the fact extractor as people carry out their normal tasks).

We take these interaction histories and visualize them on an overview representation of the entire project. Overviews provide a compact display of all the project artifacts, and allow information to be gathered at a glance. In addition, the overview representation can be overlaid with visual information about the interaction history or about changes to the artifacts. Although some tools such as CVS front-ends do limited visualization of the source tree (e.g., by colour), our goal here is to collect much more information about interaction, and provide richer visualizations that will allow team members to quickly gather awareness information.

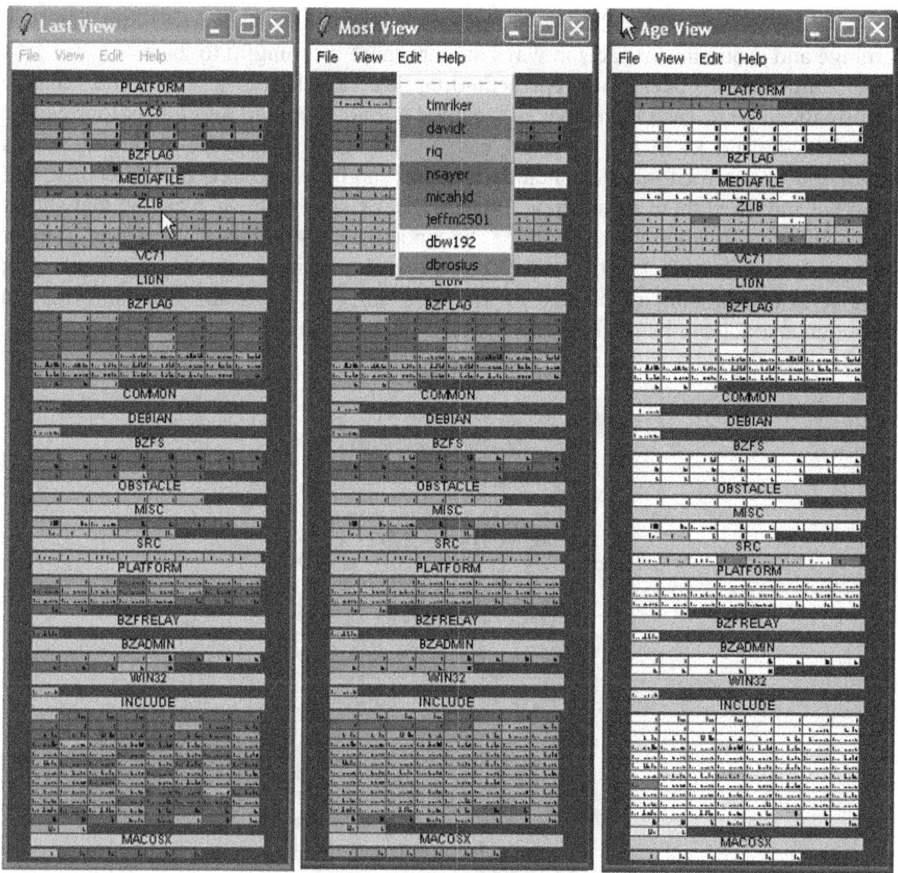

Fig. 4. Project overviews showing directories (grey bars) and files (coloured blocks) for a medium-sized game project with 322 files. Three types of filters are shown: at left, block colour indicates who changed the file most recently; at middle, colour shows who has changed the file most often; at right, grey level indicates the amount of time since last change. In each block, the bar graph shows the edit history since the start of the project. Developer colours are shown in a menu. Note that normally only one window would be used, with the filter changed through a menu selection.

ProjectWatcher uses the extracted fact base to create a visual model of what each developer is doing in the project space. Project artifacts are shown in a simple stacked fashion that displays packages, files, classes, and methods. We chose this method of organization because it is much more compact than other approaches, such as class diagrams or dependency graphs. With the stacked representation, even a small overview can completely display projects with up to several hundred files (e.g., Figure 4 shows 322 files); in larger projects, developers can collapse particular packages to save space. The drawback with the stack is that there is little contextual information available to help users determine which artifact is which. To try and reduce this problem, artifacts are always stacked by creation date, so that their location in the overview is fixed, and can over time be learned by the user. We are also experimenting with allowing users to reorganize the display, so that they can arrange and group the artifacts in ways that are more meaningful to them.

On this basic overview representation, we overlay awareness and change information. First, each developer is assigned a unique colour, and this colour can be added to the blocks in the overview based on a set of filters. Common filters that involve developer information include who has modified artifacts most recently, and who has modified them most often. Other filters exist as well, such as one that shows time since last change (see Figure 5). Second, we show a summary of the activity history for each artifact with a small bar graph drawn inside the object's rectangle; bars represent amount of change to the class since its creation. More information about an artifact can be obtained by holding the cursor over a rectangle: for example, the name of the class and a more detailed bar graph.

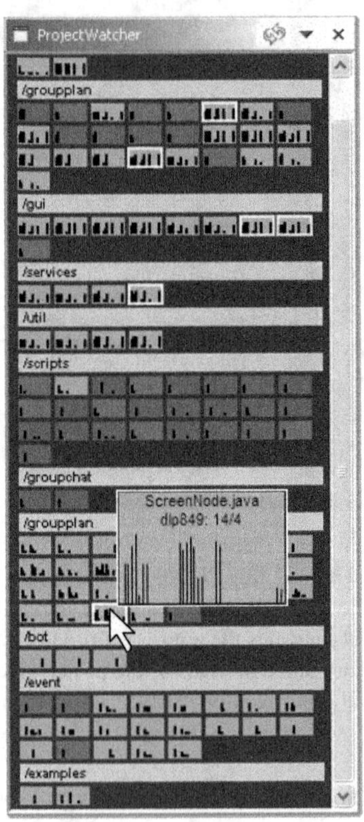

Fig. 5. ProjectWatcher as an Eclipse IDE plugin (www.eclipse.org), showing highlights (yellow borders on blocks) to indicate others' recent changes, and popup window to show more detail about a particular file.

Change information can be shown in addition to information about developers. The system highlight artifacts (using coloured borders) if they have changed recently – this provides users with dynamic information about commits to the project. When a change occurs to the CVS repository, the changed files are highlighted in the overview representation. More details about the change can be seen using the popup detail window, and further information (such as the difference between the two versions) can be seen through a context menu.

The overview displays help developers to answer a variety of questions about the project and about the activities of their collaborators. For example, it can be seen that the developers timriker (light blue) and davidt (red) are currently active (since they have each been the last to touch several files), and are core developers on the project (since they are both the most frequent committer for many files). We can also see that developers riq (green) and nsayer (dark blue) are each likely responsible for one main module in the project, since they are the most frequent for all the files in a particular directory. Two other people, dbw192 (yellow) and dbrosius (brown) are neither recent or frequent committers, since neither filter shows any files in their colour. Finally, we can see from the 'age' filter (Figure 4, right) that most of the project has recently been changed, since most of the blocks are white or light grey.

The highlights (see Figure 5) provide an analogue to the CVS-commits mailing list, but with considerably less effort. As can be seen in the figure, there are six files that have been changed since the local user last updated files from the repository. It is easy to determine how much change is occurring, and in general where it is happening. By holding the mouse cursor over any of these blocks, the developer, can get more information about what file has been changed, who committed the most recent change, and the number of lines added and deleted in the change (the '14/4' in the popup indicates that 14 lines were added, and 4 deleted).

5. Comparison to Related Work

A number of software engineering tools provide some degree of information about other members of the team (such as their identities or their assigned tasks), or provide facilities for team communication (e.g., [2,6,19]). However, only a few systems combine information about people's activities with representations of the project artifacts. Two that do this are Augur [7] and TUKAN [20,21].

TUKAN is one of the first systems to explicitly address the question of awareness in software development. The basic representation used in TUKAN is a Smalltalk class browser, onto which awareness information is overlaid. In particular, the system shows the distance of other developers in 'software space,' using a software structure graph as the basis for calculating proximity. The main difference in our approach with ProjectWatcher is in the use of an overview; where TUKAN presents relevant information about others who may be encroaching on a developer's current location, ProjectWatcher provides a general overview of the entire project.

Augur is a system similar to Ball and Eick's SeeSoft [1], that presents line-based visualizations of source code along with other visual representations of the project. The goal of Augur is to unify information about project activities with information about project artifacts; the system is designed to support both ongoing awareness and investigation into the details of project activity. ProjectWatcher also uses the ideas of edit/read wear and combining activity and artifact information; the main difference between the two systems is that Augur is a large-scale system with many views and a highly detailed representation of the project, whereas ProjectWatcher's visualization is designed only to support the two awareness questions seen in our work with existing projects ("who is who in general" and "who works in this area of the code"). In addition, ProjectWatcher is based on a much finer temporal granularity of activity than is Augur, which uses repository commits as its source of activity information. We see ProjectWatcher as more suited to day-to-day activities on a collaborative project, and Augur to specific investigations where developers wish to explore the history of the project in more detail.

6. Future Research

Our future plans for ProjectWatcher involve improvements and new directions in both the mining and the visualization components. The current version of the system primarily addresses those awareness issues that we saw in distributed projects, but the basic tools and approaches can be used for a variety of additional purposes.

First, we currently visualize source code that is in the process of being edited, and therefore the source code may be inconsistent, incomplete and frequently updated. We are investigating techniques for improving the robustness and performance of the fact extraction process, and techniques for visualizing partial information given these circumstances. Our system also only records user edits to the method level. We plan to move towards even finer grained awareness so that we can handle concurrent edits in some situations.

Second, the capturing and recording of developers' activities supports new software repository mining research in addition to supporting awareness. Developers normally change a local copy of the software under development, and periodically synchronize their changes with the shared software repository. Unfortunately, the developer's local interactions with the source code are not recorded in the shared software repository. With our finer-grained approach, the local interaction history of the developer is recorded and is available to be mined. Example software mining research directions include:

- *Discovery of refactoring patterns.* Analysing local interaction histories may be useful for identifying novel refactoring patterns and coordinating refactorings that affect other team members.
- *Discovery of browsing patterns.* Local interaction history includes the developer's searching, browsing and file access activities. Analysing this browsing interaction may be useful in supporting a developer in locating people or code exemplars.
- *Discovery of expertise.* Since the factbase contains facts from the Java API, we can determine what parts of that API each developer has used, and how often. It can now be possible to determine who has used a particular Java widget or structure frequently, and to build that knowledge into the development environment.

We also plan to refine and expand the visualization component. Short-term work will involve testing the representations and filters to determine how the information can be best presented to real developers. Longer range plans involve extensions to the basic idea of integrating information about activities with information about project artifacts. For example, we plan to extend our artifact collection to include entities other than those in source code. Many other project artifacts exist, including communication logs, bug reports and task lists. We hope to establish additional facts to model these artifacts and to use the new artifacts and their relationships in the awareness visualizations. We can also extend our use of the interaction histories to other areas. As discussed above, recording developers' interaction history and extracting method call facts from the source code provides us with basic API usage information. We can present this information in the IDE to provide awareness of technology expertise.

Finally, we plan to extend the range of awareness information that can be seen in the visualizations. As mentioned above, displaying information about refactoring, browsing, and expertise may be useful to developers in a distributed project. Other possibilities include questions of proximity – "who is working near to me?" in terms of the structures and dependencies of the software system under development, and questions of scope and effect – "how many people will I affect if I change this module?" Proximity is an important concept in software development because developers who near to one another (in code terms) form an implicit sub-team whose concerns are similar and whose interactions are more closely coupled [20]. Proximity groups are not defined in advance and change membership as developers move from task to task; therefore, it is often very difficult to determine who is currently in the group. We will address this problem by extending the ProjectWatcher visualizations to make it easier to see proximity-based groups.

7. Conclusions

We have presented a system to address some of the awareness problems experienced in distributed software development projects. ProjectWatcher contains two main parts: a mining component and a visualization system. The system keeps track of fine-grained user activities through the use of a shadow repository, and records those actions in relation to the artifact-based dependencies extracted from source code. Second, visualizations represent this information for developers to see and interact with. The visualizations present a project overview, overlaid with visual information about people's activities. Although our prototypes have limitations in terms of project size, they can provide developers with much-needed information about who is working on the project, what they are doing and how the project is changing over time.

Acknowledgements

The authors would like to thank IBM Corporation for supporting this research.

References

1. Ball, T., and Eick, S. Software visualization in the large. *IEEE Computer*, Vol 29, No 4, 1996.
2. Chu-Caroll, M., and Sprenkle, S. Coven: Brewing better collaboration through software configuration management. *Proc FSE-8*, 2000.
3. Cordy, J., Dean, T., Malton, A., and Schneider, K., Software Engineering by Source Transformation - Experience with TXL, *Proc. SCAM'01 - IEEE 1st International Workshop on Source Code Analysis and Manipulation*, 168-178, 2001.
4. Dix, A., Finlay, J., Abowd, G., and Beale, R., *Human-Computer Interaction*, Prentice Hall, 1993.
5. Dourish, P., and Bellotti, V., Awareness and Coordination in Shared Workspaces, *Proc. ACM CSCW 1992*, 107-114.
6. Elliott, M., and Scacchi, W., Free software developers as an occupational community: resolving conflicts and fostering collaboration, *Proc. ACM GROUP 2003*, 21-30.
7. Froehlich, J. and Dourish, P., Unifying Artifacts and Activities in a Visual Tool for Distributed Software Development Teams. To appear, *Proc. ICSE 2004*.
8. Gutwin, C. and Greenberg, S. A Descriptive Framework of Workspace Awareness for Real-Time Groupware. *Journal of Computer-Supported Cooperative Work*, Issue 3-4, 2002, 411-446.
9. Gutwin, C., Penner, R., and Schneider, K., Group Awareness in Distributed Software Development, to appear, *Proceedings of ACM CSCW 2004*, Chicago, 2004.
10. Herbsleb, J., and Grinter, R., Architectures, coordination, and distance: Conway's law and beyond. *IEEE Software*, 1999.
11. Herbsleb, J., Grinter, R., and Perry, D., The geography of coordination: dealing with distance in R&D work. *Proc. ACM SIGGROUP conference on supporting group work*, 1999.
12. Herbsleb, J., Mockus, A., Finholt, T., and Grinter, R., Distance, Dependencies, and Delay in a Global Collaboration, *Proc. ACM CSCW 2000*, 319-328.
13. Hill, W.C., Hollan, J.D., McCandless, J., and Wroblewski, D. Edit wear and read wear. *Proc. ACM CHI 1992*, 3-9.
14. Kraut, R., and Streeter, L., Coordination in software development. *CACM*, 1995.
15. Malton, A., Schneider, K., Cordy, J., Dean, T., Cousineau, D., and Reynolds, J., Processing Software Source Text in Automated Design Recovery and Transformation. *Proc. 9th International Workshop on Program Comprehension*, 127-134, 2001.
16. McDonald, D., and Ackerman, M., Just Talk to Me: A Field Study of Expertise Location Finding and Sustaining Relationships, *Proc. ACM CSCW 1998*, 315-324.
17. Mockus, A., Fielding, R., and Herbsleb, J. Two Case Studies of Open Source Software Development: Apache and Mozilla, *ACM ToSEM*, 11, 3, 2002, 309-346.
18. Monk, A., and Watts, L., Peripheral Participants in Mediated Communication, Proc. ACM CHI 1998, v.2, 285-286.
19. Raymond, E., The Cathedral and the Bazaar, O'Reilly, 2001.
20. Schummer, T., Lost and found in software space. *Proc 34th HICSS*, 2001.
21. Schummer, T., and Schummer, J., TUKAN: A team environment for software implementation. *Proc. OOPSLA 1999*.
22. Segal, L., Designing Team Workstations: The Choreography of Teamwork, in *Local Applications of the Ecological Approach to Human-Machine Systems*, P. Hancock, J. Flach, J. Caird and K. Vicente ed., Erlbaum, 1995, 392-415.
23. Whittaker, S., Frohlich, D., and Daly-Jones, O., Informal Workplace Communication: What is It Like and How Might We Support It?, *Proc. ACM CHI 1994*, 131-137.
24. B. Zimmermann and A. M. Selvin. A framework for assessing group memory approaches for software design projects. *Proc. Conference on Designing interactive systems*. 1997.

Discussion

[Bonnie E. John] You chose no to look at video or IM Buddy lists, is that because prior research suggests that that is not where the action is, or was it easier not to do that, or what?

> [Kevin Schneider] We were interested in the software artefacts and what we could get from that! Other people in the CSCW field are working on other aspects such as the ones you mention. The field does not really know where the bang for the buck is.

[Bonnie John] You mentioned scalability! How big does it scale and do you have ideas of how you could chunk or aggregate to allow you to scale further? Are we talking about 10 person projects with 10,000 lines of code or a 100 person project with 1,000,000 lines of code?

> [Kevin Schneider] It is a big issue! I think the visualisation might not scale and that is why we are trying to think of other metaphors! Currently 10,000 to 100,000 would probably be the limit! Currently we use relatively little screen space and the projects we have looked at does not seem to need more than that! Other studies have shown that even large projects such as Linux tends to be organised around specific parts of the code and that might help solve the scalability problem you mention! Maybe it is software architecture that will have to solve that problem!

[Peter Forbrig] I like your tool very much. What about the software developers? Did they like to be tracked in this way?

> [Kevin Schneider] Because we were looking at open source projects there was no problem with privacy. Their community is willing to publish all activities. We can combine our approach with techniques to achieve privacy, but we did not look at it up to now.

[Bonnie John] Are real people using it and would they hate you if you took it away from them?

> [Kevin Schneider] Only internal people are using it, and we do not know if they would hate us if we took it away!

Author Index

Lecture Notes in Computer Science

For information about Vols. 1–3480

please contact your bookseller or Springer

Vol. 3587: P. Perner, A. Imiya (Eds.), Machine Learning and Data Mining in Pattern Recognition. XVII, 695 pages. 2005. (Subseries LNAI).

Vol. 3580: L. Caires, G.F. Italiano, L. Monteiro, C. Palamidessi, M. Yung (Eds.), Automata, Languages and Programming. XXV, 1477 pages. 2005.

Vol. 3578: M. Gallagher, J. Hogan, F. Maire (Eds.), Intelligent Data Engineering and Automated Learning - IDEAL 2005. XVI, 599 pages. 2005.

Vol. 3576: K. Etessami, S.K. Rajamani (Eds.), Computer Aided Verification. XV, 564 pages. 2005.

Vol. 3575: S. Wermter, G. Palm, M. Elshaw (Eds.), Biomimetic Neural Learning for Intelligent Robots. IX, 383 pages. 2005. (Subseries LNAI).

Vol. 3574: C. Boyd, J.M. González Nieto (Eds.), Information Security and Privacy. XIII, 586 pages. 2005.

Vol. 3573: S. Etalle (Ed.), Logic Based Program Synthesis and Transformation. VIII, 279 pages. 2005.

Vol. 3572: C. De Felice, A. Restivo (Eds.), Developments in Language Theory. XI, 409 pages. 2005.

Vol. 3571: L. Godo (Ed.), Symbolic and Quantitative Approaches to Reasoning with Uncertainty. XVI, 1028 pages. 2005. (Subseries LNAI).

Vol. 3570: A. S. Patrick, M. Yung (Eds.), Financial Cryptography and Data Security. XII, 376 pages. 2005.

Vol. 3569: F. Bacchus, T. Walsh (Eds.), Theory and Applications of Satisfiability Testing. XII, 492 pages. 2005.

Vol. 3567: M. Jackson, D. Nelson, S. Stirk (Eds.), Database: Enterprise, Skills and Innovation. XII, 185 pages. 2005.

Vol. 3565: G.E. Christensen, M. Sonka (Eds.), Information Processing in Medical Imaging. XXI, 777 pages. 2005.

Vol. 3562: J. Mira, J.R. Álvarez (Eds.), Artificial Intelligence and Knowledge Engineering Applications: A Bioinspired Approach, Part II. XXIV, 636 pages. 2005.

Vol. 3561: J. Mira, J.R. Álvarez (Eds.), Mechanisms, Symbols, and Models Underlying Cognition, Part I. XXIV, 532 pages. 2005.

Vol. 3560: V.K. Prasanna, S. Iyengar, P.G. Spirakis, M. Welsh (Eds.), Distributed Computing in Sensor Systems. XV, 423 pages. 2005.

Vol. 3559: P. Auer, R. Meir (Eds.), Learning Theory. XI, 692 pages. 2005. (Subseries LNAI).

Vol. 3557: H. Gilbert, H. Handschuh (Eds.), Fast Software Encryption. XI, 443 pages. 2005.

Vol. 3556: H. Baumeister, M. Marchesi, M. Holcombe (Eds.), Extreme Programming and Agile Processes in Software Engineering. XIV, 332 pages. 2005.

Vol. 3555: T. Vardanega, A. Wellings (Eds.), Reliable Software Technology – Ada-Europe 2005. XV, 273 pages. 2005.

Vol. 3554: A. Dey, B. Kokinov, D. Leake, R. Turner (Eds.), Modeling and Using Context. XIV, 572 pages. 2005. (Subseries LNAI).

Vol. 3553: T.D. Hämäläinen, A.D. Pimentel, J. Takala, S. Vassiliadis (Eds.), Embedded Computer Systems: Architectures, Modeling, and Simulation. XV, 476 pages. 2005.

Vol. 3552: H. de Meer, N. Bhatti (Eds.), Quality of Service – IWQoS 2005. XV, 400 pages. 2005.

Vol. 3551: T. Härder, W. Lehner (Eds.), Data Management in a Connected World. XIX, 371 pages. 2005.

Vol. 3548: K. Julisch, C. Kruegel (Eds.), Intrusion and Malware Detection and Vulnerability Assessment. X, 241 pages. 2005.

Vol. 3547: F. Bomarius, S. Komi-Sirviö (Eds.), Product Focused Software Process Improvement. XIII, 588 pages. 2005.

Vol. 3543: L. Kutvonen, N. Alonistioti (Eds.), Distributed Applications and Interoperable Systems. XI, 235 pages. 2005.

Vol. 3541: N.C. Oza, R. Polikar, J. Kittler, F. Roli (Eds.), Multiple Classifier Systems. XII, 430 pages. 2005.

Vol. 3540: H. Kalviainen, J. Parkkinen, A. Kaarna (Eds.), Image Analysis. XXII, 1270 pages. 2005.

Vol. 3537: A. Apostolico, M. Crochemore, K. Park (Eds.), Combinatorial Pattern Matching. XI, 444 pages. 2005.

Vol. 3536: G. Ciardo, P. Darondeau (Eds.), Applications and Theory of Petri Nets 2005. XI, 470 pages. 2005.

Vol. 3535: M. Steffen, G. Zavattaro (Eds.), Formal Methods for Open Object-Based Distributed Systems. X, 323 pages. 2005.

Vol. 3533: M. Ali, F. Esposito (Eds.), Innovations in Applied Artificial Intelligence. XX, 858 pages. 2005. (Subseries LNAI).

Vol. 3532: A. Gómez-Pérez, J. Euzenat (Eds.), The Semantic Web: Research and Applications. XV, 728 pages. 2005.

Vol. 3531: J. Ioannidis, A. Keromytis, M. Yung (Eds.), Applied Cryptography and Network Security. XI, 530 pages. 2005.

Vol. 3530: A. Prinz, R. Reed, J. Reed (Eds.), SDL 2005: Model Driven. XI, 361 pages. 2005.

Vol. 3528: P.S. Szczepaniak, J. Kacprzyk, A. Niewiadomski (Eds.), Advances in Web Intelligence. XVII, 513 pages. 2005. (Subseries LNAI).

Vol. 3527: R. Morrison, F. Oquendo (Eds.), Software Architecture. XII, 263 pages. 2005.

Vol. 3526: S.B. Cooper, B. Löwe, L. Torenvliet (Eds.), New Computational Paradigms. XVII, 574 pages. 2005.

Vol. 3525: A.E. Abdallah, C.B. Jones, J.W. Sanders (Eds.), Communicating Sequential Processes. XIV, 321 pages. 2005.

Vol. 3524: R. Barták, M. Milano (Eds.), Integration of AI and OR Techniques in Constraint Programming for Combinatorial Optimization Problems. XI, 320 pages. 2005.

Vol. 3523: J.S. Marques, N. Pérez de la Blanca, P. Pina (Eds.), Pattern Recognition and Image Analysis, Part II. XXVI, 733 pages. 2005.

Vol. 3522: J.S. Marques, N. Pérez de la Blanca, P. Pina (Eds.), Pattern Recognition and Image Analysis, Part I. XXVI, 703 pages. 2005.

Vol. 3521: N. Megiddo, Y. Xu, B. Zhu (Eds.), Algorithmic Applications in Management. XIII, 484 pages. 2005.

Vol. 3520: O. Pastor, J. Falcão e Cunha (Eds.), Advanced Information Systems Engineering. XVI, 584 pages. 2005.

Vol. 3519: H. Li, P. J. Olver, G. Sommer (Eds.), Computer Algebra and Geometric Algebra with Applications. IX, 449 pages. 2005.

Vol. 3518: T.B. Ho, D. Cheung, H. Liu (Eds.), Advances in Knowledge Discovery and Data Mining. XXI, 864 pages. 2005. (Subseries LNAI).

Vol. 3517: H.S. Baird, D.P. Lopresti (Eds.), Human Interactive Proofs. IX, 143 pages. 2005.

Vol. 3516: V.S. Sunderam, G.D.v. Albada, P.M.A. Sloot, J.J. Dongarra (Eds.), Computational Science – ICCS 2005, Part III. LXIII, 1143 pages. 2005.

Vol. 3515: V.S. Sunderam, G.D.v. Albada, P.M.A. Sloot, J.J. Dongarra (Eds.), Computational Science – ICCS 2005, Part II. LXIII, 1101 pages. 2005.

Vol. 3514: V.S. Sunderam, G.D.v. Albada, P.M.A. Sloot, J.J. Dongarra (Eds.), Computational Science – ICCS 2005, Part I. LXIII, 1089 pages. 2005.

Vol. 3513: A. Montoyo, R. Muñoz, E. Métais (Eds.), Natural Language Processing and Information Systems. XII, 408 pages. 2005.

Vol. 3512: J. Cabestany, A. Prieto, F. Sandoval (Eds.), Computational Intelligence and Bioinspired Systems. XXV, 1260 pages. 2005.

Vol. 3511: U.K. Wiil (Ed.), Metainformatics. VIII, 221 pages. 2005.

Vol. 3510: T. Braun, G. Carle, Y. Koucheryavy, V. Tsaoussidis (Eds.), Wired/Wireless Internet Communications. XIV, 366 pages. 2005.

Vol. 3509: M. Jünger, V. Kaibel (Eds.), Integer Programming and Combinatorial Optimization. XI, 484 pages. 2005.

Vol. 3508: P. Bresciani, P. Giorgini, B. Henderson-Sellers, G. Low, M. Winikoff (Eds.), Agent-Oriented Information Systems II. X, 227 pages. 2005. (Subseries LNAI).

Vol. 3507: F. Crestani, I. Ruthven (Eds.), Information Context: Nature, Impact, and Role. XIII, 253 pages. 2005.

Vol. 3506: C. Park, S. Chee (Eds.), Information Security and Cryptology – ICISC 2004. XIV, 490 pages. 2005.

Vol. 3505: V. Gorodetsky, J. Liu, V. A. Skormin (Eds.), Autonomous Intelligent Systems: Agents and Data Mining. XIII, 303 pages. 2005. (Subseries LNAI).

Vol. 3504: A.F. Frangi, P.I. Radeva, A. Santos, M. Hernandez (Eds.), Functional Imaging and Modeling of the Heart. XV, 489 pages. 2005.

Vol. 3503: S.E. Nikoletseas (Ed.), Experimental and Efficient Algorithms. XV, 624 pages. 2005.

Vol. 3502: F. Khendek, R. Dssouli (Eds.), Testing of Communicating Systems. X, 381 pages. 2005.

Vol. 3501: B. Kégl, G. Lapalme (Eds.), Advances in Artificial Intelligence. XV, 458 pages. 2005. (Subseries LNAI).

Vol. 3500: S. Miyano, J. Mesirov, S. Kasif, S. Istrail, P. Pevzner, M. Waterman (Eds.), Research in Computational Molecular Biology. XVII, 632 pages. 2005. (Subseries LNBI).

Vol. 3499: A. Pelc, M. Raynal (Eds.), Structural Information and Communication Complexity. X, 323 pages. 2005.

Vol. 3498: J. Wang, X. Liao, Z. Yi (Eds.), Advances in Neural Networks – ISNN 2005, Part III. XLIX, 1077 pages. 2005.

Vol. 3497: J. Wang, X. Liao, Z. Yi (Eds.), Advances in Neural Networks – ISNN 2005, Part II. XLIX, 947 pages. 2005.

Vol. 3496: J. Wang, X. Liao, Z. Yi (Eds.), Advances in Neural Networks – ISNN 2005, Part II. L, 1055 pages. 2005.

Vol. 3495: P. Kantor, G. Muresan, F. Roberts, D.D. Zeng, F.-Y. Wang, H. Chen, R.C. Merkle (Eds.), Intelligence and Security Informatics. XVIII, 674 pages. 2005.

Vol. 3494: R. Cramer (Ed.), Advances in Cryptology – EUROCRYPT 2005. XIV, 576 pages. 2005.

Vol. 3493: N. Fuhr, M. Lalmas, S. Malik, Z. Szlávik (Eds.), Advances in XML Information Retrieval. XI, 438 pages. 2005.

Vol. 3492: P. Blache, E. Stabler, J. Busquets, R. Moot (Eds.), Logical Aspects of Computational Linguistics. X, 363 pages. 2005. (Subseries LNAI).

Vol. 3489: G.T. Heineman, I. Crnkovic, H.W. Schmidt, J.A. Stafford, C. Szyperski, K. Wallnau (Eds.), Component-Based Software Engineering. XI, 358 pages. 2005.

Vol. 3488: M.-S. Hacid, N.V. Murray, Z.W. Raś, S. Tsumoto (Eds.), Foundations of Intelligent Systems. XIII, 700 pages. 2005. (Subseries LNAI).

Vol. 3486: T. Helleseth, D. Sarwate, H.-Y. Song, K. Yang (Eds.), Sequences and Their Applications - SETA 2004. XII, 451 pages. 2005.

Vol. 3483: O. Gervasi, M.L. Gavrilova, V. Kumar, A. Laganà, H.P. Lee, Y. Mun, D. Taniar, C.J.K. Tan (Eds.), Computational Science and Its Applications – ICCSA 2005, Part IV. LXV, 1362 pages. 2005.

Vol. 3482: O. Gervasi, M.L. Gavrilova, V. Kumar, A. Laganà, H.P. Lee, Y. Mun, D. Taniar, C.J.K. Tan (Eds.), Computational Science and Its Applications – ICCSA 2005, Part III. LXV, 1340 pages. 2005.

Vol. 3481: O. Gervasi, M.L. Gavrilova, V. Kumar, A. Laganà, H.P. Lee, Y. Mun, D. Taniar, C.J.K. Tan (Eds.), Computational Science and Its Applications – ICCSA 2005, Part II. LXV, 1316 pages. 2005.